ASSASSINATIONS
AND THE
POLITICAL ORDER

ASSASSINATIONS AND THE POLITICAL ORDER

Edited by

William J. Crotty

A TORCHBOOK LIBRARY EDITION
Harper & Row, Publishers
New York, Evanston, San Francisco, London

CONTENTS

PREFACE

Political assassination as a factor of consequence in American politics or, for that matter, as a contender for attention in the popular mind seemed a pretty exotic concern prior to 1963. Then came John Kennedy's assassination. The events are blurred in retrospect, yet the feelings remain. Then Robert Kennedy was assassinated while seeking his party's nomination for the presidency, an assassination that followed within months the murder of civil-rights leader the Reverend Martin Luther King. The image remains of men struck down in their prime by, at least in the case of the Kennedy brothers about which more is known, singularly disturbed individuals. Basically, they were killed for no rational purpose, and to compound the tragedy their deaths served no grand end.

The public reaction in 1963 was one of shock, anger, and sorrow, a pattern clearly reminiscent of previous presidential murders. Five years later the feelings of shock were muted, and sorrow was the principal response. Assassinations were no longer quite so exotic occurrences. People had begrudgingly come to accept them as a fact of political life, deplorable, yes, but a possibility for a public figure of any stature.

One reaction to the series of assassinations and the general violence and turbulence was that society began to question itself: What was wrong with America? What did the country stand for? Where was it headed?

One hopeful outgrowth of the general confusion has been the reinvestigation of American history and the assessment of the traditions under which the nation has developed. The country has shown a willingness to reassess itself and the assumptions that have guided its public life. Part of this willingness has been the initiation of serious inquiry into the frequency of violent occurrences and the causes and consequences of such behavior. The essays in this volume represent a contribution to this effort.

A few personal comments are in order. I am not an assassination buff in any popular sense, and I was not drawn to the study through a fascination with any conspiratorial theories or the like. My reactions to the John Kennedy murder were as intense and unbelieving as any of those reported in the studies that followed his death or that are contained within this book. I watched with horror and fascination the events of the tragic weekend in Dallas and their depressing aftermath: the Ruby murder of Oswald, the sensational trial, and Ruby's eventual death; the nation grappling with its emotions; the Warren Commission hearings and the issuance of its report; the continuing controversy over the actual events. When given the opportunity, I visited Dallas and the site of the assassination.

Beyond this, like the majority of my fellow countrymen, I was content to resolve my own problem of believing that the act was the sad outcome of a single pathology. I took heart in both Lyndon Johnson's vigorous assumption of the powers of his office and in the ability of the political system to sustain itself. As a political scientist I had a particular interest in this latter aspect of the assassination's aftermath. I had a curiously objective interest in examining how the nation and its governing institutions responded to tragedy. I was impressed by the vitality of the political system and the national response. Short of a lingering wish that the tragedy had never happened, I managed to go about my business.

A second assassination struck me more closely and again disturbed me deeply. In 1964, I was a resident of Athens, Georgia, the home of the alleged murderers, when Lemuel Penn, a Washington, D.C., educator returning home from reserve duty, was killed by night riders outside the town. I followed the investigation and in particular the trial in state court of the accused murderers. I was appalled by the prosecution and the extent to which the court trial became imbedded in and reflected the worst local community values.[1] The memory of this stayed with me, but I did not connect it directly to the earlier assassination.

---

1. The defendants were acquitted. Later, they were tried in federal court under an 1870 Civil Rights Act, and several were found guilty of impairing the civil rights of Penn, a sentence that carried a maximum ten-year penalty. The outcome was considered a victory of sorts, in that the white men were held accountable for the murder of a black in the courts. This was one of the first decisions of its kind.

Then came 1968. The sequence of violent events was electrifying. A disreputable war continued; the cities were burned; the campuses smoldered; the civil-rights fight took an ugly turn; and a general sense of despair enveloped the country. Events culminated with the assassination of Martin Luther King—apparently not an act of passion and one about which little was initially known. The major hope seemed to be the on-going fight for the Democratic nomination for president. Then Robert Kennedy was assassinated.

At this point, my frustration and my feelings took more tangible form with my appointment as co-director of the Task Force on Assassination and Political Violence of the National Commission on the Causes and Prevention of Violence. This experience helped me to sort out my own ideas and gain some perspective on the forces at work that underlie events such as political assassination. It also involved me more deeply in thinking through the institutional ramifications of assassinations, a subject that continues to fascinate me. The present book is in the nature of a continuing exploration of the problem from a variety of different vantage points. It is intended to shed some light and introduce some order into an essentially irrational and senseless occurrence.

The essays that follow attempt to place political assassination in a more understandable framework. They address many of the questions most asked about assassinations, and they explore American problems, placing them within the evolution of American traditions as well as looking at them from the perspective provided by foreign experience.

Each of the essays is the contribution of a person who is knowledgeable in an area that has few experts. No single emphasis or interpretation is put forward to explain the occurrence of political assassinations. The reader will find substantial areas of agreement, however, among the contributors.

No one tone sets the essays off. They range in presentation from the theoretical to the angry, from the descriptive to the speculative. Cumulatively, they provide a provocative overview of a topic of substantial concern.

Each of the authors does hold a belief that political assassinations can share common properties and that they are open to intensive investigation and better understanding—also, that assassinations are not freak occurrences, totally unfathomable chance events. Political assassinations are part of a nation's fabric. They develop from a strain within it and are associated with the culture of violence and the institutions for resolving social tensions that distinguish one nation from another. Broadly speaking, beyond the characteristics of a country that are related to the different types of assassination and diverse levels of politically relevant violence, they are roughly predictable. While specific acts against an individual cannot be predicted in advance, certain eras and different types of social conflict are more likely to give rise to the conditions associated with assassinations. These can be anticipated. Once identifiable, they can be dealt with.

The volume is divided into four parts. Part I describes the American experience with assassinations (William J. Crotty, "Assassinations and Their Interpretation Within the American Context"), with particular emphasis on the presidential assassinations. The second piece (Ivo K. Feierabend et al., "Political Violence and Assassination: A Cross-National Assessment") comparatively analyzes political assassinations in the United States within a framework provided by the experiences of eighty-four other nations.

Part II investigates the psychology of the assassin from the vantage point of three eminent doctors, two psychiatrists and one psychologist. Dr. Lawrence Zelic Freedman ("Psychopathology of Assassination") presents a psychiatric overview of the presidential assassins, examining their psychological state within the context of today's understanding of human motivations and development. Dr. David A. Rothstein ("Presidential-Assassination Syndrome: A Psychiatric Study of the Threat, the Deed, and the Message") reports on his research about people who have threatened the president and its relevance for understanding the individual psychological processes that result in such behavior. Rothstein calls on the extensive information available on Lee Harvey Oswald to compare his mental state with the case histories of those explored in the report. Both psychiatrists put forward explanatory theories for the behavior they observe. Dr. Thomas Greening ("The Psychological Study of Assassins") reviews Sirhan Sirhan's development in light of the knowledge available on assassins and then relates this to the areas of knowledge needed by society for a broader understanding of the interaction of such individuals with their environment.

Part III concentrates on public reactions to political assassinations. The first selection (Samuel C. Patterson, "Political Leaders and the Assassination of President Kennedy") reviews the feelings of an element of the population—political leaders—curiously neglected in the rash of surveys that followed the major American assassinations. The expression of Southern school children on learning of the death of the Reverend Martin Luther King and its ramifications within the context of what we know concerning the political socialization of the child are reported on in the research by Professors James Clarke and John Soule ("Political Socialization, Racial Tension and the Acceptance of Violence: Reactions of Southern School Children to the King Assassination"). The third study (James McEvoy, III, "Political Vengeance and Political Attitudes: A Study of Americans' Support for Political and Social Violence") analyzes the returns on a nationwide survey that explored the tolerance in the United States for violence and violent acts such as assassination and the limits placed on these.

The fourth and final part looks into the implications of assassination for the political health and continuity of the entire social system. Professor Joseph Bensman's introductory piece ("Social and Institutional Factors Determining the Level of Violence and Political Assassination in the Operation of Society: A Theoretical Discussion") explores the background and nature of differing patterns of assassination. Seymour M. Lipset and Carl Sheingold ("Values and Political Structures: An Interpretation of the Sources of Extremism and Violence in American Society") provocatively review the American traditions that have proven supportive of high levels of political violence, including the continuing concern with acts of assassination. Richard E. Rubenstein ("Assassination as a Political Tradition") carries this strain of argument a step further, developing the thesis that political assassination is in itself an American tradition and one of major, and essentially unrecognized, consequence in the evolution of the United States. H. L. Nieburg ("Murder as Political Behavior") reviews the ramifications of assassinations of all levels of society and their consequences, stressing the need to assess these acts within the social framework and historical experience of a particular country. The parallel concern, yet divergent perspectives, found in the Lipset and Sheingold, Rubenstein and Nieburg chapters reward a close reading of the three in relation to each other.

The final two selections deal principally with the postassassination implications of the sudden removal of a national leader, but from quite different vantage points. Professors Murray Edelman and Rita James Simon ("Presidential Assassinations: Their Meaning and Impact on American Society") detail the policy and institutional needs for continuity and relate this to the American experience with such problems after the murder of the presidents. Dwaine Marvick and Elizabeth Wirth Marvick ("The Political Consequences of Assassination") explore a similar problem but employ examples from three different nations in varying time periods. Overall, this selection, as with the entire last section and the book more generally, attempts to assess the implications for a society of an act of murder for which we have little tolerance and often less understanding.

part I

ASSASSINATIONS IN
THE UNITED STATES AND ABROAD

Assassinations and their Interpretation within the American Context

William J. Crotty

Introductory Comments. Assassination in the United States, especially at the higher and more visible levels, has been essentially anomic, that is, committed by private individuals for personal motives. At the most critical levels of governmental decision making, there has been little evidence of broad group support or involvement. There are few exceptions to the general rule.

Political assassination in other nations has been planned more with an eye on achievable political goals. In this sense, they have been more "rational." The murder of an individual has been the result of a premeditated move toward an identifiable, and generally accomplishable, political objective. While anomic assassinations are not unknown in other nations, witness the official explanations put forward concerning the attempt on the lives of the Russian leaders in January, 1969, the principal experience in other countries has been with the politically motivated assassination act, one reason why foreigners find it difficult to credit a judgment of a government-sponsored probe of an assassination that is found devoid of all political meaning.

History. Experience with assassinations goes back to the dawn of man.[1] The practice has a long ancestry. Reportedly, the Greeks in

1. The discussion of the historical evolution of assassination was drawn principally from the following works: Richard Bunot Laney, "Political Assassination: The History of an Idea" (Ph.D. diss., University of Utah, 1966); Oscar Jaszi and John D. Lewis, *Against the Tyrant: The Tradition and Theory of Assassination* (New York: The Free Press, 1957); Joseph Bornstein, *The Politics of Murder* (New York: William Sloane, 1950); and E. I. J. Rosenthal, *Political Thought in Medieval Islam* (Cambridge: University Press, 1962).

the fifth and sixth centuries B.C. practiced tyrannacide. Philip II of Macedon, father of Alexander the Great, Tiberius Gracchus, and Julius Caesar all died by an assassin's hand before the birth of Christ. The Middle Ages claimed as victims Thomas à Becket, Emperor Albert I of Germany, and James I of Scotland. The sixteenth and seventeenth centuries witnessed a rash of major assassinations beginning with the death of Alessandro de Medici and including such notables as William I of Orange and Kings Henry III and Henry IV of France. The list of those who met death through assassination includes heads of state (Italy's King Humbert, Sweden's Gustavus III, Portugal's Carlos I, Greece's King George, France's Carnot and Doumer, Russia's Alexander II, Mexico's Madero, Carranza, and Obregón, Jordan's King Abdullah, and the Dominican Republic's Trujillo); court advisers and ministers (Rasputin of Russia, Philippe Henriot of France, Canovas del Costrillo of Spain, and Ahmed Maher Pasha of Egypt); clergymen (Cardinal Beaton and Archbishop Sharp, both of Scotland); moral leaders (Gandhi, Martin Luther King); military chiefs (France's Admiral Darlan and General Kleber); and public figures of varying renown (Marat, Francisco Villa, Jean Juares, Trotsky, Count Bernadotte). Virtually every major nation in the world has experienced one, and some very many, prominent assassinations. At least one assassination (that of Archduke Ferdinand) set in motion the events leading to war, and another ended one nation's centuries-long experience with royalty (the murder of Russia's Nicholas II and his family).

The first systematic use of assassination as a political weapon is credited to a Persian, Hasan ibn-al-Sabbah, in the eleventh century. Hasan Sabbah developed a cult centering on the concept of assassination. The *Fidais,* or assassins,[2] were specially trained to gain the trust of competing rulers and then when the opportunity presented itself to murder them. Employing assassination as a political tactic, Hasan Sabbah expanded his principality elevenfold and eventually hired his disciples out to other needy rulers. The

2. The word "assassin" was introduced to the Western world by the crusaders, who brought back tales of their exploits. It means "user of hashhish," in Arabic *hashshashin.*

motivation for the individual assassin was eternal damnation if he failed. Should he die in the line of duty, his soul escaped to heaven. To this day, the sect has survived in small numbers in the Mideast, notably Syria, Iran, Iraq, Pakistan and India, and in parts of central Asia.

The murder of kings was often encouraged in prerecorded history. Under the superstitions of the time, a ruler who began to show signs of human weakness, such as the effects of aging, invited the gods to visit catastrophe on his subjects. Thus, through a variety of ritualistic ways, the spent king would be assassinated and a more vigorous successor would ascend the throne. Taken to its extreme, one kingdom in West Africa assassinated the king the night after his coronation, thus assuring no one ever reigned and no visitation from the gods. In southern India, the obliging monarch would murder himself in a grotesque ritual, thus saving his followers of the need. The wiser king instituted proxies, killing these periodically to satisfy the gods and his people, while he himself continued in power.

The practice of assassination has not been matched by an abundance of theoretical attempts to justify its use.[3] The Greeks appeared to condone tyrannicide, as did John of Salisbury (ca. 1120–1180) in what is the first explicit philosophic rationalization of the practice. Drawing the distinction, which dates back at least to the Greeks, between the legitimate ruler and the tyrant, the latter a usurper of power who ruled for his own advantage, John of Salisbury argued that the assassin who killed a tyrant did no more than God's will. Other writers, Coluccio Salutati, William of Occam, Marsilius of Padua and Niccolò Machiavelli, in the Middle Ages and later put forward similar justifications for assassina-

---

3. There is no "theory" of assassinations per se that develops the circumstances—environmental pressures, institutional factors, personality needs—that combine to produce different frequencies and types of assassination in a nation. The chapter by Joseph Bensman, "Social and Institutional Factors Determining the Level of Violence and Political Assassination in the Operation of Society: A Theoretical Discussion," in this volume comes closer to filling this need than anything available. The related selections by the Feierabends et al. and Nieburg contribute perspective to any attempt to ᵊolve an explanatory theory.

tions. Even in the abstract, however, the act was not well received and was argued only as a measure of last resort.

The attempt to divorce temporal from spiritual affairs led to a conflict between church and state. Some fifteenth- and sixteenth-century writers, as a consequence, advocated regicide if a king transgressed in spiritual matters, broadly conceived. The conflict between Protestant and Catholic also resulted in justifications of assassination. Calvinists such as John Knox, George Buchanan, Theodorus Beza and the anonymous author of *Vindiciae Contra Tyrannos* (ca. 1648), probably the most thoughtful rationalization of assassination, assumed a king to be of conflicting religion with the majority of his subjects. Repression and execution of large numbers of the population often followed, as they had with the Huguenot slaughters in Catholic France of 1572. The murder of a king could be accepted as humanitarian in such circumstances.

Catholic theologians such as the French Jesuit Robert Bellarmine and the Spanish Jesuits Juan de Marina and Francisco Suárez argued from a different premise, assuming the secular head of state and the Pope to be in conflict. The assassination of the king in such encounters would be approved as the disposal of a heretic. Marina and Suárez did condition such removals on an implicit assumption of an agreement between rulers and subjects that had been violated and the approval by bodies representative of the people.

There are references to assassination in some of the writings of the nineteenth-century anarchists and in those on guerrilla warfare and civil disturbance of the present day.

Nonwestern thought, even less than its Western counterpart, provides little philosophical groundwork to justify assassination, although some countries, notably Japan in the pre-World War II period, found it a common political occurrence.

As a concept with philosophic underpinnings, it is poorly developed. It appears principally in tracts on church-state relations, Protestant-Catholic conflicts, and in the repeated attempts to find a means to limit the power of despots. Even in these cases it is overladen with conditions regarding its use. The act itself is repulsive, and the thinking of writers on the subject reflects their ambivalence. While employed in practice, it is little honored in the thinking of man.

ASSASSINATIONS IN THE UNITED STATES

The American exposure to assassination is a recent occurrence, or so most would like to believe. On November 22, 1963, President John F. Kennedy was murdered while on a political trip to Dallas. People were shocked. The world's mightiest government momentarily staggered. An investigation was initiated into the events surrounding the act with the intention of fixing responsibility for the murder within the limits of the evidence.

The Warren Commission report, as it became known, which followed, was a comprehensive, although not flawless, examination of the assassination. The report's conclusions, despite a continuing controversy, were generally accepted by the American people. Within five years of John Kennedy's assassination, his brother Robert was murdered while seeking the Democratic nomination for the presidency. Robert Kennedy's assassination followed by less than three months the killing of the Reverend Martin Luther King, black civil-rights leader and the adapter of Gandhian principles of nonviolence to the turbulent racial crises of the 1960's. Between the deaths of the two Kennedys and Dr. King, at least two other political leaders representing polar extremes of political philosophy, Medgar Evers, the NAACP leader in Mississippi dedicated to achieving peaceful electoral participation of blacks, and Lincoln Rockwell, a fascist and outspoken head of the revived American-German Party, were assassinated.

The continuing assassinations in concert with a decade of seemingly endless violence brought serious concern to Americans. While assassinations, it turns out, are not unknown in the United States, these acts were new to the consciousness of the vast majority of living Americans.

The immediate outcrys were ones of confusion: Was America a "sick" society? Was some sinister long-range plot wreaking its vengeance? Was the United States headed toward a new era of open political warfare and potential police-state repression? Was the delicate fabric of American social and moral behavior collapsing?

This essay will explore some of these questions, attempting to place the American experience in broad historical and comparative perspectives. In the process it will draw together the available information, at times fragmentary, in an attempt to address the most vexing considerations of a broad social nature associated with acts of assassinations.

Definition.[4] Assassinations of political consequence, as treated in this report, can be defined as the murder of an individual, whether of public prominence or not, in an effort to achieve political gain. The classic conception of the assassination act is as a tactic in struggles for political power. Julius Caesar was assassinated by a group of friends and senators, who feared the evil consequences of his great power; the legendary Rasputin was assassinated by Prince Felix Yusupov and a co-conspirator who resented his evil influence over the Czar; two premiers of Japan, Hanaguchi and Inukai, plus a number of Cabinet officials were assassinated by political opponents in pre-World War Japan; Stalin had Kirov assassinated as a pretext for the purge of opponents that followed, and Trotsky, a former rival, was assassinated, apparently on instructions from Stalin; an attempt was made on the life of Hitler by those who disapproved of his continued conduct of the war; and so on. Each of these assassinations and the bulk of the vast majority that stud the pages of history had explicitly political motives behind them.

The definition above has to be modified slightly to have meaning within the American context. The statement assumes an element of rationality in the planning of the murder *as it relates to the achievement of specified political objectives*. A killer with even the most casual concern for his victim or one who is seriously mentally ill will enter into a certain amount of deliberation about the manner in which to assault the victim—the time, the place, the weapon to be used, the nature of the encounter, and so on. The concept of rationality is not intended to convey the idea of the preplanning of the details of the act. Rather, it means that the execution of the

4. No one definition of assassination has been imposed on the studies in this volume. Any attempt at doing so would be a carping for precision rather than an attempt to understand better the acts and their consequences. All the definitions employed are within the common understanding given the term "political assassination." Each, however, fits given authors' individual needs—as with the quantitative cross-national studies, the emphasis on motivation in the psychological assessments, etc.

victim has a tangible relationship to a policy goal the conspirators wish to achieve. The act has been motivated by political concerns. The chief factor distinguishing assassinations in the United States and other countries hinges on this distinction.

Such a definition has limited applicability in the United States at the level most people are aware of, the assassination of presidents. Thus it needs modification. This review of assassinations includes the murder of politically prominent figures for personal or at best indirectly political motives. The discussion is thus broad enough to include, for example, John Schrank ("God has called me to be His instrument"), the man who attempted to take the life of presidential candidate and former chief executive, Theodore Roosevelt; Leon Czolgosz ("I thought it would be a good thing(s) for the nation to kill the President. . . . He was an enemy of the people. . . . He was always shouting prosperity and there was no prosperity for the poor man"), the assassin of President McKinley; and Oscar Collazo ("Anything that I had done I did it for the cause of liberty of my [Puerto Rico] country"), one of two who attempted to take the life of President Truman and in the history of American assassins considered to be one of the most rational. While the definition allows for consideration of these cases, it is not diffused to the point of encompassing a political figure killed for personal reasons (family squabble, lover's fight, business misunderstanding, object of a violent crime).

The study does include a limited appraisal of the murders of nonpolitical visible individuals executed for political purposes. The murder itself becomes an act with political implications. Notable examples of cases of assassination that fall within this category are civil rights slayings: the 1965 murder of Mrs. Viola Liuzzo, a Detroit housewife, killed while assisting in an Alabama civil-rights demonstration; the 1964 killings of one black and two white civil-rights workers in Philadelphia, Mississippi; and the 1964 slaying of Lemuel Penn, an educator returning to Washington, D.C., from military duty in Georgia.

The definition of the subject matter to be examined directs attention to three factors: the nature of the victim; the ends to be achieved by the murder; and the alleged motivations of the killer. Each of the second two factors, and especially motivation, is based on inference—one reason it is difficult to explain with certainty acts such as Oswald's—in which post facto evidence and official police reconstructions of the event represent the principal type of evidence. Assassinations, similar to politically oriented violence more generally, are best understood within the vortex of environmental circumstances in which they occur, the latter resulting from a series of historical, social, and individual psychological factors.

It can be argued with some limited support that the assassinations of prominent American political leaders, or at least of presidents, are best understood as individual acts that result from the pathological drives of the killer. All the presidential assassins have been lonely figures, mentally unstable, and through these murders have acted out inner fantasies. Such explanations may be partially acceptable for explaining *simple* acts; they are of little value for understanding the persistence of the murders over a period of time or their broader implications. Why should an individual choose a public personage as his target if he is irrationally responding to internal needs? Why after seemingly peaceful interludes do assassinations reoccur? Why are assassinations more frequent in one nation than another? An approach that focuses on the peculiarities of a given assassination or number of assassinations can not begin to address such questions. Assassinations are social acts with grave political consequences. They will not be treated as isolated phenomena and thus not subject to systematic, comparative analysis or interpretation. Rather, they will be viewed as reflections of a variety of cultural forces and social conditions that culminate in bizarre forms of political behavior.

A classification of assassination acts helps refine the data and can serve to introduce the explanation of the patterns of assassination in the United States as it compares to other nations. Such a typology permits more explicit comparisons.

Assassinations can be divided into five categories.

1. *Anomic assassination.* Already introduced, this is the murder of a political figure for essentially private reasons. The justification for the act is couched in broadly political terms, but the relationship between the act and the advancement of the political objectives specified is impossible to draw on any rational basis. The connecting link then is assumed to be the fantasies of the assassin.

This type of act is the most familiar to those concerned with presidential assassinations.

2. *Elite substitution.* The murder of a political leader in order to replace him or those he represents in power with an opposing group at essentially the same level. The palace-guard assassination of a dictator or the power struggle among groups for governmental leadership would result in this type of assassination. The continuing blood struggle between the Karageorgevich and Obrenovich dynasties in Serbia is a case in point. During the period 1817 to 1945, of the nine national leaders, four were assassinated, two deposed, and one abdicated. Transfer of power through elite assassination became almost a matter of court routine in nineteenth-century Turkey.[5]

3. *Tyrannicide.* One of the oldest forms of assassination, and the one with the greatest philosophical justification, the murder of a despot in order to replace him with one more amenable to the people and needs of a nation. The assassination of Czar Alexander II of Russia is such a case, although the results were not as intended. His successor, Czar Alexander III, turned out to be even more ruthless and repressive than his predecessor. The philosophic justifications of assassinations concentrate mostly on cases of tyrannicide.

That assassination developed beyond the simple act to the preoccupation with tyrannicide and regicide in particular can be traced to the latter half of the nineteenth century. The struggles in Russia against the czar developed the systematic and tactical use of assassination as a broad-scale political weapon. The intention was to punish the government or its minions for specified acts, to decentralize and weaken it, and eventually to incapacitate it. This, in turn, developed into a fourth type of assassination.

4. *Terroristic assassination.* Terror through assassination can be employed on a mass basis to demonstrate a government's incapacity to deal with insurgents, to neutralize a populace's

5. Feliks Gross, "Political Violence and Terror in Nineteenth and Twentieth Century Russia and Eastern Europe," in J. F. Kirkham, S. Levy, and W. J. Crotty, *Assassination and Political Violence* (Washington: U.S. Government Printing Office, 1969), p. 449; and Gross, *The Seizure of Political Power* (New York: Philosophical Library, 1958). See also Bensman's contribution to this volume.

allegiance to a government, to enlist their support in a revolutionary movement, or, more ambitiously, to allow a minority to suppress and subjugate a population. Examples of mass terror in history are many: the era of mass terror associated with the French Revolution; the Inquisition; the Russian purges of the 1930's; the Mau Mau rebellion in Kenya during the 1950's; the Nazi persecutions; the American South following the Civil War; and the terror used by the Viet Cong in the rural provinces of South Vietnam are examples of the systematic use of assassinations by an organized group within a population to achieve political goals. From the point of view of the terrorists, as Gross points out, ". . . the fear of the survivors . . . is survival. The fear of suffering, humiliation, loss of life and liberty influences their behavior. . . . the terrorized submit to the decisions of the terrorists, and obey their orders."[6]

The terror can be random; targets are chosen for no reason indigenous to the victim. The intention is to erode any faith in the government and intimidate the population. In this, the terrorists are willing deliberately to murder innocents to achieve their broader objectives.

A case study in random mass terrorism was the Algerian nationalists' fight against the French. According to Laney, in the first three years of the terrorism (November, 1954 to November, 1957), the Algerian rebels assassinated 8,429 civilians, of whom only 1,126 were Europeans. The rest were brother Moslems. Curiously, the OAS, the Secret Army Organization of French Algerians, resorted to mass terror when it became apparent that the De Gaulle government was willing to accede to an independent Algeria. During the latter part of 1961 and early 1962, the OAS was credited with responsibility for 500 deaths in Algeria.[7]

Terroristic assassinations directed toward specified categories of civilians or officials represent a more limited and systematic attempt to achieve the same ends as mass-terror assassinations. The Viet Cong focused on village leaders, reportedly killing or kidnaping over 2,400 officials in the period 1957–1959, with an additional 7,982 civil officials assassinated and 40,282 abducted in

6. "Political Violence . . . ," *Ibid.,* p. 428.
7. Laney, *op. cit.,* pp. 193–197.

the period 1961–1965. These figures illustrate the nature of this form of assassination and, if they are close to being accurate, indicate a successful (in numbers at any rate) example of its use.[8] The underground resistance to the Nazis during World War II, and the Macedonian, Armenian, and Bulgarian terror directed against their Turkish rulers at the turn of the century are other examples of more discrete, highly specific assassination strategies.

5. *Propaganda by deed.* This type of assassination is employed to direct attention to a broader problem, for example the subjugation of a people, with the hopes of bringing some alleviation. The assassinations during the 1950's by the Algerian nationalists were of this nature, although the volume of political murders would have to place them in the category of mass terror. The French colonial OAS organization in the early 1960's attempted to assassinate military figures and journalists in Paris to direct the attention of the French people to their difficulties. The assassination of Czar Alexander II was in part for propaganda purposes, as was the assassination attempt directed against President Truman and the explanation given for Senator Robert Kennedy's assassination. In Truman's case, the Puerto Rican nationalists hoped to publicize their cause, independence for Puerto Rico, through their attack on the President. Sirhan Bishara Sirhan, the Jordanian immigrant who murdered Robert Kennedy, wanted to emphasize the plight of the Arab nations and the supposed favoritism shown Israel by Kennedy. The murder of Archduke Ferdinand of Serbia represents a spectacular example of an assassination for propaganda purposes that badly misfired, distressing even the assassin.

The United States in World Perspective

A comparison of the level of assassinations in the United States with other nations reveals a disquieting fact: the United States has a disturbingly high level of political assassinations. By virtually

8. *Ibid.,* p. 201. The Viet Cong targets were chosen with unusual deliberation in a procedure closely akin to that of an official judicial determination of guilt. A meeting was held to hear charges *in absentia* against a village official. He would be condemned and notified of his sentence. He was then sought out and assassinated. The effect was to lessen any reliance on a central government and to demonstrate in dramatic form the power of the guerrillas to enforce their own sense of legitimacy on rural officials.

any measure, the country ranks near the top of any list of political assassinations. For the fifty-year period 1918–1968 information on assassinations and attempted assassinations reveals that the United States ranked thirteenth of the eighty-nine nations studied. In another study of the frequency of assassinations in the two decades (1948–1867) immediately following World War II, the United States ranked fifth among the eighty-four nations analyzed.[9]

9. For the period 1918–1968, the thirteen countries with a greater number of high-level assassination attempts (successful or unsuccessful) than the United States were: Mexico (51 attempts, 42 succeeded); France (40 attempts, 10 succeeded); China (21 attempts, 9 succeeded); Japan (21 attempts, 10 succeeded); Italy (18 attempts, 5 succeeded); Bulgaria (18 attempts, 10 succeeded); Egypt (17 attempts, 4 succeeded); Germany (17 attempts, 6 succeeded); Iraq (13 attempts, 10 succeeded); Cuba (12 attemps, 1 succeeded); Iran (11 attempts, 7 succeeded); Poland (10 attempts, 6 succeeded); and the United States (10 attempts, 5 succeeded).

For the period 1948–1967, the five countries with the greatest number of assassination events (successful attempts, unsuccessful attempts, and assassination plots) were: Cuba (28): Korea (20); Iran (19); Morocco (17); and the United States (16).

The data for the period 1918–1968 include only what are considered high-level assassination attempts: heads of state and heads of government or former holders of these positions; Cabinet ministers; ambassadors; vice-presidents; leading judges, bureaucrats, and legislators; and high military officers. Governors, local political officials, most United States Congressmen and Senators and prominent political figures not holding office would not be included in these listings.

The rankings for the period are based on these high level assassination attempts. When all recorded assassination attempts are calculated for the fifty year period, the United States is unfortunate enough to rank very close to the top of the list of the thirteen most assassination-prone nations of those identified above. The more comprehensive totals include, in addition to the high level assassination attempts, those directed at second and third level office holders and politically prominent private individuals. The figures for each of the thirteen countries for the period are as follows: Mexico, 104 attempts, 83 succeeded; France, 103 attempts, 55 succeeded; China, 44 attempts, 25 succeeded; Japan, 30 attempts, 15 succeeded; Italy, 41 attempts, 19 succeeded; Bulgaria, 58 attempts, 45 succeeded; Egypt, 22 attempts, 8 succeeded; Germany, 59 attempts, 35 succeeded; Iraq, 17 attempts, 14 succeeded; Cuba, 49 attempts, 20 succeeded; Poland, 37 attempts, 28 succeeded; and the United States, 88 attempts, 52 succeeded.

The data for the period 1948–1967 are inclusive and cover all assassinations directed at politically prominent figures.

The data for the period 1918–1968, collected by Professor Carl Leiden and his associates at the University of Texas, are reproduced in the Eisenhower Commission report, *Assassination and Political Violence*, pp. 243–267. The study by Professor Ivo Feierabend and his associates at San Diego State College, "Political Violence and Assassinations: A Cross-National Assessment," is the next selection in this volume. Both studies drew pri-

When the United States is compared with British Common-wealth countries with whom it shares a common ancestry, it does poorly. America's ten major attempts at assassination between 1918 and 1968 compare unfavorably with one for its neighbor to the north, Canada, five for the United Kingdom, one for Australia, and none for New Zealand.

The average number of high-ranking public figures assassinated in Europe by country was 6.4. Correspondingly, the figure for Asia was 5.8, for South America 6.1, for the Middle East 6.0, and for ten countries in Africa for which information was available, 1.9. The only democratic country with an established political tradition that consistently ranked as high as the United States was France.[10] The period 1918–1968 in Europe includes the painful aftermath of World War I, the economic decay and eventual collapse of the European economy during the twenties and early thirties, the failure of democratic governments to sustain themselves, most notably Germany, the political turbulence that preceded World War II, the war itself, and the postwar readjustment. Yet despite the forces at work on the Continent, these countries on the average had less incidence of assassination than the United States. Also, one country, France, accounted for more than twice the number of any other European country, including Germany, during the fifty-year period. If France is excluded from the total, the number of assassinations falls to virtually half that of the United States, averaging 5.1.[11]

---

marily on newspaper accounts. (The sources of data and their limitations are discussed in Feierabend below and would apply to both the Feierabend et al., and Leiden et al., repositories.) Both studies come closer to indicating the minimum number of assassination attempts, rather than being an exhaustive catalogue of the efforts.

10. The United States and France ranked atypically high in the number of assassination attempts they experienced for the twenty-year period 1948–1967 (United States 16; France 14). The European non-Communist nations averaged only .9 assassinations for the years 1948–1967 (Greece, Spain, and Portugal alone accounted for 60 per cent of these). The Communist nations of Europe also did considerably better when compared with the United States and France for these years averaging only one assassination per country.

11. For the period 1948–1967 there were 409 assassination events recorded, an average of 4.9 per country. For those two decades the regions ranked as follows: Middle East, 8.2 average; Latin America, 6.2 average; Asia, 6.0 average; and Europe, 1.6 average. Africa was excluded because of the highly limited number of countries for which information was available.

Ivo Feierabend and his associates,[12] in their comparative study of assassinations cross-nationally during the period 1948–1967, reveal a number of interesting relationships. They demonstrate, for example, an association between a high incidence of political assassination and socially disruptive and politically unstable nations. Assassinations were also related to less-developed nations and those in transitory economic situations, cases to which both France and the United States proved to be curious exceptions. There was a strong relationship between assassinations and politically violent acts more generally; in fact, the occurrence of specified types of politically violent occurrences represented one of the most consistent predictors of assassination. The link between violence—both violent acts directed against other nations and internally violent events of political significance—was clear cut.

Carl Leiden and associates, in reviewing assassinations over the entire fifty-year period, argue much the same relationship between political stress in a nation, as manifested in politically violent events, and a high level of assassinations. In noting that four periods accounted for 70 per cent of the assassinations that took place over the entire five decades, they point out that each was a time of unusual political turbulence. The years 1919–1923 represented the immediate post-World War I period; 1932–1934 encompassed the heart of the Great Depression; 1946–1951 witnessed the readjustment after World War II; and 1963–1966 highlighted the midpoint of a decade known for its political unrest. The authors draw attention to the fact that each of the periods was "characterized by turbulence, political systems in revolution, and, in general, political instability."[13] And, as indicated, each was characterized by excessively high numbers of political assassinations.

A Case Study of the Middle East

Assassination began as a systematic political weapon in the Middle East with the murder of one Nizam al-Mulk in 1092, and the area has continued to be associated with assassinations ever

12. The full study can be found below.
13. See Murray Clark Havens, Carl Leiden and Karl M. Schmitt, *The Politics of Assassination* (Englewood Cliffs, N.J.: 1970), Chapter II.

since. The average number of political assassination attempts per country in the region for the twenty years between 1948 and 1967 was a world high of 8.2, a figure that compares unfavorably with the overall single-country average of 4.9. A slightly extended review of the area's experience assists in isolating the factors commonly associated with high levels of assassination.

The area's record is unenviable. The list of those assassinated includes some of the region's most impressive and influential men of their times: the moderate King Abdullah of Jordan, father of King Hussein, in 1951; Iraq's King Faisal II, his uncle and the former regent Abdul Ilah Ilah, and General Nuri al-Said in a 1958 coup led by General Abdul Karim Kassem, who himself was assassinated in 1963. Egypt's premiers Butros Pasha (1910), Ahmed Maher Pasha (1945), and Nukrosky Pasha (1948) were all assassinated. To retaliate for the last murder, the government ordered the killing of Hasan al-Banna, leader of the zealot Muslim Brotherhood, in the streets of Cairo. King Farouk, after his dethronement in 1952, was almost murdered—a time-honored means of handling an opponent who falls from grace. Britain's representatives in Egypt, in particular Sir Lee Stack in 1924, have been the objects of assassins intent on promoting nationalism. The British exacted a fearful retribution for these murders. Yet despite these occurrences and twenty-two known assassination plots since 1918, Egypt represents one of the region's less assassination-prone countries.

The Jewish efforts to establish an independent state in Palestine led to uncounted numbers of murders of Arabs by Jews and Jews by Arabs and the British by both. The most notable were Britain's Lord Moyne in Cairo in 1944 and the United Nations' Count Folke Bernadotte in Jerusalem in 1948, allegedly both by members of a Jewish extremist organization.

Lebanon has experienced nineteen assassination attempts against leading political figures over the last fifty years, one of the most recent being the unsuccessful effort directed against Premier Camille Chamoun in the spring of 1968. Syria had a spate of assassinations in the late 1940's and early 1950's, and assassinations continue at the lower levels of government there. Iran has witnessed many high-level assassinations including those of Prime Ministers Ali Razmara in 1951 and Ali Hassan Mansour in 1965.

Few assassinations have been reported (two to be exact, one successful) in Saudi Arabia over the last five decades, although reliable information is even more difficult to obtain on this country than the others in a region noted for government censorship of the press and generally inadequate reporting.

The smaller countries on the Saudi Arabian peninsula have had extensive exposure to assassinations. The rulers of Yemen have repeatedly been targets for assassins, one of the last men to die in this manner being Ahmad in 1962. During the 1960's, overall, there were eight known assassination attempts, three of which resulted in deaths. Aden has seen more than its share of political violence in the 1960's, much of it directed against the British overseas forces—a provocative object for the area as a whole in the twentieth century. Aden counted nine assassination attempts in 1967; eight were successful. The South Arabian Federation, of British manufacture, was incapacitated and eventually dissolved under the threat of continued assassination of principal office-holders.

Turkey, Afghanistan, and Pakistan have had less experience with assassinations, although men in these countries, principally government leaders, have been felled—Bey Ali Chukri (1923) and Nevzat Tandogan (1946) in Turkey; Khan Habibullah (1919) and Shah Nadir (1933) in Afghanistan; and Liaquat Ali Kahn (1951) and Sahib Khan (1948) in Pakistan.

The traditions of the area appear more supportive of assassinations than elsewhere. As a political weapon, assassinations have been employed since the time of the early caliphs (three of the four successors to Muhammed were killed in this manner) and continue to be employed in domestic and international politics. The tradition is a curious one in many respects. Assassinations play a prominent part in internal politics, usually in the form of one elite group attempting to substitute its control for another's. Internationally, however, they also play a role. The ruler of one country will publicly call for the assassination of the chief of state of another. Nasser of Egypt, during periods of strained relationship, espoused the assassination of King Hussein of Jordan in public broadcasts directed to other nations. King Saud of Saudi Arabia has been accused of investing in the vicinity of two million dollars in attempts to murder Nasser. Assassinations become accepted weapons of foreign policy in such cases.

Another part of the tradition is equally strange. Participants are not reluctant to claim part in assassination plots. Nasser's memoirs reveal that as a junior army officer he took part in an assassination attempt, although he admits relief that it failed. Other leaders like to publicize the number of attempts made on their own lives, seemingly events that would discredit them with their followers. Yet the government-controlled Egyptian press reported at least two main attempts, 1954 and 1966, against Nasser. The years 1960–1968 alone witnessed sixteen attempts against the chief of state of these nations. One country, Yemen, reported, in addition to the three attempts against its ruler, four assassination plots directed against ranking political figures. The leader believed he fed the myth of his invulnerability by publicizing the number of unsuccessful attempts on his life. Iraq's Kassem, for example, made a point of drawing attention to the number of aborted attempts on his life up to the coup that did not fail.

Beyond a receptive tradition, the institutions of government are highly inadequate vehicles for handling social conflict. The theorizing on assassination in Western thought flourished in the period when men attempted to find alternative means of replacing absolute rulers. Assassination continues to be practiced in the Middle East, where no effective means of mobilizing dissent or organizing the opposition to gain control of the government has been devised. Governmental structures are highly centralized, culminating often in the rule of one man. Dissent is difficult if not impossible. Leadership is most often highly personalized, revolving around the whims and abilities of one person. The rule of law remains virtually unknown. The institutionalized forms and specified procedures necessary to restrain the use of power, to guide policy making and to enlarge its consensual base, and to channel alternative policies and personnel enjoy no currency. The alternative to one man in power is another, usually with much the same background and views. The way to place him in power is to assassinate the one holding office and to install your man. The less open the governmental hierarchy is, the more personal the centralization of power in the hands of one man, the greater the attention directed to him and the more endangered he is by assassination.

In addition to closed political systems, the Middle East has been and continues to be plagued by extensive turmoil conducive to spawning assassinations. The two world wars overlaid the continuing fight for control of the Palestinian areas that remains a bitter source of friction and bloodshed till this day. Underdeveloped economic systems refuse to support experiments with modified forms of democracy—even if the rulers were willing—schemes for more equitable shares in the economic output, better health conditions, and generally upgraded educational opportunities. Intense and primitive notions of nationalism, religious fanaticism, and the continuing instability and weakness of often erratic governments and one-industry economies have all done their part in providing the elements for a climate hospitable to assassinations.

The death by assassination of Jordan's Abdullah came at a sensitive time in that nation's attempt to evolve a strategy for living with the emerging Israeli nation. Quite conceivably, the King's death profoundly affected the course of future policy.

Such cases, however, are the exceptions. The more common occurrence is quite different. Assassinations ordinarily lead to the replacement of those in power; they seldom go beyond this to represent any fundamental changes in the course of a nation's policy or in the restructuring of its government.

As Leiden points out in his overview of the politics of the area, the assassination of a political leader is likely to result in serious change only under specified conditions,[14] namely:

1. When extreme centralization characterizes governing institutions

2. When a victim generates essentially personal support, held together by his own combination of specialized abilities, his

14. Treatments of assassinations in the Middle East can be found in Carl Leiden and Karl M. Schmitt, *The Politics of Violence* (Englewood Cliffs, N.J.: Prentice-Hall, 1968); Carl Leiden, "Assassination in the Middle East," in *Assassination and Political Violence,* pp. 545–552; and Bernard Lewis, *The Assassins* (New York: Basic Books, 1968). The Marvicks' chapter in this book deals with the long-run implications of political assassinations while the selection by Edelman and Simon traces the specific policy consequences of such acts at the presidential level in the United States. Assassination as a weapon of foreign policy also may not be unknown in the United States; witness the conflicting accounts concerning the role of the United States in overthrowing the Diem regime in South Viet Nam. See, for example, the reports by Betty Flynn, "LBJ Tried to Discredit JFK: Aide," *Chicago Daily News* (June 23, 1971), p. 1, Morton Kondracke and Thomas B. Ross, "More Viet Secrets: Anti-Diem Plotter Told U.S. Aides in Advance," *Chicago Sun-Times* (June 24, 1971), p. 1 and David Kraslow, "Diem's Last Pleas to Lodge," *Chicago Sun-Times* (June 24, 1971), p. 5.

charisma, and fear of his power, rather than any institutional forms or ideological beliefs

3. When the "replaceability" of the victim poses severe difficulties, when the mechanisms for developing leadership succession are inadequate, when the pool of potential substitutes is limited, or when a new ruler fails to command the allegiance of his predecessor

4. When an internal crisis confronts a governmental system caused by problems arising from an accelerated social or political change

5. When the death of a chief of state places the country in confrontation with other nations

These conditions would apply to any political system. The veneer of civilization and the light years that appear to separate the United States from its feudal sisters in the Middle East may not be as irrevocable as they appear. In dealing with political assassinations, the social factors that condition its use as well as those that serve to limit its effect have some obvious and other perhaps less apparent parallels in the American experience.

NONPRESIDENTIAL ASSASSINATIONS

Political assassinations below the level of president receive relatively little attention. Exceptions to the rule are possible: the murders of Huey Long and Martin Luther King invited wide attention, and both continue to be subjects of controversy. For the most part, however, public attention focuses on assassinations at the highest level of government. It is fair to say that the number of assassinations below the most visible position in public life are not known. Systematic studies at these levels are infrequent. Beyond this, the press has often reported political assassinations of local officials as simple murders resulting from personal causes or perpetrated by unknown people for reasons that are unclear. They have been treated as normal police matters devoid of political content and as a result have escaped the attention of researchers. Also, the difficulties in communication in early times and the lack of interest in local affairs shown by the national newspapers—the researchers' normal source for information on these acts—have tended to depress the number of lower-level political assassinations that come to public attention. Overall and including presidential attacks, eighty-one assassination attempts have been recorded. (See Table 1.)

In reviewing these cases, Professor Rita James Simon has been able to isolate several trends.[15] First, the higher the office—the

TABLE 1

Assassinations and Personal Attacks, by Office and Year

Office	Number of Cases	Year
President	9	1835, 1865, 1881, 1901, 1912, 1933, 1950, 1963, 1968*
Governor	8	1868, 1873, 1877, 1900, 1905, 1908, 1959, 1963
U.S. Senator	7	1856, 1859, 1873, 1917, 1921, 1935, 1947
U.S. Congressman	9	1868, 1870, 1890, 1924, 1954(five)
Mayor	10	1885, 1893(two), 1910, 1913, 1926, 1933, 1939, 1947, 1949
State Legislator	17	1867(three), 1868(two), 1869(two), 1870, 1874, 1875, 1881, 1892, 1896, 1936, 1945, 1947, 1958
Judge	11	1867(two), 1868(two), 1870(two), 1873, 1875, 1889(three)
Other	10	1865, 1867, 1868, 1871, 1873(three), 1875(two), 1935
(Cabinet (1)		
Tax Collector (2)		
Sheriff (1)		
Custom Inspector (1)		
Alderman (1)		
Territorial Secretary of State (1)		
Prosecuting Attorney (3))		

Source: "Deadly Attacks Upon Public Officeholders in the United States," J. F. Kirkham, S. Levy, and W. J. Crotty, *Assassination and Political Violence* (Washington, D.C.: U.S. Government Printing Office, 1969), pp. 9–47.

* Total includes Robert Kennedy, candidate for the Democratic Party's presidential nomination.

15. "Deadly Attacks upon Public Office Holders in the United States" in *Assassination and Political Violence*, pp. 9–47. The argument put forward by Rubenstein in his essay in this volume should be consulted in this context.

more centralized, focused, and personalized the power in one man—the greater the probability of attack. For example, nine assaults (six of them resulting in the death of the victim), including that on Robert Kennedy, who was a candidate for his party's presidential nomination and whose death resulted from the opportunity presented and the comments he made in the campaign, and Theodore Roosevelt, a former President seeking to return to office as the nominee of a third party, have been recorded against Presidents or presidential candidates. The number of people who have sought the presidency is not known. Thus, if we confine the argument to the thirty-five men who have held the office, four have died and two others, Truman and Jackson, survived attacks. Eight Governors, eight United States Senators (including Robert Kennedy), and nine United States Representatives have been objects of assassination attempts. Correspondingly, the number of individuals holding each office between 1790 and 1968 amounted to 1,330 (Governor), 1,140 (United States Senator), and 8,349 (United States Representative). The odds on an incumbent experiencing an attack then would be 6:1 for president, 167:1 for governor, 143:1 for senator, and 1,000:1 for congressman. The ratio of officeholders to attacks tells its own tale. Exact figures are not forthcoming for the total number of sheriffs, city councilmen, state legislators, district attorneys, and local judges, but the advantage appears to lie with the lower-level office: they are less likely to draw the attention of the prospective assassin.

The higher the office, the less personal the antagonism and the greater the likelihood that political reasons will be put forward to explain the assaults. It appears that the further removed the individual is from the officeholder, the more apt he is to channel his rationalizations for killing along strictly political lines. The office, not the man, assumes importance. The presidential assassins had no personal association with their intended victims and no grievance against them as individuals. On the local level, personal feelings play a far more significant role in motivating assaults.

A few cases can illustrate the nature of the personal interaction of some lower-level political assassinations. The *New York Times* of July 15, 1869, for example, reports the case of a Georgia Senator who, although verbally abused in front of his family, refused to be goaded into a gun fight. He was assassinated anyway in a plot involving a number of people. Although he identified his murderer before dying, civil authorities failed to take action. Another case in Washington, D.C., reported by the *New York Times* of October 13, 1873, is more complex. The case involved an attempt on the life of a former Senator by a distraught husband, who took offense to the gentleman's intercession in obtaining his wife a government job. The *Times*'s account describes the wound, the chipper nature of the intended victim (he survived easily), and the paper prophesies that the assailant "is destined to spend some time in a prison or a mad-house." The newspaper does mention in closing that an *affaire d'amour* had been rumored between the victim and the assailant's wife, a fact that might have had some bearing on the case. Other examples would include a South Carolina legislator's murder of an opponent and his brother in a fracas resulting from continuing incidents of mutual slander (1896) and a near shoot-out in a St. Louis court between an attorney and a judge, both armed, after a bitter argument over the testimony of "four women . . . with questionable characters" (1898). And then there was the case in Pensacola as reported in the *Washington National Intelligencer* of October 16, 1833: "A most horrid and cold blooded murder was committed on the body of the Mayor of this City on Saturday evening last, by a vagabond." The "vagabond" turned out to be a grog-shop operator whose unlicensed saloon was closed by order of the mayor. Such is the lot of the local official. It may be that he is accessible to the badly angered individual and that an attack thus can be overlaid with a variety of personal emotions. When assassinated, also, he receives comparatively little attention. The presidential attack, on the other hand, brings forth a different type of person, a more calculating and impersonal assailant, and he achieves extended public review.

Another pattern in the broad range of assassination attempts entails the heavy emphasis on elective officeholders to the virtual exclusion of appointive and administrative posts. This result may be a function of the inadequacy of the data and the limits imposed on the study. Assassination attempts at lower governmental levels, which would include appointees such as judicial officers, law-enforcement personnel, prosecuting attorneys, and tax-enforcement specialists, are underreported in the press. Also, the definition employed in setting the boundaries for the research exclude nonpublic officeholders such as Martin Luther King, Joseph Yablonski, and the victims of the civil rights disturbances, thus potentially overemphasizing the role of the elected public official.[16] Nonetheless, the pattern among the public officials examined remains clear: those not elected to their public trusts have greater immunity from assassination.

The cases reported in Table 1 merit a few additional comments. The one Cabinet official almost assassinated, William Seward, was a victim of the Booth plot to kill Lincoln and immobilize the Union. Similarly, Lee Harvey Oswald, charged with murdering John Kennedy, is held responsible for one of the gubernatorial attacks, that of John Connally. One of the mayors, Anton Cermak, also was killed mistakenly in the attack on Franklin Roosevelt. Puerto Rican fanatics, in addition to being responsible for one assault on the president, also accounted for five of the attacks on United States Congressmen. Three of the eight gubernatorial attacks resulted from disputes over the legality of election outcomes. One California judge, David Terry, was involved in three of the personal attacks recorded. Two occurred in a short stretch of time in 1889: one in which Terry attempted to murder a fellow judge and shortly after that when a marshal assigned to protect the judge, who among other grievances had decided an inheritance case against Terry's wife, killed Terry when he again assaulted his charge. Over thirty years earlier, the vigorous Justice Terry had killed another Californian, a Senator, in a duel resulting from campaign exchanges between the two. Election disputes figure prominently as explanations for a number of personal attacks on officeholders. Other common reasons put forward to explain the assassination attempts at lower levels include the bitterness over the slave question, the Civil War and Reconstruction; quarrels over editorials; women; money; gangsters; and the esoteric, e.g., anger over the extension of a city's limits.

The only known feud in the United States akin to the fratricide of the Middle East and resulting in a number of related political assassinations was the war between Democrats and Republicans in New Mexico. Only the peaks of the iceberg are visible, but it

16. Simon's definition reads as follows: "All reported deadly attacks upon public officeholders or aspirants to public office without regard for motive for the attack." *Ibid.,* pp. 9–10.

appears that leaders of both political parties employed assassination and encouraged others to do so. Murder became a political weapon to be directed against opponents, a practice that lasted for approximately thirty years, ceasing around the turn of the nineteenth century.[17]

PATTERNS IN THE PRESIDENTIAL ASSASSINATIONS

Many commonalities appear in the assassination attempts directed against presidents or presidential candidates. A convenient way of examining those factors that exist is to divide arbitrarily the assassination acts into similarities common to the intended victims and those associated with the assailants.

The Targets. One explanation for the assassinations, which has enjoyed some vogue, develops the assumption that certain types of politicians attract would-be assassins. The argument really breaks down into two subthemes, one stressing a psychological interpretation of a politician's approach to life and the other dealing with the nature of political demands and the officeholder's reaction to these.

Some contend that certain personalities entertain an implicit death wish. These individuals are attracted to high-risk occupations. While politics does not compare with auto racing, it does represent a precarious calling and does prove attractive to adventuresome types. "High-risk" politicians are characterized by a willingness to extend themselves—really overextend themselves—in seeking to advance their careers. They are willing to expose themselves to dangerous situations, subconsciously possibly even seek out such encounters, assumedly to satisfy internal psychological drives.[18]

Robert Kennedy purportedly represents a prime example of this thesis. The Senator's "death wish," or at least his willingness to

17. S. M. Lipset and C. Sheingold perceptively articulate the role of political parties in deflecting and channeling controversy, in effect acting to sublimate political violence and manage social conflict, in their "Values and Political Structures: An Interpretation of the Sources of Extremism and Violence in American Society" in this volume.

18. Dr. Thomas Greening, a psychologist, and Dr. David Rothstein, a psychiatrist, put forward this argument. See Greening's "The Psychological Study of Assassins" and Rothstein's "Presidential Assassination Syndrome: A Psychiatric Study of the Threat, the Deed, and the Message," both in this volume.

open himself to personal hurt, was evident in his private life in such treacherous pastimes as mountain climbing, precariously navigating waterways like the Amazon, and shooting the rapids of western rivers. He was known for his love of physically taxing sports. In public life, the same drive surfaced in the pushing to the limits of physical stamina, the incessant campaigning, the tumultuous motorcades, and the large and engulfing crowds regularly featured on the candidate's itinerary. This strain of argument contends that an individual places himself in situations that if not inviting attack permit the conditions that make it a possibility. Similar contentions were heard after John Kennedy's death. In retrospect, Theodore Roosevelt would fit this mold rather nicely also.[19]

The validity of such arguments defy casual assessment. They depend for verification upon an in-depth analysis by experts of the psychological mechanisms that motivate individual personalities. It is unlikely that explanations of this nature can serve to develop a general understanding of political behavior as it relates to violent personal attacks. Whether such an explanation applies to the Kennedys is a moot point. McKinley, Garfield, Franklin Roosevelt, and Truman do not appear to fit the theory.

At best, it is a discrete explanation sufficient for understanding individual cases. Yet the explanation directs attention away from broader and more important themes that focus on an interlocking network of circumstantial and situational factors that at least offer hope of remedy.

A second type of argument directs attention to the image and intentions of the victim rather than his psychological drives. This school of thought claims that the presidents most prone to physical attack are those who challenge the *status quo*. The movers, the doers in office, and those seeking election who associate themselves with change invite controversy and become targets for the frustrations of those inclined toward political murder.

This line of reasoning seems plausible and has appeal for under-

19. T. R. insisted on making his speech after being shot by Schrank. Carrying the bullet in his chest and bleeding profusely, he succeeded. Possibly Roosevelt's flamboyance represents an equivalent American case to the Middle Eastern fascination with invincibility.

standing an act that is virtually incomprehensible. It represents a popular approach to an implausible event.

Robert Kennedy, a leader of the "new politics," the champion of the Negro, Mexican-American, and the young could appear as just such an individual. John Kennedy may have seemed an innovator to his contemporaries. Franklin Roosevelt certainly introduced basic changes into American society. On the other extreme, Herbert Hoover and Dwight Eisenhower represented complacent, less innovative Presidents. They were not attacked.

The argument claims a superficial credibility. It does not hold up under examination, however. John Kennedy, while a personally glamorous figure, does not appear to have been a particularly rash or disruptive President by present assessments. Also, it appears that his reputed assassin, Oswald, attempted previously to kill retired General Edwin Walker, a hero of the Far Right. It is difficult to ascertain the link between Oswald's two targets, unless it lies within the killer rather than his victims.

Robert Kennedy was a product of the "old politics" more than the new, as was his brother. A more reasonable target, if this line of reasoning is extended to its logical end, was Eugene McCarthy. Senator McCarthy successfully mobilized and personified throughout the 1968 presidential-nomination campaign the politically charged elements of dissent within the United States. Further, Robert Kennedy's assassin, Sirhan, offered a different explanation for his attack. Senator Kennedy's support of Israel, a minor point in his prenomination campaign, was Sirhan's stimulus to attack. Beyond this, the love-hate relationship with the politician attributed to the murderer, offers another explanation of Sirhan's behavior, but again it is one that deals with the psychological working of the assassin and is difficult to relate to his victim.

Franklin Roosevelt was an unquestioned mover, a prime molder of the domestic economic system of modern America. His achievements were profound, far outlasting his stewardship. Certainly, he is the most powerful example to be offered in support of this line of contention.

Yet Zangara attacked Roosevelt after his election but prior to his inauguration, well in advance of any indications of the impact the President-elect would have on the country. The Democratic Party platform that Roosevelt had run on in the 1932 election was a conservative document, and Roosevelt's campaign oratory was not designed to alarm anyone.

Zangara was concerned with the office, not the man. He believed it—and other such positions—to be a symbol of oppression and disregard for the problems that beset the ordinary citizen. Zangara justified his action as a blow struck on behalf of the poor men of the world against capitalism. That Roosevelt, given his place in history and the contemporary groups that opposed him, should symbolize the rejection of the common man is anomalous.

Zangara was an immigrant. By his own admission, he desired to assassinate King Victor Emmanuel III before leaving Italy, for the same reasons he later employed to justify his attack on Roosevelt. He also intended to assassinate Presidents Coolidge and Hoover, hardly symbols of change. He never received the opportunity. The factor that distinguished Franklin Roosevelt as a target for assassination from either Hoover or Coolidge, or for that matter the King of Italy, was not his personality, his politics, or his potential impact on national politics, but the opportunity that he accidentally gave Zangara. Roosevelt happened to appear in Miami for a speech while Zangara was residing there. While not a chief-of-state at the time, he was the President-elect, which was good enough for his assailant.

Zangara made the point unmistakably clear at his own trial. When asked if he would have attacked President Hoover, he replied:

I see Mr. Hoover first I kill him first. Make no difference. President just the same bunch—all same. No make no difference who get that job. Run by big money. Makes no difference who he is.[20]

It is difficult to envisage Garfield or McKinley as significant threats to the *status quo*. The classification of Presidents Jackson and Truman and, at the time, presidential candidate Theodore Roosevelt, would depend on one's interpretation of their role in and contribution to the political development of the United States. Lincoln certainly must be regarded as a President who had a fundamental impact on his society. Overall, however, the evidence

20. Robert Donovan, *The Assassins* (New York: Popular Library, 1964), p. 145. Donovan's book is a good introduction to the presidential assassination attempts.

for this particular line of reasoning is not persuasive. The argument has an intrinsic popular appeal, but it is not substantiated by what is known concerning the assassinations.

THE ASSASSINS

Discernible patterns do emerge when the focus shifts from the victims to their assailants. First, and of greatest importance, only two of the nine attempts on the lives of Presidents or presidential candidates (see Table 2), can be considered the work of a conspiracy. And of these two, the Booth plot was a pickup conspiracy involving friends and acquaintances of his, and the attempt on Truman was little more. The attack against Lincoln was not known or supported by the Southern Confederacy, which it was intended to help, and only conjectural evidence can be cited to implicate Secretary of War Stanton, directly or indirectly, in any *coup d'état.*

The attempt by Oscar Collazo and Griselio Torresola to storm Blair House, the temporary residence of the President, and attack Harry Truman was a conspiracy, but a poorly conceived and ineptly executed one. The potential executioners were members of a Puerto Rican liberationist group centered in New York. They traveled to Washington with the intention of murdering the President as a symbolic propaganda act designed to draw attention to Puerto Rico's subjective status. The scheme was born of blind fanaticism. Truman had done more than any of his predecessors in recognizing the island's difficulties and in attempting to stabilize its political and economic conditions. Nonetheless, he was the intended victim by virtue of the office he held. What tangible public benefit could be expected to accrue from the attack is difficult to conceive. The attempt was not designed to gain control of the government, quite obviously, or to give an opposition leader or party political advantage, classic objectives in traditional assassination conspiracies.

The conspirators themselves had only the most freewheeling plans for gaining access to the President and engaged in the sketchiest preparatory planning. The effort resulted in a wild gun battle leading to the death of one Secret Service agent and Torresola, the wounding of two other agents and Collazo, and the eventual imprisonment of the latter for life.

TABLE 2

Information on Presidential Assassinations and Assaults

Assailant	Target	Date of Attack	Outcome	Activity of Victim at Time of Attack	Assailant's AGE	Assailant's OCCUPATION	Assailant's WEAPON	Assailant's PLACE OF BIRTH
ASSASSINATIONS:								
John Wilkes Booth	President Abraham Lincoln	4/14/1865	Lincoln's death 4/15/1865	Attending *Our American Cousin* at Ford's Theatre, Washington, D.C.	26	Actor	Pistol	U.S. (first generation born in U.S.)
Charles Julius Guiteau	President James Garfield	7/2/1881	Garfield's death 9/19/1881	Waiting to board train for vacation trip, Washington, D.C.	38	Lawyer, Lecturer, Evangelist	Pistol	U.S.
Leon F. Czolgosz	President William McKinley	9/6/1901	McKinley's death 9/14/1901	Standing in receiving line, Pan-American Exposition, Buffalo, N.Y.	28	Mill Worker	Pistol	U.S. (first generation born in U.S.)
Lee Harvey Oswald	President John F. Kennedy	11/22/1963	Kennedy's death 11/22/1963	Motorcade through Dallas, Texas	24	Worker in book depository	Rifle	U.S.

TABLE 2 (continued)

| Assailant | Target | Date of Attack | Outcome | Activity of Victim at Time of Attack | Assailant's | | | |
					AGE	OCCUPATION	WEAPON	PLACE OF BIRTH
ASSAULTS:								
Richard Lawrence	President Andrew Jackson	1/30/1835	Pistols misfired, Jackson unhurt	Leading funeral procession for deceased Congressman, Washington, D.C.	36	House Painter	Pistols	England
John Schrank	Presidential Candidate Theodore Roosevelt	10/14/1912	Roosevelt wounded, but survived	Leaving hotel to make campaign speech, Milwaukee, Wisc.	36	Bartender, Landlord	Pistol	Bavaria
Guiseppe Zangara	President-Elect Franklin Roosevelt	2/15/1933	Missed Roosevelt, killed Mayor Anton Cermak of Chicago standing near	Speaking at political rally, Miami, Fla.	32	Construction Worker	Pistol	Italy

Name	Target	Date	Result	Situation	Age	Occupation	Weapon	Nationality
Oscar Collazo and Griselio Torresola	President Harry S Truman	10/31/1950	President unhurt; 1 Secret Service agent killed, 2 wounded; Torresola killed; Collazo wounded	Assassins stormed Blair House, temporary residence of President, Washington, D.C.	25	Polisher None	Pistols	Puerto Rico
Sirhan Bishara Sirhan	Senator Robert Kennedy, candidate for Democratic presidential nomination	6/5/1968	Kennedy's death 6/5/1968	Returning from talk claiming victory in Calif. Democratic primary, Los Angeles, Calif.	24	Stableboy, Clerk	Pistol	Jordan

People find it difficult to understand how one lone, demented gunman can bring down the most powerful leader on earth. A pressing necessity exists to explain the murder in broader and more acceptable terms. Rather than a quirk happening, the act is reconstructed as part of a well-conceived plan with important ramifications. Thus Oswald was a Communist agent, a representative of a right-wing hate group, or the tool of the CIA. His confused background could be interpreted to lend support to each of these possibilities. Lawrence was the gunman of a Whig conspiracy designed to intimidate Jackson. Booth and his accomplices were agents of the South. Guiteau represented the Republican Party faction, the Stalwarts, that opposed Garfield. Czolgosz reportedly executed the wishes of the Anarchists, a group that paid dearly for this assumption. And Zangara carried out the orders of mobsters; one rumor had it that his intended victim was Cermak, whom he killed, and not Franklin Roosevelt.[21]

An element of psychological reassurance resides in attempts to attribute assassinations to conspiracies. However, these speculations are fed by more than the individual's desire to relieve his mental anguish. The nature of the American presidency has grown in the mythology of the times far out of proportion to the presumed abilities of one man to fill it. The president assumes the attributes of a god, a king, a political leader without equal, the super-American in every respect. By contrast, the British take the opposite approach. They divorce the traditional and symbolic roles from the seat of actual political power. Furthermore, they discourage interpretations of the prime minister as the sole mover of events. He ranks as the "first among equals." A collective, as against a highly personalized, responsibility for governmental decisions prevails. The continuing accountability of the prime minister to the cabinet and both to their political parties and the parliament

21. Schrank was not associated with fringe groups or conspiracies. His "visionary" explanation and his reliance on the "third-term" tradition to explain his attack may have proven too much for all concerned. His victim did not die, Schrank was immediately apprehended, and he was adjudged insane, all of which served to deflate wild speculation. The manner in which such speculations are fed into on-going controversies over policy objectives is adeptly traced by Edelman and Simon in their chapter below. Specific reactions by different groups to the most recent assassinations are analyzed by Patterson, Clarke and Soule, and McEvoy in their contributions to this volume.

and through these agencies to the voters receives constant re-emphasis. The office and the man who occupies it are low-keyed, professional, and businesslike. The position is one of low visibility, at least by contrast with its American counterpart. The presidency has been "humanized" through a media incredibly intrusive into every aspect of the occupant's life. The president begins to assume dimensions other than human.

The protective paraphernalia that surrounds the president enforces an image of invincibility. All are familiar with the much-publicized Secret Service and their role in providing for the safety of the president and his family. Television constantly exposes even the casual viewer to the presidential guardians in the supposedly unobtrusive execution of their duties. The president's car with its various gimmicks, including the famed, and as it later turns out, non-bullet-proofed "bubble-top" is well publicized, an object of curiosity every time he appears in a motorcade. Certainly with such an office, such a man, and such protection, one sick gunman could not be the total explanation for the assassination.

As with most erroneous beliefs that large numbers of people persist in subscribing to, there must be some credibility attached to them, some reason for believing. The ineptitude surrounding the immediate events following President Kennedy's assassination[22] and the history of occurrences since then lends support to a wide range of conspiratorial theories. The events developing out of the assassination were poorly handled. Without straining, a variety of questions can be put forward for which no satisfactory answers exist. Why did not a Secret Service man drive the route immediately preceding the presidential motorcade seeking trouble spots? Why did not any of the spectators who saw Oswald with a rifle in the window awaiting the presidential party mention it to the police officers standing with them? Why did the President's car slow down after the first shot rather than speeding away? Why was the hospital not prepared to receive the mortally wounded President? Why weren't contingency plans immediately available for implementation? Why was the Texas School Book Depository not sealed off, if not immediately, then as soon as the police had an indication

22. The portions of the Warren Commission report dealing with the Secret Service deserve study. *The Warren Commission Report on the Assassination of John F. Kennedy* (New York: Popular Library, 1964), pp. 571–615.

the shot had come from there? Why was a record not kept of Oswald's interrogation (in which the Secret Service, the FBI, the Texas Rangers, the county prosecutor's office and the Dallas police all participated)? Why was Oswald not allowed legal counsel? Why was Oswald not given over to the Dallas sheriff's office immediately after he was remanded to their custody in the hearing before the judge? Why were both of Oswald's preliminary hearings, one for Officer Trippett and the second for John Kennedy, held *in camera?* How could a civilian, known to the police, kill Oswald while he remained in police custody? Etc., etc.

The later reluctance of the government to make available the full autopsy reports and the delicacy with which some witnesses were treated by the Warren Commission, while others were never requested to appear, reveal a laudable but misplaced sympathy for the sensibilities of the individuals involved. A chief intention of the Warren Commission was to restore a sense of legitimacy and trust to the government. This concern also had to influence their deliberations. Placing the burden of the investigation into the assassination on the FBI, an agency facing judgment about its own responsibilities in the sequence of events leading to the murder, invites distrust. The price paid for all this was high, a series of reflections made on the credibility of the official explanation put forward. Such reports are always suspect. Those who frame them should extend themselves to insure skeptics no basis for argument that can be avoided. The procedures employed and the evidence collected should be characterized by the greatest objectivity. The one objective should be the most comprehensive and accurate report of the events as they occurred.

Within such a vortex of contrasting influences—the psychological need for reassurance, the overpublicized and personalized nature of the office, the invincible security arrangements and the official bungling in the handling of the murder and its ramifications—the desire to believe in a conspiracy appears not so erratic a response.

The assassins enjoyed several other things in common besides being nonconspirators. Most were fringe members of society. Virtually all were mentally unstable.[23] Few had succeeded in any

23. The psychological state of the assassins is assessed and the relevant literature summarized in the Freedman, Rothstein, and Greening analyses in this volume.

walk of life. Oswald, Sirhan, and Torresola had no professions; Czolgosz, a factory worker, quit his job three years prior to McKinley's assassination and did not work regularly after that; Guiteau was an itinerant lawyer and lecturer of no great renown; Schrank, a bartender and tenement landlord, spent the bulk of his time reading, scribbling notes, and wandering around Manhattan in the years preceding his attack on Theodore Roosevelt; John Wilkes Booth was a noted actor, not of the caliber of his father or brothers, but with declining opportunities to work and in jeopardy of having to give up his career altogether because of a throat ailment; Zangara was a bricklayer and contractor, although he held no job for any length of time in the two years preceding his attack on FDR; Lawrence, a house painter, worked infrequently in the two years leading up to his attempted murder of Jackson; and Collazo, the exception, held a variety of jobs but was employed steadily preceding his trip to Washington.

Collazo was an exception in other respects. He had a wife and a settled family life. The others had difficulty in establishing and maintaining mature emotional relationships. Collazo was proficient at his job and respected in his community, a type of recognition that eluded the others, except Booth. Collazo's fanaticism, and again the parallel to Booth is appropriate, placed a cause above life. Excepting Collazo, the others gave demonstrable evidence of emotional instability in the years immediately prior to their assassination attempts. Oswald, for example, was institutionalized while in his teens for three weeks of psychiatric observation because of his chronic truancy. The report by the eminent psychiatrist, Renatus Hartogs, reads in part: "Lee has to be diagnosed as [having a] 'personality pattern disturbance with schizoid features and passive-aggressive tendencies.' Lee has to be seen as an emotionally, quite disturbed youngster who suffers under the impact of really existing emotional isolation and deprivation, lack of affection, absence of family life and rejection by a self involved and conflicted mother."[24]

Unfortunately, Marguerite Oswald removed Lee from the New York City schools before any therapy could result. Obvious parallels exist between the assessment of Oswald's family relationships

24. *Warren Commission Report,* p. 510.

as a youth and the similarly stark emotional experiences of the other assassins.

Even with today's inadequate mental facilities it is unlikely that individuals as poorly adjusted to life as Guiteau, Czolgosz, Lawrence, Zangara, Sirhan, Oswald, and Schrank, in particular, could escape being isolated as disturbed in psychological tests administered in school, the military, or a part of work-placement programs. Still, even if judged in need of psychiatric help, the effectiveness of the treatment that might follow such a diagnosis remains moot. The effort needed to compensate in later life for the depressing emotional deprivations of the earlier years would be enormous.

Other common strains also distinguish the assassins. Most were either new to the United States or born of parents who had immigrated, thus placing them in the twilight area of reconciling the pressure caused by different life styles and conflicting values. Each of the assailants, with the exceptions of Collazo and Booth, were essentially loners, and this approach carried over into the planning and execution of their act. Each was relatively young at the time of the attack, in his twenties or thirties. Most were not superior shots or avid gun enthusiasts but found weapons easy to acquire and minimal training sufficient for the job. All except Oswald employed pistols in their attacks, depending on opportunities to come physically close to their victims, which they received.

The irrationality of their motivations would also have to rank as a factor shared by the assailants. The curious logic underlying the Puerto Ricans' attack on Truman has been commented on.

Other assassins were not shy about claiming credit for their acts. Guiteau, fearing that he might be killed by angry citizens after his assault on Garfield, left a package of materials to explain his act. Included was a note stating that Garfield's removal was "an act of God." His death would "save the Republic, and . . . create a demand for my book, The Truth." Evangelism combined with the need to spare the country the Republican Party's factionalism were the wellsprings of his act.

Lawrence appears to have been totally irrational. He had threatened assassination before. He saw himself as a king, believed the United States was subtly persecuting him, as he felt it had his father before him, and that the country owed him large amounts of money. Hence he wrought his retribution.

Czolgosz felt McKinley "was the enemy of the good people— the good working people" and reported feeling no sorrow for his crime. Schrank coupled Theodore Roosevelt's try for a third term (actually Roosevelt served the major part of McKinley's second term after his death and was elected to only one full term on his own) with McKinley's ghost in a bizarre explanation. According to Schrank, "God . . . called me to be his instrument." Apparently the deceased McKinley did also, appearing before him in a dream and declaring, "This is my murderer [pointing at an apparition of Roosevelt], avenge my death." And finally, Schrank argued that "every third termer [must] be regarded as a traitor to the American cause . . . it [is] . . . the right and duty of every citizen to forcibly remove a third termer."

Zangara wanted to strike a blow on behalf of the worker and to ease a pain in his abdomen (for which no physical explanation could be found in his autopsy), caused, he felt, by the capitalists. In his words: ". . . I have trouble with my stomach and that way, I make my idea to kill the President [President-elect Franklin Roosevelt]—kill any President, any king."

Booth wished to gain immortality, to be remembered as the man who toppled the colossus. Vaguely, he intended his plan to aid the South also.

Two strains run through the Warren Commission assessment of Oswald's motive. One is that Oswald needed to overcome feelings of impotency, to assume the heroic proportions he fantasized for himself. The second is that he, like Booth, craved historical notoriety.

One thing is also clear: the assassins struck at the office, not the man. They had no personal relationships with their victims, no animosity directed against them as individuals, and frequently even no knowledge of their personalities or actions when in office.[25] Zangara typified the majority when he stated his lack of concern over assassinating Coolidge or Hoover rather than Roosevelt, or for that matter, the King of Italy.

Most of the assailants felt they acted under divine inspiration. And although post facto diagnosis has its risks, most would have to be classified as patently unbalanced.

25. If there is an exception, it would be Booth who severely disliked Lincoln, apparently because of what he saw him doing to the South.

The presidential assailants share similar fates also. If they failed in their attacks on the presidents, they were dealt with humanely. Collazo, Schrank, Lawrence, and Zangara in his first trial, which took place prior to Cermak's death, were institutionalized for life.

If the assassins succeeded, however, vengeance became the dominant public mood. Neither the courts specifically nor the legal safeguards provided by the society as a whole has stood up well under the attack. Neither Oswald nor Booth came to trial. Both were killed. Oswald died within forty-eight hours of John Kennedy. Booth succumbed in a fiery barn within twelve days of Lincoln's death, killed either by his own hand or the bullet of a Union soldier. Four of Booth's co-conspirators were tried and hanged, at least one on questionable evidence. Four others were imprisoned on the Florida Keys, one dying from disease before and one shortly after all were pardoned by Andrew Johnson in 1869. The lot included the boy who held Booth's horse outside Ford's Theatre.

Zangara's second trial took place three days after Cermak's death. Within twenty-four hours he was judged guilty, and thirty-three days after his attack he was electrocuted. Czolgosz was tried four days after McKinley's death. His trial lasted eight and one-half hours over a two-day period. The jury took thirty-four minutes to deliver the verdict, and Czolgosz was electrocuted forty days after McKinley's death. Sulfuric acid was poured into the coffin, apparently a custom of the time. Guiteau's trial—the exception—was a circus that lasted almost three months, although the results ultimately were the same.

Lawrence's treatment, the first trial in the series, represents a noteworthy gauge against which to assess the others. Lawrence pleaded insanity. The prosecutor, Francis Scott Key, in his introductory remarks drew attention to a British precedent in a related case. Scott dismissed the prevailing criteria about an individual's capacity to judge right from wrong and thus to remain legally responsible for his crime. The prosecutor argued that a defendant who acted on the basis of a delusion, and where the crime was a direct result of the delusion, should be judged insane and treated accordingly. The defense's responsibility was to prove the defendant suffered delusions that led to the attack against Jackson, which they did with ease. Lawrence was imprisoned for life and died in a mental institution.

The atmosphere surrounding Lawrence's trial remained as tense as that of Czolgosz, Guiteau, or Zangara. The conduct and outcomes of the trials, however, were quite dissimilar. Neither Czolgosz nor Zangara pleaded insanity. None of the three sets of defense lawyers argued the precedent put forth in the Lawrence trial. Czolgosz did not have legal representatives until two days before his trial. They put forward no defense witnesses on his behalf. The most eminent medical authorities concluded that Czolgosz "unqualifiedly" was sane, and the court assumed this was the case unless proven otherwise. The contention was not challenged. A thorough reanalysis of his life, begun a year after his death by two highly competent psychiatrists, came to a quite different conclusion.

A board of two court-appointed psychiatrists examined Zangara but made no determination as to sanity. No psychiatric witnesses were called to testify on his behalf, and his sanity was assumed, although one of the psychiatrists who examined him declared to author Robert Donovan twenty years later that "medically, he was not sane."[26]

Guiteau did plead insanity. He had a determined if unspectacular set of lawyers, and testimony by experts was presented to the effect that he was insane. His outbursts and consistently unpredictable behavior during the trial should have been sufficient to convince disbelievers of his illness. The court persisted in crediting him with being sane, partly because Guiteau wanted to be judged mentally incapable and threatened God's personal intervention on the court if any other verdict was delivered. The public demanded blood. The court convicted Guiteau, and an appeal to the Supreme Court was rejected. President Arthur refused clemency and, to the satisfaction of a large crowd of onlookers, Guiteau was hanged.[27]

One last similarity in the assassination attempts deserves mention. Collazo and Torresola chose to attack Truman while he resided in Blair House, across Pennsylvania Avenue from the White House, then undergoing renovation. The other assailants found their victims most vulnerable while on some form of cam-

26. Donovan, *The Assassins,* p. 152. The differing evalutions in Part II of this book are again relevant in this context.

27. Charles E. Rosenberg's *The Trial of the Assassin Guiteau* (Chicago: University of Chicago Press, 1968) presents a provocative analysis of the trial and its implications.

paign trip to show themselves to voters and to rally support (John and Robert Kennedy, Franklin and Theodore Roosevelt and, depending on your interpretation of ceremonial functions, McKinley). Lincoln and Garfield were taking breaks from their official routines, and Jackson was leading the mourners for a deceased congressman.

The difficulties of adequately protecting the president outside the White House are considerable. Campaign tours, in particular, compound the problems, exposing the candidate to a variety of uncontrollable situations and placing him at the whim of assailants. The need to be discreet in planning the number and nature of such outings would seem apparent. Conversely, it is important for a president to travel and to be personally exposed to local political figures and their views, to regional media, and to the everyday problems that confront most Americans. This is one beneficial means of breaking through the insulation that characterizes the White House. Still, a skillful communication of presidential views to the public through extended use of television would prove infinitely preferable to the raucous campaign rallies, consisting mostly of the faithful, and the highly dangerous political motorcades and parades that have persisted since the time of William Henry Harrison. These could be reduced and possibly even eliminated without constricting the movement of the president across the country or his continuing education to the needs of the people.

THE AMERICAN CULTURE OF VIOLENCE

A five-factor sequence of events can illustrate the interrelationships between social conditions and high levels of violence and political assassination in a culture (Figure 1). These include the traditions of the nation involved, a constant exhortation to violence, examples in the country's past or in its contemporary society of group ends sought through violent means, historical experience with assassinations, and some type of reaction that results in consequences that serve to reinforce or deflect assassinations.

Tradition. America has a violent background. The point need not be belabored except for the fact that recognition of this strain in American history has been repressed. If not admitted, then it

FIGURE 1

A Heuristic Interrelationship of Cultural Violence and Political Assassination

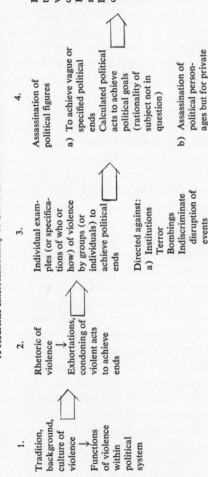

1.

Tradition, background, culture of violence
→
Functions of violence within political system

2.

Rhetoric of violence
→
Exhortations, condoning of violent acts to achieve ends

3.

Individual examples (or specifications of who or how) of violence by groups (or individuals) to achieve political ends

Directed against:

a) Institutions
   Terror
   Bombings
   Indiscriminate disruption of events

b) Specific individuals

4.

Assassination of political figures

a) To achieve vague or specified political ends
   Calculated political acts to achieve political goals (rationality of subject not in question)

b) Assassination of political personages but for private reasons: lovers' quarrel, family argument, etc.

5.

Impact of assassinations (and political violence) on political system
Readjustment mechanisms
Long- and Short-run consequences:
Social Change
Policy re-distributions
Institutional modifications

need not be dealt with. The horrible consequences can be blocked out, except for the few painful moments when the reality of the situation intrudes into daily life, most dramatically with the assassination of a Martin Luther King or a Robert Kennedy, the bombing of a Negro church or a university mathematics building, the sniper death of a police officer, or the state police or National Guard slaying of college students. At that point, politicians arise to denounce the trend away from "law and order" and the permissiveness of modern society. They call for a return to the old traditions. If public vengeance is possible, it is obtained through the courts, and after a proper interval the incident is forgotten.

Unfortunately, the ways of the past include a high level of disruption. Violence is part of the American heritage, and worse, a major part. The dominant ideologies in the United States do not emphasize a sophisticated appreciation of procedural necessities or the collective needs of a highly interdependent society. Boldness, individuality, responsibility to self, action, material success come closer to representing the ideals with which Americans are inculcated. In large part, these have evolved from the conditions facing the nation during its formative years, in settling vast stretches of geographical wilderness, and in evolving the industrial giant that rules the twentieth century. Calvinism, Lockean philosophy, Jeffersonian idealism, and even such later movements as Populism, the Progressives, and Western radicalism have constantly reemphasized the need for work, self-advancement, personal responsibility, and individualism. The industrial philosophy of *laissez faire,* pre-eminent in social, economic, and legal thought from the 1860's to the 1930's, condoned a ruthless economic war of all against all with the survivors reaping the gains.

The western hero has fed into the tradition and has proven to be an amalgam of most qualities Americans admire. Highly independent, self-contained, righteous, and administering an austere justice of personal vengeance, he has emerged from the fog of history to saturate the folklore and especially its modern conduits, television and motion pictures. Yet, as Professor Joe B. Franz has pointed out, the cowboy represented a curiously asocial and unloved figure in the Old West.[28] Wild Bill Hickok, Frank and

28. Joe B. Franz, "The Frontier Tradition: An Invitation to Violence," in H. D. Graham and T. R. Gurr, eds., *Violence in America: Historical and Comparative Perspectives* (New York: Bantam Books, 1969), pp. 127–154.

Jesse James, Ben Thompson, and John Wesley Hardin come down to the present day as very bloody heroes. More important, the values they espoused have limited applicability to the demands of a highly complex, socially and economically integrated society of today. As Franz illustrates, the subtleties of the law found no home in the West. "The frontier placed a premium on independent action and independent reliance. The whole history of the American frontier is a narrative of taking what there was to be taken. . . . [A] Decision was made on the spot, face to face. The questions were simple; the solutions equally simple."[29]

The assumptions underlying the heroes of American folklore and the traditions still employed to justify individual actions need explanation in light of twentieth-century demands on the individual and the society. The violence that permeates the history of the United States—the endless vigilante movements, the bloody Indian repressions, the immigrant battles to survive the ghetto, the labor violence, the crime and homicide rates, the urban uprisings, the summary police violence, the racial conflicts, and the engagement in war every generation—has bred a climate hospitable to violent acts, yet one that has ignored its past.

To begin to deal with the problem it is necessary to recognize its dimensions. Self-awareness has to be in the first step in any therapy.[30]

Contemporary society manifests a high level of concern with violence. People are aware of it in their own lives. Most have experienced violence in some form: service in the military, corporal parental disciplining (93 per cent in a nationwide survey), fist fights during their youth (55 per cent), or even being the object of a personal assault with a knife (14 per cent) or a gun (12 per cent). How relevant such personal exposure is remains difficult to say, given the lack of comparable data for other nations. Still, one in nine in the population claiming to be the object of an assault with a gun seems alarmingly high.

Nonetheless, despite a history of violence and a personal aware-

29. *Ibid.*, pp. 128–129. Lipset and Sheingold in their chapter in this volume contrast the American tradition as it relates to western conventions and the procedural regularities of the law to those of Canada, a country with much the same type of frontier but a quite dissimilar experience.

30. Surveys of America's violent past are available in Richard Maxwell Brown, "Historical Patterns of Violence in America," in Graham and Gurr, *Violence in America*, pp. 45–84, and in the entire volume more generally.

ness, the vast majority of Americans would *not* resort to violent activity, almost regardless of the provocation. In a nationwide Harris poll, respondents were asked the type of political activity in which they had engaged.[31] Conventional forms of political communication were the dominant conduits for views. Ninety-seven per cent of the respondents discussed political issues with friends; over one-half (53 per cent) had signed a political petition; and one-third or less had written a letter to a newspaper or to an elected official (32 per cent), contributed funds to a politically relevant group (32 per cent), or expressed a personal opinion directly to a political figure (27 per cent). Only 8 per cent had organized a group or participated in a political demonstration—more demanding forms of personal involvement. While the figures do not indicate an overwhelming concern with political participation, they do suggest a relative satisfaction with the established means for influencing government. In contrast, only a meager 3 per cent had ever participated in an "illegal" demonstration, and less than one-half of 1 per cent were associated with a riot.

To further test Americans' tolerance for violence and willingness to resort to violence, the survey posed four hypothetical situations: one in which discriminatory taxes were enacted by the Congress; the second in which criticism of the government (free speech) was outlawed; the third in which innocent Negroes in a community were imprisoned; and the fourth in which the government shot innocent people, including members of the respondent's family, in order to maintain its authority. Each respondent was asked if he approved of the action and how he would respond to it.

From two-thirds to almost nine out of ten voiced strong disapproval of the government's actions. The greatest disagreement was evidenced in the summary actions to maintain government control (87 per cent strongly disapproved), although more people vehemently objected to the discriminatory taxation than they did to the limits placed on free speech or the arbitrary arrests.

31. All the results of the nationwide surveys are taken from the report by Louis Harris and Associates, *The American Public Looks at Violence* (New York: A Poll Prepared for the National Commission on the Causes and Prevention of Violence, November, 1968). An analysis of these data appears in James McEvoy, III, "Political Vengeance and Political Attitudes: A Study of Americans' Support for Political and Social Violence," in this volume.

TABLE 3

Reactions of Individuals
to Four Hypothetical Political Situations

	REACTION OF INDIVIDUAL			
			Could Personally	
	Strongly Disapprove	*Physical Attack*	*Engage in Physical*	*(Percentage of Total*
Action	*of Action*	*Justified*	*Attack**	*Population)***
Tax Change	74%	3%	43%	1%
Free Speech	68%	9%	71%	6%
Negro Arrest	65%	9%	59%	5%
Innocents Shot	87%	48%	86%	41%
Speech by Senator	—	1%	14%	0.3%

Source: Louis Harris and Associates, *The American Public Looks at Violence*
(New York: A Poll Prepared for the National Commission on the Causes
and Prevention of Violence, November, 1968).

* Percentage is from total who would condone act.
** This column represents the total percentage of the population of those who
both condone act and are likely to engage in it.

When asked if physical assault or some type of armed action
was justified in any of the cases, 3 per cent said yes in reaction to
taxes, 9 per cent responded favorably in opposing abridgement of
speech or arrests of blacks, and one-half (48 per cent) would
oppose through personally violent acts the shooting of civilians.
This line of questioning was carried one step farther and the
respondents were asked if they personally would be likely to
engage in some form of personal violence. Forty-one per cent said
they would if the government executed large numbers of the
population, 5 per cent if blacks were arrested, 6 per cent if speech
were curtailed, and only 1 per cent if arbitrary taxes were imposed.

One other aspect of willingness to resort to violence was examined in the survey. Respondents were asked what they would do if
a senator who had blocked legislation "essential to protect the
rights of every citizen" appeared to give a speech in their community. One in twenty would resort to some physical measure to
indicate their disapproval: throwing objects such as rotten to-
matoes at the senator (5 per cent); throwing harder objects such

as bottles at the speaker (2 per cent); taking a gun or other weapon and personally attacking the man (1 per cent).

Individual temperament might color the interpretation of these poll results. Most Americans are satisfied with standard procedural outlets for registering discontent and would respond with violence only under the most extreme provocations. These findings are reassuring. Conversely, on the most extreme end of the pendulum, 1 per cent of the population, roughly 500,000 people, believe personal assaults directed against a public officeholder are justifiable. This number of potentially violent people introduces a level of stress into a society that would be extremely difficult to neutralize. If the stimulus to violence were there—the use of violent symbols within a political context—then the chemistry is appropriate for an emotionally unstable individual, or one who believes he is acting in the name of God, the best interests of his country, or the advancement of a group to which he believes himself attached, to act.

Unfortunately, the needed justifications are often available for anyone willing to do the least amount of homework. Perhaps unfairly, Dallas can serve as an example. It is a city where the western traditions of violence have been enshrined. For many, manliness and a gun are synonymous. A man is not held accountable for murdering another who alienates the affections of his wife. Weapons are easily available. The rhetoric of violence rages unfettered. Assassination jokes reportedly were the topic of the day in some cocktail circuits preceding John Kennedy's visit. The Dallas morning newspaper printed an advertisement on the day of the President's visit proclaiming that the chief executive was "wanted for treason." The bill of particulars made against him included a right-wing litany of favoritism to Communists, anti-Christian tendencies, and unrestrained lying to the American people (including his version of his alleged secret marriage and divorce). As volatile and disreputable as such charges are, they gain respectability when printed in a legitimate newspaper. Anyone needing a justification for his actions, no matter how extreme they might be, can find it in just such unbridled rhetoric.[32]

32. The Warren Commission report states that: "The Commission has found no evidence that the extreme views expressed toward President Kennedy by some right-wing groups centered in Dallas or any other general

Dallas is an unhappy example of unrestrained vilification, but not the only one. A reading of the pamphlets of the fringe groups of the left or right reveals an alarming fascination with the symbols of violence. Such rhetoric sets a climate hospitable to violence. In many cases, it goes beyond even this stage, providing a justification for the act, pinpointing a target, and advising about the weapons best suited to the attack. A few examples can illustrate the tenor of these materials. One theme permeates it all, the need for violent actions. On this score, the call to violence, the polar left and the polar right are indistinguishable.

A traditional hate group, the Ku Klux Klan, can serve as a starting point.[33] A California National Knight of the K.K.K. presents a crude but classic attempt to dehumanize the enemy, thus justifying any violent act toward them. He wrote: "Encouraged by 'liberals'—plus Washington's weakling stand—America's black primates have waxed ever more vicious and kill hungry. Anthropoids of their ilk will fear and obey one thing only—Force, in the form of Hot Lead. Mow them down without mercy—carpet the streets with their dead—and the remainder will become 'good niggers.'" Atlanta attorney James R. Venable admonished his followers in a 1964 circular that "blood will surely flow in the streets." He added: "Let it flow! Let us arm our homes to make sure that Negro-Jew blood flows—not ours." As a prod he recommended twelve-gauge shotguns, high-powered rifles with telescopic sights "for distance shooting," and hollow-nosed bullets that "go clear through your game whether two-legged or four."

---

atmosphre of hate or right-wing extremism which may have existed in the city of Dallas had any connection with Oswald's actions on November 22, 1963." They admit there is no way to judge the effect of the general political ferment in the city, they cite evidence of Oswald's awareness of the climate, and they relate several previous incidents in Dallas. Any evidence of a broader conspiracy associating the city's right-wing groups and Oswald does not exist. The contention here is that a climate of violence, uncontrolled rhetoric, and vindictive and debasing personal attacks provide cues and a receptive background for anyone who wishes to act on his own sick impulses.

33. The examples cited are taken from *Political Extremism and Violence in the United States* (New York: A Report by the Anti-Defamation League of B'nai B'rith to the National Commission on the Causes and Prevention of Violence, November, 1968). The Anti-Defamation League culled their materials from published accounts, usually newspapers, journals, or the hate group's own literature.

Connie Lynch, an organizer for the National States Rights Party, speaking to a 1963 K.K.K. rally after warning against Negroes and Jews, commented on the Birmingham church bombing that killed four black children: "Little niggers ain't little children. Children are human . . . so if there's four less niggers tonight, then I say good for whoever planted the bomb. We're all better off." Lynch then attacked a local black dentist, "who ought not to live . . . He ought to wake up tomorrow with a bullet between his eyes. . . . If you were half the men you claim to be, you'd kill him before sunup." The man did see the next sunrise, but in the hospital, the victim with three Negro companions of a severe beating.

The rhetoric is totally unrestrained. If such explosive words had a cathartic effect, if they led to a lessening of tensions, then they conceivably could serve a purpose. The evidence indicates the opposite; calls to violence serve as a spur to violence. The rhetoric condones violent acts and spurs men to commit them. A popular young schoolteacher, a woman reportedly "adored" by student and parent alike, was shot to death by Mississippi police while she and another Klansman attempted to dynamite the home of a Jewish businessman. Overall, in the period 1962–1965, the Anti-Defamation League reports 122 incidents associated with the Klan, ranging from cross burnings to murders, and the list does not claim to be complete.

George Lincoln Rockwell, leader of revived Neo-Nazism in the United States, employed the same themes prior to his assassination. Rockwell proclaimed the need for "utterly destroying all individuals" who aided the Communist conspiracy, that "the only cure for Judaism is Dr. Hitler's cure," and—concerning Negroes— "it is going to take violence and killing to solve this problem." Rockwell warned his followers to arm: "Whites must keep guns! Gun control must fail!" And lest his death appear to ameliorate their emphasis, his successors warned Jews in the organization's publication, *White Power,* to "keep it up, kikes—you're talking yourselves right into the ovens!"

The Minutemen, another right-wing organization of guerrilla fanatics, eschew conventional political activity. The group, through their publication, *On Target,* couple their alarms with specific advice on the cost, utility, and serviceability of different types of arms. In a now classic example of extremist exhortations to violence, the organization's publication in 1963 listed the names of twenty congressmen who voted against the House Un-American Activities Committee and warned: ". . . patriots are not going to let you take their freedom away from them. They have learned to use the silent knife, the strangler's cord, the target rifle that hits sparrows at 200 yards. Only their leaders restrain them. Traitors beware! Even now the cross-hairs are on the back of your necks."

The groups and the rhetoric proliferate. The right extremists interchange with the left. The late Malcolm X, who also experienced death by assassination, said, ". . . it's ballots or bullets. In order to start casting the ballot, you've got to have some bullets." Robert Williams, a black racist who defected to Cuba and China, has called for "kill-ins." After extolling the use of Molotov cocktails, hand grenades, acid, machine guns and the like, Williams warns his supporters that "not only does freedom require the will to die, but it also requires the will to kill." A black liberation group, the Revolutionary Action Movement (RAM), reputedly goes by the slogan, "Kill, Baby, Kill," and advocates widespread black revolution. The Black Panthers, now allegedly the object of summary police justice themselves in some cities, advocate self-armament ("every black man should have a shotgun, a 357 magnum or a .38 in his pad to defend it . . . every woman should understand that weapon") and the efficacy of violence ("Power only comes out of a barrel of a gun!").

The rhetoric of violence seems endless. And it does result in the intended consequences. Of specific relevance to assassinations, the following can serve to illustrate the point. The Georgia Klan, for example, contained a small group of six "enforcers" who reportedly intended (the plan was not executed) to assassinate three major opponents, Morris Abram, a Jewish lawyer, university president, and candidate for the Democratic nomination for United States Senator from New York; Sam Massell, Jewish mayor of Atlanta; and a Southern clergyman. The Klan also were publicly associated with several plots to assassinate Martin Luther King prior to his death, although each was aborted for various reasons. Two alleged members of RAM were convicted of conspiracy to murder Roy Wilkins of the NAACP and the late Whitney Young, Jr., of the Urban League. The trial of the conspirators also revealed that

Robert Kennedy was considered for assassination. The Minutemen have been associated by the government with plots to murder Senator J. William Fulbright, former Vice-President Hubert Humphrey, former Chief Justice Earl Warren, and Governor Nelson Rockefeller of New York.

Extremist rhetoric makes explicit the association among rhetoric, means, and victim. As a final example, an assumedly far-left flier pictures a Defense Department official under a caption "Wanted." The poster cites the man's background and his work in military research and ends by giving the man's place of work, the Pentagon naturally, and his home address. The implication is clear for those who wish to draw it.

CONCLUDING OBSERVATIONS

No easy answers exist to political assassinations. They are intertwined with American history, and they feed on a variety of social forces. Remedies can range from the highly specific to the more subtle. All would be of some help. The recommendations put forward, for example, by the Warren Commission and such authors as Jim Bishop and William Manchester, who dealt intimately with the John Kennedy assassination, are relevant.[34] The majority of these focused on improved protection, greater communication among relevant government agencies, and an increased weight given to security concerns. Yet these represent a very small aspect of the total picture.

Severe gun-control legislation would be helpful but is politically impractical. Any politician who proposes limitations on guns and ammunition runs afoul of one of the nation's most powerful and best organized interest groups. Serious legislation remains unlikely to become a reality and the politician who proposes it is in danger of losing his next election.

The office of the presidency has been the target of assassins because of its power and visibility as the kingpin of American government. A depersonalization of the office and its incumbent would be helpful as would an emphasis on the complex responsi-

34. *The Warren Commission Report,* pp. 615–637; Jim Bishop, *The Day Kennedy Was Shot* (New York: Funk & Wagnalls, 1968); and William Manchester, *The Death of a President* (New York: Harper & Row, 1967).

bilities of competing centers of governmental power, the Congress, the state capitals, and the mayor's office.

A number of studies and presidential commissions have dealt with violence in American society with particular focus on some of its more unpleasant aspects, the urban riots, crime, the assassinations and death and disorders on college campuses. Main themes in all the reports are the need for greater tolerance and understanding, less rhetoric, more equitable distribution of society's resources, and truly representative governing bodies. The commissions have helped society to re-examine its past, and they have done commendable jobs of explanation. The net practical results measured in legislative gain and changed governmental procedures, however, emanating from the work of the Warren, Kerner, Eisenhower and Scranton Commissions are niggardly.[35] The public and its representatives content themselves with a good deal of broad discussion of the problems involved and accept with appreciation but grave reservation the work, and especially the recommendations, of the commissions. Thus little of substance is accomplished.

The public attitude toward political assassination is fatalistic. The vast majority of Americans completely disapprove, but when in 1963 they were deeply shocked and expected nothing of a like nature to happen again, five years later they were resigned to believing that assassination represents a necessary risk of political life.[36] It need not. Such an assessment is disheartening, but the opportunities have arisen, and yet nothing appears in progress to substantially counter the conditions that give rise to such acts.

35. Murray Edelman and Rita James Simon in "Presidential Assassinations: Their Meaning and Impact on American Society" deal with short-run political responses to presidential assassinations, and Dwaine and Elizabeth Wirth Marvick in "The Political Consequences of Assassination" treat some of the broader reactions in their chapters in this volume. On the efforts to make political institutions more representative, see William Crotty, *Party Reform* (San Francisco: Chandler, forthcoming).

36. In the nationwide poll on political violence conducted by Louis Harris and Associates, one-half (51 per cent) of the respondents agreed with the statement that "if people go into politics they more or less have to accept the fact that they might get killed," and slightly over one-half (55 percent) agreed that "a lot more people in government and politics will probably be assassinated in the next few years."

Political Violence and Assassination: A Cross-National Assessment[1]

Ivo K. Feierabend, Rosalind L. Feierabend,
Betty A. Nesvold, and Franz M. Jaggar

INTRODUCTION

This study scrutinizes internal political violence and assassination on a broadly comparative cross-national basis. As many as eighty-four nations are examined in a search for global patterns of violence, assassination, and their underlying conditions. The advantage of this method lies in its scope. The examination of many cases can reveal relationships that may be obscured in the unique circumstances of specific political systems. On the other hand, it also has its disadvantages. Undoubtedly important detail and depth are lost in such a broad overview, which would be more thoroughly preserved in intensive study of one country or one assassination.

Within this approach, we seek to answer several related questions concerning the occurrence of assassination. What are the countries, or groups of countries that most frequently suffer this aberration of the political process? Which countries are less prone to such behavior? The first section presents a global overview of national and regional patterns of assassination. The second section asks a very basic question concerning the reliability and validity of these national profiles. How adequate is our information? To what degree can we trust our conclusions regarding global patterns of violence?

1. A related examination of these data appears in a report prepared for the Task Force on Assassinations of the National Commission on the Causes and Prevention of Violence, November, 1968. We wish to thank Rosemary J. Roth, who helped to collect and code the assassination data, as well as Robert Kaufman, K. Lynden Smithson, and Antonia E. Williams for their help.

Subsequent sections go beyond cross-national description and seek to discover underlying conditions, correlates, or predictors of political violence and assassination. One set of variables that is analyzed consists of different manifestations of political violence. What other occurrences of political instability tend to be frequently associated with assassinations and which are infrequently associated? How internally violent are the countries that experience assassinations? In the third section of the report, we inquire into the general structure of political violence to see where assassinations fit within the pattern.

The fourth section probes selected environmental variables of political systems. Among these, the measures of social and economic modernity are especially stressed. Are modern and developed nations less prone to violence and assassination than the developing nations? Does rate of change toward modernity affect violence and assassination? In addition, relationships are sought between assassination and selected political and social conditions. The relationship between the degree of coerciveness (tyranny) of political regimes and assassination frequency is examined, as well as the relationships of internal and external violence, rates of homicide and suicide, minority tensions, and systemic frustration.

In an effort to answer these questions, the study relies on statistical compilations of empirical, cross-national data. The analysis thus employs a quantitative and correlational approach.[2]

2. Cross-national quantitative analysis of political and social variables is a relatively recent development. For an overview see: Richard L. Merritt and Stein Rokkan, eds., *Comparing Nations: The Uses of Quantitative Data in Cross-National Research* (New Haven: Yale University Press, 1966). Two large-scale cross-national data collections and analyses are: Arthur S. Banks and Robert B. Textor, *A Cross-Polity Survey* (Cambridge: M.I.T. Press, 1963) and Bruce M. Russett, and Hayward R. Alker, Jr., Karl W. Deutsch, Harold D. Lasswell, *World Handbook of Political and Social Indicators* (New Haven: Yale University Press, 1964). Among the few cross-national analyses of internal political violence are: Harry Eckstein, *Internal War: The Problem of Anticipation* (A Report Submitted to the Research Group in Psychology and the Social Sciences, Smithsonian Institution, Washington, D.C., January 15, 1962); Ted Gurr with Charles Ruttenberg, *The Conditions of Civil Violence: First Tests of a Causal Model*, Research Monograph No. 28 (Princeton: Princeton University Center of International Studies, April, 1967); Rudolph J. Rummel, "Dimensions of Conflict Behavior Within and Between Nations," *General Systems Yearbook* 8 (1963), pp. 1–50; Raymond Tanter, "Dimensions of Conflict

CROSS-NATIONAL ASSASSINATION PROFILES
OF EIGHTY-FOUR NATIONS: 1948–1967

For the specific purpose of scrutinizing assassinations on a global basis, assassination events were collected for eighty-four countries for a twenty-year period, 1948–1967. The data for this collection were drawn from the *New York Times Index*. There are presently more than eighty-four countries in the world, but we selected our sample to consist of nations that were independent states in 1948. Also, many of our existing cross-national data collections apply to this group of nations.[3]

An assassination event was defined as an act that consists of a plotted, attempted, or actual murder of a prominent political figure (elite) by an individual (assassin) who performs this act in other than a governmental role. This definition draws a distinction between political execution and assassination. An execution may be regarded as a political killing, but it is initiated by the organs of the state, while an assassination can always be characterized as an illegal act. A prominent figure must be the target of the killing, since the killing of lesser members of the political community is included within a wider category of internal political turmoil, namely, terrorism. Finally, we used a minimal definition to distinguish assassination from homicide. The target of the aggressive act must be a political figure rather than a private person. The killing of a prime minister by a member of an insurrectionist or underground group clearly qualifies as an assassination. So does an act by a deranged individual who tries to kill not just any individual but the individual in his political role—as president, for example.

Behavior Within and Between Nations, 1958–60," *Journal of Conflict Resolution* 10 (March, 1966), pp. 41–65; Douglas Bwy, "Political Instability in Latin America: The Cross-Cultural Test of a Causal Model," *Latin American Research Review* (Spring, 1968); Ivo K. and Rosalind L. Feierabend, "Aggressive Behaviors Within Polities, 1948–1962: A Cross-National Study," *Journal of Conflict Resolution* 10 (September, 1966), pp. 249–271; and Betty A. Nesvold, "A Scalogram Analysis of Political Violence," *Comparative Political Studies* (July, 1969).

3. The other data collections on instability and violence are a portion of the "Systemic Conditions of Political Aggression" project, funded by the National Science Foundation.

This definition nevertheless excludes an accidental killing of a king during a hunting party or a *crime passionnel* committed against him.

There are additional aspects to our definition. We included assassinations carried out by agents of foreign governments and assassinations perpetrated against a political figure while he was visiting on foreign soil. Furthermore, we counted assassination plots and alleged plots within our data, although they are distinguished from assassination attempts. It is not always possible to determine, in the case of alleged plots, whether the plot in fact existed and was discovered by the regime, or whether it served as an excuse for a wave of political persecution.

Definitional clarity is important in the study of assassinations, as well as in the task of collecting data. It also must be obvious that definitions may be conceived in narrower or wider terms. In our specific case, for example, the distinction between terrorism and assassination could be abandoned in favor of a broader definition. Or assassination threats could also be counted among assassination events. Or the definition could be narrowed to include only clearly politically motivated killings by organized insurrectionists. We use a definition that circumscribes the target in a fairly narrow fashion: only the murder of a prominent political person is included. On the other hand, our definition is quite broad in characterizing the political act. We chose this definition for several reasons. Our data source made this choice the most advisable, since killings of prominent persons are most likely to be reported through the news media. On the other hand, although the victim is always known, the assassin and the nature of his motivation may not be clear from available accounts. In fact, in some cases the assassin may remain unknown. For this reason, it seemed that a broader definition only minimally circumscribing the term "political" would be less prone to error during the data-collection phase.

Within the notion of prominent public figure, we counted all top governmental officeholders, heads of state and government, presidential candidates, cabinet members, legislators, and judges. We also included military figures, chiefs-of-staff, generals, and occasionally colonels if they seemed to play an important role in the political arena. Some important local officials, such as mayors of cities or chiefs of police qualified in our definition of prominence.

Beyond governmental officeholders, we included leaders of political parties, large trade unions, social and religious movements, leaders of minority groups and other prominent members of important, visible social institutions.[4]

Let us look at the near-global frequency pattern of assassination events for the twenty-year period. In Table 1, countries are rank-ordered, starting with those that experienced the greatest number of assassinations and ending with countries that had no assassinations at all. The first column of the table shows the frequencies of all attempted assassinations, successful and unsuccessful, as well as assassination plots. The next two columns count actual assassination attempts, separating successful from unsuccessful ones. The fourth column indicates assassination plots. The subsequent four columns report the same information but only for assassinations of top government officials, while the last four columns report on the assassinations of chiefs of state.

The totals reported in the table show that 409 assassination events are recorded for the period. This may seem a staggering number, and yet perhaps it is not entirely unexpected. Looking selectively at other totals, column 10 reports the loss of life of the most important political officeholders, the chiefs of state. The other columns show the totals for the other subcategories of assassination for the eighty-four nations. It may also be seen that twenty countries, or approximately one-fourth of the sample, experienced no assassination events during this period. The largest group among these nations are the Western democracies (ten), but there are also five European Communist countries, four Latin American countries, and one Asian country within this group. Seven countries experienced only one assassination event, and thirteen additional countries, no more than two. This still com-

4. The information derived from the *New York Times Index* was coded and transcribed onto an IBM card format, making the data available for computer analysis. This card format includes the country name, the date of occurrence and the outcome of the assassination attempt (successful or unsuccessful, or plot only). The card also specifies the number of persons killed or wounded in the act. The format includes the name of the victim and his official position, as well as the name of the assassin and the social or political group that seemed to be implicated in his action. Furthermore, the nature of the tension responsible for the act is noted where possible. Also included is the reference to the *New York Times* issue, page and column.

TABLE 1

Frequency of Assassinations for 84 Nations, 1948–1967[a]

	All Persons			Top Government Officials Only				Chiefs of State Only			
Total Events	Attempts		Plots	Total Events	Attempts		Plots	Total Events	Attempts		Plots
	Successful	Unsuccessful			Successful	Unsuccessful			Successful	Unsuccessful	
Cuba	28	10	6	12	12	1	1	10	11	—	1	10
Korea	20	5	5	10	11	1	3	7	8	—	1	7
Iran	19	8	6	5	12	2	6	4	7	—	3	4
Morocco	17	7	7	3	5	—	4	1	3	1	2	1
United States	16	5	9	2	3	1	1	1	3	1	1	1
Tunisia	16	9	4	3	5	—	3	2	3	—	1	2
Philippines	15	5	2	8	8	—	1	7	5	—	—	5
France	14	1	6	7	11	—	4	7	9	1	3	6
Egypt	14	2	5	7	9	1	3	5	8	1	2	5
Venezuela	12	1	6	5	6	1	2	3	4	1	2	1
Lebanon	12	6	6	—	9	3	6	—	5	—	5	—
Guatemala	12	9	1	2	4	3	—	1	2	1	—	1
Brazil	12	3	3	6	3	—	2	1	1	—	—	1
Laos	10	8	2	—	4	3	1	—	—	—	—	—
Japan	9	2	3	4	5	1	2	2	3	—	2	1
Bolivia	9	1	6	2	4	—	2	2	2	—	—	2
Argentina	9	—	3	6	8	—	2	6	5	—	1	4

TABLE 1 (continued)

Frequency of Assassinations for 84 Nations, 1948–1967[a]

	All Persons				Top Government Officials Only				Chiefs of State Only			
	Total Events	Attempts Successful	Attempts Unsuccessful	Plots	Total Events	Attempts Successful	Attempts Unsuccessful	Plots	Total Events	Attempts Successful	Attempts Unsuccessful	Plots
India	8	3	4	1	6	1	4	1	4	—	3	1
Syria	7	4	2	1	1	1	—	—	—	—	—	1
Ghana	7	—	4	3	6	—	4	2	6	—	4	2
Dom. Republic	7	3	2	2	5	1	2	2	4	1	1	2
Colombia	7	4	2	1	3	1	1	1	1	—	—	1
Malaya	6	4	1	1	3	1	1	1	1	—	—	1
Jordan	6	2	—	4	4	1	—	3	4	1	—	3
Cambodia	6	2	2	2	5	1	2	2	4	—	2	2
Panama	5	2	1	2	2	1	—	1	2	1	—	1
Pakistan	5	3	—	2	2	2	—	—	2	2	—	—
Nicaragua	5	1	1	3	5	1	1	3	5	1	1	3
Iraq	5	1	3	1	4	—	3	1	4	—	3	1
Indonesia	5	—	3	2	5	—	3	2	5	—	3	2
Haiti	5	1	3	1	2	—	1	1	2	—	1	1
Greece	5	2	1	2	2	—	1	1	1	—	—	1
Czechoslovakia	5	1	3	1	4	—	3	1	3	—	2	1
Cyprus	5	2	3	1								

Country												Total
Burma												4
Turkey												3
South Africa												3
Thailand												3
Paraguay												3
Mexico												3
Italy												3
Israel												3
Ecuador												3
China-Mainland												3
Yugoslavia												2
W. Germany												2
Spain												2
Saudi Arabia												2
Portugal												2
Liberia												2
Ethiopia												2
El Salvador												2
Costa Rica												2
Ceylon												2
Australia												2
Albania												2
Afghanistan												2
Sudan												1
New Zealand												1
Libya												1

TABLE 1 (continued)

Frequency of Assassinations for 84 Nations, 1948–1967[a]

	All Persons				Top Government Officials Only				Chiefs of State Only			
	TOTAL EVENTS	ATTEMPTS		PLOTS	TOTAL EVENTS	ATTEMPTS		PLOTS	TOTAL EVENTS	ATTEMPTS		PLOTS
		SUCCESSFUL	UNSUCCESSFUL			SUCCESSFUL	UNSUCCESSFUL			SUCCESSFUL	UNSUCCESSFUL	
Hungary	1	1	–	–	–	–	–	–	–	–	–	–
Canada	1	–	1	–	–	–	–	–	–	–	–	–
Belgium	1	1	–	–	–	–	–	–	–	–	–	–
Austria	1	1	–	–	–	–	–	–	–	–	–	–
USSR	–	–	–	–	–	–	–	–	–	–	–	–
Uruguay	–	–	–	–	–	–	–	–	–	–	–	–
United Kingdom	–	–	–	–	–	–	–	–	–	–	–	–
Switzerland	–	–	–	–	–	–	–	–	–	–	–	–
Sweden	–	–	–	–	–	–	–	–	–	–	–	–
Romania	–	–	–	–	–	–	–	–	–	–	–	–
Poland	–	–	–	–	–	–	–	–	–	–	–	–
Peru	–	–	–	–	–	–	–	–	–	–	–	–
Norway	–	–	–	–	–	–	–	–	–	–	–	–
Netherlands	–	–	–	–	–	–	–	–	–	–	–	–
Luxembourg	–	–	–	–	–	–	–	–	–	–	–	–
Ireland	–	–	–	–	–	–	–	–	–	–	–	–
Iceland	–	–	–	–	–	–	–	–	–	–	–	–

Honduras
Finland
E. Germany
Denmark
China-Taiwan
Chile
Bulgaria

Number of
Countries = 84

Totals =	409	143	134	132	216	34	85	97	152	12	52	88
Means =	4.87	1.70	1.60	1.57	2.57	.40	1.01	1.54	1.81	.14	.62	1.05

a Countries are rank-ordered on the basis of the total frequency of assassinations.

FIGURE 1

Global Frequency Distribution of Assassinations

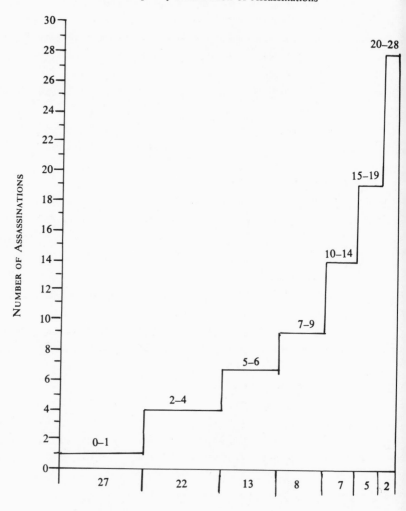

Number of Countries of each Assassination Frequency Level

paratively low number of assassinations accounts for approximately half of the entire country sample (forty nations). Then we find eight countries experiencing three assassination events; one country, four events; ten countries, five events; three countries, six events; four countries, seven events; and three countries, nine events. Finally, the first thirteen countries of the sample experience more than ten assassination events each. The United States occupies the fifth rank from the top, with sixteen assassination events, and Cuba figures as the country with the highest frequency of all, twenty-eight assassination events. It is interesting to note that these thirteen countries, representing about 15 per cent of the sample, contribute more than half of the assassination events in the global picture. If one plots these frequencies of assassinations against the number of countries, the findings appear as a staircase with steps that are growing continuously shorter and steeper.

If we look at the frequency of assassination events by year rather than by country, we see that they fluctuate over time. Figure 2 identifies some four striking peaks of high frequencies of assassinations in 1948, 1949, 1963, and 1965, and four "lows" in 1952, 1960, 1961, and the lowest in 1967. Looking impressionistically at this graph (that is, trying to draw a line that would best fit these scattered points), one would find a gently sloping downward trend. Hence one could assert that on the average, through the years, assassination events are almost constant in their volume of occurrence or, if anything, they may be slightly declining. However, from one year period to another, the fluctuation is quite considerable, as the peaks and the valleys of the line attest. If one compares the volume of assassinations for the first half of the time

FIGURE 2

Assassination Frequency by Year, 1948–1967

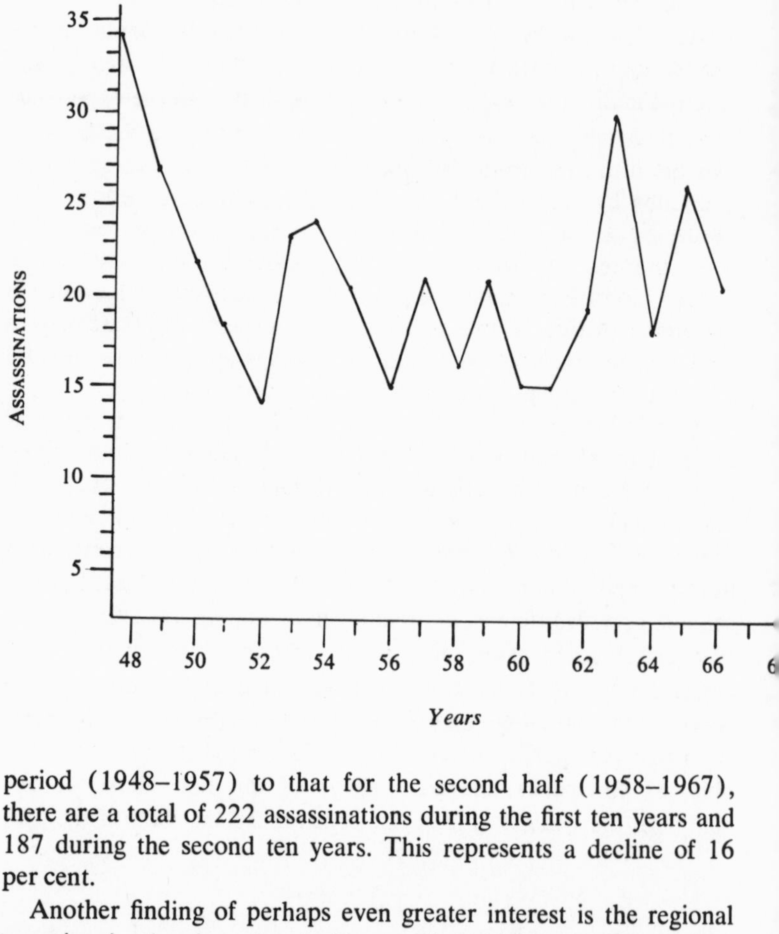

period (1948–1957) to that for the second half (1958–1967), there are a total of 222 assassinations during the first ten years and 187 during the second ten years. This represents a decline of 16 per cent.

Another finding of perhaps even greater interest is the regional grouping in the data that is illustrated in Table 2.[5] The highest average assassination frequency is found in the Middle East region: 8.23 assassinations per country over twenty years. Latin

5. The regional groupings are drawn from Bruce M. Russett, J. David Singer, and Melvin Small, "National Political Units in the Twentieth Century: A Standardized List," *American Political Science Review* LXII (September, 1968), pp. 932–951.

TABLE 2
Regional Groupings of Assassination Data
Middle East

	All Persons				Top Government Officials Only				Chiefs of State Only			
	Total Events	Attempts		Plots	Total Events	Attempts		Plots	Total Events	Attempts		Plots
		Successful	Unsuccessful			Successful	Unsuccessful			Successful	Unsuccessful	
Egypt	14	2	5	7	9	1	3	5	8	1	2	5
Iran	19	8	6	5	12	2	6	4	7	—	3	4
Iraq	5	1	3	1	4	—	3	1	4	—	3	1
Israel	3	1	1	1	2	1	1	1	1	1	—	1
Jordan	6	2	—	4	4	1	—	3	4	1	—	3
Lebanon	12	6	6	—	9	3	6	—	5	—	5	—
Libya	1	1	—	3	1	1	—	1	—	—	—	—
Morocco	17	7	7	1	5	—	4	—	3	—	2	1
Saudi Arabia	2	1	—	—	1	—	—	1	1	—	—	1
Sudan	1	—	1	1	1	—	1	—	1	—	1	—
Syria	7	4	2	1	1	1	—	—	—	—	—	—
Tunisia	16	9	4	3	5	—	3	2	3	—	1	2
Turkey	4	—	3	1	4	—	3	1	3	—	2	1
Number of Countries = 13												
Totals =	107	42	38	27	58	9	30	19	40	2	19	19
Means =	8.23	3.23	2.92	2.08	4.46	.69	2.31	1.46	3.08	.15	1.46	1.46

TABLE 2 (continued)

Latin America

	All Persons				Top Government Officials Only				Chiefs of State Only			
	Total Events	Attempts Successful	Attempts Unsuccessful	Plots	Total Events	Attempts Successful	Attempts Unsuccessful	Plots	Total Events	Attempts Successful	Attempts Unsuccessful	Plots
Argentina	9	—	3	6	8	—	2	6	5	—	1	4
Bolivia	9	1	6	2	4	—	2	2	2	—	—	2
Brazil	12	3	3	6	3	—	2	1	1	—	—	1
Chile	—	—	—	—	—	—	—	—	—	—	—	—
Colombia	7	4	2	1	3	1	1	1	1	—	—	1
Costa Rica	2	1	—	1	1	—	—	1	1	—	—	1
Cuba	28	10	6	12	12	1	1	10	11	—	1	10
Dom. Republic	7	3	2	2	5	1	2	2	4	1	1	2
Ecuador	3	—	2	1	2	—	1	1	2	—	1	1
El Salvador	2	—	2	—	2	—	2	—	1	—	1	—
Guatemala	12	9	1	2	4	3	—	1	1	1	—	—
Haiti	5	1	3	1	2	—	1	1	2	—	1	1
Honduras	—	—	—	—	—	—	—	—	—	—	—	—
Mexico	3	3	—	—	—	—	—	—	—	—	—	—
Nicaragua	5	1	1	3	5	1	1	3	5	1	1	3
Panama	5	2	1	2	2	1	—	1	2	1	—	1
Paraguay	3	—	—	3	2	—	—	2	1	—	—	1
Peru	—	—	—	—	—	—	—	—	—	—	—	—
Uruguay	—	—	—	—	—	—	—	—	—	—	—	—
Venezuela	12	1	6	5	6	1	2	3	5	1	2	2
Number of Countries = 20												
Totals =	124	39	38	47	61	9	17	35	44	5	9	30
Means =	6.20	1.95	1.90	2.35	3.05	.45	.85	1.75	2.20	.25	.45	1.50

Asia

	All Persons				Top Government Officials Only				Chiefs of State Only			
	TOTAL EVENTS	ATTEMPTS SUC-CESS-FUL	UNSUC-CESS-FUL	PLOTS	TOTAL EVENTS	ATTEMPTS SUC-CESS-FUL	UNSUC-CESS-FUL	PLOTS	TOTAL EVENTS	ATTEMPTS SUC-CESS-FUL	UNSUC-CESS-FUL	PLOTS
Afghanistan	2	–	1	1	2	–	1	1	1	–	–	1
Australia	2	–	2	–	–	–	–	–	–	–	–	–
Burma	5	5	–	–	1	1	–	–	–	–	–	–
Cambodia	6	2	2	2	5	1	2	2	4	–	2	2
Ceylon	2	1	–	1	1	1	–	–	1	1	–	–
China-Taiwan	–	–	–	–	–	–	–	–	–	–	–	–
China-Mainland	3	–	1	2	3	–	1	2	2	–	–	2
India	8	3	4	1	6	1	4	1	4	–	3	1
Indonesia	5	–	3	2	5	–	3	2	5	–	3	2
Japan	9	2	3	4	5	1	2	2	3	–	2	1
Korea	20	5	5	10	11	1	3	7	8	–	1	7
Laos	10	8	2	–	4	3	1	–	–	–	–	–
Malaya	6	4	1	1	3	1	1	1	1	–	–	1
New Zealand	1	–	–	1	1	–	–	1	1	–	–	1
Pakistan	5	3	–	2	2	2	–	–	2	2	–	–
Philippines	15	5	2	8	8	–	1	7	5	–	–	5
Thailand	3	–	1	2	1	–	–	1	1	–	–	1
Number of Countries = 17												
Totals =	102	38	27	37	58	12	19	27	38	3	11	24
Means =	6.00	2.22	1.59	2.18	3.41	.71	1.12	1.59	2.22	.18	.65	1.41

TABLE 2 (continued)

Europe

	All Persons				Top Government Officials Only				Chiefs of State Only			
	TOTAL EVENTS	ATTEMPTS		PLOTS	TOTAL EVENTS	ATTEMPTS		PLOTS	TOTAL EVENTS	ATTEMPTS		PLOTS
		SUCCESSFUL	UNSUCCESSFUL			SUCCESSFUL	UNSUCCESSFUL			SUCCESSFUL	UNSUCCESSFUL	
Albania	2	2	–	–	1	1	–	–	–	–	–	–
Austria	1	1	–	–	–	–	–	–	–	–	–	–
Belgium	1	1	–	–	–	–	–	–	–	–	–	–
Bulgaria	–	–	–	–	–	–	–	–	–	–	–	–
Cyprus	5	2	2	1	3	1	2	–	–	–	–	–
Czechoslovakia	5	1	3	1	4	–	3	1	3	–	2	1
Denmark	–	–	–	–	–	–	–	–	–	–	–	–
E. Germany	–	–	–	–	–	–	–	–	–	–	–	–
Finland	–	–	–	–	–	–	–	–	–	–	–	–
France	14	1	6	7	11	–	4	7	9	–	3	6
Greece	5	2	1	2	2	–	1	1	1	–	–	1
Hungary	1	1	–	–	–	–	–	–	–	–	–	–
Iceland	–	–	–	–	–	–	–	–	–	–	–	–
Ireland	–	–	–	–	–	–	–	–	–	–	–	–
Italy	3	2	1	–	–	–	–	–	–	–	–	–
Luxembourg	–	–	–	–	–	–	–	–	–	–	–	–
Netherlands	–	–	–	–	–	–	–	–	–	–	–	–
Norway	–	–	–	–	–	–	–	–	–	–	–	–
Poland	–	–	–	–	–	–	–	–	–	–	–	–
Portugal	2	1	–	1	1	–	–	1	1	–	–	1
Romania	–	1	–	1	1	–	–	1	–	–	–	1
Spain	2	1	–	1	–	–	–	–	–	–	–	–
Sweden	–	–	–	–	–	–	–	–	–	–	–	–

	All Persons				Top Government Officials Only				Chiefs of State Only			
	Total Events	**Successful**	**Unsuccessful**	**Plots**	**Total Events**	**Successful**	**Unsuccessful**	**Plots**	**Total Events**	**Successful**	**Unsuccessful**	**Plots**
Switzerland	—	—	—	—	—	—	—	—	—	—	—	—
United Kingdom	—	—	—	—	—	—	—	—	—	—	—	—
USSR	2	2	—	—	2	2	—	—	—	—	—	—
W. Germany	2	—	1	1	—	—	—	—	2	—	1	1
Yugoslavia	2	—	—	2	—	—	—	—	1	—	—	1
Number of Countries = 28												
Totals =	45	17	14	14	24	2	11	11	16	—	6	10
Means =	1.61	.61	.50	.50	.87	.07	.39	.39	.57	—	.21	.36

North America

	All Persons				Top Government Officials Only				Chiefs of State Only			
	Total Events	**Successful**	**Unsuccessful**	**Plots**	**Total Events**	**Successful**	**Unsuccessful**	**Plots**	**Total Events**	**Successful**	**Unsuccessful**	**Plots**
Canada	1	—	1	—	—	—	—	—	—	—	—	—
United States	16	5	9	2	3	1	1	1	3	1	1	1
Number of Countries = 2												
Totals =	17	5	10	2	3	1	1	1	3	1	1	1
Means =	8.50	2.50	5.00	1.00	1.50	.50	.50	.50	1.50	.50	.50	.50

TABLE 2 (continued)

Africa

	All Persons				Top Government Officials Only				Chiefs of State Only			
	TOTAL EVENTS	ATTEMPTS SUCCESSFUL	ATTEMPTS UNSUCCESSFUL	PLOTS	TOTAL EVENTS	ATTEMPTS SUCCESSFUL	ATTEMPTS UNSUCCESSFUL	PLOTS	TOTAL EVENTS	ATTEMPTS SUCCESSFUL	ATTEMPTS UNSUCCESSFUL	PLOTS
Ethiopia	2	–	1	1	2	–	1	1	1	–	–	1
Ghana	7	–	4	3	6	–	4	2	6	–	4	2
Liberia	2	–	1	1	2	–	1	1	2	–	1	1
South Africa	3	2	1	–	2	1	1	–	2	1	1	–
Number of Countries = 4												
Totals =	14	2	7	5	12	1	7	4	11	1	6	4
Means =	3.50	.50	1.75	1.25	3.00	.25	1.75	1.00	2.75	.25	1.50	1.00

America and Asia have approximately comparable average scores of total number of assassination events: 6.2 and 6.0 respectively. All three of these regions are significantly higher on average number of assassinations than the European countries, for which the average assassination figure is 1.6. The average number of assassinations among African countries in our sample is 3.5. Little can be said regarding this region, however, since only four countries are included. As for the North American region, it comprises only the United States and Canada, which differ strikingly in assassination frequency.

Groupings of nations based on additional criteria discriminate even more significantly among the regional groups (see Table 3). Thus if a group of generally democratic Western states is considered, we have an average assassination score of 2.2. Omitting France and the United States, since both countries are true "mavericks" for this group, the average score is lowered to 0.7. Also among the remarkably low scorers are the Communist bloc of nations, with the exception of Cuba. The mean score for this group, excluding Cuba, is 1.1.

The national and regional profiles presented in Tables 2 and 3 are based on the total count of assassination attempts and assassination plots perpetrated against prominent public figures. Similar profiles could also be constructed based on the subcategories of assassination. These profiles would differ in some respects, and yet the similarities would also be striking. The correlations among all of these profiles may be seen in Table 4. Looking at this table, we find a very high degree of agreement among total frequency of all assassination events (T) and total frequency of assassination attempts (A), successful attempts (S) and plots (P). These correlation values range from .8 to .9. Furthermore, comparing assassinations directed against chiefs of state (COS) and top government officials (TGO) to assassinations of all prominent persons, we also find a high level of agreement for assassinations of all types (T). These correlations are .8 and .9. Thus we may conclude that analyzing the data in terms of any one of these subcategories would not significantly alter the findings. Other subcategories, however, such as the number of successful assassinations carried out against chiefs of state and top government officials, present a different picture, as may be seen in the lower correlation values

TABLE 3

Political System Groupings of Assassination Data
A. Western Democratic Nations

	All Persons				Top Government Officials Only				Chiefs of State Only			
	Total Events	Attempts Successful	Attempts Unsuccessful	Plots	Total Events	Attempts Successful	Attempts Unsuccessful	Plots	Total Events	Attempts Successful	Attempts Unsuccessful	Plots
Australia	2	–	2	–	–	–	–	–	–	–	–	–
New Zealand	1	–	–	1	1	–	–	1	1	–	–	1
Canada	1	–	–	1	1	–	–	1	1	–	–	1
Israel	2	1	1	–	1	–	1	–	–	–	–	–
United States	16	5	9	2	3	1	1	1	3	1	1	1
Austria	1	1	–	–	–	–	–	–	–	–	–	–
Belgium	1	1	–	–	–	–	–	–	–	–	–	–
Denmark	–	–	–	–	–	–	–	–	–	–	–	–
Finland	–	–	–	–	–	–	–	–	–	–	–	–
France	14	1	6	7	11	–	4	7	9	–	3	6
Iceland	–	–	–	–	–	–	–	–	–	–	–	–
Ireland	–	–	–	–	–	–	–	–	–	–	–	–
Italy	3	2	1	–	–	–	–	–	–	–	–	–
Luxembourg	–	–	–	–	–	–	–	–	–	–	–	–
Netherlands	–	–	–	–	–	–	–	–	–	–	–	–
Norway	–	–	–	–	–	–	–	–	–	–	–	–
Sweden	–	–	–	–	–	–	–	–	–	–	–	–
Switzerland	–	–	–	–	–	–	–	–	–	–	–	–
United Kingdom	1	–	1	–	–	–	–	–	–	–	–	–
W. Germany	2	2	–	–	–	–	–	–	–	–	–	–
Number of Countries = 20												
Totals =	44	13	20	11	17	1	6	10	14	1	4	9
Means =	2.20	.65	1.00	.55	.85	.05	.30	.50	.70	.05	.20	.45

B. European Communist Nations

	All Persons				Top Government Officials Only				Chiefs of State Only			
	TOTAL EVENTS	ATTEMPTS		PLOTS	TOTAL EVENTS	ATTEMPTS		PLOTS	TOTAL EVENTS	ATTEMPTS		PLOTS
		SUC-CESS-FUL	UNSUC-CESS-FUL			SUC-CESS-FUL	UNSUC-CESS-FUL			SUC-CESS-FUL	UNSUC-CESS-FUL	
Albania	2	2	–	–	1	1	–	–	–	–	–	–
Bulgaria	–	–	–	–	–	–	–	–	–	–	–	–
Czechoslovakia	5	1	3	1	4	–	3	1	3	–	2	1
E. Germany	–	–	–	–	–	–	–	–	–	–	–	–
Hungary	1	1	–	–	–	–	–	–	–	–	–	–
Poland	–	–	–	–	–	–	–	–	–	–	–	–
Romania	–	–	–	–	–	–	–	–	–	–	–	–
USSR	–	–	–	–	–	–	–	–	–	–	–	–
Yugoslavia	2	–	1	1	2	–	1	1	2	–	1	1
Number of Countries = 9												
Totals =	10	4	4	2	7	1	4	2	5	–	3	2
Means =	1.11	.44	.44	.22	.78	.11	.44	.22	.56	–	.33	.22

TABLE 4

Interrelationships Among Assassination Measures
(Product-Moment Correlations)

		All Persons				Top Government Officials				Chiefs of State			
		T	A	S	P	T	A	S	P	T	A	S	P
All Persons	T	–											
	A	.94	–										
	S	.81	.89	–									
	P	.83	.60	.46	–								
Top Government Officials	T	.88	.77	.57	.83	–							
	A	.70	.76	.58	.43	.82	–						
	S	.47	.57	.67	.18	.45	.64	–					
	P	.76	.53	.38	.95	.85	.39	.12	–				
Chiefs of State	T	.81	.66	.43	.84	.94	.69	.30	.88	–			
	A	.51	.52	.26	.35	.69	.82	.41	.35	.73	–		
	S	.19	.16	.18	.17	.15	.16	.49	.09	.23	.35	–	
	P	.77	.56	.42	.93	.84	.41	.14	.98	.89	.35	.08	–

KEY: T—Total assassination attempts; A—Assassination attempts; S—Successful attempts; P—Assassination plots (ranging from .2 to .5). The number of successful assassinations of chiefs of state shows a very small range across countries (see assassination frequencies in Table 1). Most countries score zero on this dimension; a few score one, and only one country out of eighty-four scores a two. Furthermore, there are only twelve cases of successful assassinations of chiefs of state in the entire sample of eighty-four countries for the twenty-year period. The limitations of this particular category of assassination thus make it relatively useless for cross-national inquiry. We may say, then, that while the type of analyses that we have performed could be repeated using several other subcategories of assassination data, we have chosen in this study to confine our attention to the total frequency of assassinations of all types.

THE RELIABILITY OF THE ASSASSINATION DATA

Looking at these tables and scrutinizing the national assassination profiles, a nagging question of doubt must also be raised and discussed. How accurate are these profiles? Could they perhaps contain serious errors? And, if they are inaccurate, can we estimate the nature and extent of the error? The question can be rephrased in more general fashion: How reliable and how valid is this analysis of cross-national violence and assassination?

The most obvious answer is that these profiles are only as accurate as the *New York Times* reporting on these matters. The *New York Times,* among all the world's newspapers, is sometimes asserted to be the most representative and detailed single source of world political affairs.[6] And yet, even the best newspaper or chronicle of events must be expected to be selective in its reporting. If omission of news occurs, it could be of a random nature, more or less equally distributed among all countries. In such a case, one could conclude that our country profiles are a conservative estimate of a true situation. That is to say, countries actually experience more assassinations than is apparent from the data, but nevertheless, the comparative frequencies attributed to the sample of nations are accurate. For example, if the error in fact is

6. See William A. Gamson and Andre Modigliani, "On the Measurement of International Tension" (Paper prepared for the annual meetings of the Society for the Study of Social Problems, Chicago, August, 1965).

random, the rank-order of countries as presented in the previous section should not substantially differ from profiles that would be constructed from a perfect data source. We may only hope that this hypothesis of random error is true. A foolproof test is not realistic, since it would entail collection of data from all available news sources, together perhaps with consultations of as many as eighty-four experts on the internal political violence of particular nations.

A less satisfactory but an available test is to compare the national profiles derived from the *New York Times Index* to profiles derived from other sources. Among such available data collections are those amassed by Rummel and Tanter for the years 1955–1960.[7] These researchers collected their data from several sources (the *New York Times Index, Deadline Data on World Affairs,* and *Facts on File*). Comparing the total frequency of assassinations for this time period, we find that Rummel and Tanter have recorded a total of eighty-six events, while we have a total of 112. This discrepancy is undoubtedly a function of definition rather than of data source. Whatever the reason for the discrepancy, however, if we compare the relative number of assassinations per country from their data and from ours for the same time period, we find considerable agreement. The correlation is Pearson $r = .76$.

The limitation of this comparison lies in the relatively short period of time scrutinized. Another data collection from *Deadline Data on World Affairs* and the *Encyclopaedia Britannica Yearbook* is available, previously collected by the authors. This covers the identical sample of nations for the 1948–1965 time period.[8]

7. See Rummel, *op. cit.,* and Tanter, *op. cit.* See also, Raymond Tanter, "Dimensions of Conflict Behavior Within and Between Nations, 1958–1960" (Evanston: Northwestern University: monograph prepared in connection with research supported by National Science Foundation, NSF GS224, 1964).

Rummel and Tanter also inquired into questions of error and bias, specifically in the context of their cross-national conflict data. Rummel determined that there was minimal systematic error in the data due to censorship and newsworthiness of country. See Rummel, "Dimensions of Error in Cross-National Data in Mid-1950s" (Honolulu: University of Hawaii, mimeographed, 1964).

8. Ivo K. Feierabend and Rosalind L. Feierabend, *Cross-National Data Bank of Political Instability Events* (*Code Index*) (San Diego: Public Affairs Institute, January, 1965).

Deadline Data on World Affairs is a news-abstracting service that relies for its information on the world's leading newspapers and magazines. However, in its coverage it is more concise and selective by far than the *New York Times*. In fact, from *Deadline Data,* supplemented by information from the *Encyclopaedia Britannica Yearbooks,* we were able to ascertain, for the same sample of nations and a comparable time period, only 122 successful and unsuccessful assassinations, as compared with 381 assassination attempts counted from the *New York Times Index.* Even with this discrepancy, however, the comparative images of the world sample, as seen through the eyes of the two data sources are highly similar. When one compares the *New York Times Index* data on total assassination events with that recorded from *Deadline Data,* the correlation coefficient is .80. When only successful assassinations are compared, the coefficient is .83.

Furthermore, and this point will also be illustrated in the following section of this paper, the findings of world patterns and relationships between violent behaviors and ecological, social, economic, and political variables are substantially the same if we rely on *Deadline Data* or on the more abundant data of the *New York Times Index.* In other words, the results of the analyses are comparable, using either source.

This finding then gives a certain degree of credibility to the comparative and correlational findings of the cross-national study of violence and assassination. At the same time, the actual information that pertains to each separate country must be taken with great caution. Perhaps in this context one could reiterate an assertion made previously that cross-national analysis can discover meaningful world patterns but must not be mistaken for the findings of a thorough and detailed case study. To put these conclusions another way, we would expect clearer and more precise information and less ambiguous patterns from a perfect data source. This would mean higher correlation coefficients but it would not substantially alter the direction of the findings emerging in the present analysis.

Beyond this somewhat encouraging sign regarding the validity of the present undertaking, one could further speculate about some more or less obvious data errors and data biases. It would seem that newsworthiness and press censorship are very likely sources of discrepant information reporting. The United States and other large, powerful, or pivotal nations have higher visibility and news-worthiness than small countries tucked away in quiet backwaters of the international arena. The flow of information from the former could be presumed to be more abundant than from the latter. Also, countries that enforce stricter press censorship may well prevent information from reaching the pages of the *New York Times* or *Deadline Data,* while this will not be true of countries without such censorship.

One way to discover whether this double bias is operating in the source material is to find a substantial positive relationship be-tween large countries and a high frequency of assassinations and a negative relationship between press censorship and assassination frequency. This cannot be considered a perfect test, however, since the correlations may well reflect relationships in the real world rather than merely the world of reporting. One could reasonably assume that larger countries actually have more assassinations and other acts of violence. Since they are more populous, they may harbinger more potential assassins, as well as more officeholders. On the other hand, there is some evidence to suppose that per-missive countries—those without censorship—will be less prone to violence of any kind than more restrictive and oppressive coun-tries. Political tyranny, especially at mid-points of intensity, seems to lead to more, rather than to less, political violence.

The actual relationships obtained between population size, press censorship, and assassination frequency are indicated in Table 5.[9] As may be seen, the relationship between frequency of assassina-tions and size of population is zero, using both raw and logged data.[10] Perhaps another note of cautious data optimism could be

9. Population data are reported in Russett et al., *op. cit.* The press censorship data collection relies mostly on information from John C. Mer-rill, *A Handbook of the Foreign Press* (Baton Rouge: Louisiana State Uni-versity Press, 1959); I.P.I. Survey, *The Press in Authoritarian Countries* (Zurich: The International Press Institute, 1959), and semiannual Associ-ated Press Surveys of World Censorship. The ratings apply to a ten-year period, 1951–1960. A six-point scale was devised, ranging from least-censored to most-censored press.

10. Since the distribution of assassinations across the eighty-four nations is so highly skewed (see Figure 2), we used a log transformation $(X + 1)$. This technique makes the data more closely approximate the assumption of normality that underlies Pearson r. This procedure minimizes the possi-bility of distortion in the size of the correlation coefficients.

TABLE 5

Relationship Between Population Size of Nations, Press
Censorship, and Frequency of Assassinations

ASSASSINATIONS	POPULATION SIZE	PRESS CENSORSHIP
New York Times Index		
Total Events	.05	.03
Log Transformation	.09	.14
Attempted Assassinations	.05	.03
Log Transformation	.07	.10
Deadline Data		
Total Events	.05	.07
Log Transformation	.04	.12

interjected at this point. It would seem that acts of serious internal turmoil, certainly civil war and revolution, *coups d'état* and guerrilla warfare, are newsworthy items for all countries. This logic is also applicable to successful assassinations, especially of heads of state and other top governmental officeholders. Any discrepancy in the reporting of assassinations, if it is found, is more apt to be associated with plots or assassination attempts on lesser public figures.

Also, the relationship between press censorship and assassination frequency is negligible, using both logged and unlogged data. In this sense, then, the biases of newsworthiness in reporting and press censorship, if indeed they are still assumed to be present, may be said to minimize a real pattern rather than to mistakenly identify an illusory one.

This evaluation of our data base should not be interpreted as an enthusiasm for imperfection. We would feel more confident with better data. On the other hand, this study employs one of the more extensive cross-national data collections of assassination presently available. The reader should also bear in mind that error exists in all cross-national research, in the reporting of ecological, behavioral, and social indicators. It may be argued, however, that research based on cross-national comparisons can tolerate a considerable amount of random error and still not lose its validity, although similar error would be inexcusable in the analysis of a single case.[11] In this conviction, but also with this caveat, we proceed to the analysis of the factors associated with the cross-national incidence of assassination.

POLITICAL VIOLENCE AND ASSASSINATIONS

Assassinations, no matter how narrowly or broadly conceived, belong among a larger class of politically aggressive and violent behavior. As such they undoubtedly bear some relationship to other acts of internal political turmoil. Attempts to determine this relationship constitute an inquiry into the structure of violence and political aggressiveness in an effort to discover where assassinations fit within the pattern. Two universes of aggressive events were chosen for this purpose. One is defined very broadly and includes not only severe indications of internal political conflict, but also lesser acts of political aggression that in some way may convey the impression that the political system is laboring under strain. Thirty variables of internal conflict make up this first universe of political-instability events: elections, vacation of office, significant change of laws, acquisition of office, crisis within a nongovernmental organization, organization of opposition party, repressive action against specific groups, microstrikes, general strikes, macrostrikes, microdemonstrations, macrodemonstrations, microriots, macro-riots, severe macroriots, arrests of significant persons, imprisonment of significant persons, arrests of few insignificant persons, mass arrests of insignificant persons, imprisonment of insignificant persons, assassination, martial law, execution of significant persons, execution of insignificant persons, terrorism and sabotage,

11. For a discussion of data-error problems and suggested techniques for handling error see: Russett et al., *op. cit.*, and Ted Gurr, *New Error Compensated Measures for Comparing Nations* (Research Monograph No. 25, Princeton University, Center of International Studies, May, 1966), and Donald V. McGranahan, "Comparative Social Research in the United Nations," in Merritt and Rokkan, *op. cit.* Insofar as the ecological indicators are concerned, these are drawn from collections of aggregate data, primarily United Nations statistical compilations. By their very nature, aggregate data tend to oversimplify reality. They are mean calculations of such variables as caloric intake per day, the distribution of wealth, or mass communications. While they cannot be considered good descriptions of individual conditions within a nation, comparisons across nations seem a valid enterprise.

guerrilla warfare, civil war, *coups d'état,* revolts, and exile.[12] The second universe of political turmoil is restricted to the expression of the more violent instances of political aggression and includes the following variables: riots and demonstrations, boycotts, arrests, repressive action against specific groups, sabotage, martial law, *coups d'état,* revolts, guerrilla warfare, assassination, execution, and civil war.[13]

As is true of the assassination events, these political turmoil data were collected for the sample of eighty-four nations for the period 1948–1965 from *Deadline Data on World Affairs* and the *Yearbooks* of the *Encyclopaedia Britannica.* Altogether, some 8,000 events are contained in this data collection.

The first concern of this inquiry, one that has also interested other researchers,[14] is to discover whether there is any pattern of association among these events. Do some events commonly occur with others, while appearing less frequently with still a third type of internal political turmoil? The statistical technique for identifying such a structure, or set of underlying dimensions of political aggressiveness, is factor analysis.

Factor analysis is a statistical procedure designed to isolate empirical clusterings in the data. Events that have a strong tendency to occur in conjunction with each other are grouped together and analytically separated from other events. These events are considered as members of a single dimension. Once an independent dimension has been determined, a search is made for a second dimension, using the identical procedure. This searching for clusterings—for dimensions—continues until no further groups can be found that meet the preselected level of statistical explanation. The obvious advantage of this technique lies in the reduction of a large set of complex data to a much smaller number of dimensions. In our analyses, thirty different types of instability events were re-

12. For a definition of these events see Ivo K. Feierabend and Rosalind L. Feierabend, *Cross-National Data Bank of Political Instability Events (Code Index)* and Francis W. Hoole, *Political Stability and Instability Within Nations: A Cross-National Study* (Master's Thesis, San Diego State College, 1964).

13. Betty A. Nesvold, "Turmoil to Civil War: A Cross-National Analysis" (Ph.D. diss., University of Minnesota, 1968).

14. See the previously cited work of Bwy, Eckstein, Hoole, Gurr, Rummel and Tanter.

duced to nine dimensions by this procedure. Once these dimensions, often referred to as factors, are isolated, the researcher is responsible for interpreting or labeling them.[15]

The results that are reproduced in Table 6 display the nine factors that emerged when the instability data were factor analyzed. If one looks at the high loadings (50 and above) in each column, some interesting groupings emerge. On Factor 1, high loadings are associated with those events that indicate turmoil and mass participation in the political system: strikes, riots, and sabotage. The second factor is one in which revolt is present or seems imminent: repressive action against specific groups, arrests, martial law, *coups d'état*, etc. The variable of particular interest in the present analysis, assassinations, may be found in Factor 9, where it occurs in conjunction with instances of guerrilla warfare. Assassinations also show a reasonably high association with the Revolt Factor (a loading of 40). On the other hand, they are not associated, or only negligibly, with the other dimensions of political turmoil. Thus there is evidence in these findings that assassinations occur predominantly in those nations that are subject to these serious forms of civil disturbance. The nations experiencing primarily lesser-turmoil events experience only a modest number of assassination events.

A second factor analysis was performed with this data bank, using only those events that denoted violence in the system.[16] The purpose of this second analysis was to determine whether the relationships would be clarified by using only events indicating more severe strain in the political system: strikes, riots, arrests, executions, assassinations, guerrilla warfare, revolt, etc. Four factors were found that isolated increasingly stressful clusters of events: (1) turmoil, (2) revolt, (3) guerrilla warfare, and (4) civil war. This served to verify the findings of the larger matrix presented in Table 6. Assassinations loaded highly only with guerrilla warfare. There was little tendency for assassinations to be associated with the other types of events.

15. See Benjamin Fructer, *Introduction to Factor Analysis* (Princeton: Van Nostrand, 1954); Harry H. Harman, *Modern Factor Analysis* (Chicago: University of Chicago Press, 1960); and Fred N. Kerlinger, *Foundations of Behavioral Research* (New York: Holt, Rinehart and Winston, Inc., 1964).
16. Nesvold, *op. cit.*

Additional factor analyses of internal conflict data have been performed by other researchers. Both Rummel and Tanter have factor analyzed a set of conflict data quite similar to our own data collection.[17] Their results cannot be considered a complete verification of ours, however. Rummel's analysis grouped assassinations with guerrilla warfare, but Tanter found no relationship between these two events. In his results, assassinations occurred more frequently with lesser turmoil in the political system (riots, demonstrations, strikes).

The dimensions of aggressive political behavior determined by factor analysis are only one way to look at the underlying structure of internal political turmoil. Another way is to try to sort these events in terms of their intensity of aggressive behavior. It takes no more than common sense to recognize that some events indicate far greater aggression than do others. For example, a peaceful demonstration is by far a lesser event than, let us say, a civil war. Sorting events in this fashion becomes an exercise in scaling aggressive behaviors. At first, the ordering of specific instability events into a scale was approached from the viewpoint of both construct validity and consensual validation. A seven-point instrument was devised, ranging from 0 (denoting extreme stability) through 6 (denoting extreme instability). Each point of the scale was observationally defined in terms of specific events representing differing degrees of stability or instability. An illustration may be given of one item typical of each position on the scale. For example, a general election is an item associated with an 0 position on the rating instructions. Resignation of a cabinet official falls into the 1 position on the scale; peaceful demonstrations into the 2 position; assassination of a significant political figure (but not a chief of state) into the 3 position; mass arrests or assassination of a chief of state into the 4 position; *coups d'état* into the 5 position; and civil war into the 6 position.

Consensual validation for this intensity scale was obtained by asking judges to sort the same events along the same continuum. The level of agreement among judges on the distribution of items was fairly high (Pearson $r = .87$). A second exercise was con-

17. Rummel, "Dimensions of Conflict Behavior"; Tanter, *op. cit.* See page 87 for a discussion of the national conflict data collected by these researchers.

TABLE 6

Rotated Factor Matrix of Domestic Conflict Measures for 84 Nations, 1948–1962

FACTORS

Variables	Mass Participation Turmoil	Palace Revolution Revolt	Power Struggle Purge	Riot	Election	Demonstration	Imprisonment	Civil War	Guerrilla Warfare
1. Elections	29	-02	09	-18	70*	-10	-17	-05	-23
2. Vacation of Office	38	08	74*	-14	20	-11	-15	-25	09
3. Significant Change of Laws	38	41	41	-01	31	15	-16	-23	-11
4. Acquisition of office	29	06	75*	-19	15	-04	-25	-19	22
5. Crisis within a nongovernmental organization	40	13	12	-21	04	-09	62*	07	-23
6. Organization of opposition party	08	10	-02	02	56*	36	19	-39	-10
7. Repressive action against specific groups	46	61*	27	01	-03	16	12	04	12
8. Micro strikes	67*	00	-15	-26	-16	05	12	03	23
9. General strikes	73*	13	04	-42	09	-06	03	08	-18
10. Macro strikes	43	-22	-11	-35	15	-17	-33	-12	-19
11. Micro demonstrations	61*	19	-02	02	20	59*	10	03	02
12. Macro demonstrations	73*	-01	00	26	06	19	18	-21	03
13. Micro riots	46	11	-06	68*	27	-03	-03	-15	11
14. Macro riots	69*	28	-04	33	20	02	04	-08	-05
15. Severe macro riots	64*	-03	-04	53*	11	-19	-02	-20	14
16. Arrests of significant persons	09	64*	54*	07	-14	-06	23	-10	-01
17. Imprisonment of significant persons	-14	12	49	17	-05	16	38	-33	-22
18. Arrests of few insignificant persons	42	09	05	-08	07	75*	07	07	21

FACTORS

Variables	Mass Participation Turmoil	Palace Revolution Revolt	Power Struggle Purge	Riot	Election	Demonstration	Imprisonment	Civil War	Guerrilla Warfare
19. Mass arrests of insignificant persons	52*	33	14	54*	−12	−02	−01	05	01
20. Imprisonment of insignificant persons	26	−08	09	08	−12	34	64*	−03	−14
21. Assassination	17	40	23	06	24	23	−07	−10	56*
22. Martial law	11	71*	03	03	15	09	−27	−06	−08
23. Execution of significant persons	−08	01	54*	31	−26	14	−04	31	05
24. Execution of insignificant persons	01	−10	63*	32	−07	12	−02	47	−02
25. Terrorism and sabotage	62*	28	12	−21	13	−01	10	07	38
26. Guerrilla warfare	04	42	07	−19	19	−35	25	21	55*
27. Civil war	−14	25	31	14	45	08	−08	60*	02
28. Coup d'etat	03	69*	07	01	−02	12	−40	07	−32
29. Revolts	06	75*	−01	11	07	−01	−10	32	16
30. Exile	−09	40	00	03	−36	32	−19	−13	04
Percentage of common variance	23.37	16.30	13.20	9.67	8.33	8.00	7.99	6.76	6.40 = 100.0
Percentage of total variance	23.33	11.11	7.52	6.77	5.89	5.32	4.18	3.82	3.62 = 71.46

* Asterisks indicate loadings > .50. Decimals omitted from loadings.

ducted with a different group of judges, who placed events on a 100-point calibrated scale. This scaling correlated to a high degree with the original scale (Pearson $r = .94$). Other checks performed on the reliability of the method were a comparison of the assignment of items to positions on the scale by two independent raters. Their level of agreement on these scale values involving data from eighty-four countries for a seven-year time period, was very high (Pearson $r = .94$).

It should be noted that assassinations fall into the third and fourth positions of the scale. This positioning is indicative of a considerable degree of internal conflict and crisis, yet it is not sufficiently intense to qualify among the categories of greatest violence within national political systems.[18]

This seven-point instrument has the advantage that it can be used as a scale on which to weigh the internal aggressiveness and violence of each nation. Scaled aggressiveness profiles of the eighty-four nations were calculated for the years 1948–1965. In one technique countries were assigned to groups on the basis of the most unstable event that they experienced during this eighteen-year period. Thus countries that experienced a civil war were placed in group 6; countries that were prey to a *coup d'état* were placed in group 5; countries with mass arrests were assigned to group 4, and so on. The purpose of this assignment was to weight intensity (or quality) of instability events as well as frequency (or quantity) of events. Following the allotment to groups, a total of each country's stability ratings was calculated. Countries were then rank-ordered within groups on the basis of this frequency sum total.

This particular scaling of instability yields a highly skewed distribution. Instability is more prevalent than stability within the

18. For a more extensive discussion of the measurement of political instability and violence, as well as the construction of national aggressiveness profiles, see Ivo K. Feierabend and Rosalind L. Feierabend, "Aggressive Behaviors Within Polities," and Betty A. Nesvold, *op. cit.* See also Ivo K. Feierabend and Rosalind L. Feierabend, "Systemic Conditions of Political Aggression: An Application of Frustration-Aggression Theory," a manuscript awarded the Socio-Psychological Prize of the American Association for the Advancement of Science, December, 1966; and Ivo K. Feierabend, Rosalind L. Feierabend and Darlene L. Boroviak, "Empirical Typologies of Political Systems: Aggressive Prototypes" (Paper presented at the annual meeting of the International Political Science Association, Brussels, Belgium, September 1967).

sample of nations, and the largest proportion of countries are those experiencing an instability event with a scale weighting of 5. Furthermore, there is an interesting combination of countries at each scale position. The most stable scale positions, by and large, include modern nations but also a sprinkling of markedly under-developed polities and some nations from the Communist bloc. Again, the group of extremely unstable countries at scale position 6 comprise nations from Latin America, Asia, the Middle East, and the Communist bloc. The United States is at scale position 4, just below the median position of the group of eighty-four.

Another way of computing the national profiles is presented in Table 7. In this case, country instability profiles were calculated separately for three subperiods of time (1948–1953, 1954–1959, 1960–1965) using the grouped scoring method described above. These three profiles were then summed to obtain the nation's score for the total eighteen-year period. Comparing the differences in country profiles between the two techniques leads to a better understanding of the patterning of violence during this eighteen-year period. In Table 7, the distribution of countries across the scale is less skewed, with most countries falling at position 4 on the scale. Only one country, Indonesia, falls at scale position 6, indicating that it experienced a civil war during each of the three six-year subperiods. No country is at scale position 0, but a few (Ireland, Luxembourg, and the Netherlands) are at position 1. Thus the many countries that experienced some highly violent events during one six-year period have their scores tempered in Table 7 if they had relatively nonviolent experiences in some other six-year period. Some of the Communist-bloc countries fall into this category. They experienced turmoil at the time of Communist seizure of power during the 1940's but, with the exception of Hungary, did not undergo further violence of this magnitude in the ensuing years. The United States does not shift positions from one profiling method to the other. In both techniques it is at scale position 4 and at rank-order position 38 or 39, just below the median rank position of 42. Thus the level of political violence in the United States during this eighteen-year time period is higher than that experienced by approximately half of the nations in the sample, but lower than the internal violence characterizing the other half.

TABLE 7

Political Instability Profiles of Eighty-Four Countries (1948–1965)
(Stability Score Shown for Each Country is Grouped Score, Summed)

1	2	3	4	5	6
Netherland 04021	U.K. 07112	Belgium 10162	France 13435	Argentina 16445	Indonesia 18416
Luxembg. 03012	Ghana 07106	Chile 10156	U. of So. Africa 13422	Bolivia 16318	
	Austria 07057	Mexico 10111	Brazil 13209	Cuba 16283	
	Denmark 07030	Uruguay 10100	Morocco 13194	Iraq 16274	
	Iceland 07026	Israel 10064	Portugal 13190	Colombia 16244	
	W. Germany 06087	Liberia 10036	Turkey 13189	Burma 16213	
	Finland 06056	Ethiopia 10034	Poland 13179	Venezuela 15429	
	Taiwan 06039	Italy 09192	Thailand 13152	Syria 15329	
	Australia 06026	Libya 09069	Jordan 13145	Korea 15291	
	Sweden 06020	Romania 09060	Cyprus 13123	Haiti 15205	
	Ireland 05031	Costa Rica 09058	Hungary 13113	Peru 15196	
	S. Arabia 05018	Afghan. 09029	Philipp. 13105	Greece 14236	
	N. Zealand 05015	Canada 09029	Czech. 13100	Guatem. 14234	
		Switzer. 08042	China (M) 13086	Lebanon 14212	
		Norway 08034	Cambodia 13071	Egypt 14152	
			India 12360	Paraguay 14141	
			Iran 12237	E. Germany 14138	
			Pakistan 12231	Laos 14129	
			Sudan 12189	Tunisia 14126	
			USSR 12165	Honduras 14105	
			Ecuador 12117	Panama 14101	
			Nicaragua 12096	El Salvador 14079	
			USA 11318		
			Spain 11284		
			Dom. Rep. 11195		
			Ceylon 11152		
			Japan 11123		
			Malaya 11108		
			Yugosl. 11077		
			Bulgaria 11071		
			Albania 11067		

A third way of computing these national profiles is presented in Table 8. Instead of grouping scores so that one weights for the most serious event experienced by each nation, a simple summation of all instability scores for the eighteen-year period is used. Most of the nations remain in relatively the same rank-order position, yet there are some major shifts. The United States, in particular, ranks as one of the highly unstable nations of the world by this method.

The universe of exclusively violent events was scaled in yet another way. A Guttman scalogram was used, a technique that avoids the subjective judgments that typify the placement of aggressive events on consensually derived scales. Events were first clustered according to their pattern of occurrence among the eighty-four countries studied. Four groupings were discovered in the data. The first group includes riots, demonstrations, and boycotts, arrests, government actions against specific groups, and sabotage. The second comprises martial law, *coups d'état* and revolt. The third consists of guerrilla warfare and assassinations, and the fourth, executions and civil war.

Analyzing the data in reference to these groupings, we find that countries experiencing events listed in group 4 also experienced events in groups 3, 2, and 1. Other countries experienced events in groups 3, 2, and 1, however, without experiencing the most extreme events listed in group 4. Similarly, the patterning of violence for still other countries was limited to events in groups 2 and 1. Finally, there were countries that experienced events from group 1 only, or others that were beset by no events of this violent a nature. These empirical findings show that political violence is an ordered and scalable universe rather than an arbitrary and random occurrence.[19] They suggest that the occurrence of assassination usually denotes a high degree (point 3), although not necessarily the highest degree (point 4), of internal political turmoil. This is essentially the same patterning of variables that was isolated by factor analysis, as well as by consensually derived scales. All techniques uniformly suggest that in the global assessment of assassinations, those countries that experience this political aberration

19. The Guttman scaling of violence data revealed an intensity ordering of the events to a high degree of reproducibility ($r = .97$).

TABLE 8

Political Instability Profiles for Eighty-Four Countries, 1948–1965
(Summed Scores)

Country	Score	Country	Score	Country	Score
Luxembourg	12	West Germany	87	Turkey	189
New Zealand	15	Nicaragua	96	Portugal	190
Saudi Arabia	18	Czechoslovakia	100	Italy	191
Sweden	20	Uruguay	100	Morocco	194
Netherlands	21	Panama	101	Dom. Republic	195
Iceland	26	Honduras	105	Peru	196
Australia	26	Philippines	105	Haiti	205
Afghanistan	29	Ghana	106	Brazil	208
Denmark	30	Malaya	108	Lebanon	212
Ireland	31	Mexico	111	Burma	213
Ethiopia	34	Hungary	113	Pakistan	231
Norway	34	United Kingdom	116	Guatemala	234
Liberia	36	Ecuador	117	Greece	236
China (Taiwan)	39	Cyprus	123	Iran	237
Switzerland	42	Japan	123	Colombia	244
Finland	56	Tunisia	126	Iraq	274
Austria	57	Laos	129	Cuba	281
Costa Rica	58	East Germany	138	Spain	284
Rumania	60	Paraguay	141	Korea	291
Israel	64	Jordan	145	United States	319
Albania	67	Ceylon	152	Bolivia	323
Libya	69	Thailand	152	Syria	329
Bulgaria	71	Egypt	153	India	360
Chile	71	Chile	156	Indonesia	416
Cambodia	71	Belgium	162	Union South Africa	427
Yugoslavia	77	U.S.S.R.	165	Venezuela	429
El Salvador	79	Poland	179	France	435
Canada	83	Sudan	189	Argentina	445
China (Mainland)	86				

are generally the ones that also experience widespread, highly intense violent activity.

If one looks at the instability trends over time in the United States, it may be argued that this generalization applies to this country as well. Twelve assassination events in the United States stem from the 1960's, with only four occurring in the 1950's. This is also the time of increased turmoil in the United States, especially where riots and demonstrations are concerned. While the United States in the 1950's reached only the third position on the seven-point scale, in the 1960's it is in the fourth grouped scale position.

The national profiles that utilize the scale positions of the Guttman scalogram are presented in Table 9. They are the summed Guttman scale scores of all events that occurred within eighty-four countries during 1948–1965.

It should be noted that all four estimates of national aggressive-ness are in substantial agreement, although they use different tech-niques to measure political instability and violence, and although the positioning of some countries is shifted from table to table. The intercorrelations among the four techniques range from .5 to .8, as may be seen in Table 10. This indicates consistency among these methods in isolating a common underlying dimension.

A further test was made of the validity of the measurement by selecting a shorter time period that coincides with a separate re-search project investigating essentially the same variable. Ted Gurr's study of Total Magnitude of Civil Violence scores nations on this dimension for the period 1961–1965.[20] Our measures and Gurr's show a similar patterning as indicated by the correlation coefficients of .6 to .7 between his measure and our three profile techniques.

The last and most important question regarding the violence data is to ascertain the degree of relationship that may obtain between the assassination profiles and the general violence profiles of the eighty-four countries. One such relationship is presented in Table 11. Here countries are dichotomized into those experiencing high frequencies and those experiencing low frequencies of assassi-nation events. The cutting point is between two and three assassi-

20. Ted Gurr, "A Causal Model of Civil Strife: A Comparative Analysis Using New Indices," *American Political Science Review* (December, 1968), pp. 1104–1124.

TABLE 9

Political Violence Profiles of Eighty-Four Countries, 1948–1965
(Scores Derived from Guttman Scalogram)

Country	Score	Country	Score	Country	Score
Finland	0	Yugoslavia	27	Dom. Republic	70
Luxembourg	0	China (Mainland)	28	Sudan	71
Denmark	1	El Salvador	28	Laos	72
Iceland	1	Belgium	31	Greece	73
New Zealand	1	Albania	32	Paraguay	74
Saudi Arabia	1	Japan	32	Haiti	77
Netherlands	2	Czechoslovakia	33	Pakistan	77
Norway	3	Mexico	33	Portugal	77
Sweden	3	Ghana	35	Morocco	79
Australia	4	Malaya	36	U.S.S.R.	81
Afghanistan	7	Chile	38	Lebanon	83
Austria	7	East Germany	39	Burma	87
Ireland	7	Cyprus	41	France	95
Switzerland	7	Ecuador	41	Colombia	96
Israel	8	Jordan	41	United States	97
China (Taiwan)	9	Honduras	42	Guatemala	109
Canada	10	Panama	42	Syria	111
Liberia	15	Hungary	45	Iran	114
Uruguay	16	Nicaragua	48	Bolivia	120
United Kingdom	17	Ceylon	51	Iraq	120
Ethiopia	19	Philippines	51	Spain	121
Italy	19	Poland	54	Cuba	123
Rumania	20	Tunisia	54	India	124
West Germany	20	Egypt	56	Korea	125
Costa Rica	21	Brazil	57	Argentina	134
Cambodia	24	Peru	64	Venezuela	153
Bulgaria	25	Thailand	65	Union South Africa	158
Libya	25	Turkey	65	Indonesia	190

TABLE 10

Interrelationships Among Political Instability and Violence Profiles
of Nations, 1948–1965 (Product-Moment Correlations)

	1	2	3	4
1. Violence, Guttman Summed Values	–			
2. Instability, Summed Values	.65	–		
3. Instability, Grouped Values (Three Periods Summed)	.56	.82	–	
4. Instability, Grouped Values (Total Period)	.60	.79	.72	–

nations. These are the countries listed in the rows of the table, while the columns show the same eighty-four countries distributed among the six scale positions of political instability calculated in Table 7. As may be seen, there is a definite relationship. Countries with high frequencies of assassination fall predominantly at positions 4 and 5 on the instability scale. None falls at scale position 1, and only one country is at scale position 2. (Only one country falls at scale position 6—Indonesia. Cf. Table 7.) Countries low in assassination frequency, on the other hand, come primarily from scale positions 2, 3, and to some extent, 4. None is from position 6, and only four are from scale position 5.

Table 12 shows the same relationship using other methods of measuring political instability. In Table 12A, instability is measured by the grouped scoring method (not averaged). Table 12B uses the summed scale values given in Table 8, and Table 12C is based on the Guttman scale scores given in Table 9. These tables show a high degree of relationship between assassination frequency and level of political instability.

The strength of association between the two variables is also expressed in the correlation coefficients shown in Table 13. As can be seen, the values of the several correlations indicate a range from a moderately low to a moderately high degree of association between the several measures (Pearson $r = .4$ to $.6$). To repeat a point made in a previous section, the correlational patterns based on *Deadline Data* are not particularly divergent from the patterns based on the *New York Times Index*.

To summarize these findings, it appears that the general level of political violence is one of the more efficient predictors of assassi-

TABLE 11

Relationship Between Frequency of Assassination and Level of Political Instability*
(Grouped and Summed for Three Periods)

Instability

	1	2	3	4	5	6
ASSASSINATIONS HIGH (THREE AND ABOVE)		Ghana (7)	Italy (3) Israel (3) Mexico (3)	Malaya (6) Japan (9) Dom. Rep. (7) United States (16) Nicaragua (5) Ecuador (3) Pakistan (5) Iran (19) India (8) Cambodia (6) China (main) (3) Czech. (5) Philippines (15) Cyprus (5) Jordan (6) Thailand (3) Turkey (4) Morocco (17) Brazil (12) Union South Africa (3) France (14)	Panama (5) Tunisia (16) Laos (10) Paraguay (3) Egypt (14) Lebanon (12) Guatemala (12) Greece (5) Korea (20) Haiti (5) Syria (7) Venezuela (12) Burma (5) Colombia (7) Iraq (5) Cuba (28) Bolivia (9) Argentina (9)	Indonesia (5)
	0	1	3	21	18	1

Instability

ASSASSINATIONS Low (TWO AND BELOW)	1	2	3	4	5	6
	Ireland (0)	New Zealand (1)	Norway (0)	Albania (2)	El Salvador (2)	
	Luxembourg (0)	Saudi Arabia (2)	Switzerland (0)	Bulgaria (0)	Honduras (0)	
	Netherlands (0)	Sweden (0)	Canada (1)	Yugoslavia (2)	East Germany (0)	
		Australia (2)	Afghanistan (2)	Ceylon (2)	Peru (0)	
		China (Taiwan) (0)	Costa Rica (2)	Spain (2)		
		Finland (0)	Rumania (2)	U.S.S.R. (0)		
		West Germany (2)	Libya (1)	Sudan (1)		
		Iceland (0)	Ethiopia (2)	Hungary (1)		
		Denmark (0)	Liberia (2)	Poland (0)		
		Austria (1)	Uruguay (0)	Portugal (2)		
		United Kingdom (0)	Chile (0)			
			Belgium (1)			
	3	11	12	10	4	0

* Values in parenthesis indicate the number of assassinations.

TABLE 12

Relationship Between Assassination Frequency
and Political Instability

A. ASSASSINATIONS	Stability (*Grouped scores*)		
	Low (1–4)	High (5–6)	
High (3 and more)	8	36	44
Low (2 and less)	30	10	40
	38	46	84
Chi square = 25.06	p < .001		

B. ASSASSINATIONS	Stability (*Summed scores*)		
	Low (012–125)	High (126–445)	
High (3 and more)	13	31	44
Low (2 and less)	30	10	40
	43	41	84
Chi square = 18.38	p < .001		

C. ASSASSINATIONS	Stability (*Guttman Scale Values*)		
	Low (0–41)	High (42–190)	
High (3 and more)	12	32	44
Low (2 and less)	31	9	40
	43	41	84
Chi square = 21.16	p < .001		

nation. That is, if we were to single out one characteristic of a national system, without knowing the country's assassination profile, the general violence-instability profile would give a strong clue whether the political system is assassination prone. To illustrate the point from Table 11, if we were to predict high and low frequency of assassinations occurring in the eighty-four countries, we might be right in sixty-six cases, and probably wrong in eighteen cases. This is an informed guess rather than reliance on chance alone. The probability that the relationship demonstrated in Table 11 would occur by chance is less than one in a thousand.

TABLE 13

Interrelationship Between Level of Political Instability
and Frequency of Assassination
(Product-Moment Correlations)

Assassinations

	New York Times Index	New York Times Index Transformed	Deadline Data	Deadline Data Transformed
Violence, Guttman Summed Values 1948–1965	.57	.61	.45	.48
Instability Summed Values 1948–1965	.53	.63	.50	.57
Instability Grouped Values (3 Periods Summed) 1948–1965	.50	.56	.38	.46
Instability Grouped Values (Total Period) 1948–1965	.44	.57	.37	.46

VIOLENCE, ASSASSINATION, ECOLOGICAL, AND POLITICAL VARIABLES

The findings of cross-national empirical studies suggest that political violence is not a random occurrence. Violence appears to be related to a number of conditions that stem from the environment of political systems. If this is the case, the occurrence of assassination may also be pinpointed within broader patterns of national behaviors and characteristics.

A few hypotheses are suggested as guidelines for the identification of relevant aspects of national systems, which might aid in the understanding of political violence and assassination. They derive from a broader theoretical base and a more elaborate theory of

internal war and civil disorder.[21] One insight suggests that social
discontent, socioeconomic frustration and relative deprivation are
important preconditions of political unrest. These conditions may
be typified as those in which levels of social expectations, aspirations, and needs are raised for many people for significant periods
of time, and yet remain unmatched by equivalent levels of satisfac-
tion. The notion $\dfrac{\text{social want formation}}{\text{social want satisfaction}}$ = systemic frustration
indicates this relationship.

A variety of social conditions may satisfy or leave unsatisfied
the social wants of different strata of the population within social
systems. In our present century the process of modernization is
certain to create new wants and aspirations in the less-developed
countries. The acquisition of modern goals, however, is not synonymous with their attainment, and an inevitable lag between aspirations and achievements is likely in the transitional nations. The
expectations of higher standards of living, improvement in social
organization, and increased status in the community of nations is
rarely matched by the realities. The arousal of the transitional
society to awareness of modern patterns and organization brings
with it a desire to emulate these patterns. Often change falls short
of success or is not sufficiently widespread to produce social satisfaction.

The transitional society thus experiences considerable discrepancy between social wants and social satisfactions. This is less apt
to be the condition in modern states in which high levels of wants
are matched by comparable levels of satisfactions. In highly traditional societies, on the other hand, as yet little exposed to modernity, wants and satisfactions are matched at equally low levels.
Furthermore, in these transitional nations an increased participa-

21. Reference is made to a very considerable body of literature on political violence, internal war, and revolution. For a summary, as well as a discussion of the many and often contradictory insights, see Harry Eckstein,
"On the Etiology of Internal Wars," *History and Theory*, LV, No. 2
(1965). For a systematic and elaborated theoretical restatement of the
topic, relying on the frustration-aggression model in social psychology, see
Ted Gurr, "Psychological Factors in Civil Violence," *World Politics* (January, 1968) and, by the same author, "The Genesis of Violence: A Multivariate Theory of the Preconditions for Civil Strife" (Ph.D. diss., New
York University, 1965).

tion in modern life implies the growth of newly awakened strata of politically participating persons. These are in contrast to the quiescence and apathy of more traditional strata and their weaker inclination to political activity.

A second broad insight encountered in the literature on development is that rapid social change breeds crisis, disorder, and violence. All social change may be so implicated, no matter what its roots. International war or the rampage of a foreign occupation may be the source of change, or a severe inflation or depression, which plays havoc with the social structure. It may also be spectacular technological achievement. Today, in global perspective, the broad process of modernization itself may be viewed as bringing historically unprecedented change. It is a process during which former patterns of behavior, culture, and beliefs, outdated technology, territorial units, identification, established roles, statuses and norms, all must give way to new, unfamiliar patterns. The transitional personality is frustrated by his breakoff from the past and the uncertainty of the present and the future. The faster the process and the more abrupt the change, the greater is the likelihood of social disorder.[22]

These two broad hypotheses regarding the preconditions of violence need not be confined to the transitional nations. Even nations that are modern in their aggregate image may harbor pockets of underdevelopment. Traditional and underprivileged strata of the population may just be emerging into the light of modern culture in many aspects of aspiration, expectation, political participation, and rapid social change. This hypothesis is applicable to a variety of ethnic, racial, linguistic, and religious minority groups; the emergence of American Negroes since the Civil War, a process accelerated in the 1950's and 1960's, serves as an illustration.

---

22. There is a vast literature in all of the social sciences dealing with the modernization process, exposure to modernity, participant society, and political development. The theme of massive social change, instability, and political crisis is commonly acknowledged. Lucian W. Pye, in *Aspects of Political Development* (Boston: Little, Brown, 1966), for example, identifies six such crises that hamper smooth political processes: the identity crisis, the legitimacy crisis, the penetration crisis, the participation crisis, the integration crisis, and the distribution crisis.

A further set of hypotheses points to the influence of political conditions on the occurrence of violence. For example, coerciveness of political regime, the severe and consistent use of force, threat and repression, undoubtedly serve to curb overt expressions of political unrest in spite of the preconditions for such behavior present within social systems. On the other hand, unpopular, arbitrary, and repressive regimes, especially regimes that are perceived as lacking in legitimacy, must also be presumed to create social discontent as well as fear, apathy, and political withdrawal. Thus it could be hypothesized that both permissive and very oppressive totalitarian regimes will experience fewer acts of political violence, including assassinations. Regimes that are at mid-levels of coerciveness and only sometimes or erratically resort to oppression will experience higher levels of political violence.

Several other national characteristics may also be relevant to the occurrence of violence and assassination. One of these is the level of tension between ethnic minorities and majority groups. This indicates a specific mode of instability within the political system and hence could also be considered as a possible predictor of assassination. With ethnic minorities the question is raised: To what degree does the presence of minorities within nations and minority-majority tension contribute to assassination frequency?

Two additional conditions that may relate to political violence in general and to assassination in particular are international hostility, and homicide/suicide rates. The notion that external conflict is related to internal turmoil is a time-honored hypothesis. Governments internally threatened by the wrath of their own populace are said to look for external adventure as a diversionary technique. The foreign enemy may bring a new cohesiveness to a restless, dissatisfied people and serve as a target on which to vent the pent-up aggressive impulse and anger. Or the direction of relationship may be the reverse. In this case, it is the involvement in external conflict that leads to a rise in popular dissatisfaction and political instability. Level of external conflict may thus relate over time to level of internal conflict and serve as an additional predictor of violence and assassination.[23]

23. An example of the view that involvement in external conflict serves as a means of diverting popular dissatisfaction may be found in Sigmund Neumann's discussion in Taylor Cole, ed., *European Political Systems* (New

Homicide and suicide may also be considered as either reinforcing or providing alternative outlets for the aggressive impulse. Furthermore, since assassinations are only a special case of homicide, it may be that societies with high homicide rates are prone to claim their victims from political as well as private strata. In this respect, assassinations may be considered as a violent breakthrough from the social sphere into the political arena. If this is the case, a high frequency of assassinations would also correspond to high rates of homicide recorded for the social systems of the eightyfour nations. Suicide, on the other hand, may be considered as an internalized mode of aggressive response. This can be hypothesized to indicate a milieu in which frustration leads to apathy and withdrawal rather than to protest and violence. Thus one would predict a negative relationship between the suicide rates of nations and their level of violence and assassination.[24]

In the remainder of this paper all these potential preconditions of violence and assassination are examined empirically. For this purpose, specific ecological and political indicators were selected to assess each nation for its level of development, rate of socioeconomic change, level of permissiveness or coerciveness of political regime, involvement in external conflict, level of ethnic-group conflict and homicide/suicide rates.

York: Alfred A. Knopf, 1959). The empirical linkage between external and internal conflict has been both asserted and denied by different researchers. Rummel claims that the two dimensions are unrelated (Rummel, "Dimensions of Conflict Behavior Within and Between Nations"). And Tanter finds only a very small relationship between them (Tanter, *op. cit.*). On the other hand, the following researchers all find some patterning between the two types of conflict: F. H. Denton, "Some Regularities in International Conflict, 1820–1949," *Background,* 9 (1966); Michael Haas, "Some Societal Correlates of International Political Behavior" (Ph.D. diss., Stanford University, 1964); Jonathan Wilkenfeld, "Domestic and Foreign Conflict Behavior of Nations," *Journal of Peace Research,* No. 1 (1968), pp. 56–70; and Ivo K. Feierabend and R. L. Feierabend, "Level of Development and International Behavior," in Richard C. Butwell, ed., *Development and Foreign Policy* (Lexington: University of Kentucky Press, 1970).

24. Some of these notions are elaborated in Emil Durkheim, *Suicide* (New York: The Free Press, 1963). They have been explored empirically by Robert W. Winslow, "Social Integration, Political Instability, Suicide and Homicide: A Cross-National Study" (Paper delivered at the annual meeting of the Pacific Sociological Association, San Francisco, March, 1968).

LEVEL OF DEVELOPMENT AND POLITICAL VIOLENCE

Level of development, or modernity level, may be indexed in several ways. In previous studies we devised a modernity index based on eight indicators: GNP per capita, literacy level, radios and newspapers per 1,000 population, rate of urbanization, caloric intake per person per day, number of persons per physician and per cent of population having telephones.[25] Standard scores for each country on each of these indicators were averaged to yield an overall estimate of level of attainment on these aspects of modern, industrial society. The resulting distribution of countries was divided into three groups. The twenty-four countries scoring the highest on this dimension were designated modern. The twenty-three countries falling at the lowest end of the continuum were called traditional, although perhaps low development would be a better designation. The thirty-seven countries falling between the modern and traditional groups were termed transitional.

What is the relationship between modernity level and level of political violence? Are less developed countries more or less prone to violence and assassinations? The answers to these questions may be found in Table 14. Table 14A shows the relationshp between modernity level and political violence.[26] There is a definite tendency for the modern group of countries to fall predominantly at a low level of political instability; three-fourths of the countries in this group are stable compared with one-fourth, which are unstable. On the other hand, a preponderance of transitional countries give evidence of instability. Slightly over twice as many transitional countries are unstable rather than stable. Among the traditional group of countries the tendency toward stability is about equal to the tendency toward instability. The probability of obtaining this result by chance is less than one in a hundred (Chi

25. These indicators, which are based primarily on U.N. statistics for 1948–1955, are further discussed in: Ivo K. Feierabend and Rosalind L. Feierabend, "Aggressive Behaviors Within Polities"; Betty A. Nesvold, *Turmoil to Civil War,* and Betty A. Nesvold, "Modernity, Social Frustration, and Stability of Political Systems: A Cross-National Study" (Master's thesis, San Diego State College, 1964).

26. Level of political instability is measured by the summed scoring method shown in Table 8. This measure of political instability is used in this and all subsequent tables.

square = 13.71). The correlation coefficient for this relationship is —.38. (See Table 22 for all correlation coefficients between instability and assassination and the selected set of ecological, political and social predictor variables.)

A somewhat similar pattern obtains between level of development and frequency of assassination (Table 14B). Only five of twenty-four modern countries, or 21 per cent, experience a high frequency of assassination. This relationship is reversed for both transitional and traditional countries, however. Well over half the countries at both of these lower levels of development have had more than three assassinations in the past twenty years. The likelihood of this pattern occurring by chance is less than five times in a hundred (Chi square = 7.76). The correlation coefficient for this relationship is —.40.

We may say, then, that there is a definite relationship between level of development and incidence of political violence, including assassination. Developed countries tend to experience lower levels of political unrest and assassination; less developed countries tend to experience higher levels of political unrest and assassination. There are also exceptions to this tendency at all three levels of development. Among modern countries the United States and France are notable exceptions, as has been pointed out earlier in this report. Among nations at the two lower levels of development, about one-third are exceptions to the trend. It also must be noted that no difference in trend is apparent in Table 14B, and only a small difference in Table 14A, between the incidence of political violence in traditional and transitional countries. Both groups of states show a tendency toward political instability and assassination.

We may also examine assassination frequency in relation to a more detailed breakdown of level of development. The results are indicated in Table 15. The five different levels of development labeled in this table are taken from the *World Handbook of Political and Social Indicators.*[27] The division into five groups is based on one indicator: GNP in United States dollars, in 1957.

In Table 15 a tendency is shown for countries at the lowest level of development, traditional primitive societies, to experience a low

27. Russett et al., *op. cit.*, pp. 293–298.

TABLE 14

A. Relationship Between Level of Modernity and Political Instability

	I. Traditional	II. Transitional	III. Modern	
UNSTABLE (126–445)	Bolivia Burma Haiti India Indonesia Iran Iraq Jordan Laos Morocco Pakistan Sudan	Brazil Ceylon Chile Colombia Cuba Dom. Republic Egypt Greece Guatemala Italy Korea Lebanon Paraguay Peru Poland Portugal Spain Syria Thailand Tunisia Turkey Union South Africa Venezuela	Argentina Belgium East Germany France United States U.S.S.R.	
	12	23	6	41
STABLE (012–125) Chi square = 13.71 p < .01	Afghanistan Cambodia China (Taiwan) China (mainland) Ethiopia Ghana Liberia Libya Malaya Philippines Saudi Arabia	Albania Bulgaria Costa Rica Cyprus Ecuador El Salvador Honduras Hungary Japan Mexico Nicaragua Panama Rumania Yugoslavia	Australia Austria Canada Czechoslovakia Denmark Finland Iceland Ireland Israel Luxembourg Netherlands New Zealand Norway Sweden Switzerland United Kingdom Uruguay West Germany	
	11	14	18	43
	23	37	24	84

	I. Traditional	II. Transitional	III. Modern	
HIGH FREQUENCY OF ASSASSINATIONS (3 OR MORE)	Bolivia (9) Malaya (6) Burma (5) Morocco (17) Cambodia (6) Pakistan (5) China (Mainland) (3) Philippines (15) Ghana (7) Haiti (5) India (8) Indonesia (5) Iran (19) Iraq (5) Jordan (6) Laos (10)	Brazil (12) Lebanon (12) Colombia (7) Mexico (3) Cuba (28) Nicaragua (5) Cyprus (5) Panama (5) Dom. Republic (7) Paraguay (3) Ecuador (3) Syria (7) Egypt (14) Thailand (3) Greece (5) Tunisia (16) Guatemala (12) Turkey (4) Italy (3) Union So. Africa (3) Korea (20) Venezuela (12) Japan (9)	Argentina (9) Czechoslovakia (5) France (14) Israel (3) United States (16)	
	16	23	5	44
LOW FREQUENCY OF ASSASSINATIONS (2 OR LESS) Chi square = 7.76 p < .05	Afghanistan (2) China (Taiwan) (0) Ethiopia (2) Liberia (2) Libya (1) Saudi Arabia (2) Sudan (1)	Albania (2) Portugal (2) Bulgaria (0) Rumania (0) Ceylon (2) Spain (2) Chile (0) Yugoslavia (2) Costa Rica (2) El Salvador (2) Honduras (0) Hungary (1) Peru (0) Poland (0)	Australia (2) Netherlands (0) Austria (1) New Zealand (1) Belgium (1) Sweden (0) Canada (1) Norway (0) Denmark (0) Switzerland (0) East Germany (0) United Kingdom (0) Finland (0) Uruguay (0) Iceland (0) U.S.S.R. (0) Ireland (0) West Germany (2) Luxembourg (0)	
	7	14	19	40
	23	37	24	84

TABLE 15

Relationship Between Level of Development and Frequency of Assassination

	I. Traditional Primitive Societies	II. Traditional Civilizations	III. Transitional Societies	IV. Industrial Revolution Societies	V. High Mass Consumption Societies
HIGH FREQUENCY OF ASSASSINATIONS (3 OR MORE)	Burma (5) Laos (10)	Bolivia (9) Cambodia (6) China— Mainland (3) Haiti (5) India (8) Pakistan (5) Thailand (3)	Dom. Rep.(7) Ecuador (3) Egypt (14) Ghana (7) Guatemala (12) Indonesia (5) Iran (19) Iraq (5) Jordan (6) Korea (20) Morocco (17) Nicaragua (5) Paraguay (3) Philippines (15) Syria (7) Tunisia (16) Turkey (4)	Argentina (9) Brazil (13) Colombia (7) Cuba (28) Czecho- slovakia (5) Cyprus (3) Greece (5) Italy (3) Israel (3) Japan (9) Lebanon (12) Malaya (6) Mexico (3) Panama (5) Union So. Africa (14) Venezuela (12)	France (14) United States (16)
	2	7	17	16	2	44

	I. Traditional Primitive Societies	II. Traditional Civilizations	III. Transitional Societies	IV. Industrial Revolution Societies	V. High Mass Consumption Societies

	Afghanistan (2)
	Ethiopia (2)
	Libya (1)
	Sudan (1)
		Liberia (2)	Albania (2)
			Ceylon (2)
			China—
			  Taiwan (0)
			El Salvador (2)
			Honduras (0)
			Peru (0)
			Portugal (2)
			Saudi Arabia (2)
				Austria (1)
				Bulgaria (0)
				Chile (0)
				Costa Rica (2)
				East
				  Germany (0)
				Finland (0)
				Hungary (1)
				Iceland (0)
				Ireland (0)
				Poland (0)
				Rumania (0)
				Spain (2)
				Uruguay (0)
				USSR (0)
				Yugoslavia (2)
					Australia (2)
					Belgium (1)
					Canada (1)
					Denmark 0
					Luxembourg (0)
					Netherlands (0)
					New Zealand (1)
					Norway (0)
					Sweden (0)
					Switzerland (0)
					United
					  Kingdom (0)
					West Germany (2)

High	4	1	8	15	12	40
Low FREQUENCY OF ASSASSINATIONS (2 OR LESS) Chi sq. = 16.57 p < .001	6	8	25	31	14	84

level of assassinations. This is interesting, since in our measure of modernity, the so-called traditional group of states showed the highest incidence of assassinations. Unfortunately, the total number of traditional primitive societies is very small. Two-thirds of them, however, experience few assassinations. The trend is strikingly in the opposite direction at the next two levels of development. Among so-called traditional civilizations, the ratio of countries with a high frequency of assassinations, compared with those with a low incidence of this form of political violence, is 7:1. In transitional societies, the same ratio is slightly in excess of 2:1. At the fourth level of development, however, among Industrial Revolution societies, countries are equally divided between those that are high and those that are low in assassination frequency. Finally, at the highest level of development, among high mass-consumption societies, the trend is markedly in the direction of a low frequency of assassinations. Only two countries are exceptions to the trend, the United States and France. The patterning evidenced in Table 15 would be expected only one time in a thousand by chance (Chi square $= 16.57$). The correlation coefficient for the relationship between GNP/capita in 1957 and political instability, 1948–1965, is $r = -.36$. The coefficient for the relationship to assassinations is $-.28$. (See Table 22).

SYSTEMIC FRUSTRATION-SATISFACTION AND POLITICAL VIOLENCE

Another condition that we have selected as potentially related to level of political unrest is the degree of systemic frustration experienced within a society.[28] The notion of systemic frustration, as explicated earlier, is closely related to level of socioeconomic development. It refers to the gap or ratio between social wants and social satisfactions within a society, and is postulated to be curvilinearly related to modernity level: traditional and modern societies should both be relatively satisfied, while transitional societies should be relatively unsatisfied, since they have been awakened to a desire for a new way of life but are only beginning to achieve it.

28. See Feierabend and Feierabend, "Aggressive Behaviors Within Polities."

In order to measure level of systemic frustration, a Frustration Index was devised by forming a ratio from the eight indicators used in the Modernity Index. Literacy and urbanization comprised the numerator of the ratio, indicating level of want formation within society. This choice was based on notions of social mobilization, in which literacy and city life are two media through which persons in underdeveloped societies may gain knowledge of new patterns. The remaining six indicators, GNP/capita, caloric intake, radios, newspapers, physicians, and telephones, were regarded as measures of want satisfaction, forming the denominator of the ratio.

Once countries are ordered on this frustration-satisfaction dimension, relationships can be determined between this ecological condition and general political instability level, as well as incidence of assassination. Table 16A gives the relationship between systemic satisfaction level and level of political unrest, while Table 16B relates systemic satisfaction to assassination frequency.[29]

The relationships shown in these tables indicate that satisfied countries are less prone to political instability and assassination than are frustrated societies. Two-thirds of the countries that are low in systemic satisfaction are politically unstable; 60 per cent of countries high in systemic satisfaction are politically stable. The likelihood of obtaining this relationship by chance is less than five times in a hundred (Chi square = 4.07). We find a similar relationship indicated between systemic satisfaction and frequency of assassination. Seventy-eight per cent of the countries that are low in systemic satisfaction have experienced three or more assassinations in the past twenty years; 60 per cent of countries that are high in satisfaction have had two or fewer assassinations. Again, this relationship could be expected to occur by chance less than one time in a hundred (Chi square = 7.84). The correlation coefficients indexing these relationships are $r = -.57$ between satis-

29. The cutting points on the variables in this table, as well as in all of the two-by-two contingency tables presented in this report, were set at the median values on each dimension, thus equalizing the number of cases in the marginals. Also, Yates's correction for continuity was used in calculating the Chi square values for all two-by-two tables. If we were to manipulate the cutting points, we would discover threshold values of the predictor indicators, as well as increase the values of the Chi Squares.

TABLE 16

A. Relationship Between Level of Systemic Satisfaction and Political Instability

	Low Satisfaction		High Satisfaction		
UNSTABLE (126–445)	Bolivia Brazil Ceylon Chile Colombia Cuba Dom. Republic Egypt Greece Guatemala Haiti India	Iraq Italy Korea Paraguay Peru Spain Syria Thailand Turkey Venezuela	Argentina Belgium France Indonesia Iran Lebanon Morocco Pakistan Portugal Tunisia Union of South Africa United States	Netherlands New Zealand Norway Sweden Switzerland United Kingdom Uruguay West Germany	
		22		12	34
STABLE (012–125) Chi square = 4.07 $p < .05$	Bulgaria Cyprus Ecuador El Salvador Japan Panama Philippines Mexico Nicaragua Yugoslavia		Australia Austria Canada Costa Rica Czechoslovakia Denmark Finland Iceland Ireland Israel		
	10		18		28
	32		30		62

B. Relationship Between Systemic
Satisfaction and Frequency of Assassination

	Low Satisfaction	High Satisfaction	
HIGH FREQUENCY OF ASSASSINATIONS (3 OR MORE)	Bolivia (9) Brazil (12) Colombia (7) Cuba (28) Cyprus (5) Dom. Republic (7) Ecuador (3) Egypt (14) Greece (5) Guatemala (12) Haiti (5) India (8) Iraq (5) Italy (3) Japan (9) Korea (20) Mexico (3) Nicaragua (5) Panama (5) Paraguay (3) Philippines (15) Syria (7) Thailand (3) Turkey (4) Venezuela (12) 25	Argentina (9) Czechoslovakia (5) France (14) Indonesia (5) Iran (19) Israel (3) Lebanon (12) Morocco (17) Pakistan (5) Tunisia (16) Union South Africa (3) United States (16) 12	37
LOW FREQUENCY OF ASSASSINATIONS (2 OR LESS) Chi square = 7.83 p < .01	Bulgaria (0) Ceylon (2) Chile (0) El Salvador (2) Peru (0) Spain (2) Yugoslavia (2) 7 32	Australia (2) Austria (1) Belgium (1) Canada (1) Costa Rica (2) Denmark (0) Finland (0) Iceland (0) Ireland (0) Netherlands (0) New Zealand (1) Norway (0) Portugal (2) Sweden (0) Switzerland (0) United Kingdom (0) Uruguay (0) West Germany (2) 18 30	25 62

faction and instability and $r = -.43$ between satisfaction and assassination frequency (see Table 22).

We may say, then, that the level of systemic satisfaction within a society shows a relationship to the degree of political instability experienced by that society, as well as to the incidence of assassination.

RATE OF SOCIOECONOMIC CHANGE AND POLITICAL VIOLENCE

A third measure of the socioeconomic environment that may be related to level of political unrest and assassination frequency is the rate of socioeconomic change experienced within a society. The rationale for this expectation has been given earlier and leads to the hypothesis that a high rate of socioeconomic change will entail a high level of political violence. Conversely, less rapid change will mean a more stable society.

In order to measure rate of socioeconomic change, data on nine economic indicators were collected for a twenty-eight-year period, 1935–1962. The indicators were: literacy level, primary and post-primary education levels, infant mortality rate, caloric intake, radios, urbanization level, national income, and cost of living. Rate of change was calculated in percentage terms, thus showing the countries with a high base level (modern industrialized states, by and large) as having a low rate of change and countries with a low base level (underdeveloped societies) as having a higher annual percentage rate of change.[30]

The relationship between rate of change and political instability is shown in Table 17A. Again we find evidence of considerable patterning. Approximately 70 per cent of the countries that experienced a high percentage rate of change in the twenty-eight-year period are politically unstable. And 63 per cent of the countries with a low rate of change are politically stable. This patterning would occur by chance less than five times in a hundred (Chi square = 5.68).

30. For a more thorough discussion, see Feierabend and Feierabend, "Aggressive Behaviors Within Polities"; and Wallace W. Conroe, "A Cross-National Analysis of the Impact of Modernization Upon Political Stability" (Master's thesis, San Diego State College, 1965).

We find evidence of an almost identical relationship between rate of socioeconomic change and frequency of assassination. As shown in Table 17B, approximately 70 per cent of the countries with a high rate of socioeconomic change had three or more assassinations, while 61 per cent of the countries with a low rate of change exhibit a low frequency of assassination. The likelihood of having this result by chance is five times in a hundred (Chi square = 5.96).

The correlation coefficient for the relationship between rate of socioeconomic change and level of political instability is $r = .52$. The correlation between rate of change and assassination frequency is $r = .42$.

NEED ACHIEVEMENT AND FOREIGN MAIL

Two additional ecological characteristics are included, because each shows a considerable degree of relationship to political violence and assassination. The first is a psychological variable expressing the degree of need for achievement experienced within society.[31] This psychological variable is postulated as the antecedent condition for economic development: countries with elites high in need for achievement show rapid economic development; countries low in this need do not. In previous research we have found need for achievement, and especially an increase in the level of this need over time, to relate to political violence.[32] In Table 22 we find a correlation of .65 between change in need-achievement levels and general level of political instability, and a correlation of .51 between this variable and frequency of assassination. Unfortunately only twenty-three countries have been scored on need for achievement for two time periods (1925 and 1950), so these relationships are based on a small country sample. The implications of this relationship relate to the findings regarding rate of socioeconomic change and instability: if a rise in need for achievement implies a desire for economic development—as well

31. This variable is discussed and measured in David C. McClelland, *The Achieving Society* (Princeton: Van Nostrand, 1961).
32. See Rosalind L. Feierabend, Ivo K. Feierabend, and David A. Sleet, "Need Achievement, Coerciveness of Government and Political Unrest: A Cross-National Analysis" (Paper presented at the annual meeting of the American Psychological Association, September, 1967).

TABLE 17

A. Relationship Between Rate of Socioeconomic Change and Political Instability

	Low Rate of Change	High Rate of Change	
Unstable (126–445)	Argentina Belgium Chile Cuba France Greece Guatemala Italy Pakistan Paraguay Spain Union of South Africa United States	Bolivia Brazil Burma Ceylon Colombia Dom. Republic Egypt Haiti India Indonesia Iraq Korea Morocco Poland Peru Portugal Syria Thailand Tunisia Turkey U.S.S.R. Venezuela	
	13	22	35
Stable (012–125) Chi square = 5.68 p < .05	Australia Austria Bulgaria Canada China (Taiwan) Denmark Ecuador Finland Hungary Iceland Ireland Israel Luxembourg Mexico Netherlands New Zealand Norway Philippines Sweden Switzerland United Kingdom Uruguay West Germany	Cambodia Costa Rica El Salvador Ghana Honduras Japan Panama Yugoslavia Malaya	
	23	9	32
	36	31	67

B. Relationship Between Rate of Socioeconomic Change and Frequency of Assassination

	Low Rate of Change	High Rate of Change	
HIGH FREQUENCY OF ASSASSINATIONS (3 OR MORE)	Argentina (9) Cuba (28) Ecuador (2) France (14) Greece (5) Guatemala (12) Israel (3) Italy (3) Mexico (3) Pakistan (5) Paraguay (3) Philippines (15) Union South Africa (3) United States (16) 14	Bolivia (9) Brazil (12) Burma (5) Cambodia (6) Colombia (7) Dom. Republic (7) Egypt (14) Ghana (7) Haiti (5) India (8) Indonesia (5) Iraq (5) Japan (9) South Korea (20) Malaya (6) Morocco (17) Panama (5) Syria (7) Thailand (3) Tunisia (16) Turkey (4) Venezuela (12) 22	36
LOW FREQUENCY OF ASSASSINATIONS (2 OR LESS) Chi square = 5.96 $p < .05$	Australia (2) Austria (1) Belgium (1) Bulgaria (0) Canada (1) China (Taiwan) (0) Chile (0) Denmark (0) Finland (0) Hungary (1) Iceland (0) Ireland (0) Luxembourg (0) Netherlands (0) New Zealand (1) Norway (0) Spain (2) Sweden (0) Switzerland (0) United Kingdom (0) Uruguay (0) West Germany (2) 22	Ceylon (2) Costa Rica (2) El Salvador (2) Honduras (0) Peru (0) Poland (0) Portugal (2) U.S.S.R. (0) Yugoslavia (2) 9	31
	36	31	67

as change in the direction of modernization—then we would anticipate that it also entails political violence.

Second, we find that the volume of foreign mail received and sent by a nation is related to the level of internal violence and assassination experienced.[33] Volume of foreign mail indexes the relative degree of participation or isolation of a country in the international arena. Relevant factors are: geographical size, level of development, and former colonial status. The correlation between this variable and political instability is $r = -.52$, indicating that greater isolation coincides with more instability. Similarly, the correlation is $r = -.41$ between foreign mail and incidence of assassination.

COERCIVENESS OF POLITICAL REGIME

In order to measure the elusive and complicated notion of permissiveness-coerciveness of political systems, the following general questions were formulated and then applied as a yardstick against which to rate the various nations: (1) To what degree are civil rights present and protected? (2) To what extent is political opposition tolerated and effective? (3) How democratic is the polity?

These broad questions were then refined in terms of some fifty specific rating criteria. A six-point ordinal scale was devised to assess the aggregate image of each of the eighty-four countries for the time period 1948–1960. Point 1 on the scale was defined as highly permissive, point 6 as highly coercive.[34] This is undoubtedly a rough procedure to estimate a complex variable, yet the profiles find considerable support in works of other authors interested in analyzing similar aspects of political regimes.[35]

33. The data derive from Russett et. al., *op. cit.*
34. For greater detail see Ivo K. Feierabend and Rosalind L. Feierabend, "The Relationship of Systemic Frustration, Political Coercion, International Tension and Political Instability: A Cross-National Study" (Paper presented at the annual meeting of the American Psychological Association, New York City, September, 1966); and Jennifer G. Walton, "Correlates of Coerciveness and Permissiveness of National Political Systems: A Cross-National Study" (Master's thesis, San Diego State College, 1965).
35. The coerciveness profiles show a correlation of $r = .67$ to the Political Development Index developed by Phillips Cutright, "National Political Development: Measurement and Analysis," *American Sociological Review*

The relationships between coerciveness of regime, political instability and frequency of assassination are presented in Tables 18A and 18B. These tables are subdivided to indicate the six different levels of permissiveness-coerciveness. Both tables show very much the same pattern.

Coerciveness levels 1 and 2 (permissive states), as well as 6 (highly coercive states), are conspicuously more populated by countries experiencing low levels of political unrest and a low frequency of assassination. In both tables there are twenty-six countries showing this combination compared to seven countries in the deviant direction. On the other hand, coerciveness levels 3, 4, and 5 show a far greater preponderance of unstable countries and countries experiencing a high frequency of assassination. Thirty-four countries at these mid-levels of coerciveness are unstable, compared with seventeen that are stable; thirty-seven countries experience a high frequency of assassination and only fourteen, a low frequency.

These tables demonstrate the previously hypothesized relationship that assassinations and political violence are more likely to occur at mid-levels of coerciveness (3, 4, 5) rather than under highly permissive (1, 2) or highly coercive (6) regimes. Only extremely coercive systems (totalitarian states) are able to deter assassins and expressions of political violence, although there is some evidence of a deterrent tendency at coerciveness level 5. Permissiveness appears to bear the lowest relationship to violence, while the opposite is true of the range of moderate coerciveness of political regimes. Again, the United States appears as a notable exception.

This curvilinear relationship between coerciveness, political in-

---

(April, 1963). This index uses as its criteria the extent of opposition in national legislatures and the mode of acquisition and tenure of office by chief executives.

The types of political systems classified by Coleman in Gabriel A. Almond and James S. Coleman, *The Politics of Developing Areas* (Princeton: Princeton University Press, 1960) also show similarity to our coerciveness index, as do the nation typologies emerging in Arthur S. Banks and Phillip M. Gregg, "Grouping Political Systems: Q-Factor Analysis of A Cross-Polity Survey," *The American Behavioral Scientist* (November, 1965). For more detail, see Walton, op. cit. and Norman M. Howard, *Modernity, Rate of Change and Coerciveness of Political Systems: A Cross-National Study* (Master's thesis, San Diego State College, 1966).

TABLE 18

A. Relationship Between Level of Coercion of Political Regime and Degree of Political Instability

	Permissive					Coercive
	1	2	3	4	5	6
Unstable (126–445)	United States	Belgium Italy	Brazil Burma Ceylon Chile France Greece India Pakistan Turkey	Bolivia Colombia Guatemala Indonesia Iran Iraq Jordan Laos Lebanon Peru Syria Sudan Thailand Tunisia	Argentina Cuba Egypt Haiti Korea Morocco Paraguay Portugal Spain Union South Africa Venezuela	Dom. Republic East Germany Poland USSR
	1	2	9	14	11	4	41
Stable (012–125) Chi sq. = 18.69 p < .01	Australia Canada Denmark Netherlands Norway Sweden Switzerland United Kingdom	Costa Rica Finland Iceland Ireland Israel Luxembourg Mexico New Zealand Uruguay West Germany	Austria Cambodia Japan Malaya Panama Philippines	Cyprus Ecuador El Salvador Ghana Honduras Liberia Libya	Afghanistan Ethiopia Nicaragua Saudi Arabia	Albania Bulgaria China—Mainland China—Taiwan Czechoslovakia Hungary Rumania Yugoslavia
	8	10	6	7	4	8	43

and Frequency of Assassination

	Permissive					Coercive
	1	2	3	4	5	6
HIGH FREQUENCY OF ASSASSINATIONS (3 OR MORE)	United States (16)	Israel (3) Italy (3) Mexico (3)	Brazil (12) Burma (5) Cambodia (6) France (14) Greece (5) India (8) Japan (9) Malaya (6) Pakistan (5) Panama (5) Philippines (15) Turkey (4)	Bolivia (9) Columbia (7) Cyprus (5) Ecuador (3) Ghana (7) Guatemala (12) Indonesia (5) Iran (19) Iraq (5) Jordan (6) Laos (10) Lebanon (12) Syria (7) Thailand (3) Tunisia (16)	Argentina (9) Cuba (28) Egypt (14) Haiti (5) Korea (20) Morocco (17) Nicaragua (5) Paraguay (3) Union South Africa (3) Venezuela (12)	China—Mainland (3) Czechoslovakia (5) Dom. Rep. (7)
	1	3	12	15	10	3	44
LOW FREQUENCY OF ASSASSINATIONS (2 OR LESS) Chi sq. = 22.24 p < .001	Australia (2) Canada (1) Denmark (0) Netherlands (0) Norway (0) Sweden (0) Switzerland (0) United Kingdom (0)	Belgium (1) Costa Rica (2) Finland (0) Iceland (0) Ireland (0) Luxembourg (0) New Zealand (1) Uruguay (0) West Germany (2)	Austria (1) Ceylon (2) Chile (0)	El Salvador (2) Honduras (0) Liberia (2) Libya (1) Peru (0) Sudan (1)	Afghanistan (2) Ethiopia (2) Portugal (2) Saudi Arabia (2) Spain (2)	Albania (2) Bulgaria (0) China—Taiwan (0) E. Germany (0) Hungary (1) Poland (0) Rumania (0) USSR (0) Yugoslavia (2)
	8	9	3	6	5	9	40
	9	12	15	21	15	12	84

stability, and assassination is also demonstrated in the lower correlational coefficients (.20 for assassination and .31 for instability), since this technique assesses linear relationships. On the other hand, the use of a correlational technique designed to ascertain curvilinearity, eta, yields the value .57 for assassinations and .55 for instability.

EXTERNAL CONFLICT, MINORITY TENSION, HOMICIDE, AND SUICIDE

These four variables denote behaviors that provide additional outlets for the expression of a violent aggressive impulse. For this reason, they deserve scrutiny. The data on homicide and suicide rates are derived from United Nations statistical compilations. In order to assess level of minority tension a special data collection was previously compiled from *Deadline Data* involving some thirty countries for the time period 1955–1965.[36] The data on external conflict are drawn from the work of Rummel and Tanter and cover the time period 1955–1960.[37] These external-conflict and minority-tension events were scaled in very much the same fashion as the political-instability data. The scaled values were then used to profile the nations of the sample. Some sixty different types of events were distinguished in the minority-tension data collection. These included the thirty events used to denote political instability as well as events having specific reference to ethnic minority groups, such as granting of autonomy, banning of institution, police or military escort, etc. The external-hostility events included: protests, accusations, threats, anti-foreign demonstrations, diplomatic officials expelled, mobilizations, negative sanctions,

36. The minority data were collected by the authors as a portion of the Systemic Conditions of Political Aggression project.
37. This data collection comes from Rummel, "Dimensions of Conflict Behavior," and Tanter, *op. cit.* For the scaling of the data and other information, see Feierabend and Feierabend, "The Relationship of Systemic Frustration, Political Coercion, International Tension and Political Instability," and Frank W. Scanland III, "International Conflict and Internal Frustration: A Cross-Polity Study" (Master's thesis, San Diego State College, 1966), and John Stuart Chambers, Jr., "Hostility and Amity in International Relations: A Transactional Study" (Master's thesis, San Diego State College, 1966).

troop movements, diplomatic relations severed, and military actions.

The relationships between these variables and political instability and assassination are presented in Tables 19 through 21. Nations involved in external conflict tend to be more politically unstable and to experience high assassination frequency compared with nations with less hostile relations (see Table 19). The correlation coefficient between external conflict and political instability is .41; between external conflict and assassination it is .32.

The relationships between level of minority tension within society and both general political instability and assassination frequency are shown in Table 20. The correlations for these relationships are .44 between minority conflict and instability and .35 between minority hostility and assassination. These analyses are based on a sample of thirty-one countries with minority groups of sufficient strength to experience either actual or potential conflict of this type.[38] Table 20 divides minority conflict into the six positions of the minority hostility scale. The patterning in the table shows a skewed distribution of minority conflict, with most countries falling at scale position 5 on the minority hostility scale. This group of countries is also high in both political instability and frequency of assassination. Forty-two per cent of the thirty-one countries experience a high level of both minority group conflict (scale positions 5 and 6) and political instability. Thirty-eight per cent show high levels of ethnic group conflict and experience frequent assassinations. The overall patterning in Table 20 indicates that among countries with sizable minority groups, almost two-thirds experience high-scaled instability and a high frequency of assassination.

Looking at the variables of homicide and suicide, we find the correlation coefficient for the relationship between homicide rate and political instability is $r = .43$, and between homicide and assassination it is $r = .38$ (see Table 22). There is evidence,

38. The selection of these countries was based on a Minority Strength Index that weighted cultural history, language, religion, separatist tendencies, endogamy and numerical strength (proportion of population). See R. L. Feierabend, "Inter-Group Conflict: A Cross-National Analysis" (Paper presented at the annual meeting of the American Political Science Association, New York, September, 1969).

TABLE 19

A. Relationship Between Level of External Conflict and Political Instability

	Low External Conflict	High External Conflict
UNSTABLE (126–445)	Belgium Bolivia Brazil Ceylon Colombia Dom. Republic Greece Italy Peru Poland Portugal Spain Thailand	Argentina Burma Chile Cuba East Germany Egypt France Guatemala Haiti India Indonesia Iran Iraq Jordan South Korea Lebanon Pakistan Paraguay Turkey Union of South Africa U.S.S.R. United States Venezuela
	13	23
		36
STABLE (012–125) Chi square = 3.56 $p < .06$	Afghanistan Bulgaria Canada Czechoslovakia Denmark Ecuador El Salvador Ethiopia Finland Ireland Japan Liberia Netherlands New Zealand Norway Panama Philippines Rumania Saudi Arabia Sweden Switzerland Uruguay	Albania Australia Cambodia China (Mainland) China (Taiwan) Costa Rica Honduras Hungary Israel Mexico Nicaragua United Kingdom West Germany Yugoslavia
	22	14
		36

and Frequency of Assassination

	Low External Conflict	High External Conflict	
HIGH FREQUENCY OF ASSASSINATIONS (3 OR MORE)	Brazil (12) Bolivia (9) Colombia (7) Czechoslovakia (5) Dom. Republic (7) Ecuador (3) Greece (5) Italy (3) Japan (9) Panama (5) Philippines (15) Thailand (3)	Argentina (9) Burma (5) Cambodia (6) China (Mainland) (3) Cuba (28) Egypt (14) France (14) Guatemala (12) Haiti (5) India (8) Indonesia (5) Iran (19) Iraq (5)	Israel (3) Jordan (6) Lebanon (12) Mexico (3) Nicaragua (5) Pakistan (5) Paraguay (3) South Korea (20) Turkey (4) Union South Africa (3) United States (16) Venezuela (12)
	12	25	37
LOW FREQUENCY OF ASSASSINATIONS (2 OR LESS) Chi square = 6.70 p < .01	Afghanistan (2) Belgium (1) Bulgaria (0) Canada (1) Ceylon (2) Denmark (0) El Salvador (2) Ethiopia (2) Finland (0) Ireland (0) Liberia (2) Netherlands (0) New Zealand (1) Norway (0) Peru (0) Poland (0) Portugal (2) Rumania (0) Saudi Arabia (2) Spain (2) Sweden (0) Switzerland (0) Uruguay (0)	Albania (2) Australia (2) Chile (0) Costa Rica (2) East Germany (0) Honduras (0) Hungary (1) China (Taiwan) (0) United Kingdom (0) U.S.S.R. (0) West Germany (2) Yugoslavia (2)	
	23	12	35
	35	37	72

TABLE 20

A. Relationship between Level of
Minority Conflict and Political Instability

	Low Minority Conflict				High Minority Conflict		
	1	2	3	4	5	6	
Unstable (126–445)			Chile Haiti Thailand	Egypt Lebanon Syria	Belgium Ceylon India Indonesia Iran Morocco Pakistan Peru Tunisia Turkey Union South Africa United States	Iraq	
	0	0	3	3	12	1	19
Stable (012–125)	Mexico New Zealand	Netherlands	Bulgaria Czechoslovakia Philippines United Kingdom Yugoslavia	Canada Switzerland	Israel	Cyprus	
	2	1	5	2	1	1	12
	2	1	8	5	13	2	31

Chi square = 12.08
p < .05

B. Relationship between Level of Minority Conflict and Frequency of Assassination

	Low Minority Conflict				High Minority Conflict		
	1	2	3	4	5	6	
HIGH FREQUENCY OF ASSASSINATIONS (3 OR MORE)	Mexico (3)		Czecho-slovakia (5) Haiti (5) Philippines (15) Thailand (3)	Egypt (14) Lebanon (12) Syria (7)	India (8) Indonesia (5) Iran (19) Israel (3) Morocco (17) Pakistan (5) Tunisia (16) Turkey (4) Union South Africa (3) United States (16)	Cyprus (5) Iraq (5)	
	1	0	4	3	10	2	20
LOW FREQUENCY OF ASSASSINATIONS (2 OR LESS)	New Zea-land (1)	Nether-lands (0)	Bulgaria (0) Chile (0) United Kingdom (0) Yugoslavia (2)	Canada (1) Switzer-land (0)	Belgium (1) Ceylon (2) Peru (0)		
	1	1	4	2	3	0	11
	2	1	8	5	13	2	31

Chi square = 4.76
p < .50

therefore, that homicide rates are positively related to both level of political instability and assassination frequency. The direction of these relationships is reversed in the case of suicide rates. The correlation coefficients relating suicide rates to political instability and assassination frequency are $r = -.38$ and $r = -.32$, respectively. Thus countries high on suicide show a low tendency toward political violence.

Table 21 combines homicide and suicide rates and compares them to both political instability and frequency of assassination. If we look only at the two center columns of Tables 21A and B, we see a marked tendency for inverse patterns of homicide/suicide to relate to incidence of political instability and especially of assassination. Among countries demonstrating the syndrome of high homicide–low suicide, 80 per cent have a high incidence of assassination. Conversely, among countries showing the reverse pattern, 86 per cent have a low incidence of assassination. The pattern for countries either high or low on both homicide and suicide is not clear-cut. All show a greater tendency toward a low frequency of assassination. The United States is an exception, however, since it is high on homicide, high on suicide, and high on assassination.

Conclusions

In summary, what can be said regarding the cross-national pattern of violence and assassination? Do our findings help to explain the incidence of assassination in the United States? Perhaps the broadest generalization we may offer is that violence, viewed cross-nationally, is not a random or isolated occurrence. There are political, social, and ecological factors associated with it in sufficient degree to pay heed to our findings. From a knowledge of these associated variables, we can improve our prediction of violence beyond the chance level. On the other hand, the relationships are not sufficiently persuasive to claim that we have provided a complete explanation. Insufficient information, imperfect data manipulation and measurement contribute error and interfere with the results. Also the occurrence of other variables that we did not take into account would undoubtedly improve predictability.

The second broad generalization is that assassinations show a similar patterning as internal political violence and instability. In other words, whatever is related globally to violent and aggressive behavior within polities is also related, by and large, to the occurrence of assassinations.

A more detailed set of propositions regarding the cross-national incidence of assassination events includes the following generalizations:

A high rate of assassination is positively related to systemic frustration, external conflict, minority tensions, and homicide rates, as well as to political instability and violence. The higher the levels of systemic frustration, external conflict, minority tension, homicide rates and general political violence within a society, the higher the assassination rates.

A high rate of assassination is inversely related to measures of modernity and suicide. Thus the higher the level of modernity and the higher the level of suicides within a society, the less likelihood there is of assassination.

Frequency of assassination is curvilinearly related to coerciveness of political regime. Permissive, democratic societies, as well as highly coercive regimes, are less prone to assassination than are countries at mid-levels of coerciveness.

It is important to stress the fact that these relationships also obtain for aggregate measures of internal political aggression and violence. Also, these findings fit the theoretical insights outlined in the previous section of the report, with one possible exception. A curvilinear relationship was postulated between frequency of assassination and level of modernity. Instead, it seems that traditional as well as transitional societies are equally apt to experience this aberration of the orderly political process. On the other hand, it would be hasty to claim that this hypothesis was definitely overruled by our findings, since our sample of countries is probably devoid of truly traditional societies, as yet completely unexposed to modern ways. Only a very few nations of this type remain in the contemporary world. It is more likely that the nations which we labeled traditional, although certainly among the most underdeveloped countries, nevertheless may be on their way to transitional stages of development.

The previous section scrutinized the global patterning of violence in reference to each selected variable taken singly. It is of equal interest to look at the combined pattern. In Table 23 six

TABLE 21

A. Relationship Between Combined
Suicide and Homicide Rates and Political Instability

	Low Suicide Low Homicide	High Suicide Low Homicide	Low Suicide High Homicide	High Suicide High Homicide		
UNSTABLE (126–445)	Greece Italy Spain	Belgium France Poland Portugal	Burma Chile Colombia Dom. Republic Egypt Guatemala India Jordan Peru	Brazil Ceylon United States		
	3	3	4	9	3	19
STABLE (012–125) Chi square = 33.84 p < .001	Canada Ireland Netherlands New Zealand Norway	Austria China (Taiwan) Czechoslovakia Denmark Iceland Luxembourg Sweden Switzerland United Kingdom West Germany	Costa Rica Ecuador Mexico Nicaragua Panama Philippines	Australia Bulgaria Finland Hungary Japan Uruguay		
	5	8	10	6	6	27
	8		14	15	9	46

B. Relationship between Combined Suicide and Homicide Rates and Frequency of Assassination

	Low Suicide Low Homicide	High Suicide Low Homicide	Low Suicide High Homicide	High Suicide High Homicide	
HIGH FREQUENCY OF ASSASSINATIONS (3 OR MORE)	Greece (5) Italy (3)	Czechoslovakia (5) France (14	Burma (5) Colombia (7) Dom. Republic (7) Ecuador (3) Egypt (14) Guatemala (12) India (8) Jordan (6) Mexico (3) Nicaragua (5) Panama (5) Philippines (15)	Brazil (12) Japan (9) United States (16)	
	2	2	12	3	19
LOW FREQUENCY OF ASSASSINATIONS (2 OR LESS) Chi square = 14.59 p < .01	Canada (1) Ireland (0) Netherlands (0) New Zealand (1) Norway (0) Spain (2)	Austria (1) Belgium (1) China (Taiwan) (0) Denmark (0) Iceland (0) Luxembourg (0) Poland (0) Portugal (2) Sweden (0) Switzerland (0) United Kingdom (0) West Germany (2)	Chile (0) Costa Rica (2) Peru (0)	Australia (2) Bulgaria (0) Ceylon (2) Finland (0) Hungary (1) Uruguay (0)	
	6	12	3	6	27
	8	14	15	9	46

TABLE 22

Interrelations Among Ecological Indicators, Political Instability, and Frequency of Assassinations (Product-Moment Correlations)

| | Assassinations | | | | Instability (Summed Scores) (1948–1965) |
| | New York Times | | Deadline Data | | |
	RAW	TRANSFORMED	RAW	TRANSFORMED	
Level of Modernity (84)	−.229	−.402	−.207	−.319	−.382
GNP Capita (84)	−.136	−.275	.083	−.198	−.359
Level of Systemic Satisfaction (62)	−.261	−.431	−.133	−.253	−.569
Rate of Socioeconomic Change (67)	.269	.415	.279	.445	.517
Change in Need Achievement Level, 1925–1950 (23)	.349	.511	.329	.463	.647
Foreign Mail (51)	−.322	−.410	−.358	.418	−.515
Level of Coerciveness (84)	.153	.198	.128	.169	.311
Level of International Conflict (72)	.318	.319	.226	.176	.409
Level of Minority Hostility (31)	.300	.346	.383	.376	.440
Homicide Rate (46)	.278	.377	.426	.407	.427
Suicide Rate (46)	−.265	−.319	−.272	−.318	−.378

variables are examined simultaneously. The rows of the table combine three forms of political aggression: assassination frequency, political instability, and international (or external) conflict. Each variable is dichotomized, yielding eight possible intercombinations. The rows are ordered from the most peaceful combination (low frequency of assassination, political stability and low level of external conflict) to the most aggressive combination (high frequency of assassination, political instability, and high level of external conflict). The columns of the table combine three ecological variables: modernity level, rate of socioeconomic change, and level of permissiveness-coerciveness of regime. Again the variables are dichotomized, yielding eight combinations. The columns are ordered from highest systemic frustration (low level of modernity, mid-levels of coerciveness, and high rate of socioeconomic change) to highest systemic satisfaction (high level of modernity, permissiveness levels 1, 2, or 6, and low rate of socioeconomic change).

There is a very pronounced patterning in this table, which identifies syndromes of political aggression and nonaggression in the contemporary world. Eleven countries appear in the upper right-hand corner of the table. They are modern states with permissive regimes that experience a low rate of socioeconomic change and are also low on the three measures of political aggression. They have experienced few assassinations and enjoy low levels of internal and external conflict. Nine of these eleven nations may be identified as Western-style democracies. One country, Uruguay, is a Latin American state and the other, Bulgaria, is from the Communist bloc. The latter is not permissive but rather comes from the other extreme of the permissiveness-coerciveness dimension (scale value 6). Also, there are three additional Western democracies that fit the nonaggressive syndrome with the exception that they are high in external conflict.

At the other end of the table, in the lower-left-hand corner, the opposite syndrome is in evidence. Nine countries are high on three forms of aggression (assassination, general political unrest, and inter-nation hostility) and also high on three types of systemic frustration. They are low in modernity, at mid-levels of political coerciveness, and experience high rates of socioeconomic change. These countries are drawn from three areas of the world; Asia,

TABLE 23

Relationship Between Level of Development, Coerciveness of Regime, Rate of Socioeconomic Change and Assassination Frequency, Political Instability, External Conflict

	Modernity-Low / Coerciveness-Mid / Change-High / 3-4-5	Modernity-Low / Coerciveness-Mid / Change-Low / 3-4-5	Modernity-Low / Coe.-Low-High 1-2-6 / Change-High	Modernity-High / Coerciveness-Mid / Change-High / 3-4-5	Modernity-Low / Coe.-Low-High 1-2-6 / Change-Low	Modernity-High / Coerciveness-Mid / Change-Low / 3-4-5	Modernity-High / Coe.-Low-High 1-2-6 / Change-High	Modernity-High / Coe.-Low-High 1-2-6 / Change-Low	Totals
LOW ASSAS. STABLE LOW EXT.	El Salvador							Bulgaria, Canada, Denmark, Finland, Ireland, Netherlands, New Zealand, Norway, Sweden, Switzerland, Uruguay	12
LOW ASSAS. STABLE HIGH EXT.	Honduras				China-Taiwan		Costa Rica	Australia, United Kingdom, West Germany	6
HIGH ASSAS. STABLE LOW EXT.		Ecuador, Philippines		Japan, Panama				Italy	5
LOW ASSAS. UNSTABLE	Ceylon, Peru								

UNSTABLE HIGH EXT.				Chile			USSR		2
HIGH ASSAS. STABLE HIGH EXT.				Mexico			Israel		2
HIGH ASSAS. UNSTABLE LOW EXT.	Colombia Bolivia Brazil Thailand		Dominican Republic			Greece			6
HIGH ASSAS. UNSTABLE HIGH EXT.	Burma Cambodia Haiti India Indonesia	Iraq Korea Turkey Venezuela			Egypt Guatemala Pakistan Paraguay	Argentina Cuba France Union of South Africa			USA	18
TOTALS	18	6	1	2	2	7	2		18	56

Latin America, and the Middle East. An additional four countries have the same high levels of systemic frustration and exhibit a high frequency of assassination and a high level of general political unrest, but are low in external conflict. Three of these nations are in Latin America; one is in Asia. Four additional states are high on all three forms of political aggression, while high on two of three types of systemic frustration. These countries are also from Asia, Latin America, and the Middle East. We thus have fourteen countries that come close to fitting a nonaggressive syndrome and seventeen that approximate an aggressive syndrome. There are fifty-six countries in the table; hence 55 per cent of the sample may be accounted for in terms of these two syndromes. Furthermore, forty-one cells are empty, indicating that two-thirds of the potentially possible combinations of variables do not occur in the real world. If chance alone were operating and there were no relationship among these six variables, these cells would not remain unpopulated.

There are also exceptions to the pattern sprinkled throughout the table. The largest group of deviants are the four countries that are high on all three forms of political aggression, yet are satisfied on two of three indicators. The most completely deviant countries in the table are El Salvador and the United States. The former is nonaggressive despite experiencing all of the preconditions supposedly conducive to political violence. And the United States is high on three forms of violence, despite internal conditions that should be predisposing to political quiescence. Furthermore, in view of the high frequency of assassinations in the United States, it cannot even be claimed that we are a case of only borderline deviancy. The United States is the fifth highest country among the eighty-four in terms of the total number of assassination events experienced, although this high rank is somewhat reduced in the other subcategories of assassination. Among the group of Western democracies, it has a score of sixteen assassinations, where ten countries have a score of zero. It is in this respect that the deviant nature of the United States is most dramatically illustrated.

If we contemplate the associational patterns of internal instability events as demonstrated in the factor analytic, Guttman scalogram, and consensual scaling techniques, there is a strong suggestion that in the global pattern assassinations tend to occur with other events of a rather high intensity of violence, and specifically that they occur in conjunction with guerrilla warfare. In the United States, however, the events of the highest intensity of violence are riots and demonstrations and, of course, assassinations. Hence, again, not only is the United States a deviant case in terms of excessive frequency of assassinations, but also the pattern of violence is atypical in comparison with that of other nations. Since the United States is clearly a deviant in these respects, it may be difficult to arrive at an adequate explanation in terms of the variables we have chosen for this cross-national analysis. There must be other circumstances which we have omitted that are responsible for this country's political behavior. These circumstances may be presumed to be largely absent from the comparable group of nations, that is, the modern, Western democracies which on the whole experience a low assassination rate. This argument is plausible if we remember that none of the correlation coefficients between our selected set of ecological variables and the occurrence of instability and assassinations is so high as to provide a set of clear-cut determinants.

Granting that additional variables may be responsible, the findings nevertheless suggest dimensions to be explored further in seeking explanations for this country's assassination rate. It will be remembered that assassination rate is a concomitant of level of general political aggression. In the case of the United States, as was pointed out earlier, assassinations occurred predominantly during the 1960's. This is also the period of heightened political violence in this country. In the 1956–1960 period, for example, the United States experienced no events that registered higher than position 3 on the 6-point instability scale. From 1961 to 1965, 12 per cent of this country's events were at scale position 4.

Another domain of explanation could be identified within the covariation of assassination and external conflict. In this respect also the United States is no deviant. In very specific terms, considering American foreign policy and internal responses to it, the war in Vietnam undoubtedly is a strong factor in creating politically anomic behavior. A somewhat comparable case can be seen in France's controversial involvement in Algeria. The Algerian war and assassination events appear to be related. Nine of France's fourteen assassination events, or 64 per cent, took place during the years 1957–1962 (30 per cent of the total time period).

In addition, the high rate of homicide in the United States also serves as a partial explanation of political violence. The relationship cross-nationally between homicide and assassination rates gives credence to explanations based on notions of violent social and political culture. There are, of course, other circumstances that we did not include and hence do not discuss, despite their potential importance and relevancy. Historical precedents of violence are among the dimensions we were unable to analyze in this limited cross-national assessment.

There is one circumstance in the United States, as well as in many other nations, that must be judged a powerful explanatory factor in increasing political violence. This is the level of tension that exists among ethnic, racial, linguistic, religious and other groups within society. Among the sixteen assassinations that occurred in the United States during the last twenty years, seven can be attributed to this problem. Furthermore, of the twelve assassinations occurring in the 1960's, six stem from the minority problem.

The factor of minority hostility is one of the variables in the present study that is not sufficiently refined to yield a more accurate picture and perhaps a more persuasive pattern of association. Too much is left unexplicated regarding the nature of the minority, the goals, the type of country, and the response of the majority that develops minority-majority tensions. Yet even in this early stage of cross-national investigation, it belongs among the predictors of internal violence and assassination. It should be pointed out that the United States fits the expected patterns as presented in Tables 20 A and B, relating to minority hostility.

It probably needs no more than common sense to assert that this particular sphere is of great importance in assessing political instability in this country, as elsewhere. It is not only the domain of minority conflict but also the notion of modernity and participant society that may be involved in the crucible of minority-majority tensions in the United States. We can perhaps think of the current "Black Revolution" as a previously isolated but now politically significant and politically participant stratum of the population reaching toward modern, satisfied, stable, permissive, democratic Western society at an increasingly accelerated rate of speed (high rate of change).

The present analysis is comparative and cross-national in conception rather than a cross-sectional analysis of social strata within a single society. Hence the aggregate image of the United States as a highly modern nation does not register the transitional societies in its midst, among which must be included the American Negroes. Yet these social substrata could be conceived in similar terms to the stratum of transitional emergent nations in the global pattern. They are equally subject to the revolution of rising expectations and the feeling of systemic frustration. In this sense, then, the American Negro community could be conceived as largely transitional, frustrated, and at present subject to a rapid rate of social change. Even the aggregate permissiveness of the dominant political regime may be considered at mid-levels of coerciveness in its relationship to this social segment. Furthermore, the emergence of transitional societies in its midst also forces rapid social change on the rest of society. Thus the United States should perhaps be considered a "high change" society at present. In conjunction with some other selected characteristics, this fits rather well the picture of the violent or assassination syndrome.

While this assessment of the domestic scene in the United States might seem persuasive, it is but a speculative generalization in the perspective of the broader global picture. In relying largely on aggregate data, the present analysis does not reach the subtleties inherent in specific case studies. This will remain the task of future microscopic cross-national research. The present effort can only hope to discern the more salient patterns, as well as to note the more striking deviations. Furthermore, macroscopic cross-national analysis is at a stage of development where one must be sufficiently humble to proclaim that patterns are discerned only through a haze of imperfect information, as well as imprecisions of data manipulation and measurement error. The pattern that we have determined by cross-national investigation indicates that the characteristics of an assassination-prone society are very similar to those of a society beset by a high level of political unrest. This is to be expected since assassinations are one facet of a politically unstable behavior pattern.

In summary, the syndrome of traits that have been isolated in this analysis to describe the aggressive nation are: a low level of modernity, high systemic frustration, a high rate of socioeconomic change, a high level of need for achievement, a low level of international interaction (foreign mail), mid-levels of coerciveness of political regime, a high level of involvement in external conflict, a high level of minority hostility, a high level of homicide and a low level of suicide. This is a general pattern from which individual nations may deviate to greater or lesser degree. The United States shows a high frequency of assassination, without exhibiting the low level of development traits characteristic of other assassination-prone societies. On the other hand, it does show a high level of external conflict, a high level of minority hostility, and a high incidence of homicide. Furthermore, it shows an increasing tendency toward political unrest. All of these traits are themselves aggressive behaviors. Also, the typical low-development sources of political aggression found cross-nationally may exist within substrata of the total United States society.

part II

THE PSYCHOLOGY OF THE ASSASSIN

Psychopathology of Assassination

Lawrence Zelic Freedman

There has been much speculation and controversy concerning the mental stability of killers of presidents. Such diagnosis, of course, is important. But it is important, also, to ascertain what social generalities they represent. For no man is free to create either himself or his environment. Even the most creative, even the most demented, is a composite of generalities—unique, as are all human beings—in relative proportions of comparative intensity. The political murderer, therefore, may be expected to reflect in however a distorted and fanatic form some part of the arc of the spectrum of forms of social organization, existent or anticipated.

In the United States no organization seeking to change the structure of government or the leadership of government has used assassination as a weapon. Guerrilla attacks, riots, rebellion, secession, creation of other governments, and refusal to recognize the authority of the existing one, as well as civil war, have been the reactions of groups within the United States who were opposed to its government. But no political organization has yet physically attacked the head of government to attain its political goals. However, individuals who have identified themselves with the aspirations of alternatives to the American capitalist democracy have individually assaulted the head of government. Booth struck down Lincoln in the name of the Confederacy, a governmental alternative to the United States resembling it in its structure but reflecting a quite different life style: agricultural, rural, aristocratic, and slave-holding. Guiteau killed Garfield, he said, in the name of the Stalwart faction of the divided Republican party. The struggle, which was harsh, was between President Garfield and powerful leaders of his own party: Grant, Conkling, and Arthur, the Vice-President. It was a struggle to dominate the party. It was a struggle as well over the spoils system—the utilization of selective power to provide jobs and contracts to the party faithful, even when the jobs were superfluous, their functions obsolescent or contrary to the national interest. All parties to this internecine battle were committed to the same principles of federal or republican democracy, to the same principles of socioeconomic ideology, and to the traditions of political parties that had evolved since the original ratification of the Constitution. They fought, and vigorously, over the control of the two dominant parties within the Republic. Guiteau declared that he had killed the President to advance the Stalwarts, the branch represented by Chester Arthur, President Garfield's Vice-President.

Both Booth and Guiteau came from the socially and economically privileged sector of the community. Although Booth murdered in the name of an autonomous government, which by April 14, 1865 was virtually powerless and extinct, that government was a reflection in form and formal ideology of the traditional government. Guiteau's violence reflected the vigorous altercation going on between powerful men within one of the main political parties of that traditional government. Neither of the first two assassins of American Presidents reflected a political movement that differed substantially from the one of the social class from which they sprang.

At the start of this century, when Czolgosz murdered McKinley, he killed to express his opposition to the construct of government itself. Czolgosz, like Oswald after him, was a product of the lower socioeconomic strata. Guiteau and Booth, the nineteenth-century assassins, had been well educated and had family and personal connections with high-status individuals. Czolgosz and Oswald, the twentieth-century assassins, were poorly educated and emerged from low-status backgrounds. Until he murdered the President, Czolgosz had had no contacts with men in powerful and prestigious positions. Oswald had petitioned and negotiated, but never associated with them.

In 1963 Oswald murdered John Kennedy as the professed advocate of Marxism, a theory that economic control by the proletariat should supplant the Lockean principles of private property and competition. An alternative autonomous government and an alternative party faction were the expressed ideals of the first assassins. An anarchist social system and a Marxist political organization were the declared aspirations of the second two assassins. The first two assassins were from rural, upper-class families. The second two assassins were from urban, lower-class families. The first two assassins killed to change the locus of power. The second two political murderers killed to change the forms and processes of economic, social, and political organization. The first two struck before industrialization and urbanization were significant in the lives of most Americans. The third attacked when industrialization and its accompanying urbanization had become a dominant factor in American life. The fourth struck when industrialization, urbanization, and fractioning of human communal existence had become an established part of civilization.

Booth, despite his professed sympathies for the South, never became a citizen of the Confederacy or a resident within its short-lived boundaries. Czolgosz, a factory worker until three years before his attack, had for a while belonged to a socialist group. When he later identified himself with the anarchists he was unsuccessful in becoming part of their movement. Tentative inquiries by him were shunted aside when he asked not only about the philosophy of anarchy but also about the plans to use violence in order to achieve it. Anarchists considered him an *agent provocateur* or possibly a deranged crank. Guiteau was the son of a man who managed to maintain a distinguished role within the conservative, if confined, community of Freeport, Illinois, while he immersed himself in revolutionary, religious, and mystical schemes for the improvement of mankind. He was especially taken with the theories of Noyes, who preached and wrote first in Putney, Vermont, and later in small communities which he established in upstate New York and Connecticut. He based his radical interpretations on the Old and New Testaments. The Bible, Noyes taught and his communities practiced, required a life of Christian communism. Within these Christian-communist communities the boundaries of private identity yielded to a social identity: an immersion into the entire community. The examples and constraints of the family as the primary unit yielded to the total community as the primary unit. Profound sexual and economic variations from the modes of nineteenth-century America were preached and practiced. Possessiveness was the prerogative only of the entire community, not the individual. In the individual it was sin.

This inderdiction against privacy of possession was raised not only against exclusive authority and access to the inanimate, the machinery of production and the structures for habitation, but to the animate as well. "Amativeness" was pejoratively equated with "acquisitiveness." Sexual access between the sexes was considered desirable as the deepest form of human intimacy. But exclusive sexual access, the continuing relationship between one man and one woman, was forbidden. The exclusive sexual possession of another person was regarded as just as exploitive and antisocial as the exclusive economic possession of the means of production or distribution by one person. The conception of children was decided not through private wills and passions but by community representatives, whose decisions were based on considerations of the community welfare and the needs and capacities of the community for raising children. Even the sexual intimacies between two adults were required to be arranged through an intermediary. Copulation and procreation were quite separate concepts. The community decided who would be the most desirable sires and mothers; the community was in overall charge of raising the children. In such an "Oneida" community, Guiteau lived for a total of six years as a young man. Once, he left in dismay after almost three years but returned for an equal period. Finally, he left disillusioned with "Oneida" but still influenced, as he had been since childhood, by its concepts and constructs. Noyes had achieved his influence through much publication and eloquent sermons. Guiteau, after Oneida, tried both evangelical writing and speaking, but failed. Noyes justified his radical interpretations of Biblical injunctions by claiming for himself, and for every man, divine direction. So when he was tried for assassinating the President, Guiteau claimed that he had been directed by Christ, that God would protect him, and that God would punish any who punished him.

Oswald, during his puberty, had been so anxious to emulate his brothers by joining the authoritarian Marines that he managed to enlist a few months before he had reached the required age. However, just a few months before the term of his enlistment was to have been completed, he obtained a hardship discharge, claiming that his mother needed his help. He sailed for Soviet Russia, applied to obtain Soviet citizenship, and attempted suicide when this was denied him. He abruptly renounced his American citizenship, but failed to fill out the papers that could have accomplished this. He was granted permission to remain in Russia on an annual basis and was provided a job, one of the best apartments in Minsk, and a special monthly subsidy by the Russians, which gave him a special privileged status. He fell in love and proposed to a Russian-Jewish girl, who refused to marry him. Suffering, he began to see an attractive Russian pharmacist and proposed to her, mainly to revenge himself on the girl who had rejected him. She accepted. Already, however, he was disillusioned with Soviet Russia, and within a month after his marriage he had started negotiations with the United States Embassy to return to America.

Guiteau and Oswald had both experimented with communal forms of living. Neither had succeeded in overcoming his private miseries. In environments that emphasized community rather than private ideals and aspirations, in which sexual and economic arrangements were at least nominally different, each had become disillusioned and had remained sexually dissatisfied and unfulfilled by economic security. But neither Guiteau nor Oswald gave up these seemingly erratic but tenacious efforts to solve his private horrors by associating himself with community-centered activities that might reward him with leadership. In fantasy each challenged and defeated the persons who controlled their society, through alteration of the structure of society.

The psychotic delusion that one is a great and powerful person is far less common than laymen believe it to be. For several generations the professional humorists' image of a lunatic was a man dressed like Napoleon, one hand thrust into his jacket at mid-abdomen level, as Napoleon is frequently represented, but with his Napoleonic hat worn sideways. Such complete delusions do exist, but most of our more than one-half million hospitalized mental patients are unable to create so complete a world and so exalted a position for themselves within that world. The experienced misery of the residents of a mental hospital could not be quantified, but is, certainly, overwhelmingly greater than the private unhappiness, the "quiet desperation," of the "average" or "normal" person. The less severely maladapted who are treated by psychotherapists, and the overwhelming majority of people who get along more or less successfully without psychiatric assistance do so with latent paranoid and grandiose projections.

James Thurber's description of Walter Mitty, a mild-mannered, well-balanced, henpecked husband, who in the privacy of his fantasy was the hero of great dramas, rapidly became part of our common language. In Mitty, the delusional daydreams of the well-adjusted had been superbly depicted and, therefore, immediately recognized. On the opposite end of this continuum is the psychotic individual who miscasts himself and misinterprets his surroundings so successfully that he maintains his delusions in the face of the evidence of his own sense perceptions and the efforts of his family, friends, and therapists to disabuse him of them.

The socially adapted person who is always deluded in fantasy and never accurate in his perceptions of and responses to reality is certainly rare. Probably he does not exist. Every human being, however, periodically perceives himself as the center of some constellation of human relationships when in fact his role is peripheral or nonexistent. This "normal" person often senses that he is being criticized or snubbed when the person or group in question is doing neither. Less frequent, but nonetheless common, are periods when this stable individual may, in a mood of elation, underestimate and not perceive actual critical attitudes. The sense of being criticized actually or potentially is very common. The sense of being elevated in the eyes of those around him is comparatively rare. It is this unusual proclivity to suffer from the disapprobation of others that is the "normal" paradigm of the paranoidal projections of the deluded.

In one sense, in the light of these considerations the political murderer grapples with his dilemma more concretely, even more practically or realistically, than the normal, "the neurotic," or the deluded psychotic. However horrible his deed, however pathological his interpretation of events, the assassin is a man who has politicized his private miseries. He has attempted to become part of a social institution that promises him freedom from his overpowering self-loathing. Guiteau and Oswald had actually experimented with life in systems that seemed to promise escape from themselves and their fantasies and frustrations. Each eventually turned against the community he had sought out to free himself from his constant anxiety, fear, and self-accusation. When each found that he carried his private miseries and his public disaffections with him wherever he went, he turned against the new community that he had hoped would relieve him of himself. But the psychic mechanism of projecting to a political alternative different from the Midwest of the late nineteenth century for Guiteau, and the mid-twentieth century for Oswald, persisted. Booth, who did not fight for the Confederacy or become a citizen of it, nevertheless first saw himself committing an act of war by capturing Lincoln during the Civil War so that he might be exchanged for Confederate prisoners held by the Union. Since the Confederacy was far outnumbered by the Union, "capturing" the President was then a military-political act. Czolgosz, like Oswald, had come to regard himself as the victim of a political and economic system that caused him and his family to suffer. Although both included the victimization of their families as part of their rationale for hating their government, both had become estranged from their families in the years preceding their acts of assassination.

Indeed, in the objective concreteness of his projective model, in the deliberateness of his ratiocination, in the paranoidal acuteness and precision of the logical steps or imperative forces leading him to this act of political murder, the assassin grapples with the terrible reality of his life with a concreteness of image and comprehensiveness of scope that is neither unrealistically "mad" in the Napoleonic sense nor as divorced from reality as the heroic fantasies of "normal" men. The act of killing does not in itself distinguish the assassin from his fellow man. In all recorded history the overwhelming majority of men have killed willingly when the community of which they were a part, whether clan, tribe, or national state, was engaged in violent conflict with another community. Killing for private motives and in violation of the mores and laws of the surrounding community is less frequent, but nonetheless ubiquitous through time. A minority of men in every history of record have killed other men for personal reasons. Killing for personal motives is endemic; for political purposes it is cyclic and repeatedly epidemic.

To locate the assassin along the continuum from "normalcy" or "sanity" to abnormality or psychosis, we must add this second dimension to our model. The private murderer commits a sin or a crime for which he often feels guilt or shame. The soldier in an official, that is, governmental, army kills other men, men who are strangers to him without guilt or shame, often with pride. The political murderer in American history has been an obsessed, fanatical, and deluded man. But he has murdered a stranger, as soldiers kill strangers, impelled by a cause that goes beyond his own personality. No more than a soldier does he regret his act. The assassin acts politically not only in the sense that he kills a political figure, but also in the sense that he acts and feels as though he were a soldier in an opposing community, or perhaps that he was himself an army.

Antisocial deviance, including violent criminality, is never a comprehensive personality characteristic. Personal murderers and assassins have not been typically assaultive before or after their homicidal attack. Similarly, violent fantasy is far more common than violent threats. The former is common, the latter comparatively unusual. The quantitative prevalence of political threats is far, far greater than the occurrence of political violence. No "syndrome" of potential presidential assassins can be based on writers of threatening letters. Indeed, so far as we now know, the threat may be inversely rather than directly related to the act. The threat, expressed by letter or voice, may be an end state; it may be the action that reestablishes equanimity.

No United States presidential assassin has ever written directly to threaten the President, as did Rothstein's subjects, or make verbal threats before government authorities, as had Foy's and Sebastiani's subjects.[1] Rothstein's subjects had been in military service and had been imprisoned. Oswald alone of presidential assassins had been in military service. If they resembled Oswald in this factor they resembled only Oswald, for no other presidential killer had served militarily. Nor did he share with any of them a history of a written threat to the President. Foy and Sebastiani found an unusually high percentage of "threateners" had been in mental hospitals. But no presidential assassin had been previously hospitalized.

Those great crimes are never committed for self-consciously evil

---

1. See Rothstein's "Presidential Assassination Syndrome: A Psychiatric Study of the Threat, the Deed and the Message" in this volume and the references to his work contained therein; and Joseph A. Sebastiani and James L. Foy, "Psychotic Visitors to the White House," *American Journal of Psychiatry*, 122 (March, 1965), pp. 679–686.

purposes. The perpetrator sees himself as the instrument of justice. Political murder is an act of conscience. The personal murderer violates his conscience. The political murderer who kills a stranger after careful, secretive planning does so for an ideal. Not all personal murderers are convinced of their right to deprive another person of human life. Most, indeed, kill an intimate, one whom they have loved, propelled by a passion which extinguishes for that time rational calculation. After the homicide has been committed, the personal murderer often feels remorse, suffers from guilt, seeks punishment by turning himself in to the authorities, attempts suicide, forgets what he has done, and not infrequently becomes converted to a religion that will grant him absolution.

The assassin is not consciously aware of love or hate toward his victim. He is not aware of emotional impulsivity. After his deed he feels neither remorse nor guilt. He never blots out memory of his act. Since the motive that preceded his decision was, so far as he knows, an abstract ideal, it had the fanatical quality of a religious zealot. He does not turn to another form of spiritual escape after his murder, but before it. The political murderer resembles a large proportion of personal murderers in the virtual certainty of punishment, which he not only accepts but anticipates.

But whether he is alone or representative of a group, real or fantasied, he commits his murder in the name of justice, impelled by a divine influence or humanistic altruism, or the requirement that he lay down his own life and destroy that of a political figure for some sort of political ideal. The Confederacy fulfilled for Booth his ideal society of a cultured aristocracy. Guiteau was driven by God to heal the conflict of party strife in a political organization. Anarchism, the claims of individual freedom against any formal governmental restrictions, drove Czolgosz. Marxist economics, the rescuing of workers from capitalist exploitation, was Oswald's conscious "motive."

The assassin has a political ideal. His murderous paroxysm promotes it. When Sirhan shouted after shooting Senator Kennedy, "Let me explain, I can explain," he almost certainly believed that his murder in the service of Jordanian nationalism would be persuasive. When Booth melodramatically shouted, "Sic semper tyrannis," he was explaining. Oswald "explained" in his historic Diary. Czolgosz, when he said, "It is not right for one man [the

President] to get so much attention and another to get so little," was explaining.

Unlike the personal murderer, the assassin does not believe that his victim has committed a private wrong against him. He does not feel overwhelmed with irrational, irresistible impulses. When he slays a key figure who carries out sociopolitical operations affecting the entire community, his act is ideological, not personal. His sense of righteousness is unassailable. In each case, however, the political murderer has struck the wrong target. The political murderer, like the personal killer, strikes the mirror. He obliterates an intolerable image of himself that he himself has when he strikes out at his victim.

The assassin is a moral masochist, one whose capacity for social adaptation is seriously defective. His assault on a major political figure in the name of a generalized abstraction seems to be self-injuring. His gratifications are narcissistic. His act and its punishment are in their violence, significance, and finality, insurance that he will suffer no longer the humiliations of a sense of failure, and that he will establish his future identity, ineradicably linked with the identity of his victim.

The political murderer is a man who resembles the personal murderer in the inadequacy of his private identifications, for whatever reasons, during his development. But the political murderer differs from the personal murderer by generalizing his identification with a vastly augmented, abstracted political environment. When subject to experience, this most fragile of identifications has failed to fulfill its promise. When Oswald defected to Russia, he felt embittered by the capitalist competition and exploitation of the United States. But his frustration, outrage, and dismay were no less in Russia, and he returned. When experienced, the Christian communism in Oneida enraged Guiteau no less than the "non-Christian" environment he forsook for six years to live there. But neither man gave up his emotional investment in the values. Oswald became disgusted with Russia, but he still felt that in a truly Marxist state he might find his identity. He turned to Cuba, which he had never seen. Guiteau turned against Oneida and its Christian concerns but clung to the vision of theological salvation through direct communication with God. In 1879 he wrote a book called *Truth: A Guide to the Bible,* which he tried to popularize and sell in evangelical lectures by expressing as principles virtually the same ideals that he had found unbearable in practice. All assassins are killers. In this they are alike. Each resembles the others in the political context of his killing. As political murderers they were alike and, when tried, they were subject to the usual criminal code applying to murder. In law their intent when they shot was legally identical: to kill. Although they reflected different political facets of opposition to the head of government, they were alike also in their political rather than personal rationale for their assault. They were most similar in the personal motives that impelled them and the concatenation of circumstances which from their birth onward culminated in those motives. The evidence for psychological motive is less obvious than for the legal act and intent. But the underlying motives of the political aggressors have more in common with each other than do the superficially more convincing outward and legal parallelisms.

Human aggression, assault, and killing are so ubiquitous in all the recorded histories of men that we need not attempt here to discuss the putative factors predisposing to this aggression. We are concerned with three special qualities of assassination, logically related to each other, but in terms of the psychological significance of the event for its perpetrator, serving psychologically distinct, if interdependent, purposes. The assault is political; its victim is a head of government. The assault is against a stranger toward whom no personal animosity is felt. The victim is a celebrated figure.

We need not here ruminate about the propensity of the species man for violence and killing. Whether instinctually propelled or environmentally goaded, whether for national welfare or for family protection, self-protection, or self-gratification, we cannot avoid the terrible certainty that man's history has never been free of men acting alone and in consort aggressively and violently against other men.

In the United States the comparatively small number of men who have behaved violently and have been imprisoned are quantitatively infinitesimal when compared with the large mass who willingly, or with some grumbling, leave their families and their jobs as farmers or clerks, workers or executives, to become soldiers. Few soldiers, whether their governments be democratic, monarchical or totalitarian have felt that their consciences forbid the killing of other men whom they do not know, have never before seen, and with whom they have no personal quarrel. Soldiers, like police and executioners, purveyors of governmental power, violence that is sanctioned, are praised and rewarded in their own society and feel not guilt, but virtue in their assaultive tasks.

We are concerned with different sorts of aggressors. The assassin is one man who assaults a head of government with a sense of virtue and without guilt. He, although alone, shares the same type of feelings as the many whose violence is socially demanded, sanctioned, and praised. Why does the assassin choose a political target? Why does he assault the most powerful figure possible?

These politically homicidal men, impelled, as they believe, by ideological imperatives, are in fact ambitious men who, however sincerely they may deny that they have any plan of organization for a state with which to supplant the one they seek to destroy, do seek to supplant the leadership of the state, even if they aspire to a human society which is an aggregate of individuals. Nechayev, whose principles of *The Revolutionary Catechism* served as the talisman of late nineteenth-century regicides, himself killed only one man. That man was a fellow rebel who balked at carrying out one of Nechayev's relatively unimportant instructions. He had challenged Nechayev's authority. Nechayev's final principle epitomized the anomaly of the enemy of the state. It demanded the ultimate in human group cohesion. "To knit the people into a single force which is wholly destructive and wholly invincible— such is our organization, our conspiracy, and our task." Not only Lenin, Stalin, and Hitler, but also leaders of nominally democratic governments have sought to implement this principle of all-encompassing social cohesion at the sacrifice, if necessary, of its subjects or citizens in the service of the state.

It would be surprising if it were otherwise. There are attributes, not only physical but psychical as well, which are shared by all human beings. We can recognize ourselves in the maddest of men, the vilest of criminals, the most radical of revolutionaries, the greatest of creative geniuses, only if we recognize that the factors of character present in ourselves are selectively developed, albeit quantitatively atrophied or hypertrophied among those who seem to be so unrecognizably different.

These observations or speculations are not any longer seriously questioned in the mid-twentieth century. But even if true, they do not respond specifically to the problem of the politically violent man who destroys the head of state.

There are some who see the head of government solely in his vocational role as the man who merely implements the direction of governmental policy. Historical necessity, political pressure, and contemporary challenges make his acts inevitable. His economic policy is the expression of impersonal imperatives that can be calculated statistically. The assassin, lone or conspiratorial, is the active expression of political currents of his time. But the assassin, if only because of his rarity, must be viewed as a man. Every man is a repository of the generalities that he has inherited and that he shares with others of his time and generation, community and station. His individuality, like the uniqueness of every man, lies in the combination of these generalities which are within him, peculiar to him alone. Most men will pull a trigger and intend to kill a stranger at the command of legally, governmentally, or socially empowered officers. Most men then share with the assassin the capacity to fire a gun to destroy a stranger. But in two centuries of our national history only four men have felt impelled by their own order to kill the head of their own state.

The soldier's uniform guarantees to its wearer that his violence is commanded by his country. He is the anonymous instrument of national policy. The uniform of the assassin is his anonymity. The assassin escapes his own anonymity by his homicidal attack on the most celebrated and authoritative figure in his own society. The man whom the assassin kills has won from his fellows an expression of his special, separate, dominant, authoritative, and awesome celebrity. The assassin has seen himself as special, as separate, but ineffectual, despised, not rewarded to the measure of his merit. Helpless and humiliated, he kills to relieve his knowing sense of nonentity.

Why does the assassin choose a violent political act to achieve self-realization? We do know the general categories of needs that must be fulfilled to increase the probability of a sense of fulfillment and the stability of personality which we call normality. Reciprocally, we are aware of the nature of deprivations that predispose to psychopathology. We may, indeed, correlate the nature of deprivation with the form of the ensuing psychopathology.

Since man is a biological being, it seems reasonable, even

inevitable, that more penetrating investigations of his tissues will yield more understanding and more powerful protection and remedies against psychic assaults. Nevertheless, the seeming discrepancy in the level of understanding man's soma and his psyche may be more apparent than real. We more readily accept the weight of evidence that we can see, weigh, smell, taste, or hear, the evidence of our perceptive and exteroceptive senses, than we do the evidence that rests on selective construct perception and concept formation. There is good reason for this difference. The replicability and availability of sense evidence is steadier and stronger than concept evidence. Nevertheless, even when concepts differ, one may be accurate and seeming discrepancies may be semantic rather than substantive. Moreover, there exists considerable consensus concerning the malignant effect of certain environmental stresses on the developing child.

During the trial of Guiteau, the greatest weight of psychiatric authority supported the prosecution.[2] Mental illness, they said, was a disease of the brain. Guiteau had no such disease. Disease, furthermore, denoted change. Since, in their view, Guiteau had always been a scoundrel, this evil act reflected not his mental illness but his wickedness.

The major influences on American psychiatric thinking during the nineteenth century came from German and French authorities. The Germans saw human feelings and acts as epiphenomenon of the human brain, intact and healthy, degenerated, or diseased. Gall and Spurzheim had concluded that the external conformation of the skull reflected the shape of the brain within, and that the relative largeness or smallness of different anatomical segments of the brain were correlated with qualities of specific traits in corresponding quantitative measures. Lombroso, influenced by evolutionary biology, saw the criminal as an atavistic throwback to an earlier stage of human development. Not only skull conformation but facial appearance seemed to him to be correlated with various sorts of criminality. It was accepted as well that illness of the brain was one facet of illness of the body, so that Kraeplin described the

2. For a contemporary analysis of the psychiatric aspects of the trial see Charles E. Rosenberg, *The Trial of the Assassin Guiteau* (Chicago: University of Chicago Press, 1968).

most serious mental disease, dementia praecox, as both physically and mentally progressive, ending in death.

The French did not entirely reject these identities of physical and mental states. They recognized, however, that moral states, what we would today call psychological factors, were significant in their own right. Pinel abolished shackling at Salpêtrière bath as a humanitarian act, but also from his professional observation that men chained like wild beasts were less likely to behave like human beings than men free to move about as other men. Patients treated with dignity responded with their own inner restraint. Esquinol observed that there were manias confined to a single aspect of a man's life: monomanias, an irrestible impulse to commit certain acts with no other stigmata of mental disease. Morel, like these great clinicians, conceived of a *manie sans délire,* an insanity without deliriums, an insanity that consisted of a persistent misperception and misapprehension of the world around the patient, even when his thinking processes and even his moods seemed not to be remarkable. These and similar views became in the English and American psychiatric literature "moral insanity," a form of insanity in which in a few or even one sphere, behavior and perspective were so distorted as to constitute a distinct form of psychopathology.

Hate is an emotion experienced subjectively, associated with a feeling of aggressive tension, which the hater aims to discharge by attacking some appropriate object. When aggressive tension is discharged by attacking, injuring, or killing a political person, the source of this tension is related to the victim's office. Such organic factors as psychomotor epilepsy, or some form of somatic intoxication which the aggressor did not himself cause, a severe mental deficiency based upon pre-natal factors, or a degeneration of brain tissue were, particularly during the nineteenth century, the most frequently suspect. When, through organic inadequacy or mental deficiency, the range of adaptive responses to what is perceived as stress is limited, the range of maladaptive responses is potentiated. The threat of social or environmental assault when perceived by a person who is, either through physical or psychical development, unprepared to defend himself with socially appropriate defense techniques may result in attack. The two primary defenses available to man are assault and withdrawal. Most murderers have not been arrested before for violating any serious law. Rarely have they been chronic delinquents.

Psychosomatic symptoms like Zangara's stomach-ache may be concrete painful feeling coming from within which serves as the organic, inner proof that the world outside is dangerous, threatening, and suspicious. As Zangara could suffer intensive pains in his bowels, in the absence of discernible physical pathology, so too may some feel driven to end their body's functioning completely, to wish for death. The world's affliction may evoke an aggressive sense of mission to avenge by assault single perpetrators of this harm, or on groups, or on the self by suicide.

Is aggressiveness a general trait of a personality? May a person's aggressive potential be stated quantitatively, without reference to specific situational variables? Is an individual who is aggressive in one kind of personal relation aggressive in others? Aggressive potential may in some ways be seen as parallel to the sexual. The probability of aggressive activity may be altered, for example, exacerbated during puberty, adolescence, and early childhood, and muted during old age and senescence. If excessively inhibited by external pressures, violent potential may be increased or, paradoxically, reacted against with almost complete inhibition of overt evidence of the existence of either aggressive or sexual drives. Even when acted out, certain forms of violence may be valued as serving socially constructive goals and more intimately socially integrating ends. Anxiety may be the primary, prepotent reaction for both. Violence, even when viewed as incidental to the achievement of a socially desirable goal is, invariably, the reaction to a basic, personal threat. The violent offender pays scant attention to self-preservation.

Booth tried to engineer the mass murder of Lincoln and his closest advisers. Oswald had shot at General Walker. The assassin resembles the mass murderer by mortally striking down persons who are strangers to him. In August, 1966, Charles Joseph Whitman, 25, a student of architectural engineering at the University of Texas perpetrated the worst mass murder in twentieth-century United States. Ten days earlier Whitman, accompanied by his brother, had visited the 307-foot-high tower that overlooks the huge campus of the university. On the fatal day he killed thirteen people and wounded thirty-one others, all strangers to him. He had, earlier that day, killed his wife and his mother to prevent them from suffering for his deed.

Whitman had seemed to be an exemplary boy and young man. Like Oswald, Whitman had enlisted in the Marines. After successfully completing his tour of duty, he entered the university. Oswald is thought to have gained his skill as a marksman in the Marines. Oswald's older brothers had preceded him as Marines. But Whitman had been trained to use guns as soon as he was old enough to hold them, as his two brothers had been, by his father. His father described himself as "a fanatic about guns." "I raised my boys to know how to handle guns." Whitman had qualified as a Marine sharpshooter, but not for its highest rank: expert. Oswald, too, had demonstrated proficiency but not of the highest order as a marksman. Whitman, again like Oswald, had been punished and busted in rank once for illegal possession of a pistol and once for a brawl with a fellow Marine.

Oswald's biological father had died two months before his birth. Whitman had a father for a time, a father who was an authoritarian perfectionist, who demanded absolute obedience from his son, and who quarreled with and beat his mother. In march of the spring preceding his mass murder, Whitman's mother had called him home from school to assist her in leaving her husband. Charles dutifully returned, called the police to protect them from his father's violent wrath, and assisted her in moving. She moved to Austin to be near Charles. That spring John, a seventeen-year-old younger brother, broke a storefront window with a rock and paid a twenty-five dollar fine rather than return to his father. However, Patrick, twenty-one, worked for his father and continued to live with him.

Deeply upset, one of the first things that Charles Whitman did when he returned to school was to talk with Dr. Maurice Heatly, a university psychiatrist. He spoke for two hours. He was concerned about his temper and about the danger that he might explode. Deeply as he had resented his father's beating his mother, he had, he told the doctor, beaten his own wife. He was "thinking," he said, "about going up on the tower with a deer rifle and start shooting people." Although the doctor described him as a massive, muscular youth who seemed to be oozing with hostility, the doctor was not troubled by this fantasy. It was "a common experience for students who came to the clinic to think of the tower as the site for some desperate action." Five persons had in fact died by falling from the tower since it was built in 1933. Three seemed to have been suicides.

The Whitman massacre in Texas, following so soon after the Speck mass killings in Chicago, was deeply troubling to the nation. The governor of Texas, John Connally, who had been wounded by the assassin of President Kennedy, urgently pressed the legislators to pass a law which required that anyone found "insane" in a murder or kidnaping be placed in an institution for the rest of his life. Governor Connally did not ask for any registration or control over the private ownership of guns. Since Whitman had possession of a small armory, and since he had never been accused of either murder or kidnaping, the response of the Governor was peculiarly tangential. Senator Robert Kennedy, who in 1968 was to die from an assassin's bullet as he sought the presidency, offered a more moderate suggestion. Any person, he urged, found not guilty of any federal crime by reason of insanity should be committed for psychiatric treatment. Senator Kennedy explained that had Whitman lived to face trial he would "undoubtedly" have been acquitted because "he was so clearly insane." When the Governor and the Senator spoke, Whitman himself was dead. Whitman proved to have had a brain tumor about the size of a pecan in the region of his hypothalamus. But the pathologist who had performed the autopsy was certain that this lesion had neither caused the headaches from which he suffered nor triggered his murderous acts. Dexedrine tablets were found in Whitman's possession, but they detected no evidence that he had taken any before he climbed the tower.

Behavioral scientists have debated the role of the tyrannical father whose son hated, feared, and emulated him, and the clinging, victimized mother whom the boy so adored that he murdered her to spare her the agony of witnessing his violence. Whitman and the mother he had killed were buried together with full Catholic rites in hallowed ground, because the officiating priest explained Charles was so obviously deranged that he could not be held responsible for the sin of murder.

Presidential Assassination Syndrome:
A Psychiatic Study of the Threat,
the Deed, and the Message

David A. Rothstein

BACKGROUND OF THE STUDY

At the time of the assassination of President Kennedy I had just begun my tour of active duty in the United States Public Health Service that October and was stationed at the United States Medical Center for Federal Prisoners (M.C.F.P.) in Springfield, Missouri. The M.C.F.P. is a sort of centrally located institution to which physically and mentally ill prisoners are sent from all over the federal prison system.[1]

By virtue of a strange legal paradox, while the assassination of the President of the United States by Lee Harvey Oswald violated no federal law, there were federal statutes that applied to make it a punishable federal offense to threaten the life of the President. The statutes relevant at the time were found under Title 18 of the United States Code (1958). Chapter 41, Section 871 proscribed threats against the President, President-elect, and Vice-President, while Section 875 prohibited interstate commerce or communication of threats and ransom or extortion demands, and Section 876 prohibited mailing of threatening communications. Therefore, there did exist in 1963 federal prisoners committed under these

1. Studies based on my stay at M.C.F.P. or related to it include: David A. Rothstein, "Presidential Assassination Syndrome," *Archives of General Psychiatry,* 11 (September, 1964), pp. 245–254; "Presidential Assassination Syndrome, II: Application to Lee Harvey Oswald," *Archives of General Psychiatry,* 15 (September, 1966), pp. 260–266; and "Report and Testimony to National Commission on the Causes and Prevention of Violence," Task Force on Assassination and Political Violence, Washington, D.C., October 3, 1968. These ideas will be developed more extensively in my forthcoming book, *Presidential Assassination Syndrome* (Englewood Cliffs, N.J.: Prentice-Hall).

statutes. In view of the bizarre nature of the offense these individuals tended to be concentrated at the M.C.F.P. in Springfield.

At the time of the assassination I had already had contact with a few of these patients and was in a position to observe their reactions. It occurred to me that the Medical Center could serve as an excellent resource for investigation in this area. Although there would be obvious defects in trying to generalize from studies of those who had only threatened the President, as I will discuss below, I felt that investigation of the history and course of each of these patients could be useful. In addition, it seemed that an evaluation of the reactions these patients demonstrated in response to the actual assassination would be highly informative and would yield additional insight into their psychodynamics.

Although I was able to find and review a number of much earlier papers concerning psychiatric aspects of previous presidential assassins, for example, papers written by expert psychiatric witnesses (alienists) who had examined the assassins of Presidents Garfield and McKinley, there was not much on the subject in the more recent literature.[2] It seemed important, therefore, both to make available general descriptive information concerning this type of patient and to make some attempt at psychiatric formulation of the developmental and psychodynamic factors involved.

THEORETICAL CONSIDERATIONS

My aim was primarily to see whether an indirect approach of this nature could be of assistance in understanding Lee Harvey Oswald. It was not primarily directed at the problem of estimating the degree of dangerousness of the individuals studied, although the importance of this practical problem quickly became obvious, as did its difficulty of solution. The value of this indirect approach was heightened by the subsequent killing of Oswald by Jack Ruby, which substantially eliminated the possibility of any direct psychiatric examination of Oswald, except for the earlier examinations performed when he was an adolescent.[3] As I indicated, I knew

2. An able exception is Robert J. Donovan, *The Assassins* (New York: Popular Library, 1964).
3. See *Report of the President's Commission on the Assassination of President Kennedy,* (Washington, D.C.: U.S. Government Printing Office, 1964); *Investigation of the Assassination of President John F. Kennedy:*

that the study of individuals with obvious pathology might be open to question with respect to general applicability of the findings, but I also knew that it is not an unusual technique in medical sciences to study pathology for clues to more general understanding. Just as the study of anatomical pathology has often contributed to our knowledge of normal anatomy and the study of biochemical disorders has enlarged our understanding of normal biochemistry, so too do psychiatrically disturbed patients, particularly schizophrenic patients, often present on the surface and open for observation material that is usually unconscious and unavailable. I also knew that these patients had not actually committed assassination, but had, through their threats, removed themselves from circulation, and that no one could definitively say whether they really would or would not have actually assassinated the President.

As I look back at the studies of assassination, it becomes clear that two issues have not been kept sufficiently separate and distinct.[4] The first is the issue of understanding the psychodynamics, the psychological mechanisms, the developmental factors, etc., of the assassin. As is usual in many scientific investigations, I had chosen a small, workable, available system to study which was recognized not to possess all characteristics of the real situation, but did possess enough similarity to serve as an analogous model from which to draw inferences, which could then be tested for applicability to the situation of primary interest—the real assassination and the assassin.

Today man is observing and studying many things previously outside his realm of experience: microscopic bacteria, submicroscopic viruses, subatomic particles, close-up views of the moon and even of Mars, radar echoes from Venus, X-ray images of astronomical objects, and even his own intrapsychic processes. We often forget that much, even most, of this investigation is highly indirect and/or occurs in highly artificial conditions.

Hearings Before the President's Commission on the Assassination of President Kennedy (Washington, D.C.: U.S. Government Printing Office, 1964); and Renatus Hartogs and Lucy Freeman, *The Two Assassins* (New York: Thomas Crowell, 1965).

4. These beliefs result from my meeting with members of the President's Commission on the Assassination of President Kennedy, Commission staff, and psychiatrists, July 9, 1964.

Employing this approach, I looked at a group of individuals who had threatened the President in order to see what clues could be discovered to reconstruct the psychology of the individual who had assassinated the President. Members of this group would have as a necessary consequence of the one selection criterion, one common characteristic, ideation of a violent nature centering around the President, which had been expressed at least at the level of an implied or actual threat, but possibly in more serious ways. Thus the group could include among its members presidential assassins or potential assassins, but also threateners who might or might not have a potential for carrying out the act. I did not assume that all these individuals were necessarily potential assassins, and I avoided using that term, in order not to imply that they were.

This leads to the second issue, which deals with the problem of evaluating the degree of dangerousness of an individual who has come to the attention of the authorities. The problem involves deciding which individuals actually are potential assassins and under what circumstances they would be most dangerous, perhaps even including new ways of identifying such individuals who might not otherwise have come to the attention of the authorities. This is a more practical problem than the first, especially relevant to officials whose concern is not so much to understand why an assassination occurred as to stop it from happening again. The distinction is something like the distinction between basic science and applied technology.

But we should not overlook the value of knowledge and understanding for its own sake. The human mind unceasingly seeks to make order out of the universe. Psychiatrists and neurologists are familiar with the sympton of confabulation which occurs in individuals whose memory is impaired for one reason or another. The person unconsciously and involuntarily creates false memories to fill the unexplained gap. Psychiatrists are also familiar with the fact that a paranoid individual may unconsciously build up elaborate delusional systems to explain experiences which seem otherwise incomprehensible to him (in this case because the true explanations involve unacceptable feelings).

It seems to me that this same human effort to seek order in the universe lies behind so many of the conspiracy theories about the assassination. In the absence of an explanation, or in the absence of an explanation acceptable and believable to the person involved, it becomes necessary to generate one. Moreover, the idea of a conspiracy may seem to some to offer more order and predictability in the universe, since it would involve a group acting on rational motives in a manner understandable to the average man. While the idea of a lone assassin, acting from irrational, apparently unpredictable, motives would seem more threatening and would appear to leave the universe more random and capricious. But science, too, seeks order in the universe. It is a tenet of modern psychiatry that apparently irrational behavior can indeed be understood, that the unconscious sources from which it springs can, to a large extent, be elucidated. Thus the search for an understanding of an event such as the assassination of President Kennedy must be differentiated as a goal in itself, separate from the practical applications of that knowledge—although the minor consolation gained from comprehending the event is, in a way, a practical result too.[5] Studies of assassination, hopefully, help meet the needs of the community at large in furthering its understanding of the situation and in dealing with its own responses.

CASE HISTORIES

At the time of the study, there were in the M.C.F.P. nine patients whose offenses involved threats to the President. One additional patient, who had disclosed presidential-assassination fantasies during psychiatric examination and verbalized threats against the President while at the Medical Center, was also included. These ten patients formed the basis for the conclusions, supplemented by data on an eleventh patient who was committed in connection with a threat against President Johnson after the

5. Dr. Bruno Bettelheim, in describing his experiences in a concentration camp, has commented that studying, observing, and understanding a traumatic situation is one means of dealing with it. *The Informed Heart* (Glencoe: The Free Press, 1960). The comments of the editors of a study of children's reactions to the assassination of President Kennedy make the same point, as I noted in a review of the book. Martha Wolfenstein and Gilbert Kliman, eds., *Children and the Death of a President* (New York: Doubleday, 1965), and my review "Children and the Death of a President," *Archives of General Psychiatry*, 15 (July, 1966), pp. 106–107.

main portion of the initial study was completed. Among these patients, seven had threatened President Kennedy, two had threatened President Eisenhower, one of them had also threatened President Truman in the past, and several had also threatened other officials and/or relatives at one time or another. All these patients were at the United States M.C.F.P. for psychiatric reasons. Five were unsentenced patients, having been found by the court to be incompetent to stand trial and committed until mentally competent or until pending charges were disposed of according to law. The remainder were sentenced prisoners, two of whom had been originally sentenced, in part for psychiatric study and observation in order to make recommendations to the court that would be helpful in determining disposition.

Background data were obtained from the institution records, which included prison classification studies, social history, psychiatric and general medical examination, psychiatric staff conferences, and in some cases, psychological testing. I had had previous contact with several of the patients in doing the original psychiatric examination or in participating in the staff evaluations. In addition, I interviewed each of the patients included in this study in order to gain a firsthand impression of the individual.

The following summaries of the relevant case material are presented in detail, although information that would identify the subjects is excluded. Representative material concerning estimates of the potential dangerousness of the individuals has been included.

PATIENT 1

This young man, who was admitted to the M.C.F.P. in October, 1963, had written the following letter to President Kennedy the previous May: "Dear President Kenney (sic). The reason I wrote this letter (sic) I am going to kill you. Don't me lie (sic) but there is one reason I don't like to do this. Forgive me but you have to die." (signed with name and address.)

The patient related that earlier in the year he had broken up with a woman friend. He had attempted sexual relations with her, and because she had some vaginal bleeding, he felt he had harmed her and tried to turn himself in to the police. He said he felt guilty, and that letting a woman see so much of his emotions had made him feel like a "little kid." He subsequently felt rejected by her and became quite depressed. He suffered from sleeplessness, loss of appetite, and weight loss. Shortly before the final breakup he had taken an overdose of proprietary sleeping pills, with a strong implication of suicidal fantasies. After the separation he was unable to work consistently, roamed around the country without any real attachments until he returned home to his parents where the letter was written. During this period he had become convinced that the only way to handle the situation would be to get back into the military service, from which he had been discharged thirteen years previously after an apparent suicide gesture. He had already tried unsuccessfully to get back into the service many times. Finally, he decided that if he wrote a letter threatening the President, this would get some action. He later indicated that some of the anger in the letter was really directed at this woman friend, to whom he had written a threatening letter three days prior to the presidential threat. After writing to the President, he waited around for the "results," but finally left for another state where he had previously worked and was apprehended there. He also indicated that he had really wanted to get caught and that he had been willing to accept death as punishment, although he felt guilty that his death might hurt "her" (the woman friend).

Past History

The patient had no previous criminal history. He had been born and raised in a rural Appalachian region in a family of limited resources, one of fifteen siblings, eleven of whom had died. He felt that his father, a foundry worker, had been closer to an older brother, who seemed to think along the same lines as the father and had similar interests, and that the mother, an "alcoholic but a good woman," also "loved the older brother more" and had "spoiled him." The patient often felt that his military discharge had dishonored him in comparison with the older brother, who had been in the military service for almost twenty years.

The patient had attended school through ninth grade. At age seventeen he joined the service. After visiting home the following year, he became depressed and climbed up a fire escape indicating that he intended to jump off. He later expressed confusion about whether he really would have jumped or whether he had "faked it" in order to be discharged. He also expressed confusion about the general discharge under honorable conditions that he had been given after this suicide gesture, often considering it a dishonorable discharge. He had always been very uncomfortable with women, even remembering running from a girl who had wanted to go out with him. He had married about twelve years before the offense. The wife was described as immature and promiscuous, and had frequently taunted him about his military discharge. Repeated separations culminated in a final separation four years prior to the offense, when the wife left him refusing to return. The marriage had produced four children, the oldest of whom had been "given away" by the wife to a couple in another state. The patient described feeling lonely since separation from the wife.

Clinical Appearance

The patient appeared to be a rather naïve, uneducated, simple-appearing young man, but conveyed a certain warmth in his manner. He communicated an exceptionally strong feeling of guilt. He stated that the experience in prison had "sobered him up" and that he now realized the seriousness of his offense. Clinical findings were consistent with a diagnosis of schizophrenic reaction, simple type, with depressive features. Evaluation by the psychiatric staff indicated virtually no danger that he might put the threats into action and that he could be expected to do well in a controlled, supportive out-patient setting.

Reaction to the Assassination

At the time of the assassination the patient appeared depressed and said that he was getting the feeling of being the actual murderer himself. He had watched television all four days subsequently. He later said that if he had known such a thing would actually happen, he would never have written the letter. He said that he felt particularly sorry for "her" (Mrs. Kennedy) and that "seeing her standing there by the coffin, with the children" had brought home the full significance of the event. He indicated that he had respected President Kennedy, although he had not voted because he had no stable residence. He felt that Jack Ruby had no right to shoot Oswald any more than he himself had a right to send the letter and that both he and Ruby had to be taught a lesson because "the officials just can't let that kind of thing go on." He said that other patients had teased him, asking if he was now going to write to President Johnson. He worried that the assassination might adversely affect the authorities' attitude toward him and also his chances for getting a job outside prison. What bothered him most, however, was the thought that, had he been out of prison at the time, he might have been blamed and he almost felt as if the actual fact of his being in prison at the time was the only concrete evidence, even to himself, that he did not do it.

PATIENT 2

This young man was admitted to the M.C.F.P. in 1960. During January of that year he had written a letter to President Eisenhower containing a threat against his life and the lives of his grandchildren, including a notation that he had in his possession a .22-caliber pistol. His father mailed the letter for him under the impression that it was a request for information regarding his previous discharge from the service. The patient later denied any real intent to kill the President or any member of his family. He said he had initially planned to write the President asking him to change his military discharge from undesirable to honorable medical, but had become more and more "worked up" while writing the letter, and finally added the threat. He apparently never quite got around to telling the President just what he wanted and instead described the misery he felt he had gone through because of the undesirable discharge. He felt the President had never heard of him or his case, but that as head of the government the President is responsible for everything the government does and should be informed about his case, so he (the President) could "make them do right." When arrested at the home of his parents he had the revolver, which he had purchased a week earlier, in a bag that he had packed in preparation for a trip to Washington if he did not get a reply to his letter. He claimed, however, an intention to use it for suicide rather than against the President. The court-appointed psychiatrist who first saw him felt he did intend to use the gun as a threat to frighten people but would not have shot anyone.

Past History

The patient was born and raised in a rural community in an eastern state, the youngest of four children. The father had at one time worked as a janitor in a state government building that the patient tended later to remember as the Capitol building in Washington, D.C. The mother was a housewife but had also done domestic work. One brother was a career serviceman. One sister was married, and the patient noted that her children were about the same age as the President's grandchildren whom he had threatened.

The patient claimed to have suffered an attack of polio as a child, which he felt left him with a permanently underdeveloped left side from the waist down. (Physical examination revealed mild atrophy of the left leg and hip with compensatory scoliosis [curving of the spine], a slightly atrophic right testicle, and an undescended left testicle.) He had been arrested as a juvenile for arson and also as a runaway but was returned to his parents both times. Almost immediately after graduating from high school, he enlisted in the service, serving for some time in Korea. In the service he became increasingly concerned about the left side of his body, which he felt hampered him in his duties and was a source of embarrassment to him. He made several unsuccessful attempts to obtain a medical discharge, and then when his father suffered a heart attack, unsuccessfully attempted to obtain a hardship discharge in order to help his parents financially. After being AWOL on several occasions he received a court-martial, and was given an undesirable discharge.

Following his discharge he led a "semitransient, solitary, and brooding life," and was unable to hold steady employment. He was able to get several jobs but kept comparing himself to those who had had honorable discharges. He would soon begin to feel that people were talking about him and did not want him around, that he was unworthy to stay and work with "honorable" men, and so he would quit one job after another. Suicide was also a recurring thought and he was hospitalized at one point after a suicide attempt. The concern over the left side was gradually replaced by his feeling of inferiority as a recipient of an undersirable discharge.

Clinical Appearance

The patient initially was a sloppy-appearing, bewildered-looking man. He was quite distractable and continually returned to the theme that if the military service had treated him properly he would not have been in this difficulty. He also expressed mild feelings of being persecuted by that earlier examiner. He described how he had always felt that the other children in school had disliked him because of his "deformity" and that he had been surprised when the military service accepted him. Notably, the parents shared with him a great deal of hostility toward officials and continually reiterated that he should not have been accepted in the first place and that "the doctor that passed him should be examined himself." He complained about his sister's husband, whom he considered to be a ne'er-do-well, compared her children to the President's grandchildren, and inquired whether the examiner felt it was wrong for him to want to go and live with his sister and support her when he was released.

He also requested permission to write to the Russian Embassy in order to complain about the prison officials because he felt the Russians would cause his "mistreatment" to be stopped. He contemplated moving to Russia when released, because the United States government "mistreated" him so much, and he felt that everyone in Russia is treated fairly.

He received a diagnosis of schizophrenic reaction, paranoid type. During his course at the M.C.F.P. he slowly improved to the point where he was able to function at a much more appropriate level and was no longer considered potentially dangerous. His obsessive-compulsive defenses seemed to have been reinstated. He was scheduled for discharge shortly after I interviewed him.

Reaction to the Assassination

The patient's first reaction was disbelief when told of the event by another patient. He thought the other patient was teasing him in connection with his own offense. He said he had never thought such a thing would happen and asserted again that he himself had intended only to complain to the President. He said he felt some similarity between himself and Oswald, feeling that both should have received psychiatric treatment in the military service. He did not feel people would have any resentment against him for threatening the President, but worried that it might affect the decision of the authorities at the M.C.F.P. with respect to his impending discharge from prison. He felt that he now understood much better how to handle his feelings, planned to live with his parents, had no plans to consider marriage and hoped he could get a job, although he felt he might have some problems as an "ex-con" and "mental patient." He related at this time in an appropriate manner, though without much recognition of the intensity of the public's reaction to the assassination.

PATIENT 3

This late-adolescent patient had been transferred from a federal reformatory to the M.C.F.P. in October, 1963 for psychiatric reasons, which included a poor behavioral adjustment, bizarre sexual and sadistic fantasies approaching hallucinatory quality, suicide potential, and a bizarre escape attempt which resulted in his hiding all day under a manhole cover. He had been sentenced originally for interstate transportation of a stolen motor vehicle. His fantasied intentions to assassinate the President, which were revealed in the course of psychiatric examination, were the reason for his being included in this study. When asked who the President was, during a mental-status evaluation, he said that not only did he know who the President was but that he intended to assassinate the President as soon as he got out of prison because he (the patient) was a socialist. He described how he would get up on a roof and use a high-powered rifle with a silencer and that it would be impossible for the President to protect himself against such an attack.

Past History

The patient was brought up in the Great Lakes area by foster parents, who had adopted him at the age of three. He had apparently lived previously in the maternal grandparents' home. He stated that he had never really accepted his foster parents. For example, whenever they bought him presents, he would sell them. He related, perhaps unreliably, that his real father was approaching middle age and his real mother was an unmarried adolescent at the time of his birth. He expressed a compelling need to search for and find his real parents. He felt that his foster sister and foster brother were treated better than he. He described a lifelong problem of bed wetting and mentioned having seen a psychiatrist briefly about age thirteen, centering around fairly extreme passive-aggressive behavior.

The patient stopped school at age seventeen, after the tenth grade. He had disliked school because he felt the teachers were "riding" him. He attempted to join the military service at this time, but was rejected, whereupon he left home for several weeks, his foster parents presuming he had been accepted by the service. He claimed later to have rented an apartment and to have supported himself during this time, but actually had lived with some relatives. He subsequently joined the military reserves but received a general discharge under honorable conditions after only a few months of unsatisfactory performance and difficulty with the law. During the same period he also received a state sentence for car theft. He showed much confusion about his name, having utilized various aliases, and also about his age, claiming to be about five years older than his actual age. In fact, he had fantasied a life during this imaginary five years, which included a love affair with an imaginary girl who jilted him to marry someone else with his ring in his apartment. The fantasied five years also included a common-law marriage to another imaginary woman, who carried a revolver and stiletto to protect herself from men. He claimed that she had a daughter by him and that she now suffered from leukemia. He said hostilely that he did not care if she or every woman in the United States died. Verification of his history was rendered difficult by his use of more than one name and by the presence of much fantasy material, which in some of the records seemed to have been accepted at face value.

Clinical Appearance

The patient described that he felt depressed, said there was nothing to look forward to in life, that his birth was an accident, and that all he could do now was to pass time, which he would like to do by living in the wilderness like a pioneer. He described bizarre fantasies and dreams. He expressed a bizarre interest in anatomy and felt he could be helped by a brain transplant. He described a recurring dream like a western movie in which he would go into a store, order something, and then shoot everyone in the store. There was much confusion in his self identity and in his sexual identity. He claimed to be writing the definitive textbook on homosexuality. Indeed, some of his turmoil seemed to be relieved when he eventually accepted an overt homosexual role. This seemed to relieve a good deal of conflict and also to meet some of his needs for affection and contact. He was superficially rebellious and got into conflicts with male authorities but seemed to respond well to a recognition of the underlying depressed, dependent feelings. Pointing out these feelings would often result in temporary evaporation of the provocative behavior.

He seemed to derive a good deal of secondary gain from the attention to his threats. He at one point complained that the Secret Service was not paying enough attention to him and demanded replacement of "his" agent because the agent had not visited him recently. In addition, he derived a good deal of gratification from the prospect of being retained at the Medical Center because of potential dangerousness. Thus the threats were one way of attempting to insure that he would continue to be taken care of. Paradoxically, the patient felt that he was putting one over on the staff by appearing dangerous in order to maintain himself in his new-found home at the Medical Center because he consciously felt that he was not dangerous. The staff, however, believed his assertions that he would go to any length to prove his threat, including carrying it out if the authorities "called his bluff" by releasing him.

He received a diagnosis of schizophrenic reaction, schizoaffective type.

Reaction to the Assassination

The patient professed to be reacting to the assassination with pleasure and enthusiasm. He told the custodial officers on his unit how happy he was about it. He insisted that he was overjoyed and would not "get" President Johnson. He immediately expressed sympathetic concern for Oswald when he was arrested and felt Oswald was being mistreated. He seemed to identify strongly with Oswald. Despite his professed pleasure, his behavior over the weekend betrayed some turmoil raised by the event. He set up conflicts with the custodial officers, demanding special privileges and engaging in minor but provocative infractions of institution rules. He expressed bitter complaints about the custodial officers whom he maintained were undesirable because they worked for the United States Government. He said he had not voted in the election for or against Kennedy because he would not make such a concession to the United States Government (though in any case he would have been too young).

PATIENT 4

This patient was a young man transferred to the M.C.F.P. as a late adolescent in 1960 from a federal youth institution to which he had been committed two months earlier for interstate transportation of a stolen motor vehicle. This offense had occurred only shortly after his release from the same institution for a similar motor vehicle offense. About a month prior to his transfer to the M.C.F.P. he had managed to send threatening letters to several federal judges and United States attorneys and to the President. His letter to the President read in part: "Dear sir: Have you ever contemplated suicide? If so, please let me know. I wish to be the one that pulls the trigger of the gun that blows your brains out. When and if I get out of prison, I am going to kill you! . . ." It went on with threats to the rest of the President's family, some sadistic, sexual and homosexual threats, and was signed with the patient's name and prison number. The contents indicated that he really knew practically nothing about the President's family. Apparently he had been influenced by the fact that a "fad" had developed among the inmates to write threatening letters. The "fad" had been aborted during the previous year. It was felt by the staff that the patient had written the letters in order to force a transfer to the M.C.F.P., but that he could be dangerous and carry out the threats. He also had a record of previous suicide gestures while incarcerated.

Apparently a reciprocal rejection between the patient and his adoptive parents had been building up and had culminated in a final break after his incarceration in 1960, with the parents refusing any further correspondence with him. Following this he became increasingly disorganized and wrote the threatening letters.

Past History

The patient was raised in a Southwestern state. He was the older of two children adopted by his foster parents, the other being a girl. He led a rather lonely, isolated life as a child. The adoptive father had been described as having little insight, particularly regarding his own dependency needs and inadequacies against which he developed a defense with a stern and brusque external manner, projecting on to others his own dependencies and inadequacies. The adoptive mother was the dominant figure in the household. She was better educated than the father, meticulous and compulsive, rigid and demanding in her expectations for her children, and apparently attempted to fulfill her own unmet needs and ambitions in life through them. She approved of the sister because she excelled in school, in music, and was a favorite of her peers, while the patient did poorly in school, was frail and unsuccessful in social and athletic areas, and was not respected by his peers. By the time he entered high school, he had begun to feel that his parents were not really interested in him. The patient early began to experience the rejection by the parents subjectively in the form of ideas of reference, feelings that the parents were talking about him, and began to run away from home at age fifteen. However, he could not really break away from them and continued at times to extend requests for interest, succor, and love. He became increasingly involved with local, state, and finally federal law authorities.

Clinical Appearance

On initial examination, the patient appeared co-operative, forthright, and honest, but soon gave evidence of being hyperalert, suspicious, hostile, and manipulative. He was noted to be feminine in his mannerisms and evidenced confusion of self-identity. He was described as feeling weak and insecure, while relying on bravado and lying to impress himself and others with his capabilities. He seemed to have particular difficulty in handling his feelings in areas connected with dependency and relating to his parents. His diagnosis was schizophrenic reaction, paranoid type, and sexual deviancy. The schizophrenic reaction was considered to be in remission by the fall of 1963.

Reaction to the Assassination

The patient said he was watching television at the time. He said that at first the reality did not register, but when it did he felt "very bad." He denied that it made him feel guilty and he believed that no resentment had been shown toward him by other prisoners in connection with his having threatened the President. He did not expect that it would affect his own future. He said that he felt he had been suffering from a "nervous breakdown" when he wrote the letters and that when he saw them later he thought they were "silly, asinine threats" which he was sure he had not intended to carry out. He felt Oswald and Ruby were both "sick," that Oswald had "delusions" and that Ruby was "overconcerned." He was sorry for the Kennedy family and he felt that Kennedy had been a great man and a good person. He had not voted because he had not been old enough. He had been classified 4F by the Selective Service, but said he would like to get into the service and might see about getting his draft status changed after his discharge from prison. I did not inquire into how he planned to go about doing this.

PATIENT 5

This patient had written a threating letter to the President in 1962 which read in part: ". . . if necessary or expedient, I'll trim you and your Goddamn Secret Service with machine gun bullets. You're a cunning son of bitch (sic) Kennedy. . . . violent attacks have been made upon me . . . causing more bitterness from me towards the Federal Government . . . outrages perpetuated (sic) by the United States (military service) . . . be prepared to accept full responsibility." He denied any intent to carry through with the threat and said he had written letters of this type to family members throughout the past three or four years as his primary means of "releasing tension." In fact, family members would at times receive four or five letters a day cursing and abusing them. He also said that since his bad-conduct discharge from the military service, he had directed his feelings of hostility and his conviction that the world had not treated him right into what he described as "animosity toward whomever was President." He recalled, however, writing two cordial letters before the present offense, warning President Kennedy about potential assassins. He knew that President Kennedy was due to visit his home town the next day and seemed to think the letter would bring some help for him, as he recalled reading of another man being hospitalized after writing such a letter. A court-appointed psychiatrist considered him potentially dangerous.

Past History

The patient, the third of four surviving sons, was raised in a Southern state. He considered himself "lonesome as a kid." The family home was disrupted by the separation of the parents and the death of the father in an auto-accident fire when the patient was about six years old. His only clear recollection of the father is that of seeing him in his casket draped so that the burned areas would not be visible. The children were split up, with the three older ones going to the grandparents and the youngest staying with the mother. The patient reacted badly to the grandmother but could not obtain affection from the mother, who was described as having been subsequently wrapped up in her own problems of seeking male companionship and drinking heavily after the husband's death.

After his brother left school to join the military service, there appeared to be some change in the patient's personality, an estrangement from people. He did not "feel right," so, after repeatedly begging the grandparents to let him join the service, he finally stopped school in the ninth grade, lied about his age, and enlisted. During his World War II service he had striking feelings of guidance and delusions of special powers. He felt, for example, that he had saved an officer's life by magically diverting the path of a shell. After an honorable discharge he re-enlisted within a month, but subsequently began to decompensate, though he refused psychiatric treatment. After an unauthorized absence, during which he had gone home to visit his mother, he was given a bad-conduct discharge. He later claimed that he had been mentally ill prior to the discharge and that *his* request for hospitalization had been denied.

Following his discharge, he wandered widely and worked at various odd jobs, with no stable home. He had few heterosexual experiences and some homosexual experience. He recalled episodes of depression and had made one suicide gesture accompanied by a note to his mother and brother. He later evaluated this as a "half-try."

Clinical Appearance

The patient appeared as a quite tense, hyperalert and anxious man who passively sought help for many physical complaints. He was somewhat sheepish about describing the letters. He initially expressed feelings of persecution in relation to his court-appointed attorney, who he felt was in collusion with the prosecuting attorney. He showed extreme suspiciousness toward women, expressed a fear of retaliation for his hostile letter, and during his stay at the M.C.F.P. he wrote numerous litigious, inappropriate, and obscene letters to his social worker and to the warden. He claimed to have been offered the captaincy of the "longest and fastest" United States passenger ship and he offered the warden, a physician, a position as ship's surgeon. He was noticeably more disorganized in his letters than in his personal contacts. He was later able to see himself as chronically ill, to accept consciously his need for help, and to express his wish for the "security of being cared for." He received a diagnosis of schizophrenic reaction, paranoid type.

Reaction to the Assassination

At the time of the assassination the patient showed extreme agitation, to the point of near panic. He said he was shocked but not surprised by the assassination, since he had felt all along that the President had not been taking adequate precautions. He said he was quite upset "not out of fear, but out of genuine sympathy for the President and his wife and small children." He said he had been a Kennedy supporter, though he did not vote because of moving around. He said that just before he wrote the threatening letter he had been upset by reading derogatory articles about President Kennedy, and by reading about the treatment of Japanese on the West Coast during World War II. He felt the assassination "hadn't helped" his own situation and that he would elicit resentment from the public if he talked about his offense, but he had experienced none from other patients. He said that he was later ashamed of what he had written and that he wrote an apology after his commitment. He said he had been drinking when he wrote the threat and would not have mailed it if he had reread it. He said he had been thinking about his discharge at the time but now minimized its contribution to writing the letter.

Concerning Oswald, he said he was wondering about a conspiracy, but had decided Oswald was insane. He felt Communism had more of an effect on Oswald than the undesirable discharge, because his own discharge had been similar, but it had never occurred to him to correct it by shooting the President (?!). He seemed unaware of the contradiction in this line of reasoning.

PATIENT 6

This middle-aged man was received at the M.C.F.P. in 1962. His letter to the President read: "Dear Sir, I will come to Washington and put a bullet between your eyes. I thank you." (Signed with his name.) When arrested, he denied memory of writing the letter, stated that nothing could be done for him and that he would just as soon be dead. It appeared to the court-appointed psychiatrist that he might have written the letter in an attempt to get help and possibly to get himself hurt. He stated that he frequently thought of suicide and had often thought of attacking a policeman with a club so that the policeman would then kill him.

Four years prior to the offense, while in the military service, the patient had developed depressive, suicidal, and paranoid symptoms, was hospitalized for several months, and then given a medical discharge. He became very agitated and bitter, feeling that the amount of disability compensation was too small after his record of almost twenty years in the service. Shortly after the discharge he married his second wife but was unable to work, and since then had lived on his pension and his wife's income. There were repeated periods of depression, agitation, and hallucinations, with several hospitalizations. To one psychiatrist he had verbalized a threat to put dynamite on the desk of one of the Senators from his state.

Past History

The patient was born and raised in a rural Southern community, the youngest of seven children. He completed only sixth grade but finished high school after joining the service at age 20. He had married for the first time one year after joining the service, had one child, but was divorced after six years of marriage. His parents died when he was an adult. He had spent most of his adult life in the service, served a number of consecutive enlistments, and saw combat during World War II. He had always been rather quiet and seclusive.

Clinical Appearance

The patient appeared frightened and distant, but rapidly became depressed and tearful when talking about his difficulties finding a job and his feelings of low self-esteem. He described auditory and visual hallucinations. It was noted that the patient seemed preoccupied with his guilt and was a potential suicide risk, that his desire to provoke someone into killing him caused him to be dangerous and in need of close supervision, and that, although he was unlikely to be dangerous to the President, he might, in a depressive episode, attack some other authority figure nearer at hand. During his course at the M.C.F.P. his symptoms abated somewhat, but the prognosis was felt to be poor.

Diagnosis was schizophrenic reaction, paranoid type.

Reaction to the Assassination

The patient complained of inability to sleep because of the assassination. He said he had disturbing dreams but did not remember them. He said he was feeling sorry for the President, that he had voted for President Kennedy and had always liked him. He still had no memory of writing the letter. He later indicated that he had been "shocked" and "torn up," could not sleep or eat, but had recovered in about a week, and, in fact, quickly "forgot" his reaction to the event.

He was quite guarded and suspicious and wanted to be sure his comments would not be used against him. He said he did not expect any resentment from people and had not experienced any so far. He felt that the assassination was a plot and that Ruby had killed Oswald to keep him from talking.

PATIENT 7

This older European-born man had been arrested in 1962 after having written a letter in his native language that contained the following statement (when translated): "I wish to advise that if the President of the United States resists my commands, I will bash his brains in alive; and as for his guards, I will bury them alive." He had previously been sentenced after sending a threatening letter and an obscene telegram to President Truman. The letter told the President that he had too much of an army and that he would send someone over to cut his heart out. The telegram called President Truman a "son-of-a-bitch" because he was not assisting in placement of the patient's children. Subsequently, he had written to the Pope expressing negative feelings, to the Supreme Court, and had also sent a letter to Russia with the comment that ". . . the capitalists are the Big Fish in the sea who eat up the people," but the letter was returned because of insufficient address. The patient later said he felt it is wrong for our government to allow some people to eat steak while others do not have enough to eat.

He said he was only trying to indicate to the President that if he had the power to remove the President's brain, he would give him a different brain so he could understand how it feels when people do not have enough money to clothe and feed themselves properly. He said that his letter to President Truman only referred to removing the heart and giving him a heart that would understand the problems of the people. He claimed that he had not intended to carry out his threats but only wished to get himself before the court to make his ideas public.

Past History

The patient was born in a small village in Europe and grew up in a religious home. He reportedly escaped World War I military service by shooting himself in the arm and migrated to the United States shortly after the war. He married an immigrant girl at age twenty-nine after a "romance-by-mail courtship," but was divorced after five years. The wife and the two daughters returned to Europe. The wife soon came back to the United States. One daughter returned to the United States shortly before his letter to President Truman. She described him as having been obviously disturbed at the time. He had assumed the role of an apostle and prophet and was convinced that most meats were made from ground cadavers. He made a serious suicide attempt while in prison after that offense and also had a history of numerous state mental hospitalizations, which included several escapes. His daughter indicated that he had had surgery for a hernia and removal of one testicle in the 1950's and that he seemed to feel worthless afterward, as if he had serious doubts regarding his masculinity.

Clinical Appearance

The difficulty in communicating with this patient was increased by his poor command of the English language, but he refused to use interpreters. He expressed many well-fixed delusions, particularly of an oral nature. These included his cannibalistic delusions about cadaver meat. While in prison he sent a letter in his native language to a Washington official, in which he enclosed a piece of bacon, perhaps as "proof" of his contentions. The letter, but not the bacon, was returned to the staff for informational purposes.

Possibly in connection with these delusions he stated that he did not wish to be embalmed at death but to be buried in a lake, yet he also predicted that he would never die.

He continued much the same throughout his course at the M.C.F.P. When seen in October, 1963, he indicated that he had expected to be either sent back to Europe or killed for his offense, which he felt any reasonable government would do. He refused to discuss very much of anything, insisting he wished to tell it only to the court. The staff considered him to be potentially dangerous. The diagnosis was schizophrenic reaction, paranoid type.

Reaction to the Assassination

Nursing notes of November 22, 1963 indicate that the patient had become very belligerent to the custodial officers that day. When interviewed he said he felt nothing about the assassination, since it was not his brother, cousin, etc. Further efforts to elicit information produced only increasing agitation, complaints that he was being treated like a pig or monkey, and a final angry comment to remember that some day he would be the boss.

PATIENT 8

This young man was committed to the M.C.F.P. in 1962 after having written a letter threatening to kill the President with his "bare hand" (sic), a wording related to the patient's obsessive concern with masturbation, if the President started a war.[6]

The patient had also written letters to other people, including former teachers, with vague threats, each signed with a different name. He said he wrote the letter to the President because he was angry at many people but just expressed it to the President. At other times he did say that people in power had mistreated him,

6. The material in the patient's record quoted the patient's statement as using the word "hands," which I originally accepted. Dr. Edwin Weinstein, who was studying threatening letters that had been turned over to the Secret Service, pointed out to me in a personal communication that the correct quotation was "hand." Although this point may appear to be inconsequential, Weinstein has pointed out in an article that employs the methodological technique of content analysis to assess threats to kill Presidents that the nature of this reference indicates a preoccupation with masturbation. Edwin A. Weinstein and Olga G. Lyerly, "Symbolic Aspects of Presidential Assassination," *Psychiatry*, 32 (February, 1969), pp. 1–11.

and he felt he should get even with them. When examined by a psychiatrist at the request of the court, his comments about the offense were: "The trouble is that I play with myself too much. . . . It puts pressure on my head. . . . I don't know what's wrong with me, but everything just seems like it is dead or stopped. . . ." He went on to describe somatic delusions, which he attributed to masturbation. The psychiatrist felt he might prove to be a danger to himself (suicidal) and to others.

Past History

The patient was one of four siblings born and raised in a small Appalachian community. According to the mother, from an early age he suffered from a fear of darkness, fear of animals, "excessive masturbation," and "considerable daydreaming." The father had had several psychotic episodes and reportedly still manifested symptoms. During his school years his hypersuspiciousness interfered with acceptance by his peers and by his teachers. He was unable to continue school after the eighth grade, at which time he had become more withdrawn, and had begun to experience auditory hallucinations. Beginning at age sixteen he was hospitalized in state-hospital facilities several times. He received electric-shock treatment on at least one of these occasions.

Clinical Appearance

The patient was quite regressed and also expressed paranoid ideas with respect to his family, the police in his home town, his teachers, the federal government, and the President. Many somatic delusions were present. He received a diagnosis of schizophrenic reaction, chronic undifferentiated type. Initially, he was considered dangerous and in need of long-term hospitalization. Later, while long-term hospitalization was still felt to be indicated, he seemed to be so disorganized that there were no more systematic delusions; he seemed timid and was no longer considered to be a specific danger to anyone. It was then felt that writing the letters would be the most aggressive act that he would commit.

Reaction to the Assassination

This patient gave the simplest, yet perhaps most eloquent description of his reaction, with the statement "I cried." He expressed sorrow for Mrs. Kennedy. He had an increase in his somatic delusions at the time. He said he had had nothing against President Kennedy and did not know why he picked him. He said he had wanted to join the military service but failed the entrance requirements. He did not know why Oswald had acted, felt Ruby was getting even, but was unable to communicate any further information about his subjective reaction. He expressed the hope of being sent back to a state hospital, which he preferred to the M.C.F.P., and, indeed, was returned to a state hospital a few months later.

PATIENT 9

This older man was received at the M.C.F.P. in December, 1963. During October he had written extortion letters, implying that he intended to use the money to finance an assassination plot against the President, and had also written a number of abusive letters to President Kennedy. He told the court psychiatrist that he did not remember writing the letters but that he had reason to threaten the life of the President "because I would do the country a service; there are so many people talking so badly about him." He felt the letters were "silly" when he read them. The court psychiatrist felt he was potentially dangerous to himself (suicidal) and others.

Past History

The patient was the seventh of eight children born and raised in a small Southern town. The father, a schoolteacher, and later a school official, provided a comfortable living until he went into a business venture that failed in the Depression. The patient did not get along well with him, considering him too severe. The mother also taught school, taking time off when the children were young. At age eighteen, the patient had just begun his freshman year in college when his mother died, whereupon he dropped out of school, attributing it to lack of funds because of the Depression.

He never married, although he considered it once during the Depression. He gave up the idea, also because of "financial reasons." He served almost two years in the military service during World War II and received an honorable medical discharge relating to "asymptomatic neurosyphilis and arterial hypertension." He then lived with his brother until first admitted to a Veterans' Administration hospital in 1948. Since then he had been in and out of V.A. and other federal and state hospitals many times. He said he had had every kind of treatment, including insulin, electric shock, tranquilizers, and treatment for his syphilis. He made several suicide attempts during these years.

The patient's criminal record began only during the last three years before commitment to the M.C.F.P., beginning with several local police-department arrests. In 1962 he received a sentence for attempted extortion by mail, but the judgment and sentence were set aside and he was released by court order to a V.A. hospital. He said he had been writing threatening letters for some time for the purpose of being sent to prison to get treatment for his mental illness. He remained at that hospital only briefly, was released, and then signed into another V.A. hospital, where he stayed until release in October, 1963, and almost immediately committed the present offense.

Clinical Appearance

The patient acted quite unconcerned and attempted to be casual. He seemed to be attempting to appear more disorganized than he was felt to be. He manifested poor and inaccurate memory which was increased by his evasiveness, described hallucinations, and insisted he must be psychotic because so many authorities had told him so. He professed to be "in no position to dispute their diagnosis." He was afraid that he would die of a "syphilitic stroke." Diagnosis was schizophrenic reaction, chronic paranoid type, and chronic brain syndrome on the basis of his previous (but presently inactive) neurosyphilis.

Reaction to the Assassination

The patient said he was in the local jail at the time. He said the assassination had been just another news event to him. He was sorry it had happened but had worries of his own and could not go worrying about other people and their problems; after all, he had bigger things to worry about. He said Oswald must have been crazy and filled with hate. He commented that Oswald had a gun but that he, the patient, did not and made a great point to stress that he himself was harmless. He said that he was not a criminal, did not lead a life of violence like "those people," had never robbed anyone or held up anyone. He did not feel the assassination had influenced his disposition by the authorities or his relationships with other patients.

PATIENT 10

This middle-aged man was transferred to the M.C.F.P. in 1961 from a penitentiary for psychiatric reasons. He had been sentenced in 1959 for making threatening remarks relating to President Eisenhower. When stopped by police officers for questioning as he was walking down an expressway, he had begun to threaten the President, finally declaring that he would pull out the President's teeth and slit his throat. He later said that he had made the threatening remarks in order to express his views about a government that "does not take care of and feed people like me." He also indicated that he had made the remarks so that he would be institutionalized and thereby receive desperately needed food, care, and protection, as had resulted from a previous threat.

The patient had served an earlier sentence for a similar offense. When he had been questioned by officers in connection with vagrancy at that time, he had called them "capitalist lackies" and had indicated he would like to put a bullet in the President's head.

Past History

The patient, the younger of two sons, was brought up in the Great Lakes area. His mother died when he was three years old. The father remarried when he was five, and when he was seven, the father sent him away to be brought up by an aunt and uncle. He considered the aunt very strict and said the uncle never spoke to the children.

The patient finished high school. At age twenty-three, when the father died, he began to live the life of a hobo. In his late twenties he joined the military service. He received an honorable discharge after World War II. Shortly afterward, he re-enlisted, but was honorably discharged before expiration of his enlistment, due to "unsuitability." During his service career he had received five courts-martial for disobeying orders, one of which almost resulted in a dishonorable discharge.

After discharge from the service he returned to the life of a hobo. Although he expressed radical socialistic views, he was apparently not involved in any socialist organization.

Clinical Appearance

The patient received a diagnosis of schizophrenic reaction, paranoid type. His course at the M.C.F.P. was variable and marked by exacerbations and remissions. His behavior fluctuated between withdrawal and explosive acting out, including attacking a custodial officer. He did show a favorable response to electric-shock treatment. When the question of discharge approached, he became more disturbed, worrying about where he would go. He seemed to feel guilty, which he evidenced by constantly washing his hands in scalding hot water.

Psychiatric evaluation at one point indicated that he would confine his hostility to verbalizations, and that if it became over-whelming, he would be more likely to turn it in on himself and commit suicide than to express it physically toward others. Later, the staff did feel that if he were not in an institutional setting, at some future point his dependency needs might impel him again to resort to threats and that if verbal behavior did not achieve results he might engage in more actively assaultive or dangerous behavior.

Reaction to the Assassination

The patient was seen quite some time after the assassination. He said he had liked President Kennedy because he felt Democrats did more for poor people. He said that he himself had threatened President Eisenhower because he was unemployed and had wanted a place to stay during the winter, i.e., prison. He felt that both he and Oswald had committed the acts because they had been "demoralized by poverty and inability to get a good job" so that "the future looked bleak and hopeless." He partially attributed his own inability to hold a job to a hemmorrhoid operation which he felt a V.A. surgeon had "fouled up."

PATIENT 11

This late-adolescent boy was the first patient admitted with a charge of threatening President Johnson. He was admitted after the main portion of the initial study had been completed. He had been arrested after calling to inform a newspaper that he was surrendering to the FBI because of his involvement in the assassination of President Kennedy. When interviewed by FBI and Secret Service agents, he claimed to have paid Oswald to assassinate the President and allegedly stated that if President Johnson continued President Kennedy's political programs (particularly civil rights) he would consider the assassination of President Johnson to be necessary for the good of the country and would pay another person to do it.

The patient's involvement with this situation had begun in August, 1963, at which time he had attempted to found an anti-civil-rights, Nazi-type, but "nonviolent" "party." During that time he wrote, but did not mail, a letter to President Kennedy with threatening implications. After failing to secure a satisfactory identity through this group, he gave it up to join the military service. He said he had decided that joining the service would raise his self-esteem and his image in the eyes of his family. His highest hope was to atone for his guilt over his Nazi-type ideas and his intended letter to President Kennedy by rising in the service to the point where he would some day, in uniform, shake the hand of President Kennedy. This hope for atonement quickly received its first blow with the assassination of the President. The patient became very upset, tried to arrange to go to the funeral, but finally was calmed by the idea that he could still atone by rising in the service to the point of meeting President Johnson.

His hope for atonement received its second blow when the assassination precipitated further investigation of his background by the FBI and Secret Service. This resulted in a psychiatric evaluation followed by an honorable discharge from the service as a security risk, termed "at the convenience of the Government." A schizophrenic break followed, during which he committed the offense the day after his discharge. He later said he had merely wished to get even with the FBI and Secret Service for his discharge by "making them feel bad" as a result of his statements.

Past History

The patient was extralegally adopted and had a sequence of two inadequate foster fathers, the second of whom had been hospitalized several times in a state hospital. The patient recognized that the foster mother was immature and undependable. A recommendation by a grammar-school psychologist that the patient be placed in a special class was violently opposed by the mother. He left high school to support his foster parents.

After the death of the foster father, the patient had frequently "playfully" hit the foster mother. She was warned by at least two people that they feared the patient would eventually kill her. Following her incarceration after repeated arrests for driving while her license was suspended, the patient left her to attempt to form the above party. He had been continually losing the money he had been putting up for her bail bond, which she repeatedly forfeited.

FORMULATION OF PRESIDENTIAL ASSASSINATION SYNDROME

Similarities to Oswald. The first thing I noticed in reviewing these histories was the number of striking similarities between them and the fragmentary outline of the life history of Lee Harvey Oswald that was available from the news media at the time.[7] Except as I indicate below, the information utilized was essentially verified in the more authoritative report of the Warren Commission.[8] Moreover, as I will discuss later, some information not known to me at the time was, in a sense, predicted by the study.

Prior to publication of the Warren Commission report, Oswald had been reported to have already received diagnoses of schizoid personality and "schizophrenic tendencies" at age thirteen, and it

7. Unfortunately, because of the space limitations of scientific journals, which make great condensation necessary, and since evaluating degree of dangerousness was not the primary issue, I left out of the final published version what little information there was on the extent to which the degree of dangerousness of these individuals had been estimated. See, for example, *US News & World Report,* 55 (December 16, 1963), pp. 60–61; *New York Times,* 112 (December 4, 1963), p. 18; *Newsweek,* 62 (December 9, 1963), p. 36; *Time,* 82 (December 6, 1963), pp. 33–34; *Time,* 82 (December 13, 1963), pp. 26–27; *Time,* 83 (February 14, 1964), pp. 16–21; *Life,* 55 (November 29, 1963), pp. 37–39; *Newsweek,* 62 (December 2, 1963), p. 27; *Time,* 82 (November 29, 1963), pp. 27–28; *US News & World Report,* 55 (December 9, 1963), pp. 68–71; and Donald Jackson, "The Evolution of an Assassin," *Life,* 56 (February 21, 1964), pp. 68–80.

8. *Report of the President's Commission on the Assassination of President Kennedy,* and *Investigation of the Assassination of President John F. Kennedy: Hearings Before the President's Commission on the Assassination of President Kennedy.*

was reported that institutionalization was recommended. Actually, according to the Warren Commission report, when examined at Youth House in New York in 1953, Oswald had received a diagnosis of "personality pattern disturbance with schizoid features and passive-aggressive tendencies." Institutionalization was not recommended by the psychiatrist but by the probation officer. All the patients in this study were schizophrenic. We do not know whether Oswald's problems reached this degree of intensity. It would not be warranted to generalize from these data that all individuals who threaten to or actually do assassinate the President are schizophrenic, because these patients were transferred to the M.C.F.P. for psychiatric reasons, and therefore do not represent an unselected sample. Nevertheless, pathology of a schizophrenic nature does seem to be important in the constellation of factors present in these patients.

It was reported that Oswald's mother was unable to meet his emotional needs. A probation officer for Oswald when he was a chronic truant has said in retrospect that the mother seemed "so wrapped up in her own problems she never really saw her son's. . . . What the boy needed most was someone who cared." This was a not uncommon finding with these patients. For instance, the examiner at a child-guidance center had commented early with respect to Patient 4 that he was desperately in search of a strong parental figure who could accept him and give him support for his dependency needs. Patient 5 was noted to have been unable to obtain affection from his mother, who was absorbed in her own problems, seeking male companionship and drinking heavily after her husband's death. Further, Oswald's mother did not seem to be able to recognize, or found it necessary to deny, the pathology. She had apparently refused to co-operate when psychiatric treatment was recommended for her son, being convinced that there was nothing wrong with him. Some of the comments attributed to her sounded like participation in a *folie à deux,* notably: "My boy couldn't have killed the President. I know him. Nobody else knows him. He's been persecuted so long"; and "I've been persecuted, and he's been persecuted." Similarly, the mother of Patient 4 had shrugged off serious misconduct in school as "normal misbehavior." So, too, did the parents of Patient 2 tend to project responsibility and seem to participate in the paranoid pathology, as, for example, their oft-repeated remark that the doctor who passed him for the service should have been examined himself. Some comments were probably incorrectly attributed to Mrs. Oswald by the news media, for example, a comment concerning her wire to President Johnson, ". . . Mr. Johnson should also remember that I am not just anyone and that he is only President of the United States by the grace of my son's action." The Warren Commission staff members to whom I spoke seemed to believe her denial of having made this comment.

Oswald's father died several months before his birth. Fathers do not seem to be very prominent in these patients' histories, except by their death, ineffectiveness, or the virtual absence of significant memories concerning them. Behaviorally, however, resentment toward male authorities does stand out. Oswald was reported to have had a "hatred for authority—fixed on a father symbol; was resentful of persons who had fathers." These patients, too, were repeatedly in difficulty with male authority figures. This could be noted most currently in the case of Patient 3 with respect to the extreme anger and rebelliousness toward the male custodial officers.

Oswald quit school at age seventeen to join the military service. He had an unenviable service record, with a poor relationship to authorities and two courts-martial. Eight of the eleven patients in this study (1, 2, 3, 5, 6, 9, 10, and 11) also had military service records. Though not mentioned in detail in the case histories, disciplinary problems of a similar nature and difficulties with authorities were present during the military careers of these patients even before their final discharges. Oswald obtained a hardship release in connection with an injury his mother had suffered, but this was later changed to an undesirable discharge after he moved to Russia and attempted to become a citizen. Oswald was resentful over his discharge and wrote to John Connally, who he thought was still the Secretary of the Navy. His letter, "I shall employ all means to right this gross mistake or injustice to a bona-fied (sic) U.S. citizen and an ex-service man . . . ," if written a little more strongly and sent to the President, might almost have put him in prison with these eleven patients. As in Oswald's case, these patients' military discharges occurred under less than optimal conditions and also seemed to have some relationship to their parents. Patient 1 made his suicide gesture after returning from a visit home. Patient 2 had attempted to obtain a hardship discharge to support his parents after his father had suffered a heart attack. Patient 5 was discharged after being AWOL to visit his mother. All three, and also Patient 6, were bitter about their discharges, had made previous attempts to have them changed, and their threatening letters seemed directly related to this dissatisfaction.

Oswald was a wanderer and seemed to be searching everywhere to find a place for himself, a fact again common with these patients. Oswald had attempted to find a utopia in Russia and had identified himself as a Marxist. A similar interest in Russia, Communism, or socialism turns up in patients 2, 3, and 7.

Oswald's act resulted in his own death. I felt that he must have been aware of the fact that all three previous presidential assassins died as a result of their acts. It seems important that in addition to schizophrenic symptoms a history of depressive and suicidal symptoms was virtually universal in this group of patients studied. The letters combined an implicit plea for help with an invitation for punishment. While it seemed that a prominent conscious or unconscious fantasy was that the President would recognize this plea and respond by providing help, a concomitant expectation of retaliation was present, even to the point of hopefully expecting to be killed for the offense. Patient 2 demonstrates an equation of the assassination weapon with a suicide weapon. Patient 6 illustrates clearly the wish to provoke his own death by attacking an authority figure, such as a policeman. Patient 7 manifested an ambivalent expectation of either being sent back to his homeland or being killed as a result of the letter. It is, of course, possible for another person to respond at an unconscious level to the implicit meaning communicated by the act of a psychotic individual. It would seem that Jack Ruby responded to Oswald's invitation for self-destruction. A short-range response to the plea for help might have been the directing of attention toward those who are unable to meet the requirements of military service, including draft rejectees, which received some attention shortly after the assassination. The group of patients who have entered the service and failed is only a step removed from the group of those who are rejected outright.

Some of the same factors that made the patients in this study unable to succeed in the service may be present in many draft rejectees.

Formulation of a "Typical Case." Based upon the similarities among these patients and the similarities between their histories and the information about Lee Harvey Oswald, it was possible to postulate a reasonably coherent syndrome, with the threateners at the less severe end of the same continuum on which Lee Oswald represented the most severe example. The exact place of each threatener on the continuum cannot be determined with precision. It is obvious that estimates of degree of dangerousness, the likelihood of putting the threat into action, were very imprecise and differed from time to time and from examiner to examiner. Most important, it is likely that degree of dangerousness varied with changes in the patient's psychiatric condition and the circumstances in which he might find himself. Not every feature in the history of each patient, of course, was identical to the history of Oswald. However, the presence of so many features in common would indicate that they play a significant role in the development of this syndrome, which I call the presidential-assassination syndrome. On the basis of this material, a set of factors involved in the genesis and development of an "ideal" or prototype case can be established. Contrary to the readily apparent explanation of these individuals' acts as derived primarily from hostility and rebellion against male authority figures, with the threatened or actual assassination representing patricide in an Oedipal context, the study indicated that the original and deepest difficulty involved rage at the maternal object, which was only later displaced onto male authorities. Dependency needs and concern with rejection were paramount, and there was little to indicate that these patients had reached a developmental level at which true Oedipal conflicts would operate. These patients, further, had not been generally subjected to oppressive masculine authority in formative years, and the apparent resentment toward male authority was best explained as a displacement deriving from the maternal relationship. Identity confusion, particularly with regard to sexual role, played a significant part, with various earlier unsuccessful attempts to handle this problem.

Perhaps of quite crucial import in directing the focus onto the President was an "institutionalization" of the problem, frequently, although not invariably, accomplished through joining the military service in adolescence. The men unrealistically expected in this way to meet developmental needs which should have been met earlier in the family setting—an expectation bound for disappointment and one that led to the replacement of the parents by military service and the United States Government as the rejecting and frustrating object.

The immediate meaning of the action was seen to combine a plea for help with an invitation for self-destruction.

FURTHER STUDY

After completing my original research, I continued to examine each patient subsequently admitted to the Medical Center in connection with the offense of threatening the President and also a number of patients who had made threats against the President but were not presently committed in this connection. These include, for example, two patients who, while incarcerated, wrote threatening letters that were never sent. One letter contained a threat to kidnap the President's daughter since the patient felt the loss of a loved one would be worse than death. Also examined were several "borderline" cases who had not explicitly threatened the President but who, by virtue of behavioral manifestations and total clinical picture, can be taken to represent "borderline" examples. Included in this group were a very dependent young man who wrote a letter requesting the President to arrange for him to enter military service after expiration of his sentence despite his prior criminal record and homosexuality, and an extremely belligerent patient who expressed in a violent context his intention to get rid of the President, though maintaining enough sense of reality to state when questioned that he intended only to obtain politically embarrassing information. I also examined a number of patients who had threatened other individuals, particularly officials. These last patients were chosen because of similarities to the President-threateners. A typical example was a patient who wrote a threatening letter to a military officer who he somewhat paranoidly felt was responsible for his separation from active duty.

The formulations appeared to have some value in predicting the likely background and dynamics of later patients. The rough predictive value was borne out with regard to the newly admitted patients. The study of these patients also provided some further information of relevance to understanding Oswald, particularly with respect to shedding additional light on the question of how the matricidal impulse comes to take the superficially Oedipal configuration of killing an apparent father figure. This appears to be conditioned by certain factors that can be termed "pseudo-Oedipal" because they are essentially more primitive than their Oedipal appearance. For one thing, there appears in some cases an intense need for achievement and success beyond the patient's actual capacity, which has the Oedipal connotation of a sexually immature child wishing to be immediately sexually capable like the father and unable to accept his present limitations. However, this intense need to accomplish success in one drastic jump probably relates more basically to the infantile ego's magical attempts to manipulate the environment directly without regard to reality limitations. The patient would seem to have difficulty in accepting the need to reach goals in reality through a number of intermediary steps, expecting instead to have his goals materialize immediately by merely thinking about them, as if there were no distinction between the external world and his own internal mental life. The possible presence of a reading and spelling difficulty in Oswald's case, which has been considered by Weinstein and Lyerly[9] to fall into the class of congenital or developmental dyslexias, might have contributed to this by having actually made it more difficult to put his thoughts into externally communicable and effective form so that the early infantile omnipotent fantasy of direct mental control of the environment was never tempered by the experience that he could reach goals in reality by a succession of small intermediary steps.

There also appears to be, in addition to maternal deprivation, a good deal of intrusive seductiveness, even if in a castrating way, on the part of many of the mothers. The resulting ambivalent attachment has sexual and Oedipal connotations. It again basically represents a continuing symbiotic attachment to the mother as is

9. Weinstein and Lyerly, *op. cit.*

found in the earlier period of infancy and childhood and in disorders stemming from this period, such as schizophrenia. There would also appear to be some attempt on the part of the patient to conceive of the maternal deprivation in an Oedipal framework, in which the father is blamed for depriving the patient of the mother. This would spare the patient from experiencing the full force of his rage at the mother. Later, in an analogous way, the patient may attribute the parental dereliction to an "exploitative," "capitalist" government, which is considered to have made it impossible for the parents to meet the patient's needs, thus diluting the intensity of the experienced rage at the parents. Although I have not particularly attempted to include comparisons with former attempted or actual assassins in this presentation, the case of Zangara who attempted to assassinate then President-elect Roosevelt certainly comes to mind here. His mother died when he was two. After two months of school at age six, his father took him out of school to work. He resented capitalists who he felt made his working necessary and resolved to give vent to his resentment by killing a president or king.

The formulations have proved of some predictive value when applied to Oswald also, predictive at least in the sense that facts I was not aware of concerning Oswald could be anticipated on the basis of the patients I examined.

In formulating the typical case, I commented on the possible importance of an older brother's more successful military career. I was not at the time aware of the military careers of each of Lee's older brothers. The importance attached to them by Lee (his admiration for his brother Robert was said to have influenced him to join the Marines) underscored the point.[10]

I was also impressed with the question of suicidal tendencies. Based upon the prevalence of earlier suicide gestures or attempts by the patients studied, upon the fact that Oswald must have known that all previous presidential assassins died as a result of their offenses and that Oswald did indeed die as a result of his action, the importance of the suicidal equivalent of the act was

10. Robert Oswald later quoted some of my comments in his book with approval, specifically those relating to the military service. Robert L. Oswald, with Myrick Land and Barbara Land, *Lee, a Portrait of Lee Harvey Oswald by His Brother* (New York: Coward-McCann, 1967).

stressed in formulating the typical case. It was not until later, with the appearance of his diary, that I learned of his actual previous suicide gesture or attempt.[11] (It may be significant that he expected to be found dead by his *female* Intourist guide and was in fact rescued by her.)

A third significant factor, which in this same sense was predicted, was the series of events of the preceding week, and particularly of the preceding night, with respect to his relationship with his wife. In contrast to the conclusions of the Warren Commission, I believe that these events were extremely important in the complex of precipitating factors. Study of the threateners points to the importance of rejection by a female as a precipitating event, which mobilizes the underlying rage at women. Almost exactly one year earlier Oswald had been rejected by his wife when she was temporarily "liberated" from him by friends. He was currently, in a sense, being rejected by his wife, who had recently had another child and was living away from him, and he apparently felt rejected when she did not wish him to come to visit on the weekend prior to the assassination. Even if he did have some thought of assassinating the President before he returned home on Thursday night, the experienced rejections were already occurring. Further, it is not inconsistent with a view that human behavior is overdetermined to consider the conflict with his wife Thursday night as one precipitating factor. Notably, he left his wedding ring at home, so that thoughts of separation from his wife were on his mind. The fact that a separation from or rejection by a significant female occurred just prior to the act is consistent with the rough predictive value. In their excellent study of the symbolic aspects of presidential assassination Weinstein and Lyerly, while not agreeing with all of my conclusions, do provide additional confirmation for many, including the suicidal aspect and the significance of rejection by Oswald's wife as a precipitating factor. Also, in this paper and in earlier communications, Weinstein has introduced two valuable terms from the vocabulary of writers in other fields: "pseudocommunity" to refer to the groups of which these actually isolated individuals fantasied themselves to be members; and "institutional-

---

11. *Report of the President's Commission on the Assassination of President Kennedy,* and *Investigation of the Assassination of President John F. Kennedy: Hearings Before the President's Commission on the Assassination of President Kennedy,* and *Life,* 57 (July 10, 1964).

ization" of the problem for the process by which the problem becomes displaced or translated from a personal into a political idiom.[12]

The results of the study of President-threateners have direct applicability to an understanding of Oswald in two ways: (1) by helping to pinpoint which factors in the voluminous material about Oswald are of psychiatric significance, using the material about these patients as a guide; (2) by lending support to psychiatric conclusions about Oswald, since observations drawn separately from this analogous group of patients are similar to those concerning Oswald, thus removing attempts to explain Oswald's act from the realm of speculation. They also lend credibility to the conclusion that it was indeed a single disturbed individual, Oswald, who carried out the assassination.

APPLICATION TO WARREN COMMISSION INFORMATION ABOUT OSWALD

My experience in reviewing and discussing psychiatric aspects of the Oswald case with Warren Commission members, staff, and other psychiatrists gave me the opportunity to assess the voluminous amount of material available on the psychiatric aspects of the assassination. The best way to organize the material would be to comment upon items which appeared relevant to me in these particular documents and to present some of the inferences that I drew from the material. For the purposes at hand, it is helpful to take the same approach that I would in examining a patient. However, I do not intend to render any actual diagnoses in the usual medical psychiatric sense. The comments contained herein are tentative formulations put forth only for the purpose of understanding the assassination. The personality descriptions must be recognized as hypothetical reconstructions derived from the written material and are not presumed to be of the same order of validity as reports of direct clinical evaluation.

Review of Testimony of Marguerite Oswald. In view of the psychiatric formulations, the testimony of Lee Oswald's mother,

12. Personal communication from Edwin A. Weinstein, and Weinstein and Lyerly, *op. cit.*

Marguerite Oswald, provides an important perspective. The verbal record gives evidence of her attempting to manipulate the Warren Commission, one example being the request to have the power to subpoena witnesses delegated to her. This is noted by the chairman early in her testimony when he states that she ought not to "try to tie our hands in a way that would be contrary to the manner in which commissions normally proceed." Lee was probably much less adept than the commission at avoiding entrapment.

Evidences of grandiosity and projection occur in the transcript. An underlying thread, however, ties together most of the apparent irrationality. This is her own severe feeling of rejection and inadequacy, which is not surprising. Lee's problems in this area probably stemmed not only from inadequate parental support and attention in his childhood, but also from a constant exposure to his mother's concerns with the same problems. At one point, she expresses disappointment that although other people were being questioned and taped she was not: "They were not interested in any papers that I had. They were not interested." She claims to have insisted so much that they finally talked to her. At another point she states, "And I have many stories, gentlemen. I have many stories that I am sure you do not have," apparently wanting to create the illusion that she has something that other people would be interested in, a gambit to avoid rejection. So, too, does she appear to promise continually significant information, yet evades being pinned down and withholds what she alludes to in an effort to maintain tension and keep the interest of the commission.

Her reasoning about a "conspiracy," Lee's being an "agent," etc., appears at first glance to be simply illogical, but there is a pattern. The things that to her imply a conspiracy all have a connotation of rejection: the Secret Service men were not treating her as being important enough; her daughter-in-law, Marina, does not wish to live with her; Lee had wanted to leave her to join the Marines; Lee defected to Russia instead of staying with her; Lee got married, etc. The point can be illustrated. When asked what she bases a charge of a conspiracy to assassinate President Kennedy in which she vaguely involves Marina and the Secret Service, she responds, "I base that on what I told you, the attitude of this man and . . . [a Secret Service agent's] attitude also." Because Marina was offered another place to live, Marguerite feels that there is some sort of a conspiracy about that involving the Secret Service agents, Robert, and Marina. She states, "Robert was part of this conspiracy that they were going to let her go to a home and they didn't tell me. . . ." She later says, "So, gentlemen, Marina is taken care of; Robert is taken care of—I am not feeling sorry for myself, believe me, because I can take care of myself. But here is a mother who has come to the rescue, lost her job, offered her good love and insurance money, and nobody has wondered what is going to become of me." When further pushed to explain why she feels Marina conspired to assassinate the President, she responds, "Because Marina now is not happy. Marina was very happy . . . the month she was with me. . . . And Marina now has become discontented with me . . . when she has somebody else, you are pushed aside." There is also a pathetic quality to her comment about how, when apparently not invited to be with the family at Christmas, she ". . . stayed home crying, hoping against hope that the Secret Service would come and let me be with my family for Christmas time, waiting there patiently." Her explanation of why—". . . there again, I am excluded,"—is to blame it on the Secret Service.

She probably felt less rejection in believing that it was the Secret Service which was keeping Marina away. It was probably less of a blow to her self-esteem to feel that her son was joining the Marines because of some important duty, such as being an agent of the United States Government, rather than, as John Pic indicated, to get away from her. Such an explanation would also help to rationalize the humiliation and rejection that she must have felt when Lee defected. Evidence of such a feeling occurs in her comments about how the lady for whom she was working asked her to leave on a very cold winter night when she heard about Lee's defection. The fact that Marguerite apparently thought that Lee had come home to her would certainly compound the feeling of rejection when he left. With respect to his marriage, something which she might also take as a rejection, she says, "Here is a very important thing why my son was an agent. . . . Now, why does a man who wants to come back to the United States five weeks later . . . marry a Russian girl? Because I say—and I may be wrong—the U.S. Embassy has ordered him to marry this Russian girl."

Thus we can see in Marguerite a model from which Lee might have learned to externalize his dependency conflicts and feelings of rejection by projection into an institutionalized political area. One cannot really blame Marguerite for causing the difficulty in Lee, but rather one can see a repetition of the previous pattern of her life. She states, "My mother died when I was quite young, and my father raised us with housekeepers. . . . I was a child of one parent, and yet I have had a normal life, a very hard normal life that I had been able to combat all by myself, sir, without much help from anyone. . . . There are many, many children with one parent who are perfectly normal children, and I happen to be one myself."

Perhaps a significant clue to why the disturbance focused more on Lee than on his brothers is found in her comment, "Now Mr. Oswald was a very good man. There was the only happy part of my life." If so, this might have fostered a wish to continue the happy relationship through Lee, with her both tending to cling to him and also unconsciously directing depression and hostility at him.

Appreciation of these factors in Marguerite is relevant, not only in understanding the development of Lee's personality, but in evaluating the credibility of her allegations of conspiracy. That her reasoning is faulty and shaped by unconscious emotional factors does not, of course, prove there was no conspiracy, but if there was one, she would have been only coincidentally right.

Review of Testimony of Robert Oswald. Before turning to the second important woman in Lee Oswald's life, his wife, the testimony of his brother, Robert, is relevant. Robert did not develop into a disturbed person similar to his brother, a fact that led several Eisenhower Commission members to doubt psychiatric explanations for Lee's behavior.[13] Some insight into Robert's development is obtained from Marguerite's comment above and from Robert's explanation that "my mother didn't actually bring me up too much. The orphan home and the military academy, and I believe there my basic philosophy was formulated." Significantly,

13. National Commission on the Causes and Prevention of Violence, Task Force on Political Assassination. Discussion and questions following testimony on psychiatric aspects, Washington, D.C., October 3, 1968.

he indicates that he became "used to being disciplined by men, and not used to having a woman around the house." His conflict with his mother did not become channeled into a rebellion against male authorities. Robert's early environment was not identical to Lee's. Moreover, innate, constitutional differences no doubt existed.

Robert's testimony also gives an additional picture of the mother's attitude toward the children: "She is rather persistent to the extent that . . . we have never really gotten along, she tries to dominate me and my wife, and I might say that applies to John and his family, and . . . that it applied to Lee and his wife. . . ." Robert feels that "it appears as though Lee was able to put up with her more than I or my older brother John could." Perhaps Lee was less able to express himself directly except through his later, more frantic actions, possibly because of an ambivalent desire for attachment. Robert states, "I objected quite strongly to the apparent efforts of our mother to control me completely in all respects." He agrees that John, he, and Lee had difficulties in their relationship with the mother, particularly with reference to their desire at eighteen to lead independent lives, a fact that, he also agrees, may have effected Lee's joining the Marines.

Apparently Marguerite interpreted her children's independence as a rejection of her. However, Lee's own desire for almost symbiotic attachment, or oceanic union, with schizophrenic undertones, may be revealed in his letter of November 26, 1959 to Robert in which he states, "Happiness is taking part in the struggle, where there is no borderline between one's own personal world, and the world in general." This is reminiscent of what has been termed "loss of ego boundaries" in schizophrenia, a breakdown in the sense of identity as a distinct individual separate from others and from the environment. It is given as part of his explanation to Robert of what he expected from life in Russia, indicating that his expectations from Russia or Communism were conditioned by such unconscious factors.

That Marguerite felt rejected by Lee's marriage is supported by Robert's comment that she was not favorable to the idea of his own. He believes she expressed the general view "that I was leaving her alone, that both Lee and John at this time were in the service, and she would be alone, and that she would like for me to live with her. . . ."

Robert also indicates that Marina's method of showing resentment toward Lee's lack of consideration was to remain silent, symbolizing a rejection of his comments and, by implication, him.

Review of Testimony of Marina Oswald. Lee's interaction with his wife, Marina, has already been explored somewhat. One might expect Lee Oswald to choose a wife who was similar to his mother, relating to him in the same depreciating and exploitative manner. Further, a woman who married a man as disturbed as Lee Oswald might well have been guided by unrealistic and unconscious motivations. Marina's attitude toward Lee could be characterized as castrating. Some witnesses reported that she depreciated him, especially in such sexual ways as complaining about his adequacy as a husband or that he "was not a man." Some felt she had married him primarily to leave the Soviet Union.

On the other hand, in reviewing her testimony one gains a good deal of respect for her. Her tendency to ridicule and depreciate Lee does not seem to have been done in an entirely hostile manner, but could have been a genuine desire on her part to correct his faulty perception of reality and to influence his behavior along more rational lines. She had a better perception of reality than he and may have been attempting in the best way she knew to have him act appropriately. Of course, she still may have had an underlying need to depreciate men, which could influence the manner in which she chose to correct Lee's behavior.

While the impression of Marina may not fit the stereotype of a rejecting or "castrating" woman in all particulars, it is apparent that she is an intelligent person and able to handle herself quite well. It is entirely possible that her degree of competence and self-assurance was threatening to an insecure man like Lee Oswald. In her testimony she at first presents the appearance of a naïve girl who knows little about "man's business," yet is later able to respond to questions with fairly clever and sophisticated barbs. When asked whether in Russia Lee had a rifle or a shotgun, she naïvely responds, "I don't know the difference. One and the other shoots. You men. That is your business." She states that she thought he had "gone crazy" when he had her photograph him with his pistol and rifle, but says, "This was not my business—it was man's business." A hysterical-type naïve façade, as this might well represent, could be used manipulatively, leaving the man involved to feel impotently unable to counter it. The naïve-appearing girl would really be the one in command.

Such a mode of relating might not be thoroughly consistent, however, and the underlying competence might surface at times. When asked if he had a small or large sum of money when he returned from Mexico, Marina answers, "What would be a large amount for me would not be a large amount for you." Then after estimating the amount, she explains her previous statement with the comment, "It is sometimes necessary to make a joke. Otherwise, it gets boring." This seems to me to be a rather sophisticated and self-assured way of relating to the chief counsel of such a distinguished commission, especially for a girl who earlier appears so naïve. If she "played" with Lee in the same way, she may have been surprised when he, unlike the chief counsel, crumpled. Lee may have been taken in by the superficial naïveté, only to find that he had gotten more than he bargained for.

Marina's comment, "I always tried to point out to him that he was a man like any others who were around us," seems consistent with the idea that she was basically trying to correct his faulty perception of reality, i.e., his defensively inflated opinion of himself, rather than to simply deflate his ego. But her own unconscious needs may have impelled her inadvertently to choose a depreciating way of doing it. To deter him from some of the ideas that he confided to her, she laughed at them and made fun of him. She comments that she "taunted him about this [his use of the name Hidell] and teased about this and said how shameful it is that a person who has his own perfectly good name should take another name. . . ." Referring to her angry attitude toward Lee the night before the assassination, she indicates that she perceived that when she refused to make up, Lee was very upset. She further states, "I wasn't really very angry. I, of course, wanted to make up with him. But I gave the appearance of being very angry. I was smiling inside, but I had a serious expression on my face." This would seem to indicate a little more than just a realistic desire to correct his inappropriate behavior. It would indicate the possibility of some internal pleasure at agitating him.

Consistent with Robert Oswald's observations, Marina showed her anger at Lee through silence, a form of rejection. For example, on the night before the assassination, she indicated to him that she was angry with him "by not talking to him . . . He was upset over the fact that I would not answer him. He tried to start a conversation with me several times, but I would not answer." Lee would be particularly sensitive to such rejection.

There are experiences in the history of Marina that could have led to unconscious hostility toward men, which might have unwittingly surfaced in her relationship with Lee. She states, "I had a stepfather. I had no father. I never knew him." As a child she lived with her stepfather, with her mother, and sometimes with her maternal grandmother. She indicates that she did not get along well with this stepfather, because "I was not a good child. I was too fresh with him." She states that she later left her stepfather's home in Leningrad because "it is not very pleasant to be a sty in the eye of a stepfather."

Aside from whether or not Marina was in fact rejecting and hostile to Lee, it appears that Lee felt she was rejecting him. His aloof and distant attitude expressed only one side of his ambivalence. At various times he evidenced a desire for close relationships. In speaking about the separation in November, 1962, Marina tells how Lee called to see her: ". . . he came that evening and he cried and said that he wanted me to return home because if I did not return he did not want to continue living." His dependent expectations from the relationship are illustrated by Marina's account of how angry he became over such things as not having butter on the table. His indignant expression, "Why is there no butter?" was probably equivalent to a communication, "You are not taking care of and feeding me properly." Marina also notes his jealousy and his complaints that she preferred others to him. She also notes that Lee called her twice daily when he was in Dallas and she in Irving, another indication of a desire for contact in spite of a concomitant need to remain distant.

Apparently, it was not solely Lee Oswald's idea for Marina to live at Mrs. Paine's. Marina comments, "I did not really want to be with Lee at that time, because I was expecting, and it would have been better to be with a woman who spoke English and Russian." Although Lee wanted to come as usual to visit her on the weekend prior to the assassination, Marina told him "that he shouldn't come every week, that perhaps it is not convenient for

Ruth that the whole family be there, live there." Oswald's response was, "As you wish. If you don't want me to come, I won't." His answer indicates that he perceived this as a rejection. She was already angry about his use of an assumed name and further communicated this by hanging up on him when he called subsequently.

One of Lee's chief ways of getting back at Marina also involved the threat of rejection. She explains a comment about Lee's "sadistic streak" with an example that whenever she did something that did not please him, he would make her sit down at a table and write letters to the Russian Embassy stating that she wanted to go back to Russia. "He liked to tease me and torment me in this way . . . he just liked to torment me and upset me and hurt me. . . ." But his ambivalence was manifest in that although he wanted her to return to Russia, he did not want a divorce. Marina states, "I told him that I would go to Russia if he would give me a divorce, but he did not want to give me a divorce."

There is evidence that Lee had a desire for closeness with Marina on Thursday night, November 21. "He said that he was lonely because he hadn't come the preceding weekend, and he wanted to make his peace with me. . . . He was not angry—he was upset. . . . He tried very hard to please me. . . . And he said that he didn't want me to be angry at him because this upsets him. . . . He said that he was tired of living alone . . . that he didn't want me to remain with Ruth any longer, but wanted me to live with him in Dallas." When Marina refused, "he said that once again I was preferring my friends to him, and that I didn't need him." When asked whether she thinks the fact that Oswald went to bed very upset had anything to do with the assassination the next day, she comments, "Perhaps he was thinking of all of that." Her earlier reference to Oswald's "sadistic streak" reveals her perception that elements in at least one of his actions analogous to the assassination were directed at her. Referring to the circumstances around the "Nixon incident," she states, "Possibly he didn't want to go out [to shoot Mr. Nixon] at all but was just doing this all . . . to simply wound me, to make me feel bad." She later adds, ". . . now I think it was just rather a kind of nasty joke he was playing with me . . . my husband had a sadistic streak in him. . . ."

In reading over the transcript, a certain amount of sympathy is evoked for the various individuals involved. The diary that Robert made after the assassination portrays very graphically the reactions of a reasonably average person whose brother becomes directly involved in such an unbelievable event, and one can sympathize with his predicament. One can also have sympathy for Marina, Marguerite, and even Lee, and still recognize their actions and their unconscious contributions to the total situation. In fact, any serious attempt to comprehend the situation demands an objective recognition of their contributions, not so much to inculpate them as to understand the total field in which the event occurred. This applies both to the original contribution of Lee's mother to his basic personality formation and to the ongoing relationship with his wife. There are indications that Marina may have obtained some unconscious gratification from Lee's erratic behavior. Certainly she did not want Oswald to shoot anyone with his rifle or pistol, but she did seem to obtain unconscious gratification from his interest in them and there does seem to be points at which she might otherwise have taken more definitive action. Although she insisted on moving to New Orleans from Dallas to get Lee away from General Walker, more effective actions come to mind. Since she "thought that he had gone crazy," there was the possibility of obtaining medical or psychiatric help. She did ask Lee to get rid of the rifle, but she might have insured that he did not take the gun to New Orleans. She also might have taken more definitive action when he expressed his fantasies of hijacking an airplane. One of the most likely times at which Marina could have shed the rifle was in connection with her move to Mrs. Paine's. She says she knew that Lee loaded the rifle onto the station wagon in which the household goods were moved and she was aware that the rifle was stored in the garage. Since Lee was away much of the time, she probably could have disposed of the rifle herself. Naturally, it is easier for us to notice in retrospect missed opportunities. Perhaps Marina was frightened, like either one of two female members of the immediate families of two of the M.C.F.P. patients, a sister in one case and a daughter in another case. They requested prison officials to conceal from the patients that they had co-operated in providing information on the family histories for fear that the patients would be angry and physically harm them. Of course their own fears might have been based less on any realistic danger to them than in their own fantasies. They may have gained some unconscious gratification from the fantasy of being attacked by father or brother and might thus have unconsciously played into eliciting the earlier abusive behavior that the patients had directed toward them. The point of the above comments is to illustrate the possibility that Marina was unconsciously ambivalent about these matters. With reference to the "Nixon incident," for example, Marina indicates that she could deter Lee when she was resolved and collected all her forces. He did not retaliate physically, although, of course, in that instance he may not have had serious intentions. Marina's ineffectual actions at the other times might have been taken by Lee as an implicit consent.

That Marina could have derived some unconscious gratification from his having a rifle may have been a small factor that lent encouragement to him to continue this activity. She may have obtained some gratification by talking about the things her "crazy one" did such as buying a rifle. Perhaps the most significant clue in this respect is another comment of Marina's. Although, when asked whether she feels that she was becoming more impatient with all these things her husband was doing, she states, "Yes, of course. I was tired of it." Nevertheless she goes on to say, "Every day I was waiting for some kind of a new surprise. I couldn't wait to find out what else would he think of." At an unconscious level, Lee might have perceived in Marina an element of pleasurable expectation for some new surprise that would encourage him to attempt new episodes. Marital equilibrium based upon complementary relationships of this sort have been well recognized by psychiatrists, as, for example, in the case of alcoholics or wife-beaters.[14] It is possible that the same behavioral event might be simultaneously an act against the mother or wife and also an acting out of a repressed impulse. An analogous fusion of motives may have been present when Lee, as an adolescent, threatened Mrs. Pic during a quarrel in which he hit his mother. Ironically enough, despite Lee's hostility to his mother, he may have revealed his attachment to her by acting out through the assassination his

14. J. E. Snell, R. J. Rosenwald, and A. Robey, "The Wifebeater's Wife," *Archives of General Psychiatry*, 11 (1964), pp. 107–112.

conception of her own wish to become famous (much as his action toward Mrs. Pic may have been an acting out by Lee of his mother's attitude toward her). Despite his attempt to drastically assert his own identity by the assassination, he may have really let it be submerged by his mother again.[15]

Review of Youth-House Reports and Testimony. The reports from the youth house where Lee was examined as an adolescent are valuable. For one thing, they provide a source of professional psychiatric and social-background information and evaluation obtained from direct contact with Lee. In addition, these observations were made at a time when the more superficial defenses of aloofness, distancing, rebelliousness, and the like were not yet crystallized. Therefore, they give some clue to the deeper layers of his personality.

It is significant that the report of the psychiatrist, Dr. Hartogs, concludes that "no finding of neurological impairment or psychotic mental changes could be made" and that Lee received a diagnosis of "personality pattern disturbance with schizoid features and passive-aggressive tendencies." However, even more important are the descriptive comments. Dr. Hartogs comments on Lee's "low degreee of selfevaluation (sic) and selfesteem (sic) . . . mainly due to feelings of general inadequacy and emotional discouragement." He writes, "Lee claims that he can get very angry at his mother and occasionally has hit her, particularly when she returns home without having bought food for supper. . . . He feels that his mother rejects him and really has never cared very much for him." These observations are consistent with the hypothesis that the basic anger is at the mother in relation to unmet dependency needs. In fact, the importance of his disturbed relationship with his mother was well recognized at that time. Dr. Hartogs states, "Lee has to be seen as an emotionally, quite disturbed youngster who suffers under the impact of really existing emotional isolation and deprivation, lack of affection, absence of family life and rejection by a self-involved and conflicted mother." The youth house psy-

15. Robert Oswald notes in his book that he was particularly struck by my comments to this effect in one of the earlier papers. See Robert L. Oswald, with Land and Land, *op. cit.*

chologist, Irving Sokolow, reports, "There is some indication that he may relate to men more easily than to women in view of the more mature conceptualization. . . . He exhibits some difficulty in relationship to the maternal figure suggesting more anxiety in this area than in any other."

Dr. Hartogs continues, ". . . we gained the definite impression that Lee can be reached through contact with an understanding and very patient psychotherapist. . . ." He did show some capacity to reach out and relate, so that he might really have been in more excruciatingly uncomfortable conflict than if he simply had been withdrawn and isolated. This intense discomfort generated by the conflict between his tendency to reach out, his need for and ability to respond to affection, on the one hand, and his concomitant need to protectively withdraw, distance, and isolate himself, on the other, may have contributed to his being more likely to act out, to desperately seek relief.

The report of Evelyn Strickman Siegel, the social worker, contains information consistent with this interpretation. She comments, "What is really surprising is that this boy has not lost entirely his ability to communicate with other people. . . ." She indicates that "Lee was able to respond to expressions of understanding and sympathy for his lonely situation which I offered, although he denied that he really ever felt lonely." While such a capacity to respond could be a good prognostic sign enabling him to benefit from therapy, it may have also provided the energy to push him in the opposite direction, toward a violent solution. This would be similar to the case of some of the M.C.F.P. patients, notably Patient 3, whose belligerent attitude would melt away when we would address ourselves to the underlying needful depressed feelings. Such patients are more able to be worked with, but also more acutely uncomfortable, and possibly more dangerous.

John Carro of the youth house throws further light on Oswald's desire for publicity. He describes how some delinquent children commit a violent act as "a crying out . . . to say that they exist and they are human beings . . . just to get their one day in the sun, the day when all the papers will focus on them, and say, 'I am me. I am alive.' " In other words, Lee's need for publicity might have been a necessary means of expressing his existence and his own identity, rather than just simply exhibitionism. As Carro comments, "Many a boy . . . will do things like this to attract attention to themselves, that they exist, and they want somebody to care for them."

Additional observations are of relevance to his confused sexual identity. He expressed discomfort about being with other boys at the youth house, disrobing in front of them and taking showers with them. He felt he would have to steel himself to this if he joined the service. The mother's desire to have Lee receive a complete medical examination and her indication that she had been worried for fear something was wrong with his genitals are indicative of subtly castrating fantasies and an inappropriate intrusive attitude toward him, particularly in view of the observation that "when she was told that our examination had reveals (sic) nothing unusual, she looked at once relieved and disappointed." She bathed all her children herself until they were eleven or twelve and it is noted that she commented in an embarrassed manner that at that age they got a little too old for her to look at. All of this has a sexual connotation, as does the fact that she slept with Lee until a reasonably advanced age. However, observations recorded in the Youth House reports such as, "She didn't seem to see him as a person at all, but as an extension of herself," illustrate the more primitive symbiotic aspect underlying the superficially sexual seductiveness.

While the reports of the various youth-house staff members, and particularly the report and testimony of Carro, indicate that the mother withdrew Lee from the help offered by the New York social agencies, because of her resistance to becoming involved in meaningful therapy, another aspect of the case arises. There was great difficulty in finding suitable placement facilities for Lee. John Carro states in his testimony, ". . . it may have been a threat to her to want to involve her in the treatment of the boy. . . ." But he also says, ". . . we certainly were coming back to court each month, you know, with the judge saying, 'Well, try Children's Village. Try Harriman Farms, try this place and try that.'" He goes on later, ". . . the next almost nine months I spent in making referral after referral to the various institutions, the various clinics, to see if they would be able to service this boy either at home or within the institutional confines . . . and I mentioned that the tragedy of the whole thing was in this instance . . . the facilities that we had here in New York were taxed, and somehow one factor or the other kept us from getting him the kind of help that he needed." Although Carro comments that Mrs. Oswald probably believed that they were going to take the boy and place him, it may well be that her reaction was based upon factors other than those which appear on the surface. Certainly, whatever the realistic reasons for the difficulty in obtaining placement or treatment, she was bound to perceive this as a rejection of herself and her son. Her typical reaction might well have been something in the nature of "I can handle this myself, and I don't need any help," which would permit her to assume the position of the rejecting person rather than the rejected one. Carro states that as a last resort they contemplated seeing Lee on an outpatient basis in the court psychiatric clinic. Thus it was at a time when they were not planning to remove the boy from the home that the mother left. The idea that the mother may have felt that she and the son were being rejected by the delay in placement or treatment offered and that the court clinic was considered a last resort makes it easier to explain why she would choose to withdraw him at exactly this point. Many psychiatrists have seen this type of reaction in patients, or in their mothers, when they are unable to find appropriate community facilities.

PROJECTED RESEARCH AND BROADER IMPLICATIONS

This section considers the broader implications of this field of study, beginning with observations on the psychology of public figures and ending with implications for the study of such large-scale and maladaptive violence as war, which now threatens the whole species.[16]

Today, mankind is faced with two incongruous concerns. On one hand, advances in the exploration of space permit us to reach, and contaminate, other planets. On the other, we face the possibility of exterminating terrestrial life on our planet, because advances in nuclear science have outrun our understanding of how to handle

16. Marshall F. Gilula and David N. Daniels, "Violence and Man's Struggle to Adapt," *Science*, 164 (April 25, 1969), pp. 396–405.

our own human aggressive impulses. We have not caught up with the far older technology of gunpowder, as Lee Harvey Oswald demonstrated so well, much less the nuclear technology of 1945.

The approaches developed in the study of assassination do not have to be limited to this issue alone.[17] The psychiatric study of individuals offers a potential for extrapolation to broader areas of public concern. In a paper on Woodrow Wilson, Weinstein[18] commented on the issue of understanding "the way 'private' disturbances of behavior may be manifested in the world of public affairs." In Oswald's case, the private determinants of behavior, evidenced so forcefully in the world of public affairs, can probably be adequately conceptualized as disturbances. However, I would focus on the larger question of understanding how private *determinants* of behavior are manifested in the world of public affairs. In other words, such determinants of behavior should be approached in a neutral way, rather than labeling them a priori as pathological or categorizing them as disturbances.

It has been contended by some writers that the victims of aggression, violence, and even accidents have often unconsciously played a part in eliciting that violence.[19] The awareness of this led me to consider whether unconscious factors in the psychology of those who become Presidents or great leaders might make them more prone to assassination and whether such considerations might be more pronounced in some Presidents or leaders than in others.[20]

17. David A. Rothstein, "The Assassin and the Assassinated—As Non-Patient Subjects of Psychiatric Investigation" (Chicago: Presented at Midwest Regional Meeting on Violence and Aggression, co-sponsored by the American Psychiatric Association and the American Medical Association, November 15–16, 1968).

18. Edwin A. Weinstein, "Denial of Presidential Disability: A Case Study of Woodrow Wilson," *Psychiatry,* 30 (November, 1967), pp. 376–391.

19. Norman Tabachnick, et al., "Comparative Psychiatric Study of Accidental and Suicidal Death," *Archives of General Psychiatry,* 14 (January, 1966), pp. 60–68; Robert E. Litman, and Norman Tabachnick, "Fatal One-Car Accidents," *Psychoanalytic Quarterly,* 36 (April, 1967), pp. 248–259; and Edwin S. Shneidman, "Orientations Toward Death: A Vital Aspect of the Study of Lives," *International Journal of Psychiatry,* 2 (March, 1966), pp. 167–188.

20. Gilula and Daniels, *op. cit.;* Alfred E. Weisz and Robert L. Taylor, "The Assassination Matrix," *Stanford Today* (February, 1969), pp. 11–17;

In studying public figures we might begin with the assumption that public figures, similar to other human beings, have reacted to crises in their life situations. We might then search for the occurrences psychiatrists know to affect people and in manners that are to an extent established. The traces of these reactions in their public lives might then be examined in their handling of official functions. Occurrences that fundamentally affect people are, for example, serious or life-threatening personal illnesses, physical disability, marriage, marital strife, divorce, the birth of children, the deaths of children, parents, siblings, or wives, important events in the lives of their children, and so forth.

President Roosevelt had had an extremely serious illness and subsequent physical disability. President Kennedy reportedly almost always had some pain from his back problem.[21] Presidents Eisenhower and Johnson both had past histories of heart attacks, and both had surgical operations while in office. President Wilson had a stroke while in office. Winston Churchill's medical condition was worse than was publicly revealed at the time.[22] The principal negotiator for the North Vietnamese in Paris, upon which negotiations many lives depend, reportedly has had leukemia, and there was recent concern over a possible recurrence.[23] Governor Rockefeller and Governor Stevenson both were divorced. The mayor of Detroit was having serious marital difficulties at the time his city was torn by riots.[24] Premier Kosygin's wife died shortly before his historic and important meeting with President Johnson in New Jersey.[25] Governor Wallace's first wife was operated on for a malignancy and she later died while he was seeking the presidency—and she was fatally ill herself while Governor. President

---

and Alfred E. Weisz and Robert L. Taylor, *American Presidential Assassination* (in press); and the chapter by Thomas C. Greening, "The Psychological Study of Assassins," in this volume.

21. Theodore Sorensen, *Kennedy* (New York: Harper and Row, 1965).

22. Jonas Robitscher, "Doctors' Privileged Communications, Public Life, and History's Rights," *Cleveland-Marshall Law Review*, 17 (May, 1968), pp. 199–212.

23. Paul Ghali, "Hanoi Hints Quitting Talks," *Chicago Daily News*, July 26, 1968; and Paul Ghali, letter to the editor of November 15, 1968.

24. "Cavanaghs Trade Charges," *Chicago Daily News*, July 17, 1968, p. 6.

25. "Aleksei Kosygin: The Compleat Apparatchik," *Time*, 89 (June 30, 1967), p. 13.

Kennedy lost his newborn child shortly before his assassination. Governor Rockefeller's son met accidental death during the Governor's term of office. Senator Percy's daughter was brutally murdered while he was a candidate. Senator Robert Kennedy's brother had been assassinated, as he reminded a group of black people after the assassination of the Reverend Dr. Martin Luther King. Senator Edward Kennedy had two brothers who were assassinated. Others lose close relatives who succumb to natural death.

We would be naïve to conclude that these events left no traces whatsoever in the official functioning of these people. Could Premier Kosygin have had no feelings or thoughts whatsoever about his wife's recent death while he was meeting with President Johnson? Could he have kept those feelings isolated from his participation in the talks? Could there be no effect whatsoever upon the attitude of the North Vietnamese ambassador toward the war he is negotiating, toward killing and death, as a result of possibly having a fatal illness himself?

At the other end of the spectrum, psychiatrists also know that individuals occasionally become depressed paradoxically at times of success, such as, for example, job promotion. These feelings result from an unconscious emotional guilt concerning the triumph over their rivals. We know that those individuals who react with clinical illness are predisposed to this paradoxical reaction by earlier experiences and inner attitudes, by a feeling that their triumph is symbolically equated with destruction of their competitors, or by other such emotions. There is reason to believe that even well-functioning, well-adjusted people, Presidents included, have the potential to feel guilty as a result of success. Such feelings may remain at an unconscious emotional level exhibiting only an indirect relationship to overt behavior. When detected, it is usually much to the individual's surprise.

Early childhood experiences and the exposure to attitudes of parents are also important determinants of later attitudes and personality. The father of Alexander Dubcek, the former leader of Czechoslovakia, reportedly lived in America for some time, and his older brother was born here.[26] It is possible that the father's exposure to democratic ideals as transmitted to the young Alex-

26. "Dubcek's Father Lived in Chicago," *Chicago Daily News,* August 12, 1968, p. 2.

ander helped to foster an appreciation for democracy. The Vietnam War, on the other hand, a project intended to promote such ideals, will probably exert such a disrupting psychological effect on the children of a whole generation as to render them less capable of governing themselves in the future.[27]

In approaching the question of whether there might be indications in the personalities of Presidents and/or other leaders which make them more prone to assassination, a concept akin to the idea of subintentional death in accident cases or in victims of aggression,[28] several factors at least warrant a follow-up. There are recurrent indications of what one might view as unconscious fantasies of omnipotence of counterphobic elements. There seems to be a tendency to take chances involving some danger as if failure were not a consideration and to enter situations the average prudent individual might avoid, possibly to court danger for its own sake. This could be viewed as an unrealistic belief in one's indestructibility, a feeling that could result in taking unwarranted chances. It might even be viewed as a tendency to take a risk for the sake of the risk.

Yet it might also be seen as heroic. It could indicate that the particular leader has come to terms with and accepts his own mortality. In fact, the very same attribute that could be viewed as unrealistic might in another light be seen as an important factor leading to success. The attitude is reminiscent of that frequently necessary for a soldier in combat.[29] He may, in a sense, feel he is

27. Martin Waugh, "A Psychogenetic Factor in the Recurrence of War," *International Journal of Psycho-Analysis*, 49, parts 2–3 (1968), pp. 319–23; Robert E. Anderson, "Where's Dad? Paternal Deprivation and Deliquency," *Archives of General Psychiatry*, 18 (June, 1968), pp. 641–649; Thomas L. Trunnell, "The Absent Father's Children's Emotional Disturbances," *Archives of General Psychiatry*, 19 (August, 1968), pp. 180–188; and Ira L. Mintz, "Unconscious Motives in the Making of War," *Medical Opinion and Review*, 4 (April, 1968), pp. 88–95. Those concerned that the generation raised on Dr. Spock's book are now the dissenters may take heart that it has been introduced to Russia.

28. Edwin S. Shneidman, "Orientations Toward Death: A Vital Aspect of the Study of Lives," *International Journal of Psychiatry*, 2 (March, 1966), pp. 167–188.

29. Otto Fenichel, *The Psychoanalytic Theory of Neurosis* (New York: W. W. Norton and Co., 1945); Silvano Arieti, *American Handbook of Psychiatry,* Vol. I (New York: Basic Books, Inc., 1959); and Roy R. Grinker and John P. Spiegel, *Men Under Stress* (New York: McGraw-Hill, 1963).

omnipotent. He temporarily denies the reality of his potential death and of the danger to himself, in order to function and avoid being killed. If the full impact of the danger were recognized, he would likely be paralyzed with anxiety and the chances of his being killed would increase.

It appears that a successful leader may have to be an individual who acts as if he is, and perhaps in some ways believes himself to be, incapable of failure. For example, Wedge, after reviewing information collected by the CIA relating to Nikita Khrushchev, characterized him in a letter to President Kennedy as a "stable hypomanic character (chronic optimistic opportunist)."[30] This assurance of success may have to be communicated to the public nonverbally by confident action. The Warren Commission commented on a President's frequent lack of concern for personal safety and his disregard for Secret Service advice in order to allow more direct public contact. Presidents have even been known to attempt to elude their protection.[31] The same attitude that conveys confidence to the public may make safety more difficult.

The dual nature of this is illustrated by Winston Churchill's trips across the North Atlantic to enlist American support early in World War II. He made the crossings despite the threat from German submarines, a danger that could not be eliminated despite the precautions taken. The ship used on his summer, 1941 trip was sunk shortly before the December, 1941 trip.[32] A more prudent man might have stayed in safety. Perhaps it took someone with an unrealistic faith in his own indestructibility to take the chance. Yet it was no doubt this very faith in ultimate success that made him a great leader, rallied public support, morale, and enthusiasm, and gave the British people the faith in themselves to fight on. It was interesting to note, in view of this, that when Juan Bosch responded to the possibility of assassination during the election campaign in the Dominican Republic by walling himself off from the public, he unexpectedly lost the election. The impression of

30. Bryant Wedge, "Khrushchev at a Distance—A Study of Public Personality," *Trans-action*, 5 (October, 1968), pp. 24–28.
31. Frank J. Wilson and Beth Day, *Special Agent* (New York: Holt, Rinehart and Winston, 1965).
32. Winston Churchill, *The Grand Alliance* (New York: Bantam Books, 1962).

excessive concern with security during the 1968 Democratic Convention in this country seemed to result in a decrease in its candidates' chances for election. And the assassination of Senator Robert Kennedy does seem to represent a sad confirmation of the ideas expressed.

The study of assassination has led me to a concern about the importance of a President's attitude toward death. But a President's attitude toward death has been pointed out to be a factor in another even more serious area, that of war.[33] The imminent threat of nuclear destruction makes it imperative that we understand as much as possible about all factors that might influence its realization.

It is fascinating how many of the considerations which have become apparent in studying assassinations turn out to converge upon the major issues of our times: domestic violence with its underlying social causes, and the international violence that diverts needed resources from domestic concerns and which threatens us all with the possibility of elimination. Perhaps it was no coincidence that Patient 7 complained that the President had too large an army and needed a heart to understand the problems of the people, or that Patient 8 threatened the President not to start a war.

It seemed irrational when so many of these deprived patients were individually demanding to have their needs met by the government, by the President, and were underlining the demands with threats of violence to make sure the message got across—and it was probably irrational because the times when *their* needs could have been realistically met were long since past. But this is not necessarily so with respect to alleviating the conditions that gave rise to their problems and to similar ones in others. Today, not just individuals but groups are demanding the meeting of these same human needs and the alleviation of the conditions that gave rise to them. And they are threatening or actually engaging in violence to underline their message. At least some people are listening. If Jack Ruby could respond to Oswald's unconscious suicidal request, others may be responding unknowingly to his plea for help. It is

33. Ira L. Mintz, "Unconscious Motives in the Making of War," *Medical Opinion and Review,* 4 (April 1, 1968), pp. 88–95.

especially unfortunate that those who make the demands have felt it necessary to follow Oswald's example of punctuating the messages with exclamation points of violence, but it is equally unfortunate that the messages without the exclamation points, like Oswald's earlier distress signals, were so long ignored.

A cogent argument can also be made that, as in the case of individuals, the threat of violence in international relations and even its use in warfare serves in large measure a communicative function to underline concretely the symbolic communication going on at another, more abstract level.[34] It seems to me that while the domestic violence of assassinations and riots obviously differs in many ways from the international violence of warfare, all manifestations of violence are interrelated, and the study of one cannot entirely exclude the study of the others. One cannot realistically separate the forms of violence to the extent attempted by President Johnson in condemning violence after various domestic outbursts,[35] while simultaneously accepting its use to achieve international aims in Vietnam. One cannot successfully communicate verbally that there is no excuse for the resort to violence, while communicating nonverbally by action a belief that there are justifications for its use. The contradiction between the verbal message and the simultaneous nonverbal message is known in psychiatry as a double bind. It is bound to cause unrecognized confusion.

---

34. Dr. John Spiegel has distinguished, by virtue of its explosive "outburst" quality, collective violence and organized collective aggression—as in war, revolution, or conspiracy. Reportedly, a psychiatric advisory group for the Eisenhower Commission also recommended a narrow definition of violence, stressing its explosive nature, although a later paper indicates that Spiegel, in a report to the commission, has expanded its definition to include war. At any rate, Webster's dictionary includes war under its definition of violence.

See, in order: John P. Spiegel, "Psychosocial Factors in Riots—Old and New," *American Journal of Psychiatry,* 125 (September, 1968), p. 5; "Psychiatrists Prepare Data for Violence Commission," *Psychiatric News,* 3 (September, 1968), p. 5; Frederic W. Ilfeld, "Overview of the Causes and Prevention of Violence," *Archives of General Psychiatry,* 20 (June, 1969), pp. 675–689; and *Webster's Third New International Dictionary of the English Language,* Unabridged (Springfield, Mass.: G. & C. Merriam Co., 1966).

35. *Report of the National Advisory Commission on Civil Disorders; Chicago Daily News,* April 5, 1968, pp. 1, 8; and *Newsweek,* 71 (June, 1968), p. 32.

Indeed, in following up the study of assassination, the pieces fall together like a giant jigsaw puzzle. The study of the assassin leads to study of the leader and his attitude toward death. Converging upon the same point is Mintz's contention that a President's attitude toward death may be a factor in the area of war.[36] The communicative function of violence may be common to all its manifestations. Eight of the eleven patients whom I have described had been in the military service, and this experience seemed to be important in the genesis of the syndrome. Of the remaining three, two wrote the letters just referred to containing references to war or the army. One of these two had gone to a violent extreme to avoid military service. The third told me he would like to join the service after discharge. Ideation about military service and war thus seems present in one way or another in all of these eleven patients.

The comments of Dr. Freedman in this volume, that the assassin functions like a soldier, put this in a new light. A recent paper examining psychiatric hospitalizations among Vietnam returnees is illuminating.[37] The authors' descriptions of the patients' reactions to killing are most valuable. They comment that, "The first 'blooding' may stress the soldier, but apparently he soon becomes inured to what he is doing." One patient "finds himself worrying about the parents of the people he killed." Another suffered "hurt" feelings with his first killing. "Later he shot at . . . Viet Cong 'taking a crap in the field' and experienced 'fun' as they ran." Another "was proud that he had killed many of them." He remembered "seeing their bodies with flies about them and 'laughed at 'em.' " He now wanted to help people, but "stated that he would go back to Vietnam 'to kill 'em all.' " One "killed lots of 'em," he continued. "I just do my job . . . killing was part of the job." He had been " 'scared' with his first killing." Another had not wanted to shoot at the enemy originally, but seeing the deaths of comrades changed his attitude to active hatred. "He became aware of a desire to torture them." For yet another "a particularly disturbing memory was his deliberate shooting of a six-year-old girl when his unit was sweeping a village. . . . He has recurring nightmares about the

36. Mintz, *op. cit.*
37. William Goldsmith, and Constantine Cretekos, "Unhappy Odysseys, Psychiatric Hospitalization Among Vietnam Returnees," *Archives of General Psychiatry,* 20 (January, 1969), pp. 78–83.

shooting of the little girl." The authors conclude with a comment that hospitalized psychiatric patients may bring to psychiatrists' attention patterns of reaction to war that are actually common to all who have gone.

I think it might well be argued that these patterns are common, not only to those who have gone to war physically, but even to those whose participation is less direct, those who live in a psychological climate designed to prepare them to go to war. Can we realistically expect to continue to prepare our young men to be good soldiers, glorify their bravery, and then demand that they function like soldiers only in the way we want them to? It gives one pause. Perhaps we too are making an unrealistic demand.

The Psychological Study of Assassins

Thomas C. Greening

INTRODUCTION

This chapter will discuss some of the reasons why psychological studies of assassins should be done, some obstacles that tend to discourage such studies, an eleven-point outline for analyzing assassins and their acts, and some psychodynamic hypotheses about assassins, with particular reference to Sirhan Bashir Sirhan.

The nation has reacted with shock, grief, anger, guilt, and blame to the assassinations of John Kennedy, Martin Luther King, and Robert Kennedy. As we become caught up in these natural human reactions to such tragedies it is easy to lose sight of the opportunity and profound responsibility to salvage wisdom from such waste of life. Tragedies are a time to learn as well as mourn. To learn, we must resist the temptation to oversimplify the personalities and motivations of the assassins. Anger, defensive self-righteousness, and our craving to explain the unknown may tempt us to label hastily an assassin as "insane," a "political radical," or a "hired gunman." Some or all of these labels may be applicable, but they are still merely labels; we use them to avoid confronting the challenge and the horror we must face if we recognize that each assassin is a fellow human being who can be understood in human psychological ways. If we pigeonhole him in some category safely separate from ourselves, we deny that he is our brother and lose a precious opportunity to learn. We owe it to the victims, to ourselves, and to the potential future assassins who now walk the streets to use all the means at our disposal to understand what produces an assassin. We have already paid an exorbitant price for this lesson; now it is up to us to study it.

At the time of Robert Kennedy's assassination, President Lyndon Johnson, Governor Ronald Reagan of California, and Mayor Sam Yorty of Los Angeles stressed that ours is not a sick society and that America as a whole is not responsible for the deaths of John Kennedy, Martin Luther King, and Robert Kennedy. President Johnson stated that one assassin and not 200 million Americans shot Robert Kennedy. Governor Reagan emphasized that Sirhan was a Jordanian and that this was not an American crime. Mayor Yorty said: "What's happened in Los Angeles is that some of the bitterness of the conflict in the Middle East has been transferred to our city by an alien who came here embittered . . . whose bitterness did not subside, even though living here in this free country where we don't have the type of bitterness that is historic in the area from which he came. . . ."[1] One is reminded of the smug words of William H. Seward, Secretary of State, over a hundred years ago: "Assassination is not an American practice or habit, and one so vicious and so desperate cannot be engrafted into our political system."

Reagan and many others found the assassination an appropriate stimulus to call for stricter police enforcement and obedience to law and order. Emphasis on punishment and control that neglects psychological understanding as a basis of prevention is a dangerous example of the overtly civilized but covertly inhuman forces in our world which help produce such tragedies. We must be wary of our self-destructive tendency to aid and abet criminal psycho-

1. *Los Angeles Times,* June 7, 1968.

pathology by contenting ourselves with labeling and punishing the results while blinding ourselves to the sources. Hellman and Blackman studied eighty-four prisoners and found patterns of childhood behavior that would have served as a basis for predicting an adult life of crime. They conclude that "the prevention of serious criminal acts in adults will ultimately be accomplished not merely through punishment or withdrawal of freedom of the perpetrators of violence. It will be accomplished by the community's response to the cries of the desperate. . . ."[2] Back in 1941, when Frederic Wertham wrote the following statement, he was not referring specifically to assassins, but his comments are highly relevant in this context:

> For to say that a man is insane, and therefore he has committed certain acts, is to explain nothing at all. Such an evasion of real causes for human behavior may well be the results of a dim feeling that they are too near our own thresholds. Often a criminal is a man who does what other people merely think. We all like to believe that crime is entirely the result of a quirk in the other fellow's mind. This attitude removes us from any danger of feeling responsible for what is, after all, a social ill."[3]

We can all reassure ourselves with the fact that assassins and murderers such as Sirhan, Lee Harvey Oswald, James Earl Ray, Leopold and Loeb, Benny Smith, Dick Hickock, Perry Smith, Richard Speck, and Charles Whitman were strangers, loners, odd and unique individuals sick in their own way and quite independent of our society. If it is reassurance and righteousness we want, that is the approach to take. But if we want understanding and prevention, we must evaluate what the forces are in American society, in human families throughout the world, and in the basic human condition that produce and will continue to produce such men.

Insight into the feelings and behavior of others in part requires an ability to identify with them and to discover in oneself similar tendencies. A person who has never faced in himself his own

2. D. S. Hellman and N. Blackman, "Enuresis, Firesetting and Cruelty to Animals: A Triad Productive of Adult Crime," *The American Journal of Psychiatry,* 122, No. 12 (June, 1966), pp. 1431–1435

3. Frederic Wertham, *Dark Legend* (New York: Doubleday, 1941), pp. 20–21.

feelings of envy, helplessness, despair, and rage toward more powerful men will be at a disadvantage trying to comprehend the dynamics of an assassin. If we can be more in touch with the latent murderous aspects of ourselves and assist others to do the same, it may be that we can find new ways to reach out and rehabilitate the potential assassins of the world before they hurt us again. In his chapter in this volume, Dr. Lawrence Freedman makes a similar point: "We can recognize ourselves in the maddest of men, the vilest of criminals, the most radical of revolutionaries, the greatest of creative geniuses, only if we recognize the factors of character present in ourselves are selectively developed, albeit quantitatively atrophied or hypertrophied amongst those who seem to be so recognizably different."[4]

Discovering and learning from the assassin who dwells in each of us is a personal, individual task, but we can help each other with it. More open and empathic sharing of our thoughts and feelings in this taboo area can help us develop a sophisticated awareness of the deeper issues involved. Rather than turn away in repulsion from individuals who violate our most basic laws, we can risk letting ourselves be moved by them as people, without any implication of condoning their acts.

Fortunately, a number of sensitive and penetrating studies have been made of murderers, suggesting ways to approach the study of assassins. A boy named Benny Smith killed five women in an Arizona beauty parlor. Rod Wood, the Phoenix attorney who defended him, said: "Putting this boy to death is like putting a head of cabbage to death. Executing him will do nothing at all to help us understand why people like him or Oswald or Speck go out and murder perfect strangers. We can't just kill these people and try to forget that things like this happen. Instead we should be studying these killers and applying what we learn to public mental health programs, or else crimes like this will be repeated, over and over."

Reporter Dave Smith of the *Los Angeles Times* wrote the kind of perceptive article on Benny Smith for which Wood might have hoped, and concluded it as follows:

4. See the chapter in this volume by Lawrence Zelic Freedman, "Psychopathology of Assassination."

Can some value be salvaged, even from mass butchery of innocent strangers? It may be hopeless to wonder why this person or that was chosen for random slaughter, but what if we try to understand why anybody should have to die this way? The killers know why. Can we ever understand them? Some day if someone can understand, a sensitive teacher, neighbor, or parent might possibly do just a little extra, say a few words of love and encouragement, and perhaps change the course of a lonely 13-year-old who had begun to hate the world. But if no one understands or says those words, who knows . . . ? He might grow up to spend his hate on women in a beauty shop, or nurses in a dormitory, or students on a campus. He might even kill a president.[5]

Dave Smith published this article on April 15, 1968. Had he known that in two months he would be writing about a man named Sirhan he might have ended his article, "Right now there exists a man much like Benny Smith whom it is too late to understand and help, who is already embarked on the inexorable course that will lead him to kill Robert Kennedy."

As you read this chapter you can be sure there exists an individual who silently and slowly is moving toward the moment when he will attempt the next assassination in our history. Why will he try to kill? Why will he aim at a national leader? And when will we know enough to diagnose and deter him? We are not learning fast enough to keep up with the production of killers in our society. Between Robert Kennedy's assassination and his burial the following events occurred:

A Lakeland, Florida tombstone maker charged from house to house, blazing away with a pistol and killing his mother, brother, a nine-year-old girl, and wounding two other persons before taking his own life. Police said that Roy Lee Waldon, 53, took 35 minutes to leave a trail of death. His victims included a seven-year-old girl who was wounded and possibly paralyzed, and a pregnant woman in her twenties who was shot in the stomach, losing her child. Police said Waldon ended the spree by firing a shot at the husband of the wounded pregnant woman, then he reloaded the .38-caliber gun and shot the woman again. Finally, he turned the gun to his head and killed himself. No motive was immediately disclosed.[6]

5. Dave Smith, "Dark Valley of a Boy's Mind," *Los Angeles Times,* April 15, 1968.
6. *Los Angeles Times,* June 9, 1968.

A girl was killed and a youth wounded when a gunman opened fire into a crowd of teenagers in an East St. Louis, Illinois dance hall. Barney F. Crisp, 18, was charged with the shooting which cost the life of Brenda Foster, 17, Madison, Illinois, and wounded Samuel Martin, 18. Witnesses said Crisp had been sitting in the dance hall more than two hours before he drew a .25 caliber pistol and opened fire.[7]

A Negro service station attendant was charged Monday in the fatal shooting of a Jordanian grocer in what police said may have been retaliation for the assassination of Robert F. Kennedy. Aron Myers, 19, appeared in boys court and was ordered held without bond in Cook County Jail in the slaying of Abden Rayyan, 51, father of nine, in his south side grocery Saturday.[8]

Each of these murders is a tragedy calling for study and effort to prevent future repetitions. An assassination is a special form of murder which may grow out of sources common to murders in general, but which also has additional causes necessary to produce such an extreme tragedy with world-wide impact. We may be able to learn something about assassins from the study of murderers, and I will draw upon some research on murder in the course of this chapter.

Let us consider for a moment, however, the special features that usually distinguish an assassination, at least those attempted in the United States since 1800. This crime is committed by a man against another man. It is a violent, publicly dramatic attack with a gun. The assassin runs a very high risk of being caught and executed or imprisoned for life. The victim is more politically prominent and more successful in general than his killer. One way of putting it is that in an assassination a man who has won a popularity contest is killed by a man who has repeatedly lost popularity contests. The assassin destroys not only a human life but a leader upon whom a large segment of the population depends. Thus the crime is not merely against an individual, but against a group or entire nation. In most cases the assassin is younger, poorer, shorter, and skinnier than his victim. His stated motives are usually political, but in actuality neither he nor his

7. *Los Angeles Times,* June 9, 1968.
8. *Los Angeles Times,* June 11, 1968.

cause stand to gain much from the assassination in any direct political sense. He often believes he is an agent of God but has not found support for this belief from other religious laymen or leaders. Diagnostically, his personality is typically that of a paranoid schizophrenic. He denies that he is insane, however, and is insulted that his act might be thought of as pathological.

These facts, similarities, and categorizations may begin to suggest some patterns in assassins and assassinations. To pursue this exploration in more detail and depth, however, we need a systematic summary of the causative factors that should be studied in attempting to understand each assassin and his act. This type of analysis has a different focus from the studies that may be made by the defense or prosecution in connection with the legal trial of an assassin. Such trials reflect a variety of factors such as conflicting factions in psychiatry, public sentiment toward the victim and the assassin, the prevailing national mood regarding violence, legal precedents, and semantics. Society, through its judicial process, and often through its newspapers and public discussions, decides how it wants to categorize each assassin and what it wants to do for or to him. Below is a summary of the nine men involved in the eight attempts to kill United States presidents, and a description of how society dealt with them.

Richard Lawrence, 1835 (Jackson). Francis Scott Key, prosecuting attorney, encouraged defense to plead insanity. All the doctors who examined Lawrence agreed he was insane. He was acquitted and hospitalized as insane until he died twenty-six years later.

John Wilkes Booth, 1865 (Lincoln). Had psychotic episodes, but committed suicide or was shot before he could be brought to trial.

Charles J. Guiteau, 1881 (Garfield). Although he clearly was a paranoid schizophenic, the jury took only sixty-five minutes to find him sane and guilty, and he was hanged.

Leon F. Czolgosz, 1901 (McKinley). Entire trial, including impaneling of jury, took not quite eight and one half hours. Jury took thirty-four minutes to find him guilty. Defense never raised insanity question in spite of ample evidence that he was. From the time of McKinley's death it was only forty-five days until Czolgosz had been tried, found guilty, electrocuted, and had sulfuric acid poured in his coffin.

John N. Schrank, 1912 (Theodore Roosevelt). Sanity commission of five psychiatrists unanimously agreed he was psychotic. The trial was stopped, and Schrank spent the thirty-one years until his death in mental hospitals.

Guiseppe Zangara, 1933 (Franklin Roosevelt). No defense of insanity was made, in spite of Zangara's blatantly psychotic symptoms, and he was electrocuted.

Oscar Collazo, 1950 (Truman). Refused to plead insanity, was examined by one psychiatrist and judged sane, found guilty and sentenced to death. Truman commuted sentence to life imprisonment.

Griselio Torresola, 1950 (Truman). Killed in attempt.

Lee Harvey Oswald, 1963 (Kennedy). Diagnosed as having incipient schizophrenia with paranoid features at age fourteen. Killed before he could be tried.

The purpose of this chapter is to explore what can be gained from studying Sirhan and other assassins from the standpoint of psychological causation rather than legal adjudication. A basic principle of depth psychology is that all acts are multilaterally determined by a complex configuration of forces within the personality and environment. For example, no one single factor, however powerful, can adequately explain Sirhan's killing of Robert Kennedy. Much has been made of the fact that he was an angry, revengeful Jordanian who saw Kennedy as a political enemy of his people. The relative importance of this one motive remains to be demonstrated by more thorough study of Sirhan. It is a fact, however, that not all Jordanians in the United States or in Jordan viewed Robert Kennedy as an enemy. We must therefore explain how Sirhan came to hold that view so strongly. Furthermore, if there do exist Jordanians who viewed Robert Kennedy as an enemy, we must still explain the fact that Sirhan, not some other Jordanian, killed Kennedy. The sources of the extra motive power that led him to act upon his anger and belief may have roots deeper in his character and go far beyond political feelings.

A special problem is always presented by the psychological study of a crime. Often we can retrospectively or even predictively explain why a given person might commit a given crime. Psychological analysis of motives, choice of victim, and impulse control can demonstrate how a past or future murder would perfectly express the murderer's personality. But what is more difficult to explain is why and when the psychological *potential* for an act is finally transformed into the act. There are many men with political beliefs, personality problems, murderous hostility toward national leaders, and loaded guns equivalent to Oswald's, Ray's, and Sirhan's. Which ones will act, and which ones will be content to elaborate their paranoid fantasies? Wertham quotes Freud as saying, after reading a psychoanalytic study of a murder case, "Now we know everything—except why the murder was actually committed."

In his study of Gino, a boy who killed his mother, Wertham addresses this problem of the psychology of action: "Often no analysis of motives, impulses, and repressions, however complete, permits us to predict in the long run whether or not a given thought may be transformed into actual action."[9] Wertham's answer is to include but go beyond this level of analysis. He focuses on Gino's transition from a boy who loved his mother to one who vowed to kill her, and finally to one who carried that vow into action. Wertham states his purpose this way: "If, in the fantasies and actions leading up to the crime of murder, we can distinguish some which differ from those of other patients, who have not murdered, we may learn a great deal about the mechanism which differentiates the neurotic fantasist from the man of action."[10]

Our study of assassins may be motivated originally by our desire to comprehend the psychology of these very unusual and destructive men who commit such a rare crime. Our findings may take us beyond the specific focus on assassins, however. Inevitably, in looking at assassins we are faced with basic questions regarding personality development in general. These men are more than assassins—they represent an ultimate form of human pathology.

9. Wertham, *op. cit.,* pp. 22–23.
10. Wertham, *op. cit.,* p. 22.

Even more than men who commit murder, suicide, treason, or become hospitalized psychotics, assassins manage in one act to violate most of our fundamental concepts of what a man should be.

Below are listed eleven factors that may combine to make a man want to assassinate someone, carry his fantasy into action, and succeed. Because an assassination is an extreme act requiring great motivation and concerted action, it is postulated that most or all eleven of these sources must contribute to it. The psychological study of an assassin ought to consider all eleven contributing factors before concluding which ones were predominant. Similarly, programs to reduce the future production of would-be assassins, to detect the ones who exist, and to prevent the unknown ones from succeeding should take into account all eleven factors.

INGREDIENTS OF AN ASSASSINATION

1. VALUES AND PRINCIPLES

Assassins frequently make statements before or after their acts expressing a value system that justifies and even requires the death of their victims. Just as Sirhan shouted after shooting Kennedy, "Let me explain, I can explain," each assassin has been convinced his act had a rational explanation. By definition, assassination means the killing of a politically important figure; consequently, the conscious motives announced by an assassin usually involve *political* values. Religious duty, patriotism, revenge for perceived injustice, social progress—all may be proclaimed by an assassin as virtuous explanations for killing a leader. An assassin may find support from a group of people with similar values; he may even be chosen by lot or other means to express the group's decision to assassinate someone. Or he may believe he represents such a group without being in direct contact with it. Often, however, he operates alone and depends heavily on his own inner values and sense of "mission." Booth, for example, began to plot the kidnaping of Lincoln with a group of conspirators for allegedly political reasons, but eventually moved ahead on his own to kill Lincoln for a new and bizarrely personalized set of "political" motives.

It is conceivable that a hired killer might be motivated purely by money and a chance to express aggression without claiming to have a high moral and historical purpose. This is one theory about James Ray. In some countries, crass political opportunism might motivate a politician to assassinate a rival. (This has never been the case in the United States.) But usually some pretext of ethical justification is offered and assassins often believe they are uniquely destined to perform a morally imperative act, sometimes as an agent of God.

It is not the purpose of this paper to judge the values used to justify various assassinations. Clearly, in this culture we have a value system that condemns private, nongovernmental killing, especially of our leaders. Consequently, we are inclined to view the motives of Oswald, Ray, and Sirhan as pathological or evil. Some other cultures do not condemn murder as strongly, especially in a political context, and might be more inclined to view an assassin as a "normal," although vicious, enemy. Furthermore, the values and personality of an assassin may seem more "normal" and even laudable if his victim is an enemy of our own culture, such as Hitler. Sirhan has been claimed as a hero by the Palestine Liberation Organization which praises him as "a commando not an assassin" who was acting sanely and rationally. The essential point here is that a well-conceived, strongly held value system can be one important factor motivating, permitting, and even requiring an assassination. Unfortunately, this factor is often given so much attention by the assassin and his captors that it obscures analysis of other important, possibly hidden, factors.

In his article summarizing data on the nine men who successfully and unsuccessfully have attempted to assassinate United States Presidents, Hastings concludes that all were psychotic except Collazo and Torresola.[11] These two men tried to kill Truman, supposedly because they were members of the fanatical Puerto Rican Nationalist Party and wanted complete independence for Puerto Rico. This simplistic theory of their motivation was accepted by the court and is not challenged by Hastings. No evidence was found, however, to indicate that they were acting with the consent and direction of their party. Nor is it very clear how they thought Truman's death would advance rather than damage

11. D. W. Hastings, "The Psychiatry of Presidential Assassination," *The Journal Lancet*, 85 (1965), pp. 93–100, 157–162, 189–192, 294–301.

their cause. Why was it that these two men, rather than one or more of the other 500 members of their party, appointed themselves as assassins? The possibility still exists that a more thorough study of Collazo and Torresola might reveal that some of the eleven factors described here besides conscious political values may have contributed to their action. If mental illness was involved, it may have been less easily diagnosed than Sirhan's and the other assassins', or considered more "normal" in terms of their subculture.

Sirhan, too, might be regarded as "normal" in some contexts. A veteran Arab-affairs specialist was quoted as saying, "There has been an awful lot of testimony at the trial in Los Angeles about Sirhan's sanity, but if you go into one of those Palestinian refugee camps in Jordan, you will find a lot of people with the same mental makeup as Sirhan."[12] So even if we accept political values as a conscious motive, we are still left with the question of whether someone who holds those values and expresses them by assassination is sane and rational, or driven both to those values and to killing by irrational, unconscious, pathological forces.

In his analysis of Gino, the matricide case, Wertham very astutely demonstrates that the boy's great emphasis on "honor" was in fact a way of hiding from himself the more basic motive for his crime. Gino killed his mother supposedly because she took several lovers after his father's death. He says, "About my honor I don't forgive. In this world honor is more important than the word of God."[13] As Wertham points out, "We are apt to rationalize when we act from motives not approved of or repressed by one part of our personality. The French proverb, *Il faut se faire une raison* (One must make oneself a reason), expresses this. Gino rationalized whenever he spoke to me about family honor. He gave himself an explanation for an impulse which otherwise would have seemed incomprehensible even to him . . . behind that façade of family honor lay a deeper, more primitive impulse of which he himself was unconscious."[14] Gino, however, was so set on the

12. *Los Angeles Times,* April 9, 1969. An exhaustive account of the Robert Kennedy assassination can be found in Robert Blair Kaiser, *"R.F.K. Must Die!"* (New York: E. P. Dutton & Co., 1970).
13. Wertham, *op. cit.,* p. 121.
14. Wertham, *op. cit.,* p. 153.

conscious value of honor that he insisted he was sane and responsible, thus making it difficult for the defense to have him certified insane.

Several parallels to Sirhan stand out. Sirhan, too, killed someone who he felt had betrayed him, and believed so strongly that he was sanely affirming his honor that he made it difficult for his defense staff to prove he was insane. Psychiatrist Pollack, an expert witness for the prosecution, went along with Sirhan's claim and testified that the assassination was "triggered by political reasons with which he was highly emotionally charged."[15] Whether Sirhan's primary emotional charge was attached to political reasons or more personal issues will be discussed in a subsequent section.

2. INTELLECTUAL ASSESSMENT OF REALITY

In addition to his values the assassin has various specific perceptions of reality and intellectual ideas about what he perceives. Sirhan valued the cause of the Arabs against Israel, came to perceive Kennedy as pro-Israel, and concluded that Kennedy's death would strategically advance, or at least avenge, the Arab cause. He also presumably believed that he expressed the wishes of other Arabs when he killed Kennedy.

An assassin's degree of contact with reality can be measured in part by the degree to which he (1) correctly selects a victim who is in fact an enemy of his cause, (2) correctly predicts that the enemy's death will advance the cause, (3) correctly perceives that as an assassin he will be affirming the wishes and values of the group he believes he represents. Assassins are often out of touch with reality in these respects, but selectively perceive reality in a way that serves deeper drives.

Assassins may vary in the extent to which they work out a logical, conscious rationale for assassination as a politically expedient act. Some may jump illogically from a value system into impulsive action without reasoning out the choice of victim and the rationalization for killing. Others may take the time and effort to think up a documented and intellectually coherent "proof" of the soundness of their act.

Sirhan apparently based his assessment of Robert Kennedy as an enemy on two pieces of data that drastically and rapidly

15. *Time,* April 4, 1969.

changed his previous perception. He saw a television documentary showing Kennedy in Israel in 1948, and he learned Kennedy supported sending jet fighter planes to Israel. His reasoning process was obviously hasty and subjective. He did not review further information regarding Kennedy's position on the Arab-Israeli conflict or give him time to elaborate that position. Nor did he reason out a theory of just how the Arabs would be better off if an Arab killed Kennedy and other men came into power. But his rationale was good enough for Sirhan and served its purpose of giving him a pseudological explanation for his act to go along with his value system.

3. CULTURAL CLIMATE

The general, prevailing climate regarding persecution, revenge, brutality, violence, hatred, extremism, war, and killing may help determine the extent to which the latent murderousness of individuals is aroused. Killing by criminals, soldiers, police, reckless citizens, etc. may contribute to an atmosphere that says life is cheap and killing is justified or commonplace. Other men who kill provide impulse arousal, identification models, and sources of intellectual and moral rationale. The current climate in the United States, Jordan, Israel, Vietnam, and the rest of the world certainly supports the acting out of murderous impulses. Wertham has written a whole book on violence and its roots in contemporary civilization.[16] The cover picture on the *Los Angeles Times, TV Times* section the week Sirhan shot Kennedy showed a close-up of a man's hand aiming a pistol.[17]

Sirhan had been directly exposed to an atmosphere of revenge and killing in his early childhood years. Subsequent events apparently confirmed rather than extinguished his view of the world as a place where one kills to accomplish goals and avenge oneself. Similarly, Gino, the subject of Wertham's *Dark Legend,* had been brought up in a culture that clearly recognized physical violence as an appropriate retaliation for personal offense. He knew his family used violence against each other, and he had been

16. Frederic Wertham, *A Sign for Cain* (New York: Paperback Library, 1969).
17. *Los Angeles Times, TV Times,* June 2, 1968.

beaten himself. On the night he murdered his mother he saw a movie in which the rejected "good guy" devoted years to destroying his enemies, using illegal means to get final revenge.

Booth's view of the role of violence was undoubtedly strongly influenced by his father's manic-depressive psychotic episodes and the Civil War. The cultural climate in which Guiteau lived and killed is illustrated by the fact that after his arrest he was shot at twice, once by one of his guards. Following Czolgosz's electrocution, sulfuric acid was poured into his coffin after it had been lowered into the grave in a triumphant gesture expressing official American violence. Oswald explicitly pointed at the cultural climate in the United States during an interview in Moscow: "People hate because they're told to hate, like school kids. It's the fashion to hate people in the United States."[18]

While I was in the process of writing this chapter, Frank Kulak, an ex-Marine (like Oswald and Whitman), killed two policemen and injured five other people in Chicago. He was a Purple Heart veteran of World War II and Korea and was quoted as saying, "They wanted me for the Goldblatt's bombing. I did it. I did it to show how awful war is." He was referring to a tragedy in which a woman had been killed and eight people injured by a bomb placed among the military toys in a department store.[19] In Kulak's mind, at least, there was a direct connection between the violence he had experienced in war and that which he inflicted in peace.

Of course, it is usually possible to find some evidence of culturally approved violence and killing in an individual's environment. What must be demonstrated in the case of each assassin, however, is how this climate specifically influenced his personal predilection to resort to violence. The actual connecting links between a cultural climate and one individual's mental state are not always easy to demonstrate. In Sirhan's case, however, the evidence within his family and on the streets outside was so extreme that it had formative impact not only on Sirhan but also on at least one of his brothers, Sharif, also causing him to resort to

18. As told to Aline Mosely, reporter for United Press International. Reported in D. Jackson, "The Evolution of an Assassin," *Life*, February 21, 1964, pp. 68–80.
19. *Los Angeles Times*, April 15, 1969.

impulsive and planned aggression when frustrated. He was convicted for sawing through the brake lines in his girl friend's car, made telephone threats to his family and the defense staff during Sirhan's trial, and was arrested on an assault charge for bursting into the hospital ward to berate personnel where another brother was in intensive care.

4. PSYCHODYNAMIC MOTIVATION

At an unconscious, repressed level, it is postulated that each assassin harbors psychodynamic motivations to kill that are hidden from himself and probably from people close to him. Depth psychology and psychoanalysis, in particular, specialize in studying the contribution to adult personality and behavior made by early traumas, family tensions, Oedipal conflicts (love, envy, hatred toward parents), sexual problems, self-concept, and identity formation. The childhoods of assassins are full of painful experiences such as losing one or both parents, being put to work at age six, being beaten, seeing bodies blown apart by bombs, etc. As the poet A. E. put it in "Germinal,"

> In ancient shadows and twilights
> where childhood had strayed
> The world's great sorrows were born
> And its heroes were made.
> In the lost boyhood of Judas
> Christ was betrayed.

Psychologists and psychiatrists have demonstrated their ability to make substantial contributions to the understanding of the life histories and resultant motivational patterns of killers. Armchair, after-the-fact psychodynamic explanations, however, must always be tested by applying the theories developed to other cases, by integrating them with alternative or supplementary explanations, and by using them to predict and modify behavior. It is too late to predict or modify Oswald's, Ray's, and Sirhan's murderous aggression, but it is possible to compare data gathered about their unconscious inner life and formative childhood experiences with data gathered on other assassins and murderers. It is this area to which psychology is especially relevant. Consequently, the psychodynamic motivation of assassins will be discussed at greater length in a later section.

5. MOTIVATIONAL ESCALATION

A man's values, his conscious perception of reality, the cultural climate in which he lives, and his unconscious psychodynamic drives may make him a potential assassin. Many men have these ingredients, however, but do not actually move toward acting them out. The final plotting of an assassination requires building up to a heightened state of motivation during the months, weeks, and days prior to the final act of killing.

In Sirhan's case, for example, there are several factors that apparently escalated his basic dynamics in the period leading up to June 4, 1968. A loved sister died of leukemia in 1965. Shortly thereafter, Sirhan's college grades, which had been good, dropped to a failing level and he withdrew from college. In 1966, he fell from a horse, sustaining a head injury and career frustration. In March, 1968, he left his job as delivery boy after an argument with his boss. The June 5 anniversary of the Arab-Israeli war was approaching. Kennedy had expressed support of Israel in his campaign against Senator McCarthy and had been campaigning aggressively on the West Coast, ending up in Los Angeles. The accumulation of these aggravating factors built upon Sirhan's long-standing underlying motivation to spur him closer to action.

6. DEFICIENCY OF RESTRAINING FORCES

This section and the next describe the *absence* of factors that, if present, might prevent the act of assassination even if other factors were pushing the assassin toward it. Assassins frequently seem to suffer from an absence of values, group loyalties, and close personal relationships that would be destroyed by killing and being caught. In effect, each assassin must feel that he has a great deal to gain and very little to lose. He may even be hopeful that he will not lose his life. (This may be the reason for Sirhan's intense interest in the fate of Jack Kirschke who is appealing his conviction for murdering his wife and her lover.) Or he may assume he will be executed and accept or desire that end.

Sirhan certainly had no wife and children with whom he would lose a close relationship, and apparently he had no really personal friends. He would not risk ostracism from any political or social group in which he valued a membership. He was not comfortably close with his family and therefore would not lose a bond he valued if he were imprisoned or executed. It could be argued that he was close to his mother, but to the extent that was true it was an ambivalent closeness of an overprotective, puritanical mother with an emasculated, restless son who needed to break free and find his manhood.

In spite of Sirhan's exposure to the Christian religion, he apparently did not feel he would lose a valued relationship with God if he killed a human being. In fact, strict religious upbringing has not deterred a number of killers and may even have been a factor in producing their murderous rage. Wertham's case history of Robert Irwin clearly documents the role played by his mother's fanatical religious restrictions.[20] Brussel correctly predicted that the "Mad Bomber" of New York City would turn out to be a regular attendant at Catholic Mass.[21] The case described by Wittman also featured extreme religious influences.[22]

Studies have been made attempting to trace the complex relationships among parents' religious views, their child-rearing practices, and the ways their children express aggression.[23] Some religious families with strict moral standards about aggression produce children who are sporadically violent. This seems to be more likely to occur if the parents use physical punishment to enforce their standards. Their children may acquire a tendency to be harshly intropunitive up to a point and then flip over into outwardly directed anger, possibly modeled after their parents' physical punishment of them. The child-rearing practices used by

20. Frederic Wertham, *The Show of Violence* (New York: Bantam, 1967).
21. James Brussel, *Casebook of a Crime Psychiatrist* (Bernard Geis Associates, 1968).
22. P. Wittman, "Psychological Investigation of a Homicidal Youth," *Journal of Clinical Psychology*, 5 (1949), pp. 88–93.
23. T. C. Greening, "Moral Standards and Defenses Against Aggression" (Ph.D. diss., University of Michigan, 1958), and A. L. Kovacs, "Some Antecedents of Denial in Fantasy as a Defense Against Anger" (Ph.D. diss., University of Michigan, 1958).

the parents of assassins should be studied extensively as a source of further knowledge about how children in general and assassins in particular learn to handle anger. Effectively internalized moral standards against killing apparently do not always result from parents' disciplinary efforts to teach such standards.

The development of a healthy conscience and impulse controls depends to a large extent on the individual having close relationships with mature people. Many assassins have been noted for being "loners" or so disturbed that they alienated people with whom they attempted to be close. Guiteau had left his family and the substitute family of the Oneida Community, had been divorced by his wife, and had drifted around after failing in a law career. Czolgosz's mother had died when he was twelve, he had quit his job, and never had a girl friend. Schrank's father died, his mother left when he was seven, and his girl friend had been killed in a steamship tragedy. Zangara had never dated. Oswald's father died before he was born and Oswald was separated from his wife. Ray was a typical restless loner.

None of these men had much to lose and they may have reached a point of desperation where assassinating someone famous represented a warped, last-ditch attempt to establish a connection with society and save themselves from total alienation. The inner restraining forces of conscience or fear were either deficient to begin with or temporarily overpowered by their more powerful craving for revenge and contact.

7. DEFICIENCY OF ALTERNATIVE OUTLETS

Assassins typically lack alternative outlets for their frustration, competitiveness, anger, and assertive masculine identity development. Sirhan was not able to release his hostile impulses sufficiently by writing them down or by shooting his gun at targets, at animals, or at unknown humans from a distance. He did not succeed in using athletics, competition for money, sexual aggressiveness, manual labor, verbal debate, or political action as an outlet and sublimation for his aggression. He made some effort to use intellectual achievement and work with race horses to assert and develop his power, but these were not sufficient to satisfy him. He was handicapped in his development of a confident, powerful, and aggressively masculine self-concept by his small size, by the over-whelmingly hostile world of his childhood, and by the lack of a relationship with his father. The one Sirhan brother who has not been in trouble with the police is Adel, and he has the expressive outlet and occupational skill of being a musician.[24] Further study is needed of assassins' developmental difficulties in the areas of body image, physical aggression, identification with supportive masculine figures, expressive outlets, and sexual adequacy.

Previous studies of murderers have demonstrated drastic defi-ciencies in these areas. Satten et al., for example, found that the four murderers they studied "had ego-images of themselves as physically inferior, weak, and inadequate, and the histories re-vealed in each a severe degree of sexual inhibition. To all of them, adult women were threatening creatures. . . . All of them, too, had been concerned throughout their early years about being considered 'sissies,' physically undersized, or sickly."[25]

Aside from physical aggression, symbolic aggression through words may also be insufficient for a murderer. Wertham points out that Gino did not confront his mother and verbally attack her for her sexual behavior as some angry sons might have done. Nor did he engage in the aggressive sexual exploits against women other slum boys might have used as a displacement. While some men have murderous feelings toward the President, which they express by writing letters threatening to kill him, no assassin has ever used this symbolic outlet. Booth had used his acting as an outlet for his intense aggressiveness and craving for recognition, but lost this outlet when his voice cracked and his career declined. Oswald had failed or given up attempting to assert himself in his political romance with Russia and in his sexual relationship with his wife. His efforts with political propaganda appear to have been ineffec-

---

24. After this chapter was written, Adel Sirhan did clash with the law. On August 7, 1969, he was arrested for drunken driving, speeding, driving without a license, and driving on the wrong side of the road. Although he had been able to find work as a musician after his brother's conviction, he reported feeling like an outcast. The precarious success of his prior adjust-ment may have been over-burdened by the stress of having to face the world as Sirhan Sirhan's brother.

25. J. Satten, K. Menninger, I. Rosen, and M. Mayman, "Murder Without Apparent Motive: A Study in Personality Disorganization," *American Journal of Psychiatry*, 117, No. 1 (1960), pp. 48–53.

tual. Similarly, Czolgosz's attempts to get involved with the anarchist movement had been rejected. The clinical description of Oswald as a disturbed child might well apply to all assassins: he had "given up hope of making himself understood by anyone about his needs and expectations."[26]

8. PHYSIOLOGICAL FACTORS

The physical state of the assassin at the time of the assassination may also be a contributing, precipitating factor that deserves study, although there is no precise way to determine that state retrospectively. Factors such as lack of sleep, exhaustion, physical pain, low blood sugar, drunkenness, neurological impairment, or stimulus satiation from a noisy crowd may impair the assassin's reasoning, decrease his fear, and loosen his impulse controls to the point where his reactive irritability and underlying hostility are more easily triggered.

Much was made in Sirhan's trial of the effects of his purportedly having drunk four highballs and been dazed by the lights and mirror reflections in the hotel. No conclusive evidence was found of brain damage produced by his fall from a horse or other causes. Dr. Richardson's report stated that his psychological assessment of Sirhan provided "minimal or equivocal evidence of the presence of brain damage." He concludes, "Tests did not give strong evidence of the presence of organic brain damage; however, it has been noted that the possibility of a brain damage factor exacerbating or amplifying the schizophrenic process found by psychological testing cannot be ruled out."[27]

Whitman was found to have a brain tumor and had Dexedrine pills in his possession, but neither factor was proven to have a causative role in his killing spree. The recent controversy about chromosomes and murder is similarly inconclusive. Although the word "assassin" is based on the fact that an ancient group of killers used hashhish, American assassins so far have not been high on drugs.

After Guiteau's execution by hanging, an autopsy was per-

26. Renatus Hartogs, quoted in D. Jackson, "The Evolution of an Assassin," *Life* (February 21, 1964), pp. 68–80.
27. *Sirhan v. State of California*, 79 Richardson 6341, 6351 (1969).

formed in an attempt to settle disputes that had dominated his trial about whether he had an organically determined mental illness. Some signs of degeneration of gray cells and small blood vessels were found, but the results could not conclusively be linked with Guiteau's personality and crime. Charles Rosenberg, author of *The Trial of the Assassin Guiteau,* asked a distinguished pathologist, Dr. Esmond Long, to review the original Guiteau autopsy report in the light of modern medicine. He, too, found the feelings inconclusive, while noting some evidence of chronic malaria and syphilitic involvement of the brain.[28]

Weinstein and Lyerly point out that Oswald's type of phonetic misspelling in his letters clinically falls into the class of the congenital or developmental dyslexias.[29] They refer to an analysis by Lecours and state that this pattern is "commonly associated with behavior disturbances, including outbursts of violence, impulses to kill, and episodic hallucinatory scenes of death and violence. In some cases, abnormal electrical activity of the brain has been found, and episodes may be touched off by emotional stress."[30]

In general, however, it seems that physiological factors have not been isolated as important determinants of assassination. Further study may provide more information about their role, for example in the type of dissociative trance Sirhan was alleged to have had.

9. COMPETENCE

An assassin must possess considerable skill and intelligence to plan and implement his deed, unless he is desperate or dumb enough to rely on chance and fortuitous opportunity. This skill and intelligence may function under conscious control, or it may guide him in an intuitive, automatic way. If he plans to use a pistol, for example, he must be able to obtain one that works reliably, conceal it, get within firing range of his victim, draw it quickly, aim it

28. Charles E. Rosenberg, *The Trial of the Assassin Guiteau* (Chicago: University of Chicago Press, 1968), pp. 239–240.

29. E. A. Weinstein and Olga G. Lyerly, "Symbolic Aspects of Presidential Assassination," *Psychiatry* (April, 1969), pp. 1–11.

30. A. R. Lecours, "Serial Order in Writing: A Study of Misspelled Words in Developmental Dysgraphia," *Neuropsychologia,* 4 (1966), pp. 221–241.

accurately, and fire it. Depending on the strictness of gun controls, adequacy of police protection, and the predictability of the victim's physical location, this can be a difficult or easy task requiring various levels of physical and mental competence. Even if luck presents the assassin with an opportunity for which he had not specifically planned, he must be clever and skillful enough to capitalize rapidly on the opportunity.

Sirhan was able to obtain a gun and practice shooting it until he obtained some degree of skill. He practiced his marksmanship the afternoon before the assassination. He was also able to conceal his gun, get within firing range, and shoot accurately. His plan was deficient in that Kennedy might have taken another route and that .22-caliber bullets are less lethal than those previously used in American assassinations, but these deficiencies were not sufficient to defeat the plan.

The assassin's planning may be casual, his act opportunistic, and his skill rudimentary, but to succeed he cannot be frozen with fear, conspicuously violent prior to his assault, or emotionally blinded to the basic logistics required. A disorganized psychotic would risk drawing attention to himself and probably become confused and inept. A physically handicapped individual or someone with a phobia of crowds would have difficulty getting within range.

The recent introduction of rifles into assassination attacks adds to the requirements of competence. Oswald had developed good marksmanship in the Marine Corps (as had Charles Whitman) and used a 4 power scope to hit John Kennedy with rapidly fired shots at a range of seventy-five to ninety yards. James Earl Ray also used a rifle to kill Martin Luther King and confirmed that assassination is no longer limited to daredevil assaults at close range. The planning, calm, and steadiness required of an expert rifle marksman may mean that this type of assassin is distinguishable in some respects from the more suicidal, directly assaultive, close-range killers. Ray and Oswald also demonstrated competence in planning successful escapes from the scene of assassination, something few other assassins have managed. They present quite a contrast to Lawrence, who had two pistols misfire, Zangara, who shot wildly and missed Franklin Roosevelt entirely, and Collazo, whose gun also failed.

10. VICTIM'S ROLE

An assassination victim may unintentionally collaborate with his assassin in several ways to make himself a tempting, highly visible target. He may do this through naïvely optimistic trust in the populace or a well-meaning underestimation of the murderous rage some people may feel toward him. He may be provocative in personal style and openly aggressive toward opponents. He may simply be too busy with other issues to be aware of threats to his safety.

Some political figures, such as Robert Kennedy, may be well aware of the risks they are running and consciously choose to run them anyway in order to have close public contact and freedom of movement. *Time* quoted Kennedy as saying, "If anyone wants to kill me, it won't be difficult,"[31] and, according to Romain Gary, he said, "There is no way to protect a candidate during the electoral campaign. You must give yourself to the crowd and from then on . . . you must take your chances. . . . I know that there will be an attempt on my life sooner or later."[32]

As quoted, Kennedy's calculated risk-taking appears to have been motivated not primarily by an attraction to risk-taking per se but by his desire to pursue other goals that necessarily entail risks. It may still be worth examining, however, whether an attraction to risk-taking has contributed to the vulnerability of some assassination victims, possibly even including Kennedy. Some public figures do seem motivated toward risk-taking as an end in itself and thus engage in provocative, challenging, or negligent behavior beyond that which is essential to pursue their other life goals. Theodore Roosevelt, after he was shot, insisted on giving his speech as planned. Risk-taking of this sort may be motivated by a desire for excitement, adventure, mastery, and proving oneself. It could also have a component of what Shneidman has called subintentional suicide in which the victim unconsciously courts death because of grandiose fantasies, guilt and self-destructive impulses, identification or competition with dead loved persons, and the like.[33]

Robert Kennedy, for all his dedication to life, may also have

31. *Time,* June 14, 1968.
32. *Los Angeles Times,* June 7, 1968.
33. E. S. Shneidman, "Orientations Toward Death," in R. W. White, ed., *The Study of Lives* (New York: Atherton Press, 1963), pp. 200–228.

had some impulses to flirt with death. A correspondent described him after his brother's assassination as follows: "There was in those days a sense of urgency about him, almost as if he were sliding off some horrible precipice toward some faraway disaster. There was an irresistible compulsion to do everything and try everything. That is when he began to shoot rapids and climb mountains."[34] On a 1965 canoe trip down the Amazon, he is reported to have insisted on swimming in piranha-infested waters against the warnings of local Indians. His self-esteem seems to have required direct mastery of danger and of death. His need to prove himself and his dedication to his goals gave him a dramatic, idealistic, but somewhat provocative and potentially self-destructive style. Thus Kennedy's style and personality, as well as his political stands, may have provoked Sirhan to aim his envy and grievances at him as a symbolically appropriate target. That same style of Kennedy's made him an easily accessible victim because of his disdain for police protection and his desire to be directly in contact with the public.[35]

11. TRIGGERING

Even if all the above-mentioned factors are present and have brought the assassin to the threshold of his act, a final ingredient is still needed: the immediate, precipitating, triggering stimulus situation. We will never know how many men have been on the verge of killing political figures but held back at the last moment because the final push did not occur. The Secret Service is reported to have names of 100,000 possible assassins programmed into its computer.[36]

34. *Time,* June 14, 1968.
35. Since writing this paper I have discovered that David Rothstein has also discussed this issue. In a section titled "Can a President be Assassination Prone?" he refers to "unconscious fantasies of omnipotence or counterphobic elements" in presidents, and points out in some "a certain tendency to take chances involving some danger as if there were no chance of failure, to get into situations the average prudent individual might avoid, possibly to court danger for its own sake." David A. Rothstein, "The Assassin and the Assassinated—as Non-Patient Subjects of Psychiatric Investigation" (Paper presented at Midwest Regional Meeting, American Psychiatric Association, Chicago, November 15, 1968). See also the discussion in this volume by David Rothstein, "Presidential Assassination Syndrome: A Psychiatric Study of the Threat, the Deed, and the Message."
36. *Time,* June 14, 1968.

Guiteau passed up several opportunities to kill Garfield, and Schrank had an earlier opportunity for a shot at Roosevelt. Zangara had a prior plan to kill the King of Italy, but was scared off. In Sirhan's case, the June 5 anniversary arrived at midnight, Kennedy won the California primary, made a victory speech, received enthusiastic support from the crowd, and was about to leave the hotel, radiating success, confidence, and good spirits. For Sirhan, the physical closeness to Kennedy, his once-loved and now-hated victim, may have been the final stimulus needed to precipitate the shooting.

Previous studies have demonstrated the importance of the triggering interpersonal event which finally tips the balance already weighted so heavily toward murder. Blackman and his colleagues found that an insult or provocation usually provoked the twenty-one "sudden murderers" they studied.[37] Frequently this was a personal rejection. Satten et al. studied four sudden, apparently senseless murders and found that being mocked, made fun of, or nagged played a triggering role.[38] Similarly, Sydney Smith's study of eight adolescent murderers found that being nagged, laughed at, or rejected had precipitated latent murderous rage based on a deep sense of parental deprivation.[39]

These sudden, impulsive murders are different from carefully planned assassinations, or even poorly planned ones, where the victim has been selected long in advance as the result of an accumulation of clearly focused hostility. It may be, however, that the sight of the victim, often looking confident and cheerful in the midst of an admiring crowd, may be in itself the stimulus that vividly and painfully reminds the assassin of his own alienation and triggers his anger.

The following excerpt from Dr. Richardson's testimony at Sirhan's trial appears to support this point:

It seems particularly meaningful that Mr. Sirhan's paranoid feeling of envy, bitterness, vengefulness and his strong sense of external threat, may be elicited by events which have the meaning of great

37. N. Blackman, J. Weiss, and J. Lamberti, "The Sudden Murderer," *Archives of General Psychiatry*, 8 (March, 1963), pp. 289–294.

38. Satten et al., *op. cit.*

39. S. Smith, "The Adolescent Murderer," *Archives of General Psychiatry*, 13 (1965), pp. 310–319.

success for others. On card eight of the Rorschach, for example, an ink blot characterized by a variety of pastel colors, Mr. Sirhan expressed marked disturbance and discomfort, saying that the colors reminded him of happiness, jubilation and triumph. The card stimulated a memory of colored, pictorial magazine articles depicting the 20th anniversary celebration of the State of Israel; an article stressing in pictures and words the great sense of victory, happiness and success of the Israeli State at that time. The bright colors of the card reminded him of the victory celebration of the Israelis and the defeat of the Arabs. He said, 'It meant to me the Israelis were saying we beat the Arabs! It burns the shit out of me.'[40]

PSYCHODYNAMICS OF ASSASSINS

The psychological study of assassins is relevant primarily to factors (4) Psychodynamic Motivation, (5) Motivational Escalation, and (7) Deficiency of Alternative Outlets, although it can shed some light on the other factors as well. In the preceding section examples of psychological speculation, theory, and research were presented. This section will go into further detail regarding the psychodynamics of assassins, with particular reference to Sirhan.

Paranoid Schizophrenia. All but one of the ten psychologists and psychiatrists who testified about Sirhan's mental status concluded that he had pronounced paranoid characteristics. All seven defense psychologists and psychiatrists agreed in diagnosing Sirhan as a paranoid schizophrenic. The prosecution claimed he was a paranoid personality with borderline schizophrenia. (Only one witness, Dr. Olinger, denied the presence of paranoia and claimed that Sirhan was suffering from "pseudoneurotic schizophrenia," had good contact with reality, and had normal rather than paranoid suspicions.)

Sirhan appears to be a fairly typical assassin diagnostically. Hastings' review of the data on the nine would-be or successful assassins of presidents led him to the conclusion that all but two (Collazo and Torresola) were paranoid schizophrenics, or, in Booth's case, a paranoid personality with psychotic episodes.[41]

40. *Sirhan* v. *State of California,* 79 Richardson 6333–6398 (1969).
41. Hastings, *op. cit.*

Rothstein studied ten patients who had made threats against the lives of presidents and found that all ten were schizophrenic, with seven of the ten being paranoid.[42] Hastings says "the causes of this disease are not known" and limits himself to listing circumstances that are often present in the life histories of paranoid schizophrenia: "parental rejection, broken homes, lack of a strong male figure with whom a boy can identify, and emotional stresses strong enough to prevent the developing child from dealing successfully with his fellowmen." He does mention that "repressed homosexual drives have been assumed to be psychological constituents in paranoid illnesses, but the relationship is not known to be certain."

It is striking that in all the newspaper accounts of expert witnesses testifying that Sirhan was paranoid, none of them discuss Freud's classical psychoanalytic interpretation of paranoia. Freud described his theory in his account of the famous Schreber case, a German judge who developed bizarre paranoid delusions of his grandiose mission to save the world, and of persecution.[43] In his case, the sexual theme was more apparent, but Freud used the case to illustrate his basic theory of paranoia which he believed was also applicable to cases where the sexual theme was more disguised. In fact, the paranoid delusions are alleged to be primarily a defense against homosexual wishes. The transformation of unacceptable wish into conscious and acceptable thought supposedly proceeds as follows:

1. Unacceptable, unconscious wish: "I love him and want sexual relations with him."
2. Reversal of wish, but still unacceptable: "I hate him and want to eliminate him."
3. Projection of wish away from self: "He hates me and wants to eliminate me."
4. Conscious, acceptable idea: "I am morally justified in eliminating him."

42. D. A. Rothstein, "Presidential Assassination Syndrome," *Archives of General Psychiatry*, 2 (September, 1964), pp. 245–254, and his chapter in this volume.
43. S. Freud, "Psychoanalytical Notes Upon an Autobiographical Account of a Case of Paranoia," *Collected Papers*, Vol. III (London: Hogarth Press, 1953), pp. 390–472.

There is some evidence that Sirhan went through a struggle somewhat like this. At least one of the psychologists who evaluated him referred to homosexual signs in the test data, but these tendencies were probably never acted out. His sporadic heterosexual contacts were mainly pickups and did not provide sustained or emotionally intimate sexual release. He did feel love and admiration for Robert Kennedy and wanted to shake his hand. Referring to seeing the television documentary in May, 1968, he stated, "Up to that time I loved Robert Kennedy; I cared for him very much." And only two nights before he shot Kennedy, when he saw him in person for the first time, Sirhan said he was "really thrilled. . . . He looked like a saint to me. I liked him." Of course Sirhan is not referring to a consciously sexualized love. If present, that component would be repressed and might help account for the extreme intensity of his ambivalent feelings toward Kennedy.

It is also significant that Sirhan developed strong affection for one of the policemen who originally interviewed him, and for Parsons, one of his defense attorneys. His manner of reaching out to Parsons had the touching quality of a hurt and frightened little boy seeking comfort and reassurance from a protective father. This is reminiscent of his father's account of one of the many traumatic events of Sirhan's childhood in war-torn Jerusalem. Father and four-year-old son were walking to the post office via the Damascus Gate when a bomb went off nearby. "The ground shook, the walk shook. Sirhan cried from his heart. He fell down. I thought he was dead, finished. I waited and after 20 minutes he opened his eyes. 'Daddy,' he said. . . . 'Can you walk?' I asked him. He could not walk but he didn't want me to carry him lest I get tired. Imagine! We saw the yard full of blood—about 40 or 50 killed. The yard was full of pieces of meat. 'Daddy, I don't want to see it,' he said, and I covered his eyes until we passed the sight. He was so frightened he spent two days in bed."[44] The father's memory and honesty are not always reliable, but such events did occur in Sirhan's childhood environment, and he is known to have witnessed some of them. The combination of trauma, anxiety,

44. R. Toth and D. Smith, "Sirhan—The Wanderer—Never Found His Way," *Los Angeles Times,* January 5, 1969.

search for reassurance, and puritanism about sex with women can often produce a dependent and eventually sexualized attraction to men.

Unfortunately, Sirhan's father may also have been a frequent source of brutality rather than comfort, for he is reported to have beaten his wife and children often. This could have contributed to Sirhan's volatile mixture of affectionate dependency and sudden reversals into paranoia and rage. He demonstrated this mixture not only in response to Kennedy, but also toward his attorneys, whom he attempted to fire in a fit of distrust and anger. A predisposition to expect betrayal has been observed in other murderers. Sydney Smith reported that among one group he studied, "the more common denominators in these cases are a sense of disappointment with a hyperalertness to the possibility of a recurrence of the experience of loss. There is a readiness in these individuals to cast others in the role of depriving figures. . . ."[45] This distrust and vigilant readiness to jump to pessimistic conclusions about having been betrayed are characteristic of Sirhan. After seeing the television documentary showing Kennedy in Israel in 1948 (when Sirhan was four), Sirhan's love turned to hate, and he said at his trial that was the first time he had known Kennedy "was doing a lot of things behind my back I didn't know about."

This same paranoid vigilance was noted in Sirhan's psychological test data by Dr. Richardson, who saw ". . . an unstable, ambivalent oscillation between hope in a good, magical, helping figure, a powerful and good father, on the one hand; and on the other, a persisting suspicion of an alien, powerful, magically influencing enemy, whose intention is to harm, punish or exploit him."[46]

Childhood abandonment and vulnerability may thus especially predispose a boy to become paranoid and a potential assassin. Let us review briefly the facts about the seven American assassins presumed to be psychotic:

> *Lawrence:* Both parents alive during childhood, but on the way to jail after the assassination attempt he stated that the President had killed his father.

45. S. Smith, *op. cit.*
46. *Sirhan v. State of California,* 79, 6345.

Booth: His father had violent psychotic episodes. Father and brothers were often away pursuing acting careers. Father died when Booth was fourteen.

Guiteau: Mother died when he was seven. His father was heavily involved in religious beliefs to a delusionary extent. His father believed Guiteau to be insane and rejected him.

Czolgosz: Mother died when he was twelve, and he grew up in poverty.

Schrank: Father died when Schrank was seven. His mother re-married and moved away.

Zangara: Both parents alive during childhood. His father put him to work at age six and Zangara resented this all his life.

Oswald: Father died before he was born. At age three his mother put him in a boarding school. At age five his mother remarried and brought him home to live. At age nine this marriage ended in divorce.

In summary, only two of these seven men escaped the developmental difficulties presented by growing up in a broken home, and these two suffered problems related to immigration and poverty.

Millions of children have grown up in this country under similar hardships without becoming assassins, however. It is still difficult to isolate the particularly powerful combination of childhood stresses that provide the groundwork for such crimes. Potential assassins somehow refuse to allow themselves to be overwhelmed by such stresses. They do not deteriorate into hospitalized schizophrenics, delusional bums, or "hollow men" scraping out a marginal existence in society. They are not sick or beaten enough for that, although for periods they teeter on the edge of such fates. These are men determined to strike back, who are able to focus their anger, frustration, and precarious competence in one direction.

Self-Concept. Assassins, like all murderers, seek to assert and prove something, and to deny and repress something else at the same time. The more unusual, violent, or destructive the act, the more complex and intense are the killer's motives to assert and prove and to deny and repress. Below is a summary of the qualities assassins seem obsessed with:

What does the assassin seek to assert and prove?	What does the assassin seek to deny and repress?
That he is:	That he is:
Superior	Inferior
Publicly important	Anonymous
Accepted	Lonely
Brave	Cowardly
Patriotic	Homeless
Inspired by God	Agent of Devil
Strong	Weak
Tough	Vulnerable
Masculine	Homosexual
Aggressive	Passive
A man	A mamma's boy

Escape from a humiliating dependency and Oedipal attraction to his mother may have been an additional motive for Sirhan. Dr. Richardson's psychodiagnostic report on Sirhan mentions his "sense of inferiority and inadequacy relative to other males" and his determination "to condemn and to struggle against the needy, dependent, passive aspects of his personality . . . as weak, cowardly and unmasculine."[47] His father had failed to help him become a man and he had reason to feel that his mother was dominating him and fostering his dependency. During his trial, he often appeared hostile and condescending during his mother's emotion-laden testimony and he and she had often clashed about his use of the money he received as compensation for his injuries when he was thrown from a horse. In one of his psychological test responses, Sirhan told a story of a man who had just had intercourse with a woman and was going home to tell his mother.

Oswald had slept in the same bed with his mother for years and he may have had a similar need to assert his masculinity in an extreme manner. His wife had accused him of sexual inadequacy in their fights and his telling her about his assassination attempt on General Walker may have been a way of saying, "You see, I *am* a man!" Shortly before the assassination Oswald's wife had refused to reunite with him.

47. *Sirhan v. State of California*, 79, 6344.

In its coverage of the Sirhan trial, *Time* mentioned this theme of precarious manhood fanatically asserted: "What the Latin American male calls *machismo,* a hypersensitive awareness of his own masculinity, is *rujuliyah* to an Arab."[48] *Time*'s writer suggested that this was a factor in the assassination and in Sirhan's frantic insistence that passages in his diary about girls he hardly knew should not be read in court. Sirhan's sensitive pride was also apparent in his need to assert soon after his arrest, "I am not a mendicant." His narcissistic investment in his own image was apparent throughout the trial and was reminiscent of Guiteau, who, like Sirhan, made frequent outbursts during his trial, tried to fire his attorneys, was insulted at the idea he might be thought insane, and whom the judge threatened to gag if he would not be silent.[49]

Symbolic Meaning of Victim. Previous studies of murderers[50] have stressed the symbolic meaning that each victim has for the murderer. If he does not kill someone in his immediate family who is the original source of his feelings of pain, loneliness, inferiority, and deprivation of love, he may select a substitute person who symbolizes the object of his hatred.

Frederic Wertham described assassination as "symbolic patricide" in 1941 and subsequent assassinations seem to bear out this interpretation.[51] At Sirhan's trial Dr. Martin Shorr presented evidence from psychological testing of Sirhan to support this view. Unfortunately, he weakened a valuable line of analysis by "borrowing" heavily from James Brussel's *Casebook of a Crime Psychiatrist.* (The trials of assassins have often presented opportunities to view the misguided ambitions of many people in addition to the man on trial.) Weinstein and Lyerly reject any reductionistic view of the assassin's victim as simply a father substitute, pointing out that the President has many symbolic roles and that assassination cannot be explained simply in terms of a transfer of family

48. "Death Without Dread," *Time,* March 14, 1969.
49. Rosenberg, *op. cit.*
50. G. R. Bach, "Intimate Violence, Understanding and Prevention," mimeographed (Los Angeles, 1967); Brussel, *op. cit.;* S. Smith, *op. cit.;* Wertham, *The Show of Violence.*
51. Wertham, *op. cit.*

dynamics into the political realm.[52] Even if we grant that an assassin may be doing much more than merely killing a substitute for a hated parent, it is still worthwhile to search for a major source of his motive power in his family dynamics.

In his study of eight murderers, Sydney Smith concludes, "In the present sample of cases, it can be stated categorically that in every instance it was a parent or parent symbol who became the murder victim."[53] By killing the president or an important political figure the assassin deprives the nation of a leader and a source of strength. It is as if the assassin were bent on eliminating the "father" of the country so that everyone else would suffer the same deprivation he has felt.

The assassin is then no longer a solitary victim; he has become an active agent, and the entire nation becomes the victim. His private pain is now shared by millions. With one act, the assassin kills a symbolic substitute for his own father, a real leader whom he envies, and the hopes of the nation. Assassination seems to him to be the one thorough remedy for his sense of alienation and inequality. After he kills, he ceases to be obscure and alone and his feeling of being fatherless is no longer his own private anguish.

Although a president is clearly a father figure in many respects, symbolizing masculine political power and possibly physical and sexual potency, he may also be experienced at a deeper level as a mother figure by some assassins. Rothstein, in particular, has presented convincing arguments for this interpretation. From his study of ten patients who made threats against presidents, Rothstein concluded that for these men ". . . it is unlikely that the personality organization progresses to a point where true oedipal conflicts would be a primary factor. At the deepest level, these patients' anger at the male parent is a derivative of, and is strongly reinforced by, the rage at the depriving mother. Rather than being the primary difficulty, the paternal lack would seem merely to open a channel for displacement of this rage from the depriving mother on to the father. In addition, absence of a strong father and the rage at women seem to result in a defective masculine identification."

52. Weinstein and Lyerly, *op. cit.*
53. S. Smith, *op. cit.*

Rothstein followed up this study with a second in which he applied his theory to subsequently available data about Oswald and found confirmation for it in Oswald's relationship to his mother.[54] Independent corroboration of Rothstein's theory can be found in Dr. Richardson's report on Sirhan in which he placed more emphasis on basic dependency deprivation than on frustrated masculine strivings or Oedipal rivalry. He found evidence of ". . . a long-standing sense of frustration and rejection in his basic needs for maternal affection and attention, with hostile, resentful feelings to the maternal figure. The picture is of an affection-starved individual with chronic feelings of deprivation in terms of his needs for 'mothering.' He remains in a position of angry, demanding dependency on the mother, which precludes development to more independence and adequate levels of adjustment."[55]

In approaching the study of assassination from the standpoint of the rage and violence he has seen occur in therapy groups, Gerard Haigh concluded, "Violence is the ultimate desperate attempt to overcome separation. . . . The assassin's bullets fly across the interface between the outsiders and the insiders, carrying the message, 'Hey, hear me! Look at me! I want in!' "[56] Similarly, an hypothesis presented by Slomich and Kantor suggests that political leaders with charismatic magnetism appear at crisis points in American history and, because of their dynamic hopefulness, attract the wrath of dispossessed, alienated men who are frustrated sexually and interpersonally.[57] George Bach studied the dynamics of seventy-four spouse killers in five countries.[58] Among the factors he found to be significant, several seem relevant to the psychodynamics of assassins:

1. The murderers had rigid expectations and narrowly pre-scribed role demands for the spouse-victims. "Their fury

54. See the chapter in this volume by David Rothstein, "Presidential-Assassination Syndrome: A Psychiatric Study of the Threat, the Deed and the Message."
55. *Sirhan* v. *State of California*, 79, 6343.
56. G. V. Haigh, "Does Rage Require Violence" (Address to the Group Psychotherapy Association of Southern California, Los Angeles, April 27, 1969).
57. E. J. Slomich and R. E. Kantor, "Social Psychopathology of Political Assassination," *Bulletin of the Atomic Scientists* (March, 1969), pp. 9–12.
58. Bach, *op. cit.*

and bitterness are correspondingly intense when, thanks to some misconduct of the spoiler . . . their dreams are shattered."

2. The murderers tended to avoid impulsive, open displays of anger. Conventional ways of marital fighting were frightening and embarrassing to them. They were not good at aggressive negotiation. "Our subjects were on the whole, very secretive. When they felt disappointed in what the mate had done or failed to do, it was hard for them to show openly in full measure the depth of their pain, of their despair and their disappointments."

3. Rage was especially provoked by the spouse-victim being more socially popular than the shy, stay-at-home killer, or by the spouse-victim being seen as blocking the wish of the killer to "swing."

Envy. Hostile envy of the victim for having specific socioeconomic, political, and sexual advantages is a powerful motive for assassins. For example, the Kennedys are successful and honored in the political life of one of the most powerful countries in the world. The family is renowned for its warmth, cohesiveness, ambition, power, wealth, and tangible success. The Sirhans were unsuccessful and unknown in the political life of a small, ineffectual country. Sirhan's family has disintegrated. Of thirteen children, five are now living. The parents are divorced, and three of the brothers besides Sirhan have police records. Of his father it is said, "That under a façade of politeness and meekness . . . the father is a complex individual given to fits of temperament." "Neighbors remember that Sirhan's father, Bishara, beat his children with sticks and fists when they disobeyed him and once held a hot iron to one of Sirhan's heels." Of his mother, an old acquaintance in the Middle East said, "She loved her children, but she was a terribly harsh, narrow-minded and rigid woman."[59] Sirhan's sister died of leukemia in 1965, a loss which Sirhan felt deeply and which seems to have led to his poor grades and leaving college.

Robert Kennedy was known for his charm, aggressive outgoing personality, and physical prowess. He was married and had ten

59. *Life* 64 June 21, 1968, No. 25, pp. 25–34.

children. Sirhan had none of these assets or accomplishments. Robert Kennedy had mutually supportive, loving adult relationships with his wife, father, mother, sisters, and brothers; Sirhan lacked such relationships.

A similar case can be made for the relationship of Lee Oswald to John Kennedy. Oswald also lacked a father and was a supporter of a small country, Cuba, which he saw as the victim of unjust aggression from a large successful country, the United States. One source claims that both John Kennedy and Lee Oswald were fans of James Bond and were reading novels about him the night before their deaths. If true, this would demonstrate a common preoccupation with physical violence, sexual conquest, and romanticized international intrigue. But whereas John Kennedy, being powerful, successful, and rewarded might read Bond stories for entertainment and relaxation, Oswald's own powerlessness would make him an angry, jealous reader eager to turn a Bond fantasy into a violent reality.

Physical mobility and power were clearly important dimensions in the identities of John and Robert Kennedy and Sirhan. Sirhan's choice of race-horse exercising as a job and being a jockey as a career goal suggests that he was searching for a way to feel physically powerful. But he repeatedly fell from horses and finally received a head injury from an especially bad fall, which marked the end of that career. In contrast, Robert Kennedy was a public success in physical expression as well as in politics. He received much publicity for playing touch football, skiing, shooting rapids, etc., and he fathered eleven children. Rapid, powerful physical movement was a striking aspect of the six-day Arab-Israeli war with its dramatic plane and tank strikes. Sirhan's feelings of physical helplessness and vulnerability at the hands of his sadistic father, his physical injury and failure to become a jockey, his country's humiliating defeat by Israeli armor and air power, and his short stature and sexual inadequacy presumably burdened him with acute feelings of frustration and anger.

These comparisons suggest that assassins such as Sirhan and Oswald consciously or unconsciously felt acute hurt, envy, and loneliness to a degree that might provoke murderous rage. Each may have experienced the Kennedy family and Robert Kennedy as intolerable symbols of all that he lacked. Psychiatrist Frederic Wertham has used the term "magnicide" for the killing of somebody big, and sociologist David Riesman says that democracy, with its promise of equality, leaves many with the question, "Why are you so big and why am I so small?" Columnist Joseph Alsop describes "the hatred of excellence" that led at least one Athenian to want Aristides the Just ostracized and which he believes produced the assassinations of John Kennedy, Martin Luther King, and Robert Kennedy.[60]

In summary, the evidence suggests that the wish for tender caring and loving closeness and for athletic, aggressive, and sexual power were vitally important frustrated strivings in Sirhan and that they served as the basis for admiration, love, sexual attraction, bitter envy, outraged sense of betrayal, and finally murderous hostility toward Robert Kennedy.

Comparisons with Other Murder Cases. Truman Capote in *In Cold Blood* presented a moving and detailed picture of Dick Hickock and Perry Smith who murdered the Clutter family in Kansas.[61] Their conscious, self-declared motive was robbery and the wish to eliminate witnesses. The Clutters were a prosperous family who lived in an impressive house. Mr. Clutter and the children were known in the area for their success and active participation in the community. The Clutters may have represented for Dick and Perry what the Kennedys represented for Sirhan.

From Capote's descriptions of the life experiences of Dick and Perry, it seems clear that their motivations for killing were far deeper than those they stated. Again, extreme lack of love and practical support from parents contributed to their being grossly unprepared for close personal relationships and appropriately socialized, aggressive, masculine competence.

Physical prowess and motility were dominant themes in both their lives. Dick had been a high school athlete; Perry had been a motorcycle fan. Just as Sirhan had been injured falling from a horse, Dick had been disfigured in an automobile accident and Perry had been partially crippled by a fall from a motorcycle. The desires for the various symbols of love and power play important roles in the development of all men. But for Dick and Perry, these desires were frustrated, intensified, and perverted by a chain of

60. Joseph Alsop, "The Hatred of Excellence," *Los Angeles Times,* June 7, 1968.
61. Truman Capote, *In Cold Blood* (New York: Random House, 1965).

humiliating and enraging events, driving them to the point where robbing and killing the Clutter family took on tremendously overdetermined significance.

History and literature, of course, are replete with core myths and narratives about the killing of powerful fathers, father surrogates, and successful rivals. Physical mobility was the basis of the clash between Oedipus and Laius. When Laius tried to force Oedipus off a road, Oedipus retaliated. In the fight that followed, Oedipus killed his opponent whom he later discovered was his father. In ancient times, in Jordan today, and in some subcultures in the United States, the horse is a central symbol of physical power. Perry Smith's parents had been rodeo riders; Sirhan aspired to be a jockey. Perry crippled himself riding a motorcycle, his equivalent of his parents' horses; Sirhan repeatedly fell from horses and thus was finally defeated in his hopes of becoming a jockey. The interplay of these themes of deep hatred toward father figures and frustrated attempts to attain physical potency by means of cars, motorcycles, and horses further illustrate the role played by body image and sexual self-concept in killers.

A novel by Camus, *The Stranger*,[62] has become a modern classic because of the compressed, graphic way in which fundamental themes are presented. Sirhan has been described as "a loner" by classmates and by himself and certainly has his counterpart in Meursault, the stranger. Both men shot their victims with a pistol at close range, firing all the bullets they had. An apparent difference is not as real as it at first seems: while Sirhan shot Kennedy, a successful political figure, for overtly political reasons, Meursault shot an unknown Arab for no overt reason. Careful analysis of *The Stranger* reveals, however, that Meursault's motivation was in fact very similar to that postulated for Sirhan: repressed rage in response to a punitive and/or deserting father and. mother, coupled with a sense of physical and sexual fear and inadequacy.[63] Both men lacked healthy emotional relationships

62. Albert Camus, *The Stranger,* trans. S. Gilbert (New York: Vintage Books, 1954).

63. T. C. Greening, "Albert Camus: Authenticity Versus Alienation," in James F. T. Bugental, ed., *Challenges of Humanistic Psychology* (New York: McGraw-Hill, 1967, pp. 303–310); and N. Leites, "The Stranger," in W. Phillips, ed., *Art and Psychoanalysis* (New York: Criterion Books, 1957, pp. 247–270).

with their mothers and fathers, both were strangers and loners, both were unable to establish a loving, sexual relationship with a woman. Meursault's "unmotivated" murder of the Arab was in part a flight from intimacy with his girl friend Marie and an expression of his need to fight and kill a masculine figure he viewed as powerful and threatening.

The Assassin's State of Mind. Much of the testimony at the Sirhan trial, especially that of Dr. Bernard Diamond, dealt with the possibility that Sirhan was in a dissociative trance when he killed Kennedy. Fatigue after a hectic and frustrating day, confusion from the crowds, four drinks, and brightly lighted chandeliers reflected in floor-to-ceiling mirrors were cited as factors that could help trigger such a trance in someone with Sirhan's susceptibility. Dr. Diamond testified that he had been able to hypnotize Sirhan and induce him to re-experience the contorted rage, the shooting, and the choking when he was captured. Sirhan had supposedly paved the way for such episodes by intense Rosicrucian meditation while staring into a mirror flanked by flickering candles. During one such session he had seen the face of Robert Kennedy and had written over and over, "Kennedy must die."

Dr. Richardson found that Sirhan suffered from "erratic fluctuations" in his grasp of reality and from "vulnerability to ego states" in which he became paranoid and psychotic. Sirhan's Rorschach-test responses gave clear evidence of "sudden, gross breakdown in emotional control" and "sudden paranoid psychotic behavioral response"; "his personality structure or organization is highly fragile, so that his best and most adequate level of functioning is not stable or reliable, but subject to episodes of acute and rapid deterioration."[64]

The whole development of Sirhan's personality and crime clearly fits the clinical category of "catathymic crisis." The term "catathymic" was first used by Maier in 1912 to describe normal and abnormal complex-determined thinking; it had nothing to do with action. Wertham in 1937 and 1941 used the term "catathymic" to describe a new clinical entity, which he called "cata-

---

64. *Sirhan* v. *State of California*, 79, 6347–6349. See also Kaiser, *op. cit.*

thymic crisis."[65] Wertham ends his analysis of Gino, the matricide case described in *Dark Legend,* by diagnosing the boy's pathology as an instance of a catathymic crisis.

Catathymic crisis is a circumscribed mental disorder, psychologically determined, non-hereditary, without physical manifestations, and not necessarily occurring in a psychopathic constitution. Its central manifestation consists in the development of the idea that a violent act—against another person or against oneself—is the only solution to a profound emotional conflict whose real nature remains below the threshold of the consciousness of the patient.

This idea that a violent act must be committed appears as a definite plan accompanied by a tremendous urge to carry it out. The plan itself meets so much resistance in the individual's mind that he is apt to hesitate and delay. The violent climax is reached as a direct result of the inner tension. There is usually no provocation at all, or provocation which is utterly insufficient, in the outer situation. In some cases the victims are asleep. The patient's thinking may have delusional character in its rigidity and inaccessibility to logical reasoning. The violent act itself has a symbolic significance over and above its obvious meaning. . . .

The clinical development is usually as follows: an injurious life experience precipitates an unbearable and seemingly unsolvable inner situation leading to persistent and increasing emotional tension. The individual holds the outer situation entirely responsible for his inner tension. His thinking becomes more and more self-centered. With apparent suddenness, a crystallization point is reached in the idea that some violent act against another or against himself is 'the only way out.' After a prolonged inner struggle leading finally to extreme emotional tension, this violent act is carried out or attempted. It is followed immediately by an almost complete removal of the preceding emotional tension, but the patient does not gain insight at this time.

Wertham also applied this concept convincingly to the case of Robert Irwin. With Irwin and Gino, Wertham has been able to make follow-up observations for decades that substantiate his original diagnoses.

65. H. W. Maier, "Ueber Katathyme Wahnbilding und Paranoia," *Zeitskr. f. d. ges. Neurol. u. Psychiat.,* 13:555 (1912) and, "Ueber Einige Arten der Psychogenen Mechanismen," *op. cit.,* 82:193 (1923); Frederic Wertham, "The Catathymic Crisis: A Clinical Entity," *Archives of Neurology and Psychiatry,* 37 (April, 1937), pp. 974–978; and Wertham, *Dark Legend,* pp. 225–227.

The diagnosis of catathymic crisis has thus been in use for many years and it can be traced in many violent crimes and assassinations. Although the concept fits the data regarding Sirhan very closely, the expert witnesses did not introduce it at the trial. I do not know whether this was because they considered the concept and rejected it as inapplicable or because they were unfamiliar with it. Wertham agrees that "Sirhan is explainable only as a catathymic crisis" and believes that "in the Sirhan case it exists clearly as a psychological mechanism in the clinical setting of a political magnicide."[66]

The related concept of "episodic dyscontrol" has been used by Menninger and Mayman, and Blackman, Weiss and Lamberti to explain those acts of murder that seem to erupt unpredictably in certain kinds of seemingly well-controlled individuals.[67] In summary, they view "sudden murder" as an act which "can be understood theoretically as resultant from the interplay of the following factors: (a) strong surcharge of aggressive and hostile impulses; (b) relative weakness or lack of flexibility in the delaying mechanisms of the ego; (c) somewhat disturbed reality perception; (d) disturbed capacity for positive emotional investment in people; and (e) various unconscious meanings to the murderer of the victim." They are especially interested in those murderers who are not obviously irrational, delusional, or paranoid, but instead "who seem rational, coherent, and controlled, and yet whose homicidal acts have a bizarre, apparently senseless quality." These cases frequently perplex lawyers and juries because evidence of insanity is so often balanced by a kind of sanity. This becomes unusually pronounced in cases of men such as Guiteau and Sirhan where the juries, confused by the complexity, resorted to traditional bases of judgment and found both assassins sane and guilty.

Wittman describes the case of a young murderer who was similar both to Wertham's case of Robert Irwin and to Sirhan in having a devoutly orthodox religious mother, extremely puritanical attitudes toward sex, repressed hatred toward his mother for treat-

66. Frederic Wertham, personal communication to Thomas Greening (April 11, 1969).
67. K. Menninger and M. Mayman, "Episodic Dyscontrol: A Third Order of Stress Adaptation," *Bulletin of the Menninger Clinic*, 20, No. 4 (1956), p. 153; and Blackman, Weiss and Lamberti, *op. cit.*

ing him like a child, and a proneness to dissociative trances and violent fugue states.[68] Wittman rules out the diagnoses of simple schizophrenia and psychopathic personality, preferring to interpret it as "an hysterical fugue." This patient demonstrated the build-up of tension and the focusing into a violent, symbolically determined act, but lacked the premeditated rationalization present in true catathymic crises.

The patients in the studies cited above bear many resemblances to assassins such as Sirhan as far as their life history material and the final impulsiveness of their assaults. The major difference, of course, lies in the preplanning and consciously rigid focus on one victim which typifies the catathymic crisis case such as Sirhan, but is not present in the "sudden murderers" who demonstrate "episodic dyscontrol" without any intellectual context. The patients typically came from homes where the mother was "a domineering, overprotective figure who emphasized conformity to the rules of the social system." The father had been either "hostile, rejecting, overstrict, or indifferent to the patient." "Failing in his attempt to conform because of underlying feelings of inadequacy and hostility, the murderer-to-be tended to blame other people and to wander from place to place looking for greater opportunities. As a result, he felt quite consciously alone and isolated from other people."[69] The description fits Sirhan perfectly. What distinguishes the assassin is that he combines the pathological developmental background and superficially "sane" controls of the "sudden murderer" with an intellectualized focus on a major political figure and a capacity to plan his attack. Ironically, if an assassin were insane in blatant ways he might suddenly kill a stranger rather than a president. But an assassin's insanity is more severe and yet more disguised so that it unites with and is concealed by an intellectualized pseudosanity and will be satisfied only by producing a national tragedy as well as an individual murder.

Prediction and Prevention. Prevention is the goal, and all these studies and tragedies begin to give us guidelines for the prevention and detection of potential killers. Megargee, Cook, and Mendelsohn have developed an MMPI scale that discriminates over-

68. Wittman, *op. cit.*
69. Blackman, Weiss, and Lamberti, *op. cit.*

controlled, assaultive criminals from undercontrolled, assaultive criminals, nonassaultive criminals, and normals.[70] It also appears to assess "two personality constructs which are not normally found together, impulse control and hostile alienation" and which characterize assassins such as Sirhan. Hellman and Blackman found that the triad of enuresis, fire setting, and cruelty to animals was predictive of aggressive crimes against persons and urges that further statistical studies be made linking life-history data with criminal behavior.[71] Weinstein and Lyerly studied 137 men who made threats or gestures of assassination and found several variables that might be used in developing assessment methodology to predict such behavior in other individuals.

Computers and clinical hypotheses are now available to make possible increasingly sophisticated and thorough research. Psychological-test results and life-history data on living assassins such as Sirhan and Ray can be assembled and supplemented by partial data on deceased assassins. Patterns that emerge can be compared with patterns found among murderers of various types and men who threaten but do not attempt assassination. We have come a long way since Guiteau's time when the aftermath of assassination to was mostly a tabloid orgy, a circus of expert witnesses contradicting each other, and a ritualistic conviction of the villian as sane and punishable by death. Locked up in Sirhan and Ray and buried in Oswald's grave is information we must have. If it is worth a million dollars to us to give Sirhan a fair trial, it ought to be worth that and more to give the nation a fair chance to prevent the next assassination.

CONCLUSION

Although violence has progressed at a terrifying pace, and assassination along with it, we have also seen progress in our willingness and capacity to understand man's violence and its sources. Phrenology and the Devil are no longer used to explain why unknown citizens kill their leaders. Political motives alone do not account for these politically devastating crimes. The label

70. E. Megargee, P. Cook, and G. Mendelsohn, "Development and Validation of an MMPI Scale of Assaultiveness in Overcontrolled Individuals," *Journal of Abnormal Psychology,* 72 (1967), pp. 519–528.
71. D. Hellman and N. Blackman, *op. cit.*

"insane" has ceased to be an adequate explanation of such complex personal and social acts. The childhood traumas, unconscious conflicts, Oedipal turmoils, and sexual self-concepts of assassins are now accepted by the courts and the concerned public as meaningful areas for investigation. Modern psychology and jurisprudence have reached the point where our civilization can go beyond the simple analysis, punishment, and treatment of the individual assassin. By understanding the forces that made him and seeing how they rise out of the basic nature of our imperfect community of man, we can grasp more clearly the fact that each assassin is but a symptom of mankind's violence, pain, and loneliness. Our civilization produces the assassin and he tells us how far we still have to go.

part III

PUBLIC REACTIONS TO ASSASSINATIONS

Political Leaders and the Assassination of President Kennedy

Samuel C. Patterson

The assassination of the President of the United States in Dallas on November 22, 1963, was not a unique event in American history. Presidents Abraham Lincoln, James Garfield, and William McKinley were assassinated in office and, though there can be few who remember Lincoln's murder in 1865 or Garfield's assassination twenty-five years later, there are many people still alive who recall McKinley's assassination in 1901. The death of a president in office, even those who, like Franklin D. Roosevelt or Warren Harding, died in office of natural causes, is a shocking event. It is an event of political significance that affects a large part of the population in a profound way because it strikes at the deepest political loyalties, commitments, and fears of the masses of people.

The death of the central authority figure in national political systems, whether it be Louis XVI, Josef Stalin, George V, or the American president, produces a crisis of authority. The deaths of such rulers produce in their national populations widespread expressions of shock and disbelief, deep manifestations of personal grief and the occurrence of unusual political behavior. The latter may include unusual rallying to the new authority, extraordinary deification of the dead ruler and substantial ambivalence and anxiety regarding the causes of the ruler's demise. When King Edward VII of England died, it was said to be the

> Greatest sorrow England ever had
> When death took away our dear Dad;
> A king was he from head to sole
> Loved by the people one and all.[1]

---

1. Reported in Sebastian de Grazia, *The Political Community* (Chicago: University of Chicago Press, 1948), p. 113.

And the nature of reactions to the death of kings is also interestingly illustrated by Kingsley Martin's comments about the death of George V in 1936:

When George V died . . . no one who talked to his neighbor on the bus, to the charwoman washing the steps, or to the sightseers standing on the street corner could doubt the almost universal feeling of loss. Nor could any perceptive observer fail to notice the peculiarly personal character of this emotion. People who had never even seen the King and who had only heard his voice over the radio talked about him with tears in their eyes as if he were a personal friend or near relative cut off in his prime . . . I think the clue is to be found, perhaps, in a remark that one heard very frequently at the death of George V. People constantly reiterated that King George 'was a father to us all.'[2]

ASSASSINATION OF AMERICAN PRESIDENTS

Because of its illegitimate and unexpected character, assassination of the ruler probably greatly exacerbates public reactions. In America, assassination of the president or attempts to assassinate him are fairly recurrent events. In addition to the presidents who died from wounds inflicted by assassins, attempts to assassinate Presidents Andrew Jackson, Franklin D. Roosevelt, Harry S Truman and former President Theodore Roosevelt in 1912 nearly succeeded. And the assassinations of Lincoln, Garfield, McKinley, and John F. Kennedy (and, interestingly, potential president Robert F. Kennedy) have followed a very similar pattern.[3] It is announced that the president is to make a public appearance in a crowded and accessible place. Either at that public place, or in the course of traveling there, a demented and unnoticed little man lurks in hiding with a rifle or emerges suddenly from the crowd with a pistol, and shots are fired. The president is mortally wounded.

The news of the wounding of the president flashes across the country; crowds gather and mill around in city streets. The public reaction is one of astonishment, great anxiety, and incredulity.

2. Kingsley Martin, *The Magic of Monarchy* (New York: Alfred A. Knopf, 1937), pp. 13–14. Also reported in de Grazia, *op. cit.*, pp. 113–114.
3. Robert J. Donovan, *The Assassins* (New York: Harper & Brothers, 1952), pp. 1–7.

Many think a lunatic did it but many attribute the falling of the leader to a heinous conspiracy. Conspirators are sought, sometimes ruthlessly. The president dies after herculean attempts at medical restoration. Public grief swells to crescendo. Orations, eulogies, and literature pour from pulpits, embassies, and presses. In myth, the fallen president is a hero. The trial of the assassin (or the assassin's assassin) feeds public ambivalence and the urge for retribution. But political authority, highly institutionalized, is soon restored, and reassurance and quiescence fairly quickly regained. The crisis has passed.

This is essentially the scenario for events during and after the assassination of President Lincoln by John Wilkes Booth. That event has produced a mountainous literature and is very well known.[4] Less well understood is the fact that the same scenario fits the assassinations of the less lionized American Presidents— Garfield and McKinley. President Garfield was shot on July 2, 1881 by Charles J. Guiteau, a paranoid schizophrenic (he was not, apparently, a disappointed officeseeker). Garfield was waiting for a train in Washington's Baltimore and Potomac Station on his way to attending the commencement at Williams College, his alma mater. Guiteau appeared suddenly, shot Garfield mortally, and was immediately caught. He was tried and hanged. The reactions to Garfield's death are now familiar:

Americans were deeply shocked by the assassination. Within half an hour of the shooting, crowds gathered outside newspaper offices in the larger cities, waiting for telegraphic bulletins to be posted. Along Philadelphia's Chestnut Street and in New York's printing house square, crowds filled sidewalks and despite a hot sun spilled over into roadways. At first it was assumed that the President had died, and in New York flags were lowered; at eleven, however, with the arrival of more accurate news, they were raised and public interest—if it were possible—increased. Six policemen were stationed at each of New York's newspaper offices, clearing a path for pedestrians through the dense crowd. The *Tribune* reported that streetcar drivers on Park Row had to bring their horses to a walk and then shout themselves hoarse in an effort to move through the tightly packed street. By noon,

4. For illustrations see Ida M. Tarbell, *The Life of Abraham Lincoln,* IV (New York: Lincoln Historical Society, 1895), pp. 41–58; and Jim Bishop, *The Day Lincoln Was Shot* (New York: Harper & Brothers, 1955).

extras had been set in type, printed, and sold out. By noon, as well, the President, a somewhat colorless figure a few hours before, had become a leader of towering stature.[5]

There followed a remarkable outpouring of public grief and mourning, and "Garfield's name and imposing bearded head were soon to be found embossed on trays and enamels, etched in glass, and engraved on steel."[6]

In September, 1901, William McKinley visited the Temple of Music at the Buffalo Exposition for a public reception. Late in the afternoon on the day of the reception, in the midst of a very large crowd, Leon Czolgosz, a deranged anarchist son of Polish immigrants, suddenly appeared immediately in front of the President and shot him with a .32-caliber revolver. He died a little more than a week later. Margaret Leech said, "The news of the attack on the President spread horror throughout the nation . . . Americans were wonderfully conscious of a unity which had effaced their political differences."[7] There was a search for conspirators and several anarchists including Emma Goldman were arrested.

> Never in history had the Union of the States been joined in such universal sorrow. North and South, East and West, the people mourned a father and a friend, and the fervent strains of "Nearer, My God, to Thee" floated, like a prayer and a leavetaking, above the half-masted flags in every city and town . . . Entranced and regretful, they remembered McKinley's firm, unquestioning faith; his kindly, frock-coated dignity; his accessibility and dedication to the people . . . The eulogies reverberated, as orators and journalists and poets extolled the virtue of an upright life, a death of Christian fortitude.[8]

The parallels these episodes provide cannot be lost on those who are familiar with the events in Dallas in the autumn of 1963 when President Kennedy was slain by assassin Lee Harvey Oswald. They drive us to explore the crisis of authority that is precipitated by the assassination of the chief executive. However, we need not limit our historical parallels to assassinated presi-

---

5. Charles E. Rosenberg, *The Trial of the Assassin Guiteau* (Chicago: University of Chicago Press, 1968), pp. 6–7.
6. *Ibid.,* p. 11.
7. Margaret Leech, *In the Days of McKinley* (New York: Harper & Brothers, 1959), p. 597.
8. *Ibid.,* pp. 602–603.

dents. There is ample evidence that reactions to the deaths of presidents whose demise was natural follow a pattern much like those of the assassinated presidents. Difficult as it may be to believe in historical perspective, reactions to the death of Warren G. Harding appear to have been very similar to those we have considered, except, of course, no assassin's trial or death prolonged the suspense. And it is very clear that the death of President Franklin D. Roosevelt produced public reactions much like those following the assassination of President Kennedy.[9]

THE ROLE OF THE PRESIDENT

How can the remarkable public reactions to the death of presidents be accounted for, and what do they mean? The completely frank answer is that in any full sense we do not know. It is easier to name the phenomenon than it is to explain the causes or consequences. Yet it is eminently plain that the chief executive of a nation, whether he is a president or a king, a tsar or a dictator, and even if he is thought not to be very competent while he is alive, is the linchpin of political systems in some very fundamental ways.

The American president is distinguished from other political figures and from other popular personages by his extraordinary salience in public awareness. Only a minuscule proportion of the American public is incapable of identifying the president, and his visibility far exceeds that of other political leaders. He is the centerpiece in the national public drama of events, and his "dramaturgical jousts with public problems make the world understandable and convey the promise of collective accomplishments to masses who are bewildered, uncertain, and alone."[10] The salience of the president makes him the recipient of great public respect,

9. On Harding and FDR, see Harold Orlansky, "Reactions to the Death of President Roosevelt," *Journal of Social Psychology*, 26 (November, 1947), pp. 235–266.

10. Murray Edelman, *The Symbolic Uses of Politics* (Urbana: University of Illinois Press, 1964), p. 91, and his essay co-authored with Rita James Simon in this volume. See also Fred I. Greenstein, "Popular Images of the President," *American Journal of Psychiatry*, 122 (November, 1965), pp. 524–525; William Stephenson, *The Play Theory of Mass Communication* (Chicago: University of Chicago Press, 1967), pp. 94–95; and Gottfried Dietze, "Will the Presidency Incite Assassination?" *Ethics*, 76 (October, 1965), pp. 14–32.

especially among the young. Benevolent attitudes toward political authority generally, and especially toward the president, are fundamental attributes of the political socialization of Americans.[11] Yet Presidents Truman and Lyndon Johnson illustrate that, particularly under the persistent strain of prolonged and unpopular limited wars in the Far East, the president may be the focal point for very substantial public hostility. Even so, the normal condition of public affect toward the president seems to be positive. Even the most unpopular postwar presidents have acquired low evaluations of their performance only after having been accorded extraordinary public acclaim. And there is a very pronounced tendency for Americans to rally to the support of the President in times of crisis, even if presidential action in response to a crisis is later assessed to have been in error. For instance, support for President Eisenhower actually increased substantially following the U-2 incident; and public approval of President Kennedy rose in about the same amounts following the Bay of Pigs invasion, widely thought to have been a major error, and the Cuban missile crisis, widely accorded acclaim as a correct decision.[12]

The deeper motivational significance of the president for Americans is not too well understood but it seems apparent that the symbolic role of the president in a psychic sense is vital to an accounting of the relative stability of the American political system and to an explanation of the crucial role of the president in it. The president seems to provide an indispensible cognitive linkage between the citizens and the government, an outlet for citizens'

11. Fred I. Greenstein, *Children and Politics* (New Haven: Yale University Press, 1965), pp. 27–54; Robert D. Hess and Judith V. Torney, *The Development of Political Attitudes in Children* (Chicago: Aldine Publishing Company, 1967), pp. 32–59; and David Easton and Jack Dennis, *Children in the Political System* (New York: McGraw-Hill, 1969), pp. 165–208. A major exception to the benevolent-leader image of the president among children is to be found among the children of the Appalachian poor. See Dean Jaros, Herbert Hirsch, and Frederic J. Fleron, Jr., "The Malevolent Leader: Political Socialization in an American Sub-Culture," *American Political Science Review*, 62 (June, 1968), pp. 564–575. Also, compare the attitudes of French children toward General de Gaulle analyzed by Charles Roig and F. Billon-Grand, *La Socialisation Politique des Enfants* (Paris: Librairie Armand Colin, 1968), pp. 74–84.

12. Greenstein, "Popular Images of the President," *loc. cit.,* pp. 525–526; and Fred E. Katz and Fern V. Piret, "Circuitous Participation in Politics," *American Journal of Sociology,* 69 (January, 1964), pp. 367–373.

emotional discharge, a symbolic focus for political identification and participation, and a symbol of national unity.[13] Because he can personify and reify the complexities of human events and experiences and dramatize them for civic consumption, the president can supply reassurance that things are under control, provide a symbol of aspirations and serve as a symbol of national unity.[14]

THE KENNEDY ASSASSINATION
AND THE WARREN REPORT

Public reactions to the assassination of President Kennedy clearly indicate that the president is a significant focus of a national loyalty that appears to be very deeply rooted in Americans. Reactions of shock and incredulity on the part of many Americans followed the bizarre events in Dallas in the late fall of 1963. The murder of the President was followed by the killing of the alleged assassin, Lee Harvey Oswald, by Jack Ruby before the eyes of millions of television viewers. The public reaction is partly illustrated by the sharp controversy that has not subsided over the facts of the case. The adequacy of the official report of the Warren Commission has been questioned in a variety of ways and sizable proportions of adult-population samples express disagreement with the Commission's finding that Oswald acted alone.[15] The public opinion data shown in Table 1, drawn from surveys by the Gallup poll and the Harris survey, indicate the trends in public attitudes toward the Warren Report and its conclusions. Although in every survey large proportions of Americans sampled thought Oswald was the guilty assassin, public attitudes have fluctuated considerably in regard to the conspiratorial aspects of the assassination and the completeness of the Warren Report. Just after the assassination more than half of Americans interviewed thought Oswald had had accomplices, although, with the Report of the Warren Commis-

13. Greenstein, "Popular Images of the President," *loc. cit.,* pp. 527–528.
14. Edelman, *op. cit.,* p. 78; and Erwin C. Hargrove, "Popular Leadership in the Anglo-American Democracies," in *Political Leadership in Industrialized Societies,* Lewis J. Edinger ed. (New York: John Wiley & Sons, 1967), pp. 188–192.
15. See *Report of the President's Commission on the Assassination of President John F. Kennedy* (Washington, D.C.: United States Government Printing Office, 1964).

TABLE 1

Public Attitudes Toward Oswald and the Warren Report

(in percentages)

Assassination Attitudes	November, 1963	September, 1964	October, 1964	September, 1966	December, 1966	February, 1967	May, 1967	September, 1967
Was the Assassination a conspiracy?								
Oswald acted on his own	29	45	56	34	36	35	19	24
Oswald had accomplices	52	40	31	46	64	44	66	60
Uncertain	19	15	13	20		21	15	16
Was Oswald Guilty?								
Yes	74	76	87	69	*	70	*	*
No	3	3	2	3		7		
Not sure	23	21	11	28		23		
How Adequate Was the Work of the Warren Commission?								
Full story in Report	*	*	45	32	*	30	18	24
Still unanswered questions			45	54		59	72	64
Not sure			10	14		11	10	12

* Data not available.

Sources: American Institute of Public Opinion (Gallup poll) and Harris survey.

sion, more than half of the people temporarily accepted the Report's conclusion that Oswald acted alone. But in 1966 and 1967 that conviction steadily eroded, so that by late 1967 only a fourth of the public believed there had been no conspiracy to assassinate President Kennedy. Similarly, confidence that the full story about the assassination had been unearthed by the Warren Commission declined after late 1964 (although even then less than half of the public apparently believed the report was thorough), and by September, 1967, two-thirds of the people interviewed thought there still were questions about the assassination that were not adequately answered.

The prolonged controversy about the events surrounding the assassination of President Kennedy, fed by a spate of books presenting interpretations in conflict with the Warren Commission findings (some of them patently fanatical), and centering around the so-called two assassin theory, as well as by the celebrated legal proceedings initiated by district attorney James Garrison in New Orleans, must have contributed heavily to the erosion of public confidence in the Warren Report. Speculation about and interpretation of the events of the assassination are reactions of an important kind, and these reactions are familiar to anyone who remembers or has studied the aftermaths of the assassinations of Lincoln, Garfield, and McKinley. Public interest in these speculations and interpretations reflects the permanence of the profound influence of a presidential assassination and the lasting nature of public grief. The controversial interpretations of the events in Dallas written by Epstein, Lane, Sauvage, Joesten, Weisberg, Manchester, and others are more or less useful to us as explications of eyewitness behavior, the use and abuse of evidence, the operation of *ad hoc* commissions, the reactions of the immediate presidential family and his close friends to a president's death, the adequacy of the Secret Service, the FBI, and local police forces, and some of the myth and mystique that surrounds the death of a national leader.[16] Their conflicting interpretations of the facts involved in

16. The most important critiques of the report of the Warren Commission are the following: Alexander M. Bickel, "The Failure of the Warren Report," *Commentary*, 42 (October, 1966), pp. 31–39; Thomas G. Buchanan, *Who Killed Kennedy?* (New York: G. P. Putnam's Sons, 1964); Edward Jay Epstein, *Inquest* (New York: Viking Press, 1966); Henry

the assassination, and their sharp, sometimes myopic criticism of the Warren Commission may have helped to erode public confidence in the Commission and enhance the acceptability of conspiratorial interpretations in the mass public. But they are not very useful in helping us better to understand and explain reactions to the assassination in the general public or among political leaders.

PUBLIC REACTIONS TO THE ASSASSINATION

Our understanding of the importance of the assassination of a president as it reveals some basic patterns of political beliefs and attitudes is enhanced by a body of evidence quite different from the continuing fulminations and hypothecations about the adequacy of the report of the Warren Commission. The assassination of President Kennedy certainly was unique in American history in one sense: there was set in motion with amazing rapidity, in separate parts of the country as well as nationwide, research by social scientists about the immediate reactions people had to the momentous event of the assassination. Psychologists, sociologists, psychiatrists and political scientists conducted a large number of detailed investigations of public attitudes, many of them initiated within hours or days after the Dallas event. One study involved interviews with a sample of the entire adult population of the country. Other social scientists interviewed college students, school

Fairlie, "No Conspiracy, But—Two Assassins, Perhaps?" New York *Times Magazine* (September 11, 1966), pp. 52–55, 154–159; Renatus Hartogs and Lucy Freeman, *The Two Assassins* (New York: Thomas Y. Crowell, 1965); Gerald R. Ford and John R. Stiles, *Portrait of the Assassin* (New York: Simon & Schuster, 1965); Joachim Joesten, *Oswald: Assassin or Fall Guy?* (New York: Marzani & Munsell, 1964); Mark Lane, *Rush to Judgment* (New York: Holt, Rinehart & Winston, 1966; Lincoln Lawrence, *Were We Controlled?* (New Hyde Park, N.Y.: University Books, 1967); Richard Warren Lewis and Lawrence Schiller, *The Scavengers and Critics of the Warren Report* (New York: Delacorte Press, 1967); William Manchester, *The Death of a President* (New York: Harper & Row, 1967); Sylvia Meagher, *Accessories After the Fact* (Indianapolis: Bobbs-Merrill, 1967); Richard H. Popkin, "The Second Oswald: The Case of a Conspiracy Theory," *New York Review of Books,* 7 (July 28, 1966), pp. 11–22; Charles Roberts, *The Truth About the Assassination* (New York: Grosset & Dunlap, 1967); Léo Sauvage, *The Oswald Affair* (Cleveland: World, 1966); Harold Weisberg, *Whitewash: The Report on the Warren Report* (New York: Dell, 1965); and, Stephen White, *Should We Now Beli. ve the Warren Report?* (New York: Macmillan, 1968).

children, psychoanalytic patients, television viewers and workers on the job. These investigations all help to establish the very wide and deep national identifications and commitments that were laid bare by the assassination of President Kennedy and they indicate the very personal nature of grief that follows the death of the President.[17]

The research on public reactions to the assassination clearly establishes the salience of the chief executive in a time of great crisis. Public awareness of the event of President Kennedy's assassination occurred very rapidly and was extraordinarily widespread. Within less than six hours after the President was shot very nearly every American interviewed by the National Opinion Research Center (NORC) had heard the news. Furthermore, a very unusual degree of *public* concern was exhibited by extraordinary proportions of citizens whose normal concerns center around their own private lives, their personal health and the problems of their families and friends. Grief was widespread. The grief experienced by citizens over the President's death appeared to be the kind felt at the death of a friend or member of the family and the patterns of grief did not appear to be unusual. It appears that public grief persisted for a long period of time. Two years after the event the Harris survey reported that 73 per cent of adult Americans still

17. Two books contain most of the reports of these studies: Bradley S. Greenberg and Edwin B. Parker, eds., *The Kennedy Assassination and the American Public* (Stanford: Stanford University Press, 1965); and Martha Wolfenstein and Gilbert Kliman, eds., *Children and the Death of a President* (Garden City, N.Y.: Doubleday, 1965). Other research reports include: David Kirschner, "The Death of a President: Reactions of Psychoanalytic Patients," *Behavioral Science,* 10 (January, 1965), pp. 1–6; D. A. Rothstein, "Presidential Assassination Syndrome," *Archives of General Psychiatry,* 11 (September, 1964), pp. 245–254; Lawrence S. Wrightsman and Frank C. Noble, "Reactions to the President's Assassination and Changes in Philosophies of Human Nature," *Psychological Reports,* 16 (February, 1965), pp. 159–162; Thomas J. Banta, "The Kennedy Assassination: Early Thoughts and Emotions," *Public Opinion Quarterly,* 28 (Summer, 1964), pp. 216–224; Karen Orren and Paul Peterson, "Presidential Assassination: A Case Study in the Dynamics of Political Socialization," *Journal of Politics,* 29 (May, 1967), pp. 388–404; Roberta S. Sigel, "Image of a President: Some Insights into the Political Views of School Children," *American Political Science Review,* 62 (March, 1968), pp. 216–226; and Kurt W. Back and Judith Saravay, "From Bright Ideas to Social Research: Studies of the Kennedy Assassination," *Public Opinion Quarterly,* 31 (Summer, 1967), pp. 253–264.

often felt bad about the assassination. Although few Americans associated the assassination with extremist political groups, a sizable proportion resorted to conspiratorial interpretations of the event. However, most citizens expressed the belief that Oswald's murder was to be regretted and the hope that Ruby would be treated with justice and fair play.

PARTISAN DIFFERENCES IN PUBLIC REACTIONS

While public shock and grief following the assassination probably were unprecedented, given the rapid and wide diffusion of the news, public reactions did vary. Clearly, some Americans were more touched by the death of the President than others. Research on the assassination involved attempts at partial explanations of variations in reactions in terms of differences in the sex, race, age, social class and political preference of survey respondents. In general, the varied investigations demonstrated that women were more emotionally upset by the news of the assassination than men; children were at least as upset as adults, if not more upset; there was an inverse relationship between social class and intensity of feelings and beliefs about the President's death; and Negroes grieved more than whites. Most studies found considerable differences between the reactions of Democrats and Republicans, with Democrats reporting more pronounced emotional and physical effects than Republicans. In summarizing the leading studies of public reactions to the assassination, Greenberg and Parker concluded with respect to the impact of political preferences that their effects were normal—that "political predispositions functioned almost as they function in less dramatic circumstances."[18] But they also pointed out that the research on public reactions did not sufficiently involve, nor are ex post facto studies particularly amenable to, multivariate analysis. The suggested, in the case of race differences for instance, that the greater intensity of reactions among black Americans may have been a function of the fact that a very large proportion of Negroes are Democrats and that Democrats in general reacted more intensely to the assassination.[19] Again, there

18. Bradley S. Greenberg and Edwin B. Parker, "Social Research on the Kennedy Assassination," in Greenberg and Parker, *op. cit.,* pp. 375–376.
19. *Ibid.,* p. 376.

is some evidence to suggest the possibility that attitudes toward Kennedy as a president and support of his policies affected reactions to the assassination to some extent independent from differences in party preferences.[20]

It does not detract from analysis of the integrative role of the American presidency and the psychic importance of the president in sustaining national unity to observe political cleavages, especially differences between the two parties, in attitudes toward the president and indeed to his assassination. What our research on the role of the presidency in American national life lacks is careful analysis of the effects of significant conflicts about that role, and the research on public reactions to the assassination of President Kennedy unfortunately does not help very much to answer questions about cleavage effects.[21] Evaluation of the president is a very partisan matter. Although President Kennedy was a very popular President, his popularity was largely due to his being held in very high esteem by Democrats. Support for President Kennedy was much lower among Republicans throughout his presidency and dropped particularly among Republicans on the eve of the assassination (see Figure 1). If Republicans were relatively less touched by Kennedy's death than Democrats, it seems possible that this partisan difference occurred in part, at least, because they held him in lower esteem while he was alive.

Although the research on partisan differences in reactions to the assassination are not amenable to convenient summary, some illustrations of them can be supplied.[22] Sheatsley and Feldman, whose

20. See Lee F. Anderson and Emerson Moran, "Audience Perceptions of Radio and Television Objectivity," and Norma Feshbach and Seymour Feshbach, "Personality and Political Values: A Study of Reactions to Two Accused Assassins," in Greenberg and Parker, *op. cit.,* pp. 142–146 and 291–293.

21. David O. Sears, "Effects of the Assassination of President Kennedy on Political Partisanship," in Greenberg and Parker, *op. cit.,* pp. 305–326; and Philip E. Converse and Georges Dupeux, "De Gaulle and Eisenhower: The Public Image of the Victorious General," in Angus Campbell et al., *Elections and the Political Order* (New York: John Wiley & Sons, 1966), pp. 330–333.

22. The following items of information are drawn from Greenberg and Parker, *op. cit.,* pp. 158–159, 186, 211, 292, 342. Compare party differences in reactions to President Roosevelt's death in Dorothea E. Johannsen, "Reactions to the Death of President Roosevelt," *Journal of Abnormal and Social Psychology,* 41 (April, 1946), pp. 218–222.

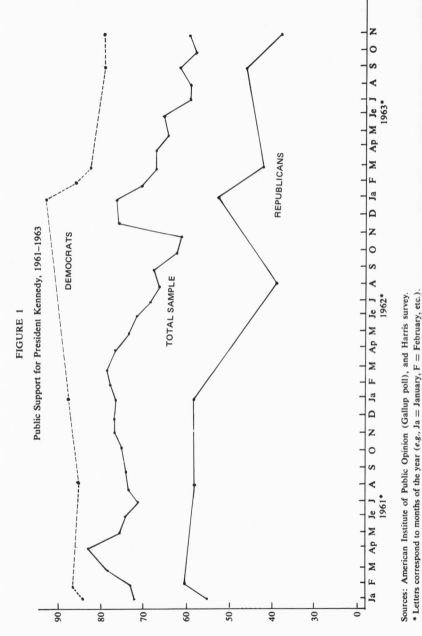

FIGURE 1

Public Support for President Kennedy, 1961–1963

Sources: American Institute of Public Opinion (Gallup poll), and Harris survey.
* Letters correspond to months of the year (*e.g.*, Ja = January, F = February, etc.).

data came from an NORC national sample of 1,384 adult respondents, did not use the customary party identification categories. However, their analysis did indicate that pro-Kennedy respondents reported physical and emotional symptoms stemming from the assassination much more than did non-Kennedy supporters. For instance, more than half of the pro-Kennedy respondents, but less than a third of the non-Kennedy respondents, reported that they did not feel like eating during the four days after the assassination. About 70 per cent of the pro-Kennedy respondents reported they felt very nervous and tense, compared with only about 56 per cent of the non-Kennedy respondents. Again, two-thirds of the pro-Kennedy respondents reported they felt sort of dazed and numb, while only about 46 per cent of the non-Kennedy respondents reported this immediate reaction. Bonjean, Hill, and Martin found differences of the same kind between Dallas respondents who had preferred Kennedy and those who had preferred Nixon in 1960, although the Dallasites' political differences were more muted than was the case in the national sample data. Sigel found that children in Detroit exhibited partisan differences in their emotional reactions to the assassination, though not very marked differences overall. Feshbach and Feshbach found a sharp party difference among college students in those who were "extremely upset," largely because of great difference between Democratic and Republican female students. Sears was able to show from an investigation of the effects of the assassination on the partisanship of a small sample of students that "the clearest effect of the assassination was a weakening of Republicans' partisanship."[23] Hurn and Messer demonstrated sharp differences in grief responses between Chicago college students and parents who highly approved of Kennedy's presidency and those who exhibited relatively low approval, regardless of the respondents' levels of political involvement. Finally, Pratt and Lane found sharp party differences among male and female students at three Eastern colleges, with Democrats much more likely still to be "in mourning" in the January, 1964 interviews than Republicans.[24]

23. Greenberg and Parker, *op. cit.*, p. 316.
24. Carolyn Pratt and Robert E. Lane, "Patterns of Closure: College Students' Return to Political 'Normalcy,' " in Wolfenstein and Kliman, *op. cit.*, pp. 164–165.

In addition, some studies suggested that immediate beliefs and attitudes about the events of the assassination were affected by differences in party identifications. Coleman and Hollander "found that people who had voted for Nixon formed less extreme beliefs, and subsequently changed them less, than those who had voted for Kennedy."[25] Nationwide and Dallas surveys provided data indicating that the death of President Kennedy was, to Democrats, a more personal matter than for Republicans and that Democrats worried more than Republicans about their own lives and the country's future. And Anderson and Moran showed that significant party differences existed in perceptions of bias in the coverage of the assassination events by the mass media.

POLITICAL LEADERS AND THE ASSASSINATION

Interparty differences in reactions to political events, and preeminently in reaction to the assassination of a very partisan leader, should have been greater among political leaders than in the mass public. We already have substantial evidence of the significant differences over political issues that can be shown to separate Democratic and Republican leaders in ways that do not so notably distinguish rank-and-file partisans.[26] It seems reasonable to think that political leaders responded to the assassination of President Kennedy in a more partisan way than would have been true in the general population. Unfortunately, variables discriminating among different political strata were not utilized in most analyses of reactions to the assassination. If the highly politicized strata of the population, the politically active subculture, has a particularly critical role to play in national political integration, it would be theoretically important to know if their reactions to crises like that of a presidential assassination differed from the response of the mass public. Woefully, the time has passed when the kinds of data we would like to have about political leaders' reactions to the assassination could have been gathered. For this purpose, we have

25. Greenberg and Parker, *op. cit.,* p. 374.
26. For instance, see Herbert McClosky, Paul J. Hoffmann, and Rose-mary O'Hara, "Issue Conflict and Consensus Among Party Leaders and Followers," *American Political Science Review,* 54 (June, 1960), pp. 406–427; and, Herbert McClosky, "Consensus and Ideology in American Politics," *American Political Science Review,* 58 (June, 1964), pp. 361–382.

available only a very limited set of data for a very small and restricted group of political leaders. The small study of these leaders must be taken for what it is and for what it is not. The available data restrict the kinds of analyses that would be maximally desirable, because the variables are few and the frequencies are small. The data, furthermore, are not directly comparable with studies that have been based upon other samples. Regardless of their drawbacks, however, these are apparently the only data available about political leaders' reactions to the assassination.

In the late spring of 1964, the Laboratory for Political Research at the University of Iowa had occasion to interview a sampling of Illinois legislators in connection with a study of relationships between legislators and lobbyists.[27] The timing of these interviews allowed us to include a series of questions inquiring about the reactions of these legislators to the assassination. These data are unique in making it possible to allow some assessment of the reactions of some political leaders to Kennedy's assassination, since other research on the assassination had involved people in general, most of whom were not politically active. Legislators are by definition politically active and involved. We can, therefore, roughly compare legislators' reactions to those of people in the general public. We do not know to what extent Illinois legislators' attitudes reflected those of political activists or public leaders, generally, but analyzing them does provide us with one example and is useful in the absence of data for a wider sample of political leaders.

Our study of these Illinois political leaders provided the following kinds of information: (1) attitude toward the assassination,

27. The data were gathered by Ronald D. Hedlund as part of the continuing legislative research program of the Laboratory for Political Research. The interview data were acquired by the use of mailed questionnaires. Two waves of questionnaires were mailed to the House members of the 72nd Illinois General Assembly in April and May, 1964. Thirty-four per cent returned usable questionnaires. This is not a probability sample and we cannot infer from the sample to the entire House in any strict sense. This is not our main purpose; rather, we wished to compare a group of Democratic leaders with a group of Republican leaders. The sample reflects the occupational and educational composition of the House very closely, but it contains a higher proportion of Republicans than did the entire House, as well as a somewhat higher proportion of downstate (non-Cook County) legislators.

which was measured by asking them to indicate their agreement or disagreement with eleven statements; (2) the political party affiliations, occupations, and religious affiliations of the legislators; (3) ideological orientation, which was measured by asking legislators to indicate their agreement or disagreement with five statements having to do with the extent of the role of the federal and state governments in domestic and foreign affairs. We analyzed these variables in such a way as to tell us what kinds of reactions were reflected toward the assassination among those in our sample of political leaders, whether being a Republican or a Democrat affected these reactions, to what extent Catholics reacted differently from Protestants, whether liberals were different from conservatives in their reactions to the President's death, and whether differences in occupations influenced attitudes toward Oswald or Ruby. Then we wanted to know how, if at all, these variables worked together. For instance, if we found Democrats reacting differently from Republicans, was this because of their party affiliation or because (since Democrats tend to be Catholics and Republicans Protestants) of differences in religious affiliation?

LEADERS' REACTIONS TO THE ASSASSINATION

Our questions about the assassination can be divided conveniently into three more general categories. The first related to the immediate personal reactions to the death of the President as experienced by these political leaders. The second involved attitudes toward Oswald and Ruby. The third had to do with the political leaders' views regarding the implications of the assassination for the stability of the political system, for an increase in political extremism, and for the strength of the government. It is clear from these indicators that even though the interviews occurred about six months after the events in Dallas, these political leaders expressed attitudes that showed the profound effects of these events.

Figure 2 shows in graphic form the extent of personal reactions to Kennedy's death. An overwhelming proportion of these political leaders (85 per cent) reported a significant emotional reaction to the assassination. In like manner, the NORC study of a sample of the adult population of the entire country indicated that most Americans experienced some physical and emotional symptoms

FIGURE 2

Reactions to the Assassination of President Kennedy

My main feeling about the President's murder was one of sadness—I felt sick.

When I first heard the news of the President's assassination, I didn't believe it could be true.

I didn't believe anything like the assassination of the President could ever happen in this country.

When I first heard the news of the President's assassination, I felt as if the whole world were caving in.

The assassination of the President didn't particularly concern me.

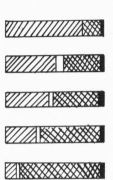

Attitudes Toward Lee Oswald and Jack Ruby

The best thing that could be done with Jack Ruby would be to sentence him to the electric chair.

The murder of Lee Oswald was just as much a disaster as the assassination of President Kennedy.

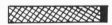

The killing of Oswald by Ruby was just as well because anyone who would murder President Kennedy deserves what he gets.

Attitudes Toward the Implications of the Kennedy Assassination

The change-over from Kennedy to Johnson proves the basic stability of our system.

The idea that the assassination of the President indicates a serious increase in dangerous political extremism is bunk.

The fact that a President was assassinated indicates a serious weakness in the governmental system in our country.

▨▨ Agree   ☐ Undecided   ▨▨ Disagree   ■ No Response

during the four days following the assassination. About two-thirds of the legislators indicated disbelief in the news of the assassination, and more than 40 per cent indicated that they did not believe anything like a presidential assassination could ever happen in this country. More than a quarter of them felt the impact of the assassination in apparently more than a personal sense—indicating that they felt this was a major disaster, that the "whole world was caving in." Only a very small number said the assassination did not concern them very much.

Only three questions in the interviews dealt with attitudes toward Oswald and Ruby and the results are not entirely unambiguous. As Figure 2 makes clear, all the legislators who responded disagreed with the notion that Oswald "got what he deserved" at the hands of Ruby. There was a division of attitudes regarding the importance of Oswald's murder, although the legislators were somewhat inclined to feel that Oswald's assassination was not as serious a disaster as the murder of the President. Half of these political leaders agreed that Ruby should be sentenced to be executed, a proportion substantially higher than was the case in the NORC general-population survey administered immediately following the assassination. These findings for political leaders can be compared with the general public by examining the following statement from the report of the NORC study:

Reactions to the shooting of Oswald himself provide reassuring evidence of the continued faith and belief of the great majority of Americans in the traditions of justice and fair play. We noted earlier that very few people indeed mentioned hatred of the assassin or a desire for revenge among their first reactions to the assassination of the President. Now, when asked to describe in their own words their feelings when they first saw or heard of the shooting of Oswald, less than 20 percent gloated over his death or expressed regret that he did not suffer more. About a third specifically stated their sorrow that he had been deprived of due process and a fair trial, while another third regretted that his death now make it impossible ever to learn the truth. With respect to his slayer, Jack Ruby, a majority (53 percent) specifically stated in their own words that he should stand trial, receive due process, and let the court decide his fate; 15 percent said he should be executed; and 20 percent that he should be punished or treated just like anyone else. Only 4 percent expressed the belief that he should be punished lightly or go free.[28]

Apparently, Illinois legislators were more inclined to believe that Ruby should be executed than people generally, though this differ-

28. Greenberg and Parker, *op. cit.*, p. 165.

ence between political leaders and the general public may have been enhanced by the passage of time.

The political leaders were in near unanimity in their belief that the transition between the Kennedy and Johnson administrations demonstrated the basic stability of the political system and widely agreed that the assassination was *not* an indication of a serious weakness in the governmental system (see Figure 2).[29] The legislators divided more on the question as to whether they felt the assassination indicated a serious increase in political extremism in the country. In the days after the assassination, nearly 80 per cent of the general population worried some about how the President's death would affect the political situation in the country and about 70 per cent felt worried about how the United States would carry on without its leader. By the time our legislator interviews were taken, the transition to the Johnson administration was successfully completed and there was perhaps in retrospect less cause for concern about the stability of the government. In the general public, there probably was a greater feeling than in our legislator sample that the assassination reflected an increase of political extremism in the country.

DEMOCRATIC AND REPUBLICAN LEADERS

As we have seen, studies of the assassination immediately following its occurrence did indicate some partisan differences in reactions to it among people generally. These differences appeared in television viewing patterns: Kennedy supporters watched television more during the days immediately after the assassination and perception of bias in coverage of the event by the mass media was affected by party preferences. More important, immediate beliefs and attitudes about the death of the President were related to party preferences. In general, Democrats were somewhat more upset emotionally and physically than Republicans, not only about the assassination of President Kennedy but also about the killing of Oswald. In Table 2, the percentages of Democratic and Republican legislators who agreed with each of the statements about the assas-

29. See Charles Aikin, "Impact of the Death of an American President on the Exercise of Executive Power," *Jahrbuch des Öffentlichen Rechts der Gegenwart* (Tübingen: J. C. B. Mohr, 1965), pp. 45–55.

TABLE 2

Partisan Differences in Leaders' Reactions to
the Kennedy Assassination

Percentage Who Agreed

REACTION	DEMOCRATS (N = 22)	REPUBLICANS (N = 38)
Feeling of sadness—felt sick	95	79
Did not believe news could be true	78	50
Did not believe anything like this could happen	50	37
Felt as if the whole world was caving in	64	5
Was not particularly concerned	5	8
Killing of Oswald by Ruby was just as well	0	0
Murder of Oswald as much a disaster as killing of Kennedy	50	37
Best thing would be to sentence Ruby to the electric chair	23	66
Change from Kennedy to Johnson proves stability of our system	95	92
Assassination indicates increase in extremism	55	40
Assassination indicates weakness of our government	5	13

sination are shown. These data do demonstrate the significantly greater impact of the assassination on Democrats. Almost all the Democrats reported feeling sick, more than three-fourths reported disbelief that the news of the assassination could be true, half were incredulous that anything like a presidential assassination could happen in this country, two-thirds felt that the "world was caving in," and only 5 per cent were not concerned. Republicans were generally less upset about the assassination of President Kennedy and less inclined to regard the murder of Oswald as a disaster of proportions roughly equal to that of Kennedy's death. However, Republicans were considerably more punitive; two-thirds of them (as opposed to less than a quarter of the Democrats) believed that it would be best if Ruby were sentenced to the electric chair.

Members of both parties reflected confidence in the stability of the political system, though Democrats were more likely to see the assassination as a reflection of increased political extremism and Republicans were more inclined to see it as a reflection of weakness in the governmental system.

The consistency of the party differences from item to item, plus the factor of simplicity of presentation, led to the combination of the first eight items in Table 2 into a single index which we will call the Assassination Index. Party differences appeared on all but one of these items. Each legislator was given a score from 1 to 5 for each item and his scores averaged. These mean scores were then grouped into three categories based on the degree to which legislators were affected by the assassination: high reaction, medium reaction, and low reaction.[30] The party differences for the combined index are shown in Table 3. As expected, Democrats tended to register a significantly higher reaction to the events in Dallas than Republicans. The use of the Assassination Index will greatly simplify the presentation of our evidence regarding the effects of religion and ideological orientations on attitudes toward the death of President Kennedy.

PARTY, RELIGION, IDEOLOGY, OCCUPATION

Of our sample of Illinois legislators, 33 per cent were Catholics, 60 per cent were Protestants, and 5 per cent were Jewish. It might be thought on a common sense basis that religion ought to have had something to do with reactions to the Kennedy assassination, given the fact that he was the first President of the Roman Catholic faith. We would presume that Catholic political leaders ought to have been more affected by the death of John F. Kennedy than Protestants. We also know that party preference and religious affiliation are related to each other: Democrats tend to be

30. The distribution of average scores was divided into three nearly equal parts, so that the highest twenty legislators were classified as "high reaction," the middle nineteen legislators were classified as "medium reaction," and the lowest twenty legislators were classified in the "low reaction" category. It was not possible to classify one of the sixty legislators. We were able to score the legislators on a 1-to-5 basis because the response categories in the questionnaire for each item provided five alternatives from "strongly agree" to "strongly disagree."

TABLE 3

Partisan Differences and the Assassination Index
(in percentages)

Party Affiliation

ASSASSINATION INDEX	DEMOCRATIC (N = 22)	REPUBLICAN (N = 38)
High reaction	64	16
Medium reaction	27	34
Low reaction	9	47
Not classifiable	0	3
Total	100	100

Catholics, while a higher proportion of Republicans tend to be Protestants. The sample of political leaders fits this characterization. Of the Republicans, one-fourth were Catholics and three-fourths were Protestants. Of the Democrats, half were Catholics, a third were Protestants, and the rest were Jewish. Since all the Jewish legislators were Democrats, they can be left out of the analysis. The question is: Is the difference between Democrats and Republicans in reactions to the death of President Kennedy really just a difference between Catholics and Protestants? The answer is set out in Table 4. It can be seen that there is some difference between Catholics and Protestants in the direction we might have expected, although the numbers are small. But it does appear that this difference is due largely to the fact that Catholics tend to be Democrats and Protestants Republicans. Catholic Democrats scored higher on the Assassination Index than did Catholic Republicans. Among Protestants, Democrats tended to register a "high reaction" while more than half of the Republicans scored in the "low reaction" category. The differences between Democrats and Republicans are not simply an artifact of the predominance of Protestants among Republicans and of Catholics among Democrats. Party differences in reactions to the assassination of the President are independent of differences in religious affiliation.

It has been shown that reactions to the assassination were heavily influenced by the party affiliation of the political leaders in the sample. And while religious affiliation contributed something to this difference, party preferances strongly withstand the test of reli-

TABLE 4

Religious Affiliation and Leaders' Reactions to the Assassination by Party
(in percentages)

ASSASSINATION Index	All Catholics (N = 20)	Democratic Catholics (N = 11)	Republican Catholics (N = 9)	All Protestants (N = 36)	Democratic Protestants (N = 7)	Republican Protestants (N = 29)
High reaction	35	55	11	28	71	17
Medium reaction	50	46	56	25	14	28
Low reaction	15	0	33	44	14	52
Not classifiable	0	0	0	3	0	4
Total	100	101*	100	100	99*	101*

* Totals diverge from 100% because of rounding.

gious differences. But it may be that the real differences are simply the result of dissimilarities in ideological orientations. Perhaps reactions to the assassination vary because liberals lamented the death of a liberal President, and conservatives reacted less strongly. Because most Democrats are liberals and most Republicans are conservatives, the real ideological difference in reaction appears, incorrectly, to be a political party difference.

The data do not support this line of reasoning, as can be seen by studying Table 5. It is true that liberals were more pronouncedly affected by the assassination than conservatives. However, the relationship between ideological orientations and assassination reactions is not very strong. In our sample 70 per cent of the Republicans were conservatives by our measurements and 77 per cent of the Democrats were liberals.[31] But within each category—liberals and conservatives—Democrats were markedly more affected by the assassination than Republicans. The party difference in the response to the assassination is not just an artifact of differences in ideological orientations. Well over half of the Democratic liberals were high in their reactions, while most of the Republican liberals were low. Most of the few Democratic conservatives were high, while two-fifths of the Republican conservatives were low, and only 16 per cent had a high reaction.

In all the available studies of the assassination, responses were influenced considerably by socioeconomic differences. In general, working-class people responded more intensely than did middle- or upper-class people. Also, working-class people were more prone to extreme recommendations for the fate of Oswald and Ruby while those with higher status offered more tempered and reasonable views regarding the punishment of the assassins. Our sample of political leaders is so heavily middle- and upper-middle class that such an analysis is meaningless. It might be thought that occupa-

31. The Illinois legislators were rated as liberals or conservatives on the basis of their responses to five questions in the questionnaire: (1) "The federal government should take a greater role in ending all racial discrimination"; (2) "The federal government should turn its social security programs over to the states"; (3) "The United States should formally recognize Red China"; (4) "The Illinois legislature should completely end Aid to Dependent Children and associated programs due to abuse"; (5) "The United States should discontinue foreign aid to all countries not willing to fight for us." Conservatives were those who made less than three "liberal" responses; Liberals were those who made three or more "liberal" responses.

TABLE 5

Ideological Orientations and Leaders' Reactions
to the Assassination by Party
(in percentages)

ASSASSINATION INDEX	All Liberals (N = 27)	Democratic Liberals (N = 17)	Republican Liberals (N = 10)	All Conservatives (N = 30)	Democratic Conservatives (N = 5)	Republican Conservatives (N = 25)
High reaction	44	59	20	27	80	16
Medium reaction	22	29	10	40	20	44
Low reaction	33	12	70	33	0	40
Total	99*	100	100	100	100	100

* Totals diverge from 100% because of rounding.

tional mobility—the extent to which individuals are on the move up in occupational status—could affect attitudes toward the assassination. The hypothesis might be that people on the move, and thus more insecure in their jobs and status, would be inclined to greater expressions of fear and extremism in their reactions to the assassination. The Illinois legislators do exhibit differences in occupational mobility, but there are no differences of any moment between Republicans and Democrats in our sample in this respect. So party differences in responses to the assassination could not be the result of differences in occupational mobility.[32]

Similarly, the distribution of lawyers between the two parties in the sample is about the same. About a third of the members of both parties are lawyers and they are the largest single occupational group in this legislature. One might well expect reactions peculiar to lawyers for at least some of the items we have used to assess attitudes toward the assassination. However, this expectation does not materialize in any important way. Perhaps the most interesting single item with regard to lawyers' attitudes is the one having to do with the question of sending Ruby to the electric chair. It might be expected that, regardless of political-party affiliation, lawyers would tend to take a more prudent position on this item than non-lawyers. But this is not the case. More than two-thirds of both Republican lawyers and non-lawyers agreed that Ruby should be sentenced and executed. On the contrary, half or more of the Democratic lawyers and non-lawyers disagreed. And, what may seem more distressing, in fact more lawyers were willing to agree to Ruby's execution than non-lawyers, but perhaps this is due to the generally stronger partisan anchorings of lawyer-legislators compared with legislators in other occupations.

PRESIDENTIAL ASSASSINATION
AND POLITICAL STABILITY

For the available research on reactions toward the assassination of President Kennedy we do not, in general, have analyses that demonstrate, or fail to show, the independent effects of differences

32. Forty-seven per cent of the sample were occupationally mobile and 53 per cent were stable occupationally. Democrats and Republicans did not differ significantly.

in partisan identifications—free of differences in such things as sex, age, social class, religion, or ideological orientations. For the political leaders in the study reported here, party differences seem to provide the major desiderata in accounting for variations in reactions to the assassination. In spite of the limited analysis of the large-scale survey studies and the small number of political leaders available for study, it does appear that variations in assassination reactions were, on the whole, not great or abnormal. Further, the party differences in reactions do not in retrospect seem to have been unusual, even though they appear to have counted for more in the responses of political leaders. In sum, the assassination of President Kennedy, though it was a very shocking and saddening event, does not appear to have evoked systemic instability by activating intensified political cleavages. Variations in reactions to it appear to have been quite predictable utilizing the normal political behavior variables. There is no significant evidence in the data for the mass public, for specialized subgroups or for political leaders that the presidential assassination contributed to political instability. Unlike political assassinations in some other political systems, American presidential assassinations have not involved organized political movements utilizing assassination as a political weapon for the purpose of seizing power. Thus, they presumably are not as threatening to public confidence in the orderly transfer of power and therefore are not productive of substantial political instability.

In some respects, it would be possible to argue that the assassination of President Kennedy had stabilizing effects. The funeral and burial of the President had most of the attributes of a national communion. It represented a tremendous outpouring of national consensus and for many Americans it probably was an experience of rededication to national symbols of a sort that strengthened national political integration. The presidential funeral, like the coronation of the monarch, provided conditions under which "people became more aware of their dependence upon each other" and citizens may have sensed some connection between this awareness and their relationship to national political authority.[33]

33. See Edward Shils and Michael Young, "The Meaning of the Coronation," *Sociological Review,* 1 (December, 1953), pp. 63–81. The quoted phrase is on p. 74.

Political Socialization, Racial Tension, and the Acceptance of Violence: Reactions of Southern Schoolchildren to the King Assassination

James W. Clarke and John W. Soule

The assassin's bullet that abruptly ended the life of Martin Luther King on April 4, 1968 evoked a public response among black Americans that remains unparalleled in our long history of such tragic events. King's death again dramatized the racial hostility and tension in this country. This event precipitated the violence that erupted in many cities and on a number of black university campuses.

One of the most important sources of tension in American society is the racial hostility that has divided this country as no other issue since the Civil War. The dimensions of this tension are well known: a persistent antipathy between blacks and whites, which is reinforced by discrimination in education, employment, and housing, as well as other areas of human concern.

It comes as no surprise that our findings confirm that racial tensions persist among black and white schoolchildren. We have documented the attitudes that might be expected from such a group in the aftermath of the violent death of this nation's most prominent black leader. More important is the fact that these schoolchildren—black and white—give indications that violence is recognized, tolerated, and in some cases, a preferred means of accomplishing one's objectives. Neil J. Smelser has suggested that "if hostility is to arise from conditions of strain [tension] these conditions must exist in a . . . setting which is either permissive of hostility or prohibitive of other responses, or both."[1] Our find-

1. Neil J. Smelser, *Theory of Collective Behavior* (New York: The Free Press, 1962), pp. 224–225.

ings indicate that significant numbers of young black and white students accept the use of violence as a legitimate alternative for political action. We are suggesting here that this acceptance of violence is an important consequence of what social scientists have called "political socialization."

For the past ten years social scientists have devoted a great deal of attention to the political socialization of young Americans, i.e., how children learn politically relevant behavior. This research has been plagued with a number of substantive or methodological problems of which we shall deal with only one. Studies of how children acquire political beliefs from their parents have been limited to only those beliefs that are supportive of the existing political system.[2]

The research to date does support generally the hypothesis that children transfer feelings they have toward their parents to political figures. However, as a result of the heavy emphasis placed upon the influence of the family and the schools as agents of socialization, we have overlooked the effect that public events, e.g., economic crises and assassinations, have on the child's acquisition of political beliefs. It is our contention that external events which are highly publicized and emotional in character interact with parental and peer-group beliefs to constitute a significant factor in the political socialization of young people. It is also conceivable that such events have an independent influence on socialization, i.e., apart from family and school influences.

The heavy reliance in previous socialization research on psychoanalytic hypotheses has directed attention away from the influence of external events.[3] We believe that the psychoanalytic focus overly accentuates children's reactions to parental authority.

2. See, for example, Lewis A. Froman, Jr., "Learning Political Attitudes," *Western Political Quarterly*, 15 (1962), pp. 304–313; R. E. Dawson, "Political Socialization." In *Political Science Annual*, Vol. 1, edited by James A. Robinson (New York: Bobbs-Merrill, 1966), pp. 1–84; Robert D. Hess and David Easton, "The Child's Changing Image of the President," *Public Opinion Quarterly*, 24 (1960), pp. 632–644; Fred I. Greenstein, "Children's Political Perspectives: A Study of the Development of Political Awareness and Preferences Among Preadolescents" (Ph.D. diss., Yale University, 1959); and Dean Jaros, "Children's Orientations toward the President: Some Additional Theoretical Consideration and Data," *Journal of Politics*, 29 (May, 1967), pp. 368–387.

3. Froman, *op. cit.*

The determination of influential agents of political socialization is an empirical question. The psychoanalytic focus ignores this point. The result is a static or *status quo* view of political socialization. It does not explain the dynamics of change in political cultures.

Our study is concerned with the impact that Martin Luther King's slaying had upon public schoolchildren. We have examined children's reaction to the assassination from cognitive and affective perspectives that include their perceptions of their parents' attitudes, their thoughts concerning just punishment (or reward) for the unknown assassin and a comparison with reactions following President Kennedy's assassination. The evidence shows that this assassination had a substantial impact on these students. Among black students, reactions indicate that this event reinforced doubt and suspicion of existing legal means of apprehending and punishing criminals. White student reactions suggest that the assassination reinforces an attitude that violence is an acceptable means to a preferred end. While our data are only suggestive, the response to the King slaying indicates the probability of important dysfunctional consequences for the American political system.

METHODS AND SAMPLE

A sampling of 165 white and 217 black students was drawn from seventh-, ninth-, and eleventh-grade classes of four public schools. The schools were located in two metropolitan communities in north and southeast Florida. With the exception of the eleventh-grade classes, these students attend schools that are essentially segregated. Questionnaires were distributed and administered to each class by the regular classroom teacher. We, two white university professors, avoided any contact with the students in an effort to minimize any bids that may have been introduced by our presence. Every effort was made to avoid any disruption of the normal classroom situation.

One major consideration in selecting the sampling was simply to include a comparable number of black and white students within each grade level. Our desire to determine the reaction to the King assassination as soon after the event as possible precluded the implementation of more rigorous sampling techniques. The data were collected within a twelve-day period immediately following the assassination. Meetings with school officials to explain and secure approval for the study accounted for this delay. No claim is made for the representativeness of our sample. It was impossible, given the nature of the event, the crucial time factor and the sensitivity of school officials, to approach the problem in any other way. Although we have no reason to believe that our respondents are atypical Southern schoolchildren, there is no attempt to generalize beyond the data reported here.

INITIAL REACTIONS

Data in Table 1 indicate a clear difference between races in their critical reactions toward King's assassination. Responses were elicited by asking students the open-ended question: "How did you feel when you first heard of Dr. King's death?" Reactions varied from a deep sense of sorrow and grief to feelings of elation and happiness. Mixed between such polar reactions were feelings of indifference, incredulity and anger. Fifty-nine per cent of the white students surveyed expressed indifference or elation. Conversely, 96 per cent of the black respondents expressed profound shock and grief. Clearly, black and white students responded quite differently to the assassination. While this finding is not surprising, the realization that a majority of white students were, at best, indifferent or unconcerned about the assassination suggests an alarming callousness among these youngsters concerning such acts of violence.

The reaction of white males and females is shown in Table 2. White males were clearly less sympathetic than their female counterparts. Seventy-three per cent of the white males were indifferent or pleased. Over half the white females registered a sympathetic response. Virtually no differences in reactions were revealed between black males and females. Black students of both sexes were greatly disturbed by the assassination.

PERCEIVED PARENTAL REACTIONS
AND SOCIAL CLASS

That parents transmit their attitudes and values to their children has been well documented in behavioral research.[4] One scholar offers the following explanation for this relationship: "The family

4. See, for example, Frederick Elkin, *The Child and Society: The Process of Socialization* (New York: Random House, 1960).

TABLE 1

Initial Reaction to Dr. King's Assassination by Race*

INITIAL REACTION	Black N = 189 %	White N = 141 %
Shocked, grieved, saddened, or angry	96	41
Indifferent or pleased	4	59
	100%	100%

* A total of 52 students did not answer these particular questions and were excluded from the analysis in computing percentages. The fluctuations in the marginals of future tables are due to "don't know" and "no responses" on the item or items being considered. In this and in future tables, no answer/don't know responses are excluded except where inclusion is specifically noted. In investigating student attitudes, particularly young students, a substantial number of "no responses" are to be expected.

TABLE 2

Initial Reaction to Dr. King's Assassination
by Sex Among White Students

INITIAL REACTION	Males N = 70 %	Females N = 71 %
Shocked, grieved, saddened, or angry	27	55
Indifferent or pleased	73	45
	100%	100%

is the most prominent environmental source not only of what may be deemed its inherent function of providing affection, but also of satisfying other needs. This is probably the central reason that the individual comes to think and act like his family more than he thinks and acts like those who are less regularly relevant to his need satisfactions."[5]

Convincing evidence of this relationship is shown in Table 3. More interesting, however, is the fact that fully 30 per cent of the sample who reported their own feelings were unable or unwilling

5. James C. Davies, "The Family's Role in Political Socialization," *The Annals of the American Academy of Political and Social Science*, 361 (September, 1965), p. 12.

TABLE 3

Correspondence Between Perceived Parental
Reactions and Children's Reactions to
Dr. King's Assassination
(combined black and white)

Perceived Parental Reaction

	FELT BAD N = 111 %	INDIFFERENT OR GLAD N = 80 %
CHILDREN'S REACTION		
Felt bad	97	17
Indifferent or glad	3	83
	100%	100%

to report their perceptions of their parents' attitudes. This finding lends support to the hypothesis that events like assassinations have an effect on young people that is independent of family influence.

The class dimensions of racial prejudice are well known, i.e., that lower-status whites tend to be more prejudiced than higher-status whites.[6] Our findings regarding the King assassination tend to confirm these views. We found marked differences in the reactions of white students whose fathers hold different occupational statuses. Table 4 shows the relationship between father's occupation and the initial reaction of white students. The data indicate considerably more indifference and pleasure among white students with fathers in clerical, skilled and unskilled occupations compared with other white students with fathers in managerial, professional and official occupations. Furthermore, 65 per cent of these children from higher-status families expressed sadness or sympathy. It seems clear from these results that there are class differences in the expected direction among white students with regard to their reaction to the assassination.

6. The explanations offered for this are complex, involving personality attributes associated with lower-class backgrounds and socioeconomic insecurity. For a more detailed discussion see George Eaton Simpson and J. Milton Yinger, *Racial and Cultural Minorities: An Analysis of Prejudice and Discrimination,* 3d ed. (New York: Harper and Row, 1965), pp. 103–108.

TABLE 4

Initial Reaction to Dr. King's Assassination by
Father's Occupational Status Among White Students

Fathers' Occupations

Students' Initial Reaction	Managers, Professionals, and Officials N = 65 %	Clerical, Sales, Skilled, and Unskilled N = 51 %
Shocked, grieved, saddened, or angry	65	18
Indifferent or pleased	35	82
	100%	100%

Further evidence of class differences are observed when race is controlled and parental reactions to the assassination are considered with regard to occupation in Table 5. Table 5, in conjunction with Table 4, shows that children share essentially the basic class biases of their parents. Sixty-three per cent of the white children whose fathers are employed in lower-level occupations were either pleased or indifferent about King's death. Fewer parents of white children in higher-level occupations (25 per cent) shared these attitudes. More disturbing is the fact that in both the upper and lower occupational categories, children's responses to the news of King's assassination were less compassionate than their perceptions of their parents' response. This finding raises some unsettling questions concerning the socialization of Southern white children. The fact that children are less compassionate than their parents suggests that some other influence—perhaps the school, the community, or the cultural milieu of the South—is affecting their attitudes.[7] These are questions that cannot be answered in this study. Again, black students were overwhelmingly saddened by the event without regard to class differences, as were their parents.

7. Also, it may be that this deviation means nothing more than that we are simply comparing people at different stages of the socialization process at a given point in time, i.e., the attitudes of these children may change substantially by the time they reach the age of their parents. At this point, we cannot predict either the magnitude or direction of attitudinal change over time.

TABLE 5

Parental Reaction to Dr. King's Assassination
by Father's Occupational Status

	Managers, Professionals, and Officials		*Clerical, Sales, Skilled, and Unskilled*	
	BLACK	WHITE	BLACK	WHITE
PARENTAL	N = 40	N = 65	N = 101	N = 56
REACTION	%	%	%	%
Felt bad	73	34	73	12
Pleased or indifferent	2	25	2	63
Not sure	25	41	25	25
	100%	100%	100%	100%

RELIGION

Another indicator of student reaction was ascertained by asking respondents: "Did you say any special prayer or attend a memorial service for Dr. King?" As expected, 70 per cent of the Negro students, compared with 17 per cent of the white students, reported that they had done so. Following the Kennedy assassination, Sheatsley and Feldman reported that three-fourths of a national sample of adults responded positively to this same question.[8] Although black students were found to attend church more regularly than whites, church attendance seemingly had little bearing on whether blacks or whites prayed following the assassination. Most blacks did pray and most whites did not, regardless of their past record of church attendance. Similarly there was no relationship between religious preference and either the black or white reaction.

WHO IS TO BLAME?

The extent to which the King assassination was viewed in racial perspectives was explored by asking: "Who or what do you think is to blame for his [King's] death?" Black and white responses to this question are reported in Table 6. It is not surprising to note

8. Paul Sheatsley and Jacob J. Feldman, "A National Survey of Public Reactions and Behavior," *Public Opinion Quarterly*, 28 (1964), pp. 189–215.

TABLE 6

Who Is to Blame for Dr. King's Slaying?
(by race)

	Race	
BLAME PLACED UPON	BLACK N = 154 %	WHITE N = 138 %
A white man	35	12
Killer's color not mentioned	34	30
King himself is to blame	4	41
A prejudiced, racist, sick society	27	17
	100%	100%

that more blacks than whites identified the assassin as a white man. Furthermore, 41 per cent of the white students felt that King himself was to blame for his own death. Only 4 per cent of the black students felt that way. The following response is typical of the white reaction blaming King. Eleventh-grade white male: "Himself [he is to blame]; he went around stirring up trouble." Most of these responses described King as a man who "started riots," "pushed too hard," or "was stupid." Twenty-five per cent of our sample refused to speculate on who the assassin might be—16 per cent of the whites and 29 per cent of the Negroes.

Some of the children in our sample viewed the assassination in a much broader perspective. After President Kennedy's assassination not one child—white or black—was reported as saying that "we are all to blame."[9] Our findings are sharply divergent. Twenty-seven per cent of the blacks blamed a "racist society" for the tragedy, as did 17 per cent of the whites. An important difference in this response was the fact that white students tended to generalize more about the ills of American society, whereas blacks tended to identify specifically the racist character of this society.

When these results were analyzed by grade level, we found that as their grade level increased, blacks were much more likely to

9. Roberta Sigel, "Television and Reactions of School Children to the Assassination," in *The Kennedy Assassination and the American Public*, edited by B. Greenberg and E. Parker (Stanford, Calif.: Stanford University Press, 1965), pp. 199–219.

blame a racist society for King's death. For example, one eleventh-grade black girl, struggling for words, expressed it this way: "I feel that the blame for his death is that white people don't want the Negroes to be said as good as they are . . . Negroes is better than white if you want my opinion of it, because we have done white people's labor long enough." Another young black ninth-grader said, "I think hate is to blame for his death . . . the hate for Negroes and thinking of them getting their freedom." Younger blacks tended to view the event in a more limited perspective, i.e., they were more likely to blame simply "a white man." Among the white students, as grade level increased, blame was increasingly attributed to King himself. Sixty-six per cent of the white eleventh-graders blamed King for his own assassination.

PUNISHMENT FOR THE ASSASSIN

A further inquiry involved the question, "What do you think should be done to the person who shot Dr. King?"[10] Again, the data reveal a clear distinction between the races about the fate of the assassin (Table 7). Sixty-five per cent of the black students responded with hostility or a desire for revenge. Typical responses were:

Seventh-grade black:	"He should be hanged by the neck on public TV."
Ninth-grade black:	"He should be shot by Mrs. King or King's brother."
Eleventh-grade black:	"He should be taken out and beaten. Why don't they set him loose on . . . [a black university] campus. We would do the job on him—but good!"

10. Responses were coded into three categories: included in the first category were those who thought the killer should be accorded the due process of law; respondents included in the second category expressed a desire that extralegal sanctions be brought against the killer; our third category contained those persons who felt the killer should not be punished, or who, in fact, felt this person should be rewarded in some way for his deed.

TABLE 7

What Do You Think Should Happen to Guilty Person?
(by race)

	Race	
	BLACK N = 198	WHITE N = 151
IMPUTED FATE	%	%
Tried, punished by courts	35	65
Death	65	18
No punishment, freed, congratulated	0	17
	100%	100%

Conversely, sixty-five per cent of the whites felt the assassin should be accorded the due process of law. More disturbing, however, is the finding that 17 per cent of the white students felt the killer should be rewarded for his deed. For example, respondents said:

Seventh-grade white: "He should go free."

Ninth-grade white: "He should get the Congressional Medal of Honor for killing a nigger."

Eleventh-grade white: "We should try him in court and find him not guilty. He did what lots of us wanted to do; he had the guts."

Moreover, among whites, sympathy for the killer increased with grade level, i.e., about 30 per cent of the white eleventh-graders favored no punishment for the assassin compared with only four per cent of the white seventh-graders.[11] An opposite reaction was noted among black students. As grade level increased, blacks were much more likely to elicit "due process" responses as opposed to extralegal, violent or revengeful responses, whereas 74 per cent of the seventh-grade blacks expressed a dsire for violent sanctions for the killer. This percentage declined to 50 per cent among eleventh-grade blacks.[12] However, it is important to note that at

11. Relationships involving grade level as a control variable are not shown in tabular form.

12. A fourth variable, father's occupational status, was added as a control in analyzing black and white responses to the killer by grade level. It was possible that occupational status was an intervening variable. While the cell sizes became very small when this control was introduced, the relationship remained unchanged.

all grade levels a majority of blacks favored some form of violent death for the assassin with no mention of established legal procedure. In their view, King's death could be atoned only through the violent and, in some cases, sadistic execution of his killer.

Two Assassinations: Some Comparisons

Studies made following President Kennedy's assassination revealed that blacks—adults and children—expressed more sorrow over the President's death than whites. A number of the same items used in Sigel's study of reactions to the Kennedy assassination were included in our questionnaire for comparative purposes (See Table 8.)

The data reveal that the contrast between black- and white-student reactions is sharp. Invariably, the white students expressed less sympathy, were less ashamed and upset and were less disturbed that such violence could occur in this country. Following President Kennedy's assassination both black and white students responded sympathetically.

The extent and intensity of the black response to King's death is evidenced by the fact that black students expressed a greater emotional loss, more anger, shame and vengeance at his death than they did when President Kennedy was killed. (It is generally accepted that President Kennedy enjoyed considerable popularity among blacks.) Again, this response indicates the decided effect King's death had upon black schoolchildren.

Conclusions

In our introduction we outlined several components of social behavior that have political relevance. Subsequently, we have shown the extent to which both racial tension and attitudes conducive to the use of violence exist among black and white schoolchildren. This volatile combination of situation and attitudes provides sufficient conditions for interracial conflict.

While Martin Luther King's death served as a precipitant for the violence that followed immediately, his death might also be viewed as an important event in the long-range socialization of young blacks. Sixty-five per cent of these children wanted revenge beyond punishment by law for his death. Some evidence of this and

TABLE 8

Reaction of Children by Race Toward Both the King
and Kennedy Assassinations
(in rounded percentages)

This Is How I Felt

	KING REACTIONS		KENNEDY REACTIONS[a]	
	BLACK N = 217 %	WHITE N = 165 %	BLACK N = 342 %	WHITE N = 1006 %
Felt the loss of someone very close	89	15	81	69
Worried what would happen to our country	88	85	74	63
Felt so sorry for his wife and children	98	63	91	94
Felt worried how the civil-rights movement would carry on	89	45	..[b]	..[b]
Felt angry that anyone should do such a terrible thing	95	47	84	81
Hoped the man who killed him would be shot	76[c]	20[c]	54	36
Felt ashamed that this could happen in my country	77	63	75	86
Was so confused and upset I didn't know what to feel	40	15	40	44
Felt in many ways it was King's (Kennedy's) own fault	10[c]	49[c]	18	15

[a] These data were taken from Roberta Sigel, *op. cit.*, p. 211.
[b] This item was not included in the study of President Kennedy's assassination.
[c] The differences between these responses and the responses presented in Tables 6 and 7 are explained by the fact that a larger number of students responded to the items that appear in this table.

other factors may be reflected in the increasing militancy of young blacks.

The King assassination has revealed also that prejudice and hostility are important dimensions of the attitudes of significant numbers of the white children studied. Fifty-nine per cent of these children were indifferent or pleased upon hearing of King's death. These children, at best, were not concerned that a man had been killed because his views were contrary to the views of many white Americans.

The revengeful attitudes of blacks and the callousness of whites suggest what may be an alarming dimension of racism in the United States. Violence appears to be increasingly recognized and accepted—by both blacks and whites—as a legitimate means of settling grievances.

Political Vengeance and Political Attitudes: A Study of Americans' Support for Political and Social Violence[1]

James McEvoy, III

Support for violence can take many forms. To explore the levels of public support for the various types of violent behavior, a national sample survey was conducted during the fall of 1968.[2] In designing the survey, the areas of personal violence, political violence, military violence, and violence in the media were isolated as conceptually independent and a number of questions were devised that we hoped would isolate verbal support for, or opposition to, force, roughness, and the unlawful exercise of force.

Additionally, we obtained a good deal of information from our respondents about their political activity and beliefs, their socio-economic status, and their personal experiences with violence. We also included short forms of the California F Scale and the Anomy

1. Without the generous financial support of the American Jewish Committee, this project would have been impossible. In particular, I wish to thank Mrs. Lucy Dawidowicz for her help. I would also like to thank James Short, J. Merrill Shanks, James Burdette, Michael Morrissey and Carl Nelson, all of whom have contributed substantially to this project.

2. The survey was conducted by Louis Harris Associates of New York City in October, 1968. A total of 1,176 completed interviews make up the study reported here. The survey was designed for the National Commission on the Causes and Prevention of Violence, and I served as consultant on the survey for the Commission's Task Force on Assassination and Political Violence. The Commission sponsored the survey and provided financial support for its initial analysis. Others participating in the survey design included Sheldon B. Levy, Sandra J. Ball and William A. Gamson. Two other papers should be consulted by the reader interested in a more comprehensive analysis of these data. These are William A. Gamson and James McEvoy III, "Police Violence and Its Public Support," *The Annals of the American Academy of Political and Social Science,* 391, September 1970, pp. 97–110; and Rodney Stark and James McEvoy III, "Middle-Class Violence," *Psychology Today,* November 1970, pp. 52–54, 110–112.

Scale in the interview schedule and also asked our respondents how they had felt when a number of nationally prominent persons had been assassinated. These measures are discussed in some detail in the following pages.

The organization of the essay is as follows: first, a discussion of the several types of violence mentioned above is presented, and data indicating the levels of verbal support and opposition to some of the relevant measures of these types of violence are analyzed. Then measures of political violence are integrated into the analysis and, finally, the dependent variable or what has been termed "political vengeance," is isolated for examination. This variable, (an index), is based upon a factor analysis of a number of items in the survey, and is offered as a general measure of support for political violence. Most of the latter part of the essay deals with the correlates of political vengeance and the extent to which violence is apparently legitimated by one's political beliefs. A brief discussion of the relationship of the findings of this study to other current stresses in the society completes the essay.

PERSONAL VIOLENCE

One factor in a person's experience that might seem logically associated with his verbal support or opposition to violence would be his prior experiences with violence. This, for example, was given prominence in the trial of Sirhan Sirhan in which the violence surrounding his childhood was often stressed by the defense as a mitigating factor in his behavior. Theoretical arguments can be made that strongly support several conflicting hypotheses about the outcome of the attitudes of persons with high exposure to violence. We therefore were concerned with the question of what, if any, difference it made in our respondents' behavior if they had had more exposure to violence than others and, further, if they had engaged in violent acts against other persons.

We asked our respondents several questions in this area, the first series of which dealt with the extent to which they had been the victims of violence and the sceond with their own use of violence against others. Table 1 presents the results of some of the ques-

TABLE 1

Personal Experience with Violence

A. *When you were a child, were you spanked?*

	%	N
Frequently	32	391
Sometimes	61	755
Never	5	61
Not sure	2	21
	100%	1228

B. *Have you ever been slapped or kicked when you were an adult?*

	%	N
Yes	17	209

C. *Have you ever been punched or beaten when you were an adult?*

	%	N
Yes	14	171

D. *Have you ever been choked when you were an adult?*

	%	N
Yes	4	51

E. *Have you ever been threatened or cut with a knife while you were an adult?*

	%	N
Yes	9	109

F. *Have you even been threatened with a gun or shot while you were an adult?**

	%	N
Yes	9	110

* Excludes military actions.

tions from the first series and Table 2 the data from the second series.[3]

The principal point that is made by examining these data is seen in the vast discrepancy that exists between the population's actual experiences with violence and its willingness to tolerate its use against unpopular and deviant individuals and to advocate violence as a necessary part of the socialization process. For example,

3. Percentages in Tables 1, 2, and 3 are taken from the initial report by Louis Harris Associates to the Commission. They are based on weighted data and the number of cases given is approximate.

TABLE 2

Personal Use of Violence

A. Have you ever spanked a child?

	%	N
Yes	84	1038
No	16	194
	100%	1232

B. Have you ever slapped or kicked another person while you were an adult?

	%	N
Yes	19	238

C. Have you ever punched or beaten another person while you were an adult?

	%	N
Yes	9	113

D. Have you ever had to defend yourself with a knife or a gun? (all responses)

	%	N
Yes	6	68

70 per cent of the sample agreed or strongly agreed with the importance of fist fights in a boy's maturation; 40 per cent with the "whipping, or worse" of sex criminals; and 49 per cent with the hitting of students. A somewhat smaller percentage was willing to tolerate the kinds of police violence proposed. A surprisingly high percentage of the sample was willing to approve of a judge sentencing someone to a year or more of hard labor if he was an "agitator." Clearly, this is an identity it would be well to avoid in America in the seventies. The only exception to this general trend in these items is found in the child-beating question where overwhelming rejection was, quite naturally, the modal response.

In general, the pattern of responses to the items in Tables 1, 2, and 3 is similar to that found between two indices of political violence discussed below. One index, Acceptance of Political Violence, has a distribution skewed in the direction of relative tolerance for, or expectation of, violence; the other index, Political Vengeance, in which advocacy and support of political violence is measured, was skewed in the opposite direction toward rejection of violence as a means of political change.

TABLE 3

Situations in Which Violence Is Perceived as Appropriate Behavior

A. *When a boy is growing up, it is important for him to have a few fist fights.*

	%	N
Strongly agree	12	153
Agree	58	711
Not sure	3	37
Disagree	25	303
Strongly disagree	2	26
	100%	1230

B. *Sex criminals deserve more than prison: they should be publicly whipped or worse.*

	%	N
Strongly agree	18	223
Agree	22	270
Not sure	8	96
Disagree	41	501
Strongly disagree	11	139
	100%	1229

C. *Are there situations that you can imagine in which you would approve a parent beating his child?*

	%	N
Yes	8	104
No	90	1114
Not sure	1	14
	100%	1232

D. *Approve of a public school teacher hitting a student?*

	%	N
Yes	49	606
No	47	572
Not sure	4	51
	100%	1229

E. *Approve of a policeman striking an adult male for saying vulgar things to the policeman?*[a]

	%	N
Yes	27	251
No	69	651
Not sure	4	42
	100%	944

F. *Approve of a policeman striking demonstrators against the war in Viet-nam?*[b]

	%	N
Yes	19	180
No	76	721
Not sure	5	45
	100%	946

G. *Approve of a judge sentencing an agitator to one or more years of hard labor?*[b]

	%	N
Yes	76	825
No	18	194
Not sure	6	64
	100%	1083

[a] Percent of these approving of policeman striking an adult, no cause specified, in this case 73 per cent of the sample.
[b] Includes only persons initially approving of a hard-labor sentence, in this case 86 per cent of the total sample.

Both these distributions and the data examined above point to a double standard with respect to the population's response to violence. On the one hand, there are clearly norms that militate against being violent personally or supporting child beating, political murder, or the like. On the other hand, Americans often seem quite ready to advocate and support violent, illegal and brutal behavior directed at unpopular persons in the society.

As part of the interview schedule, Professor William A. Gamson and I devised a series of psychological test-type items that we hoped would emerge through factor analysis and other techniques of index construction as measures of police, military, and political violence. Table 4 presents the items appearing in the five factors that emerged when these and other items were factor-analyzed using the varimax solution.

The first factor, as might be expected, emerged from items taken for the most part from previously constructed scales, the F Scale and the Anomy Scale. This factor was termed "Anomic Authoritarianism." The second factor, Political Vengeance, was drawn from three items that seemed to tap approval of politically directed

TABLE 4

Five Violence Factors*

FACTOR 1   *Anomic Authoritarianism*
ITEM
A few strong leaders could make this country better than all the laws and the talk. (F scale)

People were better off in the old days when everyone knew just how he was expected to act. (A scale)

Justice may have been a little rough and ready in the days of the Old West, but things worked better than they do today with all the legal red tape.

What is lacking in the world today is the old kind of friendship that lasted for a lifetime. (A scale)

FACTOR 2   *Political Vengeance*
ITEM
Sometimes I have felt that the best thing for our country might be the death of some of our political leaders.

The government in Washington is the enemy, not the friend, of people like me.

Some politicians who have had their lives threatened probably deserve it.

FACTOR 3   *Acceptance of Political Violence*
ITEM
If people go into politics they more or less have to expect that they might get killed.

Politicians who try to change things too fast have to expect that their lives may be threatened.

A lot more people in government and politics will probably be assassinated in the next few years.

FACTOR 4   *Police Violence*
ITEM
The police are wrong to beat up unarmed protestors, even when these people are rude and call them names.

* Factor analysis is an analytic technique that seeks out and groups items whose scores show the greatest relationship. In the table, the "A" notations refer to items from McClosky and Scharr's Anomy Scale. See Herbert McClosky and John H. Scharr, "Psychological Dimensions of Anomy," *American Sociological Review*, 30 (February, 1965), pp. 14–40. The "F" notations refer to items from the scales devised by T. Adorno and et al., in *The Authoritarian Personality* (New York: Harper & Row, 1950).

The police frequently use more force than they need to when carrying out their duties.

Any man who insults a policeman has no complaint if he gets roughed-up in return.

Sex criminals deserve more than prison. They should be publicly whipped, or worse. (F scale)

FACTOR 5   *Military Violence*
ITEM
In dealing with other countries in the world we are frequently justified in using military force.

Our government is too ready to use military force in dealing with other countries.

It is unfortunate that many civilians are killed by bombing in a war, but this cannot be avoided.

violence *and* the perception that the government as a hostile and threatening force to the respondent. The next factor, Acceptance of Political Violence, was based upon three items that suggest passive acceptance of violence rather than active anticipation of it. Factor 4, Police Violence, is based on items which measure support or disapproval of police violence. And the fifth factor, Military Violence, is based upon items with similar intent dealing with military force. Table 6 presents the interitem correlations or each of the factors.

Scales, or more properly indices, were created for each of these factors by assigning values of 1 to 5 for each response category (strongly agree, agree, not sure, disagree, strongly disagree) and then summing 1 to 5 the items in the factors. The range of possible scores for the items in Factor 1 was, then, 6–30; for Factors 2, 3, and 5, 3–15; and for Factor 4, 4–20. Each of the items was scored in such a way that a low score indicated disagreement with the assertion, a high score meant agreement. When necessary, items were reversed to retain this scoring configuration. Thus a score of 6, 7, 8 or 9 on Factor 1, Anomic Authoritarianism, indicated that a respondent was relatively low in this characteristic; a score in the 20's indicated that he was relatively high. Linear functions were used to shrink the range of the distributions and further collapsing

TABLE 5

Factor Loadings

The factor loadings for the factors were as follows (items listed in order):

FACTOR 1	FACTOR 2	FACTOR 3	FACTOR 4	FACTOR 5
.6910	.7370	.7988	.7867	.7051
.6593	.6837	.7346	.6190	.6857
.6507	.6054	.6576	.6127	.5591
.5902			.3558	
.5160				
.4674				

was often imposed in the analysis. In summary, using analysis to identify clusters of related items, the items in the factors were combined as indices and a respondent's score on any given index was based on the sum of the single-item scores for the set of items in the factor. Any missing data from the items in each factor deleted the respondent from further computation of a score for that factor.

An examination of the distributions of these indices provides a rough idea of the level of tolerance, approval, or support for the various kinds of violence they attempt to measure. Table 7 presents the distributions of four of these indices grouped in categories ranging from low to high scores on each index.

The pattern I mentioned earlier between the distributions of the Political Vengeance Index and the Acceptance of Political Violence Index is obvious: 58 per cent of the Vengeance scores are at the lowest two points of the distribution, whereas only 19 per cent of the Acceptance scores fall at this end of the index; the modal score on Vengeance is 2, for Acceptance 5.

The Police and Military Violence indices both have rather similar distributions and approximate normality. In each case the modal score is at the midpoint of the distribution. However, 32 per cent of the distribution of scores for military violence fall above the midpoint; only 24 per cent of the scores for police violence fall above this point, indicating relatively greater support for militarily related violence than for police violence in this sample.

These four indices are, of course, related to each other. The correlations between them are shown in Table 8.

TABLE 6

Interitem Correlations (Pearson R)
of Items in Factors

Anomic Authoritarianism

	16	13	I 01	14	09	15
16	–	.267	.240	.227	.243	.248
13		–	.300	.379	.308	.251
14			–	.267	.245	.259
09				–	.254	.387
15					–	.183

(mean interitem correlation = .271)

Political Vengeance

	25	22	II 07
25	–	.267	.251
22			.196
07			–

(mean interitem
correlation = .238)

Police Violence

	24	06	III 20	19
24	2	.250	–.130	–.078
06		–	.130	–.026
20			–	.283
19				–

(mean interitem
correlation = .150)

Acceptance of Political Violence

	10	IV 18	21
10	–	.441	.303
18		–	.310
21			–

(mean interitem
correlation = .351)

Military Violence

	12	V 03	17
12	–	.012	.310
13		–	.019
17			–

(mean interitem
correlation = .114)

Because of some similarities between the items in the Vengeance and Acceptance indices and because of their fairly high correlation, an attempt was made to combine them into a single index. Since the combination proved to be no better a predictor of some other measures of political violence than did the Vengeance

TABLE 7

Distributions of Scores on Indices of Violence,
Political Vengeance, Acceptance of Political Violence,
Police Violence and Military Violence*

	Political Vengeance	
	N	%
1	251	22
2	536	46
3	230	20
4	105	9
5	25	2
6	8	1
7	3	.3
	1158	100%

	Acceptance of Political Violence	
	N	%
1	25	2
2	190	17
3	243	21
4	256	22
5	338	29
6	83	7
7	26	2
	1161	100%

	Police Violence	
	N	%
1	3	.3
2	29	3
3	149	13
4	317	28
5	382	33
6	198	17
7	65	6
8	10	.9
9	4	.3
	1157	100%

	Military Violence	
	N	%
1	4	.3
2	34	3
3	241	21
4	517	45
5	291	25
6	65	6
7	8	.7
	1160	100%

* The linear function used to shrink scores was $\frac{R}{2}$ where R = ordered range of scores.

TABLE 8

Intercorrelations of Political Vengeance Index, Acceptance of
Political Violence Index, Police Violence Index,
and Military Violence Index
(Pearson R)

Political Vengeance	.300	.221	.149
Acceptance of Political Violence	. .	.295	.304
Police Violence		. .	.204
Military Violence			. .

Index by itself, the Political Vengeance Index alone was employed as the dependent variable in the analysis that follows.

Several rough methods of assessing the validity of the Vengeance Index have been explored thus far. The most impressive support for the utility of the Vengeance Index as a measure of support for actual political violence comes from an examination of an index constructed from a series of questions dealing with the respondents' feelings about five recent political assassinations (the two Kennedys, King, Malcolm X, and Rockwell). A high score on this index indicated feelings of relative *hopefulness* and *relief* at the occurrence of a particular assassination. The correlation between the Vengeance Index and this measure of support for real instances of political murder was +.226, far higher than for any other index or item in the survey. Vengeance was also strongly related to the Anomic-Authoritarianism Index ($r = +.246$), a relationship that is not in the least surprising whether one considers authoritarianism and anomy as either true psychological types or simply as measures of extreme right-wing ideology. In both cases, we would expect high scorers on authoritarianism to be high on items measuring toughness, hostility, and approval of totalitarian means of political action.

If we are willing to accept the Vengeance Index as a rough but acceptable measure of support for political violence, we can now turn to a discussion of the elements involved in the production of high scores on the index.

DEMOGRAPHIC CORRELATES OF VENGEANCE

Table 9 gives the distributions of the respondents by race, region, income, education, and other demographic variables over the Vengeance Index. In this and all other tables, the Vengeance distribution has been reduced to four categories based on the transformed distributions discussed above. The only change in the data has been in the grouping of persons with a score of 4 or higher on the transformed distribution into a single category (4) for presentation in the following tables.

Three prominent findings emerge from an examination of Table 9. First, the South contributes a disproportionate number of highly vengeant respondents to this sample; second, blacks are twice as likely as whites to be high on political vengeance; and third, declining levels of income and education are associated with increasing levels of political vengeance. Other less significant predictors of vengeance are being retired and being a Protestant. Let us consider the first three of these results in somewhat greater detail.

THE SOUTH

The South contributes twice the proportion of highly vengeant persons as the Midwest, more than twice the proportion than the West, and a third more than the East. Many commentators on the

American South have observed that it is the location of a violent culture. Martin Luther King, John Kennedy, Medgar Evers, and George Lincoln Rockwell were assassinated in the South—the scene for years of hundreds of lynchings, bombings, and other kinds of terror used to suppress the black and sometimes the white population.

The rates of certain types of violent crimes, including murder, non-negligent manslaughter, and aggravated assault are far higher in the South than elsewhere. For example, the reported rate of murder and non-negligent homicides nationally was (in 1966) 5.6 cases per 100,000 persons; in the Southern states of Delaware, Maryland, Virginia, West Virginia, North Carolina, South Carolina, Georgia and Florida the rate averaged 9.1 cases per 100,000. A national rate of 118.4 (in 1966) cases of aggravated assault per 100,000 persons compares with an average rate of 179.1 cases per 100,000 in these states.

Rank-ordering the highest ten states by their reported homicide rates puts Alaska first (12.9 per 100,000) followed by South Carolina (11.6), Georgia (11.3), Alabama (10.9), Nevada (10.6), Florida (10.3), Louisiana (9.9), Mississippi (9.7), Texas (9.1), and North Carolina (8.7). Eight of these are, of course, Southern states.[4]

While one could argue that criminal statistics such as these can be produced by a small minority, it is clear from the table that this culture of violence in the South is not a "one percenter" phenomenon. Quite the contrary, almost a fifth of the Southerners score at the high end of the Vengeance scale and, unlike the other regions of the country, only 15 per cent of the respondents from the South manifest a relatively low level of vengeance. This compares with 27 per cent of persons in the East who are relatively low on vengeance and 23 per cent who are relatively low in both the West and Midwest.

These regional differences may, of course, be in part the result of the generally lower levels of income and education that characterize the population in that region. Nevertheless, it is apparent that the South's cultural pattern of violence, so well described in

4. *Statistical Abstract of the United States, 1968* (Washington, D.C.: U.S. Government Printing Office, 1969), p. 146.

TABLE 9

Vengeance by Selected Demographic Characteristics:
Race, Region, Income, Education, Age, Sex, Religion

Occupational Category

(*Per Cent*)
Political Vengeance Score

	1	2	3	4	TOTAL[a]	N
RACE						
White	22	49	19	10	100%	938
Negro	22	35	24	20	100%	218
REGION						
East	27	42	19	12	100%	325
South	15	44	24	18	100%	326
Midwest	23	51	17	9	100%	323
West	23	50	19	8	100%	185
COMBINED FAMILY INCOME						
$3,000	15	42	23	21	100%	184
$3–4,999	21	37	28	14	100%	161
$5–6,999	17	48	21	14	100%	206
$7–9,999	22	48	19	11	100%	292
$10–14,999	31	47	17	6	100%	200
$15–19,999	33	53	9	5	100%	58
$20,000	6	81	13	0	100%	16
EDUCATION						
Fourth grade or less	8	33	38	23	100%	40
Fifth to eighth grade	16	36	27	21	100%	213
Some high school	20	45	21	15	100%	244
High school graduate	22	50	18	10	100%	363
Some college	28	53	13	7	100%	183
College graduate	25	58	18	0	100%	73
Postgraduate study	39	43	9	9	100%	54
AGE						
18–20	24	34	29	13	100%	38
21–25	26	47	19	8	100%	121
26–30	21	43	23	13	100%	125
31–35	21	54	12	13	100%	116
36–40	24	48	18	10	100%	100
41–45	24	48	15	14	100%	102
46–50	20	62	12	6	100%	101
51–60	24	43	20	13	100%	181
61–65	16	49	20	13	100%	45
65 and older	18	39	27	16	100%	229

SEX						
Male	22	46	18	13	100%	590
Female	21	47	21	11	100%	555
RELIGION						
Protestant	21	47	19	13	100%	741
Catholic	22	49	20	9	100%	296
Jewish	29	43	19	10	100%	21
Other	27	30	27	16	100%	44
Not sure	19	48	10	24	100%	21
OCCUPATIONAL CATEGORY						
(head of household)b						
Hourly wage worker	21	46	21	12	100%	374
Salaried	27	51	14	9	100%	362
Self-employed	18	51	20	12	100%	142
Retired	17	40	26	17	100%	184

a Totals do not reflect rounding errors and are fixed at 100%.
b Occupational data are not available beyond these categories.

W. J. Cash's *The Mind of the South,* is clearly manifested in these survey data.[5]

RACE

Table 10 displays scores on the Vengeance Index broken down by racial group and region. Since blacks are disproportionately low in income and educational attainment, these tabulations have the effect of partially controlling for income and educational imbalances between regions. As an inspection of the tables indicates, the basic pattern still holds. Southern whites are twice as likely to be highly vengeant than either Eastern or Western whites and almost twice as likely as Midwestern whites. The pattern changes, however, for blacks. Eastern blacks are by far the most vengeant segment of the population with 28 per cent falling at the high end of the Vengeance Index. Southern blacks are next, followed by Midwestern and Western black and Midwestern white respondents.

5. A recent and highly convincing paper by Sheldon Hackney ("Southern Violence," *American Historical Review,* 74 [February, 1969], pp. 906–925) explores ecological indicators of Southern violence and concludes that cultural rather than demographic factors are responsible for high rates of violence in the American South.

TABLE 10

Vengeance and Region by Race

Negroes

VENGEANCE SCORE	East	South	Midwest	West
1	15	22	33	4
2	35	28	37	65
3	22	28	17	22
4	28	21	13	9
	100%	100%	100%	100%
N =	68	97	30	23

Whites

VENGEANCE SCORE	East	South	Midwest	West
1	30	11	22	27
2	44	50	52	47
3	18	22	17	19
4	8	16	9	8
	100%	100%	100%	100%
N =	257	229	293	162

Negroes in the eastern parts of the United States are largely located in the great urban ghettos of New York, New Jersey, Boston, Philadelphia, and Washington, D.C. It is quite clear from many other sources of data that these ghettos are the scene of much militant political activity and it is to be expected that this activity combined with the deplorable conditions of life in these areas would yield great distrust and hostility toward the government. The riots that have occurred during the past few years in these and other cities constitute further evidence that urban blacks are disproportionately hostile to the government.[6] We do not know, of course, from these data if the relative hostility of the black population in these areas has increased or declined. But it is certain that large numbers of blacks, especially Eastern urban blacks, are profoundly hostile to the government.

6. A survey by *Newsweek* (June 24, 1969) gives further support to these assertions.

INCOME AND EDUCATION

Income and its close correlate, education, are both variables which have a strong effect on the level of support or opposition that a respondent manifests to items in the Vengeance Index. In general, the effect can be seen as a strong inverse relationship between increasing levels of income and education and support for political vengeance.

An examination of Table 9 shows that as income and education increase the proportion of respondents in the high vengeance cells of the table declines rapidly. For example, at the lowest levels of education—persons having an eighth-grade education or less—roughly 22 per cent are found in the high vengeance group. Among persons with some college, this proportion falls to about 7 per cent and declines to zero within the group of persons with a college degree. There is a slight increase in vengeance among persons with postgraduate degrees in the sample, but the number of cases is so small that this cannot be viewed as a significant finding.

The same general pattern can be seen in the table reporting combined family income. At the lowest levels of income, between 14 and 21 per cent of the respondents fall at the high end of the Vengeance Index. At the higher income levels, ($20,000 or more income) none to only 6 per cent score at that level of the Index.

It remains to be seen whether increasing levels of income have the effect of diminishing vengeance among both racial groups. Figure 1 considers only persons at the two extreme ends of the Vengeance Scale. The line labeled "Low Vengeance" is made up of responses of persons with a score of 1 on the scale and that labeled "High Vengeance" is made up of the responses of persons with a score of 4. As Figure 1 indicates, there is a strong and almost linear decline in the proportion of persons at the high and low ends of the vengeance scale as income either increases or decreases.

Figure 2 presents the mean income level of all respondents at the various scores on the Vengeance Index by race. As an examination of the figure shows, the effect of increasing income levels for blacks is by no means the same as it is for whites. Indeed, blacks at the highest levels of vengeance are slightly higher in income

FIGURE 1

Proportion of Persons at High and Low Scores on Vengeance
Index by Combined Family Income
(Per Cent)

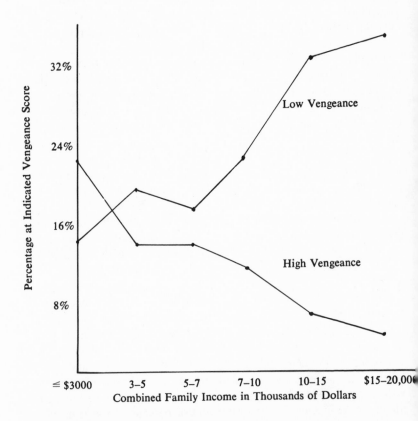

than blacks in the third quartile on the Vengeance Index. We must
ask: Why does the effect of increasing income among blacks have
so little relative effect in reducing their levels of political vengeance?

A classical formulation of the class-conflict argument suggests
that the curves for whites are what we would expect, that is, as one
moves to more and more deprived segments of the population,

FIGURE 2

Mean Income Level of All Respondents at Scores
on the Vengeance Index, by Race

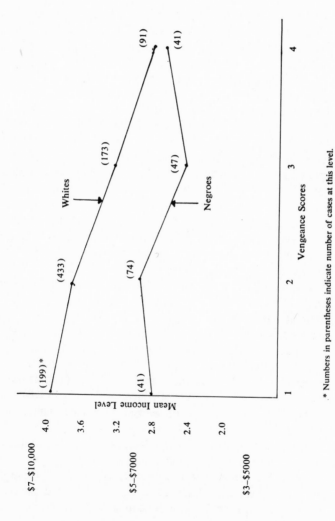

* Numbers in parentheses indicate number of cases at this level.

there should be greater and greater levels of hostility to governmental structures—except at the very lowest, or *lumpenproletariat* level, where we should find little or no revolutionary sentiment. The curves for whites in Figure 2 give some support to this argument, except for the fact that the relationship among the *lumpenproletariat* segment is not in the expected direction. While this is an extremely crude formulation of the class-conflict hypothesis and an equally crude measure of it, the argument in general is supported within the white population.

The picture for blacks suggests alternate formulations. If on the one hand the blacks be taken theoretically to form the segment of the population that in the contemporary United States is the functional equivalent of the classical *lumpenproletariat,* perhaps they should not then be expected to show any great differences in hostility toward the government despite increasing income levels. On the other hand, this argument is rather insubstantial because, as we have seen, blacks (especially low-income blacks) are much more likely than whites to be high on political vengeance and cannot, therefore, be treated as a prerevolutionary, apolitical segment in the classical Marxian sense. It seems most reasonable, therefore, to conclude at this stage of the analysis that factors more important than simple class position are operating to produce the rather generalized support for vengeance found among blacks. A number of possible factors come readily to mind: racial discrimination, relative deprivation irrespective of income level, and the presence and increasing appeal of separatist and black militant ideologies. In any case, these data argue that simply increasing blacks' income levels will not correspondingly increase their confidence in the government and the social system.

Table 11 reports the educational level of blacks and whites. The general pattern here is the same found in the data on income except that increasing levels of education appear to have a stronger effect on the attenuation of vengeance among whites than does income.

Figure 3 presents the mean educational levels of all respondents by race and their score on the Vengeance Index.

As an inspection of this figure indicates, low-vengeance blacks and low-vengeance whites have about the same proportion of respondents at each level of education, with vengeance falling off

TABLE 11

Negroes
Education and Vengeance*
(Per Cent)

EDUCATION LEVEL VENGEANCE SCORE	1	2	3	4	5	6
1	9	17	19	26	32	14
2	30	45	33	29	36	57
3	35	23	22	24	14	29
4	26	15	26	22	18	0
	100%	100%	100%	100%	100%	100%
N =	23	47	61	52	23	7

Whites
Education and Vengeance
(Per Cent)

EDUCATION LEVEL* VENGEANCE SCORE	1	2	3	4	5	6
1	6	16	20	22	27	26
2	35	34	48	54	54	57
3	41	28	22	17	13	17
4	18	23	11	8	5	0
	100%	100%	100%	100%	100%	100%
N =	17	164	178	305	159	65

* Key: 1: 1 = fourth grade or less; 2 = fifth to eighth grade; 3 = some high school; 4 = high school graduate; 5 = some college; 6 = college graduate; 7 = postgraduate work.

directly with increasing education. In the case of the high-vengeance blacks and whites, however, the two curves diverge rather sharply. As educational attainment increases among whites, the proportion of high vengeance respondents falls off rapidly. The opposite is true of higher-income blacks. As Figure 3 shows, the mean educational level of high-vengeance blacks is just slightly

FIGURE 3

Mean Educational Level of Respondents by Score
on Vengeance Index and Race

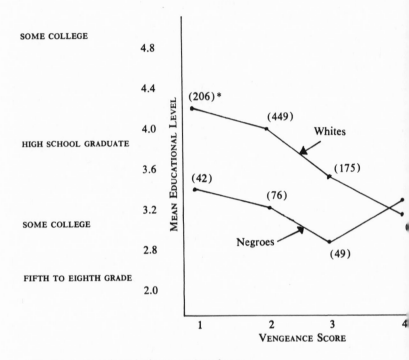

* Number in parentheses indicates number of cases.

below that of the low-vengeance blacks; only in the middle-income
range does the curve for blacks parallel that for whites.

What these data and those for income level suggest is that cultural assimilationists who argue that Negroes will become uniformly allegiant members of the society once their relative deprivation is reduced are over optimistic. Instead, the data reported here
point in a somewhat different direction: allegiance and approval of
the political order (at least as measured by the Vengeance Index)
tend to decline among high-income and high-education blacks. This
leads to the conclusion that crude social-welfare measures that
have as their principle effect an absolute increase in income levels

among blacks may, at the middle-income levels, reduce hostility to the political system. In the absence of further changes in the value structure of the society, however, such programs do not seem likely to produce an allegiant black socioeconomic elite and may, in fact, produce the opposite.

VENGEANCE AND THE POLITICAL SYSTEM

We have already seen that the Vengeance Scale has in part been constructed on the basis of an item that measures political trust and that low political trust and approval of political murder are highly related. We therefore ought not to expect that our highly vengeant respondents have "normal" attitudes about the American political system. Nevertheless, it is worthwhile giving some consideration to the question of the political attachments of highly vengeant respondents. Let us look first at the national election of 1968.

Interest in the election as reported by respondents is shown in Table 12. Presumably, lack of interest in national elections is in part an indicator of alienation from the political system. We should expect to find greater proportions of the low-interest respondents at the higher ends of the Vengeance Index and, in fact, we do. Again, however, when the data are partitioned by race, blacks are found to contribute much higher proportions of persons who are both uninterested in the election and highly vengeant. Indeed, 30 per cent of the blacks in the "not much interest" group were at the high end of the Vengeance Index compared with 14 per cent of the

TABLE 12

Interest in (1968) Campaign
(Per Cent)

VENGEANCE SCORE	Very Much Interested			Not Much Interested		
	BOTH	BLACKS	WHITES	BOTH	BLACKS	WHITES
1	24	22	25	15	15	14
2	46	41	47	43	27	49
3	18	23	17	25	28	23
4	11	14	12	18	30	14
	100%	100%	100%	100%	100%	100%
N =	576	105	471	250	63	187

whites. This is a finding that underlines our previous analyses: blacks are disproportionately alienated from the political system and express this alienation in the form of lack of interest in this major intersection of public opinion and political policy.

A rather different pattern emerges when we look at the presidential preference of our respondents in the national election of 1968. Table 13 reports these distributions for the entire sample.

TABLE 13

Presidential Choice (All Respondents)
(Per Cent)

VENGEANCE SCORE	NIXON	HUMPHREY	WALLACE	NOT SURE
1	25	26	12	21
2	50	46	50	48
3	17	20	17	23
4	8	8	22	9
	100%	100%	100%	100%
N =	509	253	144	179

While there were no substantial differences between Nixon and Humphrey supporters in the proportion of those groups located at the high end of the Vengeance Index, the persons who supported George Wallace contributed, proportionately speaking, almost three times as many highly vengeant respondents as either the pro-Nixon or pro-Humphrey groups.

As we might expect, Wallace supporters were 99 per cent white. Moreover, Wallace's campaign was not only based in large part upon appeals to racism but was also replete with numerous violent references to many of America's political elites, e.g., threatening to throw some of them in the Potomac and calling others traitors and Communist sympathizers. This tactic evidently appealed strongly to about a fourth of his supporters, and, if we consider the set of highly vengeant white respondents with a presidential preference, just under half of them (45 per cent) were found in the ranks of the Wallace supporters.

It is quite clear that Wallace was successful in mobilizing by far the greatest share of politically vengeant white persons in the national election of 1968 and that he did so on the basis of appeals that were precisely the opposite of those which have mobilized black opposition to our political system. The implications of this finding are unpleasant: political vengeance is highest in two groups in the society that have little attachment to its political system and have increasingly become the targets of militant demagogues who openly espouse violence as a means of social change.

Table 14 reports the partisan identification of the respondents in the sample. The wording of this question may have inhibited identification with Wallace's American Independent Party. It read: "Regardless of how you may vote, do you usually consider yourself a Democrat, a Republican, an Independent, or what?"

TABLE 14

Party Identification by Vengeance Score

	Republican	Democrat	Independent	Not Sure
1	23	20	24	19
2	47	46	44	46
3	20	21	19	16
4	10	13	12	19
	100%	100%	100%	100%
N =	290	584	242	38

There is little difference between the three groups in their level of vengeance, with Republicans having a slightly lower proportion of identifiers at the high end of the Vengeance Index—quite likely an artifact of their generally higher levels of education and income. The "uncertain" categories yielded the smallest proportion of the least vengeant and a higher proportion of the most vengeant.

A final measure of political attachment, party switching, produced a finding that is consistent with our expectations about the relationship of political stability to political vengeance. Table 15 reports the percentage of persons reporting party switches in a "conservative direction" (those who switched from the Democratic to the Republican Party), a "liberal direction" (those who switched from the Republican to the Democratic Party), and those retaining their initial party choice. The group contributing the

TABLE 15

Party Switching by Vengeance Score
(Per Cent)

	Now a Republican Once a Democrat "Conservative"	Now a Democrat Once a Republican "Liberal"	Stable
1	20	17	23
2	48	46	45
3	18	20	20
4	14	17	11
	100%	100%	100%
N =	108	119	559

smallest proportion of vengeant respondents was the stable
identifiers.

VENGEANCE AND POLICY

We have seen that highly vengeant respondents are predominantly located in ideologically opposite camps, and we should
therefore not be surprised to find that on selected measures of
policy preference the persons at the extremes on desired outcomes
are much higher in the proportion of respondents at the high end
of the Vengeance Index. Table 16 reports the distribution of
opinion on the issue of preferred policy in the war in Vietnam.

TABLE 16

Political Vengeance and Policy Favored by Respondents
as a Solution to War in Vietnam (October, 1968)
(Per Cent)

VENGEANCE SCORE	Pull Out Now	Stop Bombing, Remain	Continue Present Policy	Invade North Vietnam	Use Nuclear Weapons
1	20	19.	33	21	15
2	42	44	48	53	44
3	22	27	14	17	21
4	17	10	6	10	20
TOTAL	100%	100%	100%	100%	100%
N =	208	215	206	345	105

In reading his table, it must be remembered that this question was asked before the bombing halt ordered by former President Lyndon Johnson early in November, 1968. As this table shows, the proportion of highly vengeant respondents decreases as one moves toward the middle of the table, with the central column in which persons favoring a continuation of then current United States policy contributing the smallest proportion of highly vengeant respondents.

This same pattern appears in Table 17 in which respondents' views on the speed of integration are reported. Those stating that integration was proceeding too slowly and those saying it was proceeding too rapidly are both more than twice as likely to have highly vengeant respondents in their ranks than those who state that they think integration is going at "about the right" speed.

TABLE 17

Political Vengeance and
Speed of Integration—Both Races

VENGEANCE SCORE	*Too Fast*	*About Right*	*Too Slow*
1	18	27	24
2	48	45	42
3	20	22	18
4	14	6	16
TOTAL	100%	100%	100%
N =	539	250	265

On another measure of policy relating to civil rights, however, we see (Table 18) that persons favoring segregation are by far more likely to be highly vengeant than those favoring integration or "something in between." In its essentials, this is simply a replication of our earlier findings about support for Wallace and vengeance because of the extremely high proportion of Wallace supporters who are in favor of segregation.

CONCLUSION

We have now examined data which argue that certain segments of the American public are relatively hostile both to each other and to the political system. These hostilities are most likely both a

TABLE 18

Political Vengeance by Attitude Toward Segregation
(Per Cent)

VENGEANCE SCORE	*Favor Segregation*	*"In Between"*	*Favor Integration*
1	11	20	27
2	44	47	47
3	24	21	17
4	21	12	9
	100%	100%	100%
N =	190	527	397

cause and a manifestation of a larger series of stresses now present to an unusually high degree in American society. These additional stresses on the polity and their probable relationship to the findings from the survey data deserve discussion.

In March, 1968, the National Advisory Commission on Civil Disorders summarized its studies of recent American civil disorders as follows: "Our nation is moving toward two societies, one black, one white—separate and unequal." The findings of our analysis support this basic assertion of the Kerner Commission. Blacks in the United States, particularly those in urban ghettos, are manifesting their distrust in America's political institutions and political system in ways that are strongly supportive of political violence. Whites, particularly those opposed to equality of opportunity for blacks, are also responding with violent opposition to this same political system. The net result of this condition is the formation of groups in the society that are at once violently antagonistic to each other and, at the same time, hostile to the political order as we know it.

The National Advisory Commission on Civil Disorders also reported that the origins of rioting were caused in part by political variables, specifically extreme distrust of the government and a high sense of political efficacy on the part of the rioters. Our data confirm that this level of distrust was evidently high among urban blacks more than twenty months after the great wave of rioting that occurred in this country during the summer of 1967.[7]

7. Again, see the *Newsweek* survey mentioned above for the data on this point, and Jeffery M. Paige, "Collective Violence and the Culture of Subordination" (Ph.D. diss., University of Michigan, 1968).

Added to this racial cleavage, the increasing hostility to the government's policies on the war in Vietnam by significant sectors of the public has resulted in an internal conflict that has seriously split a major political party and has caused a massive defection of American intellectuals and students from support of the government's foreign policy. From the data analyzed here, we have seen that extreme opposition to federal policy on the war in Vietnam (and, of course, on civil-rights matters as well) is a high predictor of political vengeance. By pursuing an unpopular policy in Indo-China, the government may have added many hundreds of thousands of persons to the list of the politically hostile, a significant proportion of which may also be politically vengeant.

Within a decade, the United States has had three of its most important political figures murdered by assassins; it has undergone a series of political riots of great intensity; and it is today faced with large and significant segments of the population who, as we have noted, are extraordinarily hostile to its policies in Vietnam, in civil rights, and in other areas as well. It has also experienced an added source of political strain: student rebellion. The increasing levels of rebellion present in some of America's college students, perhaps epitomized by the occupations of the buildings at Harvard and Columbia, the gassing of students at Berkeley and, most poignantly, the murder of students at Kent State and Jackson State, can no longer be considered merely as isolated phenomena, affecting merely a few students or campuses.

The basis for almost all leftist attacks on American universities and colleges lies in radical students' ability to mobilize large-scale student support based upon the institution's racism, militarism and hostility to social change and social progress. Radical students have been successful in labeling institutions of higher education as tools of the Federal Government and the larger society. Many students view the government with great distrust; if convinced of their school's "complicity" in supporting the policies of a government to which they are hostile, they have demonstrated quite clearly that they are prepared to disrupt the universities, regardless of the consequences.[8]

8. For a collection of recent articles on this point, See James McEvoy and Abraham Miller, eds., *Black Power and Student Rebellion* (Belmont, Calif.: Wadsworth Publishing Company, 1969).

At the same time, the Federal Government and many state governments and the governing bodies of colleges and universities have acted to restrict academic freedom, revoke financial aid to dissenters, limit appropriations to institutions of higher education, and more and more frequently, allow uncontrolled attacks by the police and the National Guard against students to occur. The effect of these actions has been to further increase the hostility of students, broadening the base of support for radical and sometimes violent minorities to embrace substantial majorities of a student body.

If the level of political murder continues, if racially based conflict grows, and if student rebellion (despite its recent apparent decline) emerges as the rule rather than the exception, the chances for survival of a stable, constitutionally governed society are diminished, possibly resulting in irrevocable damage to the American political order.

part IV

THE POLITICAL IMPLICATIONS
OF ASSASSINATIONS

Social and Institutional Factors Determining the Level of Violence and Political Assassination in the Operation of Society: A Theoretical Discussion

Joseph Bensman

INTRODUCTION

This chapter explores the theoretical dimensions involved in the analysis of social and institutional causes of violence. It does *not* propose and test a definitive theory of violence. Such a task may be beyond the life work of any one man. Moreover, political violence and assassination may have different meanings in evolving historical situations. A definitive theory that transcends history may thus be impossible. What we propose is a heuristic theory. It points to the necessary questions that must be asked in order to develop substantive theories of violence and political assassination. It indicates the types of data necessary to verify or reject such theories. It also suggests the range in types of violence in the last half of the twentieth century in the United States. From such a heuristic theory the outlines of substantive theories of violence and assassination relative to this era will hopefully emerge. In addition, the policy implications of such theories will be treated.

Our primary focus will be on social and institutional factors that evoke and inhibit violence and political assassination. We do not focus on purely psychological or individual factors. This self-limitation is due to the author's conviction that political violence and assassination, regardless of their individual and psychological roots, are expressed in social and political terms: such behavior represents a response to institutional, cultural, and social situations. Cultural factors govern its occurrence, the form it takes, the response to it and its consequences. A more detailed discussion of this point follows in the first section of this paper.

Similarly, violence and assassination will be discussed in terms of the total operation of society. Violence in some form, though not necessarily political assassination, represents an intrinsic and normal aspect of the operation of society. The very definition of the modern state and of sovereignty implies the normalcy of violence. The state is usually defined as that institution in society that has a *legitimate* monopoly over the use of violence in a society.[1] This includes the sole right of the state to wage war, to arrest, punish, and incarcerate criminals. It includes the *right* to repress rebellion, riots, and revolution. When the state lacks the *right* and the power to perform these functions, it ceases to be a state. The achievement of sovereignty within a territory thus historically involves the surrender by all other institutions in the society of the *right* to use violence.[2] The shift from feudal society to the modern European state witnessed the loss of access by feudal elites of the right and power to use violence on their own behalf. The change included both the surrender of judicial and police functions as well as the right to create and maintain private, i.e., feudal, armies. In the same sense, modern state building in Asia, Africa, and Latin America[3] involves a struggle on the part of the state to achieve a legitimate monopoly over the use of violence. The refusal of tribal, feudal, and party leaders to surrender their access to instruments of violence has resulted in violent confrontations. The achievement of sovereignty by the state arises from violent encounters and is usually followed by violent or potentially violent repressive action on the part of the government.

1. Max Weber, "Politics as a Vocation" in *Essays from Max Weber,* edited by Hans Gerth and C. Wright Mills (New York: Oxford University Press, 1946), pp. 77–128.

2. Harold J. Laski, *Studies in the Problem of Sovereignty* (New Haven: Yale University Press, 1917), pp. 1–26; and Harold J. Laski, *The Foundations of Sovereignty and Other Essays* (New York: Harcourt, Brace and Co., 1921), pp. 1–29.

3. As an illustration, see Seymour Martin Lipset and Aldo Solari, eds., *Elites in Latin America* (New York: Oxford University Press, 1967). The sections on "Economic Development and the Business Class" and "Functional Elites," especially the articles by Horowitz, Landsberger, and Obregon illustrate this point fully.

Historical experience shows that the achievement of a peaceful society, following the achievement of state sovereignty, is a slow process in which ideas of *trust*—between the members of society and the government, i.e., the rulers of the state, and between classes, political and ethnic groups and parties—emerges as a replacement for the continuous use of force to maintain stable government.[4]

When a *trust situation* has evolved, the society can be viewed as a political or moral community. Such a community rests upon the ideological acceptance of the state by sufficient numbers of the society to make the large-scale repressive use of force by the government, acting as agent for the state, necessary. The acceptance of the state by its membership is called legitimacy and means that the "citizenry" surrenders the use of violence as a way to achieve its goals. The citizenry develops the "trust" that legitimate, peaceful means are available for realizing their objectives.

Even when a state and its government are wholly legitimate, the state still rests upon the legitimate use of violence. The police power of a state as well as the ability to conduct war, to undertake national defense and to conduct international relations all rest on the controlled use of violence. Moreover, the *potential* to use violence by a government, once it is secure, serves to guarantee that violence need not be used. The strength of a government, measured as the probability of defeat for a challenging group, diminishes the desire of opposing groups to test its will. Violence thus is intrinsic to the routine operation of even "peaceful" governments.[5]

But, as we shall see, governmental policies and repression can induce groups, parties, or classes to engage in violence even against the government. The study of social causes of violence thus

4. Reinhard Bendix, *Nation Building and Citizenship* (New York: John Wiley & Sons, 1964), pp. 55–104. The author traces this development in Western European societies from the eighteenth century and illustrates the concept fully. William Gamson in *Power and Discontent* (Homewood, Ill.: The Dorsey Press, 1968) presents a useful summary of current political theory relevant to the concept of political trust.

5. Max Weber, "Religious Rejections of the World and Their Directions," in Gerth and Mills, *op. cit.*, p. 334.

involves consideration of the contributions of government to abnormal violence in a society.

POLITICAL ASSASSINATION
AS A FORM OF POLITICAL VIOLENCE

The discussion until now has focused upon violence rather than political assassination primarily because assassination represents only one form of political violence. Political assassination almost universally takes place within a context of political turbulence, conflict, and violence.[6] Issue conflict normally precedes political assassination. Assassination thus becomes one technique of political action, an alternative to other violent or nonviolent means. Much of our concern then centers on these questions: Why select assassination as the technique for violent political action? What social, political, economic, cultural, and ideological preconditions favor political assassination? Are there general processes that can be isolated, which predetermine the frequency with which assassination is employed as a political weapon? To what extent is political assassination self-sustaining, i.e., does one political assassination breed others? Under what conditions does political assassination, once current, recede in frequency as a means of political action? Can a society reduce its level of assassinations? If so, how?

Political assassination usually takes place within a broader framework of political violence. Thus similar questions must be asked of violence. Most of all the conditions under which significant numbers or groups within a society resort to violence to achieve their political, personal, or social aspirations will concern us. And the legitimacy of a society to its members and the condi-

6. Arnold Forster, "Violence on the Fanatical Left and Right," *The Annals of the American Academy of Political and Social Science,* 364 (March, 1966), pp. 141–148. Although he does not discuss political assassination, Coser demonstrates that lower-status groups, women, students, and the young select violent aggression as a way of dealing with their frustration during times of revolutionary normlessness, highly anomic and disorganized situations. See Lewis A. Coser, *Continuities in the Study of Social Conflict* (New York: The Free Press, 1967), pp. 53–71.

tions that inhibit or foster such legitimacy will help frame our investigation.

Assassination as an Individual Phenomenon

The current interest in political assassination stems from the three assassinations of major national political figures within a five-year period: John and Robert Kennedy and Martin Luther King. The same time period saw the assassination of Malcolm X, a black leader of increasing national prominence. Other attempts, threats, and conspiracies to commit political assassination were also revealed, resulting in indictments or retaliation.

While all the evidence has yet to be assembled, the three major political assassinations at this writing appear to be the work of individual assassins. Despite much effort, no convincing evidence has yet been presented that links the assassinations to organized conspiracies with political goals and ideology. Each of the accused assassins appears to have suffered severe psychological and emotional disturbance. The evidence, of course, is not always clearcut. The probability of political assassination is not usually considered in gathering psychiatric evidence in advance of the act. After the assassination the disinterested gathering of facts is not always possible for a variety of obvious reasons.

Because each assassination has been associated with a disturbed individual, some have come to think of political assassination as a purely individual phenomenon, an irrational act with uncontrollable consequences. Other commentators find this interpretation completely unacceptable. The total senselessness of the attacks has led them to construct theories to "make sense" of the seemingly unexplainable. Despite the lack of evidence, they have constructed theories of political conspiracy that make the assertion a "logical" outcome of its irrational assumption.[7] Such theories also result

7. Edward J. Epstein, *Inquest* (New York: Viking Press, 1966); Mark Lane, *Rush to Judgment* (New York: Holt, Rinehart & Winston, 1966); and Leo Sauvage, *The Oswald Affair* (Cleveland: World Publishing Co., 1966). These by no means represent an exhaustive list of conspiracy theories on President Kennedy's assassination or criticism of the Warren Commission Report. Other obscure books espouse "the grassy knoll" theory and "the double-Oswald" theory. The acquittal of New Orleans businessman

from a historical experience in which highly organized ideological movements employed assassinations to achieve political gain. This interpretation has been accepted primarily in Europe and in the Middle East, where it reflects the indigenous experience with assassination.

A third attempt at understanding accepts the idea that individual assassinations may be the work of emotionally disturbed *individuals,* but rejects the idea that political assassination itself is an isolated, individual phenomenon. The basic assumption of such a theory is that the assassin operates within a political, social, and historical "climate" that, despite individual emotional problems, leads him to direct his disturbance into violent political channels. Thus it is argued that the very nature of American political history as well as the current political and psychological climate lead disturbed individuals to politicize their problems by seeking emotional release through actions that fall within, although at an extreme end of, a range of political irrationality that characterizes much of the American political scene.[8]

To state this differently, there are many emotionally sick people in any society and we have no way of knowing (given differences in the willingness and ability to measure psychiatric disturbances between societies) whether America produces a larger number of these individuals than do other countries. But regardless of such difficulties in comparative assessment, the existence of mental illness does not explain how such emotional disturbance becomes politicized nor does it explain why it uses violence as a means of expression.

Clay Shaw after a highly publicized indictment that took two years to come to trial had overtones of a highly complex plot supported by little evidence. See Paris Flammonde, *The Kennedy Conspiracy: An Uncommissioned Report on the Jim Garrison Investigation* (New York: The Meredith Press, 1969); and Edward J. Epstein, *Counterplot* (New York: Viking Press, 1969). The phenomena are evaluated and the American experience discussed in more detail in William Crotty's "Assassinations and Their Interpretation Within the American Context" which opens this volume.

8. Harold Lasswell, *Psychopathology and Politics* (Chicago: University of Chicago Press, 1930). At a more institutionalized level, the same point is made by Richard Hofstadter in *The Paranoid Style in American Politics* (New York: Alfred A. Knopf, 1966). See also the contributions of Freedman, Rothstein and Greening on this point in Part II of this volume.

THE POLITICIZATION OF VIOLENCE

The politicization of violence thus appears to be the central factor in the understanding of political assassination. It is the central thesis of this paper that the politicization of violence can be understood only in social terms—that even where political assassination is the product of emotional disturbances of isolated individuals, it, by its very nature (the selection of a politically prominent person as a target), bespeaks a social and cultural matrix for the acting out of private disturbances through violent means. Thus social and cultural phenomena enter the potential assassin's definition of his world. They also help determine the plausibility of political action as a vehicle for delusional behavior and the specific goals to be achieved.

A purely individualistic or psychological theory of political violence aimed at reducing violent behavior is futile. If political violence or assassination were purely an individual, psychological problem, the solutions to the problem would be: (1) restore all potential assassins to mental health—as yet an impossible solution because of the lack of resources and diagnostic abilities; (2) confine all would-be assassins to institutions in which they would be incapable of realizing their potential—a solution which also would be impossible because of lack of resources and our present inability to predict who in fact can become a political assassin; (3) isolate all political leaders and would-be leaders from actual or potential assassins. The alternative includes the systematic containment of all violent political groups with access to a political leader, a similar identification and detaining of known fanatics and other politically disturbed individuals and the application of a host of well-developed but as yet unsuccessful security measures that isolate the leader from all public occasions in which he can become the target for a potential assassin.

This latter technique has in various ways been practiced since the beginning of recorded history and was the policy in force at the time of the current wave of political assassinations. The failure of this approach in the past becomes the occasion for an even stricter and more intensive application of such security measures. It is undoubtedly true that such measures do limit and *frustrate* attempts at political assassination (as witness the attempts on the life of President Truman), but one doubts whether such a policy can ever be completely successful. First, such security measures would need to be practiced continuously and intensively for an undetermined number of political leaders. The slightest relaxation of effort, even after periods of political peace and stability, can produce successful assassination attempts. Second, the methodology and technique of political assassination appears to develop as rapidly as the technique to frustrate it. Finally, political and social leaders resist the attempt to isolate themselves from the public, even at the risk of assassination, since such isolation is considered by them to be the surrender of their leadership, ceremonial, and public roles. Political communication and leadership "entail" the risk of assassination. Excessive avoidance of this risk means the abdication of leadership. As a result, virtually all major leaders, including the Kennedys and Martin Luther King, have rejected, despite premonitions of death, the policy of isolating themselves from the public as a means of preventing assassination.

For these reasons, policies stemming from the assumption of isolated political irrationality as cause of assassination cannot prevent assassination, although security measures will always be necessary, regardless of the other policies adopted. These other approaches must stem from the assumption of the social and cultural origins of politically violent behavior.

If political assassination flows jointly from the politicization of individual emotional disturbance and from channelization of irrationality into violent directions, then the direction of social policy should be to sever the links between personal disturbances and political violence. In concrete terms this means (1) locating the specific cultural, social, and institutional situations in American society that breed violence and the politicization of violence, and (2) attempting to create the conditions where politicized violence cannot be, or is not envisaged as, a plausible form of political action, even by the emotionally deranged.

Social Sources of
the Politicization of Violence

The argument being advanced can be outlined as follows: Violence can and does become part of the "normal" operation of society. The tension and violence from time to time builds up so that it becomes an accepted part of the society's everyday operation, in fact, to the extent that political groups may see in the use of organized violence a means to achieve their otherwise legitimate goals. Disturbed or near psychotic individuals, in responding to the "normality" of violence, conceive of violence as a plausible channel for action and deflect purely personal forms of irrationality into public forms. These public forms include political assassination.

A key to this conception is the understanding of normality of violence in the society as a whole. Social and political historians and other social scientists have located five major "normal" situations in American history and/or society that are or have been conducive to the acceptance of a violent atmosphere in American society. We shall only briefly summarize them.

1. *The frontier as a source of violence.* The expansion of the American frontier was based on violence—a violence initially directed against the American Indian and resulting in virtual genocide. In such expansion, the arming of the individual and groups of individuals became a necessity in defense, attack, reprisal, and counterattack against the Indians. Local, colonial and state militia, and federal troops were supplemented by armed bands of citizens. Violence along with bearing arms was considered natural.[9]

9. The best overall account is Helen Hunt Jackson, *A Century of Dishonor* (Boston: Roberts Brothers, 1887). For various regional accounts, see Henry Putney Beers, "The Western Military Frontier 1815–1846" (Ph.D. diss., University of Pennsylvania, 1935); Ralph K. Andrist, *The Long Death: The Last Days of the Plains Indians* (New York: Macmillan, 1964); and William H. Leckie, *The Military Conquest of the Southern Plains* (Norman: University of Oklahoma Press, 1963). For an excellent case study of this problem, see Mark H. Brown, *The Flight of the Nez Perce* (New York: G. P. Putnam's Sons, 1967).

In the expansion of the frontier, the struggle against the French and English colonists and troops and against Spanish and Mexican colonists and troops was based upon governmental and non-governmental resort to violence. As opposed to most international relations and warfare, these conflicts involved direct, violent citizen participation as much as it did participation by professional soldiers.[10] The success of Americans in such violent participatory confrontations is part of the romantic patriotism of America.

The expansion of the frontier usually outstripped the expansion of the police force. Criminals moved to frontiers and noncriminals became criminals in the absence of a stable police and military pacification of new territories. Crime was violent, including cattle and horse rustling, claim jumping, bank robbery, and armed robbery. The use of a gun was intrinsic to both crime and the resistance to crime.[11] The absence of police control led to vigilantism, lynching, and the employment of previously professional killers as law-enforcement officers. Legal procedures and law enforcement were primitive.[12]

As a result of this past, the romanticism and glorification of violence is and has been a central theme in American folk and popular culture. It is currently celebrated in American history, the movies, television, and folk music. It is further elaborated in circuses, pageants, and rodeos. It is part of the *contemporary* culture of Americans, especially in the West. The ownership of guns and their use continues to be a central fact in the culture of violence in the West and in other areas where the incidence of violent crime is high. Thus recourse to violence is not implausible to anyone who in some way participates in a culture that glorifies

10. As an illustration, see Beers, *op. cit.*, particularly Chapter VII; and Arthur P. Whitaker, *The Spanish-American Frontier: 1783–1795* (Gloucester, Mass.: Peter Smith, 1962).

11. Alfred Vagts, *A History of Militarism* (New York: W. W. Norton, 1937), pp. 93–102; and Carl Bakal, *No Right to Bear Arms* (New York: Paperback Library, 1968).

12. James H. Chadbourn, *Lynching and the Law* (Chapel Hill: University of North Carolina Press, 1933); Arthur F. Raper, *The Tragedy of Lynching* (Chapel Hill: University of North Carolina Press, 1933); and Sheldon S. Wolin, "Violence and the Western Political Tradition" *American Journal of Orthopsychiatry*, 23 (January, 1963). See also Lipset and Sheingold's comparative treatment of these points in the chapter that follows.

it; the selection of violence as a political or personal technique of action becomes acceptable.

2. *Southern violence.* Violence became institutionalized in the United States with the institutionalization of slavery. Slavery rested upon the ability of local and state law to maintain the ownership of individuals by other individuals. But since slavery involved *personal* control over other individuals, the threat of and the actual use of violence had to be given to the slave owner and his agents. Moreover, the total repressiveness in a slavery system invites fear of counterviolence, slave rebellion, and escape. Such fear necessitated the upholder of slavery to demonstrate his mastery of the situation by not permitting any threat, however mild, to his supremacy.[13] The freeing of the slaves intensified fears of retribution. The compromise election of 1876 resulted in the reinstitution of the repressiveness of slavery through both extralegal and legal means. The rise of the Klan, the restoration of white supremacy in the 1870's, and the new segregation could only be maintained by terror, by depriving the Southern Negro from even thinking of the possibility of equality. Terror was maintained by oppressiveness, by police brutality, and by lynching.[14] Thus systematic illegal violence was a major means by which an ongoing social system maintained itself. It was practiced with sufficient frequency and pervasiveness to become part of the normal tradition and social atmosphere. Negroes were "permitted" (by nonenforcement of the law) to practice violence upon each other, but not against whites. Whites in turn were "permitted" to practice violence on Negroes, but not on each other.

In effect, Negroes were taught that the police (the law) are agents of oppression and that violence is legitimate if the practitioners of violence have the power and the strength to impose their

13. John Hope Franklin, *From Slavery to Freedom* (2nd ed.; New York: Alfred A. Knopf, 1956), especially pp. 426–488; Gunnar Myrdal, *An American Dilemma* (New York: Harper Brothers, 1944), Vol. I, especially pp. 520–570; and "Lynching," *Negro Year Book, 1952* (New York: William H. Wise, 1953).

14. Allison Davis, Burleigh Gardner, and Mary R. Gardner, *Deep South* (Chicago: University of Chicago Press, 1941); W. E. B. Du Bois, *Black Reconstruction* (New York: Harcourt, Brace & World, 1935), especially pp. 670–710; and C. Van Woodward, *The Strange Career of Jim Crow* (2nd ed.; New York: Oxford University Press, 1966).

will on others.[15] The heritage of slavery and its functional alternatives—segregation, discrimination, exploitation, and brutality—
cast their shadow not only on the South, but also on all those in
the United States who have directly and indirectly been exposed to
it.[16]

The counterviolence among those who have had to repress
violent attitudes comes to the surface both as lesson and as "need"
when the former oppressors lack the strength to maintain oppression, or as the former victims gain the political or psychological
strength to express previously repressed emotions.

Thus violence breeds violence, and as a result the United States
in its race relations suffers from a generalized atmosphere of
violence, which in its Southern slave ownership and social origins
is more than 350 years old.[17]

LABOR-MANAGEMENT RELATIONSHIPS

A neglected aspect of the history of violence in American
society is in the area of labor-management relationships. The last
thirty years have produced little public violence among these

15. See my introduction to *The Black in Blue* by Nicholas Alex (New
York: Appleton-Century-Crofts, 1969). The major ideologists of all modern
American black-nationalists movements justify their "counteraggression" on
this score. See Eldridge Cleaver, *Soul on Ice* (New York: Dell, 1968);
Louis Lomax, *When the Word Is Given* (Cleveland: World Publishing Co.,
1963); and Malcolm X, *The Autobiography of Malcolm X* (New York:
Grove Press, 1966). This theme is always explicit in the work of Negro
playwright LeRoi Jones and, though less provocatively, in the works of
James Baldwin.

16. For excellent accounts of severe social repression that leads to con-
frontations between Negroes and the police, see Arthur I. Waskow, *From
Race Riot to Sit-in 1919 and the 1960's* (Garden City, N.Y.: Doubleday
Anchor, 1966); John Hersey, *The Algiers Motel Incident* (New York:
Bantam Books, 1968); Alfred McClung Lee and Norman Daymond, *Race
Riot* (New York: Dryden Press, 1943); and Robert Conot, *Rivers of Blood,
Years of Darkness* (New York: Bantam Books, 1968). Specific and impor-
tant references to the psychological consequences of such brutalization in-
clude: Kenneth Clark, *Dark Ghetto* (New York: Harper & Row, 1967), pp.
15–16, 63–74; Charles E. Silberman, *Crisis in Black and White* (New York:
Random House, 1964), pp. 36–67; Abraham Kardinier, *The Mark of Oppression* (New York: W. W. Norton, 1951); and William H. Grier and
Price M. Cobbs, *Black Rage* (New York: Bantam Books, 1968).

17. *Report of the National Advisory Commission on Civil Disorders*
(New York: Bantam Books, 1968).

groups. Yet in the North and the East, since the beginning of the Industrial Revolution, when mechanics and craftsmen first attempted to organize craft guilds and unions, violence has characterized these relations. In the period after the Civil War, industrial violence was endemic in the United States. The fight between labor and management involved the use of strikebreakers, imported paramilitary forces, labor thugs and the intervention of the police, state militia, and the National Guard.[18] It involved pitched battles, bombings, and arson. Worker organizations developed ideologies of violence in order to counter management violence. The images of the Homestead and Pullman strikes became almost as much a part of our national heritage as our Western movement.[19]

The violence in labor relations is instructive because it has declined; it becomes a case study in extending areas for peaceful resolution. The enactment of the National Labor Relations Act in 1937 gave trade-union members minimal *rights* to organize and, more important in terms of our problem, established procedures by which they could attempt to achieve their substantive aspirations by peaceful means. A new area for bargaining was established within the framework of law. Violence became unnecessary to secure these rights; violence occurs at present only when access to the law is denied to a party entitled to it.[20]

18. H. L. Nieburg, "Violence, Law, and the Social Process" in *Riots and Rebellion,* edited by Louis H. Masotti and Don R. Bowen (Beverly Hills, Calif.: Sage Publications, 1968), pp. 379–387, and Nieburg's contribution to this volume; Louis Adamic, *Dynamite* (New York: Viking Press, 1934); Thomas Brooks, *Toil and Trouble: A History of American Labor* (Boulder, Colo.: Delta Publishing, 1965); and Leon Litwack, *The American Labor Movement* (Englewood Cliffs, N.J.: Prentice-Hall, 1962), pp. 18–24.

19. John R. Commons, et al., *History of Labor in the United States* (New York: Macmillan, 1918), Vol. I, pp. 412–418, Vol. II, pp. 495–502; Philip Taft, "Violence in American Labor Disputes" in *Annals,* pp. 127–140; Leon Wolff, *Lockout: The Story of the Homestead Strike of 1892* (New York: Harper & Row, 1965); and Almont Lindsey, *The Pullman Strike* (Chicago: University of Chicago Press, 1942).

20. "The strikes that stand out for their violence are those in which employers refused to deal with employees over the terms of employment and those in which professional strike guards and strike breakers were employed." See Taft in *Annals,* pp. 133–134. This idea of using deviant means to achieve cultural goals legally or informally denied one is first developed in Robert K. Merton's "Social Structure and Anomie" in Merton's *Social Theory and Social Structure* (Glencoe, Ill.: The Free Press, 1957). The

THE IMMIGRANT

The immigrant has always been a focus of violence in American history. Immigrants have consistently been the object of discrimination, exploitation, and attitudes of racial and ethnic superiority. They have been denied full participation in American society by earlier immigrants who saw themselves as being more American because of their earlier arrival. The Germans in the early part of the nineteenth century, the Irish, Italians, Poles, Bohemians, Hungarians, Jews (all countries), Spanish, Negroes, and internal migrants have all had to face ethnic and religious slurs, housing and job discrimination, physical violence, and social exclusion.

They, at times, have been the objects of organized political movements like the Native American party, the Know-Nothing party,[21] the Ku Klux Klan, and the various hate organizations of the thirties. The focus has always been directed toward the most recent arrivals. As older objects of enmity become "Americanized," they shift from being objects of hatred to sources of it. Thus today Negro and Spanish immigrants become the objects of hate

---

discussion of the reverse phenomenon, the institutionalization of legal settlement of labor conflicts, is discussed in Rolf Dahrendorf, *Class and Class Conflict in Industrial Society* (Stanford: Stanford University Press, 1959), pp. 206–280. The problem is treated in related terms by H. L. Nieburg in his chapter in this book and in his *Political Violence* (New York: St. Martin's Press, 1969). "One of the great contributions of the National Labor Relations Board has been the virtual elimination of the old-fashioned labor war, resulting in a sharp diminution of violence in labor disputes. Not only are employers prohibited from utilizing many former devices to abort organization by their employees, but they must deal with the representatives of their workers in proper bargaining unit." See Taft, *op. cit.*, p. 140.

21. John Hingham, *Strangers in the Land* (New York: Antheneum Press, 1963); Sister M. Evangeline Thomas, "Nativism in the Old Northwest 1850–1860" (Ph.D. diss., The Catholic University of America, 1935); William D. Overdyke, *The Know-Nothing Party in the South* (Baton Rouge: Louisiana State University Press, 1950); David M. Chalmers, *Hooded Americanism* (Garden City, N.Y.: Doubleday, 1965); William P. Randel, *The Ku Klux Klan* (New York: The Chilton Company, 1965); John M. Mecklin, *The Ku Klux Klan: A Study of the American Mind* (New York: Russell and Russell, 1963); Charles C. Alexander, *The Ku Klux Klan in the Southwest* (Lexington: University of Kentucky Press, 1965); and Will Herberg, *Protestant, Catholic and Jew* (Garden City, N.Y.: Doubleday, 1955), especially pp. 152–156, 262–282.

campaigns in an extreme situation of organized and unorganized violence.

Immigrants, of course, tend to bring their own brands of violence to the countries they settle in. Characteristically, the first generation born in urban America environments have produced high rates of delinquency and crime. Each group has contributed to ethnically composed criminal groups that feed organized crime. As each group becomes assimilated, it begins to lose any purely ethnic connection to crime, i.e., crime becomes either an individual or an integrated phenomenon.

The causes of such tendencies to crime (and violence) are the dislocations caused by movement into a new and alien urban environment for which the rural, old-country background fails to prepare one. Children of immigrants reject the "un-American" background of their parents without being exposed substantially to the institutions of the dominant society. The breakdown of social controls allows a portion of these groups to organize their own version of American society—a delinquent, violent subculture that resembles neither that of their parents nor that of the dominant society, although it contributes to the latter culture. Since the process of assimilation of earlier groups occurs together[22] with the arrival of new immigrant and migrant groups and in a period in which the dominant culture is itself changing, this violent, delinquent culture is continuously in flux. It has never stabilized or solidified and never becomes in any essential way a stable feature of American life.

At the same time, the particular forms of violence of whomever occupies the urban ghetto continues to be a part of the ever-changing culture of America. Moreover, this cycle of violence and delinquency provides the changing bases for the discriminatory attitudes of more settled groups. Thus the actual and potential violence against immigrants and migrants draws part of its ratio-

22. For detailed discussions of the assimilation of various ethnic subcultures, see Albert Cohen, *Delinquent Boys* (New York: The Free Press, 1955); Herbert J. Gans, *The Urban Villagers* (New York: The Free Press, 1962); Oscar Handlin, *The Newcomers* (Garden City, N.Y.: Doubleday, 1959); W. I. Thomas and Florian Znaniecki, *The Polish Peasant in Europe and America* (New York: Alfred A. Knopf, 1927); and William F. Whyte *Street Corner Society* (2d ed.; Chicago: University of Chicago Press, 1955).

nale and imagery from the delinquent subcultures of the ghetto. And the violence in the immigrant ghetto contributes continually to the overall environment of violence in the society. It also contributes to making violence a plausible alternative for action for those who would use it.

Immigration, in addition, produces another subspecies of violence—the violence of the old country. Thus where there are distinctive patterns of violence in a country that produces millions of immigrants, they reappear in the new country. Practices are simply modified to meet new situations.[23]

The vast proportion of American immigrants were peasants. The major exceptions to this trend were the puritans, the German 1848ers, and the Jews. Peasants represent a distinctive type of person and attitudinal orientation. Wherever they come from, they tend to personalize and concretize their social relations. They reject abstract thought, impressional forces, and bureaucratic or abstract legal forms.[24] When crime occurs, it involves direct personal attacks against people or physical objects. These crimes include assault, murder, manslaughter, and armed robbery. Middle-class crime is usually abstract and impersonal, representative examples including fraud, embezzlement, and evasion of administrative law.[25] Thus the Irish and the Italians, the "Arkies," the Spanish and the Negroes brought to the urban area special forms of crime contributing to the creation of an atmosphere of violence.

Immigrant groups, in addition, can import *political* violence. One important spur to immigration was the political repression and exploitation experienced by immigrants in their former countries. In some instances, these factors constituted the economic stimulus to migration. In other cases, the failure of revolution, or its success for some, was the prime cause of migration.[26]

But in all cases, American immigrants were a favorite recruiting and funding source, and frequently an organizational base, for

23. Nathan Glazer and Daniel P. Moynihan, *Beyond the Melting Pot* (Cambridge, Mass.: M.I.T. Press, 1963), pp. 181–202, 217–229.
24. Oscar Handlin, *op. cit.,* and *The Uprooted* (New York: Grosset & Dunlap, 1951); and Gerth and Mills, *op. cit.,* p. 283.
25. Edwin Sutherland, *White Collar Crime* (New York: Holt, Rinehart & Winston, 1961). For a description of peasant crime, see Gaetano Mosca, *The Ruling Class* (New York: McGraw-Hill, 1939), pp. 11–13, 211–214.
26. Oscar Handlin, *The Uprooted,* pp. 7–36.

national liberation and political revolutionary movements that were aimed primarily at the European homeland. The relative freedom to organize outside the mother country provided the climate for American group support for European revolutions. Thus the Irish, Polish, Czech, Israeli, Italian and various Latin American national liberation movements had important organizational support in the United States. The United States housed leaders of the Russian revolution, German revolutions, anti-Mussolini Italians (and pro), German refugees, French royalists and Bonapartists and, of course, refugees from the Iron Curtain countries as well as from both left- and right-wing Latin American countries.

Such movements were often violent. The violence centered not only on the home country but often carried over into the United States. This was particularly true of the Irish in the period immediately after the Civil War.[27] Other groups demonstrated similar tendencies. Individual acts of political assassination, such as that of Carlo Treska, appeared related to that of the domestic politics of Italy. The violence among pro- and anti-Castro Cubans is a recurrent feature of the current American scene.

POLITICAL IDEOLOGIES AND VIOLENCE

These latter cases of the revolutionary and "liberation" violence are particularly important since they reveal that violence per se is not only part of the continuing atmosphere of America, but that *political* violence is a normal part of the American political climate.

Thus political violence in the American past is most closely linked to problems of race, ethnic status, political revolution and the struggles over trade unionism. Political violence, unlike crime and frontier violence, is strongly linked to explicit political ideologies that defend its use. These ideologies are utilized by organized groups as a higher law to justify violence, including political assassination. The appeal to a higher morality to defend extreme

27. Thomas N. Brown, *Irish-American Nationalism, 1870–1890* (Philadelphia: Lippincott, 1966); Oscar Handlin, *The American People in the Twentieth Century* (Boston: Beacon Press, 1963), pp. 138–139; and Glazer and Moynihan, *op. cit.,* p. 243.

actions is part of most modern political ideologies. The introduction of the philosophy of national law to justify the American revolution is a pertinent example. As we have indicated, the recent political assassinations appear not to be a part of organized political conspiracies based on an explicit ideology. But all of them had political overtones involving, variously, racism, international relations in the Near East and, in some unknown way, the cold war. In each case, the violence appears to be motivated by a political ideology expressed in terms of the higher law by a deranged but politicized assassin.

IDEOLOGIES, VIOLENCE, AND POLITICAL ASSASSINATION

Political ideologies, no matter how imperfectly understood, and even without the support of organized groups, thus provide a linkage between personal derangement and politicized assassination. The plausibility of such a linkage is provided by a generalized atmosphere of violence that pervades a whole society. When that atmosphere of violence has a political base, the linkage is even tighter.

Still these interconnections do not explain sufficiently the role of ideologies in assassination, nor do they explain the relationship of such ideologies to the normal operation and organization of a society.

There are many types of political ideologies that involve violence. Some political ideologies, such as that of passive resistance and pacifism, explicitly reject violence in all its forms, including its use as a means to achieve group-supported goals. Thus, Tolstoi's and Kropotkin's anarchism, Gandhi's civil-disobedience movement and Martin Luther King's civil-rights movement were based upon the rejection of violence. Other movements do not, in principle, reject violence as a necessary condition for state power. They do reject the use of violence as the normal means for internal change. Spokesmen for these groups emphasize the need to use the normal, peaceful means of protest—agitation and propaganda—to achieve changes in structure, policies and the definition of rights within a society. But the assumption of theories of action based upon peaceful change presumes the ability of aspiring groups in a society to achieve legitimate goals through the use of such machinery and this hope rests upon a trust that other groups in society will not block the attempt to secure justice within the framework of its institutions. A repressive society can only breed violence unless its suppression is so extreme that it eliminates even the hope for justice.[28] If a society permits its less-favored groups to aspire for equality, but gives no hope for its realization, then it breeds the potential for violence. If it allows the oppressed groups to gain awareness, self-consciousness, some organizational strength and the hope for equality, but does not provide the means by which these hopes can be actualized,[29] then violence becomes a near certainty. Ideologies are the means by which political objectives and self-awareness coupled with the desire for change are turned into a political force. Denial of hope is the means that can turn ideological aspirations into a violent force. But such ideologies look to violence as a means to realize political, economic, and social programs. Violence is viewed as a means, not an end. The use of violence is an evil necessary to transform society.

IDEOLOGIES OF PURE VIOLENCE

At the other extreme to pacifism are ideologies that glorify violence and at times seem to suggest that violence is the sole aim of revolutionary activity. Such theories would include the anarchistic theories of Bakunin, Nechayev, and the Narodniki.[30] In violent anarchism, the aim is the end of state and all coercion, to be

28. Crane Brinton, *The Anatomy of Revolution* (Englewood Cliffs, N.J.: Prentice-Hall, Inc., 1952), p. 278; and Coser, *op. cit.*, pp. 96–101 (also see Coser's "Critique of Fanon," pp. 215–222, in the same volume).

29. Reinhard Bendix and Seymour Martin Lipset, "Karl Marx's Theory of Social Classes" in *Class, Status and Power*, edited by Bendix and Lipset (New York: The Free Press, 1966), pp. 6–12; Coser, *op. cit.*; Niccolo Machiavelli, *The Prince* (New York: New American Library 1952), pp. 46–47, 54–55–62; Eric Hoffer, *The True Believer* (New York: New American Library, 1951); and Max Scheler, *Resentment* (New York: The Free Press, 1961). Ted Gurr has made relative deprivation, discontent, and the anticipation of increasing frustration the major axis of his theoretical and empirical studies on violence. See "Urban Disorder: Perspectives from the Comparative Study of Civil Strife" in Masotti and Bowen, *op. cit.*

30. Hannah Arendt, *On Revolution* (New York: Viking Press, 1963), pp. 1–12, and *The Origins of Totalitarianism* (New York: Harcourt Brace & World, 1966), pp. 328–330; David Shub, *Lenin* (New York: New American Library, abridged edition, 1950), pp. 14–20; and Edward Wilson, *To the Finland Station* (Garden City, N.Y.: Doubleday Anchor, 1953), pp. 280–288. See also in the opening chapter of this volume Crotty's discussion of the ideological justifications for assassinations.

replaced by a noncoercive, nonviolent utopian society. In other cases, the exclusive preoccupation is with the destruction of the existing order. The problem of reconstruction is one to be encountered only in the process by which the destruction of established security occurs. There is thus no concern with drawing plans, programs, and mythologies for the future, since these plans are never, in fact, implemented. All that matters is to destroy the present forms of society. It is first necessary to eradicate the evil before a rebuilding can start. Such ideologies of violence concentrate on the description of the current injustices, the necessity of destroying them, and the organization and tactics appropriate to implementing the charges. The concern with group forms and tactics and the conspiratorial community of professionals place emphasis on a total dedication to the task at hand, by assassins if need be. Ideologies of violence create an image of an elite community of assassins bound together by mystical bonds that demand total commitment—to duty, to the rejection of society, and to the risk involved in the enterprise. Dostoevski, Malraux, and Camus have best portrayed this most extreme psychology of political assassination. Only in the total rejection of all other relationships to society can the conspirators achieve the sense of mystical brotherhood, of an emotional intensity and commitment that overcomes their sense of self-alienation. Dedication to the cause serves to alleviate the anxiety, the doubts, the self-consciousness, and self-questioning. Both as a political philosophy and as a psychology, the ideology of pure violence is a philosophy of despair. The overwhelming present is viewed as so hopeless, so intractable to reason or to change, that only total destruction can restore the hope for escape. Transcending the present means, however, living in a mood of hyperexcitation at the prospect of being involved in the immediate future in violent activities. In an important sense, the deferment of discussion of long-term political goals and programs, or of the construction of idealized images of a distant future, allows this concentration on the emotional richness of the violent life to be achieved in the instant activism. Georges Sorel comes close to presenting this life image in ideological terms in his *Reflections on Violence.* Violence together with myth and poetry allows the masses to achieve a level of emotional intensity, unity of self, and a dedication that no amount of reason can achieve. Moreover, only by violence can revolutions be achieved. Only violence can result in the polarization of classes, the creation of class loyalties at an emotional level and the enthusiasm necessary to accomplish a revolution. Explicit in Sorel's work, as it is in other ideologies of violence, is the rejection of legalism and the delay, the "empty rationality" and materialism of nonviolent change. All nonviolent change necessarily involves compromise, restraint, negotiation and argument over tactics and procedure. It means at best a slow process of modification and the changes at any one time may be of small magnitude. Thus the self-consciousness, the dull rationality and the separateness of individuals is part and parcel of nonviolent change. In part, the present is accepted as a base line in the process of change. One starts from here and accepts incremental changes. One also incorporates rationally in this line of reasoning the psychological alienation of the contemporary situation into the very process of change. Thus workers and managements, according to Sorel, may be seduced away from a violent confrontation because at material and rational levels they can achieve their demands by slow change. Violence prevents such rationality and is necessary to achieve a revolution.

The ideology of violence is thus an all-or-nothing philosophy; it accepts defeat as better than small but continuous victories, because at the level of its demands true victories are achievable only by the obliteration of a sense of self. In this way, it is a philosophy of despair. One can speculate that the all-or-nothing ideology is essentially a "nothing" ideology,[31] i.e., that total defeat is the actual or psychological goal of theories of pure violence. Victory in revolution would mean a return to the politics of everyday life. This includes the nagging administrative problems, legalism, compromise with one's allies and with the new demands of the ruled. It would mean a return to self-consciousness, routine, and the politics of limited goals and commitments. To achieve a permanent escape from these forms of alienation would thus either be a "hero's death," in which self-consciousness disappears, or "perma-

---

31. Robert Payne, *The Life and Death of Lenin* (New York: Simon and Schuster, 1964), pp. 31–35; Albert Camus, *The Stranger* (New York: Alfred A. Knopf, 1946); Fedor M. Dostoevski, *The Possessed* (New York: Macmillan, 1951), trans. Constance Garnett; and André Malraux, *Man's Fate* (New York: The Modern Library, 1934), trans. Haakon Chevalier.

nent revolution," where the self-exaltation and the emotional commitment to total causes could be maintained by ritualization of violence and revolution.

This perhaps long digression on ideologies of pure violence is undertaken despite the absence of such systematic ideologies in the American scene because we feel that the psychological fundamentals of the ideology underlie all violent political movements, *even when the ideological form is absent.* Thus we feel that current confrontation politics rejects ideas of compromise, of routine, of legalism, of "rational unidimensionality,"[32] and "alienation," and strives for enriched, poetic, emotional and myth-responsive men, men who are close to the emotional and irrational sources of their being. The experience of confrontation produces an emotionally enriched sense of being. It produces a communion of "revolutionaries," and it delays participation in the alienated present and near future. The distant future does not have to be planned for; once achieved out of the poetry of violence, it will take care of itself.

Maoism, as expressed in its cultural revolution, rejects the routinization of its successful revolution and the bureaucratization of revolution with its reliance on the procedures and privileges of "business as usual." It seeks to reinvoke the enthusiasm, devotion, sacrifice and heroism of the revolution against the now bureaucratized and stabilized revolution. Violence against its own success becomes the means by which these emotional values are to be retained. Youth is the basis from which the cultural revolution is to be achieved, since youth has not been compromised by its involvement in a stable, bureaucratic order. The apparent failure of the Chinese cultural revolution, like the failure of the euphoric stages of all revolution, attests to the persistency of forces in society to routinize its social organization. Normal life functions (birth, marriage, education, work, play, the rearing of children) exert a persistent pressure for a stable order to protect their daily operation. The escape from the dullness of such a life constitutes a major value of violent political movements.

The all-or-nothing ideology, the avoidance of negotiation and

32. Herbert Marcuse, *One-Dimensional Man* (Boston: Beacon Press, 1964); and Kurt Wolff and Barrington Moore, Jr., *The Critical Spirit: Essays in Honor of Herbert Marcuse* (Boston: Beacon Press, 1968).

compromise, the glory in the drama of violence may be a component in some segments of the black militant movements.[33]

Even to the isolated individual political assassin, the commitment to violence involves the rejection of the grayness of everyday life, the rejection of any attempt to confront problems by the ordinary machinery of society. The act of conceiving a plan of assassination and carrying it out must be an act of total commitment. It commands one's complete attention and, if carried through, one's absolute enthusiasm. It is an act that enables one to transcend the ordinary isolation of existence and to gain the imagined achievement of importance and possibly even immortality. It is, however, an act of desperation, since the consequence may be death for the assassin as well as the victim. Assassination constitutes a form of self-annihilation in which the assassin joins his fate with that of a political figure.

IDEOLOGIES OF VIOLENCE
AS MEANS TO POLITICAL GOALS

Ideologies of pure violence are relatively rare,[34] although aspects of these emerge as psychological and phenomenological values in other violent political movements. Most political acts that involve violence define it simply as a means to other ends. It is part of the methodology, the tactics and strategy of revolution. As a result, the use of violence is rationally controlled. However, as has been seen, violence has its own aesthetics and psychological appeal, making the control of violence in revolutionary situations extremely difficult. Exponents of violence in revolutionary actions tend to run amok. Some revolutionists develop an enthusiasm for violent behavior that becomes separated from the goals of revolution itself.[35] They become promiscuous in its use. The freedom to perform acts of violence, once these have proven successful,

33. Cleaver, *op. cit.;* Malcolm X, *op. cit.;* and Frantz Fanon, *The Wretched of the Earth* (New York: Grove Press, 1963), pp. 203–251.

34. Hannah Arendt, "Reflections on Violence," *New York Review of Books,* 12, No. 4 (February 27, 1969), p. 28.

35. Leon Trotsky, *Stalin* (New York: Harper & Brothers, 1941), pp. 384–410; and Isaac Deutscher, *Stalin* (New York: Oxford University Press, 1949), pp. 345–385.

produces a euphoric escape from the boredom of the enforced inactivity that any long-term conspiracy entails. Once this euphoria is attained, then a limitation of violence to necessary situations becomes difficult. The "higher law" of the revolutionary ideology, in addition, permits individual revolutionaries to commit personal acts of violence. These include the use of revolutionary violence as retribution for insults or rivalry, to satisfy individual greed or ambition or to gratify personal pathologies. All of these exist, of course, in nonrevolutionary environments. However, they are restrained by the absence of a "higher law" to justify them and the cover of generalized revolutionary violence which conceals individual pathologies.

The tendency for violence to run unchecked is a problem to professional revolutionaries, a profession, coincidentally, that came into existence only after Marx began to codify[36] the laws of revolution, and Lenin defined the job specifications of the revolutionary (*What Is to Be Done?*). The job of the professional revolutionary with respect to violence is to specify the situations of necessary action and to eliminate the self defeating acts. The latter include those that invite damaging reprisal, those that alienate significant sectors of the population critical to achieving support for the cause, and those that divert the attention and resources of the movement. Adventurists, opportunists, "bourgeois romantic terrorists," and undisciplined revolutionary amateurs are threats to the objectives of the professional. Typical situations for necessary violence will be discussed below.

Regardless of the attempt to control violence, the successful revolutions (i.e., those that achieve power) almost universally overindulge in violent behavior. Opponents are eliminated or otherwise made the object of controlled or uncontrolled acts of violence. "Counterrevolutionaries" are purged. Moderate revolutionaries are discredited, often because they fail to demonstrate sufficient enthusiasm for the revolution and its excesses. Violence is directed at opposing factions in the revolutionary coalition. The

36. Lenin's *What Is to Be Done?*, trans. S. V. and Patricia Utechin, ed. with an introduction and notes by S. V. Utechin (Oxford: Clarendon Press, 1963); Hitler's *Mein Kampf*, trans. Ralph Manheim (Boston: Houghton Mifflin, 1943); Sorel's *Reflections on Violence* (New York: Macmillan, 1961) and Nechayev's *Catechism* are all in this sense blueprints and handbooks for political violence.

demands for unified co-operation among ideologically hostile factions suppress the factional infighting while the revolution is in progress. Once success is achieved, however, trouble emerges. Latecomers to the revolution may assume command and repress the original revolutionaries or alternatively be purged themselves. Administrators may attack ideologists, as in the case of Stalin's purges, or be eliminated by the ideologists, partially the cause underlying the Chinese cultural revolution.

The promiscuously violent people may be purged because such indiscriminate behavior threatens the lives of more peaceful revolutionaries. More often, the indiscriminately violent revolutionaries are contained through promotion to positions in the police administration, the security forces, and the military forces. They become defenders of law and order and confine their terrorism to enemies of the administration. Violence becomes contained by being institutionalized. The institutional co-optation of violence and officials who are addicted to it, however, results in repression which in turn produces tendencies toward counterviolence. The development of counterviolence depends upon the efficiency of the repression. Thus violence, even in successful revolutions, produces pressure to counterviolence at the point where institutionalized violence either loses its efficiency or is relaxed. It is therefore difficult to produce a nonviolent counteraction directed toward achieving the restoration of previously lost political and civil rights.

Finally, violent leaders in successful revolutions are often sent to foreign countries to further the cause by undermining hostile regimes. They are allowed to exercise their special talents in climates that do not threaten the established revolution. Thus they become exporters and breeders of violence and assassination. The use of violence is continued, even after repressive "nonviolence" is established in the homeland of the revolution.[37]

SOME SOCIAL FUNCTIONS OF VIOLENCE

From the standpoint of the revolutionary, violence and political assassination have positive functions. They are justified either in political ideologies or as revolutionary tactics.

37. Che Guevara's mission to Bolivia may well have been an example of such an exporting of revolution.

The first of these "positive" functions is to define issues, to call attention to the revolutionary group and its power and to specify the enemy. The target of the assassination attempt need not be an officeholder nor a man influential in the government structure. But he must symbolize an objective of importance; an issue, a regime, a class, or an ideology. His symbolic value is precisely that needed for revolutionary purposes. Protest demonstrations, picketing, propaganda, and agitation are, of course, alternative means to assassination directed towards achieving the same end. Assassination as a political means attempts to accomplish these purposes in a single dramatic gesture. It requires less mass organization, less broadly based social support, and is, in its illegality, more secret and conspiratorial. Political assassination, then, when employed by organized political revolutionary groups, is most likely to be used in repressive societies where the ordinary politics of protest are denied. When employed, it is used by relatively small or weak groups unable to dramatize issues by other means. Its very purpose is based upon this weakness; the assassination is used to publicize an issue, to indicate strength and to rally latent support to the cause.

In the parallel cases of political assassinations committed by isolated, deranged assassins, the same element is present. The selection of Martin Luther King appears to have been based on his being a symbol of the black civil-rights movements. The selection of Robert Kennedy as a target seems in a similar fashion to have been done in order to protest his and America's support of Israel against Jordan. Since both assassinations appear to be the work of irrational, isolated individuals, and not of an organized political group, there appears to be no political organization or machinery to "profit" from the assassination. At most, these assassinations appear to be senseless acts of "protest."

The use of assassination as a tactic for defining issues by an organized revolutionary group includes the attempt to provoke repressive countermeasures by the regime. These governmental acts are directed against not only the assassins but against any group that is a potential ally of the revolutionary cause. Thus the misdirected reprisals provoked by the assassination cause new groups to perceive the assassination as "justified." Ironically, the new repression becomes a substitute symbol for the alleged suppression that provoked the original assassination. The reprisal produces new victims and new heroes, strengthening the movement. As an example, the execution of Lenin's brother Alexander produced the most important single recruit to the ranks of the Russian revolutionary movement.

Violence as a Self-Sustaining System

All this suggests that organized, revolutionary assassinations are implicit conspiracies that involve unintended co-operation[38] between repressive regimes and violent revolutionaries. The system operates as follows: repression produces assassination (or other violent provocative action); the assassination produces counter-violence that usually spills over to groups and individuals other than those directly involved in the assassination; the counter-violence enlarges the ranks of revolutionary groups (or those sympathetic to them) who engage in further aggressive political action (possibly including assassination). The system includes the escalation of violence and repression, the polarization of the society, and the imminence of a total "confrontation" where revolutionary victory, or defeat, is achieved. Reactionary forces may encourage this process, as well as radical groups, since the escalation and polarization include the possibility of driving moderates and conservatives into their camp, giving them control of this sector of society. The escalation of violence and polarization of society also permits reactionary forces to free themselves from the normal restraints on violence and repression, allowing them to hope for an ultimate victory. They, too, accept the "all-or-nothing" logic of despair. Under such a philosophy, they may initiate political assassinations, purges, and policy programs intended to hasten confrontation. In doing so, they attempt to drive the opposition into premature acts of desperation. These actions can be controlled and their perpetrators removed because of the ill-advised desperation of the acts.[39]

38. This idea is suggested by Max Weber in his essay "Religious Rejections of the World and Their Directions," in Gerth and Mills, *op. cit.,* pp. 340–355.

39. Bayard Rustin, "The Lessons of the Long Hot Summer," *Commentary* (October, 1967); and Coser, *op. cit.*

This dynamic system of violence seems to be an essential process in all violent revolutions. It operated specifically in the Russian Revolution and in the rise of Nazism. Political assassination was an essential ingredient of both situations. The awareness of such processes becomes more widely diffused as the study of revolutionary practices is undertaken by both the practitioners and the disinterested students of politics. As such knowledge becomes disseminated, the temptation increases to apply the theory, if only to test it. It would appear that much of the politics of protest and confrontation voiced by radical youth is based upon such theorizing. Its basic assumptions have been developed by Chairman Mao, Che Guevara, Fanon, and Régis Debray. Fortunately, in recent Western radical youth movements protest demonstration, provocation, and confrontation other than assassination have been used. Political assassination is, however, the ultimate application of such theories, the one demanding the complete subjugation of the individual to the movement. In avoiding this total commitment, current Western radical movements have so far avoided equally inclusive retaliation. In other respects, the politics of confrontation in the above meanings of the terms has tended to polarize society and invite an escalated response greater than the repression that provoked it.

This is the danger of these tactics. Once initiated, they begin a process whose outcome is uncertain. They may well create the very repression that presumably is its cause. If such tactics succeed, they institute new forms of repressive violence. If they fail, they accentuate and re-create older forms of repressive violence at greater levels of intensity.

Revolutionary assassination includes the political murder of members of rival political groups. In any revolutionary situation, there are usually a large number of groups, parties, and conspiracies that compete for leadership of the same potential supporters. Many groups derive from the same ideological forebears. Many emerge as the result of splits among factions of a parent group; others emerge from the competition of leaders over differences in tactics or ideology. In a conspiratorial environment, where repression governs all political activity, the means of political argument are limited. In the same situation, assassination and similar techniques to eliminate rivals become a standard form of political action. Alternatives include the denunciation of the illegal rival groups to repressive authorities, the disrupting of meetings, and violent personal assaults directed against leaders of competing factions. Political assassination is an extreme measure, but becomes normalized by unusual situations. It is also a means of control over a community. The threat of assassination may serve to silence rivals. It may also prevent the adoption of alternatives more moderate than those advocated by the groups that threaten violence. In this sense, assassination threats neutralize moderates, contributing to the polarization of a society. The assassination of moderates by extremist reactionary groups accomplishes the same purposes. Such acts consolidate control in the most extreme groups. The political "poles" are permitted to confront each other without the ambiguity and complexity of more moderate intervening positions.

The use of violence against political rivals is, in principle, subordinate to the main effort of achieving a confrontation of force between extremes. In actual fact, however, vendettas against opponents may become the main effort. Political rivals tend to occupy the same social space and appeal to the same potential supporters. They are derived from the same social movements. As competitors, they are more salient to each other and, as potential targets, they are more accessible to attack than governmental figures. As a result, the impulse toward political violence frequently is directed against secondary and tertiary targets. Its effect, however, is always to intensify the atmosphere of violence and to legitimate violence, i.e., to make violence appear as a plausible means of action. Its use invites intervention and counteraction by repressive authorities and thus helps to escalate the system of violence.

VIOLENCE IN NONREVOLUTIONARY SITUATIONS

Our digression into violence as related to revolutionary situations is, in part, outside the immediate problem of recent political assassinations in America. But these speculations have suggested that there is a "logic" of violence and assassination, that a system of violence exists, and that there are psychological and phenomenological ties to assassination that are transferable to even such "irrational" assassinations as those that have evoked our inquiry.

In the same way, political assassinations in nonrevolutionary situations are relevant to our task.

We indicated in the introduction that political assassinations are related to the process of state building and in our discussion of revolutionary assassination that political assassination is related to the destruction and reconstitution of established states. Let us return to our original point.

ASSASSINATION IN FEUDAL AND TRIBAL SOCIETIES

In feudal and tribal societies, and in former colonial states that have not achieved the necessary political trust, violence and political assassination are the normal means of political action. In such societies, no state has achieved a legitimate monopoly on the right to violence and no universal law has been accepted that provides techniques for the achievement of personal and social aspirations without recourse to violence.

Groups of individuals normally arm and defend themselves on their own account. The political organization consists of these defensive and aggressive arrangements. The tribe, the extended family, and the armed feudal class become the units that control violence. The alliances among these groups constitute the legal order. Since neither a moral community nor a legitimized universal legal order exist, armed conflict is a normal mode of action. The vendetta becomes a way of saving personal and family honor; the duel is used to redress personal insult.

Assassination is accepted as a means of removing political rivals and of securing the functional equivalent of elections. Thus, in feudal society the incidence of political assassination was, and to the extent such societies still exist, is high. The period of the War of the Roses and the Hundred Years' War in England, the fifteenth and sixteenth centuries in France, and virtually any century in Russia were periods of political assassination. In the Italy of the Renaissance and the late feudal period, the use of daggers, politically motivated poisonings,[40] and armed bands of assassins were normal occurrences. In the Near East, tribal leaders assassinated

40. Janet P. Trevelyan, *A Short History of the Italian People* (London: George Allen and Unwin Ltd., 1956), pp. 230–257.

each other with regularity. Where statehood was imposed upon tribalistic societies by Western powers, the act of assassination in political exchanges was continued within the structure of the semifeudal states. It also appeared in relations between nations whose respective unifications replaced tribalism in form only. Thus, in the Middle East the threat of assassination and sometimes its use are normal means of conducting international relations between seemingly friendly countries.

POLITICAL ASSASSINATION IN THE PROCESS OF STATE BUILDING

In the same sense, the achievement of statehood by former colonial states, whose new boundaries reflect the administrative convenience and postimperialistic opportunities of their previous rulers, did not result in the development of a political community strong enough to preclude violence. The process of state building thus results in violence. The forms of violence include genocide, especially evident in the total elimination of tribes whose right to existence does not fall within the culture of the dominant tribe. It includes the incarceration or the assassination of leaders of rival parties and tribes. "Civil" wars are endemic. Political stability, to the extent it is achieved, is done so through the violent repression of the opposition. Of the new nations created since World War II, only India, Israel, and Somaliland have provisionally succeeded in establishing political climates based upon peace and trust in the political order.[41] The establishing of a political community is difficult. Such achievements in the West have been the result of the processes being repeated at present in the newly formed states. Civil war, murder, violence, and assassination give way to organized, authoritarian repression. New forms of violence are only gradually replaced by a respect for the law, a belief in the legiti-

41. Morris Janowitz, *The Military in the Political Development of New Nations* (Chicago: University of Chicago Press, 1964), pp. 6–10, *passim;* Eloise G. ReQua and June Stathom, *The Developing Nations: A Guide to Information Sources Concerning Their Economic, Political, Technical and Social Problems* (Detroit: Gale Research Co., 1965); and Myron Weiner, "Political Modernization and Evolutionary Theory" in *Social Change in Developing Areas* by Herbert R. Barringer, et al. (Cambridge, Mass.: Schenkman Publishing Co., 1965), pp. 102–112.

macy of the government, and a public opinion supportive of institutionalized arrangements. It took centuries for the Western nations to achieve these "civilizing" processes. And once established, they have been under almost continuous assault. Pressures that can result in the resort to violence and assassination are always present. Perhaps the major impact of the historical revolution within Western society has been to convert politically violent behavior from an accepted means of political action to one that evokes disgust.[42]

The difficulty of achieving the normalization of internal peace in Western societies might enable us to understand similar problems when encountered in the newer nations. In addition, developing nations have other challenges. The emergence of the territorial state in Western society occurred simultaneously with pacification. Thus dynastic empires were transformed to nation-states. The process was slow; for example, it did not occur in Austria-Hungary until the twentieth century. The idea of the nation preceded its realization in most Western societies. Nationalism as an intellectual and social movement helped stimulate the loyalties necessary to sustain the newly created states. Whenever states are established through the administrative decree of former rulers or of international bodies, they may come into existence without common loyalties, language, institutions, or habits of thought. The basic awareness of the existence of a "citizen" as a member of a group larger than a tribe or locality, a prerequisite of a stable national development, may also be missing. Statehood can thus be imposed upon the residents of an area only by force.

THE SOCIAL STRATIFICATION OF ASSASSINATION

The characteristic kinds of political assassination vary with the stage of political development of a nation. Three kinds of political assassinations can be specified in these regards: (1) peer assassination; (2) down-the-line political assassination; and (3) up-the-

42. Daniel Walker, *Rights in Conflict: The Chicago Police Riot* (New York: New American Library, 1968). The publication of this volume owes much to the public outcry concerning the media coverage of the confrontation between demonstrators and police during the 1968 Democratic Convention in Chicago. Also see the Kerner Commission report (*Report of the National Advisory Commission on Civil Disorders*) on the riots.

line political assassination. Up-the-line political assassination appears to characterize our era. It is, at least, the one we are most sensitive to. Up-the-line political assassination is the murder of the head of a government, of some centralized institution, or of a symbolic leader by an individual or a group with lesser influence in the society. The assassinations of Martin Luther King and the Kennedys are of this nature. Down-the-line assassination is the murder of someone with less power, influence, or symbolic importance. It is commissioned by the heads of a state or a powerful organization within the state. The assassination of Trotsky is an example. Peer assassination can occur at all social and economic levels, but by definition occurs when assassin and victim are at approximately the same social level. While examples of all three types of assassination can be found in any one period, we would hypothesize that each is more characteristic of different historical eras.

PEER-GROUP ASSASSINATIONS

Peer-group assassination is most closely associated with feudal and tribal societies. Basically, this is because the society fails to develop institutions for the peaceful transfer of power among contending groups. As a result, only relatively powerful *armed* groups can enter the political game. Down-the-line groups are disarmed and controlled by repression and military force. When repression is too severe, these down-the-line groups explode. Such uprisings occur at odd moments, as in present rebellions. The revolts are infrequent and disorganized. They rarely result in cumulative change. The repression and pacification of lower strata of the society occur at the same time that repression between elements of the upper strata is in process. Since the major segments of each strata are armed, and since no agency of the society has a legitimate monopoly on the use of violence, the politics of such societies center on the struggle for military dominance between powerful armed groups. Alliances and counteralliances and exchanges of loyalty and fealty are the means by which peace is obtained. But since all such elite groups are armed, and all major issues are settled by force, armed struggle and the preparation for warfare are characteristic of the operation of society. Peace is achieved when one faction has clear military dominance or when the probability of winning in the test of arms is low. Hence the necessity arises for some formal accommodation among competing groups. Political assassination is a major occurrence in the internal warfare that distinguishes these societies. The assassination of peers, however, is the prevalent type of political murder. The leaders of one faction assassinate their peers in rival groups.

Of course, the assassination of peers occurs in other stages of political development. We have indicated that revolutionary groups will assassinate leaders of competing groups. Reactionary groups near the centers of power will do likewise during revolutionary situations. Such assassinations are incidental to up-the-line or down-the-line struggles for power and are not the characteristic forms.

DOWN-THE-LINE POLITICAL ASSASSINATION

Down-the-line assassinations principally occur in the process of state building. An established individual or group attempts to monopolize all power in a territory by disarming competitors. The effort involves internal warfare, including attempts to destroy the economic and political bases of rival groups. It also includes the construction of centralized state machinery. Attacks are directed against the political and administrative functionings of rival groups. Other factions, previously subservient to the rival groups, are freed. Alliances between lower strata and elite groups are forged. Myths of the nation, including those emphasizing national patriotism, are created, and new loyalty structures result. The principal form of assassination in these circumstances is by members of the dominant elites against those of subordinate groups. This, again, is only one of many means of achieving complete power. Virtually every nation that emerges has a history of state-induced political assassinations. Since statehood is achieved by individual countries in varying centuries, each will have different periods when its history is besmirched by a high incidence of political assassinations. Thus a relatively powerful nation like England has a history of political assassination, many of which were state induced. These political murders continued well into the seventeenth century until nationhood was achieved. In the newer nations this process still continues.

Down-the-line assassinations almost always stimulate up-the-line political assassinations and vice versa. In part, this is true because organized political assassination becomes incorporated into a retaliatory network. In the same sense, the assassination of a peer provokes other retaliatory peer assassinations. Down-the-line political murders, however, represent more than assassinations. They are part of the attempt to destroy the elite position of powerful competitors. Thus, the target group not only protects itself against assassination but is forced to defend its total historic, legal, military, and political rights. One of the armory of techniques it has at its disposal is the assassination of the claimants of state power. As a result, a characteristic form of retaliation to down-the-line assassination is up-the-line assassination. The head of state and his supporters become the objects of assassination by conspiratorial groups drawn from those strata that previously shared power but whose position is in jeopardy. Again, this type of up-the-line assassination characterizes the process of nation building.

Down-the-line *political* assassination occurring during nation building results in another kind of down-the-line assassination. Since the would-be state builder draws into his circle of support groups previously not involved in the political scene, these new individuals become a threat to those in danger of losing power. The new groups become the target of down-the-line repression of older groups who are in the process themselves of being liquidated.

Down-the-line assassination generates counterassassination and subsidiary assassination. But the characteristic form of assassination in a particular era is related to the central historical and political drift of the society. In this sense, the primary form need not be the most frequent type, but it must be the generative type of political assassination.

Up-the-Line Political Assassination

We have indicated that most revolutionary forms of assassination are up-the-line. In addition, we have argued that the characteristic types of assassinations of political leaders in the American past have been up-the-line assassinations. And we have noted that up-the-line political assassinations occur as a response to down-the-line repression and assassinations. At this time, we can only add some comments about the general nature of up-the-line assassinations and elaborate some additional types.

In primitive societies, power is centralized among a number of rival armed groups. None of these achieves a legitimate *monopoly* of power. All other groups are pacified and controlled by repressive means. Occasionally, the level or repression may be so great that peasant groups arm themselves and revolt. The rebellion usually involves looting, burning of mansions, orgiastic behavior, drinking and rape. Peasants are usually armed with only the tools of their trade. Rarely do they have centralized political or organizational leadership or extensive resources. As a result, the revolt is suppressed and followed by even greater repression.

Alternatively, when disarmed peasants and other groups are severely repressed by feudal or tribal elites in a society that has minimal central authority, they "take to the hills," exiling themselves to uninhabited areas, and become bandits. Banditry is a response to overrepression by up-the-line groups. It is different from revolutionary activity in that it lacks any formal ideology and is not concerned with overturning the political system, but lives off it. Thus banditry becomes professionalized. It is institutionalized as a form of crime. Although its origins are political, banditry becomes professionalized rather than politicized. It forms a deviant part of the political system. It need not be considered political. It does, however, contribute to the violence level of a society and to the atmosphere that makes political violence a plausible alternative. In addition, banditry becomes a refuge for political outcasts who enter previously "institutionalized" bandit groups as a means of escaping repression.

Organized up-the-line violence and assassination in the pure case are responses to the established state. Once institutionalized, state structure and social policies reflect the interests of those who control it. At a formal level, the "state" attempts to set procedures by which its law is dominant. Forms are ordained through which its laws can be enacted. It also provides the criteria that determine who shall be eligible to modify the law. Finally, it enacts specific substantive policies that affect differentially life fates of various groupings of its citizens. *Politics*[43] represents the process by which groups influence these uses of state power. Political parties and factions organize and exert pressure to modify the access to and structure of state power and the specific policies that become law. In doing so, they also may deny access to the state machinery and the protection of state policy to other groups within the state. This refusal to allow a group whose social and economic development has proceeded to the point where it reaches the possibility of access to the institutionalized means for forming policy is the major source of violence in society. Once hope of achieving aspirations already enjoyed by others in society is denied to a group, its only redress is to attack the state and its conspicuous representatives. The denial of hope can only be maintained by repression. Thus those who control state power must use state and nongovernmental violence as the means for maintaining their monopoly.

These favored groups have at their disposal the organized forces of repression of the state: the police, militia, army and internal security forces. As a result, violence can be relatively direct and open. The challenging group, in turn, is forced to adapt clandestine means to achieve its ends. Sudden mass demonstrations, strikes and political assassination are the usual outcomes.

Once such a condition is achieved in a society, the up-the-line system of political violence is instituted and evokes reciprocal down-the-line political violence. Political assassination is both an ingredient of the system and a by-product of it. When it is an ingredient of the system, it is part of the organized struggle for power. When it is a by-product, individuals influenced by the general atmosphere of violence and their own emotional problems undertake political assassination on their own account.

POLITICAL ASSASSINATION ACROSS NATIONAL LINES

The above discussion rests upon the notion that a nation-state exists and that violence is directed by and against holders of its power. Such a contention is only partially true. In some societies— feudal, tribal, and colonial—the state in the modern sense does not

43. Max Weber, "Politics as a Vocation" (pp. 77–128), and "Class, Status and Party" (pp. 180–195), both in Gerth and Mills, *op. cit.*

exist. In addition, much political violence, and especially assassinations, occur in international situations.

Political violence and assassination is likely to appear with
relative frequency in the struggle for national liberation. Much of
the violence of central Europe and in colonial Africa was directed
against imperial powers and their agents. Such violence is likely to
occur frequently because the groups who are the objects are by
virtue of their national and ethnic differences thought to be
particularly subject to the higher laws that condone total retribution. Alien rulers justify their power by ideologies of racial and
national superiority, which in turn favor severe repressive actions.
The racial and ethnic defenses of the indigenous populations lead
to violent counterattacks. Up-the-line political assassination is
more likely to occur in situations of ethnic or national domination.
The heritage of violence is likely to continue for some time after
national liberation has been achieved because of the normalization
of such actions in preliberation eras.

Cross-national political violence, as indicated, also takes the
form of peer-group violence as battles for national liberation
spread to other nations. This form of struggle involves various
groups with different ideologies and tactical approaches to national
liberation, as well as contests between supporters and opponents of
the dominant regime in the homeland. Political assassination
between Algerian nationalistic groups occurred almost as frequently in France as it did in Algeria.

Finally, cross-national political violence, and particularly assassination, is employed when a dominant regime in the homeland
attempts to eliminate revolutionary refugees who have escaped to a
foreign country to plan continued strategies of resistance. In these
cases, legal means of repression are not available to the established
regime. It is forced to employ conspiratorial methods to achieve its
ends. Political assassination is a favorite technique.

THE PERIODICITY OF ASSASSINATION

The above discussion indicates that political assassination derives from various causes and has distinguishable meanings. But
these differences in source and meaning are not random. Rather,

there are characteristic forms of political assassination that are associated with different stages of the political development of a society. These characteristic stages of development overlap. Also, each type of political violence tends to generate counterviolence, in some cases, of a different form. Nevertheless, there are periods when one form of political violence predominates.

As has been noted, however, organized political violence is only one form of violence, a factor of special importance in relation to political assassination. There is a spillover from organized to unorganized political violence. This spillover takes many forms. In the simplest form, individual political assassins go into business on their own account. This is to say, they appropriate the issues and ideologies of organized, violent political movements and resolve them by personal acts of violence. Political assassination is a form of political action amenable to such treatment in that it can be carried out by an isolated individual.

Second, a major theme suggested by our total analysis is that the atmosphere of political violence, or even a more general violence, in a society suggests to emotionally disturbed and deranged individuals the plausibility of political assassination as a means of acting-out inner tensions. Political violence, especially, normalizes personal violence. It evokes an emotional dynamic in which the planning and execution of a violent act evokes forms of personal commitment that help to overcome the sense of alienation felt by many deranged, as well as normal, persons in a large society.

Implicit in this is the idea that each act of violence legitimatizes, i.e., normalizes, violence for others. It assumes a contagious and epidemiological character. The plausibility of violence suggests itself to individuals who are politically violent simply as "a thing to do." Thus a political assassination is rarely a unique or isolated event or, in this sense, an individual phenomenon. Each assassination stimulates others. Political assassinations appear likely to occur in sudden bursts. Organized political violence is likely to cause a series of episodes and counteractions that result in periodic violence on other grounds also.

If the pattern holds true, then the mass media can have an important role in the normalization of violence. We refer not to the presentation of violence on television and other mass media via westerns, war movies and crime programs, but to the effect of news programs.[44] Television particularly can dramatize and personalize violent characters and situations more vividly than any other media. Actual assassination can be re-created. Leaders of small violent movements can be turned into national celebrities. By so doing, the medium provides for the recruitment of followers and, conversely, the mobilization of opposition. Leaders of such movements appear larger than life. Television can dramatize local cults and styles, give them national exposure and prominence, and diffuse their culture within a few weeks.

If this is true for social movements generally, we can hypothesize that it holds also for political violence and assassination. Political violence and assassination may be made plausible by the frequency of their occurrence. The mass media can intensify the process by making more dramatic and more pervasive the fact of their occurrence.

The implications of these processes in a democratic political system are ambiguous. Some increase in the incidence of political violence, including assassination, may be one of the necessary prices of a free society.

THE REDUCTION OF THE INCIDENCE
OF POLITICAL ASSASSINATION

We have indicated that political assassinations come in spurts for a variety of reasons. The explanations include: first, the use of assassination as a technique for "solving" particular problems at a given stage of development in a society; second, a common number of assassinations, stemming from the activity of one or a number of related groups together with reprisals; and, third, a contagion or epidemic of assassinations among unorganized, isolated individuals. These individuals see the drama and "affirmation" in assassination in terms of a legitimacy based upon the occurrence of previous acts.

44. *Report of the National Advisory Commission on Civil Disorders,* pp. 366–367; Otto N. Larsen, "Controversies About the Mass Communication of Violence," *Annals, op. cit.,* pp. 38–39; and Christopher La Farge, "Mickey Spillane and His Bloody Hammer" in *Mass Culture,* edited by Bernard Rosenberg and David Manning White (New York: The Free Press, 1957), pp. 176–186. For a general review and discussion of the aggravating and stultifying effect of this process, see Otto N. Larsen, ed., *Violence and the Mass Media* (New York: Harper & Row, 1968), pp. 33–56, 115–164.

But if assassination is a self-sustaining system, i.e., one assassination stimulates another, then the incidence of assassination should continuously rise. This obviously does not happen. The reason why requires examination.

Organized political assassinations are limited because assassination is only one type of political weapon. The decision may be made to continue the struggle by other means. Quite frequently, this involves a shift from individual assassination to direct and open conflict, such as rebellion or civil war. The success of a movement that uses political assassination may reduce its incidence though, as indicated, such acts are replaced by other forms of terror.

Finally, political assassination can be eliminated by the solution of problems that evoked the murder. The achievement of statehood may resolve feudal or tribal assassination, but it does bring with it the problems of assassination within a nation-state. These assassinations, in turn, may be eliminated by the achievement of democratic or national revolutions. Even these solutions may not last. New groups emerge, claim rights they feel are theirs, and may employ violence as a means to achieve their aspirations. Between these intervals, political violence and acts of assassination subside.

There is even a periodicity to the contagion of violence. Since such violence is based on individual irrationality, it is always unpredictable. But part of the attractiveness of individual assassination is its novelty. After a number of such assassinations, we can hypothesize, assassination becomes too routine to express the need to escape from the conventional. From this perspective, individual assassinations are likely to occur in brief stretches, principally during periods characterized by high amounts of violence in a society. They run their course and subside, only to reappear at some later date when an isolated individual begins a new cycle.

SOCIAL POLICY AND POLITICAL ASSASSINATION

The above discussion has many implications for social policy. The major ramifications are discussed below.

1. Some kinds of political assassination appear to be unavoidable. These include those based upon the purely idiosyncratic behavior of irrational individuals.

2. Security measures designed to isolate the victim from the assassin can only be partially effective. This is because potential victims will not permit themselves to be continuously isolated from the public sufficiently to avoid assassins. Moreover, since the victim need only be a politically prominent individual, the isolation of one or another potential target could result in the "substitution" of targets. Logically, this practice could lead to the isolation of all political leaders. Nevertheless, security measures will be and need to be taken to protect major election officials if only to make assassination more difficult.

3. The major cause for the isolated, irrational assassination is the linkage of political assassination with the individual derangement of the assassin. This includes acceptance of the idea that violence is a normal means of expression and that politics normally involves violence.

4. Both of these connections between political assassination and personal derangements are present because of the repeated occurrence of violence in political life. "Normal" violence heats up the political atmosphere, suggests the plausibility of such acts and politicizes violence among those who do not regularly participate in the conventional politics of society.

5. The reduction of political assassination, then, is to be accomplished, if at all, by cooling off the political atmosphere. This means the reduction of violence as a means of political and social action.

6. In some historical cases this appears to be impossible, since violence is "built into" the very process of political development. This is particularly true of the violence involved in feudal societies and in the process of state building. But the reduction of violence is possible within the framework of a secure nation state.

7. Within such a state "normal" political violence occurs when some segment of the population is driven to reject the state and the normal processes by which its interests are translated into law.

8. The key to this rejection is the loss of hope by groups in the political machinery of a society. The loss of faith, we believe, is due to the failure of established groups, i.e., those that control the political institutions, to grant access to these procedures to newly emerging groups within the society. The greed of established groups results in the misuse of state machinery. It is employed to

protect and enlarge their own privileges at the total expense of "outsiders." The stupidity of these established groups is evident in the belief that once an outside group emerges it can be prevented from making claims for rights, the authenticity and attractiveness of which are validated by the fact that they are enjoyed by "insiders." Thus inside groups demonstrate the desirability of these privileges, but deny their availability to outsiders.

In peaceful political processes, the outside groups attempt to claim these rights by peaceful attempts at legislative or constitutional change. They will accept instituted processes so long as there is a hope that their society will provide them with the means to make their claim for their share of the social values. When they can no longer trust the political machinery of society or the groups that control it, then violence is almost inevitable.

9. One way to avoid such violence would be to repress totally the aspiring groups. To be effective such repression would have to be unceasing. Each letup would result in an outburst of demands for change and the release of previously developed resentments. Moreover, the maintenance of continuous repression can only be done at fantastic costs to the total society. These include both the repression itself and the subjugation of all ancillary groups opposed to the use of a state's police power in such a manner. But the greatest costs of all are the indirect, occasioned by the inability of a repressive system to evoke the enthusiasms and the work and skill potentials of the suppressed groups.

Once denial of equality of access to the state machinery is undertaken, together with the delimitation of substantive rights and privileges, the society commits itself to a system in which violence and political assassination become normal means of political action. And once violence becomes a characteristic action in the society, it cannot be confined exclusively to the direct participants. The deranged become contaminated by the atmosphere of violence and by its politicization. Political assassination, in such situations, is the by-product of a defective political process.

10. The solution of the problems of political assassination in the United States, in particular, must be based on the repairing of weaknesses in the political processes and in the structure of American society. Given the level of violence in the American past and in the present, the cooling off of the violent political atmo-

sphere appears to be a long-term task. In the meantime, recent struggles over civil rights and youth politics have accelerated the atmosphere of violence to the point that the term "law and order" too often becomes a code word for *increased repression,* the principal issue in contemporary American society. America has become increasingly polarized; racial and youth violence on the one hand has been countered by demands for increased repression by those who feel most threatened. The violence stems from the failure of established society to provide equal opportunities in the past.

11. Ultimately, the reduction of political violence and the undermining of the potentiality for political assassination depends upon the reversal of present trends to polarization. Provision must be made for means by which all groups in American society can seek rights within the framework of its legal system.

Whether this is a possibility within the present context of extremism is open to question. The polarization of sentiments may well have gone too far. Social policy is not made by social scientists or by political experts. It is made, for good or for bad, by citizens and by the groups who propagandize, educate, manipulate, and express their desires. The "best" social policy is aimed at making the best political policy possible.

Values and Political Structure:
An Interpretation of the Sources of Extremism and Violence in American Society*

Seymour Martin Lipset and Carl Sheingold

Events of recent years have given rise to considerable distress both at home and abroad concerning the current state and future prospects of the American political system. Our political parties

* This essay is an elaboration of various themes analyzing violence and extremism in the context of studies of American values and structures in Lipset's earlier work. Particularly relevant are S. M. Lipset, "On the Politics

are under intense attack from the right and the left for their seeming inability to respond quickly to changes in popular sentiment about issues of war, poverty, and race. The Democratic and Republican parties have been charged with being unrepresentative, and many Americans have recently given their energies and support to third, even fourth, party efforts. Further, there have arisen over the issues of race and war movements dedicated to achieving their ends through militant and often violent political action outside the party system—action ranging from demonstrations to illegal acts of civil disobedience. We have seen the operations of major universities halted and sections of our major cities burned to the ground. Punctuating this turmoil, and perhaps most distressing of all, has been a series of political assassinations.

Given the popular conception of America as a conservative and stable nation characterized by consensus politics, these events have suggested to many that the American system may be breaking down, that the two-party system that seemingly functioned well in the past is no longer adequate to deal with current problems. Under circumstances such as these, it is useful to put matters into some historical and comparative perspective. Even a cursory review of American political history suggests the conclusion that our current situation, at the very least, is thoroughly precedented —that moralistic mass movements characterized by the politics of conscience and extreme commitment, which on occasion have encouraged violence, have emerged on many past occasions.

The conservative image of American politics has been fostered by the fact that all efforts to create radical "third" parties, whether of the left or right, have failed. The United States remains one of the few countries without any socialist representation in its legislative bodies. The Democratic party claims correctly to be the oldest party in the world with continuous existence. And although its

---

of Conscience and Extreme Commitment," *Encounter* (August, 1968), pp. 68–71, and analyses in S. M. Lipset, *The First New Nation* (New York: Basic Books, 1963; Doubleday Anchor, 1968); and *Revolution and Counter-revolution* (New York: Basic Books, 1968; rev. ed., Doubleday Anchor, 1970). In elaborating on these ideas in a paper originally prepared in October, 1968, as a background paper for the National Commission on Violence, we have repeated a number of points directly from these earlier publications.

opposition has changed format over the years, one can trace a line of continuity among the more elitist-based Federalist, Whig, and Republican parties.

Partisan continuity in two broad electoral coalitions, which include groups that are often in conflict with each other, however, has not prevented the enactment of important changes. The clue to the flexibility of the American two-party system in policy terms has been the relative ease with which a variety of "social movements," some of which have also been third parties, have arisen and had a significant impact. These movements have included the large-scale anti-Masonic movement of the 1820's and early thirties, the abolitionist movement that rose to strength in the forties and fifties, the large nativist and anti-Catholic organizations that rose and fell with considerable support during the nineteenth century and the early 1900's, the prohibition movement that existed for over a century before its success in enacting the Eighteenth Amendment, the various radical agrarian movements of the second half of the nineteenth century, the suffragette movement in the nineteenth and early twentieth century, the multimillion-member Ku Klux Klan of the 1920's, the pro-fascist mass-based movements of Father Coughlin and others of the 1930's, the various socialist and other liberal-left organizations of this century, the McCarthyite syndrome of the 1950's, the assorted white segregationist groups of the post–World War II era, their opponents in the rising civil rights and black nationalist movements and, finally, the campus-based movement against the Vietnam war.

The politics of social *movements* as distinct from that of *parties* creates a sharply divergent image of the degree of stability and instability and of the ability of dissident groups to foster change in America. If we contrast the American political system with that of a number of affluent European nations (e.g., Great Britain and Scandinavia) with respect to the frequency and importance of major mass movements, the United States would clearly appear to be less stable, i.e., it gives rise to more movements.

The implications of the distinction between movement and party may be pointed out by a comparative look at Canada and the United States.[1] Since World War I, Canadian politics has wit-

1. This comparative theme has been discussed at greater length by Seymour Martin Lipset in *The First New Nation* (New York: Basic Books,

nessed a growth of many "third parties." These include the Progressives in the 1920's who became the second largest party for a brief period and controlled the government in a number of provinces; New Democracy, a third party that secured their 10 per cent of the vote in the mid-thirties; the socialist Cooperative Commonwealth Federation (CCF), now renamed the New Democratic Party (NDP), and Social Credit, both formed during the 1930's and still continuing; and a host of French Canadian parties that have had transient but significant electoral success in various provincial and federal elections in the Province of Quebec. If one compared a statistical table that reports on Canadian and American federal, provincial, and state elections between 1916 and 1966, one would have to conclude if he had no other information that the Canadians have been among the world's most unstable and tension-ridden people, while the United States electorate is relatively quite conservative and unmovable, except in terms of switches between the two major parties. The only significant third-party vote cast during the same fifty-year period was that received by Senator Robert La Follette in his Progressive campaign in 1924.[2] But such a conclusion could only derive from the evaluation of political stability and conservatism in terms of the rise and

---

1963), especially Chapter 7, "Value Differences, Absolute or Relative: The English-Speaking Democracies," pp. 284–313; and in *Revolution and Counterrevolution* (New York: Basic Books, 1968), especially Chapter 2, "Revolution and Counterrevolution: The United States and Canada," pp. 37–75. The following are a number of relevant works on Canada: S. D. Clark, *The Canadian Community* (Toronto: University of Toronto Press, 1962); Kaspar D. Naegele, "Canadian Society: Some Reflections," in Bernard Blishen, et al., eds., *Canadian Society* (Toronto: Macmillan, 1961), pp. 1–53; Frank Underhill, *In Search of Canadian Liberalism* (Toronto: Macmillan, 1960); Dennis Wrong, *American and Canadian Viewpoints* (Washington, D.C.: American Council on Education, 1955).

2. Of course, George Wallace made a substantial showing in the 1968 election, but it remains to be seen whether he created a viable third party, or rather a movement that called itself a party to go to the polls. It is interesting to note in this context that Wallace's "party" offered no candidates at the state and local level. For a discussion of this and other points relating to Wallace, see Seymour M. Lipset, "George Wallace and the U.S. New Right," *New Society,* 12 (October 3, 1968), pp. 477–483; Seymour Martin Lipset and Earl Raab, *The Politics of Unreason* (New York: Harper & Row, 1970), Chapters 9 and 10; and Carl A. Sheingold, *Third Party Politics in America: A Social Structural Analysis of the Rise and Fall of the Wallace Vote in 1968* (Ph.D. Thesis, Harvard University, 1971).

fall of ideological parties to the right and left of the two major moderate ones; and it would clearly, in our view, be in error.

The equivalent of new minor parties in the American context has been extraparliamentary social movements. Not being part of the normal partisan political game, they are all the more likely to be extremist in their tactics. They are not subject to the discipline inherent in the need to win the support of moderate voters which parties face. Rather, as minority-based movements they try to force the leaders of the two broad-based electoral coalitions to respond to their demands. Lacking the discipline of parties seeking to elect people to office, many of them have appealed openly to racial and religious tensions. Some of them have sought to label their opponents as agents of foreign conspiracies; or like the abolitionists, the two Ku Klux Klans, the Southern segregationists, or the current antiwar movement, they have engaged in civil disobedience, employing tactics that violate what they have held to be "immoral law," even if enacted by democratically elected governments. Some of these movements, whether extremist or not in tactics, have been radical in their objectives, e.g., seeking to upset existing concepts of property rights.

A view of American history that focuses on the role and tactics of movements, as distinct from parties, must produce the conclusion that reliance on methods outside of the normal political game has played a major role in affecting change throughout most of American history. While most of the movements mentioned here have not engaged in violence as such, it is important also to recognize that some of the major changes in American society have been a product of violent tactics resulting from the willingness of some of those who have felt that they had a morally righteous cause to take the law into their own hands in order to advance it. And by extreme actions, whether violent or not, the moralistic radical minorities have often secured the support or acquiescence of some of the moderate elements, who have come to accept the fact that change is necessary in order to gain a measure of peace and stability. To some extent, also, the extremists on a given side of an issue have lent credence to the arguments presented by the moderates on that issue. Extremists, whether of the right or left, have often helped the moderates in the center to press through reforms.

The most striking example of this sort of behavior in American history has been the successful movement to abolish slavery. The radical abolitionists were willing to violate congressional law and Supreme Court decisions to make their case before the public and to help Negro slaves escape to Canada. Some of them were even ready to fight with arms in order to guarantee that the western territories would remain free of slavery. John Brown's armed raid on Harper's Ferry played a major role in convincing both Southerners and Northerners that the slavery debate had to be ended, either by secession or by some form of manumission. Conversely, the violence of the first Ku Klux Klan after the Civil War helped convince the North that it had to desist in its effort to prevent white domination of the South. The guerrilla actions of the Klansmen played a major role in re-establishing white Bourbon power and in securing the end of Reconstruction.

The women's suffrage movement, as it gained strength, also manifested the depth of its commitment by various forms of civil disobedience such as efforts to disrupt the orderly operation of government by illegal demonstrations, women chaining themselves to buildings, and so forth. Some prohibitionists also showed the intensity of their feelings against liquor by efforts to ridicule and ostracize those patronizing saloons, and even on occasion by violent attempts to prevent dispensers of liquor from doing business.

The violence often exercised by various anti-Catholic movements both before and after the Civil War, continuing into the twentieth century, had considerable effect on local authorities in determining their policies in the schools.[3] They also activated opposition to mass immigration. The violence of the second Ku Klux Klan following World War I played an important role in

3. During the course of this paper we will be discussing various movements in American history in rather general terms, and hence we will not be providing extensive citations. With respect to movements on the right, readers may consult the analysis of the American radical right in historical perspective by Seymour Martin Lipset and Earl Raab, *The Politics of Unreason*. Detailed sources for many of the statements presented here can be found in this volume.

intimidating opposition to nativism and Protestant fundamentalism, and helped pass legislation against non-Protestant immigration.

During the Great Depression, illegal efforts were also important.
Agrarian movements brought about moratoriums on mortgage-
debt collection and changes in various banking laws by their armed
actions designed to prevent the sale of farms for nonpayment of
debt. In the cities, also, the labor movement won its right to collective bargaining in industries that had traditionally opposed it by
illegal "sit-ins" in factories in Akron, Detroit, and other places.
State governments found themselves helpless to remove workers
from factories, and antiunion employers were quite often forced to
accept unions in their plants by these actions.

Since the Supreme Court school desegregation decision in 1954,
the issue of Negro rights in the South has stimulated both sides to
engage in civil disobedience to attain their opposing moral ends.
The Southern white upholders of segregation initiated such tactics
when organizations like the White Citizens' Councils and the Klan,
and various elected officials, including governors, police chiefs,
and judges, deliberately disregarded the law of the land as enunci-
ated by the Supreme Court and Congress. Ross Barnett of Mississippi, George Wallace of Alabama, and Lester Maddox of Georgia
essentially told their followers that it was right to disregard
immoral law, that they should do all in their power to prevent the
enforcement of integration.

It is important to recognize that the tactics of civil disobedience
and even of violence in the black-white struggles in the South
were introduced by Southern conservative whites, a point made
many years ago by Gunnar Myrdal in his classic study of the
Negro problem in the United States, *An American Dilemma.*[4]
Myrdal pointed out in the forties that the conservative white
upholders of segregation endorsed law violation and engaged in
what we now call civil disobedience. The Negroes and their white
supporters learned from firsthand experience with those in authority in the South that the most effective tactic in their struggle was

---

4. Gunnar Myrdal, *An American Dilemma: The Negro Problem and
Modern Democracy* (New York: Harper & Row, 1944).

civil disobedience, that this was necessary to counter the illegal actions of their opponents. The current use of "sit-ins" in this country arose in the South in the context of the civil-rights activities and then spread to the North to struggles within universities as in Berkeley, and later in the protest movement against the Vietnam war. The recent resort to armed violence by some of the most extreme black groups parallels, in a real sense, comparable earlier efforts by Klansmen and other white segregationists.

In recent years the advocates of civil rights have shown a greater degree of commitment, of willingness to take extreme action to further moral objectives, than have their opponents. To some degree, this reflects change in the sentiments in the black and white populations. Blacks now express more bitterness about their depressed situation than in the past, while white prejudice against them has declined considerably. Even the most bigoted sections of the white population have come to accept the proposition that Negroes are entitled to various legal and economic rights, which were denied to them before the 1950's. This shift in the attitudes of the racial groups has brought about a change in "who is most likely" to resort to violence. Racial violence in American cities up to World War II largely involved actions by whites against Negroes. Essentially, the political system upheld the position of the white bigots and extremists. Currently, however, the blacks are on the offensive, although Negroes rather than whites continue to predominate among those killed, and the political structure between 1948 and 1968 adapted itself much more to Negro demands than to white resistance. Black violence, though condemned by all political leaders, has generally been followed by administrative, community, and legislative action to improve the condition of Negroes. As in the past, the movement that has shown it feels most deeply about its goals and that has been most willing to act extremely to gain them seems better able to win its objectives.

In recent years the black opposition movement has intensified, since in spite of the various legislative and economic gains the overwhelming majority of Negroes remain badly educated, ill-housed, and lowly employed. There is, however, growing evidence, most vividly expressed by the Wallace campaign, that a powerful base has emerged for a revived white anti-Negro extremist movement. Many whites see a threat to their status, and psychic security, in the success of desegregation efforts and in the rising sense that they are exposed to physical danger as a result of increased crime and violence that they have been led to blame on Negroes. During the 1968 election campaign George Wallace was quite proud to boast that his followers were ready for drastic action to counter the influence of "anarchists"—a cover term in the Wallace lexicon for all militants of the left.

It is, of course, hard to anticipate the extent to which such talk will become reality. Recent years have not been devoid of white anti-Negro violence. A number of Martin Luther King's last organizational efforts—most notably in Chicago and Memphis—were accompanied by violent reactions by segments of the white communities of these cities. Wallace has clearly toyed with the idea of transforming his electoral following into a mass movement. The fervor of his supporters—he boasted of the "hysteria" that the issue of law and order can induce in his audiences—suggests the possibility that we may be moving into a period in which white racist violence will become more prevalent than black violence. It is probably significant here that the relationship between the police and black militant groups in many cities has reached the point where both sides characterize it as a state of war. There have been many casualties on both sides of the line. A large proportion of urban policemen are recruited from those social groups which have been most prone to backlash sentiment and politics. Some of Wallace's most fervent supporters in 1968 were policemen. In any case, it is clear that the two major parties and government authorities have found themselves hard pressed to know how to react in a way that will most reduce the strain on law and order and on the operation of the political system, which the apparent increased extremism and violence among both racial groups has produced.

The success of the current antiwar movement is another example of the way in which those who feel most deeply and are willing to use extreme methods to attain their ends have an impact on the body politic. It is too early to tell what absolute measure of success the antiwar movement will have. Clearly it has not attained all of its goals. Just as clearly, the American role in the war is being reduced in advance of the achievement of the goals which guided our initial involvement. In view of America's history as a passionate and successful nation at war, this is a considerable accomplishment.

A measure of the strength of the antiwar movement is the greater tolerance for antiwar activities shown by prowar groups and by the government which has characterized this war. This is not to say that there have not been government actions which could be characterized as repressive with respect to antiwar dissent. However, the scale and intensity of such actions has been strikingly modest when compared to the situation which obtained during the Korean War (the period of McCarthyism), or the two World Wars. This reflects, in our judgment, a greater degree of self-doubt about the objectives of the war rather than a greater commitment to the political rights of dissenters. Unlike previous antiwar movements opposing ongoing wars, the current antiwar minority has been able to gain some of its objectives because it is more committed than its opponents.

WHY MOVEMENTS AND NOT THIRD PARTIES?

The propensity of the American political system to produce extra party movements rather than third or fourth parties is directly related to the nature of our electoral system.[5] Ours is, from the court house to the White House, a plurality system, i.e., constituencies elect a single representative. The point of comparison is a proportional representative system common in Western Europe within which parties elect representatives in strength proportional to the size of these groups. In plurality systems a minority parties

5. The following are some general works on the theory of electoral systems: Maurice Duverger, *Political Parties* (London: Methuen, 1954); Harry Eckstein and David Apter, eds., *Comparative Politics* (New York: The Free Press, 1963), pp. 368–375; Carl Friedrich, *Constitutional Government and Democracy* (Boston: Ginn & Co., 1950); D. Morgan, *Election and Representation* (Cork: Cork University Press, 1945); E. E. Schattschneider, *Party Government* (New York: Rinehart & Co., 1942); and S. M. Lipset, *The First New Nation, op. cit.,* pp. 286–317.

can achieve maximum power only in coalition with other groups. Minority representation is, of course, much more direct in a proportional system.

It is clear that electoral systems based upon proportional representation encourage new movements and interest groups to go into party politics. Conversely, electoral systems based upon plurality representation discourage such a course of action. Within plurality systems, the larger the size of the constituency, the more difficult it is for minority movements to compete successfully as parties. Thus when we look at examples of relatively successful third-party efforts in American history, we find evidence of considerable victory at the local level in electing mayors and congressmen and more moderate success at the state level. However, such parties have invariably met with disaster when they went national and attempted to elect a president. Two prominent examples are the Know-Nothing movement in the 1850's and the Populist movement in the 1890's.

The role of America's presidential system in discouraging and frustrating "third" party politics is highlighted in comparison with the greater prominence of such efforts within the parliamentary systems with single-member (plurality) districts, in which voters do not choose a central executive but rather cast their ballot for a local representative. Within such a system new parties with geographically distinct sources of strength (i.e., in occupations such as mining, ethnic, religious, or regional groupings) can focus their efforts on electing members to parliament in the areas in which they are strong, though they are not in a position to receive a significant national vote, nor are they ever required to test that strength in a national election. Thus we find in Canada, which has such a parliamentary system, ecologically isolated minorities such as wheat farmers and French Canadians are in a position to elect minority party M.P.'s without having to face the challenge to create a major party on the national level.

Another factor contributing to the difficulty of creating "third" parties in America is the decentralized structure of our political parties. At the constituency level this is manifested by the prominence of primary elections, which give minority interests an opportunity to express themselves within the party and thus ironically serve to legitimate their relative lack of control of the party.

A perhaps more important manifestation at the national level is the looseness of party discipline in the Congress, which allows for cross-party alignments on particular issues. Congressmen who represent minority ideologies within one party do not have to join or form another party in order to please their constituents. This factor has enabled Southern conservatives to maintain their position within the Democratic party for as long as they have. The importance of this factor is evident when we look at the Canadian case.

Canadian parliamentary parties are run with tight discipline. Whenever a Canadian region, class, ethnic group, or province comes into serious conflict with its party of traditional allegiance, it must either change over to the other party, with which it may be in even greater disagreement on other issues, or form a new "third" party. The result of combining social diversity with a rigid constitutional structure has been the regular rise and fall of relatively powerful "third" parties.

Just as the American electoral system discourages "third" parties, it has important consequences for the nature of the two parties it encourages. American parties tend to represent broad coalitions of interests and groups. Such coalitions inevitably contain potentially conflicting elements. Within such a system parties are most frequently competing for marginal groups of potential shifters among the voters. Thus party stability and viability are typically based upon a balancing act involving compromise and avoidance of interest-specific ideological postures. In general, party ideology in America tends to be very diffuse, appealing to generalized visions of the nation and vague promises for the future. Very rarely have American political parties taken what might be regarded as extreme ideological positions. On the rare occasions that they have—e.g., the Democrats with the Bryan-Populist position in 1896, the Republicans with the Goldwater-conservative position in 1964—they have suffered dramatically at the polls for it.

Given the fact that parties emphasize ideology at the peril of losing the center—that, in effect, they cannot emphasize the real differences that separate them—they often sound similar with respect to basic policy. Consequently, they stress non-policy issues. We often find electoral rhetoric in America focusing upon either throwing the rascals out or keeping the rascals out—upon efficiency, morality, integrity, corruption or Communists in high places, the personalities of leaders, etc.

The construction of party coalitions and the development of party ideologies and rhetoric appropriate to keeping such coalitions together is clearly a rather delicate task. Once the task has been completed the forces pushing for stabilization of party constituent groups, ideology, rhetoric, etc., are quite strong. Similar stabilizing forces however, are not in operation for the society as a whole. America is a highly dynamic society. Few groups within it stand still for very long, and the demands that they make upon the political system—the issues which concern them, the answers which appeal to them—move with them. Under these circumstances, groups within America often find themselves out of step with their party of traditional allegiance on specific issues, but also out of step with the alternative party on others. These issues may be more or less "legitimate" (ranging from demands for equal rights for women or blacks to demands for the head of immigrants), but they are invariably real and often preoccupying to the participants themselves. Meanwhile, the parties, particularly at the national level, are resistant to changes in their basic orientation—as are most organizations of a similar structure. Such shifts take place when changes in the society at large become so pervasive—hit so many groups—that the coalitions upon which the parties are based become patently untenable. In short, party change comes through crisis.

The current state of the Democratic party would seem to be illustrative of this phenomenon. Since the days of Franklin Roosevelt, the party's strength has been based upon a majority coalition composed, among others, of the urban white minority ethnic groups, trade unionists, and urban blacks. The Democratic program and orientation through the New Deal and most of the postwar years were satisfactory for these groups. Pledges of equal rights under the law for Negroes did not particularly impinge upon the interests of the white ethnic groups or union members. Promises of higher minimum wages and various social-welfare legislation were seen in a positive light by each group. But times have changed, and so have these groups.

During recent decades, the black American has achieved notable progress on many fronts. With respect to average income, voting rights, the easing of restrictions in employment, housing, recreation, etc., his lot has objectively improved. However, these decades have also seen a deepening of our racial crisis. A major dimension of this phenomenon is the fact that progress has taken place selectively, and it has been incomplete. For instance, the major economic avenue of advance for Negroes has not been the standard commercial, business, or political channels, but rather through professional channels—the ministry, education, civil service, entertainment, athletics, social work, etc. For many who have risen in this way, progress in other fields—most notably in housing and education—has not been commensurate.

Further, for a large percentage of Negroes, progress has been impeded by the fact that the recent economy was one that had been characterized until 1970 as having plenty of room at the top but no room at the bottom. There was a growing need for educated, trained people but little need for muscle power and unskilled work. In order to enter the higher parts of the social and economic structure, the majority of Negroes must jump from a low level of education and skill, and a low achievement motivation, to a high level. The cultural residues of slavery and caste inferiority, which have been abundantly documented in studies of the family and education, prevent many of them from doing so. This situation, in which the civil-rights movement has won almost all the victories it ever hoped to achieve politically (with considerable support from Democratic administrations)—and yet almost all blacks live in ghettos, Negro unemployment is great relative to whites, and black income is on the average much lower than white—clearly makes for great frustration, particularly among young Negroes.

Thus, while the objective position of the black American has improved dramatically, his expectation level has increased even more sharply, and consequently so has his sense of relative deprivation. Those who have risen economically are embittered because their advance on other fronts has not been correspondingly great. For those who have not advanced economically, the relative progress of their fellow Negroes provides additional basis for alienation, above and beyond their generally deprived situation vis-à-vis the white community. This kind of "crisis of rising expectations" has, of course, been the seeding ground for many protest and revolutionary movements throughout history.

Meanwhile, the white workers participated in the generally affluent economy only to experience many of their hard-earned dollars going for taxes for programs to aid the Negroes, and to see their long-sought-for position of affluence and comfort threatened by urban riots. The reasons for the greater participation in the Wallace movement by white trade-union members, compared with members of the middle class, are inherent in the fact that the former are more likely to live inside the central cities relatively close to black ghettos. Hence, they are also more likely to be directly and personally concerned with the consequences of efforts to integrate schools and residential neighborhoods.

The Democratic party thus found itself hard pressed to formulate a program—at whatever level of generality—that appealed to both of these traditionally Democratic groups. It should not come as a surprise that many Negroes found action on the street a more satisfying form of political behavior than voting Democratic at the ballot box, or that many white workers appeared to be strongly sympathetic to the Wallace third-party effort. The Democratic coalition is in the midst of a crisis, an event made manifest in the formation of movements operating outside the normal rules of the game of two-party electoral politics.

More generally, the history of the American political parties can be seen as a cyclical phenomenon.[6] There are relatively unchanging periods, during which parties sit on top of stable coalitions of voters and are responsive enough to their basic needs and concerns to make their niche in the party a comfortable one. These are followed by transition periods, in which the parties seem to be out of step with the real situation of various groups in the society. Party appeals take on an increasingly archaic flavor. Party organization becomes increasingly incapable of reaching and satisfying

6. The party systems' approach to the interpretation of American political history is now generating a substantial body of literature. An important early work in his field is V. O. Key, Jr., "A Theory of Critical Elections," *Journal of Politics*, 17 (1955), pp. 1–18. Essays by Chambers and Burnham in William N. Chambers and Walter Dean Burnham, eds., *The American Party Systems* (New York: Oxford University Press, 1967), present historical outlines of the kind of cyclical process discussed here.

important segments of their traditional constituency. It is, of course, during these periods that extraparty movements flourish and attempts are made to create "third" and "fourth" parties. Finally, there are reorientation periods during which the parties themselves are in movement, seeking new and relevant coalitions and ideologies which appeal broadly. If they are successful, a new period of stability follows.

It is only in the context of this kind of broad historical perspective that we can appreciate the importance and meaning of extraparty movements and, in general, of repeating periods of political turmoil in American history. When critics charge that the American political parties are inherently unresponsive, they are inaccurate. But it *is* an endemic part of the way our system operates for the parties periodically to become unresponsive to the needs of specific groups for limited periods of time. It is in these "transition periods" that extraparty movements not only develop but play a very positive and necessary role in insuring the continued vitality and relevance of the party system. They are signposts to the parties that change is at hand. It is precisely the forcefulness with which these movements have pressed their demands that has encouraged an accurate reading of these signposts by the parties.

Of course, when describing cyclical historical patterns of this kind, one is often misled by the simplicity and apparent calm of a smooth pattern of repetitive events. As we have already documented, the reality is far from calm. What we have dubbed "periods of transition" have also, typically, been periods of intense violence and despair. We will next address ourselves to some of the reasons for this. What, in historical retrospect, appears as a few brief years of party reorientation, appears to many of the participants as Nero-like abnegation of party responsibility. Further, the midwife to the emergence of a reoriented party system has, on at least one occasion, been a bloody civil war.

WHY VIOLENCE?

Thus far we have discussed some of the reasons for the prevalence of militant extraparty movements in American political history. However, we have not yet directly discussed the tendency of these movements to resort to violent, often illegal, tactics. The drive toward stabilized operations within the parties themselves implies the need for dramatic action on the part of those who feel themselves to be unrepresented or unspoken for. But why do Americans who wish to be politically dramatic so often resort to violence? It is worth noting, in this context, that political violence appeared in advance of the firm establishment of the American party system. The nation was founded in an act of violent revolution. The American Revolution was followed by Shays Rebellion in 1786 and the Whisky Rebellion in 1794. An important event in the founding of the first party system itself was resistance to the Jay Treaty, which peaked with mass disorders and rioting in Boston in September 1795.[7]

Once again, comparison with the Canadian experience is instructive. Both nations share similar positions on scales of industrialization, urbanization and social mobility, as well as comparable ecological and demographic conditions. However, on virtually any scale of political and related violence, ranging from ratios of those concerned with maintaining law—police or lawyers—to population, homicide and other crime rates and industrial violence or political assassinations, the United States would appear to be a significantly more violent society.[8] This difference, we would hold, is related to different national experiences with respect to political origins, religious traditions, and frontier settlement, all of which resulted in differences of degree with respect to shared value systems.

As noted on many holidays the United States of America was a result of a successful revolution. The ideology of the revolution, as spoken in the Declaration of Independence, is one of equalitarianism. This has been a most salient and pervasive American value ever since. It is to be seen in our emphasis upon education for all, in our relatively unauthoritarian parent-child relationships, and in the preponderance of elective rather than appointive civic offices in this country. A theme running through our history has been the notion that "the people" are the ultimate source of wisdom and

7. Paul M. Downing, *Acts of Civil Disobedience in American History: Selected Examples* (Washington D.C.: The Library of Congress Legislative Reference Service, 1967).

8. For some examples, see Lipset, *Revolution and Counterrevolution.* pp. 45–47; and the Feierabends' chapter in this volume.

decision and a complementary mistrust of established elites and expertise. Naturally enough, this populist ethos has led to impatience with legal due process and even disrespect for the law.

In America, unlike more status-oriented societies, generalized deference is not accorded to those at the top. Popular derision of public servants is a very old tradition in this country. Our civic discourse has always been distinguished by intemperate rhetoric coming both from those in power and those outside, which often stands in sharp contrast to the grinding reality of party processes. Canada, by contrast, had her political origins in a counter-revolution. Status distinctions have always had greater legitimacy there as have more traditional mechanisms of social control—what Russel Ward refers to as "deferential respect for the squire."[9]

An interesting aspect of the background for these differences is the varying experiences that these two nations have had with frontier settlement. In Canada, fear of American expansionist tendencies resulted in the early extension of the power of civil authority to the frontier. The Royal Canadian Mounted Police are interesting in this context, for they clearly were representative of central authority, and their presence greatly increased the respect for legal institutions on the frontier.[10] Even in mining camps— notorious in American lore as centers of volatile behavior—the Queen's peace prevailed in a fashion. On the American frontier, law and order were enforced by local authorities, who themselves embodied the distinctive values of the frontier. Respect for legal processes was by no means the rule in frontier towns. A good measure of this phenomenon is the persistent glorification of frontiersmen and outlaws like Jesse James in American folklore. Canadians have always had a somewhat more ambivalent attitude toward these rough and ready men of the West and have made a hero of the frontier police, the Mounties.

Another pervasive value in American society has been that of

9. Russel Ward, *The Australian Legend* (New York: Oxford University Press, 1959), p. 27.
10. See Edgar W. McInnis, *The Unguarded Frontier* (Garden City: Doubleday, Doran and Co., 1942); Paul F. Sharp, "Three Frontiers: Some Comparative Studies of Canadian, American and Australian Settlement," *Pacific Historical Review* 24 (1955), pp. 373–374. See also S. D. Clark, "The Frontier and Democratic Theory," *Transactions of the Royal Society of Canada*, 48 (1954), Series 111, Section Two.

achievement—a strong emphasis on an "open society," on "getting ahead." This has been linked by analysts of American society (especially the sociologist Robert Merton) with making it an "ends-oriented" culture as distinct from a "means-oriented" one.[11] In the former type, winning is what counts, not how one wins. Conversely, social systems with a more rigid status system, with a greater emphasis on the norms of elitism, are more likely to be concerned with appropriate means; the norms place greater stress on conforming to the proper code of behavior. The comment by Leo Durocher that "nice guys finish last" may be counterposed against the old Olympic motto that "it matters not who wins the game, it matters how you play." The latter, of course, is the aristocratic code of a ruling class that "won" some generations back and in effect, is seeking to prevent the "outs" from pressing too hard to replace it. The differences between an achievement- and "ends-oriented" culture as distinct from a "means-oriented" one. are subtle and hard to demonstrate in any rigorous fashion, but they are real and, in our view, contribute to many aspects of social life, including the crime rate and general willingness to rely on militant political tactics. American extremism may be seen as another example of the propensity to seek to attain ends by any means, whether legitimate or not.

This propensity is related to the equalitarian ethos that we discussed previously, i.e., upon the emphasis in America for achievement for all.[12] We can see this at work in the greater degree of union militancy in America compared with most of Europe, or even Canada.[13] In an open-class system resentment of

11. Robert K. Merton, *Social Theory and Social Structure* (New York: The Free Press, 1968), especially Chapter 6, "Social Structure and Anomie," pp. 185–214.

12. See Lipset, *The First New Nation,* especially Part I, "America as a New Nation," and Part II, "Stability in the Midst of Change," pp. 17–114, 115–237. See also, Robin Williams, *American Society* (New York: Alfred A. Knopf, 1970).

13. Lipset, *op. cit.,* Chapter 5, "Trade Unions and the American Value System," pp. 193–236. See also Louis Adamic, *Dynamite: The Story of Class Violence in America* (New York: Viking Press, 1934); B. C. Roberts, *Unions in America: A British View* (Princeton, N.J.: Industrial Relations Section, Princeton University, 1959), p. 95; and Arthur M. Ross and Paul T. Hartman, *Changing Patterns of Industrial Conflict* (New York: John Wiley & Son, 1960), pp. 141–145, 161–162.

disparities of income are more deeply felt than in a more avowedly status-bound system where labor is regarded, in the words of Winston Churchill, as "an estate of the realm." Americans eschew the notion of estates and blame individuals, should their status be low, and by implication encourage individuals to improve their status and alleviate their resentment in self-interested and narrowly defined terms. Thus we find Americans accepting conflict as a "normal" method of resolving labor disputes and violation of rules and laws as merely an unfortunate by-product of such conflict. The United States has had a higher strike rate than the other developed industrial democracies of northern Europe and Canada. When strikes have occurred in the latter group of nations, they have typically been accompanied by less violence. "The use of professional strike breakers, labor spies, 'goon squads,' 'vigilante' groups, armed militia, and other spectacular features of industrial warfare in the United States in previous decades has been absent from the Canadian scene—again with several notable exceptions."[14]

Moralism is also a source of extremism. Americans tend to be a moralistic people, an orientation that they inherit from their Protestant sectarian past. This is the one country in the world dominated by the religious traditions of Protestant "dissent," Methodists, Baptists, and the other numerous sects.[15] The teachings of these denominations have called on men to follow their conscience in ways which the denominations that have evolved from state churches (Catholic, Lutheran, Anglican, and Orthodox Christian) have not. The American Protestant religious ethos is basically Arminian. It assumes, in practice, if not in theology, the perfectibility of man and his obligation to avoid sin, while the churches accept the inherent weakness of man, his inability to escape sinning and error and the need for the church to be forgiving and protecting.

14. Stuart Jamieson, *Industrial Relations in Canada* (Ithaca: Cornell University Press, 1957), p. 7.

15. For a more detailed discussion of this and other issues associated with the American religious experience as it relates to political behavior in this country, as well as for extensive citations, see Lipset, *The First New Nation,* Chapter 4, "Religion and American Values," pp. 159–192, and Lipset, *Revolution and Counterrevolution,* Chapter 9, "Religion and Politics in the American Past and Present," pp. 305–374.

The American, therefore, as political and religious man, has been a utopian moralist who presses hard to attain and institutionalize virtue or to destroy evil men and wicked institutions and practices. He has tended to view social and political dramas as morality plays—as battles between God and the Devil—within which compromise is virtually unthinkable. This moralistic tendency in America generalizes beyond its denominational or even specifically religious base. A distinguished French Dominican student of American religion (R. L. Bruckberger) has criticized American Catholics for having absorbed the American Protestant view of religion and morality—"either virtue or a reign of terror." He expresses the fear that American Catholics are becoming more like American Baptists and Presbyterians than like European or Latin American Catholics.[16] Agnostic and atheistic reformers in America also tend to be utopian moralists, believing in the perfectibility of man and of civil society and in the immorality, if not specifically sinful character, of the opposition.

Thus, almost from the beginning of the Republic, one finds a plethora of "do-good" reform organizations seeking to foster peace, protect the Sabbath, reduce or eliminate the use of alcoholic beverages, wipe out the corrupt irreligious institution of Free Masonry, destroy the influence of the Papists, eliminate corruption, extend the blessings of education, etc., etc. Perhaps the archetypical example was the battle over slavery in the 1840's and 1850's. An essential element in the dynamics that culminated in the Civil War was the tendency of both sides to view the other side as essentially sinful—as agents of the Devil. In all these movements the intensely committed have been hard pressed to regard the "rules of the game"—legal or electoral processes—as of greater importance than their cause. Extremism and violence have often been the result.

The strength of such moralistic pressures can best be seen in the widespread opposition to almost every war in which the United States has participated, with the possible exception of World War

16. R. L. Bruckberger, "The American Catholics as a Minority," in Thomas T. McAvoy, ed., *Roman Catholicism and the American Way of Life* (Notre Dame: University of Notre Dame Press, 1966), pp. 45–47.

II. Conscientious objection to participation in "unjust wars" has been more common in the United States than in any other country in the world. Large numbers of people refused to go along with the War of 1812, the Mexican War, the Civil War, World War I, the Korean War, and now with the Vietnam War. They took it as self-evident that they must obey their conscience rather than the dictates of their country's rulers. And the same moralistic element which has fostered resistance to each war has led some Americans to press hard for those political changes that are in line with their conscience. Such extreme behavior by moralistic reformers has made the task of running this country extremely difficult. Those in authority have often found themselves in the position of Presidents Johnson and Nixon, denounced as wicked men who sponsor evil and corrupt policies. Consensus politics has never been an effective answer to moralistic politics. As a result, the moralistic reformers have often obtained their objectives by winning the agreement of the moderate majority. Outraged by their tactics, the moderates have often given in, either because they came to feel that the activists were "basically in the right," or in order to keep the peace, to reduce divisiveness and restore the broken consensus.

Again the contrast with Canada is dramatic. There, religion has retained its ecclesiastic character and strong ties with the state.[17] Thus, rather than giving encouragement to egalitarianism and complementary trends of fundamentalism and experimentalism, the Canadian Catholic and Anglican churches, with which a majority of the population are affiliated have provided the society with hierarchical models and tradition rooted control mechanisms noticeably weaker in America. The connection with the state is of particular importance. Churches with an experience of having been established have been by definition churches of the whole society and, as such, tend to be more tolerant of people who deviate on ostensibly nonreligious matters. Being securely rooted in the society, they can afford such tolerance and in general avoid a fundamentalist orientation. They also, of course, have firmer connections with the "established order" and some degree of historical responsibility for the moral tone of the present social order. For these reasons as well, established churches—and the general

17. See Clark, *The Canadian Community,* especially p. 388.

moral environment that they promote—are less likely to sponsor
or encourage extremist reform movements.

WHY ASSASSINATION OF PRESIDENTS?

There is one final topic that we have dealt with only indirectly
so far—the extent to which American presidents, and potential
presidents, have been the targets of assassination attempts. It is
important at this point to make quite clear at what level we will be
discussing this problem. In the final analysis, most acts of assassination are more psychological than sociological or political
events. When one asks, "Why did he do it?" the relevant answer
ultimately must focus upon the psychopathology of the assassin
rather than what might be construed as the social pathology of the
society in which the event took place. However, rates of assassination and attempted assassinations are sociological facts. If many
more assassinations have been committed in the United States than
Canada or Britain, the explanation must focus upon what kind of
societies they are. The fact that a man is deranged is a psychological fact. But the fact that in one society such a man is tempted to
kill a president, while in another he might be more tempted to
commit suicide is a sociological fact admitting a sociological explanation. This distinction between psychological and sociological
facts was most cogently advanced in Durkheim's classic work *Suicide*.[18] There can be no more individual and personal act than the
taking of one's own life, but, as Durkheim indicated, an explanation of the fact that, for instance, more Germans commit suicide
than Frenchmen must be a sociological one.

We will not be offering anything as grandiose as an explanation of America's tragic experience with assassinations. We can
only suggest certain factors that might be related to such an explanation. We will not repeat the obvious relevance of some of the
more general factors contributing to political violence in America,
which have already been covered. We begin again with a myth. Just
as many have believed that America has a stable and conservative

18. Emile Durkheim, *Suicide* (Glencoe, Ill.: The Free Press, 1951). The
comparative rates of assassination for nations are analyzed in the Feierabends' chapter in Part I of this volume.

polity, so have they also believed that because the American federal system is so highly decentralized the role of leaders is of reduced importance compared with more centralized systems. The truth, as usual, is somewhat more complex.

The American political system can be viewed as made up of two subsystems—the federal system and the presidential one. The former is indeed marked by decentralization and elaborate checks and balances. However, within this federal system the key elections held at the national, state, and local level are for only one man—the president, governor, or mayor. As a result, government tends to be personalized in the man who holds the key executive office. For instance, the American cabinet is responsible to the President, not to party or parliamentary colleagues.

A related factor is the nature of our parties. Most students of party systems are immediately struck, when comparing the American with, say, the English or Canadian cases, by the loose structure of American political parties. In Europe parties are more tightly disciplined ongoing organizations. In America, at the national level, they are loose electoral coalitions coming together once every four years to nominate and then to elect a president. In the European case, parties have long-term strategies that go beyond the personality or policies of any particular leader of the moment. In America such strategies are less prominent, and the general emphasis is reversed; it rests precisely upon the qualities of the leader. This emphasis is a realistic one, since the less coherence the party has, the more important the leader in fact is. This emphasis is present at all levels of government but is obviously felt most intensely at the national level with respect to the president. It is also significant to note here that the relative importance of the presidency in this sense has increased progressively through the course of American history. An interesting measure of the importance placed upon the particular individual who occupies that office is the fact that in the sixty-year period from the presidency of Jackson to that of McKinley only two out of ten presidents—Lincoln and Grant—were elected to a second consecutive term in office. From McKinley to the present day only two out of ten— Taft and Hoover—have failed to obtain re-election.

The phenomenon we have been describing is not limited to political parties but is a generalized consequence of certain organizational dynamics. A similar example is provided by Harrison in his book. *Authority and Power in the Free Church Tradition*—an analysis of the organization of the Baptist Church.[19] The Baptists are congregationalists and hence de-emphasize hierarchical systems of authority. The church's organization, on paper, is highly decentralized. But the philosophy and organizational reality of congregationalism in no way eliminates the necessity of organizational co-ordination, or of some basis for effective authority within the organization. As Harrison depicts it, these needs are met by a heavy emphasis upon personal leadership—upon what Weber called charismatic authority. This kind of authority emanates from the personal qualities of leaders rather than the bureaucratic power of office.

The analogy between the organization of the Baptist Church and that of the American political system is fairly clear. There are two prominent consequences for the problem we are addressing ourselves to. One, which we have already mentioned, is an intense emphasis upon the office of the president and upon the specific characteristics of the man who occupies that office. It is significant here that the development of the media of communication in recent decades has served to increase dramatically the intensity of this emphasis and, some might claim, distort our view of the office and the man. Contributing to this is the tendency we discussed earlier of the parties to deprecate the ideological differences between them and stress, among other things, variations in the ability, character, and personality of leaders. All these factors have the effect of increasing the intensity of our feelings about the president, be they positive or negative. It is interesting to note that social movements in the United States—and the media in covering them—have also tended to stress the personality and general importance of their leaders. When Dr. King was assassinated, many wondered whether the Southern Christian Leadership Conference could continue and were surprised to learn of the significant role that such men as Andrew Young, James Bevel and Hosea Williams, up till then in the shadows, had played.

19. Paul M. Harrison, *Authority and Power in the Free Church Tradition* (Princeton: Princeton University Press, 1959).

The other consequence is that in this kind of system it does in fact matter who is president and that the departure of a president, whether the agent of that departure is the voter at the ballot box or an assassin's bullet, does make a difference. Neither of these consequences makes the assassination of a president a rational action. However, they do very likely increase the probability that an irrational mind might be tempted to commit such an action.

CONCLUSION

We have seen that extremism, in act, if not objective, is (to paraphrase Rap Brown) "as American as cherry pie." Though contemporary reliance on civil-disobedience tactics by the civil-rights and antiwar movements clearly places a severe strain upon the operation of a democratic system, the American system has survived such efforts in the past. Movements have often played a dynamic role within the system. There is, then, little reason to fear or hope that the current unrest will topple the established order.

It is important to emphasize, however, that a review of the themes of this essay should not result in a complaisant or calm feeling for anyone concerned about this country. Our message is most decidedly not "all will work out in the end." We must recognize, on the one hand, that those who have engaged in civil disobedience and confrontation tactics have not always achieved their objectives and that sometimes these are morally bad, e.g., those of the Ku Klux Klan. By resorting to such tactics, they run the risk of turning many moderates against them, of creating a "backlash" that strengthens their opponents, and not only defeats them but helps to reverse social trends which they favor. Inherently, civil disobedience weakens the respect for the rule of law, which guarantees the rights of all minorities, of all whose opinions or traits are considered obnoxious by the majority. Hence, the use of civil disobedience as a political tactic is only justified as an extreme last-ditch measure, to be employed when there are no democratic means available to realize deeply-held moral values. Indiscriminate use of confrontationist tactics can only result in the undermining of the rule of law and the encouragement of all groups (including the military) to take the law and general power into their hands whenever they feel frustrated politically.

Ultimately, of course, it is not enough to say that the established order will survive. We must always ask, "At what price?" We have used the word "violence" rather casually in this essay, but it is not a casual phenomenon. While the political system has been reorienting itself, many have suffered and some have died. The American political system will probably emerge from the current turmoil intact. But will the individuals who have lived in the vortex of this turmoil be similarly intact? Is the loss of leaders of the caliber of John F. Kennedy, Medgar Evers, Martin Luther King, and Robert F. Kennedy a price we must periodically be prepared to pay?

Though we have been discussing violence as, in effect, a subtheme of the operation of the American political system, it goes far beyond that. It involves, as we have indicated, some of the central values and traditions of American society itself. Perhaps we must begin to question some of these. In doing so, however, we must keep in mind that everything we have discussed in this essay as a precipitant of violence—a plurality electoral system, the values of equalitarianism and achievement, the "nonconformist" religious ethos, the revolution in mass-media technology, the personalized presidency, etc.—are also precipitants of some of the best and noblest aspects of our society.

Given the fact that the tendency to resort to violence in American politics is linked to various persistent cultural and structural traits that cannot easily be changed, and that we might not even want to change, thought must be given to more concrete security measures which might be taken to reduce the toll of violence and particularly to better protect our national leaders. However, a discussion of such steps goes beyond the purview of this essay.

Assassination as a Political Tradition

Richard E. Rubenstein

THE SICK-SOCIETY DOCTRINE

"Political assassination" has at least two meanings, depending upon whether one focuses on the victim or the assassin. The phrase may suggest only that the victim played a role in the world of politics; in this sense, the murder of President Garfield by a disappointed office-seeker was a "political assassination." Or "political" may describe the assassin's role, for example, his intention to alter the political universe by his act, or his membership in a political organization. The distinction is not merely an exercise in semantics, for in describing and analyzing domestic assassinations Americans have consistently emphasized the first definition while ignoring the implications of the second. That we have had our share of political assassinations is admitted. That such events are politically significant, in the sense that they are generated by the political system, is denied.

The standard response to domestic assassinations has been to pass them off as isolated, gratuitous acts of evil or deranged personalities. The clear implication of most works of American history is that the typical assassin is both a loner and a lunatic: "President Lincoln was shot by a Southern fanatic"; "President McKinley was murdered by a deranged anarchist." After the tragic death of Senator Robert Kennedy at the hands of a "demented Arab nationalist," the statement heard most often was that the killing was "meaningless." In fact, acceptance of simplistic psychological explanations for assassination leads one to conclude that the entire subject is meaningless, politically speaking, since assassination in this context seems unrelated to the normal operation of the political system.

Thus one researcher reporting to the National Commission on the Causes and Prevention of Violence noted the prevalence of

415

psychological disorders among presidential assassins, and stated: ". . . some comfort can be taken in the fact that assassination has not become part of the American political system as has happened elsewhere in the world. . . ."[1] He attributed the increase in assassinations in recent years to the "contagion phenomenon."[2] Similarly, a recent study of American presidential assassination conducted by psychiatrists at the Stanford Medical Center concluded that ". . . with one exception, assassins have been young men with delusional thought processes who tended toward lives of alienation and socioeconomic deterioration."[3] The doctors' "preventive suggestions" were therefore limited to stronger gun laws, legislation regulating presidential exposure to crowds, creation of "homicide prevention centers," and establishment of an ombudsman system for processing complaints.[4]

This style of research reveals a profound commitment to what may be called the "sick-society" doctrine: the idea that the United States, for cultural and historical reasons, is producing more than its share of mentally disturbed or morally incompetent individuals. In this context, "sick society" is a misnomer, since the effect (if not the purpose) of this sort of psychological reductionism is to acquit the American political system while condemning American culture. Analysts under the spell of the doctrine avoid certain critical questions: Why do not the homicidal maniacs among us plot against their aunts and uncles instead of political figures? Is there a certain kind of political milieu that helps to generate or to shape these acts? Is there a relationship between "abnormal" acts of personal violence and the "normal" way our system operates? Moreover, they frequently succumb to the temptation to distort or misinterpret the historical evidence, for example, by ignoring political murders that do not rise to the dignity of "presidential" assassination and by assuming that the acts of neurotic or psychotic persons must be devoid of broader political significance.

1. Richard Maxwell Brown, "Historical Patterns of Violence in America," in H. D. Graham and T. R. Gurr, eds., *The History of Violence in America* (New York: Bantam, 1969), p. 57.
2. *Ibid.,* p. 59.
3. Robert L. Taylor and Alfred E. Weisz, "American Presidential Assassinations," in David Daniels, et al., *Violence and the Struggle for Existence* (Boston: Little, Brown & Co., in press.)
4. *Ibid.*

As a corrective to this new orthodoxy let me offer several broad generalizations that seem to me to be supported by the weight of historical evidence:

First, and most important, most assassins and would-be assassins in the United States identify themselves as members of definable political groups and believe themselves to be acting in such groups' interests.

Secondly, the political groups in question are generally *not* those thought of as "lunatic fringe" or fanatically ideological. They are large, disaffected domestic groups whose identities are based on shared ethnic, economic, racial, or sectional interests.

Thirdly, most domestic assassinations have not been individual efforts aimed at high-ranking officials in authority, but the work of organized cadres, directed against lower-level personnel representing competing groups. This pattern, describing the principal type of domestic political murder, may be called "instrumental" assassination.

Finally, what is now thought of as the usual type of assassination—the murder of nationally known political figures by assassins representing small groups or just themselves—is in fact a minority strain, a type of political murder that I will call "lost-cause" assassination. However, even "lost-cause" assassins have generally identified with political groups and attempted to act on their behalf.

TYPOLOGIES

Typologies are of limited usefulness, but it is necessary to emphasize the distinction between instrumental and lost-cause assassination, if only to draw attention to the existence of the former. A collectivized version of the "lonely-lunatic" fallacy admits that people are sometimes killed in the course of intergroup struggle or group revolt but holds that such incidents are the results of "mob violence" or "collective behavior." They are not "assassinations," i.e., conscious political acts. The proposition is false in at least two senses: (1) domestic groups like the Reconstruction Ku Klux Klan and the Molly Maguires of the 1870's employed assassination systematically as a way of ridding their territories of group enemies. Even assuming a simplistic distinction between rational and irrational acts, it is clear that these calculated murder campaigns were rational both in conception and implementation; (2) much action that may have seemed purely irrational, like the lynching of "uppity" Negroes, sometimes had a patent and conscious political purpose—for example, the destruction of potential militant leaders among Southern blacks. It seems pointless to consider the secret lynching of a black legislator by a Klan cadre as "assassination" and the open lynching of a local leader by a Klan-oriented crowd as "mob violence," when the elements of deliberation, political motivation, and political consequence are present in each case. Indeed, wherever domestic group struggles have produced a great deal of political violence, instrumental assassination has been practiced both by organized cadres and by mobs or *ad hoc* vigilante committees.[5]

For example, K.K.K. assassins in the late 1860's and 1870's struck at a wide range of alleged enemies from white Republicans like John W. Stephens of North Carolina and John H. Clayton of Arkansas to black political leaders like Mississippi State Senator Charles Caldwell and hundreds, perhaps thousands, of lesser-known men. After white supremacists regained power in the South, blacks were kept in line by a continued stream of vigilante actions (including more than 3,000 lynchings between 1882 and 1935) and what might be called "official assassinations"—judicial executions of prisoners convicted without evidence. In the modern era, when the legal balance tipped once more in favor of the blacks and against white supremacy, organized assassination—related to the revived K.K.K., the White Citizens Councils, and smaller terrorist groups—was again a response. Once more its targets ranged from nationally known figures (like Dr. Martin Luther King, Jr.) to local leaders (like Medgar Evers) and from civil-rights activists (Colonel Lemuel Penn, Viola Liuzzo, and Schwerner, Chaney, and Goodman) to random victims like the Sunday-school students in Birmingham's Sixteenth Street Baptist church. On the local level, terror was again found to be an effective method of delaying, if not preventing, the rise of antiracist political leaders.[6]

5. On the tendency to consider all collective behavior irrational, and a discussion of its causes, see the excellent critique of "collective-behavior" theory in Jerome H. Skolnick, *The Politics of Protest* (New York: Ballantine, 1969), pp. 329–346.
6. There is a voluminous literature on racist violence which establishes, *inter alia,* the political motivation and significance of much lynch-mob kill-

But the practice of instrumental assassination was by no means a Southern or racist monopoly. In the 1870's, Molly Maguires operating in the anthracite fields of western Pennsylvania murdered scores of scabs and company spies until their organization was exposed by a Pinkerton man and their leaders executed. In the sixty years of nationwide labor-management warfare that followed, murder was resorted to on both sides, most often in the heat of battle but sometimes as a result of carefully laid plans. Union men murdered scabs, sheriffs, and Pinkertons, while management forces viciously assaulted union organizers like the United Mine Workers' Lawrence Dyer:

. . . Evidence was adduced showing how the Harlan County Coal Operators Association learned through its spies of the trip planned by Lawrence Dyer, organizer of the United Mine Workers of America. As Dyer's car was passing beneath a clump of bushes, a volley of shots from the top of the cliff wounded two of the car's occupants. Later Dyer's home in Pineville, Bell County, was dynamited.[7]

Assassinations in classical form were sometimes the result of labor-management conflict. Anarchist leader Alexander Berkman tried to kill Carnegie Steel's Henry Clay Frick in 1892. Harry Orchard of the Western Federation of Miners confessed to the murder of Governor Frank Steunenberg of Idaho, allegedly at the request of union officers, in 1905. The McNamara Brothers, officials of the Iron Workers Union, A.F. of L., were convicted of bombing the *Los Angeles Times* office in 1910 in an apparent attempt to assassinate officials of that newspaper. Similarly, at the behest of management, Frank Little of the Industrial Workers of the World was taken from a room in Butte, Montana during the

---

ing, e.g., *Report of the Joint Select Committee to Inquire into the Condition of Affairs in the Late Insurrectionary States* (Rep. No. 60, 22, 42nd Cong. 2nd Sess., Government Printing Office, 1872); House Committee on Rules Hearings, *The Ku Klux Klan* (67th Cong., 1st Sess., Government Printing Office, 1921); Stanley F. Horn, *Invisible Empire: The Story of the Ku Klux Klan, 1866–1871* (Boston: Houghton Mifflin, 1939); David M. Chalmers, *Hooded Americanism* (Chicago: Quadrangle Press, 1968); Arthur Raper, *The Tragedy of Lynching* (Chapel Hill, N.C.: University of North Carolina Press, 1933); Arthur Waskow, *From Race Riot to Sit-In* (Garden City, N.Y.: Anchor Books, 1967).

7. Philip Taft and Philip Ross, "American Labor Violence," in Graham and Gurr, *op. cit.*, p. 350.

1917 copper strike and lynched by masked men. A series of "official assassinations" employed the forms of legality to do away with labor leaders like the Haymarket Square defendants, Joe Hill, Nicola Sacco and Bartolomeo Vanzetti. The initial period of labor-management killing ended with the New Deal's reorganization of labor relations and the subsequent slowdown of labor organizing in the South among farm workers and in urban ghettos.[8] In altered form, however, often involving what we now call "organized crime," assassination remained a weapon of last resort in cases of intense labor conflict.[9]

Organized crime suggests a third manifestation of instrumental assassination in the United States—murder for the purpose of obtaining or maintaining group control over the machinery of local government. Political murders frequently take place where the potential rewards/penalties of winning/losing local power are unusually great; for example, where the outcome of a political struggle will determine the fate of a territory *in perpetuo,* or where victory means economic security and defeat poverty for competing groups. To put it another way, instrumental assassinations appear to increase during political crises that are also *constitutional*—those in which a group or groups battle to determine how a political unit is initially to be organized, or whether an existing form of political organization is to be overthrown.

A good deal of killing on the American frontier, for example, although commonly dismissed as apolitical "frontier violence," can be attributed to the bitterness of such essentially institutional struggles as the undeclared war between Indians and white settlers, the battles between slavery and antislavery men in the new territories (particularly in Kansas-Nebraska), the bloody feuds between cattle and sheep raisers in Arizona and Montana, and the murderous political party struggles in New Mexico (where Republican Albert J. Fountain and other politicians of both parties "dis-

8. Existing material on labor-management violence, including assassination, is diffuse and uneven. See, e.g., Louis Adamic, *Dynamite: The Story of Class Violence in America* (Gloucester, Mass.: Peter Smith, 1963), and Samuel Yellen, *American Labor Struggles* (New York: S. A. Russell, 1956). The recent work of Taft and Ross, *op. cit.,* pp. 281–395 merits study.

9. As an example, in January, 1970, an insurgent United Mine Workers leader, Joseph Yablonski, was assassinated. Characteristically, the event provoked no comment from students of "political" assassination.

appeared"), Kentucky (where Democratic Governor-elect William Goebel was shot in 1900), and elsewhere. The stakes of victory and defeat were similarly high on the "urban frontier" during the organization and reign of old-style political machines. An over-emphasis on Al Capone and Prohibition may obscure the fact that political murders, both in the form of "mob violence" and planned assassinations, have been characteristic of ethnic-group struggles in large urban areas since before the Civil War.[10]

Much the same may be said of intragroup struggle under conditions of high politicization and low institutionalization—the preconditions of "constitutional" crisis. Large domestic out-groups coming rapidly to political consciousness and seeking to organize for eventual power are likely to be wracked by fierce internal conflict, very often including the use of assassination by one or more competing factions. American Tories were murdered by Patriots and Southern scalawags by white supremacists; Irish, Italians, and other urban fighting gangs practiced intergroup assassination along the way to becoming political organizations; and Malcolm X was apparently the victim of black-nationalist assassins. Indeed, the drive of black Americans in the face of intense internal and external opposition toward full political consciousness and internal reorganization has produced several examples of instrumental assassination, from attacks on occupying forces found on group turf to politically motivated factional murders. More common, however, has been the use of instrumental assassination *against* blacks both by white vigilantes and conspiratorial bands (espe-ally in the South) and by policemen representing competing groups or the *status quo*. It is difficult to avoid the conclusion that the murders of unarmed blacks during urban disorders, the unpro-voked armed attacks on militant organizations in several cities, the police shootouts, frameups, and "wars" against black street groups throughout the nation are part of a pattern of repression and re-prisal, one of whose consequences is the "official" assassination of militant leaders. Mounting evidence suggests that the police in urban areas are beginning to perform the functions traditionally

10. See, for example, John Higham, *Strangers in the Land: Patterns of American Nativism* (New York: Atheneum, 1963).

reserved to rural vigilantes—control of the underclass through terror.[11]

The foregoing material suggests that we can no longer be satisfied with analyses that restrict applicability of the term "assassination" to the occasional murder of famous politicians. Casting aside for the moment the traditional image of assassination (the stricken president, the furtive fanatic, etc.), one perceives a different reality—a pattern of political murder in which anonymous foot soldiers representing domestic groups strike down those representing other groups or the authorities. Instrumental assassination is thus recognized to be concomitant with intense intergroup and intragroup struggle and related therefore to the operations of the political system as a whole. Assassination, like other forms of political violence, has sometimes been *functional* for domestic political groups, a fact that can only disturb those devoted to both civil peace and justice in the United States.

The implications of this fact for policy are far-reaching. If assassination in its most common form is related to the nature of group conflict in America, patent-medicine solutions like the homicide-prevention center and the ombudsman (however appropriate as cures for other ills) will not suffice. It will not be enough to attempt to treat the potential Lee Harvey Oswalds and Sirhan Sirhans, even supposing that they have curable "diseases," so long as American society continues to be wracked by group conflicts that are, in effect, miniature wars. To reduce these conflicts below constitutional-crisis levels, political changes which are constitutional in effect must be contemplated. Examples of such potential changes are many, and I do not wish to go too far afield. But three kinds of change in particular seem to be called for, each of which would attack the problem of group warfare at a different root:

1. The United States must discover new institutional means for permitting representation of group interests. Coherent subnational communities in the United States will continue to war against each other and against the representatives of authority until new politi-

11. This assertion, which was considered fantastic when first raised by black militants and in the left-wing press, is now merely controversial. See Skolnick, *The Politics of Protest,* pp. 241ff.

cal and legal means are devised to permit such communities to govern themselves and to bargain *inter se.*[12]

2. Similarly, so long as there *are* oppressed out-groups in America, and so long as documents like the *Report of the National Advisory Commission on Civil Disorders* fail of implementation, insurgency and counterinsurgency will be endemic to the American political system, as they have been for two centuries.[13]

3. Finally, the obscene spectacle of domestic groups in the world's richest nation fighting desperately for available jobs, housing, education, medical care, and social services must be ended. If it should be found that violent conflict between lower- and lower-middle-class groups is related to a contrived or tolerated scarcity, the economic system should be altered to eliminate such scarcity. All this, of course, is more easily said than done. But until changes of this magnitude are not only contemplated but carried out, it is difficult to foresee a decline in either the intensity of group conflict or in the frequency of instrumental assassination as a function thereof.

LOST-CAUSE ASSASSINATIONS

The existence of a tradition of instrumental assassination, of course, does not negate the existence and persistence of other traditions. What I have called "lost-cause" assassination brings us closer to the accepted notion of assassination as the murder of great men by deranged individuals, but even here the political content is a good deal more significant and policy implications more complex than is commonly recognized. As the phrase suggests, lost-cause assassinations are not blows calculated to advance group interests or revolutionary acts intended to bring about a new order. On the contrary, they are most often the bitter fruit of lost or hopeless causes, which is what accounts for their aura of meaninglessness. Unlike the Klansmen or Molly Maguires, whose attacks on enemy forces were part of planned campaigns to bring groups

12. An argument in this vein is to be found in Milton Kotler, *Neighborhood Government* (Indianapolis and New York: Bobbs-Merrill, 1969).
13. This background is explored analytically in Richard E. Rubenstein, *Rebels in Eden* (Boston: Little, Brown, 1970).

to power, lost-cause assassins have lashed out at national leaders to avenge individual or group humiliation and to restore group honor. Such acts reek of vengeance, of nostalgia for dreams denied, of twisted notions of tyrannicide and Roman heroism.

In fact, there is a direct spiritual link between political murders performed under cover of the custom of dueling (such as Burr's murder of Hamilton) and modern assassinations, beginning with the "regicide" of the Southern gentleman, John Wilkes Booth.[14] The Southern tradition of effacing one's dishonor by performing heroic murder lived on into the twentieth century. Huey Long, for example, was assassinated by a genteel Louisianian who opposed him politically and to whom he made the mistake of attributing Negro ancestors. But even outside the South the notion of revenging a humiliating defeat through assassination persisted. Henry Clay Frick of Carnegie Steel was assaulted by the anarchist Berkman *after* the Homestead Strike had been lost. Governor Steunenberg was killed *after* the Western Federation of Miners had been defeated in the Idaho mining war. Similarly Czolgosz's assassination of McKinley and Zangara's attempt to kill Franklin D. Roosevelt (he succeeded in shooting Mayor Cermak of Chicago) were acts of personal and political despair. Representatives of the ruling class were attacked, not because they represented decadent capitalism standing in the way of a socialist or anarchist triumph, but because they had so thoroughly crushed and humiliated the radical opposition.

The same "lost-cause" mentality was apparent among many assassins of the 1950's and 1960's—principally racists and nationalists-in-exile. This spirit of romantic, vengeful heroism flows, it seems to me, from what the majority so frequently does to "extremist" minorities in the United States. Effectively suppressed, excluded and ostracized, there is no question of their coming to power. Consequently, the extremist assassin does not hope to take power but to avenge a prior defeat by destroying those who already possess it. The Puerto Rican nationalists who attacked

14. For an interesting treatment of dueling in the United States, including political duels, see William Oliver Stevens, *Pistols at Ten Paces: The Story of the Code of Honor in America* (Boston: Houghton Mifflin, 1940). On violence and the Southern sense of honor, see W. J. Cash, *The Mind of the South* (New York: Vintage Books, 1955).

President Truman, the anti-Castroites who plotted against President Kennedy, the Arab refugee who killed Robert F. Kennedy and the racist who murdered Martin Luther King, Jr., did not intend to "free" Puerto Rico, Cuba, the Jordanian refugees or the South. They did intend to strike heroic blows against their people's fancied oppressors and to mount the stage of history. The desire of assassins to become historical figures, by now a cliché, becomes more comprehensible when one recalls that the political groups from which lost-cause assassins spring have been forced out of political history and into obscurity of "nonnewsworthiness." Before the attempt on Truman's life, who knew the passion of the Puerto Rican nationalists? Before Senator Kennedy was murdered, who imagined that there were substantial numbers of Arab refugees in the United States longing for the destruction of Israel? These were not matters deemed "news fit to print" until assassination made them newsworthy.

This suggests that even lost-cause assassinations have political as well as psychological roots, since *these assassins are so often members of political fringe groups.* They are anarchists, die-hard racists, Communists, neo-Nazis, nationalists-in-exile, etc. Such groups are usually referred to as "extremist" or "lunatic fringe," the implication being that it is quite natural for their members to engage in assassination. But the problem is not this easily resolved, since in general the attitude of "extremist" leaders toward assassination has been negative. Jefferson Davis and other former Confederates denounced John Wilkes Booth; top anarchists like Emma Goldman strongly condemned bomb throwers and assassins; various Arab leaders disavowed the act of Sirhan Sirhan; and so forth. Therefore, we cannot define such groups as extremist because they are committed to a policy of assassination, although it seems clear that they may tend to attract potential assassins.[15]

Well, then, perhaps we may use "extremist" or "lunatic fringe" to describe an organizational style characterized by clandestine

15. Indeed, as Chapter 2 of this paper suggested, the systematic use of assassination is more closely related to serious conflict between large domestic groups than to ideological extremism. This is, perhaps, a perverse illustration of the nonideological character of American politics praised by such writers as Daniel Boorstin; see Boorstin, *The Genius of American Politics* (Chicago: Phoenix Books, 1967).

meetings, passwords and aliases, costumes, coded messages, and all the other trappings of conspiratorial, illegal politics. If they meet in cellars, wear bedsheets, or call each other "brother," we can be sure that they are up to no good! But this overlooks a crucial point: most minority political groups in America have not operated as clandestine organizations until suppressed by the majority and driven underground. Whether racist or anarchist, fascist or Communist, domestic "fringe" groups have usually attempted to operate openly and in accordance with law until the majority turned the law against them. American political organizations have seldom been conspiratorial *by nature;* the charge of conspiracy, however, has often been used to outlaw political minorities with the effect of rendering them conspiratorial.[16] A frequent tactic, as we know, has been to make use of a single plot (the Haymarket Square or Wall Street bombings or the Alger Hiss case, for example) to attack an entire group as conspiratorial, with the effect of compelling it, if it wishes to remain in existence, to resort to secret meetings, passwords, coded messages, and the rest. This development is most obvious in the case of the left, but even Southern racists first turned to conspiracy and terror during the period of disenfranchisement of ex-Confederates and occupation of the South by Northern troops. (The persistence of such tactics in the South seems closely related to the continued belief in a Southern "nation" enslaved to the North, a passion akin to that of the nationalists-in-exile.)

The implications of this analysis are clear. By "extremist" or "lunatic fringe" we really mean those political groups that are outside the prevailing national consensus—which depart too radically from the basic assumptions, attitudes, and doctrines of the center. "Extremists" may be too far to the right or the left, too specialized economically or too utopian—it matters not. Their common sin is that they are different, and threatening to the established order. If they persist in remaining in existence, and particularly if they show signs of real strength, they can look forward to persecution and outlawry, contumely and ostracism, jail or de-

16. Knowing this, the young radicals indicted for criminal conspiracy in Chicago in connection with the Democratic National Convention demonstrations of 1968 are determined *not* to be driven underground; they have organized an open defense organization called "The Conspiracy" and have invited sympathizers to "Join the Conspiracy Today."

portation. However, groups are not so easily driven out of politics. Faced with the choice of meeting in cellars or ceasing to exist, they will meet in cellars, where, to be sure, they will attract unstable people who nurture dreams of revenge and greatness. These are the origins of lost-cause assassinations.

Observers have often noted that one of the real horrors of American life is the ability of the majority of Americans to go about their daily business, priding themselves all the while on their free institutions, while dissenters are being outlawed, hunted down, and even murdered in the dark corners of the society. A particularly clear example of the process is now being played out in black ghettos across the nation, where organizations like the Black Panther party—whose chief "crime" has been to challenge the legitimacy of police tactics within the ghetto—are being systematically (and illegally) punished by law-enforcement agencies. Such organizations are labeled "extremist" and infiltrated by government agents. Their mail is opened and their telephones tapped; their offices are raided and their files confiscated or destroyed by the FBI; their officers are arrested on false charges by local police and their members harassed, humiliated, and entrapped into shootouts or driven into exile.[17] (Occasionally, as in Oakland, Chicago, and Brooklyn, even the mask of legality has dropped, and policemen have made unprovoked armed attacks on Black Panther headquarters.) It is an old pattern. The habit of discriminating against, ostracizing, and terrorizing political minorities that threaten the *status quo* is what de Tocqueville described in 1835 as the "tyranny of the majority." (He stated further, "I know of no country in which there is less real freedom of discussion than in America.")[18] It is what Louis Hartz had in mind 150 years later when he wrote, "This then is the mood of America's absolutism— the sober faith that its norms are self-evident."[19]

17. An example of these tactics (December, 1969) was the killing in Chicago of Panther leaders Fred Hampton and Mark Clark. Several special commissions and a grand jury investigated whether this was, indeed, another "official assassination," but the results, while critical of the police actions, were confused by a series of political charges and counter-charges.

18. Alexis de Tocqueville, *Democracy in America* (New York: Random House, 1966).

19. Louis Hartz, *The Liberal Tradition in America* (New York: Harcourt, Brace & World, 1955).

Again, as in the case of instrumental association, the policy implications of the analysis are complex and far-reaching. What we are really talking about is the ability of the political system to tolerate political conflict (both legal and quasi-legal) along a wide spectrum of opinion and belief. The price of suppressing such conflict (like the price of repressing psychic conflict) would seem to be an increase in seemingly irrational types of violence, like assassination. To attack the underlying causes of assassination, therefore, one must contemplate altering a system that outlaws and crushes minorities in the name of "stability."

In this connection, it is important to call attention to well-established institutional devices that permit or encourage the suppression of political minorities—not just those laws and customs that "unleash" the police against dissident groups, but those that prevent minority movements from entering the universe of everyday politics. For example, almost every state discriminates legislatively in favor of the two major parties and against potential third or fourth parties by making it exceedingly difficult and expensive to get new parties on the ballot. Practically every political jurisdiction in the United States has rejected proportional representation as an electoral technique in order to ensure that "splinter-group" votes will not be counted. Using legislative powers to determine the qualifications of their members, both the United States Congress and state legislatures have expelled elected members with whose ideas they have disagreed. The present system of campaign contributions, which the two major parties are unwilling to alter, makes it certain that nobody will be elected to office unless he is allied with powerful, monied interests. The press and mass media have unfettered discretion to ignore the activities of some groups and play up those of others; and notwithstanding the Federal Communication Commission's "equal-time" rules, there is not yet a right of access to the means of public information. Through such devices as these, the relegation of ideological extremists to a political Siberia is assured.

It is an illusory stability that is purchased at the price of creating a lunatic fringe. Indeed, I would argue when a system becomes so "stable" as to drive dissident minorities out of nonviolent politics, a turn to violent politics is predictable. It is no accident that the dozen major assassinations of recent years took place during the administration of Lyndon Johnson, whose "Great Society" was to be based upon a consensus of moderates, or that assassination seems endemic in majoritarian systems characterized by strong executive rule and weak legislatures. The last hope of a deflated political minority is representation in legislatures at various levels of government; the collapse of legislatures in modern, centralized states has helped majorities to narrow the spectrum of conflict by driving minorities out of electoral and into extremist politics. (This is equally true of certain developing nations, the Soviet Union, and the United States.) The question therefore raised (and I can do no more than raise it here) is whether the United States may not have something to learn from nations that seem to have struck a more successful balance between the demands for representation and the requirements of stability. This issue will become particularly acute, I believe, as differences of political opinion in the United States continue to intensify and the accommodative devices of the two-party system are further strained, perhaps even shattered. The great danger is that a combination of political conservatism and institutional inertia will drive new groups of dissidents into extremist politics, thereby increasing the probability, *inter alia,* of more assassinations.

CONCLUSION

For purposes of descriptive analysis, we have divided assassinations into two types or traditions—instrumental assassination, which is a function of intense group conflict, and lost-cause assassination, which is a function of suppression of minorities and consequent political extremism. In both cases, assassination (and other forms of political violence) has been produced by the inability of the political system to reflect and to satisfy group demands under circumstances in which such demands are constitutional in nature, that is, they require a redistribution not only of goods and services but of decision-making power. Both types of assassination may be seen as part of a single process that begins with a period of warfare between competing groups over the initial distribution of power, proceeds through a phase of struggle between in-groups and out-groups over maintenance of the initial pattern of authority and subjection, and ends either with the admission of out-groups to power or their outlawry. The first two phases are characterized by campaigns of instrumental assassination in the form, respectively, of cadre and mob action, the third (if outlawry results) by the politics of extremism, including lost-cause assassinations.

In simpler language, political groups begin by struggling for power and end by struggling for honor. The system that denies them both can remain stable systematically only in the sense that the eye of a hurricane is quiet. The problem of assassination in the United States cannot be correctly perceived or solved unless it is recognized to be but one manifestation of the problem of maldistributed power.

Murder as Political Behavior

H. L. Nieburg

A society faced with the prospect of the normalization of extreme forms of political behavior can no longer afford the defense reflex of pushing the unpleasant realities into the subconscious by labeling them as "blind and mindless actions of the insane." Virtually all the literature on assassination dwells upon the tortured mind of the assassin, as though his tragic action were fully explainable by the accident that created a flawed human being and gave him the proximity and weapons to act out an automatic and predestined, and therefore meaningless, murder. This is reassuring, but false and misleading; it defeats common sense and understanding and, in the present crisis of our society, it can be dangerously dysfunctional.

While we cannot hope for perfect understanding, we cannot avoid the responsibility to study political murder with the same perspective that we bring to other social phenomena. As a political scientist, I am concerned with institutional processes and public policy, not with clinical therapy. However, I cannot neglect individual motivation and behavior, the basic units of the network of relationships that constitute a social system. Individuals are the concrete monads of any larger abstraction. Private motive cannot be ignored; however, it must be seen as part of a societal process.[1] One must look to dynamic social factors rather than isolated individual motives. Murder, whether personal or political, is, like suicide, always a present possibility which society must expect and anticipate with mechanisms of defense and localization as well as prevention. Isolated or recurrent acts of political extremism, like assassination, must be analyzed within the context of functional behavior.

The definition of "deviance" always reflects normative values and is an extension of behavior which, at some level, is functional both for the deviant and for society. One of society's main functions is to minimize and moderate destructive behavior. Thus the axiom: disruptive and destructive actions are symptoms of deep social, as well as individual, problems. The symptoms of a disease are the indicators and tools of the doctor, not his enemies. It is not enough to cosmetically eradicate the symptoms. They are the friends of diagnosis and may point the way to cure. Like many forms of extreme behavior, assassination may be looked upon as society's early-warning system, revealing deep-rooted political conflicts that are gathering strength beneath the surface of social relations. In a real sense, the unbalanced individual is a sensitive telltale. The Middle Ages prized and honored the "village idiot"; Shakespeare enjoyed putting his most cogent truths in the mouths of jesters and knaves. The marginal individual suffers from social strains and cleavages that run through his very life, unlike the "well-balanced" man who is insulated by habit and social constraints and who is much slower to feel and to speak. The distraught and disturbed act and react without waiting for a new consensus. In this manner, they are both victims and the heralds of social change.

Political extremism, whether for or against the *status quo*, means pressure is building against the chain of social relationships.

---

1. Private "motive" becomes a social fact when "it is made overt by the people of the society concerned, and when their regard for it affects the actions they perform after a homicide. Studying homicide in terms of 'motive' is often only a shorthand for studying social situations in which homicide occurs." Paul Bohannan, ed., *African Homicide and Suicide* (Princeton, N. J.: Princeton University Press, 1960), p. 252.

The weakest links are the first to break and may, as has happened often in the past, precipitate events of larger crisis. The assassination of Chicago auto dealers (the Foreman brothers) by a Negro (who bought a car he could not afford) was a forecast of the smashing of loan offices and auto dealerships that erupted soon thereafter in Chicago and other riot cities. Too many individuals in crisis mean a society in crisis. Whether violent action is deliberately contrived by extremists in order to create a crisis situation or haplessly enacted by distressed individuals out of their own frenzy, the result is much the same. It is commonplace that war and revolution are great catalysts of social change. Other forms of extreme behavior may have a similar cause and effect.

DEFINITIONS

The conventional common-sense approach to assassination limits itself to acts against prominent and important political personages, who are presumably chosen as victims by virtue of their role/office rather than a personal relationship to the assassin. By this definition the world since World War II has seen at least fifty major and clearly identifiable political assassinations involving legislators, candidates, generals, ambassadors, presidents, premiers, cabinet members, etc. Other forms of murder that may in some sense be termed primarily political, but are localized, obscure, and capture little attention from national audiences, are excluded.

Ali A. Mazrui[2] eliminates the requirement of "motive," preferring to fasten upon the *importance* of the victim: "the victim need not be a professional politician, or hold a formal office of state. Neither Mahatma Gandhi in 1947 nor Malcolm X in 1964 was a politician or a state official in this professional sense. Yet we think of their deaths as instances of assassination."[3] He chooses to follow convention while broadening the notion of "political importance."

2. Ali A. Mazrui, "Thoughts on Assassination in Africa," *Political Science Quarterly*, 83 (March, 1968), pp. 40–48.
3. *Ibid.*, p. 43.

Victor T. LeVine takes an alternate route, emphasizing the role of the killer and the mode of the act rather than the status of the victim. "The difference between assassination and murder is admittedly a tenuous one; I would contend that it lies in two areas, the role of the killer, and the element of surprise. Assassins are usually hired or delegated, and they generally strike without warning to the victims."[4] There are several problems in using LeVine's definition. Assassins are not always hired or delegated, and the actual killing always requires a tactical element of surprise without which it is thwarted. Further, there are many examples of warnings and threats used as harassment prior to the actual attempt. This approach is too narrow and suffers from the same problem as the other, that is, it tends to represent a special case within a broad class. It is the broad class that should be defined.

In my view, a broader definition, internally consistent, would be preferable. This would open the way for a breakdown of more specific varieties of assassination and would emphasize the continuity of extreme behavior with normative behavior. I offer seven categories that are relevant to all forms of political behavior:

1. The object or victim (toward what or whom the behavior is directed)
2. The implementation (the way the act is carried out)
3. The motivation (deep or superficial, calculated or impulsive, etc.)
4. Association (lone act, small or large conspiratorial group, etc.)
5. Organization of the activity (professional assassin, underlings and leaders, participant haplessly induced by threat or pressure of others, etc.)
6. Culture pattern (perception or assertion of normative pattern or political behavior)
7. Political impact and effects

4. Victor T. LeVine, "The Course of Political Violence" in William H. Lewis, ed., *French Speaking Africa: The Search for Identity* (New York: Appleton-Century-Crofts, 1965), p. 68.

In trying to cover all these aspects, one may state a definition:

> Political assassination: act of murder whose purpose, choice of victim, surrounding circumstances, implementation and/or effects have political significance, i.e., tend to modify the behavior of other actors in a bargaining situation of systemic social consequences.

The categories of this definition will fit any kind of behavior, political or criminal, yet clearly separate assassination from both nonmurderous political behavior and all acts of murder that lack any significant political dimension. This definition makes it possible to differentiate and relate acts of assassination to "threats, capabilities, and attempts," all of which may have political significance. It also makes it possible to narrow every kind of special case of political assassination, requiring a clear description of the key factors involved. It steps beyond the previous definitions by including the impact and consequences of the act, the exploitation of outcomes by participants and others that may endow the activity with its most important political character. By using general categories applicable to all political behavior, it opens the way to comparative analysis.[5]

There is no reason for not dealing with political murder when it occurs within small formal or informal political groups (having the same pattern and significance on its own level of social organization as has an assassination of national or international scope). Throughout the political and social structure, threats and acts of assassination may be parallel and comparable in terms of intending or acquiring a purposive political effect. This includes retributive feuds and murder chains, acts of deterrence, compulsion, enforcement, and punishment; warfare among tribal elites, reprisals, and rudimentary systems of self-help justice; symbolic, ritual, or ceremonial acts aimed at diverting the real thing by means of a substitute that has similar effects; as a form of "propaganda of the act"; as a demonstration of group unity, individual commitment,

5. See my book, *Political Violence: The Behavioral Process* (New York: St. Martin's Press, 1969). See also the categorizations discussed in Chapter 1 and the cross-national quantitative analyses found in Chapter 2 of this volume.

or, conversely, as a test of these qualities in rival groups; as a demand for attention from a larger audience; as a claim, assertion, and testing of legitimacy; as an act of enforcing and maintaining authority; as an act of provocation falsely blamed on innocent groups in order to justify one's own actions against them; retaliation or reprisal in a bargaining relationship that moves toward settlement; as a method of terror; as a way of forcing confrontation on other issues; or as a way of avoiding such confrontation by diverting attention; as an expression and measure of group or individual commitment; as a test of the manhood and loyalty of new recruits; as a method of precipitating revolutionary conditions; etc. This is a suggestive list of the functional continuities that exist in threats and acts of political assassination encompassed by our definition.

It becomes possible to explain the otherwise meaningless and isolated act of a desperate individual: (1) marginal individuals inhabit a world in which fantasy endows them with the same legitimacy and purposefulness that gives meaning to the policy uses of assassination by organized groups; (2) it is more useful to understand how political groups use the psychotic individual or exploit his actions in their own interests than to dwell upon the etiology of his illness.

Anomic assassination, apparently meaningless, must be studied as part of a continuum of political behavior. It is always extremely difficult to separate the individualized motives, intentions, and purposes of the assassin from the social process of which his act is a part. And, indeed, it is not necessary that this be done. In fact, it is considerably more helpful and probably more realistic to admit a wide variety of motives, including those that may be contradictory: the individual's problems and values, his relationship, aspiration, or sense of identity with other groups and individuals, his structure of loyalties, including those that are divided, his *post hoc* rationalizations, etc. There is a kind of arbitrariness about who commits a political act and for what reasons. Like the simultaneity of invention, when a felt need exists, many rise to fill it from separate life situations. The historical record shows many examples of multiple assassination plots smoldering at approximately the same time but in different places and frequently with different motives. In a sense, the actual assassin is always an instrument of larger dynamic relationships. This fact may suggest the path to analysis of extremism and murder as political behavior.

SOCIAL BARGAINING

The distinctive mark of the state is its unitary sovereignty, which centralizes the authority of all the various normative systems of behavior that make possible the precarious balancing act of group life. This unitary sovereignty functions to protect private and public activity and bargaining through which men seek to achieve whatever values they contrive. The nation contains a vast multiplicity of personal lives, energies, relationships, etc., which somehow must maintain order in the midst of change, and change in the midst of order; the group must endure and grow through continuous adaptation to the parameters of the human and physical environments. The power of the state gives authority to the institutions that mediate and bind diversity with unity, freedom, experimentation, and conflict with social stability and institutional continuity. The state authority does not eliminate conflict but underpins the institutionalization of conflict and bargaining in ways that optimize consensus and values.

Political violence cannot be dealt with in terms of a "legality" that views the formal system of law and order as sacred and inviolate, a view that is easily corrupted as a *status* quo ideology. Legality supports the prevailing consensus against erratic transitions, enabling the majority of citizens to conduct their private and public affairs within a more or less stable environment. Private violence and forceful self-help are among the most important conditions which the legal institutions are intended to replace. Yet this very value endows such methods with efficacy as the last resort of political bargaining.

The essence of politics is bargaining, the classic relationship of ambivalence: love/hate, cooperation/conflict. In its early stages, a test of strength and will tends to be conducted symbolically by threat or by limited and token displays of force. When symbolic and token displays of force are despised by their target, or elicit counterescalation, then a higher magnitude of risk-cost is imposed upon all the parties. The avenue back to constructive bargaining is increasingly blocked. It is at this point that lovers kill the thing they love and college presidents call in the gendarmes, while students seek ever more provocative forms of retaliation. This explains why 38 per cent of all homicides are committed within the family, why another 40 per cent occur among close friends, why abusive parents kill more children than die from leukemia, cystic fibrosis and muscular dystrophy combined. Lone assassins generally are found to be strongly attached to their victims, having gone through periods of great love and admiration and frequently identifying with him even after a sense of rejection has led him to threaten and/or attempt an act of mad and fantastic revenge, punishment, retaliation and, in his view, purification.

The opposite of war is not peace, the opposite of love is not hate, the opposite of collaboration is not harassment; in terms of bargaining relationships, each of these dichotomies are at one end of the scale of mutual involvement and relatedness. At the opposite end of the scale lies separation, indifference, exclusion, and rejection. Failure to comprehend the model of a bargaining continuum leads directly to the description of extreme forms of behavior as "meaningless"; it disables us from understanding and appropriately responding to the drift of bargaining engagements toward the breaking point.

However, failure to assess correctly the role of bargaining is a universal and probably inevitable habit. The very failure of intelligence (which raises the risks) may confer tactical advantages in a bargaining situation. Appreciation of the dynamics of escalated and counterescalated actions generally springs from and/or reflects weakness and a willingness to make concessions. It tends to legitimize the escalated actions. Thus intelligent assessment of danger may be read by one's antagonists as an incremental advantage that assures the efficacy of further escalation. This is a fundamental paradox of the bargaining equation and a formidable challenge to hopes that mankind will find a way to avoid self-defeating wars and domestic and personal confrontations. Most of the time, men and groups grant concessions and moderate demands only in the face of grave dangers and disasters already enacted or immediately at hand. This accounts for the great melodramas and tragedies of human history, adding massively to the common woe and an ominous portent of the future. A scientist can only hope that understanding the dynamics of bargaining will eliminate at least the most asinine and unnecessary denouements, facilitating assessments of cost/risk constraints in future bargaining outcomes well before the breaking point of violent confrontation.

Social change often pursues a logic that defies prediction and is only logical in retrospect. Whether union strikers slug scabs, sit in, or quietly picket cannot always be planned or controlled by union leadership. One shove of a woman picket by a plant manager or a policeman may suddenly focus years of accumulated grievances and unrelated suffering, forcing the leadership reluctantly to follow the followership or lose the technical role of leader. The political bargaining values of an accident of violence and its ballooning aftermath are not calculable. In many situations, the escalation toward illegality and violence is one that does not have to be inspired or planned but cannot always be controlled. Yet it becomes a part of the bargaining relationship and has influence on the assessment of options available to the parties in a bargaining engagement.

GROUPS AND INDIVIDUALS

Individuals discover, learn, and achieve values as members of groups, formal and informal, at all levels of organization of the society. Without the reinforcement and the creation of normative social relations that group life affords, personal values take on a spectral sense of unreality even for the individual who holds them. Though they may originate with inspired, talented, or tormented individuals (writers, artists, managers, etc.), so long as they remain the interior vision of an isolated man, they lack the test required to give them legitimacy even for their author, that is, integration into some kind of group experience. What an artist achieves by flinging his work of art before the public, the administrator achieves by directives, memos, and reorganizations, the reformer by personal persuasion and public speaking, etc. In short, legitimacy is an attribute conferred by some kind of group consensus. Every individual with a grievance is extremely anxious to tell his story in order to find someone who agrees with him, thereby giving his complaint a scrap of legitimacy, however modest. The truism that man is a social animal is nowhere clearer than in his need to discover and reinforce his identity and self-righteousness.

Through group relationships, both face-to-face as well as remote and theoretical, life situations and experiences of individuals become inputs for the whole society. In the realm of values and morality the group is larger than the sum of its parts. Every group, however marginal, specialized, limited in size, hostile to the values of other groups, is able to generate and sustain legitimacy. Honor, justice, and group loyalty supercede and transcend individuals. Self-preservation yields to group values when the group requires it. Every group has its heroes, legends, and martyrs, whether juvenile gangs, criminal mobsters, or old folks' homes.

Studies of "why men fight" conducted after World War II and the Korean War demonstrate that "patriotism" and "indoctrination" have little to do with combat performance; rather, the best fighting men are found to be those who belonged to well-integrated small groups, squads, and companies, who valued above all things the loyalty and respect of their fellows. Spontaneous, voluntary, and informal groups are held together by the power of their legitimacy and require few negative sanctions to enforce their norms and values. Mutual reinforcement and esteem keep a futile remnant of a political party intact long after it has lost any realistic aspiration for fulfilling its original function. The admiration and respect of one's peers is a more powerful instrument for shaping and controlling the young than parents or teachers.

The group amplifies and gives meaning to the life of the individual. It shelters and protects him and not only gives him values but also makes him more effective in their achievement. It requires and for the most part receives loyalty, recognition of its leaders and service toward group-defined objectives. On the other hand, where required, every group severely punishes violation of its norms, permitting atonement and penance for small infractions, exclusion, ostracism, and even death for large. For all groups, the most deadly offense is heresy and disloyalty. The group values loyalty and conformity to group norms more highly than any kind of talent, ability, or genius.

The smaller and more embattled a group the greater the commitment required of its members. Coser: "They tend to absorb and pre-empt the whole personality of their numbers whereas larger groups require only a weaker type of participation in group activities."[6] The larger a group the more pluralistic are the residual, overlapping values represented among its members. Therefore, the more specific and limited will be group demands and consensual values. A confrontation that escalates costs and risks tends to break down the unity of action groups: members are forced to make their own assessments in terms of other values that they may not share with the group. This tendency induces counterpressure against *lukewarmness* and may lead to external provocations to force rival groups into actions which may weld the challenger's unity.

Small groups seek to enhance their power by militancy and by wholesale mobilization of the energies and resources of their members. Some small groups assume a sectlike character, demanding and receiving consensus and conformity in virtually all the behavior values of members. Even the exclusivity and separatism of romantic attachments and marriage are treated as suspect and potentially disloyal to group values and leadership. Tight-knit associations of professional criminals demand and get complete dedication and obedience.[7]

For most of humanity, the tribe or the state is the unit within which killing is murder and outside of which killing is proof of manhood and bravery. Although the modern nation-state is the technical source of sovereignty and cohesive legitimacy, the regime

6. Lewis A. Coser, *Continuities in the Study of Social Conflict* (Glencoe, Ill.: The Free Press, 1967), p. 107.

7. The Senate Crime Investigating Committee noted that "family, religion, and country are all secondary and required to be subservient. . . ." as if this fact were immoral in itself. Obviously all groups that are embattled intensify their security codes and demand the same kind of loyalty. The Senate report continues: "the penalty for disloyalty . . . is usually death . . . ordered for a variety of reasons . . . a grab for power, the code of vengeance, gangland rivalries, infidelity to the organization, or even for suspicion of derelictions, particularly for informing or aiding law enforcement officials." U.S. Senate, Committee on Government Operations; Subcommittee on Investigations, *Hearings, Organized Crime and Illicit Traffic in Narcotics,* Pts. I & II. September–October, 1963. 88th Cong. 1st Sess., 1963. Vol. I, p. 2.

that commands it at any given time may fail to establish its claim to legitimacy. Its use of the enforcement machinery of the state may only postpone, not abate, its demise. Cohesion purchased by force and repression only strengthens the cohesion and legitimacy of opposition groups and forces them into a statelike counterforce role.

At the nation-state level, violence is legitimate for the enforcement of law and order, punishment for transgressions against society, and the defense of the state and its territory against internal or external enemies. Private citizens retain the right to use violence for the defense of life, safety, family, and, in some cases, property. None of these rights is absolute but must be exercised within reasonable limits.

Within the state many private groups develop their own security codes. Among its elements are the reciprocal aid of members to each other's needs; obedience and loyalty to the recognized leaders; reaction of all members to an offense against one of them as though it were an offense against all; no appeal or alignment with outsiders in resolving internal conflict; etc. To the extent that the group moves or is forced into confrontation with the state and other groups, to the same extent is its security code intensified and the enforcement sanctions raised.

Many sociologists use the term "subculture of violence." Where the state is the enemy and lacks legitimacy, the inhabitants are thrown upon self-help in protecting themselves and maximizing their own security. Upper middle and upper social classes (whose interest is guarded by the authority of the state) abhor physical combat as a method of conflict resolution. They possess a wide variety of normative systems for conducting and resolving conflict (property, contract, direct political influence, membership in organized power groups). They regard as trivial the social and personal stimuli that provoke combat among the loser classes. Differential access to other forms of social bargaining and the omnipresence of state authority (embodied in policemen) contribute to this subculture not only because physical violence is one of the only modes of conflict available, but also because its advantages are daily demonstrated. In the ghettos, the most serious crime is "to call a cop." There is strong community sanction against this transgression, because it constitutes a challenge to the prevailing and functioning systems of legitimacy. The lower-class male is socialized by a system that places the highest value on physical courage and quick resort to combat in the face of insult.[8]

In a period of revolutionary change, all kinds of otherwise moderate groups may be forced to extreme intensification of their security codes. A period of violent confrontation poses a severe test of the viability of groups. There is no substitute for the ultimate sanction of execution, assassination, and deadly combat. The irrevocable character of death gives it unique and irreversible consequences. For the group, extreme actions commit a man symbolically, breaking his ties with his previous commitments and making the survival of the group synonymous with personal survival. "He is reborn, so to speak, through the act of violence and is now in a position to assume his rightful place in the revolutionary world of new men."[9] Between life and death is an implicit moral judgment. In the words of a Sicilian peasant commenting on a Mafia assassination in his town: "He's dead, and if he is dead he must have been wrong. I can't help seeing it like that. . . ."[10] Schelling and Hoffmann make the same point about nuclear strategy: "the act of commiting oneself irreversibly," which in fact limits freedom of maneuver and might therefore be considered imprudent, under certain circumstances becomes "a source of strength."[11]

To the extent that the legitimacy of the state is challenged, the normative use of violence will be asserted both by the regime and by many private groups. The kinds of tactics that groups adopt depend upon the available options and their reinforcement by

8. Marvin E. Wolfgang, *Patterns in Criminal Homicide* (Philadelphia: University of Pennsylvania Press, 1958), pp. 188–189.

9. Coser, *op. cit.,* p. 81.

10. Danilo Dolci, *Waste* (New York: Monthly Review Press, 1964), p. 45.

11. Stanley Hoffmann, *The State of War: Essays on the Theory and Practice of International Politics* (New York: Frederick A. Praeger, 1965), pp. 206–207. It should also be noted that irreversible commitments of high risk may generate self-fulfilling prophesies, provoke pre-emptive high-risk action by others, be cheated of efficacy by being scorned by others, etc. The threat of the ultimate sanction, death, may be deprived of any efficacy whatsoever when the intended victim either humbly accepts the risks or acts first. Thus the threat or actuality of death is not without ambiguities. Mutual threats and capabilities tend to cancel each other and create conditions of possible mutual extinction and/or a return to low-risk bargaining.

efficacy in changing the behavior of others. Extreme actions are by nature self-limiting, negative, and, beyond a certain point, counter-productive. They are therefore less efficacious than peaceable bargaining through exchange of values. However, groups that lack positive values to exchange will exploit what values they have. In a period of intense social change, the uprooting of established institutions and pluralistic challenges to the legitimacy of centralized authority, both the regime and other groups will be forced into violent actions. Extreme modes of conduct will tend to become normative for private individuals and groups of all varieties. Such unstable conditions tend to bring into prominence those groups whose existing normative frameworks already legitimize the use of violence. Extremist groups seek to use violence and forms of direct confrontation in order to create situations in which such forms of behavior become normative. Success in this objective will bring these groups and their leaderships access to the bargaining process that under peaceful and stable conditions they are denied.

To understand extreme forms of political behavior by anomic individuals or small conspiratorial groups, it is necessary to look at the ways in which such behavior may serve the interests of groups. Such uses may be deliberate and calculated actions of policy, initiated and directed by organized groups through their decision-making authorities; they may be the exploitation of nonplanned events as a substitute or complement to such policy initiatives; they may take the form of a passive threat, an active threat, a demonstration of the threat by token action, and an effort to fulfill the threat; they may be the result of anticipated action by others or a response to such action; and they may aim at provoking such action or deterring it.

In the behavioral sense, extreme tactics may be highly *rational* in terms of maximizing behavior options or preserving and augmenting bargaining assets. Just as a suicide may be interpreted as a "cry for help," so all extreme actions may be seen as a search for or assertion of legitimacy, an expression of the will to live and love, to win human sympathy and co-operation. In short, they arise out of the very same needs and glories of human community that maintain the normative structures of a tranquil and stable society.

Attention is drawn to the violent events of history and every-day life mainly because violence represents the frontier of our social experience, which, in order to insure survival, must be managed and moderated by some form of control or social reintegration. The overwhelming and commonplace reality, so omnipresent that it goes unobserved, is the nonviolence of the greater part of man's social life, the existence of vastly complicated co-operative activities and relationships, and the routine channeling of the great majority of conflicts at every level into peaceable and constructive bargaining outcomes.

Physical sanctions and violence may be the least important and are certainly the least effective methods of social control and leadership. The most common tactic of protest, dissent, and revolution is to force upon government an escalation of physical sanctions that in itself will tend to erode the legitimacy and self-confidence of prevailing power groups. One cannot educate or mold a child or a man merely by threats of terrible punishment. Such a method may achieve temporary obedience, but the costs are high. In the longer run, it will create resistance rather than compliance and will insure the inevitability of increasingly ineffective and self-defeating physical sanctions. At the first opportunity, the victim of such treatment will run away, rebel or seek the remedies of spiteful self-destruction.[12]

Within a given framework of means/ends, violent and extreme forms of behavior may be as rational and functional for individuals as they are for groups. Individual behavior cannot be understood except in relation to group values, interests and norms. Even the anomic and socially isolated individual acts in reference to groups. Such an individual seeks reinforcement and legitimacy for his actions. "Reference-group theory" has proven useful in accounting for criminal behavior. The "reference group" is defined as "that group whose perspective constitutes the frame of reference of the actor" without necessarily being the group in which he is accepted or aspires for acceptance.[13] Ralph H. Turner calls such behavior "role-playing." The individual, even though socially iso-

12. Richard T. LaPiere, *A Theory of Social Control* (New York: McGraw-Hill, 1954), p. 221.

13. Tamotsu Shibutani, "Reference Groups as Perspective," *American Journal of Sociology* 60 (May, 1955), pp. 562–563. See also Rubenstein's commentary on this point in the preceding chapter.

lated, takes the role of a member and adopts the group's viewpoint as his own.[14]

Reference-group behavior on the part of an individual (whether in or out of such groups) can be dismissed as *post hoc* alibi and rationalization. A great deal of extreme individual behavior occurs as implusive reflex to provocative stimuli not fully comprehended by an excited actor. An attempt by him to legitimize his reflex will exploit any material he may believe to be plausible to an auditor, and therefore of no diagnostic or analytic value. The dismissal of such rationalization, however, ignores a fundamental principle of *all* behavior, i.e., its causes are always imperfectly understood by the actor and he always seeks legitimacy by aligning himself with such individuals and groups as may reinforce and accept him. In other words, the process of *post hoc* rationalization is precisely the same as the process that leads individuals to identify with groups and co-ordinate their behavior with group norms. With Kenneth Boulding, we may say the fundamental principle of behavior "is much the same whether we are considering an individual acting on his own behalf or a person acting in an organizational role."[15]

One may go further and say that individual behavior always relates to group norms even when it is directed against the values and interests of majority groups. The actor of crimes always feels himself supported by a system of values of which he is the instrument of justice and truth. He seeks recognition by his peers and goes contentedly to his doom in the electric chair, the sympathy and admiration of his peers conferring a self-image of martyrdom and immortality.

Criminal homicide does not occur in a vacuum. The study of "the choice of victim" clearly indicates the vast majority of slayings (about 80 per cent) involve people who have engaged in a series of social interactions prior to the crime. The series and the

14. Discussed in Melvin Schramm, Jack Lyle and Edwin B. Parker, *Television in the Lives of Our Children* (Stanford: Stanford University Press, 1961), pp. 237–238. See also Daniel Glaser, "The Sociological Approach to Crime and Correction," *Law and Contemporary Problems* (Autumn, 1958), pp. 681–702.

15. Kenneth E. Boulding, *Conflict and Defense: A General Theory* (New York: Harper & Brothers, 1962), p. 150.

crime itself occur within an institutional setting (family, place of employment, recreational establishment, etc.) and generally occur among persons of similar social status. Homicides not of this type (20 per cent) fall into other recognizable social categories. A large portion of them are crimes of property in which homicide is incidental. Virtually all such crimes involve victims of higher social status than the slayers, which gives them a suggestion of legitimacy from the point of view of the perpetrators. In short, the individual exists and acts within a series of social matrices, all of which impinge on his behavior; his social situation and group identities are inseparable from his actions and motivations.

Social isolation for the individual is roughly comparable to lack of political access for the group. In both cases, there is unleashed a tendency to experiment with extreme forms of behavior, as if to search for an exit from a spiritual cul-de-sac and to seek a broader test of legitimacy (i.e., the ability to engage in social bargaining and the exchange of values).

The history of assassination suggests that potential assassins are frequently alienated figures not identified with organized political movements. They tend to act outside the context of prevailing cost/risk constraints that limit the tactics employed by organized groups. Lawrence, Guiteau, Czolgosz, Zangara and Schrank, all of whom killed or tried to kill American presidents, were all highly anomic in terms of their relations with organized political groups. While Czolgosz and Zangara called themselves anarchists, they were not members of any of the anarchist groups common at the time. Under conditions of general revolution their actions might have been rationalized as representing normative tactics of warfare. But such conditions did not exist at the time of their acts, which therefore must be understood in terms of a perception by the assassin that his act could create such conditions and/or his subjective perception that such conditions already existed. It is in terms of these perceptions that anomic behavior can be understood as identical to elitist behavior, but occurring in a social vacuum. The stereotype of the wild-eyed anomic individual resembles that of the leader of highly embattled social groups except for the devastating fact that there are no followers, organization, or group reinforcement. He is a leader acting as though surrounded by admiring legions. This is a kind of reference-group behavior. In some cases, an extremely bold and imaginative act will in fact cause admiring legions to materialize. The behavior could no longer be characterized as anomic, even though its form is not changed.

The completely anomic individual is little more than a theoretical construct; all individuals combine degrees of integration in various groups. More often anomic conditions are characterized by conflict-group identification and membership as well as by exclusion or isolation. It cannot be said that any individual behavior is meaningless. Freud and the whole edifice of modern psychology refutes and rejects this view. Actions that appear to others impractical, hopeless, and unrealistic may appear quite otherwise from a different value perspective.

Children of the slums, far from being anomic, are loyal members of highly integrated groups. The delinquent is a conformist par excellence. "He is actually incapable of doing anything alone."[16] He is socialized in the streets and alleys and polished in the finishing school of prison. There is a high degree of honor among thieves and severe punishment for lapses. That their values may be antisocial and self-destructive does not make them anomic. Quite the contrary. They may be extremely adaptive for those who live in the entropic boundaries of social systems that harass, manipulate, exploit them, and are totally unresponsive to their needs.

Diagnosis and analysis of extreme individual behavior must proceed on the assumption that all behavior is plausible and realistic within the framework in which it occurs. To understand how a father can murder his wife and children, one begins by asking: Under what conditions would a reasonable man consider such action acceptable? Such action *might* be acceptable under conditions of siege to save them from a certain and prolonged death, or after a nuclear attack as starvation, radioactive poisoning, crazed and predatory neighbors close in on his back-yard shelter. Transfer the analogy back to the unfortunate father: In what ways was his objective life situation comparable *for him?*

16. Arthur Miller, "The Bored and the Violent" in Shalom Endleman, ed., *Violence in the Streets* (Chicago: Quadrangle Books, 1968), p. 273.

Why did he interpret it this way? Such an approach can make extreme behavior meaningful and instructive in terms of the forms that normative behavior might take in the face of extreme stress.

Each man is the champion and the hero of his own psycho-drama of life. Whatever happens to him and whatever he does about it, he seeks to justify himself and his flawed nobility. He does this in terms that might justify him to others, because human nature is a socialized product. When Everyman is reduced to the point that he cannot salvage some scrap of legitimacy or dignity in the eyes of someone, then, by his own hand, he carries out the informal judgment of the world, punishing or murdering himself. This resolves the puzzle of the relationship of homicide and sui-cide. People who are highly socialized, who have internalized the nonviolent behavior systems by which they live, tend to commit suicide; those whose socialization is highly divided or weak tend to react to the same stimuli by killing others. Both acts are extreme and in some sense on the part of the actor are a response to an extreme situation.

Suicide may be viewed as a reciprocal of murder and similarly meaningful in terms of bargaining. Like murder, suicide is an act of killing in which the victim is oneself. Yet, taking oneself away from others can be a means of punishing them; it can be an attempt to demonstrate a threat, and a means of influencing the behavior of others. Suicide and the threat of suicide are an ancient instrument of political protest and demonstration. Hunger strikes, self-immolation, Buddhist monks and American pacifists drench-ing themselves in gasoline and striking a match—all are political acts with political motives and effects. The assassination of a prominent public man in situations where escape is impossible are acts that beg for death and may be looked upon primarily as acts of self-destruction in which the killing of others is merely instru-mental.[17]

17. Like all acts of escalated confrontation, a suicide is unfinished busi-ness for the survivors, if not for the victim. Anthropologists report that many tribal religions treat it as contagious for all who knew the dead man or had physical contact with the body and its surroundings. In Christian Europe well into the nineteenth century, the church would not permit re-moval of a suicide victim except in the dead of night and by someone en-

When someone commits suicide, all those who may sense the circumstances that drove him to it re-examine their own lives, are strengthened in convictions concerning the society in which they live. A suicide can lead to efforts to reform state and national laws, as noted in the case of the overextended installment buyer in Chicago. A suicide, apart from its real motives, will be quickly exploited by those with a social cause. In effect, a suicide resembles a resignation from a government: it challenges values and institutions evoking from all survivors a sense of the unresolved tensions that surround them, threatening the prospects for their own survival. The suicide of Marilyn Monroe led within a few days to a flurry of suicides by women, mostly blond and middle-aged. Individual suicides, however obscure and ambiguous, like other acts of escalation, threaten the world and thus change it.

Extreme acts with political significance "differ from simple crimes to the extent that collective support given to outlaws is not itself the product of coercion."[18] There is some level of collective support for even the most quixotic and disgusting acts of violence. Somebody loves every assassin and rejoices at every bombing and assassination. However, the distinction between social action and simple crime or lunacy reduces itself to one having to do with the extent of collective support for the action in the continuing conflicts between groups. Chalmers Johnson: "True revolution is contingent upon this perception of societal failure."[19] Ortega y Gasset notes the paradoxical debt to rationality paid by apparently irrational behavior: "It may be regrettable that human nature tends on occasion to this form of violence, but it is undeniable that it im-

---

tirely unrelated to the deceased. The body was unsanctified and could not be buried near the remains of those who died an honest death by pestilence, murder, or hanging. In primitive societies it was not uncommon to sacrifice a sheep or goat to pacify the spirit of the suicide, which might otherwise draw others after him. Bohannan, *op. cit.,* pp. 110–114. In many cultures suicide is considered ritually unclean, and elaborate rituals are prescribed to evade further evil. It is a common theme of literature (sometimes imitated by life) that those who feel responsible for the death are driven by remorse to take their own lives. It is not unknown in Japan for parents to commit suicide or become acolytes following the suicide of their children.

18. Reinhard Bendix, *Max Weber: An Intellectual Portrait* (Glencoe, Ill.: The Free Press, 1962), p. 45.

19. Chalmers Johnson, *Revolutionary Change* (Boston: Little, Brown, 1966), p. 12.

plies the greatest tribute to reason and justice. For this form of violence is none other than reason exasperated."[20]

As the legitimacy of the state weakens, there are a host of claimants, individuals and groups, who assert and offer their own substitute authority. Even in times of relative stability there are gaps and vacuums of state authority, where groups assume semi-sovereign roles and exercise statelike authority. In times of upheaval and crisis, the integration of the nation-state as a unifying institution undergoes major schisms. Violent confrontation involving individuals, groups, and the regime are all involved in a process of testing various claims to legitimacy. By imposing the most severe risks and costs, violence is the métier of the process, testing the resources of all the available systems of integration. This is not to say that the ability to organize and apply violence determines the outcome, or that successful use of violence is per se the basis of legitimacy. Violence is the testing instrument; it tests all the positive factors of social integration, such as the workability and success of normative systems in adapting a group to its physical and social boundaries, while providing legitimate means of internal conflict. The factors being tested are often intangible and moral. Men will endure the rigors and sacrifices of violent confrontation only for what appears to be a higher good. Violence forces a mobilization of whatever assets and resources, both human and material, a social system commands. Therefore, this gives confrontation a certain validity as a test of legitimacy.

When the legitimacy of the state is weak or divided, personal leadership and loyalty become functional alternatives. The security code of groups is accentuated and converts them into protosovereign units. Where this happens, authority structures are highly personified and personalized; therefore the challenge to that authority by other claimants also tends to be highly personal. In terms of the competition for control, succession, legitimacy, etc., political assassination becomes a highly functional instrument, whether it is actually carried out or not. Under these conditions, threats are most likely to have efficacy in imposing restraints on certain kinds of action. Actual assassinations may be committed

20. José Ortega y Gasset, *The Revolt of the Masses* (New York: W. W. Norton, 1932), p. 82.

by groups who seek to demonstrate the credibility of their threats, or by individuals inflamed by the contagions of a poisoned atmosphere.

UNLEARNING ASSASSINATION

Residual and frictional violence and extreme acts, isolated and low grade, are probably ineradicable and are not the problem. It is not the presence of violence, but rather its degree and kind, its effects in inhibiting political leadership from a creative role, the imminent deadlock of escalated and counterescalated force, the general loss of legitimacy of normative institutions, and the danger of contagion. Even the loss of a popular leader to a lone assassin's bullet is not the problem. Rather, it is the danger of divisive conditions that fomented it, which make it a pattern, and which attack and undermine the recuperative powers of the society. The problem of political violence raises virtually every other major issue in political sociology and political theory, as well as every major unresolved issue of public policy and the social system.

The scientific literature makes much of "social stress," "precipitating events," and the "contagious" quality of panic, terrorism, and other forms of extreme behavior.[21] These are useful concepts, but they need to be fixed within social and political matrices in order to be of diagnostic value.

Many studies demonstrate that social stress is a factor of cohesion rather than division. Under the discipline of external war the rate of both suicide and murder falls (although suicide falls at a sharper rate than murder). The real test of social cohesion occurs under conditions of relative stress/relief. Latent divisive forces are suddenly discharged; long-deferred demands for social change suddenly assert higher priorities than those of discipline and unity. Stress is not uniformly distributed in society and thus endows bargaining relationships with differential commitment and urgency. If the main function of government is defined as "allocating values," then the negative of that function is "the allocation of stress."

21. David Abrahamsen, *The Psychology of Crime* (New York: John Wiley & Sons, Science Editions, 1960), pp. 23–26.

Groups without access to the formal process of values always get more than their share of stress, and forms of direct action and political protest may be viewed as an effort to reallocate stress.[22]

No precipitating event is significant unless all the factors are present and ready to be precipitated, in which case, a great variety of events may be equally capable of catalytic action. Social contagion is a familiar process. When transitory, it is called "faddism," and when of enduring value, tradition. There is obvious faddism in all social behavior, including suicide, crime, and political action. Men socialize each other and continuously test new forms of adaptive behavior, some of which waz and wane peripherally and shallowly, others leaving a residue of enduring institutionalized culture. The tides of social change are always influenced by creative individual acts that process great expressiveness and communicability in terms of changing social values. Imitation and mimicry are a form of social learning having a functional effect and giving form (what might be called "behavioral direction") to emerging values that are widely shared.[23]

In analyzing contagion and precipitating events, we must look to conditions that endow them with efficacy. To comprehend and deal with a pattern of political assassination we must ask: How is assassination learned and reinforced? Why and for whom does such behavior become adaptive and functional? If indeed assassination should become a fad or a tradition, this would suggest conditions of deeply divided legitimacy, including incipient or actual warfare between large social groups. One such a pattern is established, it suggests that less provocative forms of political action have lost efficacy and that only sensational political murders are still potent as rallying symbols for some and an attack on the social viability of others.

A democratic system must preserve the right of organized action

22. Langston Hughes: "Seems like what makes me crazy has no effect on you/I'm gonna keep on doing until you're crazy too."

23. See Gabriel Tarde, *Penal Philosophy,* trans. R. Howell (Boston: Little, Brown, 1912), pp. 339–340. An important contributory condition to extreme behavior is the existence of such social or group predefinitions of situations that require and elicit extreme responses. See Alfred Lindesmith and Anselm Strauss, *Social Psychology* (New York: Dryden Press, 1949), p. 332.

by private groups and accept the risk of the implicit capability of violence. By permitting a pluralistic base, the democratic state enables potential violence to have a social effect and to bring social accommodation with only token demonstration, facilitating a process of peaceful political and social change.

The good society must learn to manage constructively some degree of violence and potential violence. Communities can endure with murder societies in their midst, provided the institutions of the whole maintain their legitimacy and are able to isolate and control the effects of antisocial actions. One can never hope to completely eliminate the ubiquity of anonymous telephone or letter threats to authors, public personalities, and people who get their names in the paper. Political assassination cannot be eliminated once and for all by preventive measures that are even more dangerous to the health and survival of the nation. Attempts to make assassination impossible are incompatible with a free political process and may in fact enhance the probability of *coups d'état*. The most anxious man in a totalitarism system is the dictator, just as the most anxious man in prison is the warden.

However, it is possible for society to manage its problems in such a way that no single man can change history with a single bullet. The inefficiency of political assassination is the best safeguard against the danger that an isolated act can begin a self-perpetuating series and provide a pattern for political success.

At all times, even in a healthy society, the whole spectrum of political options is occupied by claimants for leadership and legitimacy. The best way to keep the extremes of the spectrum from overwhelming the center is to improve the efficacy and legitimacy of such modes of political action and leadership in order to deescalate latent threats of violence and to facilitate social change and the political integration of new groups. The very success of peaceable modes of bargaining constitute a prediction of futility for extremist actions. When these do occur, the vast multitudes of the nation will support the actions of the state in limited and reasonable deterrence, localization and, when necessary, containment by appropriate and measured, rather than overreactive, means of force.[24]

---

24. George Wallace's threat to run his car over demonstrators tends to escalate and legitimize political violence. Mayor Daley's instruction to police

It is a simple matter to diagnose theoretically the conditions of and causes of political violence. It is much more difficult as a matter of practical policy to know how to avoid social trials by ordeal. How does government terminate and stabilize a period of search behavior and confrontation? How can it conserve and integrate adaptive social innovations? The way a social process starts and spreads has been studied much more than the question of how it terminates. A process may cease because it has exhausted itself or because a point of termination is institutionalized as part of the process itself. Some processes may go on indefinitely, ceasing only with the disappearance of the groups whose interests they served or opposed. In some cases, a process provides built-in opportunities, at which it can be deliberately stopped or redirected. What should be done in a situation where high-risk political confrontation is already well-established and seemingly irreversible?

It is easy to formulate verbal generalities that seem to answer these questions. One can create countertendencies to dampen extreme oscillations. This calls for highly creative political action and leadership, not only from the leaders of prevailing cadres and groups, but on every level of social and political organization in both the formal and informal polity. This may not be as difficult as it appears. There is a strong tendency in social life towards humanizing power, towards creating conditions of predictability and order in the midst of change and towards avoiding the danger created for all by efforts to apply overly extreme penalties and measures to some. One of the great facts of American response to the recent series of political assassinations has been the tendency of the community to unite against all varieties of extremism and to seek new routes of conciliation and social reform. This is a built-in corrective that, with a little luck, can see us through grave situations.

A few additional generalities may be cited. Revolutionary conditions testify to the absence or the disuse of other channels of political change. Political leaders must keep such alternatives vital and responsive to claims by previously silent groups. Behavioral research indicates that organized conflict groups tend to use less

---

to "shoot to maim" looters has the same effect. Government must learn the value of nonviolence as an appropriate tactic of control in certain conditions where violence, even the superior violence of the state, will not work.

violent means of combat and bargaining than those which lack organization; therefore, we must seek institutions which offer representation and identity to groups that might otherwise remain inchoate and unstable.

The nation-state is a complex living organism, whose growth tends to respond to the interests and desires of those who exercise political, social, and economic power. Most of the great political problems that confront us arise from the emergence of a new capability for social bargaining on the part of previously submerged groups. The custom of serving only established and prevailing power groups will always leave basic social equations to fester and writhe beneath the surface, ultimately to break through and deface the grand façade of established power. Our institutions must aim at the discovery of new constituencies and new routes of access by which they can generate their own leadership. This is a very real challenge to our ingenuity and inventiveness as political innovators.

Presidential Assassinations: Their Meaning and Impact on American Society

Murray Edelman and Rita James Simon

This chapter reviews the features common to American presidential assassinations in order to furnish a basis for examining their consequences in politics and in opinion formation. It is part of a larger study in which we tried to identify: (1) the political and social conflicts that served in each particular case as reason or rationalization for the assassination attempt and that therefore gave the attempt a broader and deeper significance than would be involved in the murder of a celebrity; (2) those elements in the social and psychological backgrounds of the assassins or conspirators that in the light of hindsight help explain their choice of this extreme form of political action; and (3) the uses made of the assassination by various groups to further their own ends.

ASSASSINATION PLOTS

Political assassination is basically different from other murders, both in its motivation and in its consequences. The ordinary killer is not likely to justify his act by claiming that it is a service to mankind, though an occasional murderer may allege that it served that function, too. He has, rather, yielded to a kind of temptation, usually for personal gain or vindication, to which all men are occasionally subjected. Frequently, it is a yielding he regrets. The political assassin, however, regards his act as virtuous and justifies it only in those terms. Rather than expecting personal gain, he knows in advance that he is making the most severe personal sacrifice for what he imagines will benefit others.

In his political opinions, the political assassin always reflects a point of view held with greater or less intensity by many other people as well, though few approve of his means for realizing their values. It is this widespread support and opposition to his political views that endows his dramatic action with more than personal meaning, that makes it a significant factor in an ongoing struggle among interests and that makes it possible for groups to use it for their own purposes. That assassins have frequently protested in their postassassination statements and confessions that they had no animus against the man they killed but only against the system for which he stood is a further clue to the nature of the fundamental distinction between ordinary murder and political assassination.

Because politics always involve conflicts over values, because leaders come to symbolize political virtues and vices, because political leaders are just as frail and mortal as anyone else, and because there are always some zealots and psychopaths about, assassination is obviously a possibility at any time. Whether it is tried against any particular president or political leader is a matter of chance and essentially unpredictable, and whether it succeeds if tried is also largely chance, though somewhat more predictable.

The key element is the state of mind of a potential assassin and not the personality, behavior, or policies of the victim.[1] American presidents who have been targets have been as strong as Lincoln and Roosevelt and as weak as Garfield and McKinley. They have been shot at when popular tensions were acute and when social conflict was minimal. The nature of contemporary public issues and the reasons offered by the assassins for their actions have covered a wide range.

The observation that in the twentieth century at least it has been the strong presidents who have been assassination victims, followed very often by the policy suggestion that the nature of the office be changed, is not persuasive. Franklin Roosevelt was shot at before he was inaugurated and certainly before he had a chance to show how strong a president he would become. There are no reported attempts on his life later in the thirties or after he announced his candidacy for a third term. And Woodrow Wilson, who was certainly as strong a president as Truman or Kennedy, was not a target.

The assassination efforts have been impressive for the consistent absence of effective political organization to carry them out. All but two have apparently been the work of single individuals, and in every case the lone would-be assassin showed strong evidence of mental disturbance. The assassins have typically been alienated figures, not identified with organized political movements and confused about the prospects and strategies of the organized movements they thought they represented. The two known plots, involving attempts against the lives of Lincoln and Truman, could have done little to bring about the triumph of the political causes the plotters favored, and the second was ridiculously inept even in its plan for killing the president. In most of the cases, therefore, the effective motivating element has been the private mental disturbances of the assassins, rather than their political rationaliza-

---

1. McKinley and Garfield were moderate conservatives. Kennedy, Truman, and Lincoln were liberals, or at least more liberal than their opponents. Roosevelt was attacked at a time when his political philosophy was not yet identifiable, although one might have classified him as a conservative on the basis of his balance-the-budget and fiscal-integrity speeches during the 1932 presidential campaign. The Crotty essay and those contained in Part II of this volume also explore the choice of victims. The pyschological studies and those by Nieburg, Bensman and Rubenstein investigate the factors contributing to a politicization of the murder impulse.

tions. Under these circumstances there is no systematic reason why the assassinations should bring about the particular changes in policy or governmental structure that the assassin favors.

In Europe and Asia, political assassinations have more typically been planned and carried out by political organizations. The plotters in these countries have viewed their desperate acts as the most promising road to achieving political change where legitimate channels for opposition have been closed to them. The comparative rarity of such plots in the United States may be interpreted as a tribute to the openness and flexibility of American political institutions. Opposition groups apparently do not often perceive the system as manipulatable only through resort to violence.[2]

PUBLIC RESPONSE

Every presidential assassination has evoked an intense sense of shock among the public generally. After each of these tragic events newspapers have reported an awesome outpouring of public emo-

2. There may also be more positive influences upon the form that American political assassinations have usually taken. In its frontier culture, its industrial order, and its political system America has consistently emphasized the irrelevance of class politics, the negation of organized pursuit of ideologies, and the triumph of individual enterprise. This has been the theme of the most widely accepted and hallowed slogans, myths and dramaturgical gestures. It should not be surprising that this climate should give its characteristic and legitimized form to deviance as well as to conformity, that even assassination should be practiced as free, individual enterprise. Taking the law into one's own hands to overthrow the wicked and establish justice has consistently been a prominent theme in several American subcultures, especially on the frontier and in the rural South and Southwest. Its virtues have been celebrated in legend and practiced in vigilantism and lynchings. The cue has been there for the alienated and deranged to follow, and at fairly frequent intervals they have done so. Daniel Bell in his essay "Crime as an American Way of Life," *The Antioch Review* 13 (June, 1953), pp. 131–154, has vividly summarized this facet of American life:

> "No amount of commercial prosperity," once wrote Teddy Roosevelt, "can supply the lack of the heroic virtues." The American was the hunter, cowboy, frontiersman, the soldier, the naval hero. And in the crowded slums, the gangster. He was a man with a gun, acquiring by personal merit what was denied to him by complex orderings of a stratified society. And the duel with the law was the morality play *par excellence*.

Lipset and Sheingold and Rubenstein add perspective to this tradition and Nieburg, in particular, broadly assesses the responsiveness of political agencies to out-group demands, all in their contributions to this volume.

tion, grief and anxiety. Public-opinion polls and sample survey studies document this response for the Kennedy assassination, but the journalistic and memoir accounts of previous ones leave no doubt that the Kennedy case was typical, not exceptional. Garfield, who had held office for less than six months, was no less the object of public grief than were McKinley and Lincoln who were serving their second terms.

What people find so intensely upsetting is not only the fact of assassination or the death of a well-known figure, but the death of an incumbent of the highest office of the state. The public's response is characterized by the awe inspired by one's native state and homeland, for it is grossly out of proportion either to people's subjective attitudes toward a president before his death or to his objective importance in history. His official position makes a chief executive a reassuring symbol against threats from potential enemies and a potentially hostile environment, regardless of whether one approves of his politics. His sudden death shocks because it removes that protection.[3]

3. Psychoanalytic theory suggests a compatible explanation for the universal and intense sense of shock, but is also more specific. Freud saw in *Moses and Monotheism* (New York: Alfred A. Knopf, 1939, pp. 170–171) the man who has risen to an exalted position as supplying the masses' need for authority:

> Why the great man should rise to significance at all we have no doubt whatever. We know that the great majority of people have a strong need for authority which they can admire, to which they can submit, and which dominates and sometimes even ill-treats them. . . . It is the longing for the father that lives in each of us from his childhood days, for the same father whom the hero of legend boasts of having overcome. And now it begins to dawn on us that all the features with which we furnish the great man are traits of the father, that in this similarity lies the essence, which so far has eluded us, of the great man.

There is scattered, suggestive, but quite inconclusive evidence in the reports of some psychoanalysts about their parents' reactions to the deaths of presidents that people do indeed identify the chief executive with their fathers and may project their wishes for a more perfect father figure onto him. See David A. Rothstein, "Presidential Assassination Syndrome," *Archives of General Psychiatry* 11 (September, 1964), pp. 245–254, and his essay in this volume; Richard Sterba, "Report on Some Emotional Reactions to President Roosevelt's Death," *The Psychoanalytic Review* 33 (1946), pp. 393–398; David Kirschner, "Some Reactions of Patients in Psychotherapy to the Death of a President," *The Psychoanalytic Review* 51

The fears an assassination of an American chief executive evoke do not center upon specific policies, but upon the foundations of the policy itself. The universality of the shocked response, including anxiety on the part of political opponents of the assassinated president, suggests that the intended response is to something deeper and more universal than policies on specific issues. A clue as to what it is that assassinations evoke can be found in an examination of the kinds of speculation to which they give rise and the kinds of official reassurances that are consistently offered to counter them.

After every assassination there has been much speculation and competing legends about the political ties of the assassin, his motives, how the assassination was really carried out, whether there was a conspiracy and its purpose, and what the event implied for the future, in short, substantial ambiguity about the meaning and consequences of the assassination, and especially about its implications for the future stability, soundness, and vigor of the state. Behind the ambiguity there has consistently been anxiety that the assassination is part of a continuing plot to subvert the constitutional system.

After Garfield's assassination, speculation arose concerning Guiteau's ties to important figures within the Stalwart camp of the Republican party. The names of Senator Conkling of New York and Vice President Arthur were mentioned as having supported Guiteau, not only by Guiteau's attorney but by the press as well. Those who interpreted the assassination as a conspiracy saw Conkling as the source of the inspiration and control of the party and the state by the Stalwarts as the goal.

Until the assassination of President Kennedy, the death of Lincoln had been the subject of the greatest number of theories, rumors and questions about the "real story behind his death." The explanations ranged from a conspiracy directed by Jefferson Davis,

---

(1964–65), pp. 125–129; and Patterson's evaluation of the reactions to John Kennedy's death and Clarke and Soule's examination of children's responses to Martin Luther King's murder, as well as the relevant literature cited in these earlier chapters.

president of the Confederacy, to treachery within his own cabinet. Secretary of War Edwin Stanton was the person most often cited in this connection. But the Southern-born Vice-President, Andrew Johnson, did not go unnoticed by the conspiracy-seeking press and public.

The story that circulated after McKinley's assassination was that it had been organized and directed by anarchists with worldwide connections. Czolgosz was merely the pawn of a highly sophisticated, international terrorist organization that had in the recent past assassinated the heads of states of several European countries.

Each of these interpretations had the effect of increasing the public's anxieties about the stability of the government and the danger to the country from internal subversion or foreign invasion.

Leading government officials always recognize these sentiments and doubtless feel some of them themselves. Thus, after every assassination there are emphatic high-level assurances that the polity is healthy, that the new president will continue to pursue his predecessor's goals, and that the assassination was the work of a psychotic or a small group of isolated conspirators whose actions in no sense reflect a widespread movement or extensive discontent. Lyndon Johnson's slogan, "Let us continue," after the Kennedy assassination and the Warren Commission's determined and repeated theme that Oswald acted alone and without foreign or domestic support exemplify the classic response of governments to the assassination of a major officeholder. It is also a response to worrisome and widely felt doubts about the assassination's meaning.

While every successor regime naturally tries to solidify its mass support and perhaps its own uncertainty with such assurances, there is reason to suspect that the effort is most likely to succeed in countries in which the mass public is not split into clearly defined segments with strongly conflicting views and interests regarding the central concerns of the state. Indeed the one time in the United States that such an effort met with least success was in the period following the death of Lincoln, when the country was more sharply split than it has ever been before or since. Try as he did, at least in the early days of his regime, Andrew Johnson was unable to rally the followers of Lincoln to his side.

In many European countries, in Africa and in Asia such splits are common, with rightist or centrist interests fairly consistently opposing leftist groups on foreign policy, economic policy, and church-state relations. In the United States, the configuration of opinion on public policy is generally unimodal rather than bimodal; the period of the Civil War is the dramatic exception. Differences in one policy area do not normally coincide with differences in other important policy areas, and the consequent overlapping in interests binds the public together. We suggest that the fact of a unimodal or a bimodal interest configuration strongly conditions people's reactions to an assassination. Where interest conflicts are deep and stable, the suspicion of a far-reaching plot is also likely to be deep and stable. In such a society, it is harder for people to accept the view that a lone psychopath, unconnected with political organizations, committed the assassination. Both inner frustrations and tensions and social reinforcement from others with common political interests function to spread the conviction that an assassination is inevitably a political plot. The difference between the great majority of Americans apparently willing to accept the view that Oswald alone planned and carried out the Kennedy assassination and the great majority of foreigners suspicious that the official explanation only masked a conspiracy is the most recent example of the distinction.

The public response is very likely more widespread and more intense where the assassination is not perceived as simply a gambit in a continuing conflict over policies and ideologies, but rather as an assault upon the fundamental constitution or legitimate symbol of the state itself. And it is, paradoxically, in a stable democracy, such as the United States, with a unimodal value distribution, that the latter view seems to recur.

The combination of perceived threat and ambiguity has some predictable consequences in political behavior. It makes it easier to influence perceptions of the meaning of the shocking event and of political institutions, to arouse or reassure a mass public, and therefore, to manipulate its political support, opposition, or quiescence. Fundamentally, it is men's anxieties and search for reassurance that are involved. In an ambiguous situation, they will perceive what they hope to find because they will read their own needs and wishes into it.

The cases we have studied suggest more specific propositions about the character of the ties among the basic elements involved in assassinations of leading political figures: the victim's symbolic role as head of state, the public issues of his time and his symbolic role in later times. In each case, the assassination widened and deepened public concern with the central contemporary political issues. After each assassination, groups concerned with current political and social issues tried to use the public shock and anxiety evoked by the event to further their causes. To some extent they succeeded in doing this, because people transferred their concern about the assassination to whatever public issues were already occasioning anxiety, with little attention to logical relevancy. Thus, the circumstances of Lincoln's assassination became entangled with the ongoing debate over Reconstruction policy; Garfield's with civil-service reform; McKinley's with suppression of anarchism and immigration policy; the attempt on Truman's life with suppression of internal Communist subversion; and Kennedy's assassination with the cold war and extremism at home.

With the exception of Lincoln, whose assassination, as we already indicated, occurred at an extraordinary time, it is doubtful that any one of the assassinations produced a dramatic policy reversal, though the timing of political action was probably affected. So far as current public issues were concerned the assassinations served as catalysts and bargaining counters in ongoing political maneuvering.

In the last section of this paper, we review the specific events that followed the assassination of each American president and analyze in summary form how the events influenced and perhaps altered public policy. The connecting theme for each case is that even though presidential assassinations did not represent direct attempts at a seizure of power or the work of an organized political opposition, each of the assassinations, nevertheless, had important political and social consequences. It is the social and political aftermaths of each presidential assassination that we now discuss.

SPECULATIONS

William McKinley was shot by Leon Czolgosz, a lonely, alien-ated figure who frequented anarchist circles in the silk-mill towns of northern New Jersey but about whom the anarchists published a warning (claiming he was a spy) only a week before he shot the President. Organized repercussions to McKinley's assassination were mainly of two types: one consisted of acts of violence by local citizens against persons with known anarchist sympathies. In some cases, individual anarchists were attacked by angry mobs; in others, vigilante committees were organized for the purpose of attacking anarchist communities. The second consisted of legisla-tion by Congress and state legislatures restricting immigration and the activities of anarchists already in the country.

There were probably fewer than 10,000 anarchists in the United States at the time McKinley was assassinated. Most of them lived in large industrial centers and in cities with large foreign popula-tions such as New York, Chicago, Philadelphia, Pittsburgh, St. Louis, and cities in northern New Jersey, particularly Paterson. There were a few scattered anarchists' co-operative communities on the West Coast, in central Illinois, and in parts of western Pennsylvania and New York.

Three days after the assassination, Emma Goldman was ar-rested in Chicago along with Abe Isaak, editor of the anarchist paper, *Free Society,* and eight other leaders of the Chicago anar-chist movement. They were charged with conspiracy to assassinate the President. In the territory of New Mexico federal agents ar-rested Antonio Maggio, an anarchist leader from Kansas City, Missouri, whom the *St. Louis Globe-Democrat* labeled as the leader of a group who sought to remove the President of the United States from office.

On September 7, the day after the President was shot, *Die Freiheit,* an anarchist paper published in New York City and edited by Johann Most, carried an editorial which included the following:

The greatest of all follies in the world is the belief that there can be a crime of any sort against despots and their accomplices. Such a belief is in itself a crime. Despots are outlaws; they are in human shape what the tiger is among beasts—to spare them is a crime. . . . Yes, the crime directed against them (despots) is not merely a right; it is also the duty of everyone who has the opportunity to carry it out, and it will be his glory if it is successful.

When Most learned of the assassination, he tried without success to recall the issue. Following its publication, Johann Most was arrested and sentenced to one year in prison.

Anarchist leaders were also arrested in Pittsburgh, Paterson, Boston, New York, and Philadelphia. In Rochester, New York, the city in which Emma Goldman's family lived, Justice Day of the New York Supreme Court ordered a grand jury investigation of the city's 100 anarchists. He ordered that "every person found to be a member of the local society was to be indicted for conspiracy to overthrow the government." In Cleveland, the police suppressed meetings of local anarchist groups, and the newspapers wrote editorials demanding that Czolgosz's father be fired from his job as a ditch digger for the city.

In localities that contained anarchist communities, riots broke out between the local citizenry and the inhabitants of the communities. Near McKeesport, Pennsylvania, at the anarchist colony of Guffey's Hollow, a community composed primarily of Italian coal miners, twenty-five anarchist families fled the community after 300 men wearing robes resembling those of the Ku Klux Klan and armed with rifles and shotguns attacked the community.

In Spring Valley, Illinois, the site of another anarchist community of about 500 members, a citizens' committee visited the general manager of the Spring Valley Coal Company and insisted that he discharge every known anarchist in his employ. At the same time, the committee also informed the manager that there were 2,000 local townspeople who were ready to assist in exterminating the *Reds*.

All over the country the atmosphere was sufficiently charged as a result of the assassination that any group which the public might associate with anarchism or with the assassin felt impelled to make a public statement denouncing the act and separating themselves from association with the assassin. Thus all five of the Polish newspapers in Buffalo unequivocally condemned Czolgosz and denounced anarchism in very strong language.

But the more significant repercussions to the McKinley assassination, as measured by long term effects, were the changes in the immigration laws that Congress passed two and a half years after the assassination. The first sign that immigration policy might be affected by the assassination appeared in an editorial in the *Washington Post* eight days after Czolgosz shot the President. The editorial stated:

We parade as a matter of patriotic pride those dangerous political dissipations which should be a cause of patriotic sorrow and alarm. We open our arms to the human sewage of Europe; we offer asylum to the outcasts and malefactors of every nation. . . .

In his first message to the Congress, President Theodore Roosevelt said:

We should war with relentless efficiency not only against anarchists, but against all active and passive sympathizers with anarchists—both the advocate of anarchy and the apologists for anarchism were morally accessory to murder before the fact.

Roosevelt urged the Congress to exclude from the United States "anarchists who extolled assassination and to deport alien anarchists who espoused the views." He also proposed that treaties be drawn up making anarchy an offense against the law of nations similar to piracy and the slave trade.

On May 27, 1902, the House of Representatives passed an immigration bill that added anarchists to the list of excluded immigrants. It defined anarchists as "persons who believe in or advocate the overthrow by force or violence of all governments or all forms of law, or the assassination of public officials."

The Senate added to the above definition a paragraph that forbade all persons who disbelieved in or were opposed to all government or who were members of or affiliated with organizations teaching such views or who advocated the assassination of public officials because of their official character from either entering the United States or becoming naturalized. The Senate version became law on March 4, 1904.

The activities of native-born or naturalized anarchists were also limited by government action. Two years following the assassination, the state legislatures of New York, New Jersey, and Wisconsin passed laws outlawing the teaching of anarchist doctrines and limiting the movements and activities of anarchist organizations within their states.

The passage of the Pendleton Act in 1882 establishing a federal Civil Service Commission is traceable directly to the assassination of James Garfield. Garfield's term in office was marked by the same intraparty strife that had characterized the state of the Republican party before his election. Garfield's nomination (on the thirty-sixth ballot) was the compromise finally agreed upon by the Conkling and Blaine camps after it became clear that neither of the two leading contenders (Grant was the Stalwarts candidate) could marshal enough votes to gain a majority. Garfield's election carried with it the expectation that he could unite the Republican party. But in the brief period that he was permitted to hold office it became clear that rather than serve as an independent force that might eventually bring the opposing factions to his side, Garfield allied himself with Blaine. He appointed James Blaine his Secretary of State. On the other hand, Chester A. Arthur, the Vice-President, spent most of his time in New York helping Conkling mend his political fences.

Charles Guiteau, Garfield's assassin, claimed when he was apprehended that he had acted under divine inspiration and that Garfield's death would unite the Republican party and save the Republic. Guiteau, it turned out, was also an embittered office seeker who had worked for Garfield's election, in return for which he believed he deserved a consulship in Paris.

Upon hearing of Garfield's assassination (his death did not come until two months later), the nation's reaction was split between profound grief and fear for its welfare. The latter emotion was aroused chiefly by the fact that Arthur would succeed to the presidency. Until this time, Arthur's reputation was based primarily on his loyalty to Conkling and on his own abilities as a political boss within the Conkling camp. It was fortunate for the country that it had greatly underestimated both Arthur's abilities and ideals.

In the three and one-half years of his administration, on a majority of occasions Arthur acted more like a statesman than a political boss and on most matters placed himself above intraparty squabbling. He advocated policies in areas such as tariffs, national defense, civil service reform and public spending that went beyond party positions and took account of broader interests.

But given the public's expectations concerning the kind of president Arthur would be, the need for a Civil Service Act seemed more urgent than ever. During his administration, former President Hayes had predicted that the Congress, which had just failed to pass a Civil Service bill, would enact such a law only in response to a determined public's demand. That demand came after the public witnessed the assassination of a President at the hands of a disgruntled office seeker. When Congress failed to respond in its first session immediately following the assassination, the voters failed to return most of the incumbent Republicans to office in the congressional election of 1882.

In both his first and second messages to the Congress, President Arthur forcibly advocated the passage of Civil Service legislation. Finally, when Congress (in December, 1882) did pass the Pendleton Act, Arthur appointed to the three-man Civil Service Commission men whose reputations assured the public that he was placing the enforcement of the law in the hands of people who would be expected to serve its objectives.

There is little doubt that passage of a Civil Service Act would have occurred before the end of the century. There had been considerable pressure for such enactment by the end of Grant's first term, and that pressure increased during the scandal-ridden period that marked his second term in office. Hayes (Grant's successor) had tried, with little success, to gain passage of an effective Civil Service Act. But it took the tragedy of a presidential assassination to dramatize the need for such reform.

The Lincoln assassination presents an especially difficult problem for the social scientist. For more than a century, references to the assassination of Lincoln have evoked some measure of awe and shock. And for at least several decades it was closely associated with opinion respecting one of the most lasting and divisive controversies in American history: Reconstruction policy. The very fact that it strongly and clearly evoked a key political issue that polarized opinion makes it impossible to trace the specific connotations and consequences of the assassination in the way that we can do somewhat more confidently for others. In the Lincoln case, the meanings to the public of the assassination became inextricably intermingled with other influences upon Reconstruction policy.

Though this analysis must therefore remain speculative to a marked extent, that can hardly be a reason for failing to undertake it. If, as we suggest below, the assassination did have significant and lasting consequences for the course of American political and social history, it seems better to have available some admittedly tentative propositions about the nature of the consequences than to ignore the issue altogether and thereby leave unchallenged a "common-sense" view that, we think, is far more speculative and based largely upon myth.

In life, Lincoln was a moderating influence upon a country polarized by civil war and by intense differences over how to deal with the defeated South. The manner of his death intensified the polarization, brought wider political support to the advocates of a radical Reconstruction policy, and served to perpetuate a political cleavage centered upon the relative status of whites and blacks. That is our hypothesis. We turn now to our reasons for believing it valid.

Lincoln's views at the end of the Civil War were far more conciliatory to the defeated South than was true of the radical Republicans who then constituted only a small fraction of the Republican party. On the key issues of Negro suffrage, probably the most revealing example of his position, Lincoln is on record as having opposed giving former slaves the right to vote and to hold office. In his Proclamation of Amnesty, he announced that when persons "equal in number to one-tenth of the votes cast in the presidential election of 1860 had taken the oath and established a government," he would recognize that government. He also offered pardons to any former Confederate who would take the oath to support "the Constitution of the United States and the Union of the States thereunder." Lincoln's plan excluded Negroes from any participation in the government of the restored states. They would not be expected to take the oath, nor would they be permitted to vote or hold office. The restored states would be governed by whites. Lincoln's influence, therefore, would have been exerted against the key provisions of the Fourteenth Amendment, against continued military occupation of the Southern states to maintain governments dominated by blacks, and for early restoration of seceded states to the Union.

There is every reason to believe, moreover, that that influence would have been substantial. As the President who had led the North to victory, who had been re-elected by a large majority, and who, as a founding member of the Republican party, was also its leader in more than the formal sense, Lincoln was the key political figure of the day. He had the skill and the experience at this climactic point in his career to handle the political aspects of his job in a manner that would attract popular support for his views on the central issues of Reconstruction policy, regarding which opinion was forming and still ambivalent and manipulatable.

The assassination, however, created quite a different set of pressures upon public opinion, and there is persuasive evidence for the hypothesis that it added substantially to the strength of those who advocated a radical Reconstruction policy. For one thing, the assassin and his fellow conspirators were avowedly pro-Southern; and that fact was lent added force by other circumstances that made this the most traumatic of American political assassinations. It occurred just as our most divisive war had finally ended. It was, and remains, the only successful American political assassination that was clearly a political plot and widely publicized as such.

As noted above, studies of the aftermaths of other political assassinations reveal a consistent kind of impact upon opinion. In each case, the combinations of shock and ambiguity about the meaning of the crime for the nation's future evoked wide and intense public concern with the central contemporary political issues. In this instance, that issue was manifestly Reconstruction policy. In each case, furthermore, the assassination made it easier to influence perceptions of the meaning of the event and to manipulate political support and opposition. In the case of Lincoln, Northern suspicion and resentment of the South could only be rendered more intense by the assassination plot and more susceptible to the argument that unless the political activities of Southern whites were forcefully suppressed, a conspiratorial plot against the Union would persist.

Thus the radicals within the Republican party, by emphasizing this reinforced perception of the continued potency of the enemy, were able to replace the leadership on behalf of moderation that President Lincoln had begun to exert. More than that, Lincoln's successor, Andrew Johnson, served less as leader of the forces of moderation than as a conspicuous and easy symbol of the alleged infiltration of the Federal Government by the still viable traitorous elements of the South. An examination of the background, political ties, and style of the new President offers added reason to believe that this assassination did indeed catalyze a dramatic change in policy.

Andrew Johnson, unlike Lincoln, was not one of the founding fathers of the Republican party. In Northern Republican politics he was relatively unknown. What was known about him was that he represented a border state in the Senate prior to secession, had opposed secession, and had served as military governor of Tennessee. He had been personally selected by Lincoln as his running mate, in part because he was one of the few loyal Southerners available, and as a reward for his service in support of the Union. Thus, when Johnson was nominated for the Vice-Presidency, he had little grass-root support within the party. After the election, his ties within the party were mediated largely through Lincoln.

Indeed, in the days immediately following Lincoln's assassination, one of the major jobs that the press undertook was to introduce the new President to his public and to reassure the public that even though Johnson was Southern by birth, family, and style of speech, he did not share either ideology or political loyalty with the South. He could be expected to behave as any other president elected by the Union States on the Republican ticket.

During the eight months that Andrew Johnson held office in the absence of the Congress, he embarked on a program of restoration that resembled Lincoln's proclamation of December, 1863 on all points except one. And on that one point he was more severe than Lincoln. Thus, between April and December, 1865, Johnson restored most of the Southern states to the Union, and when Congress reconvened in December, they found Southern representatives waiting to be admitted to their seats in the legislature.

This became the issue upon which the Radical Republicans made their first stand. On the opening day of the legislative session, when the Clerk of the House called the names of the assembled representatives, he omitted the names of the Southern members. Acting on a prearranged plan, Thaddeus Stevens, who was to emerge as one of the major forces against Johnson in the House and a leader of the Radical Republican Reconstruction Program, then introduced a motion to form a joint committee of fifteen members (nine representatives and six senators) to pass on the qualifications of the new claimants. In speaking for the committee, Stevens made it clear that it intended to make the most extensive and unhurried deliberations, not only upon membership, but also upon the entire question of Reconstruction and the adequacy of the President's policy. The ex-confederate states would be kept waiting indefinitely for readmission.

The forming of this committee was the Republicans' first collective reaction to the new executive. They acted as they did even though many of them had no objections to Johnson's first message to Congress, which was read the day after the legislative body assembled. It even received considerable praise from some Republicans for its literary merits. Substantively, Johnson seemed to be following the paths only vaguely formed by Lincoln. He argued, as Lincoln did consistently, that the states' acts of secession were constitutionally not real but pretended; and therefore null and void. He reiterated Lincoln's major thesis that the states had no power to dissolve the Union: the whole cannot exist without the parts, nor the parts without the whole! As President, he claimed that it was his responsibility to decide whether the states that had formed the Confederacy were to be held as conquered territory. He had decided "to restore the vitality of the states rather than to incur the great dangers of indefinite military government."[4] McKitrick makes the point that Johnson not only had the support of many of the leading Republicans in the Senate and House, but he also received widespread support from influential Northern newspapers including the *New York Times,* the *Chicago Tribune,* and the *New York Tribune.*

But quite aside from the external situation, Johnson was not a

4. Eric L. McKitrick, *Andrew Johnson and Reconstruction* (Chicago: Phoenix Books, 1960), p. 255.

party man; he was a loner. He saw politics largely as a matter of ideology and principles, and not as a matter of organization and bargaining.[5] He felt passionately about his plebian background and about his struggle to rise above his lowly beginnings. He hated the men whom he viewed as his social superiors and the basis for much of his support for the Unionists' cause grew out of his hatred of the Southern planters. He felt that the small landowners and the poor farmers had no chance against the large plantation economy of the Old South. His political career in the Tennessee legislature and as Governor and Senator of that state had been marked by bitter struggles against the Southern aristocracy, whom he viewed quite accurately as having organized themselves against him. He was used to bypassing "the party" and taking his case directly to the people. He felt that he spoke for the small landowners, the artisans, and the small merchants of Tennessee and the South. When he campaigned, he depended hardly at all on party organization and almost completely on his ability to persuade the people of the justness of his cause. He was awkward at party wheeling and dealing; stump speaking and direct appeals to the public were his ways of playing the political game.

In the months prior to Congress' reconvening, Johnson acted in the style that characterized his prior political behavior. He made decisions after carefully examining the issues, testing them against his own interpretation of the Constitution, and evaluating them against his own moral code. He ignored party leaders. Within three months after Congress reconvened, Johnson vetoed major pieces of legislation. Both were bills that had the support of the moderates within the Republican party, men who saw themselves as Johnson's supporters.[6]

The first act was the Freedmen's Bureau Bill, and the second was the Civil Rights Act. Both bills were eventually passed over Johnson's veto. McKitrick notes that these two occasions were the first times that major pieces of legislation had ever been passed over a president's veto.[7] Johnson paid heavily for his vetoes. They

5. *Ibid.*, pp. 87–88.
6. In the Senate: John Sherman, William Pitt Fessenden, Lyman Trumbull and James W. Grimes.
7. McKitrick: *op. cit.*, p. 323.

cost him the support of most of the Republican Congressmen who had not yet affiliated with the radical wing, and they antagonized many of the Northern newspapers who had adopted a "wait-and-see policy" toward Johnson.

At the same time that the Radical Republicans were rallying loyal party men to their cause, Johnson was seeking support for his policies from the electorate directly. After his veto of the first Freedmen's Bureau Bill in February, 1866, Johnson embarked upon a series of speaking tours and impromptu speeches. His purpose was to tell the public how Congress was mistreating him, how it was trying to wreck his programs, and how his policies, if enacted, would unite North and South and allow the bitterness created by the Civil War to be forgotten most quickly. Perhaps it was the latter theme, especially coming from a Southerner, to which the Northern audiences were most allergic. There were many groups in the North who did not want to forget the bitterness and the strife of the preceding years. Indeed, it was those memories that they were most anxious to keep in their minds, because such thoughts provided them with their most effective arguments for treating the South as a conquered province.

With the passage of the Freedmen's Bureau Bill and the Civil Rights Act over the President's veto, Congress gave formal notice to Johnson that it would enact its own program of Reconstruction. In the Senate, all but one Republican voted against the President. The Republican party thus appeared united, with Johnson on the outside. He was the "man" to be defeated, because he was perceived as "soft" on those who threatened the form of Union with which the Radicals now identified.

By March, 1867, a year and a half before Johnson's term of office was officially over, he was effectively stripped of power. Congress had completely stymied presidential Reconstruction and was on its way toward imposing its own plan. The congressional plan was to last for ten years until a later Republican President, Rutherford B. Hayes, ordered the withdrawal of Northern troops from Southern soil.

The irony in this analysis is that by their short-run success in defeating the Lincoln-Johnson presidential programs of restoration, the Radical Republicans laid the ground for the long-run domination of the South by the old conservatives. Had the assassination not occurred, the Southern planter class, the class that dominated Southern political life, might not have had the opportunity to regain the control it exercised before the war. While the Radical Republicans, the moderate Republicans, and Johnson were fighting among themselves, the prewar Southern leadership consolidated its position. Southern reaction became increasingly homogeneous and bitter, and the bitterness served as grist for the conservatives' mill. Forces and issues were polarized. Men were either loyal to the "old South" or traitors. Issues were phrased and choices offered in such a manner that Southerners either had to go along with the large landowners or cast their lot with the Negroes, the carpetbaggers, and the North. The opportunity for the development of a new class of Southern leaders was foreclosed.

Had Lincoln not been assassinated the more conservative policies that he advocated might well have been adopted. The very adoption of a more conservative program in the short run might have fostered the birth of a new ruling class in the South. A long-run effect then would have been to accomplish some of the objectives that the Radical Republicans were seeking immediately—the development of a moderate Southern middle class whose livelihoods and status were not dependent upon an agrarian plantation economy. In allowing events to move as fast as they did in the years immediately following the Civil War, a tempo was established that was then adopted by the Southern leaders who were moving in the opposite direction—a return to the older order.

The Truman case is different from most we consider because it was an unsuccessful assassination attempt. It involved a plot, and it was explicitly and dramatically tied to a particular political cause. But these distinctive features did not make its aftermath distinctive. The failure of the plot unquestionably produced a lesser impact upon public opinion than would have been true of an actual presidential assassination. Nonetheless, efforts were made to use the assassination attempt to strengthen a wide range of political causes and careers, chiefly centering upon fears of subversion and most of them unconnected with the Puerto Rican nationalism that had inspired the plotters.

The plot was largely an outgrowth of Puerto Rican politics and of the circumstance that the United States, for some Puerto Ricans, had come to symbolize opposition to Puerto Rican independence. The aftermath, on the other hand, was largely played out in terms of American politics. It became a weapon in the hands of groups using it for their own purposes.

Harry Truman was an unlikely choice for a symbol of the suppression of Puerto Rican aspiration for independence. That he nonetheless played exactly that role illustrates that it is not the nature of the symbol but the needs of men that create its meaning. The symbol must be only formally appropriate, and Harry Truman was President of the country of which Puerto Rico was a territory.

Throughout his presidency, Truman had shown sympathy for self-determination for the Puerto Ricans. On October 16, 1945, shortly after he became President, he sent a special message to Congress recommending that four proposals for change in the status of Puerto Rico, including outright independence, be submitted to the Puerto Ricans for their choice. In 1946, he appointed Jesus T. Pinnero as the first native Governor of Puerto Rico. The following January Congress granted Puerto Ricans the right to select their own governor and other national officers other than auditor and judges of the Puerto Rican Supreme Court. In 1949, Congress made provision for Puerto Rico to write its own Constitution, to be approved by a referendum among Puerto Ricans. This enabling act was signed by Truman on July 3, 1950, and as a first step in the process, a registration of voters was set for November 4 of that same year.

The date, as will appear shortly, was the reason for an abortive revolt on October 29 of the Nationalists who intended to upset the registration procedures. It probably also influenced the timing of the assassination attempt on November 1. From the point of view of the Nationalists and other advocates of Puerto Rican independence, all this legislation was a meaningless sop to the Puerto Rican people, making it possible for American influence and economic exploitation to continue. Gilberto Concepcion de Garcia, head of the Independence Party (not to be confused with the Nationalist Party), announced that his party would boycott the registration because it did not have confidence in the guarantees offered by the government.[8] Given this perspective, the violence of late October and early November in Puerto Rico and Washington

8. *New York Times,* November 4, 1950.

becomes understandable as a way of shocking public opinion into questioning the reality of the measures for Puerto Rican self-rule.

The attempt on President Truman's life occurred as the country was entering a period of intense anxiety about Communism as an internal threat, a period dominated by what was shortly to be labeled "McCarthyism." Russian-American relations had become strained shortly after V-E Day. The most conspicuous news of the late forties consisted of accounts of tense confrontations in the United Nations, of bilateral encounters and, after 1947, of American resort to the Marshall Plan and the Truman Doctrine as containment devices. The external conflict found its domestic reflection in fears of Communist infiltration or domination of various organizations, especially labor unions. The Taft-Hartley Act of 1947, for example, included a non-Communist affidavit provision; and in the late forties the C.I.O. expelled several unions for alleged Communist infiltration. By 1950 and 1951, this kind of concern was spreading throughout American society, and it was being used to curb the liberal movements that had been influential before the war under Roosevelt and again in the promises of Truman's 1948 campaign.

The Korean War, which began in 1950, facilitated the possibility of hinging a popular appeal in domestic politics upon fear of Communism and therefore contributed to the onset of McCarthyism. At the time of the attempted assassination, the war news was prominent. Sharing the front page of the *New York Times* with the assassination story on November 2, 1950, was a story about a jet attack upon a United States unit by the "Korean Reds." Though Senator McCarthy's domination of the news was just beginning, its spectacular quality was already foreshadowed. On November 11, for example, Drew Pearson's column referred to charges by Senator Schoeppel of Kansas that Secretary of the Interior Oscar Chapman had pro-Communist leanings. Another news story the same day declared that the elections just held strengthened McCarthy's hand against the State Department. The next day *This Week* magazine, distributed as a Sunday supplement to many newspapers, carried an article entitled "The FBI Wants You." It alleged that Communists had been highly effective in their work in the United States and declared that the FBI intended "when the time comes" to arrest 12,000 dangerous Communists. "With the alert help of every American, that roundup can be 100 per cent complete."[9]

In this atmosphere, every news story was likely to be examined by liberals and McCarthyites with a view to its utility as a ploy in the controversy that dominated American public affairs. Because McCarthyism was an example of the kind of issue that arouses emotion and polarizes the population through mutual threat, any news story used effectively as such a ploy had to evoke wide public attention and a deep sense of shock. In this respect, a political assassination met the test perfectly; and it was indeed used to manipulate opinion on this key issue.

On November 2, the day after the assassination attempt, Senator Kenneth Wherry of Nebraska, the Republican floor leader, said the shooting showed there was need for a "vigorous Red roundup." He called on the President to enforce the new Internal Security Act by ordering the arrest of all Communists who had failed to register. Terming the shooting the "bitter fruit of years of appeasement and coddling of Communism in and out of the federal government," he declared that it makes "mandatory" the firing of all subversives on the federal payroll.[10]

Leading American magazines similarly linked the assassination attempt to Communism. *Newsweek* referred to the assassination attempt, the revolt in Puerto Rico, and the bomb throwing in the Puerto Rican Labor Office in New York City, and noted that Governor Muñoz Marin had "characterized the violence as a 'conspiracy against democracy helped by the Communists.'" It then went on to say, "And he was not dragging a Red herring. All signs pointed to Communist participation. . . . There was evidence that the two Blair House assassins had worked closely with a Communist 'action' cell in Mexico and with Communist elements in New York's sprawling Puerto Rican colony where pro-Communist Representative Marcantonio has for years made inflammatory speeches for immediate Puerto Rican independence." Tracing recent Puerto Rican history, *Newsweek* introduced an original note by alleging that in the thirties the Nationalists had worked with the Nazis.[11]

9. *San Francisco Chronicle,* November 12, 1950.
10. *Chicago Tribune,* November 3, 1950.
11. *Newsweek,* November 13, 1950, pp. 28–29.

In bold type at the beginning of a story headed, "Why Puerto Rico Boils Over," *U.S. News and World Report* declared, "Terrorists in Puerto Rico are a ruthless band, aided by Communists."[12]

Reviewing the life of Albizu Campos, *Life* said, "While in [the Federal Penitentiary in] Atlanta (in 1943) for conspiring to overthrow U.S. rule in Puerto Rico, he undoubtedly knew his fellow inmate Earl Browder, then U.S. Communist boss." Later in its story, *Life* pointed out the moral it saw in the affair and made crystal clear for its more obtuse readers its possibilities for American politics: "The acts of violence make no sense—except to Communists who thrive on disruption in the Caribbean and elsewhere. With the plots fortunately foiled the next step was to fix the Communists' cloudy part in them."[13]

In this atmosphere, the rhetoric of Communist threat afforded a cue to those Puerto Ricans in official positions who wished to emphasize the allegedly deviant, unrepresentative character of the Nationalists. Governor Muñoz Marin took this line most strongly:

This further crime [the assassination attempt] further confirms me in my conviction that the nationalists are having their lunacy, fanaticism, and irresponsibility manipulated for the benefit of Communist propaganda and strategy.[14]

Muñoz Marin returned to this theme frequently in the following months.

Antonio Fernos-Isern, Puerto Rican Representative in the United States Congress, also recognized implications for an anti-Communist movement in the events of early November. He declared on November 2 that the assassination attempt represented an "unholy marriage" between the small Puerto Rican Nationalist party and United States Communists; both groups, he said, want to discredit both governments.

Russell Derrickson, Acting Director of the Caribbean division, Office of Territories, Interior Department, took a more tentative view. He declared that he doubted that Communists had any direct responsibility for the violence because the whole thing had been too amateurish and disorganized. Communists had no doubt en-

12. *U.S. News and World Report,* November 10, 1950, p. 22.
13. *Life,* November 13, 1950, p. 25.
14. *New York Times,* November 2, 1950.

couraged the Nationalists, however, and he said it was known through official sources that some Nationalists were Communists.

The American Communist party reacted quickly to the attempt to link it to the assassination. William Z. Foster issued a statement saying:

As is well known, the Communist Party condemns and rejects assassination and all acts of violence and terror. This can only be the act of terrorists, deranged men—a 1950 version of van der Lubbe and the Reichstag fire frameup.

Another issue much in the news just after the assassination attempt was the congressional and mayoral elections in New York City on November 7, 1950. With respect to the election, too, the assassination had its uses. In an assessment of the election picture on Sunday, November 5, the *New York Times* saw the assassination attempt as evoking widespread sympathy for Truman and heightening the effect of the only campaign speech he had made, in St. Louis, on November 4.

It was in the Puerto Rican section of New York City that the most direct impact of the shooting was felt, and there the allegations of a link to Communism may well have been crucial. James G. Donovan, the candidate who was opposing the incumbent Congressman Vito Marcantonio in the East Harlem district, directly linked the attempted assassination to the campaign. On November 4, he alleged that Mr. Marcantonio pulled one Sopo Valez from a truck paid for by Communists and helped him go into hiding. Valez had been speaking on behalf of Marcantonio. Referring to Valez as an "ex-assassin" who had been a co-defendant with Campos in Puerto Rico in connection with the recent riots there, Donovan could hardly have been oblivious of the connotations at that time either of "assassin" or of "Communist." Throughout the campaign, he charged Marcantonio with voting the Communist line. Whatever the reasons, Marcantonio lost the election to Donovan by a margin of about 14,000 votes, with approximately 85,000 votes cast.

The Republican candidate for mayor of New York City, Edward Corsi, also used the assassination attempt as the basis for an appeal in the Puerto Rican districts. In a campaign speech, he declared that the "unfortunate incident should not be looked upon as a reflection upon the Puerto Rican people." He went on to say that he was "proud of support . . . given [to me] throughout my career by men and women from Puerto Rico," and declared he would "stand firmly with them against any calumny, whatever may be done by a few Puerto Ricans who bring discredit upon their community."[15]

In foreign reactions to the assassination attempt, the pattern of reinforcement of themes long prominent appeared again. *Pravda* concentrated upon the revolt in Puerto Rico rather than the shooting at Blair House and accused the United States of provoking the revolt as an excuse to use tanks and planes to inspire "bloody terror" among those seeking independence. *Pravda* reported that "thousands" had been thrown into jail.[16]

In Latin America, the Yankee imperialist theme and the fear among friendly government officials that it would be reinforced by Collazo's execution dominated reactions. Petitions for clemency for Collazo flowed in from Guatemala, Uruguay, Argentina, Brazil, and El Salvador. Nineteen Cuban lawyers cabled President Truman asking him to commute Collazo's sentence. The legislatures of Cuba, Uruguay, and Guatemala passed formal resolutions urging commutation. In New York, a "save Collazo Committee" collected 30,000 signatures on a clemency petition, chiefly among Puerto Ricans. Governor Muñoz Marin sent an urgent telegram to the President advising him that the execution would damage United States foreign relations in all Latin America.

Concluding with a brief analysis of the last presidential assassination, we find that the deepest, most significant, and most lasting set of responses to the death of John F. Kennedy centered on the controversy between ideological extremists and moderates. The opinion polls showed that a substantial proportion of the people assumed, on hearing the news of the assassination, that it was tied to either rightist or leftist extremism. In his speech at Kennedy's bier in the Capitol rotunda, Chief Justice Earl Warren blamed hatemongers and ideological extremists as ultimately responsible for the atmosphere that had produced the murder. In striking this note, the Chief Justice sounded a motif that was to be echoed often in the succeeding months and years.

15. *New York Times,* November 4, 1950.
16. *New York Times,* November 16, 1950.

Ralph McGill, the publisher of the *Atlanta Constitution* and a syndicated columnist, declared in an article published on December 14, 1963 that "hatred knows no direction. The American Communist-oriented and right-wing extremist groups have disassociated themselves from their country. The danger comes from both." He alleged that the abuse of the President and the government have inspired many "whose disturbed minds tend easily toward recklessness and criminal action."[17] Many Southern leaders, the *New York Times* noted, voiced "a reaction against extremism from either the left or the right" as an immediate response to the assassination.[18] In a report issued February 1, 1964, the B'nai B'rith Anti-Defamation League asserted that opinion surveys showed that a majority of Americans believed the slayings of Kennedy and Oswald "were the result of organized plotting" and not of individual action, and the report declared that this view could be attributed to the psychological need for meaning rather than absurdity and to "the influence of various extreme groups, left and right, which for years have been preaching the existence of plots and conspiracies in United States life—for their own dedicated purpose."[19]

The placing of the ultimate blame upon the extremists of the right and left came consistently from liberals and moderates. Like other efforts to interpret and use the shock of assassination in order to influence public opinion, it casts the authors' adversaries in the role of scapegoat.

This relationship among accuser, accused, and public opinion was even more apparent when the extremist groups were the accusers. The charge that the assassination was a Communist plot came almost entirely from the extreme right wing. It is revealing and significant that it did not come from moderates, in spite of Oswald's widely publicized sympathy for Communism and his residence in the Soviet Union. A statement from the John Birch Society cited approvingly a statement by former Congressman Martin Dies that Oswald was a Communist and that when a Communist murders, he acts under orders.[20] Major General

17. *Saturday Evening Post,* December 14, 1963, p. 8.
18. *New York Times,* February 1, 1964.
19. *New York Times,* February 1, 1964.
20. *New York Times,* December 15, 1963.

Edwin A. Walker issued a statement declaring that "the tragic events of yesterday demonstrate the internal threat that can never be underestimated." He was also quoted as saying the assassination was a Communist plot organized by Fidel Castro.[21] Gerald L. K. Smith, long active as a right-wing extremist and anti-Semite, contended that Kennedy was killed by a Communist because he was planning to doublecross Russia and move to the right and that "a Los Angeles Jew was raising money to free Rubinstein."[22] Revilo Oliver, a member of the council of the John Birch Society, also charged that Kennedy had been killed for not following the orders of his Communist masters and that the assassination was preparation for a "domestic take-over."[23] The *National Review,* a somewhat less extreme but conservative weekly journal of opinion, published a letter from "a friend with long and intimate acquaintance with Soviet and Communist operations." It charged Kennedy with "at least the passive endorsement of Khrushchev" had planned to eliminate Castro and substitute a leftist regime in Cuba. "The probable motive for the assassination of Kennedy was that Castro wished to thwart this scheme for his elimination. . . ." The *National Review* also suggested that the American government travel-aid loan of $435 to Oswald so that he could return from Russia was a factor. "Was the crime made possible because of a misunderstanding of the nature of Communism by some of Mr. Kennedy's advisors that led to a relaxation of necessary security measures?"[24]

This sample of the responses of the extreme right makes clear not only that it concentrated upon Communism as the culprit, but also that each strain of rightist opinion singled out for blame those particular liberal institutions and groups it consistently opposed, tarring them with Communism and with a connection with the assassination. It is noteworthy in this connection that the attacks are launched less vehemently against Khrushchev and the Soviet Union than against Kennedy himself, the men around him, liberals, Jews, and Castro. Castro, like Khrushchev, was used as a foil to attack alleged liberal softness toward Communism.

21. *New York Times,* November 24, 1963 and December 2, 1963.
22. *New York Times,* February 1, 1964.
23. *New York Times,* February 11, 1964.
24. *National Review,* December 17, 1963, p. 515.

For those who saw the ideological right as the enemy, the assassination was also made to serve. One of these groups were the liberals, who suffered from the serious handicap that Oswald's ties were with the left. But the fact that the assassination had occurred in the area most closely associated with right-wing extremism was still relevant. On December 2, some ten days after the assassination, Senator Paul Douglas of Illinois was quoted as blaming "right-wingers" for having created what he described as "an atmosphere and a climate which made unbalanced people think it proper to resort to assassination if they find someone they deeply dislike."[25]

A second, more emphatic group that blamed the right wing was apparently chiefly concerned with finding a general tie among Texas oil interests, the Dallas police, the FBI, right-wing ideologists and the assassination. In a widely advertised book, one Joachim Joesten stated this view in rather blatant form:

I believe Oswald had been connected with both the CIA and the FBI. I believe that he was picked as a fall guy precisely because, as a petty, and perhaps discarded, agent of the CIA, and later of the FBI, he was an ideal scapegoat. I tend to the belief of a conspiracy of powerful men with a narrow circle of complicity in the middle echelons of the FBI and Dallas police. The conspiracy involves, I believe, some officials of the CIA and FBI as well as some army figures such as General Walker and reactionary oil millionaires such as H. L. Hunt.[26]

In another book, by Thomas G. Buchanan, the major speculation is that Texas oil interests and members of the John Birch Society conspired to bring about the assassination.[27]

Somewhat similar views, though expressed more moderately, were voiced by a number of liberals, including Leo Sauvage, a writer for the Parisian newspaper *Le Figaro,* and Mark Lane, a New York attorney who devoted himself to defending Oswald from the charges against him in the press and in the Warren Commission report.

The charge that the American right was responsible for the assassination was also a major theme in the Soviet press. To the

25. *New York Times,* December 2, 1963.
26. Joachim Joesten, *Oswald: Assassin or Fall Guy?* (New York Marzani & Munsell, 1964).
27. Thomas G. Buchanan, *Who Killed Kennedy?* (New York: G. Putnam & Sons, 1964).

extent that it was accepted by world opinion, it could be expected to strengthen the international position of the U.S.S.R. On November 24, 1963, the English-language service of the Soviet press agency *Tass* asserted in a dispatch from New York that "all circumstances of President Kennedy's tragic death allow us to assume that this murder was planned and carried out by ultra-right-wing fascist and racist circles. . . ."[28] The same day *Pravda* saw the American right using the assassination to step up anti-Soviet and anti-Cuban "hysteria," and it suggested a tie between right-wing elements and American gangsters, a charge that was to be repeated from time to time in Russian periodicals. Ten days later *Izvestia* published a front-page report featuring a charge by Mrs. Marguerite Oswald that FBI agents had shown her a picture of Ruby before he shot her son. The story suggested that the FBI was implicated in the President's death.[29]

Cuba followed Moscow's lead. On November 26, a Foreign Ministry statement declared that ". . . powerful forces of reaction in the U.S. were trying to hide the intellectual authors and true motives for the crime."[30]

Both from the left and from the right there were, predictably, efforts to counter the effects on public opinion stemming from these extremist charges. The American Communist party issued a statement on November 24 declaring:

In view of the fact that attempts are being made to link the suspected assassin with the Communist Party, we want to reiterate our complete condemnation of the dastardly assassination of President John F. Kennedy as a monstrous crime against the country.[31]

Norman Thomas of the Socialist party and leaders of the Communist, Socialist Workers, Socialist Labor, and Progressive Labor parties all declared that true Marxism opposes the use of violence against individuals.[32] Barry Goldwater used the rather different tactic of defending conservatism by dissociating the moderate from the radical right. On February 12, he told a press conference that

28. *New York Times,* November 24, 1963.
29. *New York Times,* December 3, 1963.
30. *New York Times,* November 27, 1963.
31. *New York Times,* November 24, 1963.
32. *New York Times,* November 27, 1963.

attacks on Kennedy in *American Opinion,* the journal of the John Birch Society, were "detestable."[33]

The Soviet Union and Cuba were not the only foreign powers that saw in the assassination an opportunity to do some profitable fishing in troubled waters. What is impressive is the unlikely variety of groups on the world political scene who were able to interpret the event so as to pin responsibility on their classic enemies.

On the day after the assassination, apparently before he knew the identity of the assassin, President Nnamdi Azikeive of Nigeria made a statement tying the assassination to racism in the United States:

New African states must ponder seriously before deciding whether to trust a government elected by the American electorate, because it is now crystal clear that certain influential sections of the American public neither respect human dignity now nor regard the black races as human beings who deserve to be treated with respect, decency and equality.[34]

The Arab press identified Jack Ruby as Jewish and reasoned from this fact that Zionists were behind the assassination. A headline in the *Independent Daily Al Hayat* of Lebanon read: THEY KILLED PRESIDENT KENNEDY'S ASSASSIN TO OBLITERATE AN INVESTIGATION. KILLED BY RUBY THE JEW.[35]

Juanita Castro, estranged sister of Premier Fidel Castro of Cuba and a frequent spokesman for the anti-Castro Cuban refugees in the United States, declared on the anniversary of the assassination that her brother was responsible for it, if only indirectly.[36]

There was considerable inclination throughout the world for people who were suspicious of American foreign policy to question the findings of the Warren Commission and to suggest that the official handling of the assassination and the investigation was a foreign policy tactic. Unlike some of the charges just noted, this view was shared by many highly respected people. In England, for example, a group of eminent figures including Lord Boyd Orr, Sir

33. *New York Times,* February 13, 1964.
34. *New York Times,* November 30, 1963.
35. *New York Times,* November 27, 1963.
36. *New York Times,* November 21, 1964.

Compton Mackenzie, J. B. Priestley, Hugh Trevor-Roper, Kingsley Martin, and Michael Foot joined a "Who Killed Kennedy Committee" organized by Bertrand Russell. They subscribed to the position stated by Russell that "there has never been a more subversive, conspiratorial, unpatriotic or endangering course for the security of the United States and the world than the attempt by the United States Government to hide the murderer of its recent President."[37]

But the Kennedy assassination is still too recent and too controversial for its ramifications to be fully assessed. The more detailed assessment of President Kennedy's death will undoubtedly involve analyses of the 1964 presidential election and the subsequent assassination of Robert Kennedy, all of which will occur sometime in the future.

CONCLUSION

Because American presidential assassinations occur frequently and prominently, and because they observably evoke intense, somewhat patterned, and empirically unverifiable beliefs about their meaning, it is important for social scientists to try to identify their social and political functions. Our study suggests that they serve functions for the assassin, for contemporary political interest groups and for the polity.

For the assassin, they serve mainly to displace inner anxieties onto a conspicuous political figure and to rationalize his assassination in terms of the public interest. This observation is consistent with Smith's, Bruner's, and White's idea that one function of political opinions is to externalize inner tensions.[38] The assassin has not been our chief concern, however, and we make this point only incidentally.

Our central finding, and one less possible to anticipate in the light of extant theory, concerns the functions of assassinations for public opinion and interest-group support. After each assassination, those already strongly committed to a position on a public issue perceive the assassination as related to that concern, and as

37. Harrison Salisbury, *New York Times,* November 25, 1964.
38. M. Brewster Smith, J. S. Bruner, and R. W. White, *Opinions and Personality* (New York: John Wiley & Sons, 1956).

evidence of the correctness of their position, irrespective of whether it was a logically or empirically valid inference. The combination of anxiety and ambiguity produced by the assassination also encourage interest groups to try to win wider support from the less committed public by advancing their own interpretations of the meaning of the shocking event. Cleavages already present are thereby intensified, and political attitudes on dominant current issues spread to a wider segment of the population.

Each of the assassinations thus catalyzed wide politicization and public concern about prominent issues. Typically, this effect produced no long run or basic change in policy direction, though it unquestionably widened and deepened the support for such policies as civil-service reform, restrictions on immigration, and suppression of dissent from those defined as subversives. By doing so, it probably brought earlier enactment of these policies than would otherwise have occurred, and perhaps made their enforcement more zealous for a time.

In the Lincoln case, where a prior polarization on the key issue of Reconstruction policy had already been advanced at the time of the assassination, these effects almost certainly did produce a change in long-run policy direction. In that instance, the added support for a radical policy evoked by the assassination brought greater suppression of the white Southerners than seemed politically likely had Lincoln served out his second term. In turn, that suppression produced wide support for an extremist white Southern position that has dominated the politics of the South since the Reconstruction period.

The Political Consequences of Assassination

Dwaine Marvick and Elizabeth Wirth Marvick

INTRODUCTION: THE CONCERN WITH ASSASSINATION

Political assassination means the violent death of a public figure, brought about on purpose by nonlegitimated action.[1] Since we are concerned here with consequences, it is best to leave open the question of the motives for political murder. Apparently these can be quite various. Yet we must acknowledge that assassination by members of the political elite implies a set of motives and generates a set of consequences quite different from those associated with assassination by persons marginal to elite circles.

By defining political assassination as nonlegitimated action, we restrict attention to those cases of political murder that are supported neither by public consensus nor by elite rationalizations. "Judicial murders" are not part of our agenda—whether of English monarchs or Bolshevik leaders.[2] Of course, legitimation is a relative term, and it must be tested by whether or not a particular audience accepts it. Thus being a "foreigner" may rob the death by violence of a public figure of much of the "legitimacy" that many "natives" may attach to it. The international ramifications of assassinations are best considered, however, after canvassing more polity-bound effects.

There are other forms of violent death that sometimes befall political leaders—forms that are legitimate and hence outside our

1. A public figure is one on whom attention is focused. For a discussion of the term as it is used here see Herbert Goldhamer, "Public Opinion and Personality," *American Journal of Sociology* 55 (January, 1950), pp. 346–354.

2. Political criticism is often built into definitions of assassination. One catalogue equates the fate of Henry VIII's wives and Charles I. Gabriel Peignot, *Notice Chronologique de tous les Souverains—d'Europe qui ont peri de Mort Violente*—(Paris, 1865). Another account characterizes as assassination both the Katyn massacre and the Nürnberg condemnations. F. J. P. Veale, *Crimes Discreetly Veiled* (London: Cooper, 1958).

purview. Almost all of these raise questions very similar to those raised by assassination. The massacre of St. Bartholomew's Day was a case of widespread political murder initiated by the legitimate government of the day. Its modern analogue is the "purge" taken to forestall subversion and stifle civil conflict.[3] In such cases of domestic struggle, as in international cases, the death of political leaders through "enemy action" can be of critical weight in shifting the outcome of a conflict over control of the legitimate machinery of state.

Violent deaths that come to political leaders by nonpurposively directed forces, e.g., accident or misadventure, also must be admitted to complicate analysis. Often they leave residues comparable to those of political assassination. Such mishaps appear to upset the social order of surviving elite relationships almost as much as do political murders. Indeed, attempts are sometimes made to explain such unnatural deaths as the vengeance of angry fate or the "will of God," as though the deaths had been caused by purposive human actions and needed a cloak of legitimacy.

Related also are deaths of public figures through unanticipated natural causes. Before the flowering of medical terminology gave at least the illusion that someone had clear insight into the source of most physiological ills, the deaths of major public figures were routinely suspected to be cases of poisoning. Autopsies performed on the corpses of kings rarely yielded results sufficiently authoritative to dispel suspicions of foul play.[4] The mere fact that Zachary Taylor and Millard Fillmore died in office was sufficient to excite suspicions that were still current at the beginning of ˙Lincoln's term.[5] Leaders who themselves dispose of great amounts

3. Hitler's purge of Nazis following the killing of Roehm has been called the "German Saint Bartholomew's Day." Joseph Bornstein, *The Politics of Murder* (New York: Sloane, 1951), p. 95.

4. The rapid extinction of the Capetian line in France after Philip the Fair's confrontation with the Pope's power was attributed to assassinations. On this and other suspected poisonings of French princes see A. Corlieu, *La Mort des Rois de France* (Paris, 1873).

5. John M. Potter, *Plots Against Presidents* (New York: Astor-Honor, 1968), pp. 29–30. An apparently natural death of a public figure may be later revealed as a purposive act. Such "secret assassinations" may become more important with changing techniques. For some details of these crimes in recent years see: Karl Andere, *Murder to Order* (London: Ampersand, 1965).

of unreviewed power seem especially to arouse rumors of assassination when they die, whatever the prosaic facts may be. Stalin reportedly compared Roosevelt's last illness to Lenin's, which in turn reminded the suspicious of stories about Stalin's complicity in the death of the founder of the Soviet state.[6]

In the past decade, three murders of public men have had immediate widespread impact on Americans. The assassination of John F. Kennedy eliminated the incumbent of the highest secular office in the United States. It set in motion the legal machinery for determining succession in a constitutional system and it tested the effectiveness of spontaneous attitudinal mechanisms for transferring legitimacy to the lawful heir.

On the other hand, the assassination of Martin Luther King, Jr., left a different kind of void. Unlike the President, King did not stand in a uniform legal relationship to American citizens. The role he played depended for its influence almost solely upon his charisma and hardly at all upon legal-rational authority. Insofar as his organizational role was formally defined, that role was of such small significance that no struggle surrounded its transfer to a successor. But the charismatic power Dr. King had wielded could not easily be transferred along with the formal title to the new incumbent of his office[7]. Part of it may have disappeared. Part accrued to his legend, and no doubt part went to the foremost bearer of that legend, his widow. Parts also seem to have touched other leading or emergent figures in the civil-rights movement, briefly including Senator Robert Kennedy of New York.[8]

6. Robert Sherwood, *Roosevelt and Hopkins* (New York: Harper, 1948). Like many others, Bornstein takes it for granted that Lenin was poisoned by Stalin. *Op. cit.,* p. 291.

7. The fragmentation of King's power after his murder is suggested by this respondent in a Florida study of reactions: " '. . . The people that have followed just haven't been able to carry out the movement that he started with the dignity that he was able to . . . However maybe he helped get the ball rolling, so maybe in the future we'll make it one way or another. . . .' " Philip Meyer, "Aftermath of Martyrdom: Negro Militancy and Martin Luther King," *Public Opinion Quarterly* 33 (Summer, 1969), p. 170.

8. An electoral study in Ohio showed an increase among Negroes in positive affect toward significant Negro reference groups and an increased polarization of affect toward Lyndon Johnson and the Democratic Party. See C. R. Hofstetter, "Political Disengagement and the Death of Martin Luther King," *Public Opinion Quarterly,* 33 (Summer, 1969), pp. 174–179.

The third victim of an assassin's weapon to attract universal attention was Robert Kennedy, winner of California's primary and top contender for the Democratic presidential nomination in 1968. Some portion of his murdered brother's charismatic attraction he had acquired; ever since the assassination of November, 1963, he had been urged to take his brother's place. In June, 1968, however, he was still aspirant. His party's nomination was significantly nearer, perhaps, but the presidential mantle of office was still a distant goal.

A United States senator attracts much deference in the American political system, but incumbents are eminently substitutable. The political effects of his murder were not to be seen primarily as effects generated by a vacancy in a key formal position. Rather, those effects were evident in the way the crime changed people's expectations and forced many of his fellow citizens to rearrange their posture toward the play of future political events. Many activists had been deeply involved in his presidential candidacy; some portion of the public as well were attracted by the prospect that he might take up his brother's task and fill the presidential role. For these persons—activists and citizens alike—his murder was a shock all the more traumatic because of its cumulative overtones; his followers were slow to recover from their sense of loss, and some were driven back to private pursuits in their disappointment at what could happen to public men in America.[9]

Because these three assassinations occurred in the United States within a span of five years, there is a tendency to examine their common features—the causes and consequences they all share. The brief review just made has highlighted features that differentiate each from the other two. The effects of each crime were linked to the quite different role played on the public stage by each victim. We could equally well have differentiated among these assassinations in other ways: the formality and public character of the circumstances; the character and fate of the criminal; the

9. Francine Klagsbrun and David C. Whitney, eds., *Assassination: Robert F. Kennedy, 1925–1968* (New York: Cowles, 1968). Especially interesting in this regard are the comments of one journalist suggesting that the climate of partisan competition was in part responsible for the tragedy (pp. 244–246).

evidence of conspiracy; the news coverage by mass media. Each way of differentiating one from the others calls attention to fresh avenues for examining the political consequences.

Our approach has been illustrated by the way these events have been treated. Two sets of effects preoccupy us. First, assassinations are interruptions; they are rechanneling events in the processes of political recruitment. Second, assassinations modify the perspectives of the victim's audience—that public, including elite members as well as ordinary citizens, which has given the political leader his significance by its attention. Assassinations lead to the recruitment of new leaders by eliminating a public figure from the political scene. The elimination may or may not lead to the recruitment of a successor to fill the complex role of the assassin's victim; the successor may or may not play that role in a political style and direction similar to those of his murdered predecessor. Withal, the consequences of the deed are to be found by examining the changes in leadership that it brings about. At the same time, assassinations modify the political perspectives of the victim's public. Those who have been observers of the events surrounding a political murder are compelled to change their expectations about related political questions; they must direct their attention to the surviving actors performing in modified roles. Legitimation of both formal and informal successorship is problematic; it depends upon these changed perspectives. In this legitimation process, the varied identifications of members of the audience with the murdered leader are in point. So are their effective demands upon those who step to the center of the stage.

The events of 1963–1968 are to some extent still unassimilable. For the sake of analytical clarity, let us direct inquiries to more distant cases of assassination. In the following section, three cases are examined that in time and cultural setting are far removed from modern America. Each of the three victims of assassination to be considered played a symbolic role comparable to that played by the others in its informal aspects. Each victim was a public figure of such prominence that his actions as a central political leader received maximum attention of a national scope. Similarities in the pattern of the crimes will be apparent as the analysis proceeds. In a laboratory approach to the tasks of conceptualizing the consequences of political assassinations, let us recapitulate three widely separated dramas surrounding the deaths of Henri IV, Lincoln, and Gandhi.

THREE CASES

In the modern age (that is, since the Renaissance), three charismatic leaders, each with a style that had captured popular imagination, were assassinated just as their lifelong goals seemed about to be realized. Henri IV of France, Abraham Lincoln in America, and Mohandas Gandhi of India were truly popular figures. Each was murdered at the end of a period of civil conflict in which the cause they had championed was victorious. Each had stood for policies of generosity toward the vanquished, of reconciliation with former enemies, of help for disadvantaged minorities. The "healing" role played by these men had more than once made each of them a target for a "fanatical" would-be assassin. In the final, fatal attack, each of the three was struck down by an assailant who acted seemingly from a conviction of righteousness. At the time, each of these three assassinations was widely, though by no means universally, regarded as a major political disaster. Each tragic event evoked horror at the crime, grief over the loss, and fear of the public consequences. Yet in none of these cases are those demoralizing effects on social and political life easily identified or widely agreed to by scholars. Even harder to trace are the long-run effects on public policies and on popular belief systems. Nevertheless, the circumstances and aftermaths of these three assassinations are worth further examination; they may suggest a schema for analyzing the consequences of other political murders.

1. Henri IV. On May 14, 1610, Henri IV of France was on his way by carriage across Paris to meet his finance minister. He was waylaid en route and fatally stabbed by François Ravaillac of Angouleme. It was not the first attack upon the founder of the Bourbon dynasty; no fewer than ten attempts on the life of this monarch are recorded. Nor was assassination a novel fate for French kings. Only a generation before, Henri IV's immediate predecessor had been murdered by a young Dominican. But the popular emotion evoked by Ravaillac's deed was pervasive and intense to an unprecedented degree.[10]

At the age of fifty-six, Henri IV's position as ruler of France was analogous to that of a popular leader in a modern state. He had been King of Navarre, but it was his personal abilities rather than his more doubtful lineal qualifications that had made him the choice of the Valois rulers to succeed their failing line. In his tastes—simple to the point of rudeness—and in his amiability, he had the equalitarian manner of a democratic leader.

By his policies as King, this former Protestant had conciliated the warring religious factions, ended long years of bloody civil strife, restored the finances of the kingdom, and set an example of martial bravery that helped to assure France of national autonomy. For his queen, he had chosen a consort who brought not only benevolence toward her adopted country but significant alliances as well. To crown these restorative virtues, Henri IV and Marie de Médicis provided France with the first dauphin born in more than eighty years; the queen's fertility assured for the kingdom the solace of an uninterrupted succession.[11]

Contemporaries of the assassination all report an almost universal sense of affliction produced by the regicide.[12] Frenchmen near and far treated the loss of their King as a personal and severe deprivation. The tragedy and disappointment were expressed by a poet of the day:

> *Grand Capitain, si grand Roi*
> *C'est de lui seul que l'on espére*
> *Voir au Levant florir la Foi. . . .*[13]

The verses are reminiscent of Walt Whitman's lines of mourning for Lincoln written 250 years later. Not only the tragedian but also

10. The most detailed recent account of this assassination and its aftermath is Roland Mousnier, *L'Assassinat d'Henri IV* (Paris: Gallimard, 1964).

11. Cataloguing all these assets, a contemporary remarked, "Truly, no prince in the world surpassed him"—the more remarkable since the observer was the courtier of Henri's successor. Charles Bernard, *Histoire de Louis XIII*, I (Paris, 1646), p. 7.

12. The dismay of contemporaries of all stations is recapitulated by Pierre de Vaissiere, *Henry IV* (Paris: A. Fayard, 1928), pp. 696–697.

13. Quoted by Mousnier, *op. cit.*, p. 235.

the ordinary people felt the King's loss as a heavy blow. Countless witnesses describe the stunned misery that met the news all over France. From the queen down to lowly passers-by in the streets, Parisians especially mourned their familiar leader and "good father."[14]

The murderer Ravaillac was immediately seized. Two weeks of "interrogations" grimly followed, and much of his personal history was extracted from him. About age thirty-two, he had never married. He lived alone with his mother, a woman who—at the time of his crime—had been separated for six years from his father and from her other six children, all daughters. A poorly paid schoolmaster in Angouleme, Ravaillac occasionally practiced the trade of solicitor in Paris, where he came periodically to plead cases before Parliament and before the royal court.[15] Extremely devout, at one time he had sought to enter a Benedictine order in Paris, but after six weeks he had been asked to leave. His "visions" or hallucinations led the friars to mistrust his suitability for monastic life. Repulsed by the Feuillants, he repeatedly petitioned for readmission. He sought entrance as well into a Jesuit house, also without success.

Perhaps as much as a year before the event, the idea of killing the King took possession of Ravaillac's mind. He sought relief through confession to a priest. In his obsession, he saw himself acting on behalf of a divine agency. He had been chosen for the act of tyrannicide to protect the Catholic Church, the Pope, perhaps France as well against a King who jeopardized all three. Henri IV's failure to punish the Huguenots was seen by his murderer as a policy inimical to the true church and its practitioners. In fantasy, Ravaillac saw the King bent upon attacking the Pope personally and removing the Holy See to France.

It is extraordinarily difficult to sift the kind of evidence in which every coincidence seems to portend a fatal act. A spate of supernatural or bizarre events presaging or following the assassina-

14. A detailed account of local reactions is given by Maloherbe in a letter of May 19, 1614. He reports that he believes "the people of Paris have never cried so much." *Oeuvres,* III (Paris, 1862), p. 169.

15. Ravaillac's history is based here on Mousnier's account, *op. cit.,* pp. 7–19. Contemporary accounts differ on various details.

tion was chronicled by diarists of the day. According to several contemporary reporters, premonitions of disaster were felt by the King himself and by others close to him. Such intimations were realistic enough, in light of past experience. This time, however, they may have prompted the King to an extraordinary step: two days before the murder, he caused his consort to be crowned. The possible significance of this coronation in precipitating Ravaillac's decision to act simply cannot be assessed.[16]

The death of Henri IV left his queen in full possession of state authority, and her regency was further legitimized by her position as guardian of the new King, a child of nine. In the hours and days immediately after the event, some observers feared mass panic and hysteria would lead to public disorder. Actual disruptive behavior seems to have been minimal. The few descriptions of some marauding and vandalism by bands of nobles and ne'er-do-wells do not create the impression that domestic tranquillity was unusually disturbed.[17]

After two weeks of interrogation, Ravaillac was put to death. It was the dreadful death of a regicide, carried out within sight of thousands of citizens. So vengeful were the latter, it is said, that they almost assaulted a priest who tried to utter a final prayer for mercy over the dying man.

Aside from the penalty inflicted upon Ravaillac, the immediate peripheral effects of the crime itself were rather limited. Copies of Juan de Mariana's works on tyrannicide were burned by order of the Paris court. Some Jesuit refuges were closed temporarily. The family of Ravaillac was exiled from the realm, and its name forbidden to French descendants.[18]

16. The events leading up to the coronation and the King's apprehensions are reported firsthand by Bassompierre, *Journal,* I (Paris, 1870), pp. 272–273.

17. Malherbe, who had feared disorder, notes the tranquillity of Paris a few days after the murder—"as though no change had taken place." *Op. cit.,* p. 173.

18. The connection between the wish to implicate more culprits than the assassin alone and the proceedings against subversive political works is made by a witness: "After the punishment of the detestable Ravaillac . . . the other concern of the people was with the . . . accomplices that he was thought necessarily to have had, it being inconceivable . . . that such a blow could be planned by only one man without being strengthened from without, either by some evil person or by the teaching of turbulent and abominable writings. . . ." Bernard, *op. cit.,* I, p. 10.

The workings of the judicial process—chiefly through torture of the assassin—had revealed no conspiracy. Ravaillac consistently denied that he had accomplices. From other sources, there were hints of complicity on the part of a former mistress of the King and complicity also by some of the King's associates. These charges were dismissed after a rather lengthy and seemingly thorough investigation by the Parliament.[19]

Long-term political effects are less easy to judge. In the years of Marie de Médicis' regency that ensued French foreign policy was marked by temporization and by increased conciliation of the papacy and the Habsburg powers. There were fewer fraternal links with the Protestant powers of Europe than had been the fashion under Henri IV. On the domestic scene, there was a growing failure of royal control to prevail over the nobility, especially the Protestants. From the third estate came increasingly open criticism of the crown. The finances of the kingdom relapsed into disorder, and the gains achieved by Sully were lost. In these respects, therefore, it could be said that the "policy goals" of Ravaillac, the King's assassin, were implemented. A decade later, however, Louis XIII reached his majority. Thereafter, and especially with the commencement of his collaboration with Richelieu, the policy changes temporarily effected by the removal of Henri IV were decisively nullified.[20]

2. *Abraham Lincoln.* On April 14, 1865, John Wilkes Booth gained entrance to Abraham Lincoln's box at Ford's Theater in Washington and shot the President through the back of the head. Brandishing knife as well as pistol, the assassin dropped to the stage and made his escape through the wings. Lincoln died early next morning. Rumors that a simultaneous assault had been perpetrated against the Vice-President proved to be unfounded. The Secretary of State, knifed by another attacker, was reported in serious condition, which was an exaggeration.[21]

Although a serious attack had previously been made upon

19. Mousnier, *op. cit.,* pp. 32–42.
20. For a summary description of the state of the realm between 1610 and 1630, see the essay by Gerard Walter in Georges Mongrédien, *La Journée des Dupes* (Paris: Gallimard, 1961), pp. xi–xxiv.
21. Clara E. Laughlin, *The Death of Lincoln* (New York: Doubleday and Page, 1909), pp. 67–115.

Andrew Jackson, the murder of Lincoln was the first presidential assassination scheme to succeed. It is worth noting that "Old Hickory" was the last occupant of the office before Lincoln to have infused it with a significant charismatic appeal as well as demonized it. Rumors of assassination plots against Lincoln were plentiful. Almost from the time of his nonimation as the Republican candidate, he became the target of intense hostility, as realization grew that he represented the probable triumph of a policy hostile to slavery. As President-elect, his first journey to Washington was made with extreme precautions to assure his safety from ambushes feared along the way.[22]

At the time of his murder, Lincoln was dealing with the capitulation of Southern military forces with political sagacity and in conciliatory ways. His plan was to reintegrate the South into the Union with a minimum of residual animosity, and to defer until the accomplishment of reunion the imposition of requirements to insure the protection of blacks. Against the factions in Congress and within his own cabinet, which urged a more punitive attitude and called for the colonization of the South by Northern military and civil organizations, Lincoln's strategy was one of evasion and diversion. In private conferences, he authorized his generals to accept their Southern counterparts' surrender of arms with a minimum of conditions. To give credence to the view that his aims were pacific rather than vengeful and to encourage the feeling that the opportunity existed for harmonizing intersectional relations in good time, Lincoln freely visited the late centers of resistance.[23]

John Wilkes Booth, the murderer of Lincoln, was twenty-seven at the time of his crime. He was the third surviving son of a family of actors. His father had been a famous Shakespearean performer in England as well as in the United States and had settled in the countryside near Baltimore to raise his American family. The two elder brothers of John Wilkes Booth as well as the husband of his older sister early rose to eminence as actors, but the younger brother did not fare so well. He acquired a reputation for theatri-

22. Norma B. Cuthbert, ed., *Lincoln and the Baltimore Plot* (San Marino, Calif.: Huntington Library, 1949).

23. Reinhard H. Luthin, *The Real Abraham Lincoln* (Englewood Cliffs, N.J.: Prentice-Hall, 1960), pp. 577–605. See also Edelman and Simon's chapter which preceeds this one for a review of Lincoln's policies and their implications.

cal heroics and acrobatics—emulating his father's eccentricities but not the older man's outstanding skills. At the age of nineteen, he tried his luck in the South, where his style was more congenial to the theatergoer. When the Civil War began, he was once again in the North. For a time he had some minor stage successes in provincial towns, but he was still unable to capture favorable endorsements from metropolitan critics. Openly sympathetic with the South, he was apparently not taken seriously by his Unionist family.[24]

Booth's affiliations with pro-Confederacy societies in the North seem to have been less important in the germination of his plan to kill Lincoln than his talent for securing a loyal personal following from men and women of limited judgment and experience. To his followers, Booth at first described his plot against the President as a kidnaping scheme. It was to be the means for bringing the North to concur in Southern demands. In this same period, however, Southern resistance reached a point of total collapse. Given Booth's temperament, it is not hard to understand why he transformed an abortive kidnaping plot into a theatrical murder and stage-leaping escape.[25]

Lincoln's assassination caused bitter recriminations. Northern opinion leaders, even some of those who had kept passion in check throughout the actual civil hostilities, treated the assassination as an awful revelation of the South's true nature; all its representatives were damned as irredeemable. The funeral train bearing Lincoln's body to Springfield, Illinois, wound a slow and circuitous trail through the major urban centers of the East and Midwest. It became a focal point in community after community—and perhaps it was contrived as such by certain members of the Union administration—for outbursts of oratory against Southern iniquity

24. A history of the family of Lincoln's assassin is to be found in Lloyd Lewis, *Myths after Lincoln* (New York: Readers' Club, 1941), pp. 131–175.

25. It was undoubtedly only in his imagination that Booth acted as an agent of the Southern political elite. The evidence against real Confederate complicity is summarized in Laughlin, *op. cit.,* pp. 205–210. Booth's self-delusion is found to be like those of recently studied would-be assassins of American presidents. Such "volunteers" have been seen as identifying with "pseudocommunities" rather than actually instigating groups. Edwin A. Weinstein and Olga G. Lyerly, "Symbolic Aspects of Presidential Assassination," *Psychiatry,* 31 (February, 1969), pp. 1–11; and Part II of this volume.

and demonstrations of solidarity behind the most vengeful Northern factions. In many localities, rumors spread that local copperheads were rejoicing at Lincoln's murder; some suspects were attacked by mobs. In New York, a Negro group asserted its rightful place in the funeral parade.

These disturbances were short-lived and exaggerated. Fears that the draft-riot troubles of 1863 would be renewed did not prove justified. Throughout the North, most cases of violence linked to the aftermath of Lincoln's assassination were of limited seriousness.[26]

Booth was hunted for twelve days. When he was apprehended, an overzealous noncommissioned army officer shot him dead. Eight alleged fellow conspirators were tried by a military commission in June; all were found guilty. Four were condemned to hang, and the sentences were duly executed. Among them was Mary Surratt, the mother of a supposed conspirator who made his escape abroad. John Surratt was eventually arrested and his trial was undertaken, but he was never penalized for his part in the conspiracy.

The mass trial and the hangings raised serious questions about American processes of criminal justice. The demands for speedy revenge and expiation were said to have overridden standards of judicial fairness and objectivity. Capital punishment of a woman, against whom many felt there had been an incomplete and unconvincing case for complicity in the murder plans, provoked much criticism. The motives of War Department members were questioned, especially those of Secretary Stanton. Doubts and second thoughts were increased by evidence produced in John Surratt's trial—a diary kept by Booth—that had not been presented at the earlier trial of eight.[27]

Even the lapse of more than a century has failed to quiet a

26. Victor Searcher, *The Farewell to Lincoln* (New York: Abingdon Press, 1965). In reviewing this book, Harris L. Dante emphasizes the extent to which the funeral train "inspired hatred for the South, bitterness against the Democrats and loyalty for the Republican party." *American Historical Review,* 71 (October, 1965), p. 318.

27. For a vindication of Mary Surratt, see David M. Dewitt, *The Assassination of Abraham Lincoln* (New York: Macmillan, 1909). On the nature of legal proceedings relating to assassinations, consult Crotty's review in the opening chapter of this book.

persistent volume of speculation about Lincoln's murder. For decades after the event, a plethora of publications appeared canvassing every aspect of the assassination and catering to every conceivable angle from sectional-plot disclosures to necrophiliac details. In recent years, too, investigators continue to pour over new selections of scattered facts, formerly only given passing consideration, which suggest fresh and invidious interpretations of the true identity and hidden motives of the criminals, their subsequent fate, and so forth. For example, suspicion of complicity in the assassination has been cast upon the Jesuits, the Secretary of War, the head of the Secret Service, the Vice-President, the Knights of the Golden Circle, General Grant, and others. Careful and sober historians concede that much mystery still surrounds the details both of the murder plot and its implementation.[28]

Andrew Johnson, the new President, was reputed to be sympathetic to the South's rehabilitation. But he lacked the personal esteem and political skill on which his predecessor's influence among the political elite had in part been based. Johnson was unable either to restrain Congress or to control his own administration. Lincoln's death, like Jackson's withdrawal from the political scene, presaged a long period of decline in the influence of the presidency.[29]

3. Mohandas Gandhi. On January 30, 1948, Mohandas K. Gandhi was shot to death in Delhi on his way to a prayer meeting. The leader of India's independence movement was flanked on either side by members of his household, as the assailant approached from the midst of a group that had been observing

28. One writer appears to believe Stanton was behind the conspiracy. See Otto Eisensehual, *Why Was Lincoln Murdered?* (Boston: Little, Brown, 1937). A follower of this author who elaborates on Colonel Baker's (of the Secret Service) part in the plot is Shelton Vaughn, *Mask for Treason* (Harrisburg, Pa.: Stackpole Books, 1965). The Jesuits and the Roman Catholic Church are implicated in Emmett McLaughlin, *An Inquiry into the Assassination of Abraham Lincoln* (New York: Lyle Stuart, 1963), p. 19. The Knights of the Golden Circle are held to account by Isola Forrester, *This One Mad Act* (Boston: Hale Cushman and Flint, 1937). A review of the courtroom testimony in the trial of persons accused of complicity in the assassination is to be found in David E. Harold, *The Assassination of President Lincoln* (New York: Funk & Wagnalls, 1954).

29. James Barber discusses the special handicaps of Johnson in maintaining Lincoln's role. See "Adult Identity and Presidential Style: The Rhetorical Emphasis" (Yale Papers in Political Science, No. 30, n.d.).

Gandhi's slow progress. Ten days earlier, another man's attempt to kill Gandhi had failed; this time murder was done.[30]

Acute grief and deprivation were felt by many Indians, both Hindu and Moslem. Nehru, himself suffering a sense of shock and loss, went on the air to console his countrymen and to admonish them to follow the Mahatma's lead. He urged them to conciliate potentially hostile groups and seek nonviolent resolution of communal conflicts.[31]

At the time of his death, Gandhi held no governmental position. The question of succession in office did not arise. Nor did the unique informal role he had been playing call for a successor. One of his last tasks had been that of negotiating with the British governor-general about the end of the British Raj. In these discussions, the partition of India had been projected—and agreed to. Gandhi's efforts influenced the Congress party to accept the inevitability of a Moslem Pakistan separate and apart from largely Hindu India. The ending of the colonial regime had been accompanied by widespread and sustained communal rioting; for months Gandhi's efforts had been directed toward the reconciliation of the warring religious groups.[32]

Gandhi's funeral procession to the banks of the Jumna River was an occasion for emotional outpourings from millions of spectators. And while shops, offices, and homes of those in the Hindu nationalist group to which the assassin belonged were invaded and left in ruin as expressions of rage at the deed done to the pacific leader, such depredations seem to have been largely local and disorganized.[33]

The murderer was N. K. Godse, the editor of a small Mahasabha newspaper. Described by the press as a "fanatical" Hindu, Godse apparently had been particularly outraged by Gandhi's sympathy for Moslems in Delhi who had been subjected to violence by Hindu activists. To help these victims, Gandhi had been fasting and attending meetings. Along with several supposed accomplices, Godse was immediately taken into custody.[34]

---

30. Geoffrey Ashe, *Gandhi* (New York: Stein & Day, 1968), pp. 380–385.
31. *Keesing's Contemporary Archives*, VI (1946–1948), 9077.
32. Pyarelal Nair, *Mahatma Gandhi: The Last Phase*, II (Abmedabad: Navajivan, 1958), pp. 686–746.
33. *Keesing's Archives, loc. cit.*, 9137.
34. *Ibid.*, 9077.

The trial of Godse and his accused co-conspirators before a magistrate began in early June and lasted until year's end. In his defense, Godse professed to have felt respect for Gandhi's "saintliness."[35] At the same time, he had been convinced that Gandhi's policies of conciliation and communal tolerance were bringing "sufferings and ruin to millions of Hindus." Moreover, they were now leading to the partition of India; within her former borders Pakistan was to be created. Godse had acted "as a dutiful son of Mother India," he declared. In removing Gandhi from this world, he denied the help of any accomplices. He took full responsibility for the murder: "I thought it my duty to put an end to the . . . so-called father of the nation who had played a very prominent part in bringing about the vivisection of the country."[36]

The trial resulted in a sentence of death for Godse and for two others. For most of the rest, lighter sentences were imposed, and charges were dismissed against one defendant. Not until November, 1949, were the executions carried out.[37]

There is little evidence that Hindu-Pakistani conflict at the "international" level or religious hostilities at the "local" level were significantly exacerbated by the assassination of Gandhi and its sequelae. Long-term effects are asserted but not readily demonstrated. One writer has suggested, for example, that the martyrdom of Gandhi was essential to the perpetuation of his ideals.[38] On the other hand, a Western journalist at an anniversary occasion honoring Gandhi twenty-one years later found his example "revered" but "irrelevant" to the problems of contemporary India.[39]

The removal of Gandhi by assassination left no void officially in the Indian political hierarchy. His influence was primarily moral and informal; it was exercised not by domination but by setting examples. Albert Einstein commented, "Generations to come, it may be, will scarce believe that such a one as this ever in flesh and blood walked upon this earth."[40] The Indian leader himself gave

35. *Ibid.,* VII, 10114.
36. *Annual Register* (London: Longmans, Green, 1948), p. 130.
37. *Keesing's Archives,* VII, 10349.
38. Pyarelal, *op. cit.,* pp. 781–783.
39. Joseph Lelyveld, "In the Mahatma's Centenary Year," *New York Times Magazine,* May 25, 1969, pp. 27–64.
40. Quoted in *Ashe, op. cit.,* p. xi.

signs of sharing this belief that his influence would be felt most strongly after his death.[41]

Gandhi's leadership was paralleled on the official level by Nehru, his close friend. Gandhi's death did not mark a significant milestone in the transformation of the Indian political elite. Rather, it was the disappearance of Nehru that seemingly did so:

Nehru's passing will make the end of an era for India. The last great charismatic leader from the generation that wrested independence from Britain will have gone. A new generation subject to the normal mechanics of Indian political life will come to power.[42]

Thus India's leadership "came of age" only after Nehru's death, in the sense that its key figures thereafter owed not only their origins but their early formation and education almost entirely to indigenous influences.

THE EFFECTS OF ASSASSINATION

In sketching the events surrounding any political murder, certain common features require attention. By an act of purposive violence, a leader has been slain. On the one hand, changes in the configuration of leadership and in the continuity of public policies seem likely. On the other hand, changes in attitude are to be expected in the wake of heightened levels of insecurity and mutual distrust that tend to emerge both in elite and public sectors. Political assassinations affect both practices and attitudes at various removes from the criminal scene.

Certain direct and practical results occur whenever a key public figure is removed from the scene. Like other "sudden-death" situations, assassination causes a sequence of personnel changes to occur, and a range of policies are affected in tempo, scope, and form. Not only is there a leadership void to be filled, but it is also true that the political careers of associates and functionaries are perforce rechanneled.

There are other ways of changing personnel and securing new

41. Francis Watson, *The Trial of Mr. Gandhi* (London: Macmillan, 1969), p. 275. There is abundant evidence of Gandhi's preparation for martyrdom.

42. Welles Hangen, "Succession and Personalities in India," *Journal of International Affairs* 18 (1964), pp. 21–22.

policy directions. Assassination—because it is an act of criminal violence—is treated as having distinctive effects. Yet no adequate appreciation of its significance as a political phenomenon is possible without canvassing those effects that assassination largely shares with other "sudden-removal" effects in political life: accidents, physical collapse, expulsion, unexpected electoral defeat, and so forth. In the wake of such events leaders must act. Practical problems must be faced whenever a key public figure is removed from the stage—by whatever means—and the problems are most immediately thrust upon those at the apex of the political hierarchy. Even when the removal involves murder, the practical problems of personnel and policy are largely the same.

Yet assassination is by definition purposive murder, whether it is the retributive act of a vengeful fanatic or the strategic crime of an elite faction bent on dislodging entrenched rivals and thus changing the course of major public policies. Emotional adjustments have to be made by those who watch the public stage. The fallen leader must be symbolically replaced. Whatever historical and social forces he has exemplified will probably lose the distinctive focus they have had. His successor will have his own style. In the public mind, he too will come to stand for some unique configuration of ideas, attributes, habits, and interests. The forces epitomized by the assassinated leader have been interrupted in their course. The criminal act by which the interruption has been caused underscores the crisis of legitimacy that is posed.

Nor is it only the psychological difficulties about accepting a new leader that create public tension. Mutual suspicions, group hostilities, doubts about the efficacy of channeling one's private aggressions onto political targets—these too are escalated in the wake of assassination.

Uncertainty and apprehension heighten the possibility of hasty elite actions, prompted both by a desire to reaffirm mutual solidarity and a wish to fill a power vacuum. Discharge of tensions can be vented on scapegoats as readily as on the guilty. Punishment for the crime is called for; it is necessary to show that justice will be done by the reconstituted ranks of authority. Appropriate obsequies for the dead men are expected throughout the nation. Some of those who mourn are suspected of being secretly exultant at the leader's departure; willy-nilly, all those whose political prospects have improved by his removal find themselves in some sense on the assassin's side.

No analytical model exists as yet for systematically examining the effects of assassination on the practices and attitudes of elites and the wider public. Nor can a comprehensive survey of their myriad ingredients be undertaken here. In what follows, a paradigm of significant aspects to be included in such analysis is first outlined. Thereafter, to indicate the range of variation possible within the framework for inquiry, the cases of assassination thus far considered as well as other materials on assassination are briefly reviewed.

A. PRACTICES

Practical consequences follow any assassination. For the most part, these effects seem to be shaped by elite actions, including the tactical moves of rival factions. But elite actions are also based on expectations about public responses. Leaders appraise public sentiments as indicators of dispositions to act in the future. Such responses as riots, processions, assaults, etc., in turn shape subsequent events and must be considered in the category of practical effects.

An analytical approach to the study of the effects of assassination can focus in turn on the perpertrator of the crime, the victim, the victim's colleagues and associates, interest-group representatives, and unorganized actors among the public. These actors contribute in various ways to the kinds of practical effects that occur.

1. Assassins. The identity and characteristics of the perpetrators of the crime radically affect the practical consequences. Particularly important in the immediate aftermath is the assassin's political proximity to the centers of power. If he is part of a faction within the ruling group, a *coup d'état* may be signaled. If he belongs to a fringe group somehow affiliated with the political opposition forces, his act may with varying plausibility be represented as a conspiracy rather than an act of criminal caprice.

Depending on how the assassin was recruited—whether voluntarily, or as a chosen instrument, or through solicitation channels involving organized groups—many practical features in the aftermath of the crime have a different appearance. For example, the choice of targets for "passionate" assassinations is probably quite different from the targets for "calculated" assassinations. Again, the consequences for all affected by the event probably hinge in significant ways on the strategic skills wielded by the assassin, his co-conspirators and his supporters.

2. Victims. Various attributes of the victim significantly shape the political consequences of his death. If the leader held a formal post, recruitment of a successor is necessary. If the dead leader's personal qualities importantly magnified his influence, not only is an interruption in the continuity of decision making inevitable, but it is then also true that a power vacuum is created. However easy it is to designate his "legitimate" successor, it is difficult to transfer to him the sentiments of personal allegiance to the fallen figure that have been engendered. Moreover, apart from formal role replacement, the social and historical "forces" for which the victim stood are temporarily in eclipse. The sudden termination of the symbolic role of a political personage thus can create urgent practical problems of "carrying on" for the surviving members of his entourage.

3. Associates. For the slain leader's colleagues and key subordinates, his death may portend policy shifts and personnel changes upon which they can exercise some influence. For them, the practical consequences of the assassination presumably depend on how prepared they were for the ensuing emergency. Complicity in the event, of course, implies complete foreknowledge. In such cases, presumably plans are ready to be executed in accordance with a strategy already fixed upon.

Yet for certain members of the leadership group not party to any conspiracy, tactical means designed to frustrate such plans may also be in readiness. A conspiracy may be neutralized, counteracted, or rechanneled. All degrees of contingency planning are possible. The state of preparation in specialized elite circles (e.g., military, diplomatic, bureaucratic) may be quite unrelated to foreknowledge of actual murder plans.

4. Interest representatives. Removal of a particular individual from the public arena not only rearranges the power relations among elite individuals. It also threatens the balance existing among mutually supporting and antagonistic population segments and interest sectors. Whether interest-group representatives act directly, through bargaining and persuasion processes, or simply reflect the aroused state of their rank-and-file members, articulating the claims and goals of the group, their interaction during the aftermath of an assassination period may have the net effect either of redistributing or reaffirming the community-wide influence-distribution pattern in ways set in motion by the assassination. A particular alignment of support underlies any power holder; his disappearance inescapably holds the potential for practical changes in such "support configurations."

5. *Unorganized actors.* In addition to possible realignments of the organized forces influencing the political system, assassinations may precipitate more or less spontaneous operations among unorganized persons. Riots, assaults on representatives of the legal order, or spokesmen for the antilegal order, or fellow members of a fringe group implicated in the crime, demonstrations and crowd phenomena are often features of postassassination periods. For the most part, such behavior is appropriately considered for its attitudinal aspects. But it has practical effects as well. Leaders engaged in a struggle for power and legitimation assess and try to influence the public responses to the violent loss of a central figure. At the same time, the immediate public manifestations probably set up patterns that determine the scope of practical effects in some significant measure.

B. ATTITUDES

A study of practical consequences stemming from political murders tends to focus on the apex of the elite hierarchy affected, attention to attitudes extends the scope of our inquiry to the wider public. At the elite level, initial attitudinal responses to an assassination are difficult to treat separately and hence become part of the "practical effects" to be examined. Delayed attitudinal responses by elite personnel are more readily treated in tandem with those of the wider public. An added complication arises because attention must be divided. At times, the public is seen as the object and target for communications intended to evoke, revamp, or direct popular attitudes; at other times, the public itself is the source of communications deeply affecting the public mood generated in the aftermath period.

1. Assassins. Identifying the criminal, explaining his act, and bringing him to justice are tasks that the public expects the elite to perform. Those implicated as perpetrators of the crime may appear to the public as social isolates or as conspirators within the political elite itself. In all cases, wherever they fall along this spectrum, the crisis of legitimacy that is created by the political murder can be measured by the credence the public gives to the official explanation for the crime. The explanation in turn is provided largely by the drama surrounding the investigation, the trial, and the punishment of those implicated in the crime.

2. Victims. The public image of the victim is of prime significance in assessing the attitudinal responses of the public to his assassination. Public participation in funerary observances takes a variety of forms, each of which indicates some facet of the emotions aroused by the death of the victim. Has the cause for which the victim stood also been lost with his death? Is his departure felt as a personal deprivation? If so, has it diminished the self which had derived vicarious satisfaction from identifying with the leader? Or does the loss bring grief like that experienced when a loved one dies? In the obsequies that ensue, the role of the victim is articulated in various ways. The consensus or disagreement concerning that terminated role can be shaped in significant degree by the rituals of public mourning.

3. Associates. In the aftermath of assassination, public attention is drawn to those who were the colleagues and key subordinates of the fallen leader. Public suspicion may implicate some of them in the crime. Some are likely to be turned to as figures who can cope with dangerous possibilities created by the event. Others among them may be seen as potential successors, either in a formal sense or as new champions of the victim's cause.

The attitudinal responses of the associates themselves are often extreme. The crime itself may inspire mutual distrust; the sudden death of their colleague will bring shock and dismay to some while to others its significance will lie in the public purposes and private interests that are placed in jeopardy. These strong reactions in turn may condition their appraisal of the public response. Apprehension of public disorder and fear for their own safety may lead the associates to precipitate countermeasures. Or their capacity to act may be frozen by anxieties.

4. *Interest representatives.* Organized groups and their representatives play significant roles in the public arena by labeling and interpreting the assassination. In the days that follow, the public gives special heed to spokesmen for groups with which they identify. Thus these interest representatives are in a position to challenge or to support the official version of the crime and the adequacy of the steps taken to cope with its aftermath. When a public figure without official position whose role has made him the exponent for a significant population segment is the victim of assassination, representatives of the group or interest sector are likely to be especially critical in their evaluation of the officials who must act to invoke the machinery of justice.

5. *Unorganized actors.* Both group representatives and self-appointed spokesmen for subcommunity groupings try—in the aftermath of an assassination—to guide and normalize the responses of their constituents. But spontaneous public responses to the collectively experienced event of political murder often take unplanned forms. An assassination can at times strengthen a community's level of mutual confidence, as when the whole community is genuinely saddened by the event and united in condemnation of its author. More commonly, the event weakens public attitudes of mutual confidence. Widespread signs of disorientation and/or privatization are commonly reported after an assassination. This kind of unmanaged reaction pattern to the commonly witnessed murder is difficult to trace. Popular sentiments focus almost capriciously on visible targets; patterns of "acting out" may vary from group to group and may take forms that only obscurely relate to the assassination that "triggered" them. Diffuse changes in beliefs and expectations about political leadership often appear to be punctuated by the stark event of murder; such changes are discernible only from a historical perspective, yet contemporaries often seem cognizant of them and mark them as changes associated with traumatic and evil deeds.

APPLICATIONS OF THE ANALYTICAL SCHEMA

Along these lines, then, systematic study of the factors determining the political effects of assassination can usefully proceed. Assassinations, in a dramatistic sense, are inevitably comparable.

In such comparisons, the crucial differences will emerge as differences between types of assassins, of victims, of associates, of group representatives and of publics. At this stage, it is not possible to isolate "practical" from "attitudinal" effects in a rigorous way. But it may be possible, in reviewing the cases of assassination recounted earlier, to invoke an analytical paradigm that will help to identify significant variations.

1. Assassins. Lincoln, Henri IV and Gandhi were killed by nonelite figures. In each case, the assassin was a man who did not belong to the political or social elite and who could not expect to share directly in the management of practical affairs in the aftermath of his crime. All three assassins murdered for "political" reasons, that is, their crime was rationalized in terms of the victim's political role.

A continuum is suggested. At one extreme is the wronged wife or jealous lover who unpremeditately murders the public figure out of a sense of personal injury. At the other, the murder is engineered by a clique within the ruling group which expects to seize the victim's power for itself. In between are several variants. One consists of "acts of revenge and despair without any hope of bettering existing conditions," as Oscar Jaszi says in characterizing the shooting of the Grand Vizier of Turkey in 1921 by an Armenian student seeking vengeance for his family's murder.[43] These acts are apparently not without political rationalization, but they are unrelated to a pattern of anticipated political consequences.

Another variant is illustrated by our three vignettes; in each instance, the assassin was intensely preoccupied with political events and actors. But his concern was unaccompanied by any realistic expectation of benefits to his cause or his co-conspirators that might flow from his deed. A third variant is the assassination that forms part of a planned *coup d'état,* in which, however, the actual perpetrator is not the leader but only a figure who sacrifices himself for the sake of his cause.

Within the category of "conspiratorial assassinations," in which all participants expect to share in power once the victim is dis-

43. Oscar Jaszi and John D. Lewis, *Against the Tyrant* (Glencoe: The Free Press, 1957), p. 169.

lodged, widely different kinds of personalities are potential participants. "Does not, in fact, the history of political murders prove
that there are no exceptions to the crimes which men may do, and
prosper in consequence of doing?"[44] Intensive work might dis-
close uniformities in the personal characteristics of those who
wield the murder weapon, but attention by scholars has tended to
focus rather on the social characteristics of the people who were
"involved" in the web of conspiracy.

Nevertheless, there are communities and states within which the
incidence of assassinations is so high as to make it a common—if
not the main—mechanism of elite change. In such polities, what
happens to the norms of moral inhibition that usually operate to
exclude certain psychological types from taking part in assassination plans? Presumably, such inhibitions lose their force in polities
where no tradition of change by peaceful means under constitutional rules exists and where political alignments rule out significant participation by highly politicized groups with status and
influence heretofore unchallenged. Under such circumstances, the
primacy of the question "who governs?" has seemed so important
that the scruples of even illustrious and "representative" men have
been overridden. The conspiracy against Julius Caesar by those
who wished the Roman Republic well is a much-dramatized case in
point.

In modern circumstances, the study of assassins has tended to
focus on their social, economic, and skill positions rather than on
their personalities. To those particularly interested in assassination
as a pivotal event in a *coup d'état* sequence that has recurred in
numerous, formerly colonial territories, the location of a network
of conspirators within either military or civil bureaucracies, their
technological training and the "professional ethic" generated
within such elite institutions become questions of special significance. By contrast, the personal characteristics of the "hero-
assassin" who volunteers to kill the tyrant has attracted considerable attention from historians, albeit such studies have yielded
inconclusive results. Yet the consequences can be great that flow
from the "recruitment process" by which an assassin is chosen to

---

44. Herbert Haines, *History and Assassination* (London: Royal Historical Society Transactions, 1889), p. 301.

act on behalf of conspirators bent on seizing state power. Both the efficiency and the realism of the person designated for the task can be of crucial importance. Patterns of success or failure in plotting to eliminate a ruthless leader like Hitler hinge at the last moment on the character of the assassin.

In contrast with assassins whose actions are part of a planned *coup d'état* are those outside the ruling circles who cannot reasonably expect to share personally in the personnel changes or policy revisions resulting from the murder they committed. Such were the assassins of Lincoln, Henri IV, and Gandhi. All three were self-recruited individuals from outside the political elite. Without direct access to the inner circles of leadership, Booth, Ravaillac, and Godse each chose a public place for the scene of his crime. In each case, the assassin was called a "fanatic" as a way of characterizing the weak or ephemeral conspiratorial group to which he may have belonged, as a way of emphasizing the "lone-wolf" nature of his voluntary action, and as a way of denoting the apparently spontaneous concatenation of events leading to the crime.

In all three of these cases, the mechanism through which private rage was murderously displaced onto a public figure seems to have involved rationalizing in ideological terms the supposed dangers to which the marked leader was exposing the community. The public figure selected by each of these assassins was charged with betrayal of a beloved object—the South, the church, the papacy, the mother country. The target figure was seen in each case as threatening the precious symbol with "vivisection," "prostitution" or similar defilement and violence. The assassin pictured himself protecting the endangered object from a would-be assailant.

Recent studies have suggested that a set of pattern variables may exist that is characteristic of men who entertain murderous fantasies focused upon figures of political authority. Evidence is inconclusive whether or not those who act out such fantasies are fundamentally different from those who merely entertain them. However, Rothstein has called attention to personality syndromes of real president murderers—Oswald and Guiteau—which he found were paralleled by ten cases of president threateners under his intensive professional observation. In most of these cases, evidence of pre-Oedipal rage against a maternal figure was prominent. Failure to resolve this infantile frustration was reflected in the tendency to displace affect onto political objects. Paranoid fantasies of conspiracies against the self represent in part, Rothstein suggests, maternally inspired doubts about one's own masculinity. Thus assassination becomes a means by which the longings from within the self for passive surrender and dependency may be counteracted through a complete diversion of one's bad tendencies onto a public figure. The latter is then seen as a generalized threat whose elimination will not only resolve the inner struggles of the assailant but will also rescue the populace at large from an enemy of all things good and pure.[45]

The questions of how many potential assassins goaded by motivational tensions of this kind are to be found in various communities and population segments within a modern polity is of course difficult to establish empirically. It has been suggested that patterns of politicization and simultaneous family disorganization are sufficiently common in urban places in advanced societies that it is probable that the incidence of such personality types is increasing. If so, one obvious response may be to change the methods of political-leadership protection, and this in turn could significantly affect the incidence of the events themselves. Intimate and almost continual contact with a large entourage of only partly screened subjects was the common practice for seventeenth-century rulers. This pattern has increasingly given way in the present century to formalized and carefully staged contacts between citizens and top leaders under extensive organized security rules.

At the same time, however, access to effective means of wielding long-distance violence has also substantially increased. In modern times techniques of approach by stealth and subterfuge have been improved as well. Thus even without any increase in the incidence of potential "spontaneous assassins" found among the public at large, affluence and the presence of advanced technology seem to have the effect of increasing the hazard of assassination for every conspicuous political figure. Apprehensions of this problem are

45. David Rothstein, "The Presidential Assassination Syndrome," *Archives of General Psychiatry*, 11 (1964), pp. 245–254; 15 (1966), pp. 260–266, and in the extended analysis in this volume. The Freedman and Greening commentaries are also relevant in this regard.

likely to lead to stringent and comprehensive measures of leadership protection quite different from any practiced in earlier times.

However adequate an explanation is in the aftermath of an assassination to account for the deed is always problematic. The victim's successors, anxious to enhance their legitimacy and that of the regime itself, typically make strenuous efforts to apprehend the assassin and his cohorts, if any. The whole sequence of steps taken to see that "justice is done" probably has a distinctive character when dealing with a "spontaneous assassin" rather than a "conspiratorial assassin." In the latter cases, especially when the plot implicates an inner-circle clique, explanation runs in terms of power and group interests. In the former cases, on the other hand, explanation must center on pathological needs and must cut through ideological rhetoric. Probably it is always more difficult to "convince" the attentive public that everyone who was party to a conspiracy has been brought to book than to quiet public doubts about the guilt of a "mad fanatic."

Symptoms of social pathology become most apparent in the aftermath of an assassination when irregularities interrupt the already slow judicial processes of an assassin's capture, trial and conviction. In the case of John Wilkes Booth and of Lee Harvey Oswald, where guilt seemed obvious and motives scarcely less so, the failure to bring a live murderer before a court of justice perhaps played some part in the proliferation of cults concentrating on the arcana connected with the murders of two Presidents. "Unexplained murder has for most people some uncanny quality . . .(eliciting) pronounced psychological uncertainty."[46] By contrast, in the cases of Henri IV and Gandhi, the thorough operation of the inquiry procedures of justice that were followed probably soothed rather than exacerbated public imagination. In the latter case, the measured and prolonged inquiry featured the murderer himself giving full testimony. Still, where powerful leaders are concerned, it is doubtful if any murder is fully explained. Even small cracks in the glaze of continuity can become major flaws exposing the falsity of the official story in the minds of some.

The assassin's punishment as well seems to have potentially

46. Theodor Reik, *The Unknown Murderer,* trans. Katherine Jones (New York: Prentice-Hall, 1945), p. 232.

significant effects on public attitudes. Many historical and journalistic accounts testify to unorganized demands for vengeance against those who have criminally assaulted a beloved leader. The bloodthirstiness of the public at Ravaillac's execution is only one example. The necessity to protect Godse from being murdered by the crowd that had witnessed his assassination of Gandhi is typical; similar accounts are not uncommon of the need to restrain an angry mob from committing mayhem. The fatal assault on John F. Kennedy's assassin by an apparently distraught private citizen was witnessed by millions on American television. For many of those spectators, Ruby probably acted out their own unspoken inclinations.

The failure to bring Oswald to trial in the death of President Kennedy seems to have contributed to the undulating flow of suspicion and doubt surrounding that crime. The commission of inquiry—appointed in part to provide a trial substitute and lay doubts to rest about the crime—ironically provided additional fuel for speculations about the event.

The nineteenth-century execution of the Cato Street conspirators followed medieval prescriptions for drawing and quartering traitors. It is reported to have visibly excited many in the British public. After the public execution took place, other bizarre and bloody "private" crimes were reported, allegedly triggered by the evocation of previously repressed hostile drives which the official punishment had loosed.[47] After it was learned that Senator Robert Kennedy had been murdered by a politicized Jordanian in Los Angeles, the murder of a Jordanian grocer in Chicago was attributed by the press to a man motivated by vengeful feelings in Kennedy's behalf.[48]

After President Kennedy's murder, public attitudes toward the

47. John Stanhope, *The Cato Street Conspiracy* (London: J. Cape, 1962). See also Nieburg's discussion in an earlier chapter of this book of the "periodicity" of violent events.

48. Klagsbrun and Whitney, *op. cit.,* p. 232. A murderous attack on a young radical leader in Germany was attributed by the assailant to the example of the assassination of Martin Luther King, Jr. "I read about Dr. Martin Luther King and I said to myself, 'You must do this too'." *New York Times,* April 13, 1968. The more generalized responses of adult populations are explored in the analyses reported in the chapter by Samuel C. Patterson.

assassin and toward his self-appointed executioner were for the first time systematically studied. As might be expected, young children took a more punitive attitude toward the assassin than did adolescents or adults.[49] Among adults there is some evidence that the most extrapunitive stance was taken by people of the lowest socioeconomic status and by blacks.[50] As for Ruby's execution of Oswald, it may be that murderous intentions were stimulated by witnessing the "capital punishment" of an assassin. At the same time, it can be argued that the act of retribution served to reduce anxiety among the spectators by channeling hostility outward onto the criminal-now-victim.

Being a social isolate perhaps contributed to the tendency to focus all hostile effect on outside objects—in this case on the assassin. This proposition is consistent with Greenstein's evidence that students who relied heavily on watching television while alone were also those who expressed the most vengeful sentiments toward President Kennedy's assassin.[51] Again, it might be argued that extrapunitive attitudes are modalities in a more archaic social order. Witness the widespread accounts of mass rage against traitors and assassins in unmodernized countries of the Middle East today and in western Europe at an earlier historical stage.

2. Victim. A variety of effects follow the elimination of a public figure by violent, purposeful action. Not all of these can be distinguished from effects that would be caused by a removal that is nonviolent (such as exile, electoral defeat, automatic rotation in office, voluntary retirement) or a removal that is nonpurposeful (accidental death, fatal illness).

49. Roberta S. Sigel, "An Exploration into Some Aspects of Political Socialization: School Children's Reactions to the Death of a President," in Martha Wolfenstein and Gilbert Kliman, eds., *Children and the Death of a President* (Garden City, N.Y.: Doubleday, 1965), pp. 30–61. A finding repeated with some unusual variations in the King assassination. See Clarke and Soule's report in this volume.

50. Norman M. Bradburn and Jacob J. Feldman, "Public Apathy and Public Grief" in Bradley S. Greenberg and Edwin B. Parker, eds., *The Kennedy Assassination and the American Public* (Stanford: Stanford University Press, 1965), pp. 273–286. The attitudes of blacks toward violence and assassination are also investigated in greater depth in the McEvoy chapter earlier.

51. Fred I. Greenstein, "Young Men and the Death of a President" in Wolfenstein and Kliman, *op. cit.*, pp. 172–192.

Some consequences that flow from a political assassination seem to depend upon the public role of the victim. Was his power largely a result of official status, or was it a product of unofficial resources? Did the political developments after the murder stem from the institutional aspects of the fallen leader's role, or from more personal ones?

To the extent that a public leader's power is based exclusively on beliefs and attitudes about his personal qualities, his "power" might be said to vanish almost completely on his removal. For example, the unique quality of Gandhi's influence seems to have been almost entirely charismatic. How clearly his power was delimited by his actual personal presence is suggested by the commentary after his death in an English-language daily Indian newspaper: "During his lifetime certain rules he laid down were observed to humour the Grand Old Man. But he is no longer watching us."[52]

At the other extreme, if the fallen leader's power is derived mainly from his office and from the laws and traditions governing it, changes in policy will depend on whether a successor is able to legitimise his claim to fill the same position in the same regime. Thus it is those qualities that are personal, rather than institutional, which are in point in evaluating the "victim" as a factor influencing the aftermath of assassination.

To an extent, any termination of an exalted leader's career, whether by natural death, voluntary withdrawal, or violent elimination, widely occasions a sense of shock that mirrors the charisma that institutionalized power gives to its human bearer. Belief in the proximity of kings to God led to intimations of immortality. Those beliefs have modern counterparts in the awe that attaches to the executive chiefs of modern democratic states. The half-satisfied, half-incredulous comment, *"sic transit gloria mundi,"* was widely voiced in France after De Gaulle's final resignation in 1969. It reflected the personal quality of his authority, fused with the institutional charisma of his high office. The effects in France that are linked to the loss of his person as head of state seem great; it is difficult to imagine those effects to be greatly different had he been removed by violence.

52. Quoted by Robert H. Andrews, *Los Angeles Times,* January 21, 1970, II, 7.

It is possible that assassination is a heightened risk for certain kinds of personalities who become active in political life. If so, assassination might be shown to precipitate distinctive consequences for the polity and for its policy-making elite, consequences that would differentiate it from other forms of recruitment and removal.

Are particular types of leaders lodestones for those disposed to displace murderous impulses onto public figures? Is the assassination hazard greater for leaders who play certain kinds of public roles? Observe that our three cases were among the most conspicuous of modern times because the victims were so widely mourned for their attempts to reduce violence among their fellow citizens. Henri IV, martyred by a zealot applying the monarchical doctrine against "tyrants," was the most conciliatory and reasonable of kings, as well as the most amiable. Abraham Lincoln and Mohandas Gandhi were exceptional for strong personal controls over their own rage. All three survived fratricidal wars. All three were, at the conclusion of civil strife, leaders in reconciling the parties and in healing the breach between ideological extremes. The passive stance and conciliatoriness of these leaders is in sharp contrast with the style of numerous "tyrants of history" who consistently and almost miraculously escaped fatal assaults.

Systematic observations have suggested similarities in the life histories of actual and potential assassins. Apparently, early maternal deprivation, perhaps coincident with the mother's seeming preference for other siblings, has been followed by a period of failure to adjust to a monastic order, military service or a similar institutional refuge in a pattern that is characteristic of many such persons. Following the abortive effort to adjust to an institutional life, their rage is displaced onto political leaders. Is any special type of public figure more likely than another to be chosen as a victim by such "spontaneous assassins?" Rothstein sees his observations of mental patients with assassination intentions supported by De Grazia's findings that a political leader like Franklin Roosevelt could uniformly be seen by a group of patients in psychotherapy as a primordial maternal figure.[53]

---

53. Rothstein, *loc. cit.*, and the other citations in note 45. From a different perspective, the Crotty selection, and to a more limited extent that by Edelman and Simon, address the same point.

It is plausible that such spontaneous assassins are particularly attracted to targets who play "maternal" conciliatory roles on the political stage. This was true of all three victims in the cases briefly described here. It is perhaps also relevant that the lives of our three historic figures were linked with a condition of widespread violence. The atmosphere in which they struggled for peace was redolent of war and bloodshed on an unprecedented scale.

In recent years, public figures whose careers have been characterized in analogous ways would include such diverse political leaders as Olympio, Mboya, and Robert Kennedy. The comparable roles played by Martin Luther King, Jr., and Malcolm X might also be adduced, but they are less clearly in point, since evidence suggests an organized effort by their murderers.

When private rage is murderously displaced onto a public figure, a need arises to rationalize in ideological terms the supposed dangers to which the hated figure is exposing the community—the mother country, the true religion, the precious symbol. The assassin sees himself as protecting the endangered symbol from the public assailant. The designation "fanatic" has popularly been attached to such assassins—as much, perhaps, to characterize the moderation of their victims as the immoderation of the murderers.

If public figures who characteristically seek to conciliate warring groups run a peculiar risk of attracting a certain type of assassin, an important pattern would be identified. If those leaders most skilled in the arts of healing dangerous breaches in opinion, persuading to moderation, and pouring oil on the troubled waters of civil conflict are men who by their actions make themselves more vulnerable than others to an assassin's attack, the significance of this occupational hazard would not be negligible.

Moreover, if this selection factor operates, it could well operate negatively also. For the "fanatical" assassin, strong, cruel, and ruthless heads of state would have little appeal as victims.

As for policy consequences in the wake of "spontaneous assassinations," presumably the most probable result is an increase in the polarization of opinion and policy demands that the leader selected for murder had tried to avoid. Practically, this might occur either through a weakening of moderate leadership at the institutional center, with a consequent reassertion of dissensus and social strife, or through the assumption of central authority in an arbitrary way by one of the major parties in the struggle. In our three cases, the pull of centrifugal forces on the political community was marked before the political murder took place; the assassination of a leader who had worked to conciliate and harmonize those forces could only exacerbate the conflict.

If the conciliatory "peacemaker" is liable to attract the fanatical extremist at the same time that the essence of his pacific role leaves him exposed and vulnerable to attack, the tyrant and autocrat may well have a built-in personal armor against his assailants. In addition to the institutional defenses provided by his bodyguards and his bastions, and in addition to his tactics designed to deter, confuse and expose his enemies, the tyrant has his reputation as a shield. Even when assassination is a deliberate policy adopted by a group of conspirators bent on replacing a ruthless dictator, ambivalence and hesitation may misguide the hand of the would-be tyrannicide in the presence of his implacable and conscienceless enemy. Hitler's nationally suicidal policy finally gave rise to a conspiracy aiming at his assassination. It was entered into by a set of elite figures in Germany, who were distinguished by their ability and experience in the effective management of armed violence. Yet it met with a notable lack of success, which raises the question whether the professional military conspirators may not have been unconsciously handicapped by anxieties and tensions linked to the hatred and fear that the dictator evoked. The plot against Hitler seems in retrospect to have been disastrously overelaborate. While it did not prevent its active participants from being caught and executed, it was from the beginning a less plausible way of ridding Germany of its leader than a well-placed bullet from one general officer would have been.[54] The literature on the "generals' plot" raises doubt that Hitler actually took the

54. One historian seems to draw attention to the indecision and hesitancy that appeared to plague the plotters. See Hans Rothfels, *The German Opposition to Hitler* (London: Oswald Wolff, 1961), p. 69. Stauffenberg is quoted by Trever-Roper as having said, " 'Is there no officer in the Führer's headquarters . . . capable of taking his revolver to the brute?'." Joachim Kramars, *Stauffenberg* (New York: Macmillan, 1967), p. 11. Indeed, a young officer did volunteer to shoot the dictator, and actually gained access to his presence with his revolver. Nevertheless, two historians remark, "No man visiting Hitler was allowed to carry a gun." Roger Manvell and Heinrich Fraenkel, *The July Plot* (London: The Bodley Head, 1964), p. 85.

complete precautions against assassination that his would-be murderers gave him credit for doing. Rather, the personal qualities of the detested ruler may have caused the conspirators to attribute excessive efficiency on this count to him.[55] An analogy is suggested by Rasputin's recalcitrance in the face of murderous attacks, any of which would ordinarily have been efficaciously lethal. Rasputin's apparent indestructibility would seem to be linked to the superstitious awe that his unscrupulousness encouraged even among his bitter enemies.[56] Similarly, Stalin's ability to terrorize his surviving associates may have been part of the reason why history is left with no record of attempts to eliminate him.

The sudden removal of a leader from the public arena evokes a distinctive pattern of widespread "sense of loss," which seems to be linked to the kind of role played by the leader in the mental life of audience members. Any kind of leadership elimination permits some study of the place occupied by a public figure in the private imagery of citizens. Sudden death—and especially assassination—seem to bring out most clearly the varieties of attachment that various citizens persistently have made to the central figure no longer available. One psychologist—Fritz Redl—has conceptualized the relationship between the central figure and the public in terms that highlight the intermember bonds of that public, bonds that are especially strained when the central figure is a victim of assassination.

Enlarging upon Freud's approach to the phenomenon of a public figure becoming an ego replacement for members of his group, Redl noted in his studies of group life that variations in group solidarity were linked to the emotional basis for that solidarity—whether the leader seemed primarily to be a focus of love or hate, and hence an *object* of the libido (or aggressive drives),

---

55. Manvell and Fraenkel also refer to the "strange intuitive sense of danger . . . Hitler undoubtedly possessed." (*The July Plot, op. cit.,* p. 84.) A different account has another of Hitler's enemies plotting assassination in 1942 by making use of bombs and fuses: "It would have been more to his liking to meet Hitler in the open with arms. But . . . this . . . had very little chance of success." Eberhard Zeller, *The Flame of Freedom* (Coral Gables: University of Miami Press, 1963), p. 160.
56. Leonard Gribble, *Hands of Terror* (London: F. Muller, 1960), p. 115.

or whether he was an object of identification, and hence a partial ego or superego replacement.[57]

The sudden loss of a leader by an act of violence, it can be hypothesized, will evoke responses from various segments of the public, which will reflect the relationship they bore to him, and simultaneously the relationship they bore each other *in regard to him*. When ties to the leader are suddenly severed by his violent death, they do not dangle in a vacuum. Bonds between members of the same group are placed under special strain; links between members of different groups are similarly called into question. The image of himself that has been effectively communicated by a public figure to his audience—an image that is largely a personal quality rather than a journalistic stereotype—may thus be important in analyzing the consequences of his removal by assassination.

Transferring the psychologist's observations from small-group contexts at school, at camp and in neighborhoods to the national political arena raises many difficulties. One may hypothesize, however, that the solidarity of large and loosely knit groups is initially (and perhaps persistently) reinforced by the loss of a leader widely identified with. Such a leader is one who stands *in loco parentis* in the mental imagery of many citizens. His loss is a mournful experience, but it is one that in some ways probably enhances the sense of community. The "father (or mother) of us all" is gone; one finds the orphaned children united by a grief that is shared because it is based upon a tie of kinship.

The affectionate term "Bapu" used by Nehru and many others for Gandhi designated him a leader who played this parental role. His attempts to coerce his followers peacefully into mutually harmonious relations were made through prolonged fasts that did physical harm to himself and to no others. The influence of these self-inflicted punishments depended upon the strength of the public's identification with him. It had been reported that Gandhi himself saw martyrdom as his ultimate source of power for effective leadership.

Yet there also existed a part of the Indian population for whom Gandhi was not a revered parental figure but a hated object

57. Fritz Redl, "Group Emotion and Group Leadership," *Psychiatry* 5 (November, 1942), pp. 573–596.

designing the destruction of Indian unity and the abandonment of Hindu principles. For them, his death was not an event to heighten their sense of connection with the larger community, although it may well have strengthened in-group solidarity and defensive co-operation to resist vengeful assaults from the bereaved majority.

From this viewpoint, an overall appraisal of reactions to the death of President Kennedy shows a preponderant tendency for the adult public to respond as if to the loss of a loved object—a son, husband or intimate friend—and not primarily to the loss of a person identified with. On the contrary, a parallel predominant response was for spectators to identify with the bereaved members of Kennedy's immediate family, as though the loss and grief suffered by them were one's own.[58] The public mourning response for the first time on such an occasion had been significantly shaped by television coverage, and television is a home-bound, privatized agency of communication. Yet over and beyond what information could be gleaned from home television sets, a majority of the national audience seemed to have felt a preference for isolation and for minimal communication with people outside the family.[59]

3. Associates and Successors. To the extent that a leader's choice of associates was a free choice by him, unhampered by the initiative or reaction of other power centers—interest groups, legislatures, party councils, etc.—loss of their sponsor causes those associates to be faced with precipitate loss of power. This is so whether or not their status has been legitimated formally by conferring official titles upon them. In modern democratic states, this means, among other things, that the family intimates of the dead man are left by his murder without effective formal authority. Restoration of their positions is dependent on recapture of a personal or official claim. In hereditary systems, the family members are generally the official successors; the "appointed" officeholders and counselors are the ones displaced by the leader's death. Those associates whose basis for influence is jeopardized by

58. Paul B. Sheatsley and Jacob Feldman, "A National Survey on Public Reactions and Behavior" in Greenberg and Parker, *op. cit.*, pp. 149–177; and the Patterson and Clarke and Soule contributions previously cited.

59. William A. Mindak and Gerald D. Hursh, "Television's Functions on the Assassination Weekend" in Greenberg and Parker, *op. cit.*, pp. 130–141.

the murder of a leader are displaced only to the extent that they represent interests or groupings whose position is also threatened.

In the following notes, we concern ourselves with the influence of assassination on the status and policy of associates who are either legitimate successors of the assassinated figure or competitors for his position.

Except for those associates who conspired with the murderer, and hence had guilty foreknowledge of the event, sudden death, unlike other forms of removal, leaves the successors in various states of unpreparedness. Anticipation of the natural death of an aged or ailing politician encourages his colleagues, including his successors, to fantasize the event of his death. They speculate about policy changes to come; they prepare for those changes ahead. While discussions and ruminations of this kind are not publicly staged, it is in this way that members of the elite circle "work through" in advance the grief that will be felt at the leader's loss. For them, then, the result of an "expected death" is practice in the control of emotions. When the event occurs, ceremonial activities are carried out with reduced trauma and shock.

Some surviving leaders, e.g., the heads of security forces and defense forces, are officially required to consider sudden forms of leadership removal and to take planned precautions concerning them. In the case of governments where legitimacy is a chronic problem, some members of the surviving elite closest to the military operations of the government are likely to be seen as appropriate candidates for the succession, even if this is inconsistent with the constitutional formula and even if they clearly had no basis for anticipating the event or preparing for it.

On the other hand, the disorienting effects of unexpected assassinations on the victim's legitimate successors may be disproportionately strong compared with the public's bewilderment. The very fact that potential successors have fantisized displacing the murdered leader haunts and disturbs them, leaving them disorganized when the event occurs. A sudden shift of possibilities from fantasy to reality has occurred. The elite are ill-prepared for the transfer of functions and authority. Yet since the sudden death of any figure of public responsibility is to some extent a crisis of legitimacy, the need for legitimate successors to play roles of confidence and decisiveness is proportionately greater. "Overacting" the role of leader is a possibility in such crisis situations. Policy decisions may be taken prematurely for the sake of demonstrating firmness and purposefulness. Choices of personnel also may be made with less deliberation and insightfulness than they probably would have received in the case of "anticipated removal" of the leader.

Moreover, the violence of the leader's death gives rise among his colleagues to anxieties that are often identifiable but difficult to appraise. The fear of "contagion" or of a widespread conspiracy or of a public panic may be in part apprehension stemming from the repressed thoughts of the leaders themselves, thoughts now brought closer to the surface of consciousness by the magical temptation of the "initiatory act"—an actual assassination. Repressive measures thus may be adopted by the surviving leaders in response to pressures from within themselves as well as to provocation from the outside world. The sudden reversal of values carries a nagging lesson: those with a maximum of public attention and influence can be exceptionally vulnerable to physical attack.

In cases of assassination attributed to a planned *coup d'état,* an elite that survives the event may respond by instituting policy changes represented as necessary on grounds of defending the legitimate government. Programs directed either internally or externally at the supposed conspirators may range from well-measured repression to immoderate terrorizing violence. These measures, moreover, may be applied whether or not the conspiracy was genuinely a threat to the elite's security.

The consequences that follow upon an assassination, even though its perpetrators were largely self-recruited and without influence or prospects of influence should their attack succeed, may readily be exploited by dissident forces bent upon radical change. Thus the exposure of the ridiculous Cato Street conspiracy in 1820, which apparently aimed at killing the entire British cabinet, was the starting gun for a rightward swing politically by the British elite.[60] The death of Lincoln at the hands of an allegedly Confederate-inspired cabal was exploited by that section of the Northern leadership that was determined for various reasons to ruin the South economically through punitive policies. The purge

60. Stanhope, *op. cit.,* p. 8.

of Roehm as an "arch conspirator" was the excuse by Hitler for a campaign to terrorize potential enemies through a ruthless elimination of scores of party officials.[61] The death of Kirov was the signal for the series of merciless executions and repressive acts that solidified Stalin's position as absolute ruler.[62]

Wide public responses may be separated from the immediate responses of the elite to assassinations—real, thwarted or pretended. For the political elite, such events seem often to generate the kind of atmosphere in which further violence is expected, hence normalized. Retribution for the deed need not be confined to the murderer and his immediate cohorts. The notion of a certain "magic of the initiatory act" seems relevant in seeking to account for actions taken in the wake of political murder. The series of events that were triggered by the assassination of Archduke Ferdinand at Sarajevo are not logically explained by the assassination itself. Elite claims concerning widespread public indignation are scarcely a plausible explanation for the ensuing mobilization of national armies throughout the world.

Less direct effects of assassination on the survivors who are also successors have been sketchily reported but have not been systematically analyzed for certain nonmodernized nations. In Africa, for example, one observer alludes to the consequences of assassinations as causing surviving or succeeding elite members to "pull in their horns."[63] By this is meant either a lessening of the resolution with which public policies are implemented or a loss of firmness in the way ideological commitments are affirmed, or both. Although plausible, there is little collating of evidence on this pattern. More readily subject to substantiation is the hypothesis that elimination of leaders through assassination has in African countries a more restrictive effect on later policy choices than it does in countries

61. According to the Interior Minister, many enemies of Roehm were chosen on the pretext of having been part of a planned *Putsch* by the initial victim, but actually just because they "weren't liked very well." Bornstein, *op. cit.*, pp. 95–97.

62. Hugo Dewar, *Assassins at Large* (London: Wingate, 1951), pp. 144–163.

63. Ali A. Mazrui, "Thoughts on Assassination in Africa," *Political Science Quarterly,* 83 (March, 1968), pp. 40–58. Joseph Bensman's selection in this book develops the network of ramifications these assassinations can engender.

where the elite reservoir is relatively larger and less marginal economically and socially. In a situation where political skills and talent are scarce, removal of one genuine leader is not likely to be followed by installation of a figure of comparable qualities.

Such problems of successorship are apparent even in advanced industrial countries, and especially in nongovernmental arenas— political arenas—where some contending forces have for various social and economic reasons great difficulty in recruiting enough competent leaders. Such is perhaps the case for certain clerical elites, peasant groupings, and minority ethnic and/or religious categories.

A leader's assassination may present a danger as well as an opportunity for those elite members who were competitors for his position. The danger most often derives from the possible association of former competitors with the crime. Thus Lyndon Johnson's authority as the legitimate successor to John F. Kennedy was jeopardized by the fact that at one time he had been an active political rival of the murdered President. Various fictional and popular representations of the Kennedy assassination have cast Mr. Johnson as an accomplice in the deed. Less directly, but still importantly, the position of Democratic competitors of Abraham Lincoln worsened after his assassination, although no direct evidence whatever was unearthed suggesting partisan complicity.

It is difficult to maintain that assassination can ever be a stabilizing form of "competition." The suggestion that "institutionalized" political homicide, of a kind occasionally found in Balkan countries, in Sicily and Mexico, may be consistent with a model of competitive party politics should be discounted.[64] These practices are better understood as manifestations of intertribal warfare; the concept "political assassination" would seem to lose some of its intelligibility unless it is understood to apply only to cases involving persons who share the same political community and who claim allegiance to a common political system. In countries where *coups d'état* are commonly accompanied by exile of displaced leaders rather than by their murder, the availability of the expelled leaders is a reality. Such a "presence" of potential competitors has

64. One of the most interesting accounts of such practices is Paul Friedrich, "Assumptions Underlying Tarascan Political Homicide," *Psychiatry*, 25 (November, 1962), pp. 315–327.

long been characteristic of Latin American politics; it was also common in numerous ancient polities.

On the other hand, suggestions which contend that the frequency of Middle Eastern assassinations is quite consistent with stable political systems in those countries are not convincing.[65] Even a very large supply of comparably groomed potential leaders would seem likely to be exhausted by the drain of frequent political murders. A more probable consequence would be a trend toward dictatorial rule, as an ambitious leader in one country seeks to establish his hegemony over the decimated leadership corps of the whole Middle Eastern community.

Conditions for competitive leadership selection would almost always seem to be threatened by a rise in the incidence of political murder or attempted murder.

4. Group representatives. The elimination of a public figure by violence gives rise to a rebalancing of forces supporting the political order that has been disrupted by the act. Two aspects of this disturbance need consideration. These are, first, the potential shifting of forces formerly equilibrated by the presence of the leader, and second, the possible realignment portended by the violence through which the leader was eliminated. Of these two sources of change, the first is problematic in any sudden disappearance of a leader, murdered or not; only the second is a specific aftermath of assassination.

The immediate effect of a violent, nonlegitimated act such as assassination is to thrust into prominence those agencies and group spokesmen specializing in the management of violence. Within the government this means that security officers, internal and external, receive an increased measure of attention. Organized, violent measures are directed at the assassin and his collaborators, supposed or real, and the stability of the regime may depend on the effectiveness of these measures. Nongovernmental groups occupied with the manipulation of violence may find their positions threatened or enhanced by the murder of a public figure. Vigilantism is one way in which groups controlling armed violence may increase their influence in a community as a result of assassination.

65. See Carl Leiden, "Assassination in the Middle East," *Transaction,* 6 (May, 1969), pp. 20–23.

Countermoves, i.e., efforts to control violence through public policies, may similarly result as other groups organize in defense of their "way of life." After the assassination of Robert F. Kennedy, pollster Louis Harris found an increase of ten percentage points (from 71 to 81) in the proportion of the American people who favored strict gun-control legislation.[66] To some extent, this sentiment was translated into group pressures in the national and state legislatures. To a discernible degree, in turn, the rather different sentiments of sportsmen and gun enthusiasts were also registered upon the legislative leaders.

The victim himself may be understood as a group representative. The leader eliminated by assassination had personal qualities that were doubtless important in determining his influence. At the same time, he may have been a group representative, either in some official sense or symbolically.

Assassination and other forms of unanticipated removal from office differ from electoral or deliberative replacement in that the achievement of a new political equilibrium in the absence of the once-central figure, must be effected without warning, so to speak, and during a period when the surprise of his removal keeps it in focus. Electoral defeat is evidence of a realignment that has already taken place, and which is "discovered" by the political leaders; cabinet replacement implies a reappraisal of the balance among groups in the legislature and in the country at large. Only the sudden death of a leader leaves various groups without preparation for the loss of representation or championship, and without preparation also for the unexpected opportunity thus created to augment their influence.

The removal of the leader is thus symbolic of the removal of one "representation" of historical forces. The uniqueness of this representativeness is one factor that has consequences of significance in the aftermath period. In what respect does the often-repeated statement, "We shall not see another like him," have a realistic basis? To answer this question is to describe one factor affecting the public response as well as those of colleagues, rivals and successors.

66. *Los Angeles Times*, June 23, 1968. Edelman and Simon, in particular, in the essay that precedes this one, present an admirable evaluation of the policy implications of presidential assassinations.

The disappearance of a Negro leader "born into slavery" such as Frederick Douglass may have lessened one basis for heroic leadership in the Negro community. But it also may have been a critical turning point in lightening the fettering effects of a heritage of enforced servility among the group he inspired and represented.

On the other hand, Martin Luther King, Jr., did not present himself as the "descendant of a slave." He did present himself effectively as the "son of a Christian clergyman." He was also a militant Negro leader. Although his death meant the loss of an unusually effective "militant" figure, numerous contenders for the "militant" crown appeared. In his public career, however, that militant role was fused with the role of Christian humanist. For this distinctive composite role, it was farmore difficult to find a replacement.

A different kind of fusion in roles is illustrated by Henri IV. He was the last King of France who was raised a Protestant and who included prominent Protestants in his entourage. After his death, Catholic orthodoxy became the rule for all members of the French ruling group. Official participation in the government was at an end for Protestants. But Henri IV's role as the head of the Bourbon dynasty passed readily to his son after a regency period.

We have noted that by contrast Gandhi's influence was almost entirely personal. He was by no means the only Indian leader who had been a heroic opponent of colonialism, nor the only champion of equality who derived from an upper-class stratum. Like Nehru and Jinnah, who also had these credentials and who survived him, he was educated abroad. These circumstances, coupled with his lack of an official position, combined to explain the very limited impact of his murder upon the balance of political forces within India. In spite of the profound emotional impact of his death, the assassination itself occasioned few changes in the organization of Indian politics.

5. *Unorganized actors.* The public at large responds to two aspects of an assassination—to the removal of the central figure and to the violent means by which it was achieved. These responses may be overt or invisible, directed at the self or at others, submissive or aggressive. Of the responses directed outward, the focus may be widely diffused or concentrated and channeled into predictable patterns. Immediate and spontaneous responses are

both difficult to describe systematically and hard to assess in terms of lasting effects.

After an assassination, leaders commonly fear that the public will react wildly. Panic and diffuse violence are widely anticipated, but they have often failed to materialize. Inadequate evidence about public opinion leaves doubt concerning the accuracy of historical reports of diffuse antisocial behavior in the wake of assassination. Typical of such accounts is this passage concerning popular reaction to the murder of the Austrian archduke at Sarajevo in 1913: "Assassination of the heir to the Austro-Hungarian throne had confused public opinion in all Europe, had excited the populace of Austria-Hungary and Germany to madness. . . ."[67] It is a safe assumption that "confusion" occurred; evidence of any "excitation to madness" is lacking.

That aggressive crowd behavior sometimes occurs after political murders is clear. Inaction and lethargy rather than effortful demonstration may also be the response that is widely observed. Little is known about predicting the conditions under which an assassination is a signal for mass disorder or the conditions under which the news is received passively.

The death of President Kennedy, while it was widely felt as a severe deprivation, for the most part was followed by privatized, atomistic behavior. The death of Martin Luther King, Jr., on the other hand, ushered in a week of quite extensive violence, although it was concentrated almost entirely in Negro slum districts of urban centers. More than forty deaths were somehow linked to King's murder. Many deaths happened incidental to the mass crimes against property within the ghetto areas. One investigation in Miami disclosed that the assassination of Dr. King seemed to be associated with a radicalization of former moderates.[68]

Perhaps it is not the events but rather the interpretation placed upon events by leaders that channels public response so differently. The disparate reactions to the violent and depriving event of political murder may be explained by noting when a modal interpretation is concurred in by most leaders and when many competing explanations are put forward by persons looked to for opinion leadership.

67. Bornstein, *op. cit.,* p. 4.
68. See Meyer, *op. cit.*

National political leaders decreed a complete moratorium on public business during the seven days following the death of President Kennedy. Solemn religious observances, cessation of normal pursuits and elimination of regular radio and television shows all served to channel public affect into well-behaved, self-disciplined, and even sedate modes of behavior.[69]

In the case of Martin Luther King, religious observances were hasty, widely divergent in style and often improvised. The country's national leadership was by no means unanimous in the example it gave. The President, who had not long before had serious political differences with Martin Luther King, Jr., was unable to attend his funeral. Schools and businesses throughout the country differed in their willingness to close down on the day of his funeral. Indeed, refusal to do so was the "spark" said to have ignited a number of riotous incidents in the week following King's death.[70]

What leaders predicted and expected the public to do was also a factor shaping the events that occurred. After the King disaster, various cues were given. As in the Sarajevo incident, important opinion leaders cited rage, protest, and violence as responses they expected to be forthcoming. The disruptive behavior that followed, whatever its actual meaning for those engaged in it, was thus rationalized and even "cued" in advance by such various spokesmen as Adam Clayton Powell, Stokely Carmichael, and others.

Along with disruptive action from some, there was surface indifference from others. Those who felt the loss keenly and who were now confronted by seemingly inappropriate conduct by others sometimes became aggressive. After King's death, these patterns of aggressive and destructive behavior were largely confined to the black communities of metropolitan centers, and to stores, cars, and homes rather than to people as target-objects.[71]

Immediate, spontaneous effects of assassinations are typically unorganized, unless the murder itself was part of a conspiratorial scheme aimed at stirring discontent. Typically, public responses are likely to be quite docile and easy to control.

In the case of assassinations that are part of a calculated and

69. Greenberg and Parker, *op. cit.*, pp. 29–86.
70. The account here of events following Dr. King's murder is based on the *New York Times*, April 6, 1968 through April 15, 1968.
71. *New York Times*, April 13, 1968.

not-too-far-fetched scheme for seizing power, the popular response to the event seems to depend largely on the outcome of the subsequent struggle. An elite's ability to counteract its rivals in practical ways is usually more important than how that elite tries to influence the general public's response. If hostile centers of leadership are controlled or neutralized, public response is not likely to be effectively organized and "public opinion" can be represented more or less at will.

Since the murder of a public figure is an extreme and violent event, it raises the level of mutual mistrust throughout society; feelings of insecurity are evoked, and anxieties are exaggerated. Even when the assassin is promptly caught and the explanation for his act seems clear, doubts and suspicions multiply rapidly, reflecting the activation of unconscious conflicts for many people. No matter how clear a case is made against an assassin, mystery always seems to surround murders of elite figures. One explanation for this persistent questioning of whether the full story has been revealed is that people unconsciously feel some complicity in the crime and are still unable to resolve their private tensions by accepting the official explanation.[72]

When President Kennedy was assassinated, one investigator had under his observation a number of persons who had threatened a president with violence. A second investigator observed the reactions to this same event of children who had suffered the untimely loss of a parent. Both investigators report a marked rise in the anxiety levels of their subjects. Those who had wished to kill a president found their intentions realized.[73] Anxiety arose from the primitive fear that the thought had been sufficient to cause the deed. The children's fears that their secret hostile thoughts had in some way been responsible for their parents' deaths—fears that would of course be deeply repressed—were apparently reactivated by the fate of President Kennedy.[74]

Reactions in 1963 of shock and distress to John F. Kennedy's

72. Richard M. Swinn, "Guilt and Depth of Reaction to the Death of a President," *Psychoanalytical Review,* 53 (Fall, 1966), pp. 81–82.

73. Rothstein in this volume.

74. Martha Wolfenstein, "Death of a Parent and Death of a President: Children's Reactions to Two Kinds of Loss," in Wolfenstein and Kliman, *op. cit.,* pp. 62–79.

murder were more widespread than to his brother's assassination four and a half years later. Yet the second event tended to evoke more feelings of personal guilt and more personal pledges to improve their own conduct. A Harris poll shows that no larger fraction of the public in 1968 than in 1963 felt "more against" extremist groups or "more" patriotic. But in 1968 a larger proportion of those polled did profess to feel "more considerate of other people's feelings" and more felt guilty about not doing "more for tolerance" after the Senator's death than after the President's. "There is more guilt than solid resolution," the public-opinion analyst concluded.[75]

That ambivalence toward the assassinated figure heightens the feeling of personal guilt at his murder is supported also by Greenstein's finding that college students who felt the need of a telephone conversation with their parents were most likely to have families who were politically hostile to the Democratic president.[76] The apprehensive speculations about prospects of violence that followed the death of Martin Luther King, Jr., may have mirrored a similar guilty ambivalence toward him on the part of those who unconsciously felt hostility toward him.

One way of measuring the direct effects of assassination on the level of mutual mistrust among citizens is by inquiries into the expectation of violence. An increase in apprehensions that one's neighbor may be violent and untrustworthy or a growth of fear about venturing forth at night into the community may in part be by-products of having witnessed the violent death of a famous person. A Harris poll taken after the assassination of Robert Kennedy found 93 per cent of the public willing to agree that "individual shootings can happen anytime because it only takes one madman to shoot another man."[77] This is a view that probably reflects realism rather than projective mistrust. But the same national sample of American citizens included more than 80 per cent who were willing to agree that at least "some" of the violence

75. *Los Angeles Times,* June 16, 1968.
76. Greenstein, "Young Men and the Death of a President," in Wolfenstein and Kliman, *op. cit.*
77. *Los Angeles Times,* June 23, 1968. Crotty's introductory chapter also analyzes the change in public perceptions of assassinations—as measured by a nationwide survey.

in this country was attributable to "radicals who create violence in the streets" and "too many criminals and demented people loose on the streets." Instead of these diffuse suspicions about fellow citizens and instead of a tendency to withdraw from the common life and insulate oneself against disturbing news, a more ego-oriented and "realistic" person probably would have sought to control violence—namely, through appropriate public policy changes such as the extension of gun controls. In this way, the effects of assassination would have consisted of organized and focused effort rather than uncoordinated and diffuse sentiment.

In the normal cycle of leadership—the rise to power, the days of office, the natural death—the moment of loss is an occasion for dedication to a successor usually younger, and at least temporarily less authoritative, less respected. Does assassination, and the shock that comes with violent death by illegitimate means, necessarily change this pattern of succession? In Gandhi's case, actual political power had before his death already been assumed by a younger man. Public mourning took a familiar form—grief at the loss of a benevolent parent and moral guide. Nehru presented himself as a fellow mourner for the vanished spiritual mentor.

Yet the fact that Gandhi had been murdered probably did detract from the national solidarity generated by his death. To be an ordinary citizen deprived of a respected leader because he dies of natural causes does not require one to erect defenses against one's worst impulses, because those hostile and aggressive impulses are not prompted by a violent deed. Knowing that the dead leader was murdered, even being a witness at his assassination, presumably does prompt hostile impulses for many. It is these unacknowledged and unacceptable sentiments that must be disguised; for many, the evil impulses are projected outward, onto those who have never admired or loved the lost figure but who instead have manifested indifference or hostility toward him. Political life, by its very nature committed to finding solutions to rivalry and adversary situations, is in marked degree vulnerable when competition becomes murderous. For then the level of mistrust among ordinary citizens must surely rise.

Thus the natural death of an aged leader leads to ceremonies of national mourning in which former detractors as well as admirers can experience a sense of communion. The barrier of a violent deed stands between partisan and foe and blights the funereal expression of common commitment to a larger community. The aftermath of Lincoln's murder was a time of extreme sensitivity; those who were avowedly bereaved scrutinized the manner in which others were less than zealous in their observance of the obsequies. Assassination has the power to widen the breaches already present in a society; disruptive and alienated social groups feel more isolated and at odds.

To counteract these centrifugal forces, the leader who has been physically removed from the political realm needs also to be "symbolically removed" from politics. That is, he is commonly either deified or personalized in ways that were underplayed while he was an active political figure. Efforts to place the fallen leader "above politics" tend to heighten the sense of community but efforts to picture his death as causing private tragedy within his family circle—to place his life "below politics" so to speak—tend to fragment community feeling. In the wake of John F. Kennedy's death, a notable emphasis was placed by the mass media on the picture of family tragedy—to wife and children and parents. In thus providing his political enemies with a nonpolitical basis for expressing regret and sympathy, the communal meaning of his death by violence was minimized. The common tragedy became a family tragedy.

What happens when and if the deprivation felt by the public after an assassination weakens intergroup ties more than it contributes to a sense of mutual dependence? Those parts of the public that feel intensely deprived are likely to be alienated from other subgroups whose manifestations of grief are judged to be less wholehearted. For inquiries into these relationships, studies of reactions to the murder of President Kennedy give the most abundant evidence. Three groups seem to have experienced his loss most acutely: young people, blacks, and Catholics.

YOUNG PEOPLE

Greenstein emphasizes in his findings the possibly severe effect of Kennedy's assassination for youthful members of the community. He calls attention to the special relevance of the quadrennial American election cycle in defining generations and he points out that the college students of 1963 were the Kennedy generation. The loss of a figure so closely connected with their own development was "the most unkindest cut of all."[78]

Greenstein suggests that young people of college age could scarcely look upon the youthful President as a parent substitute. Other studies of teen-age reactions, however, point out that "the President and Mrs. Kennedy were approximately the same age as their own parents."[79] This fact may have been overlooked because of how young the Kennedy children were. Studies of young people do not suggest any long-lasting effects of the Kennedy assassination. A still younger age group than these college students might be more peculiarly vulnerable to traumas from a presidential murder. Consider the dynamic forces at work in early adolescence. According to psychoanalytic formulations, the pubertal crisis that reactivates old Oedipal conflicts is simultaneously a heightening of instinctual pressures and a period of introduction into the adult world. The political events of adolescence may be expected to leave an imprint on an impressionable surface. Parental surrogates in the political world are apt to be used by young people as they move away from their families of origin.

Particular interest attaches to the effects of J. F. Kennedy's assassination on the attitudes of those children who became fifteen-to-twenty-two-years-old in 1966 and 1969. These were the adolescents within the age range of thirteen to sixteen at the time of the President's murder in late 1963. Members of this specific age group have frequently been noted to have the characteristics described by Shils and others as "antinomianism" whether on or off American college campuses in the years since 1965. Antinomianism is a mode of behavior that has stylistic elements involving an "acting out" of inner tensions through physically violent or obdurate operations.[80]

78. Greenstein, "Young Men and the Death of a President," in Wolfenstein and Kliman, *op. cit.*
79. Sylvia Ginsparg, Alice Moriarty and Lois B. Murphy, "Young Teenagers' Responses to the Assassination of President Kennedy: Relation to Previous Life Experiences," in Wolfenstein and Kliman, *op. cit.*, p. 1.
80. Nathan Adler, "The Antinomian Personality: The Hippie Character Type," *Psychiatry,* 31 (November, 1968), pp. 325–338.

Vandalism and minor criminality have always had their highest incidence among adolescents and young adults.[81] The politicization of that age group during the 1965–1969 period may owe its intensity and pervasiveness to the tragic drama on the television screens all over America in the four days beginning November 22, 1963. It is hard to design research measuring the delayed consequences of this kind of mass experience. In any particular case history, it is easy to appreciate the loss of a young president through violence as an event shaping the perspective of a young person who is of an age when Oedipal-conflict resolutions are assuming a lasting form.

NEGROES

It has been established that the Negro subgroup felt most severely deprived of any in the national sample interviewed after President Kennedy's death. They were slowest of all to recover from the symptoms of depression over the loss of a President who had been a special friend in the cause of civil equality. The murders of Malcolm X and later of Martin Luther King, Jr., and Robert Kennedy were similarly depressing to black Americans. The effects of this prolonged siege of mortal violence against protective and admired male figures may be more poignant than is generally realized, especially in a subculture where models of stable male leadership are not so frequently found in a family context. If the public models are correspondingly more important in shaping the private perspectives of Negro youths than of their non-Negro equivalents, eliminating those models through assassination clearly deepens the intensity of feelings of deprivation.

Consider the male-female differences in samples of white and black citizens reported by Bradburn and Feldman. Among Negroes, men were nearly as intense in their grief as women; among whites, men were clearly less upset than women. Group for group, Negroes were demonstrably more grief-stricken than whites.[82]

81. In Detroit in 1966, over 61 per cent of the self-reported rioters were between the ages of fifteen and twenty-four. *Report of National Advisory Commission on Civil Disorders* (New York: Dutton, 1968), pp. 129–130.

82. Bradburn and Feldman, "Public Apathy and Public Grief," in Greenberg and Parker, *op. cit.*

CATHOLICS

The third group experiencing especially severe deprivation as a result of President Kennedy's murder was the Catholic one. Lane found that the Catholics in his small sample were less disposed to work through the mourning process fully and were more likely to be classed as "nonclosers" or persons who continued to feel depressed by their memory of November, 1963. After the subsequent assassination of his brother, Senator Robert Kennedy, in June, 1968, analysis of a Harris poll showed Catholics in distinctive measure as a group rededicating themselves to the values of tolerance and community responsibility.[83]

CONCLUSION

Noting the intense popular absorption in the ceremonial aftermaths of recent American assassinations has led some social observers to emphasize the "reintegrative" effects of such rituals. The possibility exists that the traumatic events signaled by the murder of an important public figure may lead to the widespread rededication of a whole political community to the symbols that represent its basic values. Thus Verba views the funeral of John F. Kennedy in a light analogous to that in which Shils and Young saw Queen Elizabeth's coronation—that is, as a national experience akin to communion, creating and fortifying a pervasive sense of kinship and mutual identification.[84]

A number of considerations conflict with any assessment of assassination emphasizing its "functional" and "integrative" consequences. Political murders call forth feelings that people want to repress. Sentiments of fear and hostility are not typically evoked by coronations, anniversaries, inaugurals, or similar mass ceremonies. But assassinations create special problems of psychic management for the individual. The kind of solidarity generated in

83. *Los Angeles Times,* June 16, 1968.
84. Edward Shils and Michael Young, "The Meaning of the Coronation," *Sociological Review* (December, 1953); and Sidney Verba, "The Kennedy Assassination and the Nature of Political Commitment," in Greenberg and Parker, *op. cit.,* pp. 348–349.

murder's wake is built on the sand of unacknowledged mistrust and unspoken doubt. Assassinations are not the kind of occasions when people can let themselves go and can assume that only their better impulses will surface. Many people, indeed, cannot even allow themselves to display strong sentiments of revenge or loathing. Apathy and a sense of estrangement are the only ways by which they adjust to the event.

In the aftermath of political assassination, spontaneous forces largely contribute to a restoration of equilibrium. Much effort is spent on isolating the disruptive effects, clarifying the specific circumstances, reliving the event, and seeking to explain and understand what has happened. People in so doing are not consciously seeking to save society, restore consensus or generate solidarity. Yet the net effect of the personal adjustment process for most citizens is probably to re-establish the pattern of social processes much as before. In view of the sentiments aroused by the deed, it is hard to see how a political community could actually improve the level of mutual solidarity, commitment to common value, and reciprocal trust. But it is plausible that the community might be nearly as strong as before, once a period of shock and disbelief has been weathered.

But a political community does not only make a spontaneous adjustment; individuals and groups also seek to control the impact of the event. Much of this essay has been concerned with how the elite seeks to control personnel changes that follow an assassination and to manage the public's reaction to it. A simple scheme for analyzing the practical and attitudinal effects of political murder has been used. The chief actors in the drama of assassination have been described as the assassin, the victim, the victim's associates and successors, group representatives, and the wider public.

So far as the assassin is concerned, we have emphasized the question of his marginality to power centers as a pivotal determinant of the consequences. Related to his marginality is his realism, that is, the extent to which his designs are actually instrumental to his goal.

As for the victim, we have noted that the role he plays in the public arena may influence the probability of his "selection" by a certain type of potential assassin. Both recruitment into public life and performance of key leadership roles could be distorted by this kind of occupational hazard.

Critical, too, in determining the effects of an assassination is the behavior of surviving associates and possible successors of the victim. Relevant to this is their position vis-à-vis the dead leader— whether dependent or independent—and their preparedness for the event, ranging from guilty foreknowledge, through prudent readiness, to complete unpreparedness.

These actors in turn may have an impact, intentionally or unwittingly, upon the unorganized public sufficient to distort in distinctive ways both the short-run, spontaneous responses and deferred alterations in political attitudes and belief systems. Immediate public reactions may importantly shape elite strategies, while long-run transformations in public predispositions are the materials out of which emerge significant social trends.

In a modern society, more and more common effect is directed onto the major figures wielding political power. In earlier eras public figures in the arenas of business and entertainment, art and science, religion and exploration collectively and individually rivaled those in the political sphere for attention. Undeniably, ours is a pluralist society. Yet the primacy of politics is equally indisputable. The concentration of overwhelming power in the central organs of government assures this to be the case for an indefinite future. Thus discontinuity in political leadership is always a threat to intricate undertakings. The disjunctions that result from recourse to the murder of freely selected political leaders create the serious possibility of widespread hopelessness and despair.

INDEX